Making Connections

FROM THEORY TO PRACTICE IN ADAPTED PHYSICAL EDUCATION

SECOND EDITION

Janet A. Seaman
EMERITUS, CALIFORNIA STATE UNIVERSITY, LOS ANGELES

Karen P. DePauw
VIRGINIA POLYTECHNIC INSTITUTE AND STATE UNIVERSITY

Kimble B. Morton
CALIFORNIA DEPARTMENT OF EDUCATION
DIAGNOSTIC CENTER, SOUTHERN CALIFORNIA

Kathy Omoto
CLARK COUNTY SCHOOL DISTRICT

Holcomb Hathaway, Publishers
Scottsdale, Arizona 85250

Library of Congress Cataloging-in-Publication Data

Making connections : from theory to practice in adapted physical education /
    Janet A. Seaman ... [et al.]. — 2nd ed.
      p. cm.
    Includes bibliographical references and index.
    ISBN-13: 978-1-890871-75-8
    1. Physical education for people with disabilities. 2. Motor ability—Testing. 3.
Individualized instruction. I. Seaman, Janet A.
    GV445.M24 2007
    371.9′04486—dc22

2006028750

Copyright © 2007 by Holcomb Hathaway, Publishers, Inc.

Holcomb Hathaway, Publishers, Inc.
6207 North Cattletrack Road, Suite 5
Scottsdale, Arizona 85250
480-991-7881
www.hh-pub.com

10 9 8 7 6 5 4 3 2 1

ISBN 978-1-890871-75-8

All rights reserved. No part of this publication may be reproduced, in any form or by any means, without permission in writing from the publisher.

Printed in the United States of America.

Photo Credits

Front cover: upper left, FlagHouse; **middle left,** PhotoDisc; **bottom left,** PALAESTRA/Challenge Publications, Ltd./Lisa Silliman-French; **upper right:** Cal Poly Pomona Motor Development Clinic (CPPMDC); **bottom right,** Gerardo Rodriguez. **Back cover: top,** CPPMDC; **middle,** PALAESTRA/Challenge Publications, Ltd./FAYFOTO; **bottom,** PALAESTRA/Challenge Publications.

Interior photos are by authors unless otherwise noted here, by page: 1, CPPMDC; 5, Fig. 1.1, PALAESTRA/Challenge Publications, Ltd./Todd A. Teske; 15 and 28, Fig. 2.8, CPPMDC; 62, Fig. 3.10, CPPMDC; 63, Fig. 3.11, top, CPPMDC; 69, PhotoDisc; 89, Corbis Images; 91, Fig. 5.2, CPPMDC; 121, Fig. 6.2, CPPMDC; 121, Fig. 6.3, CPPMDC; 122, Fig. 6.4, CPPMDC; 124, Fig. 6.5, Ed Owen; 126, Fig. 6.8a, c, CPPMDC; 128, Fig. 6.10, CPPMDC; 129, Fig. 6.11, CPPMDC; 197, DigitalVision; 216, Fig. 9.11, PALAESTRA/Challenge Publications; 219, PhotoDisc; 223, Fig. 10.1, Ben Esparza; 224, Fig. 10.2, CPPMDC; 227, Fig. 10.4, Kathy Yasui-Der; 229, Fig. 10.5, CPPMDC; 229, Fig. 10.6, CPPMDC; 232, Fig. 10.8, CPPMDC; 233, Fig. 10.9, CPPMDC; 248, Fig. 10.12, CPPMDC; 253, PhotoDisc; 263, Fig. 11.1, CPPMDC; 266, Fig. 11.3, FlagHouse; 268, Fig. 11.4, CPPMDC; 277, PhotoDisc; 303, CPPMDC; 323, Fig. 13.5, Marnie Young; 329, Fig. 13.6, left, FlagHouse, right, CPPMDC; 330, Fig. 13.7, top, CPPMDC, middle and bottom, FlagHouse; 332, Fig. 13.8d, FlagHouse; 337, José Betancourt; 343, Fig. 14.2, CPPMDC; 353, PALAESTRA/Challenge Publications, Ltd./FAYFOTO; 419, Fig. H.1, CPPMDC; 421, Fig. H.4, CPPMDC; 422, Fig. H.5, Lyonel Avance; 424, Fig. H.6, CPPMDC; 432, Fig. H.7, FlagHouse; 434, Fig. H.8, CPPMDC; 437, Fig. H.9, top, FlagHouse, bottom, CPPMDC; 442, Fig. H.11, CPPMDC.

Contents

Preface ix
About the Authors xi

1

PHYSICAL EDUCATION FOR INDIVIDUALS WITH A DISABILITY: AN OVERVIEW   1

GUIDING QUESTIONS   1

Adapted Physical Education and Adapted Physical Activity Defined   2

Historical Perspectives of Adapted Physical Activity and Adapted Physical Education   3

Evolving Societal Context of Disability   4

Legal and Professional Contexts of Disability   5
   The Rehabilitation Act   5
   Americans with Disabilities Act   5
   Individuals with Disabilities Education Act   5
   Free, Appropriate Public Education   7
   Least Restrictive Environment   7
   Individualized Education Program   7
   The Legal Impact of Federal Legislation (IDEA '97 and Section 504) on Physical Education and Sport   7
   Amateur Sports Act of 1978   7

Categorical Thinking and the Noncategorical Approach   8
   The Effects of Labeling   8
   Categorical and Noncategorical Approaches to Programming   8

Inclusion and Inclusive Physical Education   10

Professional Roles and Preparation   10
   Physical Education Generalist   10
   Adapted Physical Education Specialist   11
   Adapted Physical Education National Standards   11

SUMMARY   11
LEARNING ACTIVITIES   12
REFERENCES   12

2

THE COLLABORATIVE TEAM: WORKING WITH FAMILIES AND EDUCATIONAL PROFESSIONALS   15

GUIDING QUESTIONS   15

The Team Approach   16
   Multidisciplinary Teams   16
   Collaborative Teams   16

Characteristics of Effective Collaborators   17
   Communication Skills   17
   Problem-Solving Skills   23
   Personal Qualities   26

The IEP Team   27
   Team Members   27

The Adapted Physical Educator as a Resource Person   33
   Roles   33
   Working with the Adapted Physical Educator   34

Integrating Students into General Programs   37
   Prioritizing Student Needs   37
   Co-Teaching   37

SUMMARY   40
LEARNING ACTIVITIES   40
REFERENCES   41

3

THE DEVELOPMENTAL APPROACH   43

GUIDING QUESTIONS   43

What Is the Developmental Approach?   44

Neurological Bases of Human Movement   44
   Growth and Development of the Central Nervous System   44
   Sensory-Integrative-Motor-Sensory-Feedback System   46

Sensory Responsivity   50
Sensory Systems   51
Reflex Activity   54
Neurodevelopment and Motor Function   55

The Developmental Model   58
Understanding the Developmental Model   63
Applying the Developmental Approach   63

SUMMARY   67
LEARNING ACTIVITIES   67
REFERENCES   68

4

UNDERSTANDING MOTOR PERFORMANCE AND IDENTIFYING SOURCES OF ATYPICAL PERFORMANCE   69

GUIDING QUESTIONS   69

Process Disorders   70
Breakdown Sites and Effects   70
Responsivity Disorders   74

Developmental Disorders   76
Reflex Activity   77
Sensory Systems   78
Motor Sensory Responses   82
Motor Patterns, Motor Skills, and Culturally Determined Forms of Movement   85

Sources of Dysfunction and Specific Impairments Attributable to Other Factors   86

SUMMARY   86
LEARNING ACTIVITIES   87
REFERENCES   87

5

THE PROCESS OF ASSESSMENT AND EVALUATION   89

GUIDING QUESTIONS   89

Testing   90
Formal Testing   90
Informal Testing   90
Rating Scales and Checklists   92
Self-Report   92

Measurement   92
Standards   93
Evaluation   93
Program Evaluation   97
Assessment   98
Purposes of Evaluation and Assessment   100
Diagnosis   100
Prediction   100
Determining Student Progress   100
Placement   100
Determining Program Effectiveness   100
Motivation   101
Individual Program Planning   101
Further Testing and Related Services   101

Using Measurement Concepts   102
Types of Scores   102
Organization of Scores   103
Measures of Central Tendency   103
Measures of Variability   104
Position in a Group   104
Standard Scores   105
Relationships Between Scores   106

Legislative Mandates   107
SUMMARY   109
LEARNING ACTIVITIES   109
REFERENCES   110

6

DATA COLLECTION   111

GUIDING QUESTIONS   111

Formal Testing   112
Criteria for Selecting an Instrument   112
Test Administration   114

Measurement at the Developmental Level   116
Reflex Testing   117
Sensorimotor Testing   120
Testing Motor Patterns   121
Health-Related Physical Fitness Tests   123

Informal Testing   127
Observational Techniques   127
Teacher Rating Scales   129
Checklists   131
Game Statistics   131

Self-Reporting 134
   Attitude Inventories 134
   Self-Rating Scales 134
   Activity Preference Inventories 135
   Portfolios 135
   Journals 136

Using Technology 136

Assessing the Whole Child 137
   Measures of Intelligence 137
   Assessing Adaptive Behavior 138
   Assessing Language 138

SUMMARY 139
LEARNING ACTIVITIES 139
REFERENCES 140

7

COMPLETING THE ASSESSMENT PROCESS 143

GUIDING QUESTIONS 143

Interpretation of Data 144

Concepts Necessary for Interpretation 145
   Performance Sampling 145
   Test Validity 146
   Test Reliability 147
   Test Specificity 147
   Tests as Indicators 148
   Test Relationships 149

Steps in Interpretation 149
   Analyze the Demands 149
   Order Developmentally 151
   Determine the Commonalities 151
   Cluster by Commonalities 151
   Describe Performance 152
   Draw Conclusions 152

Relationships for Test Interpretation 153
   Reflex Behavior 153
   Sensorimotor Measurement 154
   Motor Development Measurement 154
   Motor Ability Measurement 156
   Motor Skills Measurement 156
   Health-Related Physical Fitness Measurement 156

A Model for Interpretation 157

Reporting Assessment Results 158
   Legal Requirements 159

Considerations for Placement 160
   Eligibility Criteria for Adapted Physical Education 160

SUMMARY 161
LEARNING ACTIVITIES 162
REFERENCES 162

8

PREPARING THE INDIVIDUALIZED EDUCATION PROGRAM 163

GUIDING QUESTIONS 163

The Significance of the Individualized Education Program 164
   Types of IEPs 165

Legal Framework for the Individualized Education Program 166
   Legal Requirements of the IEP Related to Assessment 167
   Legally Mandated Components of the IEP 169

Preparing for the Individualized Education Program Meeting 170
   Referrals 171
   Assessment 171
   IEP Content 174

Completing the Individualized Education Program 176
   Preparing an IEP 176
   An Example of an IEP Document 177

Writing the Annual Goals and Performance Objectives 184
   Purposes for Writing Measurable Goals and Objectives 185
   Parts of Measurable Goals and Objectives 185
   Prioritizing Goals and Objectives 186
   Determining Achievement Dates 189
   Evaluation of Goals and Objectives 193
   Framework for Goals and Objectives 193

Determining Related Services 194

SUMMARY 194
LEARNING ACTIVITIES 195
REFERENCES 195

9

DEVELOPING AND IMPLEMENTING THE PROGRAM 197

GUIDING QUESTIONS 197

Determining an Appropriate and Meaningful Program 198
- *Philosophy, Beliefs, and Program Goals* 198
- *Curriculum* 199
- *Program Planning for Inclusion* 200
- *Determining the Appropriate Level of Programming* 202

Implementing the Program Plan 203
- *Components of an Effective Program Plan* 204
- *Sequencing Activities* 204
- *The Importance of Pivotal Skills* 205

Successful Inclusion in General Physical Education 205
- *Defining Inclusion* 205
- *Barriers to Inclusion* 207

Teaching Strategies for All Students 208

Paraeducators 215
- *Guidelines for Using Paraeducators in Physical Education* 215
- *Helping Paraeducators Assist with Physical Activity* 216

SUMMARY 217
LEARNING ACTIVITIES 217
REFERENCES 218

10

STRATEGIES FOR MEETING INDIVIDUAL NEEDS 219

GUIDING QUESTIONS 219

The Process of Learning 220
- *Laws of Learning* 220
- *Factors That Affect Learning* 220

Individualized Instruction 222
- *Part and Whole Methods* 222
- *Explanation and Demonstration* 223
- *Guided Discovery (Movement Exploration)* 223
- *Problem Solving* 223

Adaptation Techniques 224
- *Techniques for Adapting Instruction* 224
- *Techniques for Adapting the Learning Environment* 231
- *Techniques for Adapting the Activity* 234

Task Analysis 235
- *Chaining* 238
- *Partial Participation* 238
- *Successive Approximation* 238

Creating a Positive Environment 240
- *Motivation* 240
- *Class Rules* 241

Positive Behavior Support 242
- *Behavior Modification* 243
- *Analyzing Behavior* 244
- *Behavior Support Strategies* 245
- *Other Behavior Support Techniques* 248
- *The Influence of Sensory Responsiveness on Behavior* 248

SUMMARY 251
LEARNING ACTIVITIES 251
REFERENCES 251

11

EFFECTIVE PROGRAMMING: DEVELOPMENTAL ACTIVITIES 253

GUIDING QUESTIONS 253

Planning for Developmentally Appropriate Activities 254
- *Activities for Reflex Development and Inhibition* 254
- *Activities for Sensory Stimulation and Discrimination* 255
- *Activities for Enhancing Motor-Sensory Responses* 255
- *Activities for Enhancing Motor Patterns and Motor Skills* 255

Selecting Appropriate Activities for Developmental Needs 256
- *Infants* 256
- *Preschool and Primary Grades* 257
- *Elementary School Grade Levels* 257
- *Middle School and Junior High School* 258
- *Secondary or High School* 259

Transition to Adult Programs   260

Incorporating All Learning Domains into the Physical Education Program   260

Cognitive Learning   261

Language Learning   266

Socialization   270

Affective Learning   270

Incorporating Multiple Learning Domains   271

SUMMARY   274

LEARNING ACTIVITIES   274

REFERENCES   274

12

EFFECTIVE PROGRAMMING:
INCLUSIVE PRACTICES AND APPLYING MOTOR SKILLS IN CULTURALLY DETERMINED FORMS OF MOVEMENT   277

GUIDING QUESTIONS   277

Philosophical Approaches to Programming   278

Inclusive Programming   278

Noncategorical Programming   279

Universal Design   280

Culturally Determined Forms of Movement   280

Selecting Appropriate Accommodations   281

Types of Curriculum Adaptations   281

Adapting the Lesson or Game   281

An Example of Adapting Activities Based on a NASPE Standard   284

Including All Students in Culturally Determined Forms of Movement   286

Traditional Physical Education Activity Areas   286

Multicultural Games and Activities   291

Disability Awareness Activities   291

Community-Based Instruction Programs   294

Planning Activities That Develop Student Interests   298

Nontraditional Curriculum Resources   299

Instructional Tips   299

SUMMARY   299

LEARNING ACTIVITIES   300

REFERENCES   300

13

ORGANIZING THE INSTRUCTIONAL PROGRAM   303

GUIDING QUESTIONS   303

Planning and Organization   304

Orientation and Communication   304

Scheduling   304

Lesson Planning   305

Organizational Strategies   306

Safety   314

Safety Factors to Consider in the Education Program   315

Playground Safety Standards and Guidelines   317

Facilities   318

Accessibility Guidelines   318

Legislated Standards for Accessibility   320

Using Available Space   321

Outdoor Facilities   321

Indoor Facilities   322

Equipment   323

Developing the Equipment List   324

Selecting Equipment   326

Adapting Equipment   330

Working with Minimal Equipment   333

Making Equipment   333

Purchasing and Maintaining Equipment   334

SUMMARY   335

LEARNING ACTIVITIES   336

REFERENCES   336

14

CONNECTIONS AND TRANSITIONS   337

GUIDING QUESTIONS   337

Transition from School to Adult Programs   338

Individualized Transition Plan   338

Partnerships with Community Organizations   339

Advocacy Within Community Programs   340

Professional Services   341

The Role of the Family   343

Benefits of Family Involvement   343

viii CONTENTS

    Obtaining Information from the Family   343
Sharing Information with the Family   347
Methods of Communication   347
    Developing Home Programs   350
Volunteers   350
SUMMARY   350
LEARNING ACTIVITIES   351
REFERENCES   351

15 LIFELONG PHYSICAL ACTIVITY AND SPORT   353

GUIDING QUESTIONS   353
Health Promotion and Fitness   354
Sport   356
    Unified Sports   356
    Defining Disability Sport   356
    Deaf Sport   361
Disability Sport   361
    Disability Sport in the United States   361
    International Paralympic Committee   362
    International Competitions   363
SUMMARY   363
LEARNING ACTIVITIES   364
REFERENCES   364

APPENDICES

A   ADAPTED PHYSICAL EDUCATION NATIONAL STANDARDS   367

B   DEVELOPMENTAL SCHEDULE   371

C   MOVEMENT ATTRIBUTES AND ETIOLOGY OF DISABILITIES   379

D   MEASUREMENT AND EVALUATION REVIEW   397

E   ANNOTATED SUMMARY OF AVAILABLE TESTS   403

F   LIFELONG PHYSICAL ACTIVITY AND DISABILITY SPORT RESOURCES   411

G   SPORTSMANSHIP GROUP: SAMPLE LESSON PLAN   415

H   EFFECTIVE PROGRAMMING: DEVELOPMENTAL ACTIVITIES   417

Author Index   449
Subject Index   451

Preface

Making Connections: From Theory to Practice in Adapted Physical Education is based on *The New Adapted Physical Education*, the classic text by Seaman & DePauw, describing a developmental approach to working with individuals with a disability. The second edition of this new, more practical and applied book creates a truly inclusive developmental physical education model in keeping with the national standards for physical education and curriculum frameworks across the country. *Making Connections* describes how to apply a non-categorical, developmental approach to varied physical activity instructional settings and how to use it to plan and implement appropriate physical education activities and programs for individuals with a disability.

We recognize that the potential of students with a disability can be achieved in a variety of settings (from inclusive to segregated) by a physical educator who has a strong foundation in the motor, cognitive, social, and language development of children. With a clear understanding of neurological development and functional ability, disabilities and their implications for motor performance, and effective teaching techniques, physical educators can use the developmental model to help every student, not just those with an identified disability, accomplish their motor performance goals.

Making Connections introduces prospective teachers to the theoretical basis of the developmental model. We show how the model can be applied to identify sources of poor motor performance and to plan and implement physical education programs to address performance difficulties for individuals with a disability. Central to this approach is an emphasis on the individual student and the abilities the student brings to the physical education setting—focusing on ability, not disability. In particular, we center on the performance indicators that emerge naturally in the course of the student's growth and maturation, for only with an understanding of these indicators can physical educators understand atypical development and performance.

This edition of *Making Connections* clarifies the roles of general physical educators, paraeducators, and volunteers as defined in the latest reauthorization of IDEA '04. It combines an appropriate mix of content for the general physical educator with foundational resources for those students specializing in adapted physical education. Some key topics have been expanded or added, including orientation and mobility, cognitive development, and the use of technology. Chapter concepts are illustrated with brief, high-interest case studies and examples of real-life interactions taken from the experiences of the authors.

We provide updated information from the latest reauthorization of federal laws, new information on alternative models of service delivery, including the individualized transition plan and individualized family service plan, and we discuss the skills needed for consultative and collaborative work. Examples of the application of teaming concepts have been added as the role of the general physical educator has changed in the new legislation. The body of the text contains many practical examples, scenarios, and applications to assist both general and adapted physical educators in making a connection between theoretical models and practical applications to instruction. The section on lesson planning is expanded to include examples for different age groups. The examples are provided to show how to meet specific goals and objectives based on the developmental needs of each student participating within the same lesson. Additionally, more information on new legislation and the use of authentic assessment is included. New terminology, expanded health and safety information, along with additional material on positive behavior supports are included in this edition. Appendices are provided as additional support for readers.

Making Connections highlights the opportunities available for students with a disability in schools and communities, and it also explores the disability rights movement in the United States that has produced enhanced rights for citizens with a disability across the lifespan. The book brings into focus the changing roles played today by general physical educators and adapted physical educators across the country.

FEATURES THAT MAKE THIS BOOK A VALUABLE RESOURCE TOOL

Our hope is that current and future educators will find this book a valuable resource to keep and refer to throughout their careers. *Making Connections* includes numerous assessment tools, bibliographies, resource lists, and developmentally appropriate activities. Material related to the team approach, best practice recommendations, and planning for transition from school to the community also helps to make this book a valuable tool for educators. The book's special features include the following boxed features, which are titled for easy reference and contain additional practical applications, tips, examples, and pictures:

- **How Would You Respond?** boxes ask students to respond to teaching situations that they are likely to encounter, and the companion feature **The Authors Respond** presents the authors' comments and advice on the situations.
- **Teaching Tips** provide useful suggestions that will help teachers in everyday practice.
- **Making Connections** are vignettes of professionals working with individuals with a disability, bringing theories and concepts to life. Most are situations actually encountered by the authors.
- **Extend Your Knowledge** boxes provide more in-depth information about important topics for students studying to be specialists or those wanting extended information on the issue.
- **Learning Activities** are challenging activities that can be used in the college classroom or in field placements, internships, or student teaching experiences that help students make the connections between text material and real life.

In addition, an **Instructor's Manual** and **PowerPoint Presentation** are available to instructors who adopt the book for use in their courses.

We hope that the ideas in this second edition will be used as a springboard for creative teaching, allowing educators to identify and develop their students' abilities.

ACKNOWLEDGMENTS

Many people helped us throughout the writing process in development of this second edition. First, we would like to thank the staff at Holcomb Hathaway, and particularly our editor, Colette Kelly, who showed endless patience and provided considerable support for writing, organization, and communication among the four authors who were scattered across the country. We would also like to thank Rebecca Lytle, who wrote Chapter 2 for the first edition, and established the foundation for this edition's treatment of issues related to the collaborative team.

We would like to thank our reviewers, from whom we received valuable feedback and suggestions. Our thanks to (for the second edition): Curly Cox, Howard Payne University; Tim Gattenby, University of Wisconsin; Lori A. Gravish, Pennsylvania State University; Karen Hilberg, William Paterson University; Jody Rose-Dressler, California State University, Hayward; Karen Ruder, Castleton State College; Todd Russell, University of Great Falls; Judy Sloan, Southern Adventist University; Christine Summerford, San Francisco State University; and Gail Webster, Kennesaw State University; (for the previous edition): Pete Aufsesser, San Diego State University; Bill Brady, Fairfax County Public Schools; Lee N. Burkett, Arizona State University; Barry Lavay, California State University, Long Beach; Monica Lepore, West Chester University; Toni Marich, California State University, Dominguez Hills; Mary C. Marks, Fairfax County Public Schools; William T. Price, University of South Florida; and Daniel Webb, Mississippi State University.

We feel that photographs make a significant contribution to understanding the concepts, techniques, and strategies described in this text. We were very fortunate to have had help from many people in this regard. In particular, we would like to thank Perky Vetter, Mary Stegemann, Allison Apodaca, and the families and alumni of the Motor Development Clinic at California State Polytechnic University, Pomona, who so willingly gave of their time, skills, and enthusiasm. Thanks go to Cyndi and Peter Martinich for photos depicting APEAS II. In addition, thanks go to those special friends and children who added their movement skills to demonstrate our ideas.

Last, but not least, we are all grateful to our families and friends who supported and encouraged us, sacrificed and sometimes suspended life's activities so we could have the time needed to complete this project. They know who they are and know that we love them for that.

Janet A. Seaman
Karen P. DePauw
Kimble B. Morton
Kathy Omoto

About the Authors

Janet Seaman, Professor Emeritus of California State University, Los Angeles, recently retired as Executive Director of the American Association for Physical Activity and Recreation (AAPAR), one of the national associations of AAHPERD. She has been active at all levels of governance in professional AHPERD organizations for over 30 years. Seaman is a past president of the California Association for Health, Physical Education, Recreation and Dance (CAHPERD), Vice President and Parliamentarian for the Southwest District AAHPERD, and President of the Association for Research, Administration, Professional Councils and Societies (ARAPCS, now called AAPAR) of AAHPERD. Seaman was active in the Western Society of Physical Education for College Women, was Southwest District (of AAHPERD) Scholar in 1992, and received the Outstanding Professor award at California State University, Los Angeles the same year. In March 2000, she was inducted into the North American Society of Health, Physical Education, Recreation, Sport and Dance Professionals.

Seaman has a number of community and professional service appointments to her credit. She was a member of the Advisory Board for Orange County Special Olympics in California, Almansor Education Center in Alhambra, California, and the Crippled Children's Society of Southern California (now called Ability First). She received the Gold Medal Award for Innovative Programming from the National Recreation and Parks Association and the Community Service Award from the Women's Chamber of Commerce of Anaheim, California, as Coordinator of Therapeutic Recreation for the City of Anaheim. Most recently, Seaman served on the Steering Committee for the Adapted Physical Education National Standards, a project funded by the U.S. Department of Education. In 2001, she began work with FlagHouse as an advisor on products, materials, and training related to physical activity for people with a disability and the elderly. She serves on the Board of Directors for the American Association of Adapted Sports Programs and the CAHPERD Foundation.

Seaman has a national reputation in the area of motor assessment of individuals with a disability. She is an author and editor of *Physical Best and Individuals with Disabilities* along with three other books and numerous articles.

Karen P. DePauw is Vice Provost for Graduate Studies and Dean of the Graduate School at Virginia Polytechnic Institute and State University and tenured Professor in the Departments of Sociology and Human Nutrition, Foods & Exercise. Before moving to Virginia Tech, she served 22 years on the faculty at Washington State University and held several administrative positions, most recently as Dean of the Graduate School.

DePauw has earned an international reputation in the fields of adapted physical activity and disability sport. She has published extensively, presented keynote and scholar lectures around the world. She served as Editor of *Quest* and on numerous editorial boards. In addition, she has served in leadership roles in professional associations including President of the International Federation of Adapted Physical Activity (IFAPA) and National Association for Physical Education in Higher Education (NAPEHE), Speaker of the Associations Board and North American Representative for the International Council of Sport Science & Physical Education (ICSSPE), and member of the International Paralympic Committee Sport Science Committee, USOC Committee on Sports for the Disabled (COSD), and several scientific committees for Olympic & Paralympic Congresses. Among her honors, DePauw was elected as a member of the American Academy for Kinesiology & Physical Education and has received several prestigious awards from professional associations.

DePauw earned her A.B. in Sociology from Whittier College, an M.S. in Special Education from California State University, Long Beach, and a Ph.D. in Kinesiology from Texas Woman's University. She previously taught with the Los Angeles City and Los Angeles County Schools and California State University–Los Angeles.

Kimble B. Morton is the Motor Assessment Program Specialist for the Diagnostic Center, Southern California, where she works with a transdisciplinary team providing assessment and training services to the school districts in the twelve counties of Southern California. In 2002 Morton was selected as the Outstanding Adapted Physical Educator by the State Council on Adapted Physical Education of CAHPERD. In 1995 she was selected Adapted Physical Educator of the Year for the Southwest District of AAHPERD. Morton is a contributing author to the books *The Adapted Physical Education Guidelines for California Schools*, *Physical Best and Individuals with Disabilities*, and *Positive Interventions for Serious Behavior Problems*. She is the co-author of the revised edition of *Analysis of Sensory Behavior Inventory*, which is an assessment tool used to assist in understanding the unusual sensory behaviors that some individuals with a disability display. In addition, Morton has served as a part-time instructor at the University of Southern California and California State University, Los Angeles. Her numerous presentations for professional conferences, inservice trainings, and graduate seminars cover topics such as motor assessment, adapted physical education for individuals with autism and developmental disabilities, fine motor assessment and intervention, transition programs for adapted physical education, and positive behavior interventions.

Kathy Omoto is an Adapted Physical Education Specialist for Clark County School District in Las Vegas, Nevada, where she has worked since 1998. Omoto previously taught adapted physical education in several school districts in Southern California, and general physical education and physical recreation in Maryland. In 1994 Omoto was the recipient of the Outstanding Adapted Physical Educator award presented by the CAHPERD State Council on Adapted Physical Education. In 1998 she was awarded the Adapted Physical Educator of the Year from the Southwest District of AAHPERD. Omoto is a contributing author to *Physical Best and Individuals with Disabilities* and has written several articles for professional journals. She was a writer and reviewer for the Adapted Physical Education National Standards (APENS) project. In addition, Omoto was a team member for the California projects *Healthy Kids, Healthy California* and *Standards of Program Quality and Effectiveness for the Evaluation of Specialist Programs in Adapted Physical Education*. She has been a consultant for the California Deaf-Blind Project, providing training and support for assessment and activities for children with dual sensory impairments. She has served as a part-time instructor at California State University, Los Angeles, and California Polytechnic University, Pomona. Omoto often presents at professional conferences and inservice trainings on topics such as strategies for including children with a disability in physical education, preschool physical activities, incorporating sensory motor experiences in physical education, language and movement experiences, planning for transitions, adapting games and activities, and using limited and/or homemade equipment for activities.

CHAPTER 1

Physical Education for Individuals with a Disability

AN OVERVIEW

Guiding Questions

1. How are adapted physical education and adapted physical activity defined?
2. What are the origins of physical activity and physical education?
3. What are the legal mandates for physical education and sport for individuals with a disability?
4. What is the noncategorical approach to physical education for individuals with a disability?
5. What is meant by inclusive physical education?
6. What factors contributed to the changes in societal attitudes toward individuals with a disability?
7. How do the adapted physical education specialist and the physical education generalist serve individuals with a disability?

Physical activity is an integral aspect of human life. Our daily lives are sustained and enriched when we are physically active and adopt active, healthful lifestyles that will continue throughout the life span. Today, we see an increased emphasis on fitness, wellness, and health promotion through active living during one's life span. We also see a focus on the development of physically educated people and the prevention of secondary health conditions, especially among individuals with a disability. These efforts are endorsed in national reports entitled *Healthy People 2000* and *Healthy People 2010* and are being facilitated by the American Alliance for Health, Physical Education, Recreation, and Dance (AAHPERD) and the President's Council on Physical Fitness and Sport (PCPFS).

In the emerging paradigm shift from disease and disability prevention to prevention of secondary conditions in individuals with a disability, professionals will play an important role in the integration of health promotion into the fabric of a community. For example, a growing number of trained exercise specialists (e.g., physical therapists, exercise science majors) now serve as consultants to local fitness centers. Personnel is also needed in the full range of public and private facilities, including senior centers, park districts, and local youth groups.

Quality physical education plays an important role in providing formalized educational opportunities for motor development and motor skills acquisition and the application of these skills in games, sports, and other forms of physical activity. Physical education teaches movement and helps prevent secondary conditions in individuals with a disability. The physical activity patterns developed in physical education and reinforced in the home and community will provide the basis for lifelong physically active lifestyles. Today's society offers great opportunities for professionals to provide their services through educational, recreational, and community-based fitness centers to facilitate the promotion of good health practices for the more than 50 million Americans with a disability.

ADAPTED PHYSICAL EDUCATION AND ADAPTED PHYSICAL ACTIVITY DEFINED

In 1952, the scope of adapted physical education was clearly and consistently defined. This original definition established a much broader application of scientific principles underlying human movement than had been used in earlier programs. The statement of AAHPERD defined **adapted physical education** as *"[A] diversified program of developmental activities, games, sports, and rhythms, suited to the interests, capacities, and limitations of students with disabilities who may not safely or successfully engage in unrestricted participation in the vigorous activities of the general physical education program"* (AAHPERD, 1952).

The first new concept was that programs should be diversified. They should not consist exclusively of rehabilitative or therapeutic exercise, as implemented by early physician–educators, but should mirror or parallel the concepts and programs of general physical education.

Second, to ensure that such programs were diversified, the statement specified what diversification should entail. **Developmental activities** include *a broad range of movement experiences for the development of fundamental motor patterns, motor skills, perceptual–motor function, and physical fitness.* The suggestion that games, sports, and rhythms should be included in programs for students with a disability took physical education into uncharted territory. It was not until after World War II, when disabled veterans began playing wheelchair basketball and other lifetime sports, that physical educators in the schools realized how numerous were the possibilities for physical activity by students with a disability.

Third, in creating this definition of adapted physical education, the AAHPERD committee suggested that the physical education program be "suited to the interests, capacities, and limitations of students with a disability." As a result, the age-appropriate interests of students with a disability were considered for the first time. Also for the first time, it was suggested that students should be challenged to reach their capabilities.

Finally, the segment of the school population that could profit from such an all-encompassing program was identified as "students . . . who may not safely or successfully engage in unrestricted participation in the . . . general physical education program." Although early programs had been concerned with safety and the possibility of aggravating certain existing conditions, AAHPERD again ventured into uncharted waters by suggesting that students who could not be successful in the general physical education program could benefit from a program of physical education that included modification or adaptation.

Accordingly, it is incorrect now to view adapted physical education as a specific regimen of rehabilitative activities or as an explanation for "what goes on" in a particular area, room, or class. Rather, adapted physical education can be thought of as a program of physical activity designed for students with a disability. As a program, adapted physical education contributes not only to the physical and motor development of the students, but also to growth in the social, language, emotional, and cognitive domains.

The needs, interests, and abilities of students with a disability must be considered in adapted physical education programs. A program should include appropriate modifications of the instruction, environment, and activity inasmuch as they enhance participation, yet it should continue to provide a challenge to the students. Adapted physical education programs should include activities for the development of physical fitness, psychomotor functioning, fundamental motor patterns, and skills or adaptations thereof for participation in activities of daily living, aquatics, dance, and individual and group games and sports, including lifetime, recreational, and competitive experiences.

The emphasis of all adapted physical education services is to facilitate the student's participation with age-appropriate, typically developing peers, and to provide access to the general physical education curriculum. A collaborative consultation approach is beneficial because it facilitates the student's participation in general physical education and creates an environment for more inclusive types of physical education programming (see Chapter 2 for more information about collaboration and a team approach).

In the 1970s, the term *adapted physical activity* was introduced to acknowledge that the concept of adapted physical education should be expanded beyond the school setting and physical education programs. Since then, adapted physical activity has gained international acceptance (e.g., International Federation of Adapted Physical Activity) and is considered the umbrella term (Doll-Tepper & DePauw, 1996). **Adapted physical activity** is now defined as *cross-disciplinary theory and practice that attempts to identify and solve motor problems throughout the life span; develop and implement theories that support access to sport and active lifestyle; and develop cooperative home–school–community service delivery and empowerment systems* (DePauw & Sherrill, 1994; Sherrill & DePauw, 1997).

HISTORICAL PERSPECTIVES OF ADAPTED PHYSICAL ACTIVITY AND ADAPTED PHYSICAL EDUCATION

The roots of adapted physical activity (i.e., physical education for individuals with a disability) can be traced to the curative physical regimens found in China in 2700 B.C. These early regimens relied on activities such as gymnastics, preventive exercise, and therapeutic exercise to alleviate physical disorders and illnesses of the time. In the days of the early Greeks, emphasis was placed on the development of the body and a balance of mental, social, and physical training. Thus, strong and healthy bodies were valued and developed through programs of physical training as well as through the curative aspects of physical activity.

Adapted physical activity and education have been strongly influenced by both a medical and an educational perspective that emanated from the European cultures during the 1800s (Sherrill & DePauw, 1997). Per Henrik Ling (1776–1839) of Sweden advanced medical gymnastics, while sensorimotor training (an educational approach) evolved from the work of Jean Marc Itard (1775–1839) of France. Medical gymnastics, used initially by physicians to prevent illness and to promote health, provided the basis for physical education programs in the United States. The first physical educators were physicians who advocated for "education of the physical," thereby giving a medical orientation to physical education. In the mid-1900s, special educators and perceptual motor theorists in the United States promoted sensorimotor training for use with individuals with a disability. This educational approach influenced the development of physical education, particularly adapted physical education.

Prior to the world wars, individuals with physical and mental impairments received virtually no formal physical education. Little changed until after World War I, when the needs of returning war veterans allowed the structure of programs to be changed. The success of physical rehabilitation for war veterans helped promote the use of physical activity in the schools for the development and enjoyment of students with a disability. These early programs in corrective physical education functioned under the medical model, being both remedial and therapeutic in nature. During this period, which lasted from the 1920s to the 1950s, corrective physical education developed as an entity separate from physical education.

Physical education for individuals with a disability, or adapted physical education, emerged as a separate entity in the 1950s and 1960s. Prior to this time, the subdiscipline of adapted physical education was tied to the parent discipline of physical education and aligned closely with the medical orientation of corrective physical education. Beginning in the 1950s, the name and nature of physical activity programs for individuals with a disability evolved through such nomenclatures as medical, therapeutic, rehabilitative, healing, remedial, corrective, curative, special, developmental, and adapted (Sherrill, 1998). For a detailed discussion of the changing nature of adapted physical education, see Sherrill and DePauw (1997) and DePauw and Sherrill (1994).

EVOLVING SOCIETAL CONTEXT OF DISABILITY

History documents society's treatment of individuals with a disability along a continuum of exclusion to inclusion (DePauw, 1986; DePauw & Doll-Tepper, 2000). Across the centuries, individuals with a disability were killed, tortured, exorcised, sterilized, ignored, exiled, exploited, pitied, cared for, categorized, educated, and even considered divine. Although today we might judge some of these actions as harsh, the actions were consistent and must be viewed in the societal and cultural context of their time.

- Superstition and survival were key elements during the primitive and ancient periods (3000 B.C. to 500 B.C.). During this time, not only were those with physical deformities often left to face the consequences of the harsh environment, but superstition led to the treatment of those with obvious impairments as either feared or possessed.

- In the early Greek and Roman days, the treatment of individuals with a disability was based in part on their value to society. For example, those who became physically impaired in battle were honored as heroes and those with mental impairments were considered with superstition and treated accordingly through purification, exorcism, and other demonological practices. During a brief period of humanitarian reform, Hippocrates and Plato advocated care of those with an impairment, care that included physical activity, hydrotherapy, and massage.

- During the Middle Ages, individuals with physical and mental impairments who survived the harsh environment experienced limited status. The onset of Christianity helped to change previous practice, in that those with intellectual impairments were considered "innocents," free of evil and allowed to live, while individuals defined as "mentally ill" were thought to be evil or possessed by the devil and treated with exorcism and the like.

- The systematic education of individuals with an impairment began in the late 17th and early 18th centuries, when the influence of science and medicine instilled an interest in the treatment and cure of "disabling" conditions. This interest resulted in the era of remediation, during which residential "schools for the mentally retarded," "asylums for the mentally ill," and "schools for the blind/visually impaired" were developed and flourished. During the 19th century, the emphasis of treatment shifted away from "curing" the individual to educational treatment, although residential institutions and schools were often maintained as lifelong residences.

- The 20th century can be viewed as a period of social reform, increased government involvement, a categorization of "handicapping conditions," and, finally, the emergence of a concern about disability rights. The educational approach of the 19th century provided the basis for developmental programs and individualization. Federal and state legislation influenced the education, work, and civil rights of individuals with a disability.

The medical model dominant throughout history was instrumental in fostering current notions about disability as a "physical or psychological condition considered to have predominately medical significance" (Linton, 1998, p. 10) and primarily a problem of the individual (Oliver, 1990). This "medicalization of disability casts human variation as deviance from the norm, as pathological condition, as deficit" (Linton, 1998, p. 11), resulting in an emphasis upon conditions or characteristics (impairments) and the reliance upon a categorical approach (discussed later in this chapter) to treatment and intervention.

During the 1990s, the disability rights movement and the newly emerging academic discipline of disability studies challenged professionals to reconceptualize disability in the context of social relationships (e.g., Chappell, 1992; Davis, 1995; Linton, 1998) and a social theory (e.g., Oliver, 1990). At the core of this movement is the simple belief that disability is socially constructed and is not tragic or pitiable (DePauw, 1997; Shapiro, 1993, p. 20).

This understanding of disability has implications for adapted physical education and requires professionals to examine the paradigm underlying our programs and services. Condeluci (1995) challenges professionals to promote a shift from a dependence model (e.g., medical model) to an interdependence model. He identifies four existing paradigms utilized within the human services profession—medical, educational, economic, and maintenance. The approach used initially in adapted physical education was based on the **medical model,** which *tends to focus on deficits, is driven by experts, and promotes fix or change of the individual.* Although the **educational model,** used more recently in adapted physical education, *shifts the emphasis from deficits to the student's lack of knowledge and inability,* Condeluci (1995) encourages the adoption of a new paradigm of **interdependence** that *focuses on the capacities of the individual, stresses relationships, and encourages an understanding and analysis of systems.* In 1993, Sherrill proposed the **social minority model,** which *emphasizes the individual, uniqueness, empowerment, and social stigma as shared experience in contrast to the medical model of deficit and biological or psychological anomaly.*

LEGAL AND PROFESSIONAL CONTEXTS OF DISABILITY

Just as there are laws that affect society at large, so there are laws that affect specific segments of that society. Since the early 1970s, Congress has enacted several powerful and comprehensive laws regarding individuals with disabilities. The following laws, listed in chronological order, contain mandates in the areas of physical education, recreation, and sport for individuals with a disability:

- Public Law 93-112, Section 504 of the Rehabilitation Act of 1973 (also called simply Section 504)
- Public Law 94-142, Education for All Handicapped Children Act of 1975
- Public Law 95-606, Amateur Sports Act of 1978 (amended and renamed in 1998 to become the Olympic and Amateur Sports Act)
- Public Law 99-372, The Handicapped Children's Protection Act of 1986
- Public Law 99-457, Education of the Handicapped Act Amendments of 1986
- Public Law 101-336, Americans with Disabilities Act (ADA) of 1990
- Public Law 101-476, Individuals with Disabilities Education Act of 1990 (IDEA) and reauthorization resulting in PL 105-17, IDEA (IDEA '97)
- Public Law 108-446, Individuals with Disabilities Education Improvement Act (IDEA '04)

The Rehabilitation Act

Section 504 of the Rehabilitation Act of 1973, a federal civil rights law protecting individuals with a disability, reflects the government's commitment to end discrimination on the basis of disability and to bring individuals with a disability into the mainstream of society. This section implies much of the same education mandate as the Education for All Handicapped Children Act, along with the all-encompassing civil rights issues. The regulations apply to all recipients of direct federal financial assistance, including state departments of education, school districts, and colleges and universities.

All federally assisted programs and activities must be operated without discrimination on the basis of "handicap" (see Figure 1.1). The regulations forbid employment discrimination against qualified individuals with a disability. Reasonable accommodation is expected—both facilities and programs must be accessible.

FIGURE 1.1

All federally assisted programs and activities must be operated without discrimination on the basis of "handicap."

Americans with Disabilities Act

The Americans with Disabilities Act (ADA) was enacted in July 1990 with the stated purpose of increasing accessibility for individuals with a disability. Its wide-ranging mandates cover employment, public services, public accommodations, and telecommunications. The ADA is considered civil rights legislation and as such includes a section specifically prohibiting any violation of the civil rights of individuals with a disability. The ADA's protections apply primarily, but not exclusively, to individuals who are disabled and uses the following definition of an individual with a disability, found originally in the Rehabilitation Act: An individual is **disabled** if *he or she meets at least one of the following tests:*

- *Has a physical or mental impairment that substantially limits one or more of one's major life activities*
- *Has a record of such an impairment*
- *Is regarded as having such an impairment*

Individuals with Disabilities Education Act

Federal law ensures the civil right of individuals with a disability to a public education. The current law (IDEA '04) is essentially a composite of previous statutory provisions (the Education for All Handicapped Children Act, its 1986 amendments, and the 1991 amendments to the 1990 IDEA) and is a reauthorization and revision of IDEA '97. Free appropriate public education was extended to children with disabilities between the ages of 3 to 5 years by PL 99-

457. This law also created a new program for infants, toddlers, and their families that required the development of individualized family service plans. The specific purposes of IDEA '04 are:

- To ensure that all children with a disability have access to a free, appropriate public education that emphasizes special education and related services designed to meet their unique educational needs and prepare them for further education, employment, and independent living
- To ensure that the rights of children with a disability and their parents or guardians are protected
- To help states and localities provide for the education of all children with a disability, including early intervention services for infants and toddlers with disabilities and their families, and improve educational results through research, professional preparation, technical assistance and support, and assessment of effectiveness.

More so than any other legislation, the Education for All Handicapped Children Act has demonstrated the federal government's commitment to the education of all children with a disability. It outlines procedures to protect the right of these children to a free, appropriate public education in the least restrictive environment. Since the Act's passage in 1975, amendments and revisions resulted ultimately in the enactment of IDEA in 1990 and its reauthorizations as IDEA '97 and most recently as IDEA '04. In enacting this legislation, Congress has found that having a disability does not diminish the right of individuals to participate in or contribute to society and that education for children with disabilities is an essential element of national policy that ensures equality of opportunity, full participation, independent living, and economic self-sufficiency for individuals with disabilities. Although amendments have altered some procedures and mandated new provisions, the intent has not changed. The key components of IDEA are articulated in Table 1.1.

TABLE 1.1 *Key provisions, promises, and revisions of IDEA.*

PROVISIONS

- Free appropriate public education from early childhood through graduation
- Appropriate evaluation
- Individualized education program including goals for academic achievement and functional performance
- Education in the least restrictive environment
- Parent and student participation in decision making
- Procedural due process
- Highly qualified teachers

PROMISES

- Raising expectations for children with a disability
- Increasing parental involvement in education
- Ensuring that regular education teachers are involved in planning and assessing children's progress
- Including children with a disability in assessments, performance goals, and reports to the public
- Supporting quality professional development for all personnel who are involved in educating children with a disability

REVISIONS (IDEA '04)

- Provides greater flexibility for parents and schools to make minor changes to a child's individualized education program (IEP) during the school year
- Incorporates academic achievement and functional performance within a child's individualized education program
- Simplifies the rules for transition services (activities that help a student begin planning for life after high school)
- Requires teachers to be highly qualified

Free, Appropriate Public Education

The basic mandate of IDEA, while encompassing several key issues, requires a free, appropriate public education in the least restrictive environment for individuals with a disability that is specifically identified by the Act (see Appendix C for a description of each identified disability). This education must be provided at public expense, under public supervision and direction, and without charge. The education should be provided for individuals from infancy through secondary education and must be provided in conformity with an individual's education plan. Because some states' requirements surpass the federal mandates, this free, appropriate public education must also meet a particular state's standards.

Least Restrictive Environment

The education of children with a disability must be provided in the least restrictive environment. Each public agency must ensure, to the maximum extent appropriate, that children with a disability are educated with typically developing children. Special classes and separate schooling for children with a disability may still be used as alternatives to regular education only when the nature or severity of the disability is such that regular classroom education with the use of supplementary aids and services cannot be achieved satisfactorily.

Individualized Education Program

IDEA '04 requires that the free, appropriate public education in the least restrictive environment include an individualized education program (IEP) for every child served. The IEP must include goals for academic achievement and functional performance. The **IEP** is defined as *a written statement, developed and implemented in accordance with federal regulations, that must be prepared for any child with a disability who is served in public education, as well as for a child placed in a private school by a state or local educational agency.*

The IEP is jointly prepared by all persons directly concerned with the education of the child. The IEP committee must include the child's teacher, a representative of the public education agency other than the child's teacher, one or both of the parents, the child (when appropriate), and any other individual deemed necessary by the parent(s) or agency. If the child's teacher is not a general education teacher, then a general education teacher must be part of the committee as well. When the IEP includes physical education services, the adapted physical educator or general physical educator should participate in its development, revision, and review. IDEA '04 provides flexibility for minor adjustments to the IEP during the school year and allows for alternative means of communicating among the IEP team.

The Legal Impact of Federal Legislation (IDEA '97 and Section 504) on Physical Education and Sport

IDEA '97 had a significant impact on physical education for individuals with a disability. Physical education must be made available to every child with a disability receiving a free, appropriate public education. Each child must be afforded the opportunity to participate in a general physical education program unless the child is enrolled in a separate facility or the child requires an adapted physical education program as specified by the IEP. By definition, **physical education** means *the development of*

- *Physical and motor fitness*
- *Fundamental motor skills and patterns*
- *Skills in aquatics, dance, and individual and group games and sports (including intramural and lifetime sports)*

According to Section 504, physical education, athletics, and intramurals must be provided for persons with a disability when they are provided for typically developing individuals. The federal law prohibits discrimination on the basis of disability in accessibility to physical education programs, athletic competitions, athletic scholarships, and sport or physical education facilities. Separate programs for individuals with a disability are appropriate if the programs and facilities are comparable.

Amateur Sports Act of 1978

Because equal opportunity for individuals with a disability was brought to the forefront by the Education for All Handicapped Children Act and Section 504, when the Amateur Sports Act of 1978 was enacted, provisions for athletes with a disability were included (DePauw & Clarke, 1986). In 1998, the Amateur Sports Act was amended and renamed the Olympic and Amateur Sports Act (OASA) in order to broaden the scope of responsibility of the United States Olympic Committee (USOC). As a result, the Paralympics are incorporated into the USOC, clearly reflecting an equal status for athletes with a disability. Although the OASA continues the original focus of the Amateur Sports Act (to integrate disability sports with the national governing bodies), it also allows the USOC to recognize Paralympic sports organizations if integration does not serve the best interests of athletes with a disability or if a national governing body objects to integration. The USOC is officially recognized as a National Paralympic Committee for representation to the International Paralympic Committee.

Because of the Olympic and Amateur Sports Act and an increased awareness and acceptance of athletes with a disability, developmental sport programs are needed for young athletes with a disability. Physical educators must be aware of this growing need and the role that physical education can play in the development of athletes with a disability. Discussion of opportunities for physical educators to promote sport for their students is included in Chapter 15.

CATEGORICAL THINKING AND THE NONCATEGORICAL APPROACH

Our society tends to impose labels on individuals, particularly those who are perceived to be physically, mentally, emotionally, or socially different. Labeling individuals with a disability has perpetuated the earlier belief that "the problem is in the child." In various ways, society has created and continues to create many of the conditions under which individuals are "handicapped."

Terms such as *impaired*, *disabled*, and *handicapped* have often been used synonymously and interchangeably to label individuals, allowing for no real understanding of their strengths and limitations. Too often, an individual's potential—what he or she can do—is discussed but not implemented because programs, activities, and efforts focus on the person's disability and deficiency—what he or she cannot do. Often, more attention is paid to the "what" rather than the "why" of performance disorders. Although the educator should consider an individual's impairment and its implications for activity, the primary focus should be on the ability of each individual, the environmental conditions, and the interaction of the individual in the environment.

The Effects of Labeling

Labels are commonplace in our society; this is especially true when identifying individuals with disabilities. Because traditional categorical labeling has been used in federal and state legislation, this identification by categories (e.g., conditions or impairments) is easily recognizable and still considered necessary for obtaining government services and assistance. Traditional categorical labeling has few benefits, however, when weighed against the detrimental effects observed in the practical application of educating individuals with a disability. **Person-first language,** *identifying the person first rather than the disability (e.g., "individual with a disability" rather than "disabled individual"),* should be used as it communicates respect and acknowledges the dignity of a person.

Many problems are inherent to labeling:

- Labeling encourages overgeneralization about a disability and the individuals with that disability. Labeling assumes that the population is homogeneous—that all those in the population are alike—which is simply not true. Not all "blind" individuals are totally blind. Individuals with cerebral palsy vary in their motor ability, depending on the type and degree of impairment. No two individuals with an intellectual impairment are identical, any more than two without intellectual impairment are the same.

- Labeling encourages under-expectation. Research has shown that teachers' expectations can change depending on what they are told about a given student. Because of the stereotypes attributed to those with disabilities, students with a disability often are not expected to perform at the same level as their typically developing peers.

- Labels become permanent. A label and its characteristics tend to become a "possession" that an individual carries throughout life. Labeling emphasizes the condition, not the individual. In this way, disability rather than ability becomes the focus of attention. When the focus is on disability, a reading problem becomes "dyslexia," and problems encountered in learning are labeled "learning disabilities." Thus, problems are merely renamed rather than resolved.

- Both students and educators may tend to use labels to relieve responsibility for changing behavior. Labeling perpetuates the outdated concept that the problem is "in the child," relieving the educator from the responsibility for effecting any behavior change. Labeling emphasizes stability, not change, and change is what is needed in the education of individuals with a disability.

Categorical and Noncategorical Approaches to Programming

Historically, individuals with a disability have been classified, categorized, and provided with programs according to specific physical, mental, emotional, or social conditions. Basic to this **categorical approach** is *the false assumption that all those with a particular condition (e.g., impairment) have identical needs, interests, and abilities.* The failure to recognize the uniqueness of each person negates the concept of individual difference. As stated previously, there is as much diversity among those with the same condition (impairment) as there is among individuals with other conditions or with no impairment at all. Planning and programming on the basis of category (as defined by the law) must be reevaluated in deference to planning and programming on the basis of the individual and the performance of that individual in the learning environment.

As specifically applied to physical education and recreation programs, the **noncategorical approach** *focuses on individuals as they function in various types and levels of programs and activities and deals with the whole person, not with a condition that may or may not affect the person's ability to perform certain movements, skills, and activities.* As a complement to the noncategorical approach, the developmental approach emphasizes the students' abilities rather than their disabilities.

Thus, categories and conditions per se should not be the major criteria in physical education programs, although knowledge of the impairments can provide some information necessary to working with a particular individual. Acknowledging and understanding the child's impairment provides the physical educator with useful knowledge, but the condition does not provide more than a generalization when applied to a given individual with a disability. For example, the definition of mental retardation includes below-average general intelligence, below-average language development, delayed motor development, and deficits in adaptive behavior. Within this definition lies a range of variability that can only be applied generally to an individual—within below-average general intelligence, the child may function along a continuum from mild to significant mental impairment. Another example is a child with a special education designation of deaf and hearing impaired. The designation may indicate that an alternative communication method (e.g., total communication—verbal and sign language) might be necessary (depending on the level of hearing loss), but it may not inform the teacher of any additional unique abilities or limitations. In many cases, the categorical label alone does not provide adequate information for planning a physical education program.

Although information about impairments can help the educator to understand, evaluate, and develop an effective program, it should be regarded as only providing guidelines (see Appendix C for spe-

---

Teaching Tip

THE POWER OF LANGUAGE • What do you see first? The wheelchair? The physical problem—or the person? Consider some kind of change in the focus of your language. Language is powerful, and it mirrors, reinforces, and sometimes shapes our perceptions of people. Positive communication and interaction are facilitated through words that reflect a positive attitude and awareness. Using the right words can make a dramatic difference in the lives of the children we teach. It is important to:

1. Focus on the individual, not the label of the disability (e.g., instead of saying "my disabled student," say "my student, who has a disability"). It is a small difference, but one that helps to present the child as more important than the disability.

2. Be positive. Words like "helpless" or "I feel sorry" or "pity" convey negative feelings. A person with cerebral palsy is not a "CP victim." Think of the image that emotional words create. Use words that are positive and accurate (e.g., a wheelchair does not "confine" but instead allows the person to move around easily and play with others).

3. Be accurate. Remember that "deaf and dumb" and "deaf mute" are out-of-date terminology, and "spastic" refers to an involuntary muscle spasm, not a person. Avoid words that can be used as put-downs (e.g., retard).

4. Remember that the words "I can't" do not apply to students with a disability, or to their peers without a disability. All children "can do" something—even the child with visual impairment may want to be a basketball player and should be allowed the opportunity to participate in the activity when he or she has the desire (interest, motivation). It is the professional's responsibility to look at the environment and make the necessary changes or adaptations or provide the supports needed so that all children can participate to the best of their ability—to challenge them to increase their skills, especially when they are motivated or interested in specific activities. The choice of words, language, and communication used within the physical education activity setting facilitates children's participation and growth.

cific information about impairments). The emphasis should be placed on the individual's needs, interests, and capabilities. Adopting a noncategorical (and developmental) approach to providing physical education for individuals with a disability provides for a natural transition to the philosophy and practice of inclusive physical education.

INCLUSION AND INCLUSIVE PHYSICAL EDUCATION

Inclusion, along with its definition, benefits, and implementation, was the focus of much debate in the adapted physical activity arena during the late 1980s and 1990s (DePauw & Doll-Tepper, 2000), as well as in the special education arena. Much of the current inclusion debate took place in the context of "normal" or general physical education as it is socially constructed. Today, inclusive physical education programs exist in many schools, and numerous resources are available. These include books by Block (2000), Davis (2002), Hodge and colleagues (2003), Kasser (1995), and Lieberman and colleagues (1996, 2002).

The debate about inclusion, however, was primarily a dialogue in the United States. At the World Summit on Physical Education (November 3–5, 1999, in Berlin, Germany), it became quite evident that many countries' and worldwide efforts focus on integrating individuals with a disability with their typically developing peers. As a result, the Berlin Agenda, a document prepared at the World Summit, called for quality physical education for all and the development and implementation of inclusive physical education.

Inclusive physical education *must be more than a placement or a specific program; it must become an attitude or a teaching philosophy held by physical educators and adapted physical educators.* As we move toward inclusive physical education, considering the following guidelines will help us to create successful programs (adapted from DePauw & Doll-Tepper, 2000):

- All programs should be stimulating and varied.
- All expectations for students should be set at a level that challenges them individually and as a group.
- The climate should be open and affirming for everyone and conducive to learning.
- Programs should be meaningful to individuals, should focus on functionality, and should provide for a transition to an active lifestyle with family and community.
- Activities should be ability appropriate and age appropriate.

In addition to the well-known benefits of physical activity (e.g., physical, cognitive, psychological, vocational), the opportunity to be taught together with peers who are without a disability offers additional social benefits. Although applicable to all students in the learning environment, the following benefits may be of primary importance to individuals with a disability (DePauw, 2000):

- Opportunity to develop the social skills necessary to interact with others
- Opportunity to develop friendships with peers with and without disabilities
- Opportunity to interact with age-appropriate role models among typically developing peers
- Decreased isolation
- Increased expectations and challenges
- Attitude changes among peers and increased acceptance
- Increased appreciation of differences
- Greater understanding of disability rights and equity

PROFESSIONAL ROLES AND PREPARATION

The ever-changing issues and trends in our society inevitably shape the environment in which physical education must operate. The implementation of federal and state legislation places greater demands on the field, increasing the roles and teaching environments in which both the generalist in physical education and the specialist in adapted physical education must function. The need for well-qualified teachers places increasing demands on professional preparation programs (colleges and universities) and professional certification programs (national certification and state teacher licensure).

Physical Education Generalist

Due to legislation enacted in the 1970s, individuals with a disability attend general physical education classes. Although this is not a new phenomenon, the number of such students in general education classes has increased. Thus, general physical educators must have a basic knowledge and understanding of students with a disability and must possess the necessary competencies, skills, techniques, and resources to face the challenges of teaching these students in general physical education classes. Due to their increased role in the education of children with disabilities, general physical educators should be prepared to participate in the IEP meetings.

In more urban areas, school districts are able to hire both specialists in adapted physical education and physical educators. In these school districts, specialists can assist generalists who find themselves teaching physical education to individuals with a disability.

The situation in rural areas often is quite different. Specialists are often not available, and adapted physical education then falls within the job description of the general physical educator. Sometimes, the special educator is asked to provide physical education to students in special education classes. Although neither of these alternatives is the most desirable, providing physical education to *all* students is the primary responsibility of those who are trained as physical educators.

Adapted Physical Education Specialist

Adapted physical education specialists work in a variety of teaching environments. Some, trained as specialists, teach in general education, working with students with disabilities and those without. Others, itinerant teachers, are assigned to more than one school in a particular area and must travel daily or weekly to teach adapted physical education at multiple locations. Still others work in a single special education school, instructing and providing service in physical education to students with a disability. Two or three adapted physical education teachers may be assigned to one special education site (although in most states this is quite rare). Adapted physical educators are also employed by residential facilities or institutions in many states and sometimes by private schools.

Adapted physical education teachers, no matter the working environment, must usually be capable of working with any student with a disability. Their students may include individuals from infancy through transition beyond school years, those who perform across the full range of motor ability, and those with physical, emotional, learning, or sensory impairments.

The duties of adapted physical education teachers may include evaluating and advising the regular physical education and classroom teachers, participating as members of multidisciplinary IEP committees, and teaching and assessing children with a disability. In addition, they may be required to provide in-service training, demonstrations, and community or liaison services. For more information about roles and responsibilities utilizing a team approach, see Chapter 2.

Adapted physical education specialists may also become program specialists, consultants, coordinators, supervisors, and administrators of adapted physical education programs. University and community college teaching is a growing area that needs trained adapted physical education specialists, both for applied service and for teaching academic courses.

Adapted Physical Education National Standards

Recent efforts by the National Consortium on Physical Education and Recreation for Individuals with Disabilities (NCPERID) resulted in the development of Adapted Physical Education National Standards (APENS) and certification for adapted physical educators. The purpose of the project was "to ensure that physical education instruction for students with disabilities is provided by qualified physical education instructors. To achieve this end, the project has developed national standards for the profession and a national certification examination to measure knowledge of these standards" to become a certified adapted physical educator (C.A.P.E.) (Kelly, 1999).

Standards (professional competencies) were developed in 15 areas: human development, motor behavior, exercise science, measurement and evaluation, history and philosophy, unique attributes of learners, curriculum theory and development, assessment, instructional design and planning, teaching, consultation and staff development, student and program evaluation, continuing education, ethics, and communication. APENS examinations and certifications are offered annually in a variety of locations around the country (for more information about the national standards or Adapted Physical Education National Standards [APENS 2006], see Appendix A).

SUMMARY

The changes in adapted physical activity and physical education have been significant, especially in the past 15 years. Adapted physical activity programs have broadened to address the needs of diverse populations (e.g., at-risk, those with HIV and AIDS), as well as to challenge those with a disability through physical activity (e.g., competitive sport, high-risk sports such as mountain climbing and sky diving). Today's physical activity programs provide more individualized activities and offer more choices; less emphasis is placed on the disability and its limits on physical activity and more emphasis is on the individual's interests, needs, and abilities. The categorical approach (e.g., activity for specific disability grouping and segregation), which characterized much of early adapted physical education, is finally giving way to programs that take a noncategorical approach and promote integration and inclusion. Embracing a philosophy of inclusive physical education and promoting active living will not only change the programs and the delivery systems of physical education for individuals with a disability but will also provide links from educational settings to community-based programs.

Learning Activities

1.1 Visit the website of the office of the Superintendent of Public Instruction in your state to review the state laws regarding physical education for individuals with a disability. Find the state's definition of adapted physical education. Discuss with your classmates the legal mandates for physical education and sport for individuals with a disability. Identify similarities and differences across states. Compare with the federal mandates as well.

1.2 Interview a physical educator to discuss effective strategies for including individuals with a disability in general physical education. Ask about the most successful strategies. Ask about the strategies that were not as successful and find out why these were less successful.

1.3 Talk with individuals who have a disability about their experiences in physical activity and sport settings. Ask about their interests and aspirations for being physically active throughout their life span. Reflect on their answers and how they might influence you as a teacher.

References

Adapted Physical Education National Standards (2nd ed.) (APENS, 2006). Available at humankinetics.com.

American Alliance for Health, Physical Education, Recreation, and Dance (AAHPERD, 1952). Guiding principles for adapted physical education. *Journal of Health, Physical Education, and Recreation, 23,* 15.

Block, M. E. (1994). Why all students with disabilities should be included in regular physical education. *Palaestra, 10,* 17-24.

Block, M. E. (2000). *A teacher's guide to including students with disabilities in general physical education (Teachers' Guides to Inclusive Practices).* Champaign, IL: Human Kinetics.

Chappell, A. L. (1992). Toward a sociological critique of the normalization principle. *Disability, Handicap, & Society, 7*(1), 35-50.

Condeluci, A. (1995). *Interdependence: The route to community.* Winter Park, FL: GR Press.

Davis, L. J. (1995). *Enforcing normalcy: Disability, deafness, and the body.* London: Verso.

Davis, R. W. (2002). *Inclusion through sports: A guide to enhancing sport experiences.* Champaign, IL: Human Kinetics.

Department of Education. (June 21, 2005). *Individuals with Disabilities Education Act Amendments of 2004.* Volume 70, Number 118. 34 CFR Parts 300, 301, and 304. Washington, D.C.: Author.

DePauw, K. P. (1986). Toward progressive inclusion and acceptance: Implications for physical education. *Adapted Physical Activity Quarterly, 3,* 1-6.

DePauw, K. P. (1997). The (In)Visibility of DisAbility: Cultural contexts and "sporting bodies." *Quest, 51,* 416-430.

DePauw, K. P. (2000). Social-cultural context of disability: Implications for scientific inquiry and professional practice. *Quest, 52,* 358-368.

DePauw, K. P., & Clarke, K. C. (1986). Sports for disabled U.S. citizens: Influence of Amateur Sports

Act. In C. Sherrill (Ed.), *Sport and disabled athletes* (pp. 41–50). Champaign, IL: Human Kinetics.

DePauw, K. P., & Doll-Tepper, G. M. (2000). Toward progressive inclusion and acceptance: Myth or reality? The inclusion debate and bandwagon discourse. *Adapted Physical Activity Quarterly, 17*, 135–143.

DePauw, K. P., & Sherrill, C. (1994). Adapted physical activity: Present and future. *Physical Education Review, 17*, 6–13.

Doll-Tepper, G., & DePauw, K. P. (1996). Theory and practice of adapted physical activity: Research perspectives. *Sport Science Review: Adapted Physical Activity, 5*(1), 1–11.

Hodge, S. R., Murata, N. M., Block, M. E., & Lieberman, L. J. (2003). *Case studies in adapted physical education: Empowering critical thinking.* Scottsdale, AZ: Holcomb Hathaway.

Kasser, S. L. (1995). *Inclusive Games.* Champaign, IL: Human Kinetics.

Kasser, S. L., & Lytle, R. K. (2005). *Inclusive physical activity: A lifetime of opportunities.* Champaign, IL: Human Kinetics.

Kelly, L. E. (1999). *Adapted physical education national standards (APENS).* Champaign, IL: Human Kinetics.

Lieberman, L. J., & Cowart, J. F. (1996). *Games for people with sensory impairments: Strategies for including individuals of all ages.* Champaign, IL: Human Kinetics.

Lieberman, L. J., & Houston-Wilson, C. (2002). *Strategies for inclusion: A handbook for physical educators.* Champaign, IL: Human Kinetics.

Linton, S. (1998). *Claiming disability: Knowledge and identity.* New York: NYU Press.

Morris, J. (1992). Personal and political: A feminist perspective on researching physical disability. *Disability, Handicap, & Society, 7*, 157–166.

Oliver, M. (1990). *The politics of disablement.* London: Macmillan Press.

Shapiro, J. (1993). *No pity: People with disabilities forging a new civil rights movement.* New York: Random House.

Sherrill, C. (1993). *Adapted physical activity, recreation and sport: Crossdisciplinary and lifespan.* Dubuque, IA: Brown.

Sherrill, C. (1994). Least restrictive environments and total inclusion philosophies: Critical analysis. *Palaestra, 10*, 25–28, 31, 34–35, 52–54.

Sherrill, C., & DePauw, K. P. (1997). History of adapted physical activity and education. In J. D. Massengale & R. A. Swanson (Eds.), *History of exercise and sport science* (pp. 39–108). Champaign, IL: Human Kinetics.

CHAPTER 2

The Collaborative Team

WORKING WITH FAMILIES AND EDUCATIONAL PROFESSIONALS

Guiding Questions

1. Why is it important for physical educators to possess skills for working on a collaborative team?

2. What are some communication skills important to the success of a collaborative team?

3. Describe the steps to problem solving.

4. What are some personal qualities important for effectively providing service to individuals with a disability?

5. Who are some of the individuals on the collaborative team and how do they work together to serve a child with a disability?

6. What are some emerging roles for the adapted physical educator?

Thanks to Rebecca Lytle, California State University, Chico, for her contributions to this chapter.

THE TEAM APPROACH

Professionals involved in the implementation of IDEA '04 are well aware of its demands for multidisciplinary interaction. Not only are modern structures of professional interaction mandated by this legislation, but concepts for the intermeshing of professional services must also be considered. The team approach is not new to the larger arena of service delivery to individuals with a disability. Teams have been dealing with the needs of individuals with a disability for many years. These teams have primarily emanated from the medical model, such as the acute care treatment team of doctor, nurse, and medical social worker. In education, however, the need for a team approach arose with the passage of the Education for All Handicapped Children Act in 1975. Since that time the role of the multidisciplinary team has evolved.

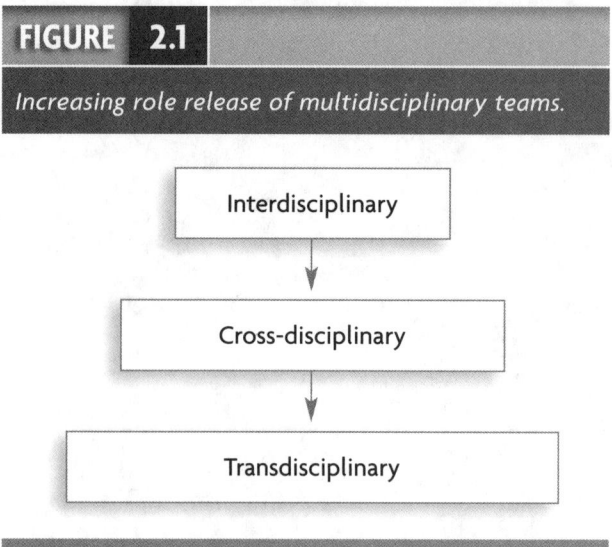

Increasing role release of multidisciplinary teams.

Multidisciplinary Teams

In educational contexts various and often confusing terms have been used to describe the multidisciplinary team, including transdisciplinary, cross-disciplinary, and interdisciplinary, without clear distinction. In general, the term **multidisciplinary team** merely refers to *a collection of professionals from varying disciplines*, while interdisciplinary, cross-disciplinary, and transdisciplinary refer more to how their interactions take place and the extent to which role release is involved. **Role release** refers to *the extent to which professionals share their ideas and interventions and allow others to implement these items that were traditionally implemented by a single professional.*

On an **interdisciplinary team,** *professionals come together to mesh their ideas.* This sharing of ideas is based on the fact that the ideas of many are better than those of just one in determining services and interventions for a child. On **cross-disciplinary teams,** *professionals "mix" job roles.* A therapist may teach a technique to the classroom teacher or physical educator, thus enabling the student to be moved through range of motion more frequently than the one or two times per week that the physical therapist sees the student directly. Finally, in the **transdisciplinary team** approach, *individuals work collaboratively in all aspects of the educational process, including assessing, designing, and determining goals jointly.* In most cases only one or two members of the team actually implement the interventions. This method is most frequently seen in early intervention and preschool programs. Figure 2.1 illustrates the increasing role release represented by the different types of multidisciplinary teams. Team members may cross disciplinary boundaries based on what is best for the child.

Regardless of the term used, the team approach involves a group of individuals from varying disciplines collaborating to determine the best possible way to provide educational services for a student with a disability.

Collaborative Teams

A broader term, **collaborative team,** applies to those specific contexts in which *multiple disciplines are being used, and* certainly suggests that *collaborative interactions are important.* From the outset of the service delivery process, IDEA '04 requires that each child have an individualized education program (IEP) team. The **IEP team** consists of *the parents, at least one general educator, at least one special educator, a representative from the local education agency, other professionals who have completed testing, and the child whenever appropriate.* The regulations further mandate the interaction of groups of personnel at least once a year for the purpose of reviewing and revising each child's IEP.

Thus, the law requires that many professionals provide input into the plan designed for each student's education, but it does not specifically require that professionals collaborate with one another to carry out that plan. However, research shows that teachers prefer a collaborative approach to the education of students with a disability (Lytle & Collier, 2002) and that successful collaboration requires formal training (Bradley, 1994; Gersten, Darch, Davis, & George, 1991). In all cases where multiple services are provided to an individual, a collaborative approach is desirable and most appropriate for delivering inter-

TABLE 2.1 *The collaborative process.*

CHARACTERISTICS OF THE MEMBERS INVOLVED IN THE COLLABORATIVE PROCESS	DUTIES OF COLLABORATIVE GROUPS WITHIN THE EDUCATIONAL SETTING
Share common beliefs and work toward common goals (working together to get the job done).	Focus on the child's individual strengths and provide support as needed.
Share group tasks, responsibilities, and leadership.	Share role release, ideas, and resources to maximize learning for the child.
Contribute unique perspectives and expertise.	Determine specific strategies to meet individual needs.
Have equal status, a nonhierarchical relationship.	Establish a working relationship in which all participants feel a part of the same team, including the parent and student.
Use consensus for problem solving and decisions (consensus is not the same as majority rule).	Use problem-solving strategies to work toward solutions for the child and family.
Strive for effective communication with others.	Document the process and ensure that everyone on the team has access to all available information.
Make a commitment to work with others.	Ensure that the needs of the child, family, and school are met.
Have an openness and willingness to share and learn.	Ensure that professionals and family are all heard and valued as part of the team.
Use good listening skills.	Create a safe environment for communication.
Be accountable for successes and challenges.	Celebrate joint successes.

ventions. To serve the best interests of the student, the physical educator must not only understand the needs of the whole individual but must also interact effectively across disciplinary boundaries.

CHARACTERISTICS OF EFFECTIVE COLLABORATORS

A collaborative team has two primary goals: to complete the task and to maintain positive working relationships among team members. Collaboration is a process in which all participants have an opportunity to facilitate the student's learning. Several skills and beliefs are important to remember when setting up the relationships within the school environment and with the parent. Each member of the collaborative team should consider the characteristics of the collaborative process as listed in Table 2.1.

In the past, interaction skills were not commonly stressed in physical education teacher preparation programs; however, more and more special education training programs are requiring a course in collaborative consultation as part of preservice training (Yocom & Cossairt, 1996). This section is devoted to a discussion of characteristics necessary for successful communication, interaction, and collaboration among professionals, including communication skills, problem-solving skills, and personal qualities.

Communication Skills

Communication skills are critical for the successful interaction of any collaborative team. Most individuals know how easily miscommunications can happen in everyday life. For this reason, it is imperative that professionals learn and practice effective communication techniques. We know from the literature that individuals who have had formal training are more successful collaborators (Bradley, 1994) and that individuals who have not had training in this area tend to avoid collaborative interactions (Gersten, Darch, Davis, & George, 1991). The development of awareness, knowledge, and skills in group dynamics should be prerequisite for participation on a team. If the school personnel serving on the multidisciplinary team do not possess the necessary skills, the educational agency should provide in-service training sessions to facilitate acquisition of these skills.

Effective communication skills are needed in order to identify goals for students and to prescribe educational priorities, sequences, strategies, implementation processes, materials, and evaluative procedures. Sharing information is an initial step toward providing a mechanism through which the collective wisdom of team members combines for the purpose of arriving at the most logical, productive, and efficient means to educate the child.

Communication implies shared meaning. This goal is possible through effective collaboration skills, including understanding each team member's frame of reference, building rapport, reflective listening, speaking skills, questioning strategies, observing nonverbal communication, and congruent message sending.

Frame of reference

In order for effective collaboration to take place, members must first understand each team member's frame of reference and appreciate, value, and encourage all contributions. **Frame of reference** refers to *the "lenses" through which an individual views the world.* An individual's perspective is based on previous experiences, values, beliefs, personal qualities, attitudes, and expectations of others. Professional training programs also influence one's frame of reference. It is important to acknowledge that each individual on the team comes to the interaction with different histories, experiences, and training. If these varying views are valued and respected, they can add to creative problem solving and provide a broader picture of the child from differing vantage points. However, if they are not valued and respected, conflicts can arise when team members expect others to embrace the same values, expectations, and views that they hold themselves.

Building rapport

Several factors contribute to establishing positive rapport. Following are some of the critical elements of creating positive relationships with the team members with whom you work:

■ Understanding the other person's frame of reference. This helps people feel valued and respected for their viewpoints and experiences, accepted for who they are, and not judged.

■ Listening patiently to others' concerns, needs, and issues. Effective listening can contribute significantly to building positive rapport and demonstrating that you understand the situation as it is presented by others (Dettmer, Dyck, & Thurston, 2004; Friend & Cook, 2002).

■ Saving suggestions until all information and ideas from others are shared. Often, new teachers feel that they must have "the answers" and want to share their expertise too soon. A new adapted physical education teacher might observe a student in a general education class and see that a change in teaching method or organization might make the student more successful. Coming to a situation with immediate suggestions for the other professional may be detrimental to establishing a positive relationship.

■ Respecting and valuing others' ideas. Listening to others' views of the situation and their concerns and ideas first will help build positive rapport and help you to understand the issues more thoroughly before making suggestions or beginning to problem solve. This is necessary even if the solutions are obvious to one of the team members. Every person must feel that his or her concerns are heard and validated.

Reflective listening

Reflective listening is an important skill to develop because it *allows the speaker to get feedback from the listener, indicating whether the meaning of what was said is clear.* An effective listener summarizes and restates the concepts presented by the speaker so that the speaker knows she or he was heard and the listener learns whether he or she has grasped the content presented. This technique further encourages the speaker to add information to the basic statements because the restatement or paraphrase tells the speaker that the meaning is being shared. Reflective listening may not be used in all team interactions, but it is often invaluable to ensure that a message is being heard and understood.

If reflective listening skills are common among team members, a typical interaction may sound like this:

Speaker: "Anytime we try to have a group game, Michael fights and gets angry and wants to quit the game."

Listener: "Michael doesn't function well in a group."

Speaker: "That's right, but when we play games such as four-square or handball, he performs well and his skills are about the same as the other students."

Listener: "He functions better in small groups."

Speaker: "Yes. He also does very well when I help him at his desk in the classroom, but when he gets into the reading group, he starts acting silly."

Listener: "He seems to lose control of his behavior when he's in a group."

Speaker: "Yes. I think he should be placed in a smaller class. We should implement a behavior modification program until he can function more consistently."

Listener: "I agree."

If all team members are competent in the use of this technique, far more communication can take place in considerably less time than is usually required for team meetings. In fact, at times individuals may resolve their own concerns through talking out loud and sharing the issues (Dettmer, Dyck, & Thurston, 2004). It is important that the listener truly listen to the content and refrain from behavior that can inhibit reflective listening such as daydreaming, rehearsing a response, or being distracted by extraneous noise or details about the speaker.

Speaking skills

After you have become an effective listener, you must develop effective speaking skills in order to reflect back what you heard, gather more information, share additional ideas, or check for understanding. Learn to organize your thoughts quickly and express them clearly. Speak loud enough to be heard but not so loud as to drown out other voices. Use words that are clear, concise, and understandable to the entire group. Be sure to use specific, concrete words when applicable instead of general or vague ones (e.g., "slouch" rather than "sit"). Whenever possible, avoid verbal clutter. Verbal clutter involves using extra words or sounds (e.g., "uh," "you know," or "if you will") or unnecessarily long phrases (e.g., "It is my opinion" instead of "I think").

As important as learning to express your thoughts clearly is learning to phrase them in a way that furthers the discussion. Two types of statements are helpful in promoting discussion: those that give information and those that seek information. The first type of statement is descriptive in nature; for example, "José is in Mr. Jones' first period physical education class" or "Kate likes to play tetherball and four-square during recess, but does not participate in physical education class." The second type of statement is used to gather more information that might be helpful; for example, "I'd really like to know more about Jack's medical history" or "I wonder what would happen if we asked the instructional assistant to come with him to physical education."

Following are some additional suggestions to help you express your point of view clearly and concisely when using statements that request or give information:

1. Use "I" statements. Talk about how you feel and how you interpret information or see the situation. Avoid "you" statements—"You didn't give me the notice in time for me to make the meeting."

2. Avoid words of absolute such as "always" and "never." For example, "Joe never dresses down for class and is always late." Chances are he has dressed down at least once and is not always late. These terms are usually exaggerations of what is actually happening and often make people feel defensive.

3. Avoid beginning a comment with "Yes, but. . . ." The word "yes" is affirming; however, as soon as you say "but" after the word "yes," you have negated the affirmation. The words "yes, but" really mean, "I disagree with you." Instead, change the word "but" to "and." This changes the meaning from negating the suggestion or comment to adding to it. It allows the previous comment to be acknowledged and affirmed and allows you to share additional ideas. For example, use "and" or "but" in the following statement and see how your choice changes the message. "I think Joe should be pulled from general physical education and receive adapted physical education." "Yes, _____ how about getting an aide for him or providing adapted physical education two days and keeping him in general physical education the other days."

4. State what you want or would like to have rather than focusing on what you don't want. No one on a team can help you with what you don't want; however, team members can work together to create a shared vision of what the team does want. For example, "I don't want to see Jan continue to be picked on in physical education" could be changed to "I'd like to see Jan feel good about participating in physical education and about her peers." This helps the team focus on what they need to do to accomplish a positive goal for Jan.

The previous examples of statements providing or requesting information are framed objectively. However, statements can also be presented in a variety of ways that reflect bias. They can attach labels, warn, advise, evaluate, or judge. Such nonobjective statements represent ineffective communication because they can inhibit discussion or provoke anger. Think about how you might feel if statements such as the following were made to you:

- All children with Down syndrome behave that way (labeling).
- If you use that teaching strategy with those children, they are going to be out of control (warning).
- You know, you really ought to talk to the counselor about that child's behavior (advising).
- Those cooperative games will never work with my class—they love competition (evaluating).
- All good teacher training programs teach you how to make modifications for different skill levels (judging).

Questioning strategies

Questions serve a variety of functions including gathering information, providing information, and clarifying or confirming information. The primary and most straightforward function of questions is to seek information. Examples include:

- Where is José's physical education class?
- When is his next IEP meeting?
- What would you like to see José working on in adapted physical education?

Another type of question is one that provides unrequested information or is advisory. This type of question may not, however, support positive interactions, such as:

- Did you know that Jan is receiving physical therapy two times a week?
- Do you think the parents will appreciate a separate placement for Jan?
- Why would you want to try teaching her how to ride a bike?

These questions may be seeking or providing more information than is necessary. Before asking a question, professionals should reflect on the purpose of the question.

Finally, questions can also be used for clarification (as indicated in the listening skills discussion). This is an effective way to ensure that you have understood what is being shared. For example:

- You want the physical education teacher to focus on eye–hand coordination skills?
- You would like to use the same behavioral intervention plan in adapted physical education?
- You will be available to meet on Tuesdays and Thursdays?

These questions help to confirm information shared.

Questions can also be open-ended or closed-ended. A closed question is one with limited responses—"Do you want to play four-square or tetherball?" or "Did Rebecca cooperate in class today?" Both of these questions give the listener a choice between two answers. On the other hand, an open-ended question allows for elaboration and a variety of responses. If we changed the two examples to open-ended questions, they might be phrased as, "What kinds of things do you like to play during recess?" and "Tell me, how does Rebecca participate during physical education class?"

Both open and closed questions are important for effective communication, depending on the nature of the information being solicited. Open-ended questions can be more effective when establishing rapport or gathering information about a new student or situation. Open-ended questions allow the speaker to respond freely and elaborate on any ideas or concerns. They provide the listener with information about what is important to the speaker and the speaker's issues and frame of reference. Closed questions are appropriate when seeking specific information—"Can you meet for the IEP on Thursday at 3:00 p.m.?"

Observing nonverbal communication

Another skill needed by team members is the ability to observe and respond to the nonverbal elements of communication. **Kinesics,** or *the body language of the speaker,* enhances the verbal part of the message considerably. A speaker who leans forward, gestures strongly, or has very animated facial expressions communicates differently than one who leans back with arms folded and has no expression (Mostert, 1997).

The physical distance between members of the team can also enhance or stifle group communication (Friend & Cook, 2002). In American culture, physical closeness during communication represents trust and commonality. Team members who are not willing to sit next to one another or who pull their chairs away from the group may be demonstrating a lack of trust or cohesiveness with the group. Individuals with a larger personal space requirement may consistently move away in any context, but this pattern is easily distinguished from a lack of trust. Even the location within the group represents various positions of power and either encourages or suppresses communi-

---

How Would You Respond?

INEFFECTIVE COMMUNICATION

How might you rephrase each of the following statements into more effective communicative statements or questions? When finished, read the authors' responses on the next page.

1. If I were you, I would never consider placing my child in that program.
2. You should have your child evaluated by a physical therapist.
3. You should have a behavior management plan in place.
4. You shouldn't feel that way.
5. If you don't change your teaching strategy, he is never going to learn to catch.
6. That specialist is always late to meetings.

cation. At a rectangular table, the seats at the ends and the middle of the sides are stronger positions and most conducive to communication because they allow for full eye contact with all members. These are also the positions of power—this is why a corporate chairman of the board sits at the end of the table, in a position to have the full, undivided attention of all other board members. The corner positions tend to be the weakest because people in those positions are closer than the accepted range of comfortable interpersonal communication with the individuals in the stronger positions; hence, their ability to take leadership may be limited. Where one feels most comfortable in a group setting and what position will most enhance one's ability to communicate are issues professionals should consider before going into a team meeting. An educator who is facilitating an IEP meeting can enhance the team members' equity by holding the meeting at a round table. This may also help the parent feel more a part of the team.

Vocal intonation, also known as *paralanguage* or *vocal cues*, is another aspect of nonverbal communication that must be understood by team members. Speech volume and pacing are important aspects of language use. Inflections implying certainty, commitment, and competence must be understood as well.

Finally, body movements such as facial expression and eye contact are also important elements of nonverbal language. For example, a teacher says, "I really like working with Kim" while rolling her eyes. This sends a very different message than if the teacher makes the same statement while looking the listener straight in the eye. Members of effective collaborative teams often ask other members for feedback regarding their communicative behaviors in a meeting. Examples of such questions might be, "Were my gestures too strong when I was making that point to the parent? Did I give enough eye contact when reporting my test results or was I reading from my notes too much?"

It is important to remember that different cultures have different expectations for nonverbal interactions. The use of eye contact, physical contact, and gestures varies greatly across cultures. In one culture, it may be appropriate to kiss each cheek of a person upon meeting for the first time, while in another a head bow with no physical contact is most appropriate to show respect. In the United States, a student looking at his shoes while a teacher is talking to him may seem like he is avoiding the interaction and not paying attention; however, depending on the child's family background, this behavior may be the child's way of showing respect to the teacher. It is important for all members of the team to value and appreciate one another's nonverbal expectations and cultural norms. Following are some suggestions that may help team members become more aware of cultural differences:

- Read about other cultures.
- Examine your values and beliefs as well as your ways of responding and interacting.
- Recognize the various cultural differences in nonverbal communication.
- Determine whether formalized team meetings tend to encourage interaction or silence from different groups of people.

Teaching Tip

VOCAL INTONATION • The same words can have very different meanings depending on where the speaker places the emphasis when delivering the message. For example, say the following sentence under two different conditions:

1. Place emphasis on the word "my."
2. Place emphasis on the word "assessment."

My assessment isn't really conclusive.

Under the first condition, the implication is that some other person's assessment may be conclusive. Under the second condition, the implication is that some other procedure or set of data is conclusive.

The Authors Respond

INEFFECTIVE COMMUNICATION

When rephrased, the statements now either seek information or provide information in a nonjudgmental way.

1. Tell me about all of the placement options available to you.
2. Perhaps you would like to talk with the physical therapist about any concerns you may have.
3. Let's see if the team can come up with some ideas or strategies to help with the behavioral concerns.
4. It sounds like you are frustrated with the situation.
5. Tell me about the ideas you have to help him learn to catch.
6. Perhaps we can wait a few more minutes and then go ahead and start the meeting. I will take minutes so those who cannot make it will know what was discussed.

- Try to understand behavior as a function of one's culture.
- Become aware of the varying beliefs about the nature of disability and how a belief might affect a family's interaction style.

As discussed earlier in the section on building rapport, it is always important to understand others' frames of reference, listen attentively and patiently, and respect and value others' ideas, perspectives, and cultures.

MAKING CONNECTIONS

Responding to Nonverbal Communication

Maria Enriquez's mother is from Mexico and does not speak very much English. Jane, the adapted physical educator, interpreted Mrs. Enriquez's facial expression to mean that she was distressed by all of the professional information that was being presented during her first IEP, even with the translator. Before Jane shared any of her report, she paused, reached over, and held Mrs. Enriquez's hand while she said, "You have the most beautiful daughter. You must be very proud of her." Mrs. Enriquez smiled for the first time since the beginning of the meeting.

Congruent message sending

Another competency needed for interdisciplinary functioning is congruent message sending (Friend & Cook, 2002). This refers to the agreement between the verbal and nonverbal aspects of the message. For example, if an acquaintance greets you with the familiar question, "How are you today?" it may be obvious from nonverbal cues that the speaker does not really want to know!

Jargon or technical language should not be used unless clearly defined. Sometimes professionals may feel the need to demonstrate their expertise by using technical phrases or jargon unique to the discipline. This is usually not good teaming behavior because it may send a message of ownership of one's discipline and an unwillingness to participate in role release. In addition, specialized language can inhibit effective communication—others may be intimidated and not ask for an explanation of terms. Unfortunately, this form of communication occurs frequently, and general and adapted physical educators should not be afraid to ask to have words defined. Likewise, when communicating, whether in writing or orally, information relative to motor performance, the physical educator should define terms as much as possible and respect those who ask for terms to be clarified. Nothing is more frustrating than to present an entire assessment report and have a parent say, "I didn't understand a word you said."

It is also important to consider individualism in communication. The meaning of a nonverbal cue is dependent on the interpretation of the message by both the sender and the receiver; for example, a speaker may sit with arms folded across her chest and legs crossed, while her verbal information is open and accepting. This can send an incongruent message to the listener of being "closed" or uninterested. The speaker, however, may be very interested, but is just feeling cold in a highly air-conditioned room. Another example might be an individual who tries to show interest by making eye contact. In some cultures or for some individuals, this may feel intrusive. Hence, the sender and receiver are viewing the nonverbal message quite differently.

To develop congruent nonverbal communication skills, it is important to reflect on one's own nonverbal behaviors and determine how they might support or hinder communication. Each team member must become familiar with the others' frames of reference and be adept at reading messages and determining individual variation. One valuable way to assess one's own congruence is by observing oneself on videotape.

To be credible members of a team, team members must be sensitive to the congruence between the verbal and nonverbal aspects of their messages. Fac-

How Would You Respond?

ELIMINATE JARGON

How could you rephrase the following sentence to eliminate jargon?

> Place the child in a prone position and have her push up into a 4-point position.

The Authors Respond

ELIMINATE JARGON

> Place the child in a prone position and have her push up into a 4-point position.

Translation: Place the child on her stomach and have her push up to her hands and knees.

tors such as being organized for the meeting and having each student's performance levels clearly in mind also lend credibility and foster communication.

Problem-Solving Skills

The purpose of most collaborative teams is to problem solve issues, such as identifying concerns, identifying the student's strengths, finding resources, and deciding what strategies and services are needed, to create the best learning environment for the student. The steps in the collaborative process include identifying needs, generating solutions, selecting a solution, implementing, and evaluating (see Figure 2.2).

1. *Identifying needs.* This step involves identifying the problems or concerns and what is needed for the student to be successful. This information can be gathered in a variety of ways such as interviewing, observing, examining medical records, or meeting with the child. Figure 2.3 is a sample form that can help determine areas of need to support a teacher in programming for a child with a disability.

At this point one should recognize the danger of getting "stuck" too long in "admiring the problem." Taking a short time for the team members to describe their frustration or the severity of the problem can bring some focus and cohesion to the team. However, it is important to shift quickly to identifying needs and begin to generate solutions.

> **EXTEND YOUR KNOWLEDGE**
>
> With some modifications, the form shown in Figure 2.3 can also be used for requesting assistance in teaching fine motor skills. In this case, the Teaching Unit and/or Curriculum Area could be listed as manuscript or cursive. The goal/objective could address increased legibility, speed, formation, size, and so forth. In the strategies and/or interventions section, the following items could be substituted:
>
> 1. Handwriting skills
> 2. Upper body strength
> 3. Hand strength (prehension)
> 4. Position in space and directionality
> 5. Perception and tracking skills
> 6. Sensory input
> 7. Manipulation skills
> 8. Self-help skills
> 9. Avoidance behaviors
> 10. Other needs or comments

2. *Generating solutions.* This step includes brainstorming all possible solutions. All team members should have an opportunity to share their ideas based on their perspectives. Team members should remain open and use effective listening skills during this process without criticizing or discarding ideas.

3. *Selecting a solution.* During this step, team members evaluate the ideas and select the ones they feel will be most effective. At this time, possible solutions that may not be available or accessible are eliminated. The team should reach a consensus to determine the best possible solution or solutions to implement.

4. *Implementing.* In this step, the most appropriate team members, depending on the issues and needs, implement the intervention. Once the solution has been selected, it is important to ensure that each team member knows who is responsible for which aspects of the plan. Without this knowledge, team members often make the assumption that someone else is responsible for a particular aspect of the plan. An adapted physical educator once shared that both she and the general physical educator thought the other was documenting the progress of the student. When the next meeting occurred, neither had the information. This was certainly an embarrassing moment for both of them. Figure 2.4 illustrates an action plan form for gathering information and can help document individual responsi-

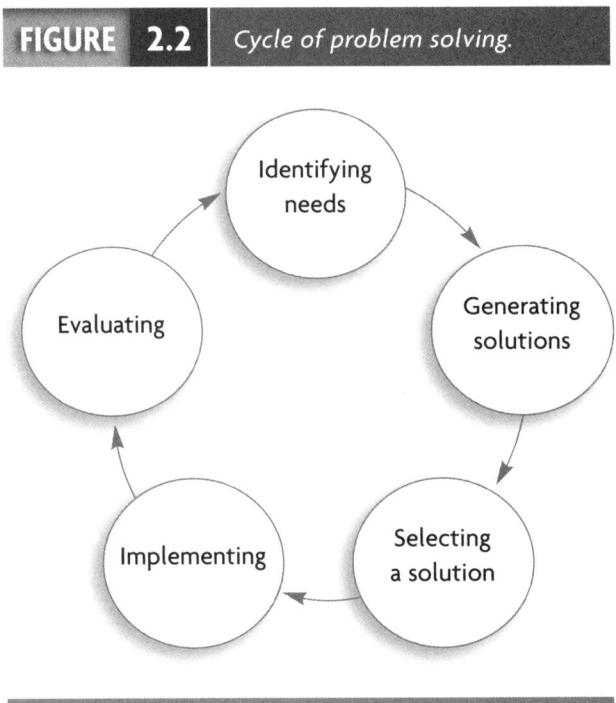

FIGURE 2.2 *Cycle of problem solving.*

FIGURE 2.3 *Request for support in teaching gross motor skills.*

ADAPTED PHYSICAL EDUCATION RESOURCE REQUEST

For physical education resources and/or support for your class and/or specific student(s), please provide the information requested below. Return the form to my mailbox and I will get back to you as soon as possible.

Thank you,

_____
Adapted Physical Education Specialist

Name _____ Grade _____

Teaching Unit and/or Curriculum Area _____

Goal/Objective _____

Number of students _____

REQUEST (be specific): _____
_____
_____

STRATEGIES and/or INTERVENTIONS:

1. Formation/boundaries

2. Equipment

3. Number of players (groups/stations)

4. Rules

5. Objectives/lesson focus

6. Language/directions

7. Modifications

8. Other needs or comments

FIGURE 2.4 *Sample action plan.*

ACTION PLAN (SAMPLE)

Date: 9-25-07 Group Name: Jim's Recreation Support Group

Purpose: Consult with after-school program staff

People Present: Sally (program director); Ernest & Marissa (program staff); Susan and George (parents); Julie (adapted physical education teacher)

Next meeting: 10-29-07

TASK	PERSON RESPONSIBLE	DUE DATE	COMMENTS, CONSIDERATIONS, REQUIREMENTS
Demonstrate prompting and limit setting strategies that are effective with Jim at home and in school.	Susan (parent)	By 10-6-07	Attend the after-school program once or twice on a Monday or Wednesday when Ernest and Marissa will have time to observe and discuss the techniques.
Teach and review game rules and procedures used in after-school program (especially tag, basketball lead-up games, and four-square).	Julie (adapted physical education teacher)	Next meeting, 10-29-07	This will be done throughout the semester beginning with tag. Report on progress and Jim's specific skills at the next meeting.
Develop a daily behavior communication form for parent and program leaders to use for communication and reinforcement.	Sally and Susan (program director and parent)	By 10-6-07	Sally and Susan meet separately to develop form. Focus on positives. Susan will make copies each weekend for Julie and put them in her box on Mondays.
Inform Julie of any new games or game rules and routines.	Ernest and Marissa (program staff)	As needed	Leave a note in Julie's mailbox. Report on progress or effectiveness of this procedure at the next meeting.

bilities. With this form, there is no mistaking what needs to be done, how it will happen, and who will do it. A team agenda can be helpful in documenting the meeting plan, results, and next meeting time.

5. *Evaluating.* Evaluation is one of the most important steps in the process and is often overlooked. Once the intervention is implemented, it is critical to determine whether the process is working. To do this, the team must collect data on the student's performance. It is helpful to get input from all team members to determine any possible challenges in the implementation. Whether the intervention is working or not, the cycle continues—identifying new needs, generating solutions, selecting a solution, implementing, and evaluating. IDEA '04 requires that the IEP describe when periodic reports on the child's progress toward annual goals will be provided and communicated to the parents.

Methods of data collection that can be used for progress reporting and documentation purposes include:

- Observation
- Rubrics
- Portfolios
- Checklists
- Attitude inventories
- Rating scales
- Journals
- Activity logs
- Direct measurement
- Formal testing

Chapters 5 and 6 expand on the assessment and data collection process in detail.

When team members have differing opinions on a problem's solution, it is especially critical to use all of the communication and problem-solving skills. Effective listening is needed to allow each speaker to explain thoroughly his or her point of view and rationale for suggested solutions. Then, an objectively determined list of possible solutions to the problem can be made, with each team member making a contribution. The group can prioritize the list into the most desirable, practical, or feasible solutions until a decision is reached with which all team members can agree. If this is not possible, any team member, including the parent, can sign the IEP form indicating disagreement with the team decision and providing the rationale for the dissent. However, so many alternatives are available for meeting the needs of students with a disability that, with effective communication, almost all problems can be resolved. An action plan, which might be modeled on the example of Figure 2.4, can contribute to efficient team problem solving by assisting with organization and tracking of team tasks.

Team members should be viewed as individuals who have insights and skills necessary to the team's functioning, rather than as representatives of a given profession. The idea that all physical therapists respond in some particular way makes no more sense than the notion that all physical educators are obsessed with competition. The skills for effective collaborative interactions must be practiced, and each of the skills should be built on the fundamental human qualities that each professional brings to the learning environment.

Personal Qualities

Several authors have identified "personal qualities" or "behavioral characteristics" that purport to be descriptive of either effective or ineffective collabo-

---

MAKING CONNECTIONS

Finding Hidden Solutions

Sometimes there is not a clear solution and team members disagree. Several team members may be unsure of what solution would be best for the given situation. In this situation, the team may agree to try one of the solutions for a specific period of time and then meet again to evaluate progress. If the solution that was tried was not effective, it can be ruled out and another can be tried.

For example, Samantha, a student with cerebral palsy, had been working on elbow and wrist range of motion in physical therapy. She was making very little progress, and the therapist thought this was due to poor motivation and interest. The adapted physical education specialist noticed that Samantha was very social and seemed to love being with other students. He suggested including Samantha in an adapted physical education group that was working on reaching for, tracking, and striking balloons, bubbles, and suspended objects, hoping that the group play would be more motivating to Samantha. After two months Samantha made no growth, and her mother thought it was because Samantha felt self-conscious about competing with the other children. The team then decided to try Samantha in a yoga class, as it would incorporate social interaction but might seem less competitive to Samantha. This increased Samantha's motivation. The yoga teacher requested consultation from the physical therapist.

rators. Characteristics exhibited by effective collaborators include openness, security, positiveness, a sense of humor, enthusiasm, patience, willingness to learn, flexibility, commitment to hard work, honesty, self-determination, and integrity (Lytle, 1999; Mostert, 1997). Friend and Cook (2002) indicate that effective collaborators value the collaborative process, trust one another, and build a sense of community through collaboration. They share resources freely and demonstrate respect and equity in their interactions with others. Collaborative team members also:

- Are reflective about the process
- Are open and nonjudgmental
- Are receptive to others
- Value others' thoughts and ideas
- View others with equal status

In addition, collaborative professionals are reflective about their own personal practices and enjoy the social interaction process. The advantages of the collaborative team are reaped by the members themselves. Team interactions enhance creativity and problem solving. Vital information for the efficacy of adapted physical education, such as behavioral strategies, learning modalities, the use of assistive devices, and much more, can come from quality collaborative interactions. Furthermore, team members share the responsibility for goal setting, obtaining resources, decision making, and outcomes, bringing the professionals closer together in working toward common goals for the child (Friend & Cook, 2002).

In contrast, ineffective collaborators may be resistant and unwilling to share resources and information, may feel uncomfortable with role release, and may lack effective communication skills. They may also:

- Be closed minded
- Be judgmental
- Be defensive and protective of their own discipline
- Focus on their own personal issues related to job function (e.g., scheduling) rather than the child's needs

Interactions in which these elements are present usually result in a lack of meaningful input and, often, a decision in which the student's best interests are not the primary concern.

When learning skills for effective collaborative interaction, you must consider what personal qualities you bring to the communication setting. Important questions to ask yourself include:

- What kind of communicator am I?
- Am I open or defensive, supportive or derisive, sincere or hypocritical, secure or insecure?
- Do I value each member of the team and respect his or her contributions?
- Am I reflective about my own practices?
- Am I threatened by differing viewpoints?
- Do I use "I" statements and avoid definitive words such as "always" and "never"?
- What type of listening and questioning skills do I have?
- How can I continue to improve my interactions with others?

Based on this introspection, the physical educator should begin working on improving in those areas in which he or she is weakest. Like effective teaching, effective communication and collaboration require constant reflection on the process and practice.

Additional desirable personal qualities that contribute less directly to effective team membership go much deeper in the educator's personality than those mentioned previously. These include a love of children, kindness, gentleness, sensitivity to others, tolerance, flexibility, empathy (not sympathy), enthusiasm, consideration of others, thoughtfulness, and patience. Whether these qualities can be acquired is debatable. Through self-evaluation, honesty, and a concerted effort to improve positive collaborative behaviors, they can be developed to some extent. Future physical educators who have none of these qualities would do well to reevaluate their career goals.

THE IEP TEAM

As described earlier in this chapter, the IEP team is a collection of individuals who come together to work toward a common goal: creating a successful educational experience for the student. Some particular individuals are mandated by IDEA '04 to serve on this team. These members are most likely individuals who work for special education and general education programs within the school. However, other community programs may also be involved. Following is a brief discussion of those members most likely to serve on the IEP team and additional community resources that may be involved.

Team Members

One of the primary purposes of the IEP team process is to maintain effective communication between the home and school. In fact, communication should take place on a regular basis, beyond the formality of the IEP process. At times in the past, communication with the home has commonly been of a negative nature—the educators have communicated to the parents, "Stay out of my domain." It is hoped that this trend has begun to change, and that the individual efforts of teachers can facilitate further change. Communication and interaction between the home and school is a two-way street, and teachers must send a clear message to parents that the primary focus of the IEP team is on what is best for the family and child.

Effective teams are critical to the educational success of the child with a disability. Team members must depend on each other and support each other in this process while playing a specific role (Lytle & Bordin, 2001). In addition to the adapted physical educator, the formal roles team members play may include parent, psychologist, special educator, paraeducator, general educator, physical therapist, occupational therapist, speech-language pathologist, orientation and mobility specialist, and nurse (see Figure 2.5). Each of these distinct roles has a clearly defined set of expected behaviors as discussed in the following section.

FIGURE 2.5

The IEP team must include the parent, at least one special educator and one regular education teacher of the child, a representative of the local education agency who is qualified to provide or supervise provision of specially designed instruction and knowledgeable about the general curriculum and availability of resources, a person who can interpret the instructional implications of the evaluation results, other individuals who have knowledge or special expertise regarding the child, and, whenever appropriate, the child with a disability (IDEA '04).

Parent/guardian/family. The parent or guardian of the child with a disability is one of the most important individuals on the team. Each team member has a snapshot of the child, usually based on his or her specific discipline, but the parent sees the child with a holistic perspective. The parent or guardian knows the child intimately: the child's sleeping and eating habits, likes and dislikes, medications, medical history, and family interactions. Parents and guardians have perspective on how a child interacts with different people and in different situations, as well as what comforts the child. They have watched the child develop over a long period of time and often have the best information on rate of progress and reaction to transitions. In addition, the family may have goals or a vision of the child for the future that should be shared and kept in mind throughout the IEP planning process. The general and adapted physical educators can obtain much valuable information from the family about their recreational habits and the functional and motor goals for their child. Team members should make every effort to help parents or guardians feel that they are part of the team. Family membership is critical to strengthening team effectiveness. However, this can be challenging. Although the professionals may see each other on a daily basis, the parents or guardians may not interact with the professionals unless invited to do so and may feel like outsiders. Figure 2.6 is a checklist that allows the professionals to evaluate elements that may help the parent to feel more a part of the team. Valuing parent involvement facilitates reciprocal relationships and mutual support.

Psychologist. Psychology is rooted in the behavioral sciences, and the psychologist is a scientist practitioner whose services are used in nearly every human service context and school program imaginable. The programs requiring the presence of a psychologist vary from state to state, as do the licensing or certification requirements. The field of psychology has grown in scope and acceptance to include such services as psychotherapy, applied behavior analysis, functional assessments of behavior, behavior modification, diagnostic evaluation, teaching, research, and career counseling. The psychologist is often a good resource for the physical educator to substantiate suspicions of neurological problems, perceptual–motor deficits, behavioral concerns, and sensory dysfunction. This individual is a great asset to the adapted physical educator in understanding and addressing behavior problems and family dynamics or concerns. Furthermore, the psychologist can help the physical educator understand the

FIGURE 2.6 *Checklist—Elements of effective teams: Including parents.*

INCLUDING PARENTS CHECKLIST

Social support: Creating an atmosphere where people can share and be offered understanding, compassion, and encouragement:

- ☐ Have you provided the parents with information about parent support groups and family resource centers?
- ☐ Do your meetings start with a list of the child's strengths?
- ☐ Have you informed the parents that they may bring a friend with them to the IEP meetings if they wish?

Proximity: The more time that people spend with each other, the more likely they are to develop a relationship.

- ☐ Have you invited the parents to volunteer in your class?
- ☐ Have you sent positive comments or e-mails to the parents?
- ☐ During IEP meetings, does the focus of the meeting remain on the child?
- ☐ Have you invited the parents to observe therapy sessions?

Distinctiveness: A sense of unity or purpose.

- ☐ Have you asked the parents to provide information about their home life to you by sharing photos or stories?
- ☐ Have you read past reports and gathered information from all sources?
- ☐ Have you shared your goals with the parents before the meeting?
- ☐ Have you asked the parents what they want for their child?
- ☐ How well do you feel you "know" the child?

Fairness: The ability to work together for the child in a spirit of camaraderie.

- ☐ During the IEP meetings, do you help the parents feel free to stop and ask questions for clarification of definitions, words, or phrases?
- ☐ Do you let parents know that their concerns are heard?
- ☐ Have you provided parents with information about the IEP process?
- ☐ Do you share information about the child's assessment report with the parents before the meetings?

Similarity: Sharing things in common with one another.

- ☐ Do you help parents to feel that you are all working toward a common goal?
- ☐ Do parents feel as though their input is heard when discussing their child?
- ☐ Do you let parents know that you value their contribution to the team?
- ☐ Have you shared with parents your curriculum and goals?

Refer to Chapter 14 for additional suggestions for involving parents.

Source: Adapted from Lytle & Bordin, 2001.

implications of cognitive and learning disabilities for physical education instruction.

Special educator. The special educator, like the physical educator, tends to focus on the acquisition of strategies for learning and progressing toward standards, problem solving, attitudes, values, active citizenship, lifelong competence, human awareness, health, and recreational habits. The special educator, however, unlike the general classroom teacher, uses different materials and modes for achieving these shared goals. The physical educator can obtain a great deal of information and help from the special educator because the special educator often spends three to five hours per day with a student (in contrast to the 30 to 60 minutes spent by the physical educator). Information such as the effect of the learning environment on learning, attention span, appropriate group size, adaptive behavior, interaction styles, preferred learning mode, cognitive level, effective reinforcement, and any unique factors affecting a student at any point in time can often be obtained through effective communication with the special educator.

Paraeducator. The role of paraeducators, also referred to as instructional assistants, is to assist the certificated staff (teachers and specialists) with providing the educational program. Within that role, there are at least three types of paraeducators:

- Those who work under the supervision of a general or special education classroom teacher.
- Those who are assigned to a particular student and follow the student through all of his or her educational settings and programs.
- Those who are assigned to a particular program and work under the supervision of a specialist, such as an adapted physical educator or speech pathologist.

Regardless of the particular type of assignment, when working in adapted physical education, the paraeducator can help by:

- Facilitating participation in movement.
- Assisting with record/data keeping.
- Setting up and putting away equipment.
- Facilitating small-group activities.
- Supervising for safety and behavior support.
- Facilitating communication with a student (e.g., sign language, picture communication).
- Facilitating communication between teachers, parents, and other staff.

General educator. In recent years, education law has placed general educators, including physical educators, in a more active role in the IEP process. General educators tend to focus on learning, problem solving, attitudes, values, active citizenship, lifelong competence, human awareness, health, and recreational habits. The general classroom teacher is responsible for helping children reach their academic goals and standards for grade-level expectations.

The general physical education teacher is the expert on the general physical education curriculum and expectations. All IEP team members must understand these expectations in order to determine the appropriate adaptations and supports needed for a particular child. The general physical education teacher should be prepared to explain the functional skills needed for the child to succeed in the physical education class. In addition to the grade-level expectancies for motor skills, these might include skills for locker room use, traveling to various activity areas, working in a large group, and using equipment safely. When the general physical education teacher is also the child's classroom teacher, he or she can provide additional information to the IEP team. For example, as the classroom teacher, the general physical education teacher may be knowledgeable about the child's learning style, peer relationships, attention span, and playground skills. The general educator is a great resource for special education teachers in determining the expectations for inclusion and any modification, accommodation, and support needs. The demands of the general education curriculum help to maintain high expectations of students with a disability.

Physical therapist. The physical therapist (PT) is involved in the examination and treatment of musculoskeletal and neuromuscular problems that affect people's abilities to move and function in their daily lives. According to the American Physical Therapy Association, physical therapists are health professionals who work with patients across their life span in various settings such as hospitals (even with critically ill patients in the intensive care unit), nursing homes, outpatient clinics, home settings, and public schools. In a school setting or children's program, physical therapists often address one or more of the following areas of performance:

- Motor control and coordination
- Sensorimotor coordination
- Postural balance and stability
- Activities of daily living and functional mobility
- Environmental adaptations and accessibility
- Use of assistive devices
- Muscular strength and endurance
- Flexibility/stretching

> ## Teaching Tip
>
> **CONTRACTURES** • A student with severe contractures may maintain functional mobility by regularly doing stretching exercises and sometimes being manually stretched by a physical therapist. School-based therapists will frequently cross-train other professionals and the parents to assist with the passive manual stretching.
>
> For the physical educator, this is important because stretching activities can be incorporated into the physical education lesson to provide more opportunities to focus on slowly moving the limbs and stretching (e.g., lying prone or supine on the floor and stretching prior to a rolling activity, sitting in a "V" or "L" position for reaching to toes, or doing forward straddle "calf" stretches against a wall).
>
> (Caution: Often the manual stretching is done only by the therapist. In these cases, the physical educator can facilitate the slow stretching movements that are part of physical activities to increase flexibility.)

For the general and adapted physical educators, the physical therapist is an excellent source of information related to proper positioning for activities and exercise; the use of personal equipment such as wheelchairs, walkers, or standers; access to the school environment for physical activity; and any contraindicated movements that should be avoided during activity. The adapted physical educator and physical therapist often work closely together when providing instruction to students who have a physical disability.

Occupational therapist. According to the American Occupational Therapy Association, the occupational therapist is a health and rehabilitation professional who helps people regain, develop, and build skills that are important for independent functioning, health, well-being, security, and happiness. Occupational therapy (OT) practitioners work with people of all ages who, because of illness, injury, or developmental or psychological impairment, need specialized assistance in learning those skills that enable them to lead independent, productive, and satisfying lives. Occupational therapists can be credentialed at either the professional (occupational therapist) or technical (occupational therapy assistant or OTA) level after completing a baccalaureate or entry-level master's degree or two-year associate degree program, respectively. These individuals work with people experiencing health problems, such as stroke, spinal cord injuries, cancer, congenital conditions, developmental problems, and mental illness, in a wide range of practice settings including hospitals, nursing facilities, home health agencies, outpatient rehabilitation clinics, psychiatric facilities, and public schools.

In the school setting or children's program, occupational therapists often address one or more of the following areas of the student's performance:

- Postural stability
- Sensory integration
- Motor planning
- Visual perception and integration
- Fine motor skills
- Activities of daily living
- Environmental adaptations and assistive devices
- Social play and organization of behavior

Occupational therapists can assist the general and adapted physical educators in the use of adaptive devices, the use of switches, fine motor skills, and sensory experiences and processing, and in some cases with assistive technology. The occupational therapist, physical therapist, and adapted physical educator can truly enhance the student's learning when they take a collaborative approach based on the vast expanse of motor knowledge they bring to the team. All adapted physical educators should get to know the therapists in their district or county who support students with a disability.

Speech-language pathologist. Speech-language pathologists (SLP) may be found on the staff of nearly every school district in the nation. Speech-language pathologists (sometimes informally referred to as speech therapists) are educated to assess communication abilities and treat speech, language, and voice disorders. Their services include prevention, identification, evaluation, treatment, and rehabilitation of communication needs. In the school setting, speech-language pathologists most often work with children who have language delays and speech problems, including children who stutter and those with voice and articulation problems (American Speech–Language–Hearing Association [ASHA], 2000). ASHA grants certification of clinical competence (CCC) for delivering clinical services, which specifies different requirements for speech pathology and audiology; however, each state sets its own requirements for delivering services in the public schools. Speech-language pathologists are a valuable resource for general and adapted physical educators in providing valuable communication information. They provide physical educators with information on the students' receptive (language input) and expressive (language output) skills and when neces-

> **Teaching Tip**
>
> **GRASPING** • A student learning how to feed himself or herself may be assisted by the occupational therapist in grasping a spoon. The therapist may also recommend special adaptive equipment to help the student hold the spoon and sit more upright, facilitating this process.
>
> For the physical educator, this is important because the techniques used for grasping can be incorporated into physical education activities for more practice (e.g., activities involving reaching, grasping for and holding objects, or using similar adaptive equipment to assist in manipulating objects for play). Examples include rackets/paddles, horseshoes, small balls and beanbags, clothespins/clips, dice, beads, rope, bars, and railings.

sary can teach sign language for terms commonly used in physical education or provide augmentative communication devices. The cognitive, affective, and psychomotor aspects of physical education are a wonderful place to enhance and incorporate language development. Including movement in speech activities and language during physical activity is an excellent way to address the needs of the whole child. Physical educators should work closely with SLPs to include speech and language development in the physical activity program. In some cases, the adapted physical educator and speech pathologist may team-teach activities.

Orientation and mobility specialist. Orientation and mobility (O & M) specialists assist individuals with visual impairment to travel more independently within their communities. According to the California Association of Orientation & Mobility Specialists, the O & M specialist is responsible for providing appropriate assessments, individualized instruction, family support, professional consultation and collaboration, and community education. Orientation and mobility assessment and instruction may include:

- Sensory awareness
- Gross motor skills
- Basic protective techniques
- Long cane skills
- Visual efficiency training
- Use of low-vision devices
- Body awareness and identification
- Spatial concepts
- Environmental awareness and identification
- Compass directions and map skills
- Information gathering
- Verbal and nonverbal communication skills
- Daily living skills
- Auditory training
- Street-crossing skills
- Indoor/outdoor travel (home, school, work areas)
- Residential travel
- Metropolitan travel
- Rural travel
- Use of public transportation
- Interaction with the public
- Skills to qualify for guide dog training

O & M specialists can provide valuable information to the IEP team and will benefit from coordinating goals and teaching strategies with other team members. Like occupational and physical therapy, the fields of adapted physical education and orientation and mobility overlap.

Nurse. The field of nursing includes a wide range of services and many individuals who have a variety of training and credentials. A registered nurse or RN is a graduate of a four-year college program and is licensed (registered) in at least one state. Technical nurses have completed a two-year training program, and practical nurses have completed a one-year program. The level of training and licensing dictates what services nurses can deliver. Most school nurses are RNs. The level of training and licensing required for practicing nursing in the public schools is determined by each state's board of education. Nurses who work with special education programs in the public schools provide a variety of valuable services including vision and hearing screening, scoliosis screening, and height and weight measurements. In addition, they may provide team members with necessary information related to tube feeding, the use of catheters, seizure management, monitoring blood sugar levels, and allergies. The nurse provides the team with critical safety information related to any medical alerts or updates for individuals with a disability. This individual is a great resource for the adapted physical educator and general physical educator regarding any medical concerns or issues. The school nurse is also a good liaison to the physicians and other medical professionals who may be seeing the student.

Administrator. Every school has an administrator. The administrator for most general education teachers is their principal. For special education staff, their administrator may be the principal of the school or

EXTEND YOUR KNOWLEDGE

HIPAA (Health Insurance Portability and Accountability Act of 1996)

You have probably signed documents related to your own medical records that are in accordance with HIPAA, which is the term used to refer to Public Law 104-191. According to the Federal Register (45 CFR Parts 160–164), the purpose of the final rule of this law is "to adopt national standards for safeguards to protect the confidentiality, integrity, and availability of electronic protected health information." Although this law primarily affects health care providers, it often pertains to health information of individual students in schools. All teachers working with students with a disability should know the requirements that this law imposes in addition to the rules for confidentiality of school records in general. The school nurse may be able to assist the general and adapted physical education teachers in understanding the requirements of HIPAA. In addition, most school districts have at least one administrator who is trained in the HIPAA law as it pertains to schools.

---

the director of special education. An administrator's role is to oversee both the facility and the individuals in that facility, including faculty, staff, and students. Most administrators must have teaching credentials, and most have taught in the public schools before going into administration. Their job is to oversee all of the operations involved in running a successful school program. They are responsible for staffing, safety, budget issues, curriculum development, and staff development, as well as compliance with state and federal educational standards and expectations. An administrator is often the representative from the local education agency in attendance at IEP meetings for students with a disability. The administrator is a very important person for both the general and adapted physical educators because she or he makes decisions about class size, caseload, equipment budgets, release time for conferences, money for instructional assistants, and transportation for special field trips. Therefore, it is extremely important that physical educators ensure that their administrators are strong advocates for their programs. For example, you may wish to invite your administrator to special events you are organizing, make sure your events receive positive media coverage to promote your school and program, and illustrate the effective implementation of strategies learned at conferences by sharing new ideas during in-service training or faculty meetings.

THE ADAPTED PHYSICAL EDUCATOR AS A RESOURCE PERSON

The role of the adapted physical educator is changing from being a direct service provider to delivering services indirectly through consulting, serving as a resource to other teachers, or a combination of these roles (Kelly & Gansneder, 1998). It is one matter to have the skills to teach children and another matter to be able to instruct, guide, and consult with other professionals who may themselves be providing the physical activity experiences for children. In most school systems, the general physical educator must rely on the adapted physical educator as the first source of information about the specific needs of individuals with a disability who are placed in his or her general physical education classes. It is incumbent upon both general and adapted physical educators to establish a collaborative relationship.

Many states have implemented the "consultant model" or have cast adapted physical educators as "resource teachers" or "specialists." Both the adapted physical educator and the general educator must take ownership of the interventions and outcomes for students with a disability (Pugach & Johnson, 2002). As more children are appropriately placed in inclusive physical education, adapted physical educators may find themselves delivering direct services only to those students with the most severe disabilities and collaborating with classroom teachers or physical education generalists on the appropriate programming for those students with a mild disability. This shift in how adapted physical education services are delivered has created a much greater diversity in the job responsibilities and roles of the adapted physical educator.

Roles

Although the role of the resource teacher or consultant is recognized as an important aspect of the adapted physical educator's job, very little research has been done to examine what this role entails (Conatser & Block, 1998; Heikinaro-Johansson, Sherrill, French, & Huuhka, 1995; Kelly & Gansneder, 1998). A recent study found that the adapted physical education consultant plays many roles in his or her interactions with other professionals, including advocate, educator, courier, resource coordinator, supporter or helper (Lytle, 1999), and source of professional resources.

Advocate. In the role of advocate, the adapted physical educator serves as a support person for students or their parents. For example, when a student moves from one grade level to another, the adapted physical educator may be the individual who has worked with the student for several years; knows specific strategies, likes, and dislikes; and can advocate for the student's needs.

Educator. As educators, adapted physical educators give information to others. This role includes sharing information from their knowledge and expertise with parents, teachers, and paraeducators. Examples include sharing curricular ideas, sample lesson plans, or information about a specific disability. This role also includes such aspects as in-service training and conference presentations.

Courier. In the capacity of courier, the adapted physical educator obtains information from a source outside the discipline to share with another—for example, obtaining information from a physician regarding any medical concerns or needs and sharing it with the IEP team or an individual teacher. Another example is sharing behavioral information from the psychologist with the general physical educator.

Resource coordinator. The adapted physical educator as resource coordinator obtains services for an individual student, class, or school or coordinates facilities. In this role, he or she is responsible for such things as providing information to parents about community programs, camps, or other opportunities that are beyond the school parameters. He or she also may coordinate assemblies such as bringing in a demonstration wheelchair basketball team or other disability sport programs or services. Finally, the adapted physical educator must work closely with administrators, secretaries, and custodians to coordinate teaching environments. Because some adapted physical educators are itinerant, traveling from school to school, they may not have a gym to work in and must coordinate their teaching environment with the staff. The school's secretary and custodian can be extremely helpful in coordinating facilities, and it is always a good idea to introduce yourself to them when entering a new school.

Supporter or helper. In the role of supporter or helper, the adapted physical educator serves within an existing program or class. Types of support include giving positive feedback to the general education teacher, assisting with equipment in a general physical education program, and bringing additional equipment to the general education teacher's classroom. This role can also include helping students in the general education class in addition to the student who is part of the adapted physical educator's caseload. The supporter or helper role is especially important when the adapted physical educator is establishing rapport and learning about the general education teacher's frame of reference.

Functioning as a consultant requires a mastery of the knowledge base known as adapted physical education. This does not mean, however, that such people have all of the knowledge stored away in their heads—only that they have a high level of understanding of the field and know where to go for additional information. Table 2.2 lists some of the skills, attitudes, and knowledge that adapted physical education specialists identify as important when fulfilling the consultant role. (See also Appendix A for APE National Standards.)

Source of professional resources. The adapted physical educator should have either a good library or the knowledge of what materials and resources are available in the school district or community. A good personal library, appropriate to the population to be served, is very helpful, as is a good set of personal resources. What journalists call a "tickler file"—a list of names, phone numbers, and addresses of those who can be called on to answer specific questions—is invaluable. Usually these resources are found in the local educational agency, but professionals at the regional or state levels, as well as those in public and private agencies, should not be overlooked. Professional agencies and organizations such as AAHPERD (American Alliance for Health, Physical Education, Recreation, and Dance), its national associations, or state and regional counterparts should be contacted for resource lists, bibliographies, and other useful materials. Professional conferences and conventions often provide opportunities for gathering resources. Speakers at such meetings may be added to a systematic file of names and addresses of those whose expertise may be needed in the future.

Working with the Adapted Physical Educator

The interpersonal skills to communicate effectively are indeed necessary for successful collaboration between a classroom teacher or general physical educator and an adapted physical educator. Effective listening allows the general educator to provide the information necessary to obtain appropriate help for a particular student or problem. The resource person should reflect, paraphrase, or summarize the information before giving an opinion or suggestion. The following is an example of an interaction between a general physical education teacher (G) and an adapted physical education specialist (A) once a positive relationship has been established:

G: "Patty has cerebral palsy and is in my swimming class. Although she can stand on the bottom of

TABLE 2.2 *Descriptors of adapted physical education consultants (Lytle, 1999).*

SKILLS	ATTITUDE	KNOWLEDGE
Communication skills	Disability awareness	Content in APE/GPE
People skills	Professionalism	Assessment
Modifying/adapting	Flexibility	Writing goals/objectives
Organizational skills	Self-motivation	Program planning
Problem solving	Enthusiasm	IEP process
Bringing a "bag of tricks"	Teamwork	Frameworks
Quick thinking	Cooperativeness	Standards
Punctuality	Positive personality	Task analysis
Time management	Collaborative attitude	Laws
Seeing others' points of view	Being able to let things go	Disabilities
Attention to detail	Even temper	Access to a professional library
Knowing where to find information	Reflectiveness	
Physical skills	Diplomacy	
	Respectfulness	
	Smiling and being pleasant	

the pool, she doesn't seem to have enough muscle control and total body control to get her hips up to float on her back."

A: "She can support her weight standing but she can't float."

G: "That's right. When she tries to float on her back, her hips and legs sink so she's almost floating in an L-shaped position."

A: "Her legs and hips sink then."

G: "Yes."

A: "Have you tried attaching flotation devices to her ankles?"

G: "No. Do you mean inflatable cuffs?"

A: "Yes, or styrofoam cylinders."

G: "No, I haven't, but we have them, so I'll try that."

With a large repertoire of experience, creative ideas, and resources, the adapted physical education teacher may easily develop a negative pattern of suggesting a technique or procedure before all of the information has been gathered. Trust, respect, and a positive rapport must be established first, followed by the gathering of information. Without these elements, an interaction like the following may occur:

G: "Patty, a student with cerebral palsy in my swimming class, can't float on her stomach."

A: "Why don't you have her try a back float first?"

G: "Yes, but she can't float on her back either."

A: "Well, then, why don't you put a life vest on her for a while until she learns to relax?"

G: "Yes, but her trunk is no problem, it's her legs that sink."

A: "Oh, have you tried flotation devices on her legs?"

G: "No, but I can."

Although this discourse may not seem to be any more time consuming than the prior exchange, this type of interaction eventually becomes frustrating and irritating. Once a relationship between two professionals becomes strained, it is very difficult to recover a positive communication setting for future contacts. Skillful communicators are not only more productive and efficient, they are also more comfortable in their working relationships with other professionals.

Asking specific, student-oriented questions is another technique for gathering information before making suggestions. Sometimes, a very vague introduction to a student is provided to the adapted physical education specialist, such as "I have this child in my class who can't. . . ." Before providing any suggestions, the adapted physical educator may need the teacher presenting this case to report some

EXTEND YOUR KNOWLEDGE

Consulting Strategy

In the scenarios between A and G, the focus was on helping the student be successful in the swimming class. Sometimes, adapted physical educators are approached with similar initial information, but the general educator is really expressing a more general frustration about the additional time, work, and safety problems that arise when the person with a disability is included in the general education class. Skillful questioning by the adapted physical educator will usually bring out these issues, but responding to them may be more complex and difficult. When this occurs, it is advisable to use the first interaction simply to focus on understanding the problem and its parts. Use restatement techniques to make sure you clearly understand the issues. Tell the general educator you will get back to him or her with resources and suggestions, and set a reasonable time frame.

This kind of request for consultation takes time and effort, but it is likely to reap positive results for all in the long term. One way to analyze the problem and approach solutions is to make a grid and write the parts of the issue in the appropriate boxes, as illustrated below.

SUGGESTIONS I CAN PROVIDE

Possible Short-Term Responses
Loan inflatable cuffs to general physical educator
Provide general information on adapted aquatics and equipment available

Possible Long-Term Responses
Set up meeting with general physical educator(s) prior to the start of each semester to discuss specific individuals with a disability
Schedule two observations per semester in GPE class

SUGGESTIONS I WILL NEED HELP PROVIDING

Possible Short-Term Responses
Request peer buddy be assigned or matched with student during general physical education class

Possible Long-Term Responses
Provide disability awareness training to general physical educators
Enlist the help of administrators in problem solving time and support issues
Consider holding a brainstorming meeting

observable behaviors. The educators should work together to answer such questions as:

1. What does the student do when he or she can't _____?
2. What does the student look like when he or she runs [walks, hops, and so on]?
3. How old is he or she?
4. Is there any diagnosed disability?
5. How would you characterize the student's language? Social skills? Intellectual functioning?

After asking open-ended questions to establish a frame of reference for the general education teacher and building a positive rapport by using effective listening, the educators can ask more specific questions to get a complete picture of the student. They then fill in information about the student's performance that will help solve the problem. Following is an example of specific questioning to gather information about a student:

G: "I have a girl in one of my classes who can't skip."

A: "How old is she?"

G: "Eight."

A: "What class is she in? Does she have a known disability?"

G: "Yes, she comes in with the third graders and is in a special day class. Jill has Down syndrome."

A: "Then she may have some gross motor delays—even typically developing children would only be learning to skip at that age."

G: "Oh, but all the other children can skip."

A: "You must be a good physical education teacher. Can Jill hop?"

G: "No."

A: "Can she balance on one foot?"

G: "No."

A: "It sounds to me like she needs to learn to balance on one foot and to hop first. Some games like Statues or stunts such as the Stork Stand could be used to work on balancing. Then, get her into some activities that require hopping, such as hopscotch or obstacle courses, where you can build hopping into the game and give her and the other children a chance to practice the locomotor patterns that are more difficult. Let me know if you would like any resources for these activities."

G: "Okay, I'll try that. Perhaps you could supply me with a few lesson plans for balancing activities."

A: "I'll e-mail or drop them by before the end of the week so you can try them next week if that works for you. Drop me a note if you need anything else and let me know how the lessons work for Jill and the other students."

Obviously, this kind of interaction between the adapted physical educator and classroom teacher is much more professional and productive than one that starts with a phrase like, "Well, anyone knows that children have to be able to hop before they can skip!" Emphasizing the equity of roles and soliciting the general educator's knowledge and expertise result in a more positive, collaborative interaction. In the preceding example, the general educator certainly knows more about Jill's current skills and the class environment, as well as her social skills during physical education. This professional knowledge is a critical contribution to problem solving. It is through valuing each person's contributions that effective consultation takes place to maximize learning for the students.

Professionals should be given the chance to "save face" if they don't know or have forgotten basic information. The adapted specialist deals with disability-specific information every day; the generalist often does not. If all educators had the same store of knowledge as the specialist, there would be no need for a specialist. By definition, the specialist is a person who has knowledge and skills that are different from the knowledge and skills of the generalist. Sharing knowledge and skills when the need arises simply fulfills the job role.

INTEGRATING STUDENTS INTO GENERAL PROGRAMS

The inclusion of students with a disability in the general education program requires planning and support from the entire collaborative team. The general and adapted physical educators play a key role in the placement of students in the general physical education class. It is the primary responsibility of the adapted physical educator to ensure that the student has a supportive environment that provides a developmentally appropriate physical education curriculum. The next sections address some of the ways in which the adapted physical educator supports the inclusion process for the general educator.

Prioritizing Student Needs

Once the unique needs of each student have been identified through the assessment process, it is a rather routine matter to match students on the basis of needs to form subgroups within a class for program planning. Figure 2.7, a worksheet used by one school district, shows how the various needs or weaknesses can be prioritized according to their frequency within a given class.

Those two or three items having the greatest frequency suggest the areas that should be the focus of the program. For example, if 20 out of 30 students in a general physical education class have weaknesses in eye–implement coordination, bilateral control, and eye–hand coordination (as measured by the district's test in Figure 2.7), then activities in this secondary program could include archery, softball, golf, tennis, and table tennis. These activities are included in this district's state-approved curriculum, but other appropriate activities might include racquetball, handball, and badminton. Within an elementary class, activities include throwing and catching progressions, four-square, group juggling, and similar games. The physical educator including students with a disability in the general class may need to vary the environment, the activity, or teaching strategies, but with practice, this can be done.

When the general physical educator continues to experience difficulty with a student with a disability, the adapted physical educator can be consulted. It will be most helpful if the general physical educator describes the problem as objectively as possible. For example, he or she should describe what the student does, what other students do, and how or when problems occur. The adapted physical educator may still need to do some observation in order to determine the needed assistance. However, specific and objective information provided by the general physical educator will assist the adapted physical educator to plan and focus the observation.

When conducting an inclusive program with students who have a disability, the teacher may not be able to identify what it is that is causing the breakdown in a lesson. Adapted physical educators as consultants must interact diplomatically, sensitively, and gently to make themselves available to teachers who need their help. Most important, they must acknowledge the general education teacher's knowledge, skills, and abilities. Adapted physical educators who come on too strong not only threaten the very people they intend to help, but also may alienate them from receiving any services at all. On the other hand, doing nothing until asked can be equally ineffective. The general educator may not know what to ask or may be afraid to ask for help.

Co-Teaching

Another strategy that is helpful in supporting general education teachers who work with students in inclusive environments is co-teaching. Co-teaching

FIGURE 2.7 Sample program planning worksheet.

School _____ Period _____

Tally the number of students in each class scoring 0 or 1 point on each of the 10 test items below. Identify areas of greatest need by observing the number of students scoring low on any given item. Using two or more areas of need, follow those lines across until an "x" is found in both need areas under an activity. The instructional unit at the top of the column is suggested for meeting the identified individual and group needs.

ACTIVITY AREA

NUMBER OF STUDENTS	PERFORMANCE AREA	Swimming	Rhythms	Stunts & tumbling	Dance	Archery	Four-square	Golf	Tennis	Basketball	Volleyball	Softball	Track & field	Weight lifting	Soccer	Football (modified)	Bowling	Batacas	Obstacle course	Table tennis	Table games
IIII	Strength (sit-ups)	X		X	X	X		X	X			X	X	X	X	X	X	X			
III	Eye–implement coordination				X		X	X		X							X			X	
*TH I	Agility (side-step)		X	X	X		X		X	X	X	X	X		X	X		X	X	X	
*TH II	Bilateral control	X	X	X	X	X	X	X	X	X	X	X	X	X	X	X	X	X	X	X	X
*TH	Eye–hand coordination				X	X	X	X	X	X	X				X	X				X	
*TH III	Balance (beam)		X	X	X		X	X	X	X		X		X		X	X	X			
III	Lower limb flexibility	X		X	X					X		X	X		X						
I	Upper limb flexibility	X		X	X					X		X	X		X						
III	Eye–foot coordination														X	X					
*TH TH	Endurance	X		X			X	X		X	X		X		X						

* areas of greatest need suggest ⇢ ↑ ↑

---

can happen in a variety of ways. Often, a child who is part of an adapted physical education specialist's caseload is included in the general physical education program. In this case, the adapted physical educator may be serving as a consultant. When this occurs, both educators are responsible for ensuring that the child is successful in that learning environment. They may use a variety of co-teaching strategies, including one teaching, one observing; station teaching; alternative teaching; and team teaching. Which strategy (or strategies) is used depends on the needs of the child and the comfort level of the teachers involved.

One teaching, one observing. With this strategy, either teacher may be the one doing the teaching or the observing. The role of the teacher is to instruct the class as a whole. The observer's role is to watch, collect data, or assist individual students. For example, the adapted physical educator may observe a student in a general physical education class to identify what needs must be met to enhance learning for the child. By observing, the adapted physical educator may be able to identify problems or needs that the instructor does not see. Once the problems are identified, the two teachers can begin the problem-solving process (as described earlier) and determine what type of intervention is needed. The roles may also be reversed—the adapted physical educator teaches the entire class while the general educator observes and assists.

MAKING CONNECTIONS

Collaboration and Inclusion

Marci is the adapted physical educator for Robby, who has rheumatoid arthritis. He is placed in Mrs. Marion's first grade class. Mrs. Marion is an excellent teacher, especially in language arts. However, during her teacher training, she was required to take only one class in physical education, and she is not very comfortable teaching in this area. Because of the demands to meet standards for reading and math, she feels she has fallen behind in the area of physical education. In addition, Robby is one of the first students with a disability she has had integrated into her class. She is enjoying him and feels comfortable teaching him, except with physical education.

Marci has offered to instruct the entire class when she comes to the school on Wednesday afternoons. Mrs. Marion is excited about having Marci come and model lessons and feels a sense of relief. This alleviates her feelings of guilt about not meeting the physical education standards, and she is excited about learning some new activities and ideas for developmentally appropriate physical education for all of her students. Marci is leaving a copy of her lesson plans with Mrs. Marion each week so she can repeat the same lesson on another day. Mrs. Marion is creating a file for Marci's lessons so she can use them in subsequent years.

Station teaching. Often used in physical education classes, a station approach allows students to work in smaller groups and on specific skills. Each teacher may instruct independently at a particular station, and additional stations may be set up to allow students to practice previously learned skills independently. In station teaching, each teacher can teach at a station, or one can instruct at a new skill station while the other moves around to assist the students as needed. With this approach, either one or both of the teachers can plan the activities. Other people may participate in station teaching to support inclusion, including parents, instructional assistants, volunteers, or older students. (See Chapter 9 for additional information on volunteers.)

Alternative teaching. At times it is appropriate for co-teachers to take small groups of students and work with them on a similar or alternative activity. Some students may benefit from pre-teaching of a skill. Pre-teaching involves providing instruction on a particular skill before it is introduced in the general physical education class. This allows the student extra time to practice and become familiar with the skill before it is introduced to everyone. This technique is beneficial for students who may need extra practice time. Another form of alternative teaching is taking a small group of students and working on similar concepts or skills in a different way.

Team teaching. With team teaching, both teachers are responsible for lesson planning and instruction. The teachers determine when and how each of them presents content. For example, one gives instruction while the other demonstrates the skill, or one writes ideas on chart paper as the students brainstorm with the lead teacher. The teachers may take turns as the lead and supporting teacher throughout the lesson. This strategy can be very successful, but it requires the most trust, respect, and planning time. This method works best when the teachers' philosophies and instructional styles are complementary. One of the advantages of this style is that teachers are often more motivated and excited by the common planning and sharing of ideas and resources. However, if both teachers are

MAKING CONNECTIONS

Modified Rules

Kate is in a seventh grade physical education class. She has cerebral palsy and uses a power wheelchair, but she has good upper body skills. Her class is currently in a volleyball unit. During skill practice, she works with her peers using either a foam volleyball or a beach ball, depending on the task. During game play, several games are set up in the gym. Students are given the choice of playing on a competitive court (5 v. 5), playing on a recreational court (5 v. 5), playing a modified game with a beach ball (3 v. 3), or staying at a skill station to continue practicing skills with a partner. The adapted physical education teacher is running the modified game and assisting with modified rules so everyone is successful. The modified rules include the option to serve from anywhere on the court and that when serving, a student may catch the ball, then toss it up and set it to another player on his or her side before it is hit over the net. Students are encouraged to try to make three hits with the beach ball on their side before hitting it over. In this smaller instructional setting, the adapted physical educator can focus on skills and form and help Kate work with her peers. In addition, her peers enjoy the benefit of additional instruction from the adapted physical education teacher.

MAKING CONNECTIONS

No One Approach Is ALWAYS Best

It is important to realize that a variety of strategies may be required for effective inclusion to take place. No one method is appropriate all of the time. For example, a student placed in a general education classroom may need to have the adapted physical education specialist teach the entire class at the beginning of the year, modeling lessons for the teacher. Later, the classroom teacher takes over more of the instruction and the adapted physical educator provides support during the lesson. Eventually, the adapted physical educator may train a paraeducator to support the student in the general education teacher's physical education instruction and observe on site only a few times per month to assist with ideas or suggestions.

---

not excited and supportive of this approach, it can be unproductive.

These strategies are just a few of the possible methods that can support successful inclusive learning environments. Regardless of the strategy used, the inclusion of students with a disability in the general physical education setting takes just as much planning, preparation, and time as providing direct service. Highly effective inclusion settings are those in which the individuals serving the student are truly collaborative in their approach.

SUMMARY

The collaborative team provides for a pooling of information so that students can be given the most appropriate education for their needs. A core of individuals (including the special educator, the general educator, the parent, and the student) serves consistently on the team, with additional professionals representing special services as needed. Specific communication skills and a clear understanding of the role and frame of reference of each team member are necessary to effective collaboration in the multidisciplinary arena.

New roles are emerging for adapted physical educators as well as for other professionals. These new roles require that educators have additional skills and knowledge to ensure effective collaborative interactions. The roles of the adapted physical education consultant include advocate, educator, courier, resource coordinator, supporter or helper, and source of professional resources. As these roles emerge, especially as implemented locally, the adapted physical educator must develop the skills necessary to provide the best physical education programs for students who have a disability.

CHAPTER 2 Learning Activities

2.1 Think of a team or group you have worked with that was highly effective. Make a list of words that describe that group. What characteristics made working with that team a positive experience? Was this group an effective collaborative team? Why or why not?

2.2 Interview a parent or an educational professional who serves on a collaborative team. During your conversation, find out about his or her philosophy and beliefs in order to understand his or her frame of reference. How is his or her frame of reference similar to or different from your own?

2.3 With a partner, first ask her or him five closed questions about what she or he wants to do after college. Then repeat the task, asking five open-ended questions. How were the responses different? How might you use each of these questioning strategies in your profession in the future?

2.4 Select a culture that you are unfamiliar with and make a list of your assumptions about this group of people. Explore the Internet to learn about this culture. What did you learn about this culture that you did not know? Were your assumptions accurate? How can this information help you work with students from this culture in the future?

REFERENCES

Al-Hassan, S., & Gardner III, R. (2002). Involving immigrant parents of students with disabilities in the educational process. *Teaching Exceptional Children, 34*(5), 52–58.

The American Dance Therapy Association, Inc. 2000 Century Plaza, Suite 108, Columbia, MD 21044, 410/997-4040, www.adta.org.

American Occupational Therapy Association (AOTA). (2005). 4720 Montgomery Lane, P.O. Box 31220, Bethesda, MD 20824-1220, www.aota.org.

American Physical Therapy Association (APTA). 1111 North Fairfax Street, Alexandria, VA 22314-1488, www.apta.org.

American Speech–Language–Hearing Association (ASHA). (2000). 10801 Rockville Pike, Rockville, MD 20852, www.asha.org.

American Therapeutic Recreation Association (ATRA). 1414 Prince Street, Suite 204, Alexandria, VA 22314, 703/683-9420, www.atra-tr.org.

Bradley, D. F. (1994). A framework for the acquisition of collaborative consultation skills. *Journal of Educational and Psychological Consultation, 5*(1), 51–68.

California Association of Orientation & Mobility Specialists. (2005). www.santarosa/~adetrick/caoms.html.

Conatser, P., & Block, M. (1998). Effective communication: An important factor in consulting. *Palaestra, 14*(3), 22–26.

Dettmer, P., Dyck, N., & Thurston, L. P. (2004). *Consultation, collaboration and teamwork for students with special needs* (5th ed.). Boston: Allyn & Bacon.

Friend, M., & Cook, L. (2002). *Interactions: Collaboration skills for school professionals* (4th ed.). New York: Longman.

Gersten, R., Darch, C., Davis, G., & George, N. (1991). Apprenticeship and intensive training of consulting teachers: A naturalistic study. *Exceptional Children, 57*, 226–236.

Heikinaro-Johansson, P., Sherrill, C., French, R., & Huuhka, H. (1995). Adapted physical education consultant service model to facilitate integration. *Adapted Physical Activity Quarterly, 12*, 12–33.

Hoover, J. D. (2002). *Effective small group and team communication.* Fort Worth, TX: Harcourt College Publishers.

Individuals with Disabilities Education Act Amendments of 2004. 20 USC, Chapter 33, Subchapter II, Section 1414 (D)(1)(B)i-viii.

Kampwirth, T. J. (2003). *Collaborative consultation in the schools* (2nd ed.). Upper Saddle River, NJ: Merrill/Prentice Hall.

Kelly, L., & Gansneder, B. (1998). Preparation and job demographics of adapted physical educators in the United States. *Adapted Physical Activity Quarterly, 15*, 141–154.

Lytle, R. K. (1999). Adapted physical education specialists' perceptions and role in the consultation process. *Dissertation Abstracts International, 60* (UMI No. 9926462).

Lytle, R., & Bordin, J. (2001). Enhancing the IEP team: Strategies for parents and professionals. *Teaching Exceptional Children, 33*(5), 40–44.

Lytle, R. K., & Collier, D. (2002). The consultation process: Adapted physical education specialists' perceptions. *Adapted Physical Activity Quarterly, 19*, 261–279.

Mostert, M. P. (1997). *Interprofessional collaboration in schools.* Boston: Allyn & Bacon.

National Association of Guide Dog Users. http://nfb-nagdu.org.

National Federation of the Blind (NFB). 1800 Johnson Street, Baltimore, MD 21230, phone: 410-659-9314, www.nfb.org.

Pugach, M. C., & Johnson, L. J. (2002). *Collaborative practitioners, collaborative schools* (2nd ed.). Denver, CO: Love Publishing.

Thomas, C. C., Correa, V. I., & Morsink, C. V. (2001). *Interactive teaming* (3rd ed.). Upper Saddle River, NJ: Prentice Hall.

Yocom, D. J., & Cossairt, A. (1996). Consultation courses offered in special education teacher training programs: A national survey. *Journal of Educational Psychology Consultation, 7*(3), 251–258.

CHAPTER 3
The Developmental Approach

Guiding Questions

1. What is the developmental approach?
2. What is the sensory-integrative-motor-sensory-feedback system and how does it apply to motor function?
3. What are the levels of the developmental model and how are they interrelated?
4. How can the developmental approach be applied in physical activity programs?

Human beings are composites of developmental levels, needs, capacities, and challenges across the cognitive, communicative, psychomotor, affective, and social domains that evolve across time. The variations of profiles require an educational approach that is flexible enough to challenge individuals to perform efficiently throughout their life span and in various cultural and social contexts. The developmental approach enables the physical educator to look at the student as a whole—the way he or she talks, plays, learns, moves, walks, throws a ball, jumps, and interacts with others. The developmental approach can serve students in any learning environment. It actively encourages the provision of meaningful movement experiences for individuals with a disability and promotes their functional performance, a new requirement of IDEA '04. Embracing the developmental approach as a philosophy ensures that educators will provide equal access to programs for all students.

WHAT IS THE DEVELOPMENTAL APPROACH?

Development, as used in this text, is defined as the process of growth and increased effectiveness through successive changes. The **developmental approach** is *a vehicle that employs a myriad of methods and techniques in a predetermined, systematic way to facilitate growth and development.* When applied to individuals with performance disorders, it enables them to approximate efficient and effective movement and achieve their maximum potential.

This definition contains several key words and phrases that deserve close attention. First, the developmental approach is a vehicle for delivering a service; it is not a sequence of activities that can be used as a recipe for the correction, remediation, or compensation of performance disorders. Rather, it provides a foundation on which theory can be put into practice.

Second, the developmental approach is not itself a method or technique. It uses an *array of methods and techniques* applied in a way that is planned, systematic, purposeful, meaningful, and developmentally appropriate.

Third, the developmental approach is used to *facilitate growth and development.* Children and young adults with a disability often have delayed or inefficient development; hence, the facilitation of developmental progress is in order. This does not mean simply an incremental change in conditions or criteria for performance; rather, it implies the process of generating a motor response with increasing complexity, appropriateness, accuracy, and specificity along the entire developmental continuum.

Finally, the developmental approach is used to assist individuals to *approximate efficient and effective movement* and *achieve their maximum potential.* Through this method, individuals with a disability are afforded every opportunity to perform successfully activities that are available to individuals without disabilities. Each person's maximum potential is unique—no two individuals perform at exactly the same level or in the same style. The physical educator must provide experiences through which individuals with a disability learn to perform fundamental motor patterns efficiently and effectively; participate in activities of daily living; pursue physical fitness activities; and participate in sports, games, aquatics, and dance.

To apply the developmental approach in physical education, it is important to understand how the sensory-integrative-motor-sensory-feedback (SIMSF) system works at the core of human performance and serves as the basis for the individual's interaction with the environment. The SIMSF system helps us to:

1. Understand the processes underlying growth and development.
2. Understand the learning process as it varies among individuals and throughout one's life span.
3. Identify sources of difficulty, to help improve the efficiency and effectiveness of motor performance.

To identify sources of difficulty requires basic knowledge of the growth, development, structure, and function of the central nervous system and its relationship to the developmental approach.

NEUROLOGICAL BASES OF HUMAN MOVEMENT

Growth and Development of the Central Nervous System

Knowledge of the growth, development, and maturation of the central nervous system (CNS) is essential for understanding the neurological bases of human movement (Drubach, 2000; Greenfield, 1998; Howard, 1994; Novitt-Moreno, 1995). Not only is it important to recognize the different structures and their functions, but it is also necessary to understand the functioning of the CNS as a whole.

A basic understanding of the CNS begins with its basic unit—the neuron. The neuron is defined as the nerve cell body and its processes, the **axons** *(pathways from the cell body)* and **dendrites** *(treelike nerve receptors conducting stimuli to the cell body)*. During the course of growth and development, the neuron undergoes major events, including cell proliferation, specification, migration, differentiation, myelination, and cell death (Williams, 1983).

1. The first stage of cell growth, proliferation, is characterized by the generation of immature neurons.
2. Soon thereafter, the cells become specified as to the type of cell and as to their final location in the CNS (cell specification).
3. Migration occurs as the cells move to different locations in the CNS.
4. On reaching their final location, the cells undergo cell differentiation. During this period, axonal and dendritic growth begins, readying the cell for transmission of nerve impulses (synaptic transmission).
5. One way to ensure synaptic transmission is through myelination, the thickening of the fatty covering (myelin sheath) around and along the nerve.
6. Early development of the CNS is complete with the death of those cells that are redundant or not needed to complete the structural makeup.

Typically, CNS maturation depends on several factors: axonal growth, maturation of neuronal dendritic systems, maturation of the synapses, and myelination. The maturation of the synapses is interdependent on axonal growth and the functioning of the dendritic systems. Myelination occurs as a separate process and is considered a measure of the maturity of the individual cell and its ability to transmit impulses efficiently. Not all nerve cells become myelinated, nor does all myelination occur at the same time. In general, myelination begins before birth and continues for nearly 30 years of life.

Structure and function of the CNS

The organization of the nervous system is hierarchical. The evolutionarily older structures are found at the anatomically lowest level (i.e., spinal cord) and are the least functionally complex (see Figure 3.1). The newer structures are found in the highest anatomical position (i.e., telencephalon or cerebral cortex) and have the most complex functions. For optimum functioning, the higher levels of the brain depend on adequate lower-level function. The following general concepts apply:

1. Growth, development, and maturation begin in the spinal cord and end in the cortex.

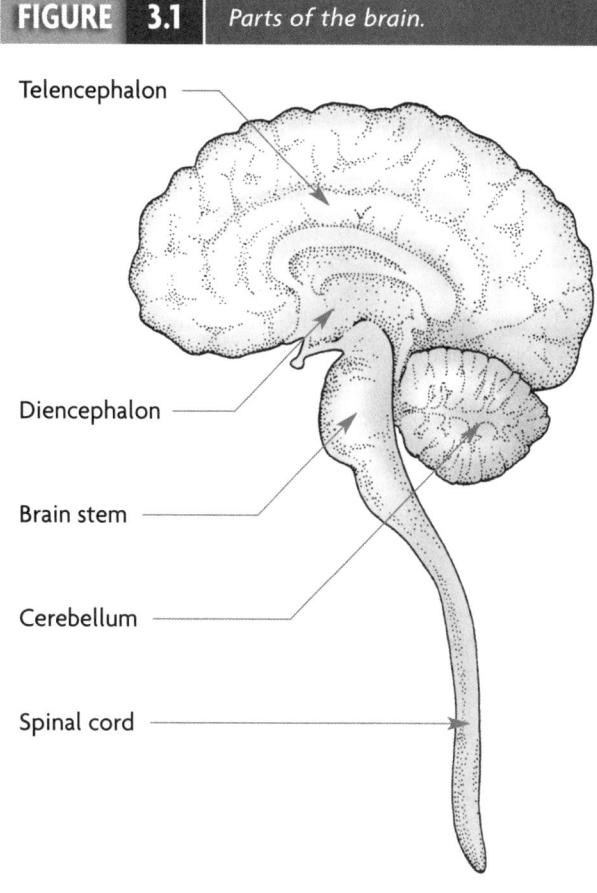

FIGURE 3.1 *Parts of the brain.*

2. Hierarchy of control and complexity of function increase with higher CNS structures.
3. Inhibitory centers tend to predominate over excitatory centers.
4. Reflexes and feedback loops become progressively more complex with higher structures.

The spinal cord is at the lowest anatomical level and is structurally and functionally the simplest in the CNS (see Figure 3.1). Its importance lies in its mediation of spinal cord reflexes and conduction of neural impulses. Located anatomically higher, the brain stem receives sensory input from many sources, handles significant and massive integration, and has widespread influence over the rest of the brain. Just as humans could not function without spinal reflexes, they would function less well without the complex sensory stimulation, integration, and motor responses mediated by the brain stem.

Within the brain stem is housed, at least in part, the **reticular formation,** considered to be *the master control mechanism in the CNS*. The reticular formation serves a general arousal and alerting function, as well as a central integrative role (e.g., inhibition, facilitation, augmentation, synthesis). It is also a selective network that decides which information is to be perceived and focused on.

The **cerebellum** is *a huge integration center, the primary functions of which are integration and regulation*. Its function has been linked most frequently to motor output, smoothing and coordinating action and influencing muscle tone.

The diencephalon and telencephalon, respectively, are the next to highest and highest levels of the CNS. Their functions are most complex. The **diencephalon** (thalamus, hypothalamus, and other structures) serves as *a relay station for sensation and movement*. The **telencephalon** includes *the basal ganglia, limbic lobe system, and cerebral cortex*. The basal ganglia assist with the initiation and execution of purposeful movement. The **limbic lobe system,** or "old cortex," is *the primary memory storage area of the brain*.

The **cortex** consists of *two hemispheres (right and left) and five lobes (two temporals, occipital, parietal, and frontal)*. The two hemispheres are connected through a bundle of fibers known as the corpus collosum, which transmits impulses between the hemispheres. These higher centers organize sensory activity at their respective levels and influence integration at the lower levels.

Processing at the cortical (cortex) level depends on subcortical (levels below the cortex) processes. As the level of function increases, behavior becomes less stereotyped and more individualized. As the level of sensory organization increases, more emphasis is placed on analysis and precise interpretation; as the level of organization decreases, more emphasis is placed on sensorimotor integration.

Sensory input (e.g., tactile, vestibular, proprioceptive, visual, and auditory) continually impinges upon the human organism, placing demands that help foster the growth of the nervous system. An individual's innate neural capacity influences responses that allow for interaction with the environment and promote development. The process begins with enhancing development at the lower, less complex levels of structure and response that, in turn, enables the individual to become more competent at the higher, more complex levels.

Although separate divisions make up the CNS, human behavior depends on the totality of brain function. The CNS divisions are merely anatomical entities; although different functions are associated with these various structures, neurological function depends on the organism's ability to operate as an integrated whole. As such, and in its simplest form, the human organism can be considered a SIMSF system.

Sensory-Integrative-Motor-Sensory-Feedback System

Human beings are essentially **sensory-integrative-motor-sensory-feedback systems.** As such, *we must receive sensory input and integrate or make sense of the sensory stimulation for a meaningful motor response. The response (output) results from the process of organizing, or integrating, sensory stimuli for use. The quality of the observable movement is related to the quality and integrity of the integration of the sensory input. The motor response results in important sensory feedback for use with subsequent motor responses or movement*. As shown in Figure 3.2, the CNS is responsible for the integration, organizing, and planning of sensory input for use in motor output.

The SIMSF system is based on sound neurological principles that provide the basis for understanding the developmental approach. The following principles underlie the SIMSF system:

1. Sequential development is an integral part of the system.
2. There is functional interdependence between the structures and related functions in the brain.
3. There is functional interaction among sensory systems.
4. There is an inseparable link between sensory input and motor output.
5. The "plastic" nature of the nervous system enables human beings to be one of the least specialized and most versatile species on earth. This plasticity allows for adaptability within the CNS.
6. The individual–environment interaction is the basis for growth, development, and learning.
7. Movement is an important and powerful organizer of sensory input. Through the motor response (movement), we can observe the degree to which sensory stimuli are integrated.

Below we discuss each phase of the SIMSF system to clarify the interaction between the sensory and motor systems. As a physical educator, you will find it useful to have a picture of how a person responds to and utilizes sensory information. This knowledge will help you apply the developmental approach and plan meaningful and appropriate programs. To understand the sequence of processing sensory information, examine the model shown in Figure 3.2. The general sequence and the related areas of the CNS are as follows:

Ⓐ Reception of sensory input
(sensory organs' receptors)

FIGURE 3.2

Sensory-integrative-motor-sensory-feedback system. See text discussion for explanation of (A)–(G).

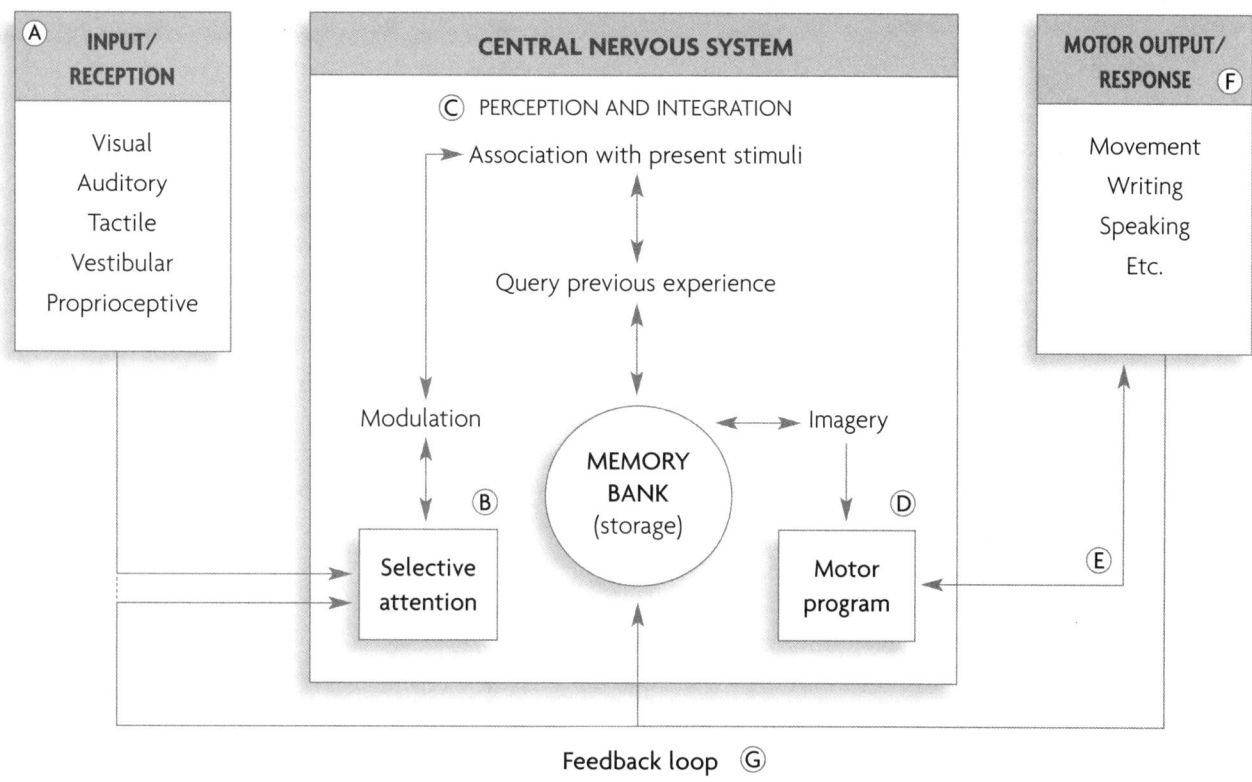

Ⓑ Selective attention and arousal
(*reticular formation [brain stem], limbic lobe system [telencephalon], cortex*)

Ⓒ Perception and integration of sensory information
(*brain stem, diencephalon, telencephalon*)

Ⓓ Translation of sensory information into a motor program
(*association and links among the areas and lobes of the cortex, premotor areas*)

Ⓔ Activation of the CNS motor centers for control of the motor program
(*basal ganglia, cerebellum*)

Ⓕ Motor response or movement
(*muscles*)

Ⓖ Feedback
(*from motor response to sensory input; from output to memory storage*)

In addition, two internal feedback mechanisms help to organize the sensory information for purposeful movement. One links the processes of perception and integration and selective attention and arousal; the other links response with control of the motor program.

Ⓐ **Reception of sensory input.** The functions of the sensory systems (tactile, vestibular, proprioceptive, visual, and auditory), along with gustatory (taste) and olfactory (smell), constitute the full complement of ways information can reach the CNS. These are sources of input; that is, as with a computer, the information is put into the CNS (central core), where it is processed.

The first step is reception. The sensory input is first received or recorded at some level of the CNS as a sensation. This is not to imply that the individual is consciously (cortically) aware of the sensory stimulation, but that some CNS structure or structures must be aware in order for the input to be processed.

Ⓑ **Selective attention.** The next step is selective attention and arousal. Before sensory input can be acted on, the CNS must become aware of and selectively attend to the stimuli. This allows for pertinent information to be conveyed to the higher levels of the CNS.

A typical person is subject to auditory and visual stimuli during most of the waking hours, and the forms of sensory input do not enter the CNS one at a time. Movement results in proprioceptive and vestibular stimuli entering the system; tactile stimulation emanates from the environment (e.g., air, clothing, equipment, and so on). A typical person can receive and process this complexity of stimuli with little difficulty. When the stimuli reach unusual levels of quantity (intensity) or quality, extreme demands for adaptation are placed on the CNS. This adaptation typically occurs when a new skill is learned. Learning the "snowplow" maneuver in downhill skiing or learning to snowboard, for example, requires that the body be placed in unusual postures, giving proprioceptive input that is intense and, at first, unusual. As learning proceeds, the position "feels more comfortable" or "more natural" as the CNS adapts to this new quality and quantity of sensory (proprioceptive) input.

Ⓒ **Perception and integration of sensory information.** This phase involves a number of functions including perception, modulation, association, memory match, and integration. The essence is the organizing of sensory information for use in motor response. This process allows individuals to synthesize sensory information in order to interact effectively with the environment. Modulation is another step, in which sensory input from several sources serves to regulate or bring meaning to the collective input. Perception, or association, takes place between present input and past input, requiring retrieval from memory in order to make the necessary comparisons.

Ⓓ **Translating perception into the motor program.** The process of translating perception to motor program involves sequencing (putting the information in meaningful and useful order), motor planning, and imaging ("picturing" what the response should look or feel like). Thus, the input is treated through a highly sophisticated mechanism and process, the end result of which is integration—bringing together all of the parts to form a whole—in preparation for a motor response.

Ⓔ **Control of the motor program.** Once the motor program is determined, the motor areas of the brain serve as the control mechanisms for action. In other words, they direct the motor response. The cerebel-

MAKING CONNECTIONS

Motor Response to Sensory Input

The physical educator may give a command to Mark, a student, to "Step up onto the balance beam, walk to the other end, and step off." Mark must first receive or hear the command and must visually receive or see the beam somewhere in his visual field (or have a mental picture of its location in his memory). There may be other sounds in the gymnasium and other objects in the field of vision, but his CNS mediates the input and allows only that input related to the task to go to higher centers for processing. At the same time, association is taking place. The words used in the verbal command must be associated with the meaning of the words retrieved from the brain's memory bank in order for Mark to understand the required task. This is coupled with treatment of the visual input to associate the words "balance beam" with the visual stimulus. Mark's brain then modulates these two primary sources of input in order to sequence and plan what the output will be. His brain is also using imagery to picture what the output will look like and feel like, before there is any observable response from Mark at all. These final stages prepare the CNS for use later. Once the input is integrated, messages are sent to the appropriate muscle groups for motor output, and Mark performs the task.

---

lum, basal ganglia, and specific motor areas of the cortex assist in the final execution of the desired motor response.

Ⓕ **Motor response.** Using the computer analogy, once the central core of the computer has processed the input data, response or output is possible. This output often takes the form of printed pages, but it may be displayed on a screen or stored elsewhere in the computer for later use. In humans, all observable behavior is motor behavior or motor output. Similar to a computer, the CNS sends messages through efferent neural pathways to motor effectors in order to create output. Whether the output is in the form of throwing a ball, writing a sentence, or speaking, central processing must occur and the control of motor program must be determined in preparation for the response.

Ⓖ **Feedback.** Feedback is a vital aspect in the SIMSF system. **Feedback** refers to *the resultant sensory information that is sent back through the CNS after the motor response.* Feedback is used in evaluat-

MAKING CONNECTIONS

Utilizing Sensory Feedback

To control Mark's walk on the balance beam, Mark's brain uses the visual, vestibular, proprioceptive, and tactile input received while he is on the beam. The challenge for Mark is that he must not only receive this new input but also modulate and associate it with the auditory input (i.e., the command) in order to generate the appropriate output—a match between what is requested and what is performed. Another function of feedback is to provide information to the brain's memory bank for future use. Had Mark not recognized the language symbols used in the command or the visual stimulus of the beam, or had he not been able to associate that information with previous experience (information retrieved from memory), he would have had difficulty planning the motor output and using the feedback (Figure 3.3).

ing the motor response and for effecting change. It is one of the most critical variables affecting the efficiency and effectiveness of motor skill learning and performance. The quality of feedback is crucial. Hazy or vague feedback can interfere with functions that enable learning. Quality feedback perpetuates the typical learning cycle; faulty feedback perpetuates the cycle as well, but it results in exaggerated or faulty performance. The quality of feedback is vitally important in motor learning because it becomes the new input used in continual central processing and refinement of performance.

As Figure 3.3 shows, without feedback, a performer has no way of knowing whether or not the performance is correct. In many situations in motor performance, however, the output appears to be the product of an open-loop system (no feedback is received) rather than a closed-loop system, as pictured here. Swinging a bat and missing a breaking pitch, making a typographical error, and missing a tennis ball that has top-spin are all examples of motor output that the performer "knows" is incorrect. In some cases, the lack of expected feedback (e.g., lack of proprioceptive feedback because the ball was missed) provides the information for correcting the performance. In other cases, the feedback from the output modulated with the new input cannot be integrated rapidly enough for the adaptation in the output to be made. Therefore, the output is incorrect.

To summarize the SIMSF system, in order for a person to move, sensory stimuli must be received (reception) and attended to (selective attention). Following neurological arousal and attention, the sen-

FIGURE 3.3 *Example of how the SIMSF system promotes learning new skills.*

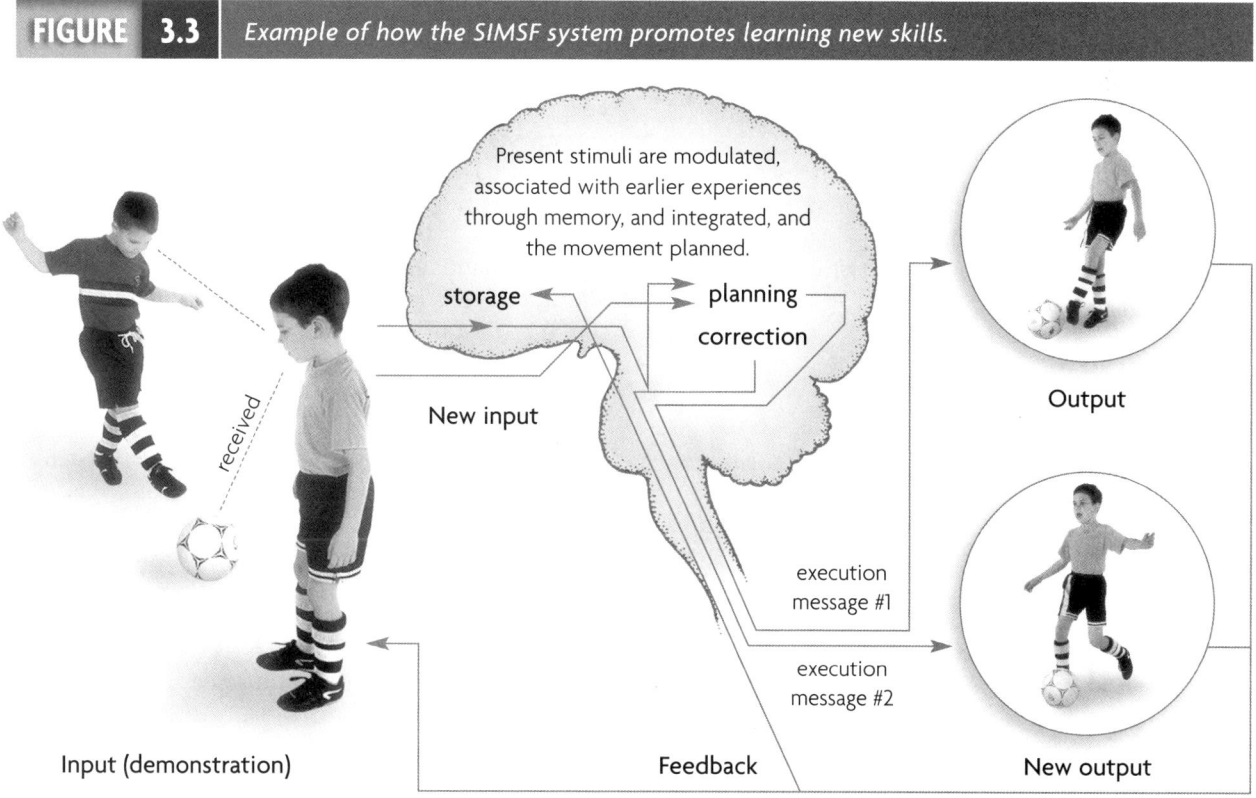

sory information is available to be modulated, analyzed, and integrated. The result is the perception or image of the desired and appropriate motor response. This is matched with memory and then translated into a motor program. The actual motor response is influenced by selected motor control mechanisms of the brain (e.g., basal ganglia, cerebellum). Once the neural impulses are sent to the muscles, the motor response occurs.

The functioning of each phase depends on the processing of the previous phase. Breakdowns, which can occur in the system, can influence the processing of the next phase and ultimately adversely affect the motor response. Breakdowns are discussed in Chapter 4. A few examples are the following:

- Without input from one or more sensory systems, greater attention to other forms of stimuli is necessary for appropriate motor output. This might be seen in individuals with a visual or hearing loss.

- With lack of attention to necessary stimuli, motor performance can appear to be random and disorganized. This might be seen in children with attention deficit disorder (ADD) or mental retardation.

- With difficulties in perceiving or integrating sensory information, atypical motor responses can be seen. This might occur in children with a learning disability or autism.

- With damage to the motor areas of the brain (e.g., cerebellum or basal ganglia), the sensory processing will be intact although the control of the motor performance will be affected. This might be seen in the scissors gait of a person with cerebral palsy.

- With damage to the muscles, input and processing are adequate although the motor response is limited to the extent of the damage. This might be seen in a person with muscular dystrophy or muscular atrophy.

The implications for programming should be obvious: educators must give attention to the sources of dysfunction and identify strategies to enhance motor performance. It is also important to note here that not all individuals with a disability have identifiable CNS dysfunction (e.g., selected physical impairments such as amputation, selected health conditions). Just as important, some individuals without a disability can show signs of dysfunction in the SIMSF system. Understanding the developmental approach advocated in this text can help physical educators provide quality physical activity programs for all students, to meet the goal of programming for all students: efficient and effective motor performance. Although seemingly simple, the SIMSF system becomes increasingly more complex throughout the course of growth and development and in relation to the specific functioning and responsivity of the sensory systems, reflexes, neurodevelopment, and motor function.

MAKING CONNECTIONS

Processing Sensory Input

Chris can sit in a college class and listen to a lecture, effectively using, for her purposes, all the auditory and visual stimuli that she needs for learning. At the same time, many other forms of sensory stimuli are entering her CNS—voices in the hall, paper shuffling in the classroom, discomfort in her muscles from a tennis game. Chris's CNS considers these sources of auditory, tactile, and proprioceptive input to be unimportant and unrelated to her learning experience at the time. Her CNS mediates and masks out the extra information as unimportant, thus allowing her to attend only to the lecture. In this way Chris is functioning at a level of homeostasis and, with the help of her CNS, is keeping her level of responsivity to sensory stimuli and her observable motor output (behavior) within context-specific limits.

Sensory Responsivity

The brain needs sensory stimulation to function adequately. Learning in and interacting with one's environment is a function of the brain, and one of the most basic demands of existence is the interpretation of and response to sensory stimuli. This action is the primary task of the nervous system.

The quality of function depends on the type and amount of sensory stimulation. The amount of sensory input is unique to each individual, and a certain level is needed for adequate brain function. Some individuals may need more sensory stimulation in one or more of their sensory systems, while others may need less sensory stimulation in selected systems.

In the process of receiving and then responding to stimuli, the human organism strives to maintain homeostasis—a state of neurological balance. As stimuli enter the sensory systems, they act as stressors and disturb homeostasis, which must then be gained anew by means of a respective, appropriate motor response. The drive toward homeostasis is inherent in humans and reflects adequate neurological function.

The influence of the quality and quantity of sensory input on motor performance has been discussed. It is the individual's CNS that determines what that influence will be. If sensory input is adequate, integrated, and appropriate, and impulses are transmitted accurately to muscles, then appropriate, correct motor responses follow. On the other hand, if one stage of this process is disordered, then some degree of motor dysfunction results.

One of the factors that can interfere with the integrity of this process is the responsivity of the CNS to sensory input. As with all aspects of human behavior, there is a range of response within which typical functioning is observed. This range is the quality that accounts for the uniqueness of each human being. Outside certain limits, human behavior is said to be atypical.

For sensory input to generate an appropriate motor response, certain minimum and maximum criteria must be met. Generally speaking, these criteria are based on the sensitivity of a nerve fiber to the stimulus, the rate of central processing, and the rate at which an impulse can travel along that fiber (or circuit of fibers). The limits set by these criteria allow the organism to function at a level of homeostasis. That is, if the stimuli stay within the limits set by these criteria, the CNS can mediate, modulate, and integrate the stimuli for appropriate and effective use.

On the other hand, an individual with a disordered CNS may display behaviors that fall outside the typical limits as a result of variance in responsivity to the sensory stimuli impinging on the CNS. Individual responses can be plotted along a responsivity continuum (see Figure 3.4). A typical response is found in the middle, at a state of homeostasis. Individuals whose systems cannot appropriately process or utilize stimuli are outside the typical range, or at either end of this continuum.

Sensory Systems

Sequential development is inherent in the sensory systems. The sequence is also hierarchical, inasmuch as the later-maturing sensory systems (visual and auditory) are interdependent on the earlier-maturing sensory systems (proprioceptive, vestibular, and tactile). At birth, the proprioceptive, vestibular, and tactile systems are almost completely mature and functional, whereas the visual and auditory systems are not as mature and consequently not as fully functional (see Figure 3.5).

Proprioceptive system. The **proprioceptive system** *detects pressure and vibration such as pushing, pulling, or squeezing.* It receives information from receptors in the muscles, joints, ligaments, and bones. Most of these sensations do not reach conscious awareness. Proprioception has tremendous importance to motor development because it is critical to the motor action of reflexes, automatic responses, and planned movement. **Kinesthesia,** the more commonly used term in physical education, is *the awareness of joint positions and movement.* Kinesthesia uses proprioceptive information for planned movement. Proprioception involves a basic subcortical awareness of body parts and their locations. Kinesthesia, then, consciously uses specific proprioceptive input to move and regulate a body segment appropriately. In physical education, individuals employ the kinesthetic sense in the acquisition of motor patterns, motor skills, and culturally determined forms of movement.

MAKING CONNECTIONS

Proprioceptive Difficulties

Suzy's class is participating in a multicultural dance unit. Her group is performing a creative adaptation of the Mexican Hat Dance. Although she can sequence the alternate heel touch pattern, she has difficulty consistently positioning her foot and leg in front of her torso. The teacher suggests that her partners connect by holding shoulders in a circle formation. This helps Suzy maintain her balance so she can use vision rather than proprioception to position her leg/foot and visually match it to the position of her peers.

FIGURE 3.4 *The responsivity continuum.*

Hyperresponsivity — Homeostasis — Hyporesponsivity

X

Typical

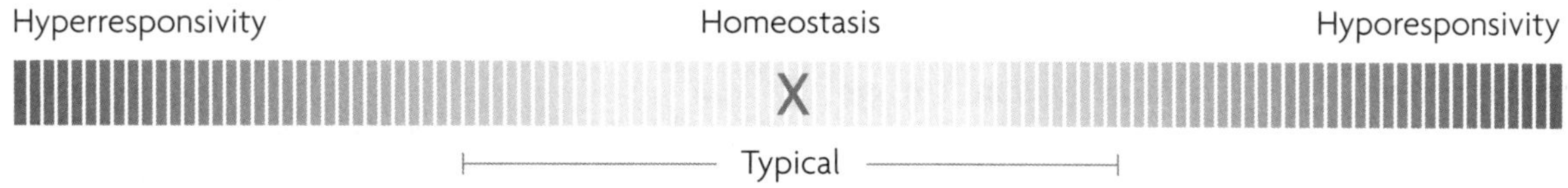

FIGURE 3.5

The CNS, showing the main flow of sensory information from each system's receptors to the brain.

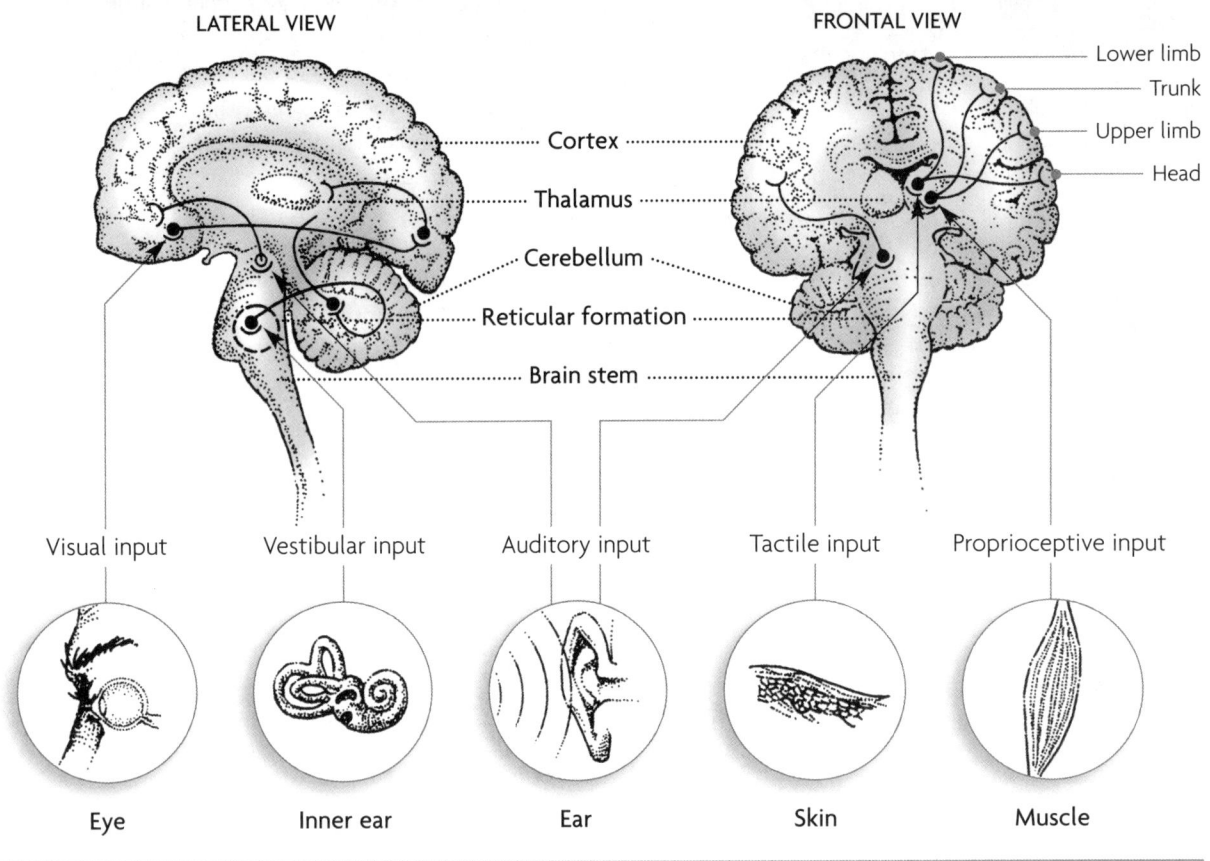

The importance of proprioception to the developmental approach is threefold: (1) it helps to maintain normal muscle contraction; (2) it influences muscle tone; and (3) it aids in space perception. Proprioception results in a basic awareness of the body's position in space and provides information for conscious, purposeful, and planned movement. The continuous flow of proprioceptive stimulation supports the motor component in maintaining muscle contraction and muscle tone. The flow of proprioceptive information through the integrative structures of the brain also contributes to visual space perception by supplying concrete information regarding the size and shape of the environment.

Vestibular system. The **vestibular system** is *a special proprioceptive system that detects whole body movement.* It functions to maintain equilibrium, muscle tone, position of the head in space, and an awareness of motion. It exerts widespread influence throughout the CNS and contributes to the coordination and timing of all sensory input for the enhancement of perception. The vestibular system responds to the influences of gravity and accelerating or decelerating movements.

Vestibular information is obtained primarily through the vestibular membranous labyrinth (i.e., the semicircular ducts, utricle, saccule, and cochlear duct of the middle ear). The vestibular system acts chiefly through the vestibular–spinal tracts and vestibular–oculomotor pathways, sending impulses to the rest of the CNS via the coordinating structure known as the cerebellum. The vestibular system develops early in life and is a highly mature system that is already functional well before birth.

Tactile system. The **tactile system,** also known as the touch-pressure or tactile-touch system, *receives stimuli from the receptors beneath the skin.* This system can be divided into two levels: touch and tactile.

MAKING CONNECTIONS

Vestibular Difficulties

Ms. Leah's class is performing a crab walk as part of their stunts and tumbling unit. Alex drops his head back and does not respond to verbal cues to keep it up. In addition, he is unable to maintain torso extension and flexes at the hips. When he tries to move forward, he performs a scooting movement rather than a sequenced "walk" with hands and feet. Vestibular difficulties are interfering with maintaining proper head position for this task. Ms. Leah recognizes this and has Alex practice performing a "table position" with the appropriate head and body position. Alex's peer partner helps him position a beanbag or small foam ball under his chin, which Alex holds in order to find the correct head position.

Touch refers to *the primary sense, characterized by the reception of nondiscriminating, nonlocalized, and generalized information.* Knowing that one's clothing is in place or that one is being touched in a crowded elevator comes from information provided at this first level. **Tactile** is *the later-developing sense able to discriminate among and localize tactile stimuli.* Distinguishing the type of fabric in one's clothing and on what body parts the elevator crowd is brushing are examples of tactile-level information. Both are important for growth and development.

Because the primary receptors for the tactile system are located in the skin, the primary function of the tactile system is to receive information from the environment. The tactile system helps in maintaining the stability of the CNS through a continuous bombardment of the brain by tactile stimulation.

MAKING CONNECTIONS

Tactile Stimulation Difficulties

Brandon likes to hold on to objects and balls, likes to touch people, often bumps into children in line, and tends to stand too close to others. These are indications that he needs large amounts of tactile input. During flee–chase games (e.g., tag), he is given a soft foam ball or beanbag with which he tags others rather than bumping into, hitting, or tackling them. This allows him to touch others and receive tactile input in a safe and acceptable manner.

Auditory system. The **auditory system** is *the hearing sense, which receives stimuli through the ear.* (It also senses vibration, in that vibrations make sounds). This is a very intricate and complex system. The stimuli enter at the ear and are routed bilaterally almost as soon as they enter. As input passes through the nervous system, it makes many different connections and travels directly or indirectly to the cortex. The indirect path leads through brain structures that contribute to the general arousal and inhibition of the CNS at the cerebellar level. As impulses travel through integrative brain structures, the auditory system becomes closely associated with the visual system. The auditory system also has a close association with the vestibular system because the receptors are in proximity to one another in the inner ear and share the same cranial nerve (vestibulocochlear). Because of this close relationship between the auditory system and vestibular receptors, hearing impairment and balance difficulties often occur concurrently.

MAKING CONNECTIONS

Auditory and Vestibular Processing Difficulties

Mr. Joe, who teaches children in first grade, wants to prepare for Jump Rope for Heart month. As a lead-up for his jump rope unit, students are going to practice jumping consecutively into five hoops (or tires) placed on the ground in front of their groups. Each student tries to jump with both feet into the middle of each hoop without stopping but maintaining a balanced and stable landing position. For the students with a hearing impairment and receptive language disorders, he instructs the leader of each group to demonstrate frequently how to bend knees, extend arms, and visually focus on landing on the poly spots that have been placed in the middle of the hoops. This provides extra visual input to compensate for their balance difficulties and inability to understand the task based on spoken language alone.

Visual system. The **visual system** *processes stimuli received through the eyes and needs light stimulation in order to develop and to ensure the maturation of vision through myelination (neurological maturation) of the optic nerve.* Vision is simplistic in nature at the lower neurological levels and becomes increasingly complex and intricate as the system matures and reaches the higher, cortical levels of functioning. Each eye

MAKING CONNECTIONS

Visual Perception Difficulties

Ivan, who has a visual impairment, has a strong interest in playing soccer with his classmates and has signed up for the lunchtime recreation activity. He is positioned as a fullback on his team and is paired with a peer buddy who will verbally direct him when the ball approaches. A game rule is that Ivan is allowed to dribble the ball for a slow count of five before opponents can tackle the ball. In "anchoring," a procedure used prior to the game, Ivan is given an explanation and "tour" of the boundary lines, goal areas, and team locations for the game.

cessing visual input (often called visual perceptual difficulty). The person may be unable to track a moving object accurately (ocular tracking), see something as separate from the background (figure–ground discrimination), or process the shape of an object that is partially hidden (visual closure). For the most part, humans are extremely dependent on adequate functioning of the complex and intricate visual system.

Reflex Activity

Reflex activity is an integral aspect of growth and development. Early reflex scholars (Bobath & Bobath, 1975; Fiorentino, 1972) identified numerous reflexes, but only those considered most important to the physical educator—spinal, brain stem, and midbrain reflexes; automatic movement reactions; and cortical equilibrium reactions—are discussed here. A more detailed description of each reflex, along with the contexts in which it may be identified, can be found in Appendix B.

sends impulses to both cerebral hemispheres, a factor that contributes to the complexity of the system. Each eye has a visual field that is divided into halves. The right visual field of each eye transmits information to the left hemisphere, and the left visual field transmits to the right hemisphere. This phenomenon, which results in accurate visual system function, necessarily involves communication between the two hemispheres of the brain.

It is obvious that good vision plays a critical role in moving safely and accurately, learning from demonstrations, and anticipating the trajectory of moving objects. However, a person who may have been tested to have good visual acuity can still have trouble pro-

Reflex development and inhibition occur along a continuum rather than in an "all or nothing" manner. Generally, reflexes that are present at birth become inhibited as the individual grows. Reflexes that are not present at birth may follow one of two paths: development of the reflex or development and then inhibition. Once the paths of the reflexes are complete, there is said to be reflex integration, which is a prerequisite to full maturity of the CNS (see Figure 3.6) and the development of voluntary movement patterns.

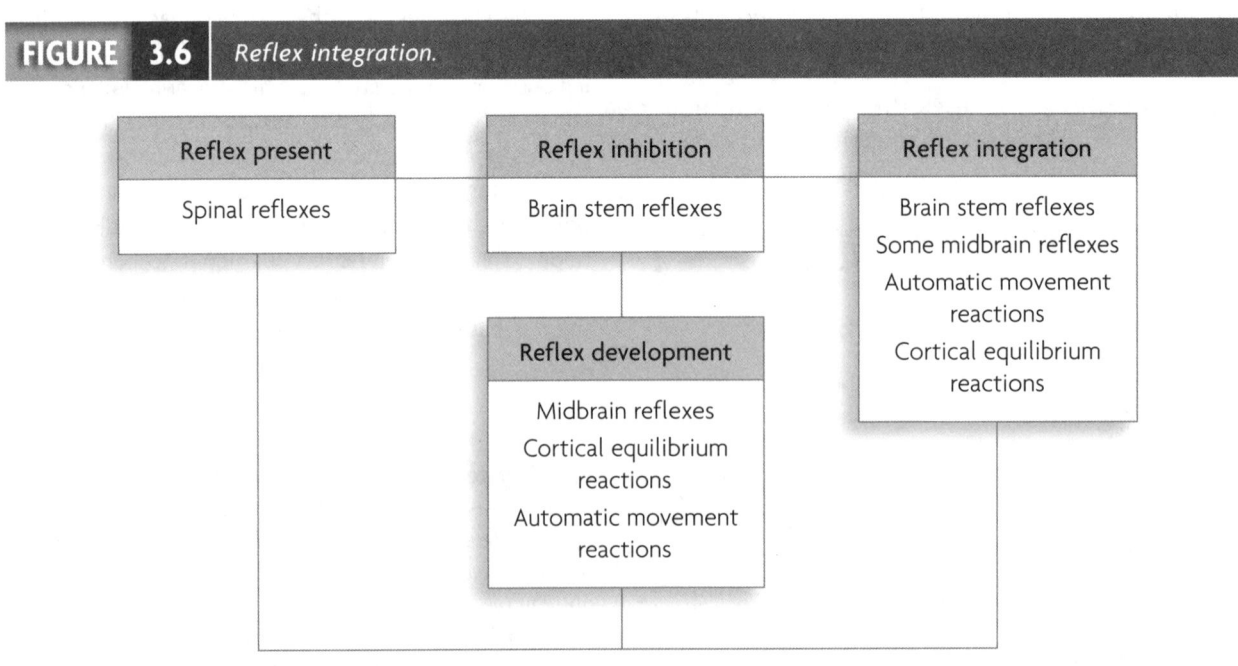

FIGURE 3.6 *Reflex integration.*

Spinal level reflexes are present at birth and become integrated into the system at two months of age. Brain stem reflexes are inhibited after four to six months of age. Midbrain reflexes slowly mature until 10 or 12 months of age and then succumb to cortical control at about five years. The automatic movement reactions and cortical equilibrium reactions begin appearing at about six to eight months and gradually bring the child to an upright posture (Fiorentino, 1972). Just as the lack of appearance of protective extension or righting reactions (i.e., automatic responses) can interfere with typical motor development, the persistence of spinal and brain stem reflexes can also delay motor development (Fiorentino, 1972).

Physical educators may see movement responses that are indicative of partially developed reflexes or of reflexes developed in stages, particularly when working with developmentally young students. The best example is the initial appearance of the protective extension reflex, evidenced by partial extension of the arm and forearm, a stage before the fully extended arms. A student may show protective extension on one side and not the other, which may also be indicative of a partially developed reflex. Reflex inhibition, not disappearance, is accomplished in stages: not discretely designated, but individually, developmentally sequenced. Consequently, throughout growth, residuals or levels of inhibition of various reflexes may become evident in motor performance and, if not fully integrated, may interfere with performance. Residuals of the tonic neck or tonic labyrinthine reflexes (TNR and TLR) adversely affect the developmental sequence leading to motor responses and motor patterns. For example, a student may lack a fully integrated asymmetrical tonic neck reflex (ATNR), which will cause one arm to flex and the head to turn when the other arm extends. Therefore, this student may have difficulty catching a ball or a beanbag with both hands. Table 3.1 shows the ages of reflex development, inhibition, or integration as cited in the literature.

Neurodevelopment and Motor Function

A thorough understanding of human development is imperative for the physical educator. A great deal of data has been gathered both empirically and experimentally for the purpose of understanding human motor development. A few basic principles will help to explain the overall process of motor development:

1. Motor development occurs in a cephalo-caudal fashion; that is, development proceeds from head to foot.
2. Motor development occurs in a proximal-distal fashion; that is, from the center of the body outward.
3. Function influences the structure of the human body; that is, the use or activity of the human organism determines to a large extent the physical growth of the body.
4. Motor development proceeds from massed, undifferentiated movements to automatic, specific, volitional motor control.
5. Among typically developing individuals, there is a great deal of variation in the age at which developmental milestones are achieved. Development does occur mostly sequentially, however, and ages of accomplishment that are cited in literature should be considered average.

Motor development follows a sequential order and refers to the acquisition and refinement of motor behavior. An individual will typically pass through the various stages of motor development, achieving the milestones along the way (see Appendix B for a comprehensive listing of developmental milestones and motor behavior exhibited in typical growth and development).

All movement is best understood as sensorimotor activity. Conscious, controlled movement depends on sensory input; therefore, all physical education can be considered to be sensorimotor training, whatever form it takes. The teacher must study both the sensory and the motor aspects of movement, and these should also be considered equally in educational programs.

Neurodevelopment and function, which occur throughout the developmental period, are discussed both in terms of structure (areas of the CNS, myelination, brain weight) and of function (sensory input–integration–motor output). Neurological development during the developmental period is characterized by changes in the structures of the brain involved with functions necessary for the survival and arousal of the organism.

Birth

Sensory input is intrasensory by nature. Usually, the somatosensory system is mature at birth. Both the tactile and kinesthetic sensory pathways are myelinated to the cortex. The visual and auditory sensory systems are relatively immature because myelination of the visual and auditory pathways to the cortex begins at birth. Sensory information, which is integrated, is primarily handled through

TABLE 3.1 *Timetable of reflex emergence and integration.*

REFLEXES/RESPONSES	WEEKS 1–4	2	3	4	5	MONTHS 6	7	8	9	10	11	12	YEARS 2–3	3–5	AFTER 5	SOURCE
Spinal																
Moro	+	+	+	±	±	±	±	±	−							Peiper
Crossed extension	+	+	±	±												Fiorentino
Grasp	+	+	+	±	±	±										Peiper
Brain stem																
Asymmetrical TNR	+	±	±	±	±	±	−									Peiper
Symmetrical TNR	+	+	+	+	+	+	−									Fiorentino
Tonic labyrinthine	+	+	+	+	−											Fiorentino
Associated reactions	+	+	+	+	+	±										Fiorentino
Positive and negative support reactions						+	+	+	±							Fiorentino
Midbrain																
Neck righting	+	+	+	±	±	±	±	±	±	±	±	±	±			Bobath
Labyrinthine righting		+	+	+	+	+										Bobath
Optical righting						+	+	+	+	+	+	+	+	+	+	Fiorentino
Body righting on the body						+	+	+	+	+	+	+	±	±		Bobath
Automatic movement reactions																
Protective extension (arms)					+	+	+	+	+	+	+	+	+	+	+	Fiorentino
Cortical equilibrium reactions																
Prone						+	+	+	+	+	+	+	+	+	+	Bobath
Supine						+	+	+	+	+	+	+	+	+	+	Bobath
Sitting							+	+	+	+	+	+	+	+	+	Bobath
Quadrupedal (all fours)										+	+	+	+	+	+	Bobath
Standing											+	+	+	+	+	Bobath

Key: **+** = age at which reflex is present; **±** = age at which reflex is beginning to be integrated; **−** = age at which reflex would normally be expected to be integrated; blank = reflex would not normally be expected to be present at these ages.

the spinal cord, brain stem, and portions of the cortex. The myelination of the somatosensory cortex takes place before that of the visual, auditory, and motor cortex. The motor output observable at birth is primarily reflexive in nature. Newborns exhibit the TNR, righting, stepping, grasp, and sucking reflexes. At birth, the human organism responds to touch and loud sounds. Visual reflexes, fixation, and eye pursuits are also apparent at this time (see Table 3.2).

One month to two years

By two years of age, the brain weight has increased from approximately 335 to 1064 grams, nearly tripling since birth. The infant still relies on intrasensory information through the tactile, vestibular, proprioceptive, visual, and auditory channels. Optic and somesthetic radiation pathways to the cortex are myelinated and functional. The auditory system is not yet fully functional

TABLE 3.2 — Neurodevelopment and motor function at birth.

SENSORY INPUT	INTEGRATION		MOTOR OUTPUT
	CNS Structures	Myelination	
Intrasensory	Spinal cord	Motor pathways to cortex	Reflex behavior
	Brain stem	Somatosensory pathways to cortex	tonic neck reflexes (TNR),
			righting, stepping,
			grasping, sucking
Somatosensory mature	Cortex	Somatosensory cortex advanced	Response to touch on body
	parietal lobe	Motor cortex advanced	
Visual immature	occipital lobe	Visual cortex immature	Visual reflexes, fixation, pursuits
Auditory immature	temporal lobe	Auditory cortex immature	Response to loud sounds

Source: Adapted from Goc Karp & DePauw (1989).

through myelination. The major motor pathway, the pyramidal tract, is functionally mature at two years of age; this is somewhat in advance of the sensory mechanisms that feed it. The reticular formation, association areas of the cortex, and cerebral commissures are in the initial stages of myelination. The spinal cord, brain stem, and portions of the cortex are primarily responsible for motor behavior during this stage. The motor behavior early in this stage is characterized by reflexive motor movements. Voluntary motor control begins with such tasks as rolling, voluntary grasp and release, head control, standing, walking, and so forth. The child is responsive to sensory stimuli and is capable of minimal attention to task. The processing of sensory information into meaningful motor output has increased in complexity but is still in the developing phase (see Table 3.3).

TABLE 3.3 — Neurodevelopment and motor function from one month to two years.

SENSORY INPUT	INTEGRATION		MOTOR OUTPUT
	CNS Structures	Myelination	
Intrasensory	Spinal cord	Motor pathways/pyramidal tract	Reflex activity
Tactile		Sensory pathways to cortex:	Voluntary motor control begins
Vestibular		optic radiation	Rudimentary movements
Kinesthetic		somatosensory	rolling, standing
Visual		auditory—incomplete	grasp/release, running
Auditory			head control, walking
	Brain stem	Reticular formation initial stage	Response to stimuli
	Cortex	Cerebral commissures initial stage	tactile, kinesthetic,
	occipital lobe,	Association areas initial stage	visual, auditory
	parietal lobe,		
	frontal lobe,		
	temporal lobes		

Source: Adapted from Goc Karp & DePauw (1989).

Two to four years

Although the most rapid period of brain growth already occurred in the previous stage, the brain weight continues to increase to 1190 grams, primarily because of the thickening of the myelin sheath. At this stage, the child is capable of processing information that is either intrasensory (through one sensory system) or intersensory (through more than one sensory system) in nature. Of primary use is visual–tactile, visual–kinesthetic, and tactile–kinesthetic information. The spinal cord and brain stem areas work in concert with the cortex to utilize sensory information. The temporal, parietal, and frontal lobes are functional; development and maturation of the hemispheres are apparent. The cerebellum and basal ganglia are functional and provide the basis for coordinated human movement. Auditory pathways are myelinated and functionally mature by the age of four. Myelination continues in the cerebral commissures (major neural pathways), association areas, and reticular formation. Locomotor, nonlocomotor, and manipulative motor patterns emerge. The child's generalized movements are becoming coordinated. The processing of sensory information and integration with motor output have become increasingly complex (see Table 3.4).

Four to seven-plus years

By this stage, the brain has reached a weight of 1245 grams, which is almost the typical adult size. All CNS structures are functional; all areas are myelinated except the reticular formation, whose myelination continues until 20 to 30 years of age. The individual is capable of processing information that is either intrasensory or intersensory in nature. Motor patterns become refined, and mature patterns are exhibited. Motor skills are developed; complex motor tasks can be performed. Motor skills are applied in culturally determined forms of movement. The process of integrating sensory information into meaningful motor output is indeed complex (see Table 3.5).

THE DEVELOPMENTAL MODEL

It is generally accepted that each developmental step depends on a certain degree of maturation at previous steps. Piaget (1952) was among the first to stress that early sensorimotor development was critical to the origins of intelligence. Early developmental stages serve as building blocks for later stages. A child inherits some innate behavior patterns, but maturation and expression depend on

TABLE 3.4 *Neurodevelopment and motor function from two to four years.*

SENSORY INPUT	INTEGRATION		MOTOR OUTPUT
	CNS Structures	Myelination	
Intrasensory	Spinal cord		Motor patterns emerge
tactile	Brain stem	Increase in reticular formation	locomotor,
kinesthetic			nonlocomotor,
vestibular			manipulative
visual	Cerebellum		Generalized movements coordinated
auditory			
Intersensory	Cortex	Increase in association areas	Response to intrasensory and
visual–tactile	parietal lobe,	Auditory pathways mature	intersensory stimulation
visual–kinesthetic	temporal lobes,	Increase in commissures	
tactile–kinesthetic	frontal lobe,		
	occipital lobe,		
	basal ganglia,		
	hemispheres		

Source: Adapted from Goc Karp & DePauw (1989).

TABLE 3.5 Neurodevelopment and motor function from four to seven-plus years.

SENSORY INPUT	INTEGRATION		MOTOR OUTPUT
	CNS Structures	Myelination	
Intrasensory	Spinal cord	All areas myelinated except	Motor patterns refined; mature
Tactile	Brain stem	association areas and	motor skills develop
Vestibular	Cerebellum	reticular formation, whose	Complex motor tasks
Kinesthetic	Diencephalon	myelination continues	
Visual	Cortex	until 20–30 years of age	
Auditory	Hemispheres, lobes		
Intersensory			Culturally determined forms
Auditory–visual			of movement
Auditory–tactile			
Visual–tactile			
Visual–kinesthetic			

Source: Adapted from Goc Karp & DePauw (1989).

individual experience. As the brain develops, growth follows a smooth, generally sequential, developmentally progressive process.

The following concepts are fundamental to understanding the developmental model:

1. Development is sequential.
2. The brain (CNS) requires sensory stimulation to function adequately.
3. An unknown amount of sensory input, unique to each individual, is necessary for adequate functioning.
4. The brain tends to function as a whole.
5. The organization of the CNS is hierarchical.
6. A human being functions as a SIMSF system.

The developmental model depicted in Figure 3.7 is a graphic representation of the sequential nature of human movement. The shaded areas of the model comprise the neurological bases of motor development and behavior (the SIMSF system). The upper portion of the model depicts the resultant motor performance. Each level of the model is described in the following sections.

Innate neural capacity. The developmental model reflects the relationship and interdependence of motor development and sensory systems. Each individual, with or without disability, is born with an innate neural capacity. This predetermined capacity undergirds development and has a potential that is influenced by experiences to which the individual is exposed. Because function and structure are inter-

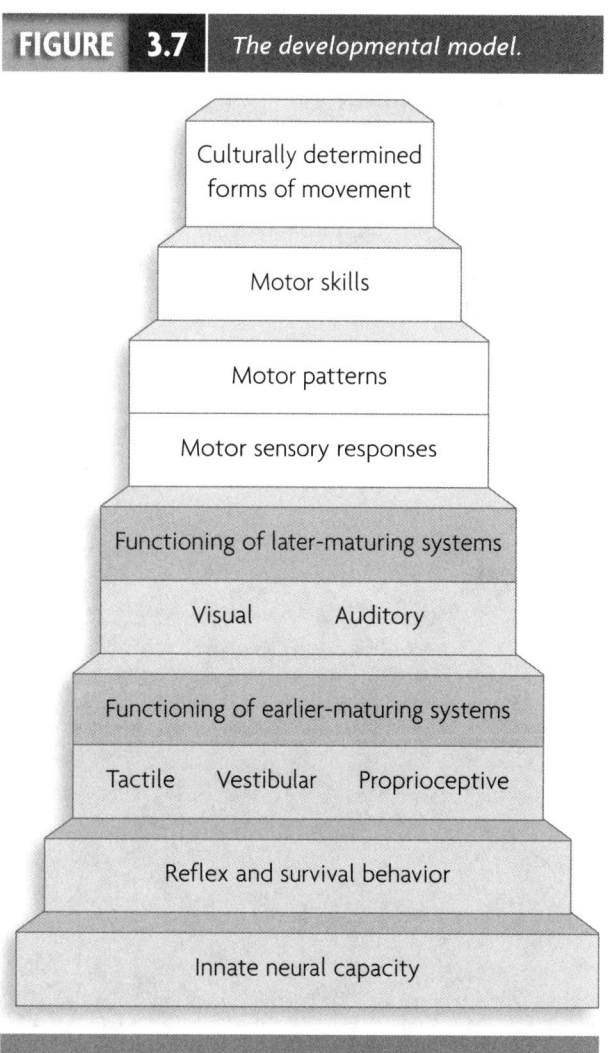

FIGURE 3.7 The developmental model.

related, the structural potential of the human nervous system, impinged on by environmental experiences, determines whether the functional potential of that innate neural capacity will be realized.

Reflex activity. Reflexive responses to various forms of sensory stimuli dominate early motor activity. The early reflexes are vital to the human drive for survival. An individual is born with primitive reflexes that are necessary for survival and that later become inhibited or integrated into the CNS for future use. Other reflexes remain with the individual throughout life, and still others must be developed in order for the individual to achieve full potential. All reflex activity is important for the further development of neuromuscular function (see Figure 3.8).

Earlier-maturing systems. Practically at birth, the earlier-maturing sensory systems (tactile, vestibular, and proprioceptive) are functioning with incredible precision. The infant's tendency to react strongly to the tactile stimulation of wetness, cold, and heat is testimony that the tactile system is delivering adequate quantities of meaningful stimuli to the brain. In turn, the brain is sending impulses to motor effectors, resulting in responses of crying, leg thrusting, and circular arm movements.

Sophisticated proprioception is also demonstrated quite early in life. Because reflex activity underlies these early-maturing systems and most postural reflexes are elicited by stimulation of the sensory end organs in the muscles and joints, it is clear that the very young infant is capable of perceiving and responding to proprioceptive stimuli. The functioning of these earlier-maturing sensory systems depends, at least in part, on the innate neural capacity and the reflex activity of the newborn child. Thus, if the innate neural capacity of an individual precludes normal reflex activity or perception of some forms of stimuli to these earlier-maturing systems (by damage or disease), functioning of the individual will be disturbed.

Later-maturing systems. The later-maturing systems are the visual and auditory systems. The immature functioning of the visual system early in neonatal

FIGURE 3.8

Interfering reflexes. This boy has an interfering reflex that causes his head and hips to flex when he kicks (left). A residual reflex that should have disappeared between four and six months of age causes this boy's right arm to flex when he turns his head to catch the beanbag (right).

life is well documented in the literature. It is common knowledge that the quality of visual stimuli entering the CNS during infancy far from matches the sophistication of that received from the earlier-maturing systems. The interdependence of the visual system with the earlier-maturing systems was first pointed out by Gesell and Armatruda (1941). They noted that infants move their hands (the active explorers) and watch them with their eyes (the learners). In this way, the eye is taught where an object is located in space. Through proprioceptive information from the hand, arm, and extraocular muscles and through tactile information from the hand, the infant learns the texture, shape, and size of an object. Thus, eye–hand coordination develops through this first step of learning hand–eye coordination (see Figure 3.9)—a motor sensory response.

The interaction between the visual system and the vestibular system, one of the earlier-maturing systems, is dramatically demonstrated by the reception of a certain type of visual stimulus. For example, if you watch a rapidly rotating object, such as a merry-go-round or a person moving under a flashing strobe light, even though you are stationary you will probably feel as though you are in motion. This sensation demonstrates that the phenomenon described as convergence of visual and vestibular stimuli probably occurs in the brain stem before it ever reaches cortical levels, causing the brain to perceive vestibular input even though the stimuli are coming from the visual modality.

The relationship between the auditory system and the earlier-maturing systems is not as well understood as the corresponding bond between the visual system and the others. Hearing, like vision, does not show an early level of sophistication. The perception of undifferentiated sounds in infants is evident when an infant shows the startle reaction, but developmentalists do not report the ability to distinguish the significance of familiar sounds, such as the mother's voice, until at least four months of age. Presumably, the infants' own undifferentiated sounds prior to this age are representative of what they are perceiving auditorily. Again, the proprioceptive system is called on to "teach" the ears to make auditory–motor associations. A baby's rattle probably serves this purpose. At about three to four months, infants use proprioceptive information to vary the pitch of their vocalizations by tensing and relaxing the muscles of the vocal folds.

Motor sensory responses. Motor sensory responses are *observable motor behaviors that specifically require much use of sensory input and that provide the basis for and are requisite to the development of motor patterns.*

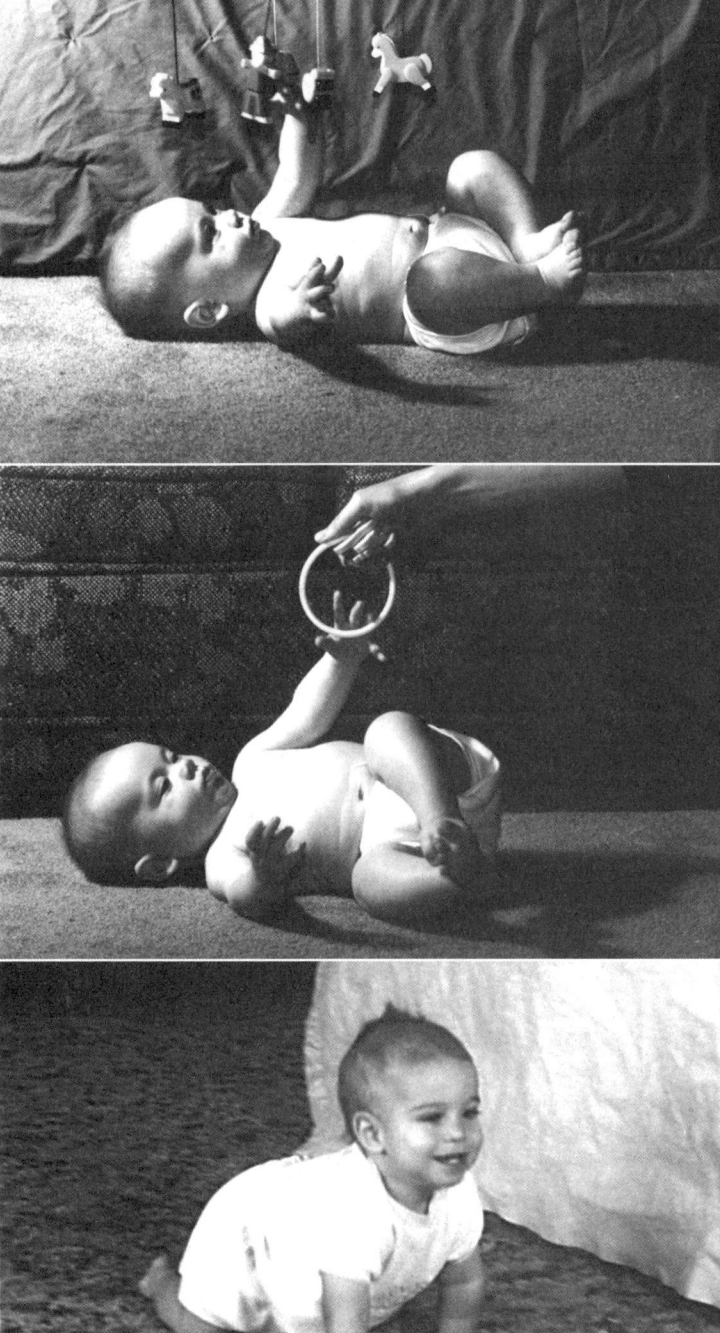

FIGURE 3.9

Eye–hand interaction. The infant sees the mobile (top) and guides hand to make contact (middle). Once the coordination between visual and proprioceptive information is learned, only proprioception is needed to enable the infant to "steer" through his or her environment (bottom).

As the infant continues to develop, more complex, appropriate motor sensory responses are observed. Although movement is observed in the infant from birth, most of this movement consists of reflexive responses to stimuli from the earlier-maturing sensory systems. As the visual and auditory systems become more sophisticated, greater quantities and an increased quality of sensory input are made available to the CNS for its use. As this occurs, more complex, appropriate, and purposeful movements are noted in the infant. These are voluntary motor responses. For example, the infant demonstrates an increasing ability to interact with objects and shows repetitive movements that later develop into motor patterns. Responses to the external environment that appear at this stage, such as reach and grasp, are evidence that integration of sensory stimuli is taking place and praxis, or motor planning, is evolving. The initial signs of volitional reaching, grasping, and manipulating are examples of the most primitive functioning of human beings as SIMSF systems. It is not until an infant's movements become purposeful and willful that we can say the infant is demonstrating a true motor sensory response.

Motor sensory responses include eye–hand interaction; eye–foot interaction; the ability to use the sides of the body together and in opposition; the ability to isolate body segments for use; the ability to cross the midline of the body; the ability to plan and execute purposeful, nonhabitual movement (praxis); and the ability to maintain balance.

Motor patterns. Motor patterns are *those major motor milestones that develop within the natural sequence of events in an individual's life, are common to typically developing individuals, and represent simple, purposeful movement.* As mentioned earlier, motor patterns evolve out of and are more accurate forms of sensorimotor responses. As infants repeatedly use a motor response as a result of sensory feedback, they demonstrate patterns such as reaching, twisting, and pulling. These patterns serve functional purposes for development, such as obtaining an object, rolling over, or creeping. Motor patterns are the foundation for more complex learning because the motor pattern provides the basis for meaningful orientation.

Motor patterns include raising the head, rolling over, crawling, creeping, climbing, walking, sliding, running, throwing, jumping, hopping, leaping, kicking, and striking. Skipping and galloping are not considered motor patterns, but combinations of patterns—skipping is made up of walking (stepping) and hopping, while galloping combines walking and leaping.

Motor skills. Motor skills, which emanate out of motor patterns, represent *a much more accurate and specific use of motor patterns and combinations of patterns.* They also represent a much higher level of integration between the sensory and motor systems. Walking, an infantile pattern, evolves into walking on a line, in a specified direction, or with a specific amount of speed—a skill. Stepping and hopping are patterns that, when combined, become the skill of skipping, a much more complex, accurate, and specific motor response. Catching emanates from the motor sensory responses of reaching, grasping, and eye–hand interaction and may involve the patterns of walking, sliding, and running (see Figure 3.10).

Culturally determined forms of movement. Motor patterns evolve into motor skills, which are ultimately applied in culturally determined forms of movement. **Culturally determined forms of movement** include *physical activities that have been influenced by or developed within one's cultural contexts.* Examples

FIGURE 3.10

This boy is just developing the catching pattern.

include individual and group games, sports, and leisure activities (soccer, tag, football, wheelchair racing, and so on). These forms of movement are influenced not only by age, socioeconomic status, gender, race, ethnicity, and other social identities, but also by the social context of family and community.

Culturally determined forms of movement are exceedingly more complex refinements and combinations of motor skills and motor patterns. Successfully receiving a forward pass in football requires appropriate reflex behavior, incredibly complex integration of sensory stimuli, and increased specificity of motor responses and patterns. An individual who has never played volleyball or participated in yoga, or whose development is impaired at any level or stage, would probably experience less success at these tasks (see Figure 3.11).

Understanding the Developmental Model

Functions at each level of the developmental model are interdependent on adequate functioning at each of the lower levels of the model. For example, free kicking a soccer ball first requires innate neural capacity that determines the capability of the kicker to conceptualize and plan the kick. Appropriate reflex activity, such as assistance from ocular, head, and neck-righting reflexes, is also needed. In addition, there can be no interference from the tonic labyrinthine or symmetrical tonic neck reflexes. Adequate functioning of earlier-maturing systems such as the proprioceptive (telling where the body parts are in space), vestibular (telling when the kicker is in motion), and tactile (giving information about when the ball is contacted) systems is necessary. Visual fixation supports the motor response of eye–foot interaction, while auditory stimuli verify contact with the ball. The sensorimotor response of balance further supports the patterns of walking, running, and kicking. The skill of kicking in a specified direction is further refined to the culturally determined skill of free kicking a soccer ball. Unless functioning at each level is appropriate, more complex, accurate skills and specific functions at higher levels of the developmental model will be impaired. Thus, motor performance can be seen to be truly complex—not as motor behavior per se, but as an observable manifestation of the inner workings of the human in motion.

Applying the Developmental Approach

As defined at the beginning of the chapter, the developmental approach is a means whereby theory is translated into practice. The developmental approach has the following functions and characteristics:

FIGURE 3.11

Culturally determined forms of movement depend on refinements of motor skills. Execution of this yoga posture depends on knowing where one's body parts are in space.

1. It allows for individualization from assessment through instruction.
2. It provides a foundation for understanding the symptoms and the causes of atypical performance by examining the sources of the dysfunction (i.e., SIMSF, developmental model).
3. It provides a natural sequence of experiences in motor learning, which enhances the growth and development of children.
4. It provides a basis for understanding the individual with a disability instead of merely the characteristics of an impairment.
5. It is noncategorical, placing emphasis on the individual's needs, capacities, and limitations.

In physical education programming for students with a disability, the teacher should be aware of the specifics of the impairments. Although these specifics must of course be dealt with in evaluating and programming, they should be viewed as aspects of functioning rather than used for categorization. Because much variation exists within and among the categories of impairments, it is imperative to focus on the individual in assessment and programming. The teacher should seek a synthesis of information, including the student's motor, social, language, and intellectual development.

The developmental model reflects sequential organization. Because optimal functioning at each level depends on adequate functioning at the lower levels, a breakdown at a lower level will cause less than optimum performance at each succeeding level. By understanding and working within the model, the educator can determine the appropriate level at which to begin programming. The teacher can use the model to identify specific sources of atypical performance, to provide a natural sequence of experiences in motor learning, and to identify appropriate levels of educational programming.

Sources of atypical performance

Because successful performance in games, sports, recreation, and leisure depends on adequate motor skills, any difficulties that a student with a disability encounters during game and sport activities should be analyzed according to the motor skills necessary for successful participation. If the student's motor skills are deficient, it is necessary to analyze the deficit in light of the prerequisite motor patterns and motor responses (see Figure 3.7). This topic is discussed in greater detail in Chapter 4, which describes the challenges to learning motor skills (also see Appendix C).

Batting and catching each require adequate eye–hand coordination for successful performance. By descending through the levels of the developmental pyramid, it is possible to ascertain that in the Making Connections example, a deficit in the sensorimotor response of eye–hand coordination adversely affected Joanne's ability to perform well in baseball (see Figure 3.12).

When the educator notices a deficit in sensorimotor responses or motor patterns, the functioning of the various sensory systems should be investigat-

FIGURE 3.12

Deficits in eye–hand interaction can contribute to unsuccessful batting (top). The use of an oversized bat can help a child who has this problem connect with the ball (bottom).

MAKING CONNECTIONS

Identifying Deficits in Performance

Joanne is having difficulty successfully participating in the game of baseball because she is unable to hit a pitched ball or to catch a batted ball. She performs adequately as a base runner. Once the ball is fielded, she has little or no difficulty throwing to the appropriate base or person. The difficulty, then, is with batting and catching. The motor skills of batting and catching can be analyzed in terms of the adequacy of motor patterns and motor responses. The fact that Joanne exhibits an adequate swinging motion and can assume the appropriate position for catching is indicative of adequate motor patterns. But analysis of the motor sensory responses of motor planning, balance, integration of the two sides of the body, and eye–hand coordination shows that Joanne has a deficit in eye–hand coordination.

ed. Continuing with the example of an eye–hand coordination problem, the educator should specifically assess the functioning of the visual and proprioceptive sensory systems. For example, Joanne may show poor figure–ground discrimination (visual system) and a lack of body awareness (proprioceptive system), both of which can contribute to poor eye–hand coordination. If necessary, the adequacy of reflex integration should also be ascertained (see Figure 3.7).

Natural sequence of experiences in motor learning

Just as descending through the model serves to address sources of atypical performance, ascending provides for a natural sequence of motor experiences. Each preceding level provides the foundation for the next level of motor experiences.

Each person is born with an innate neural capacity that is unique to that individual but basic to all humans. Reflex activity and survival mechanisms are the first observable movements of an infant. The sensory systems are functioning at birth but must mature. Reflex integration and sensory-stimulating activities make up much of the early sensorimotor experiences and learning, as reflected by the first levels of the model (see Figure 3.13).

As reflexes become integrated and the tactile, vestibular, and proprioceptive systems mature, further motor experiences include additional challenges in the visual and auditory systems. Built on a firm foundation of adequately functioning sensory systems, motor sensory responses and motor patterns emerge and continue to develop. Motor skills follow sequentially and ultimately result in culturally determined forms of movement.

Levels of educational programming

To provide physical education activities and experiences appropriate for the individual and to encour-

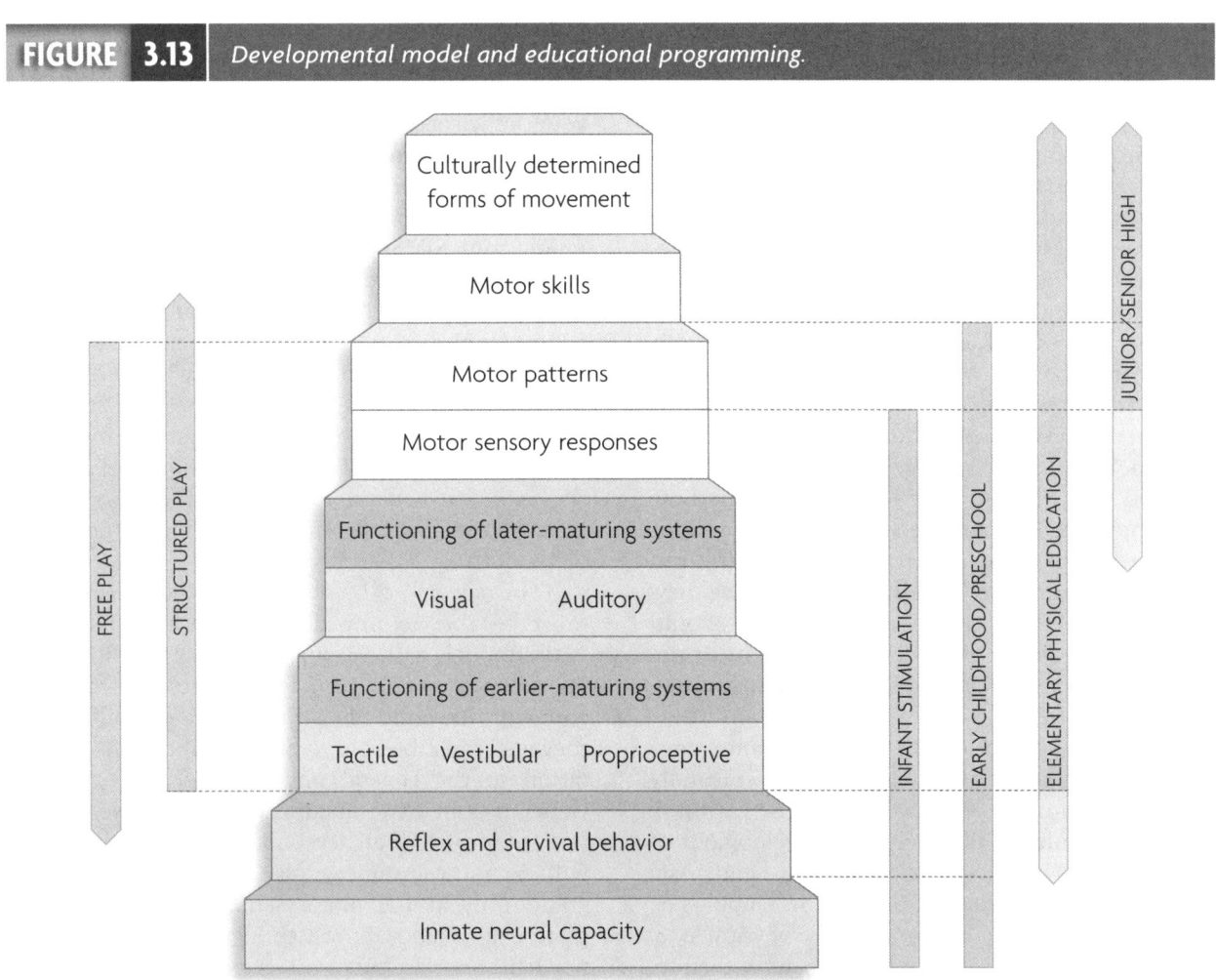

FIGURE 3.13 *Developmental model and educational programming.*

age progress through the medium of movement, the teacher must be fully cognizant of the spectrum of the motor domain. The following levels of educational programming are discussed in later chapters: infant stimulation, early childhood education/preschool play, elementary physical education, and middle and high school physical education (see Figure 3.13). In addition, lifelong physical activity and sport are discussed in Chapter 15.

The goal of a physical education program is for students to achieve their maximum potential in the motor domain through physical education experiences. Each level of the model provides a means to that end, not the end in itself. Especially when teaching culturally determined forms of movement, the physical educator must remember to teach *individuals* by providing opportunities through which students learn to move and learn about movement rather than just play "games and sports." The starting point for any given level of educational programming is, of necessity, somewhat arbitrary. The instructor should begin with activities and experiences at the lowest appropriate level of the developmental model and progress upward.

Only the first levels of the model are appropriate in an infant stimulation program. This period relies heavily on sensory input, and motor development is dominated by reflex activity and response to sensory stimuli. The goal of infant stimulation programs should be to enhance the processing of sensory input and integration with motor output, laying the foundation for further development.

Early childhood education programs usually include many types of play experiences facilitated by a structured environment. Formally structured physical education instruction is unnatural to the preschool child. Preschoolers must be actively involved in movement experiences, especially those that emphasize large muscle activity. Sensory stimulation remains quite important during this time. The child is growing rapidly and exploring new ways of moving. Activities for this level should include those designed for the development or use of sensory stimulation, motor sensory responses, and motor patterns.

Elementary physical education programs range from sensory stimulation activities to culturally determined forms of movement. The primary emphasis should be placed on the development of motor sensory responses, motor patterns, and basic motor skills. Games and some sports should be played, but only as a culmination of physical education programming and not as the focus of the program. Too often, participation in games and sports is paramount, and the program reflects little regard for the development of the prerequisite abilities and skills. The elementary physical educator must be able to task-analyze the motor performance of young students to determine their needs and abilities in the motor domain.

Although middle and high school students exhibit many differences, a similar general trend exists in both physical education programs. Generally speaking, middle and high school physical education programming assumes acquisition of motor skills. Although such programming seems appropriate, not all individuals may be functioning at this motor skill level. The focus of the programs need not necessarily be changed if activities that allow for the refinement of basic motor skills and motor patterns can be included (e.g., review of basic skills prior to learning a sport, practice of skills).

High school students usually gain physical activity experiences through sport or in pursuit of recreational sports and leisure activities such as tennis, racquetball, golf, dance, weight training, physical fitness, yoga, and the like. Physical education programs should provide the basics so that individuals with a disability can successfully participate in culturally determined forms of movement—recreational and competitive sport, dance, aquatics, fitness and wellness, leisure, and more—in community and family settings beyond their formal education years.

The developmental approach (developmental model and SIMSF system) certainly aids physical education programming for individuals with a disability. With this approach, educators determine educational placement and appropriate physical education services in accordance with the needs, interests, and performance level of each student. Students with a disability may be served by a generalist in physical education who works with them in the general physical education curriculum, by the adapted physical education specialist, or by both.

The specialist in adapted physical education must be able to provide services throughout the entire model, with varying degrees of modification. Specialists generally have more direct and frequent contact with children with a severe disability, but they also must be able to offer collaborative consultation to the general physical education teacher. Generalists in physical education must have a basic understanding of all levels of the model, but they will, in most instances, plan and implement programs only at the motor sensory response/motor pattern level and above (see Figure 3.14). These are not hard and fast rules, however.

As increasing numbers of students with a disability are included in general physical education,

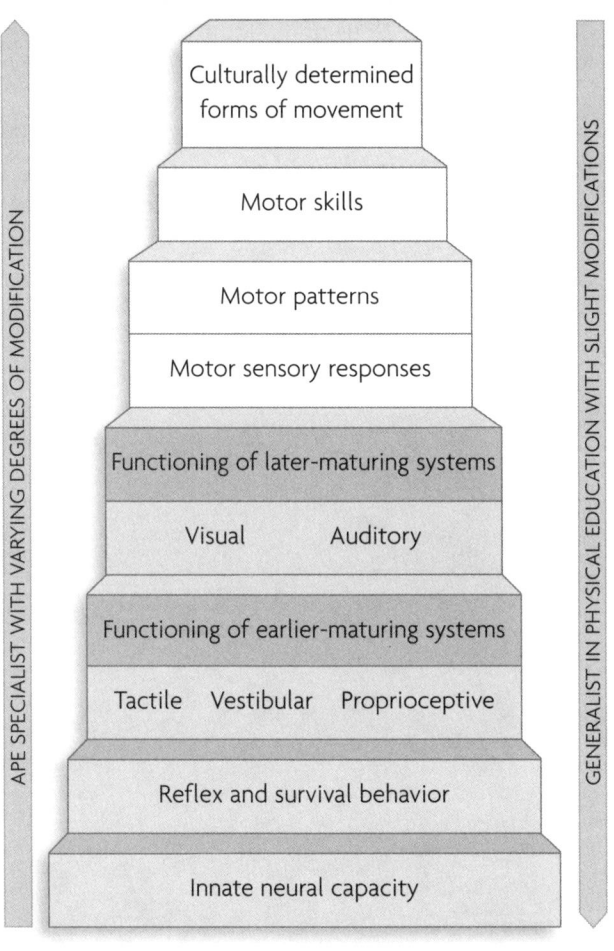

FIGURE 3.14

Programming for students with a disability provided by the adapted physical education specialist and the generalist in physical education.

physical educators will have a greater need for understanding the developmental model and its application to inclusive physical education. Physical education teachers (generalists as well as specialists) should also assist students with a disability in acquiring motor skills for use in culturally determined forms of movement for meaningful physical activity with family, within their community, and throughout their adult lives. Physical education teachers can utilize a functional approach in developing their physical education program by examining the applicability and relevance of specific activities for all students. A functional approach considers students' interests as well as their abilities.

SUMMARY

The developmental approach employs a myriad of methods and techniques in a predetermined, systematic way to facilitate growth and development among individuals with performance disorders, so that these individuals may approximate efficient and effective movement and achieve their maximum potential.

The developmental model describes the emergence of culturally determined forms of movement based on the innate neural capacity of an individual. Through understanding the neurological bases of human movement as depicted through the SIMSF system, the physical educator can provide developmentally meaningful programs for students with a disability rather than rely on educational classifications that may or may not accurately reflect the students' levels of motor performance.

CHAPTER 3

Learning Activities

3.1 Observe children of differing ages and abilities and reflect on their performance. Identify sources of sensory information and how the children attend to and process the sensory information. Watch as they use the sensory information to plan their motor output. Share this information with your classmates. Discuss your observations.

3.2 Visit an adapted physical education class for young children or those with severe disabilities. Identify the reflex activity apparent during motor performance. Discuss with the teacher ways in which the reflexes interfere with desired motor performance.

3.3 Observe children of differing ages and abilities. Identify the developmental level of the motor patterns for each child. Observe the use of the motor sensory responses that can influence the development of motor skills and their application in culturally determined forms of movement.

REFERENCES

Bobath, B., & Bobath, K. (1975). *Motor development in the different types of cerebral palsy.* London: William Heinemann Medical Books, Ltd.

Drubach, D. (2000). *The brain explained.* Englewood Cliffs, NJ: Prentice Hall.

Fiorentino, M. R. (1972). *Normal and abnormal development.* Springfield, IL: Thomas.

Gesell, A., & Armatruda, C. S. (1941). *Developmental diagnosis.* New York: Harper & Row.

Goc Karp, G., & DePauw, K. P. (1989). Neurodevelopment bases of human movement: Implications for learning. *The Physical Educator, 46,* 77–85.

Greenfield, S. (1998). *The human brain.* New York: Basic Books.

Howard, P. J. (1994). *The owner's manual for the brain: Everyday applications from mind–brain research.* Austin, TX: Bard.

Novitt-Moreno, A. (1995). *How your brain works.* Emeryville, CA: Ziff-Davis.

Ornstein, R., & Thompson, R. (1984). *The amazing brain.* Boston: Houghton Mifflin.

Peiper, A. (1963). *Cerebral function in infancy and childhood.* New York: Consultant's Bureau.

Piaget, J. (1952). *The origins of intelligence in children.* New York: International Universities Press.

Restak, R. (1991). *The evolution of consciousness: The origins of the way we think.* New York: Simon & Schuster.

Williams, H. J. (1983). *Perceptual and motor development.* Englewood Cliffs, NJ: Prentice Hall.

CHAPTER 4

Understanding Motor Performance and Identifying Sources of Atypical Performance

Guiding Questions

1. What is the difference between process disorders and developmental disorders?

2. What are the sources of dysfunction in the sensory-integrative-motor-sensory-feedback (SIMSF) system?

3. What is the significance of atypical reflex behavior and sensory responsivity to motor behavior?

Understanding the developmental influences and the neurological bases of motor performance is necessary for providing appropriate physical education for all students. Many individuals with a disability experience difficulty in motor performance and demonstrate "atypical" motor behavior. Therefore, it is important that physical educators understand the role of development in motor skill acquisition and motor performance (i.e., developmental disorders), understand the neurological processes underlying movement (i.e., process disorders), identify sources of atypical motor behavior, and understand other factors influencing motor performance (e.g., anatomical, biomechanical, and physiological factors).

Process disorders—atypical processing within the central nervous system (CNS)—are related to *impaired learning or motor behavior resulting specifically from a breakdown in the SIMSF system including sensory responsivity*. **Developmental disorders**—atypical development—refer to those *disorders of development that result in abnormal reflex behavior, dysfunction in the various sensory systems, and specific deficits in motor sensory responses, motor patterns, or motor skills*. Although developmental disorders are often associated with process disorders, this is not always the case. There are developmental disorders in which processing is fine but difficulties in typical motor performance exist. For example, the effects of polio (post-polio) can leave one with decreased muscle tone in a limb that can influence the development of motor patterns—the processing of sensory stimuli is fine, but the development and performance of motor skills are affected. On the other hand, process disorders may be seen in atypical development (motor sensory responses, motor patterns) or atypical performance (motor skills and their application in culturally determined forms of movement).

Some individuals with a disability (e.g., muscular dystrophy, arm amputation) demonstrate what we identify as "atypical" motor performance (e.g., waddling gait during walking, catching a ball by trapping it). These individuals can "process" sensory information appropriately (SIMSF), but their motor output is not considered "typical." It is important to note here that this "atypical" motor performance is likely to be their "typical performance," and, thus, the physical educator's task is to improve the efficiency and competence of the individual's "typical" motor performance.

For more information on the impairments mentioned in this chapter, see Appendix C.

PROCESS DISORDERS

A process disorder in the SIMSF system may have as its source any one or a combination of possible breakdown sites. As stated in Chapter 3, breakdowns in this system can adversely affect motor performance. It is important to understand the possible sites of breakdown (sources of dysfunction) and the breakdown effects on resultant motor behavior (see Figures 4.1 and 4.2).

In the SIMSF system, the adequacy of the motor response depends on adequate processing at each phase. To produce motor behavior, an individual must receive the sensory stimulation, selectively attend to the stimuli, perceive (integrate, interpret, and match with memory) the sensory stimuli, and translate them into the motor program. Once the motor program is "determined," the areas of the CNS responsible for controlling movement must be engaged in order for the motor response to occur. When the source(s) of dysfunction (areas of the brain responsible for the specific functions) are identified, the implications for physical education programs become evident. That is, to help students perform the desired motor response, the strategies used in physical education should take into account the source of dysfunction in processing disorders.

Feedback loops contribute to the efficiency and effectiveness of motor behavior. Feedback between perception and selective attention and arousal is necessary for adequate translation of sensory stimuli into meaningful perception. Feedback is also needed between control of the motor program and motor response, to refine the movement. After the motor response, sensory feedback is provided in accordance with the ongoing processing of the dynamic SIMSF system.

Breakdown Sites and Effects

Ⓐ **Input/reception.** Structural or functional impairment may prevent sensory stimuli from reaching the CNS. As a result of damaged or dysfunctional transmission routes, the neural impulses may not be transmitted or may be transmitted in such poor quantity or quality that the CNS cannot effectively utilize the information. Inasmuch as the learner would be expected to perform based on inadequate sensory information, the resultant motor response would be less than desired, considered atypical, and perhaps inefficient or ineffective. Individuals with sensory impairments (vision, audition) must rely on sensory information from other channels to aid in the processing of information needed for motor performance.

FIGURE 4.1

Breakdown sites in the sensory-integrative-motor-sensory-feedback system. See text discussion for explanation of Ⓐ–Ⓖ.

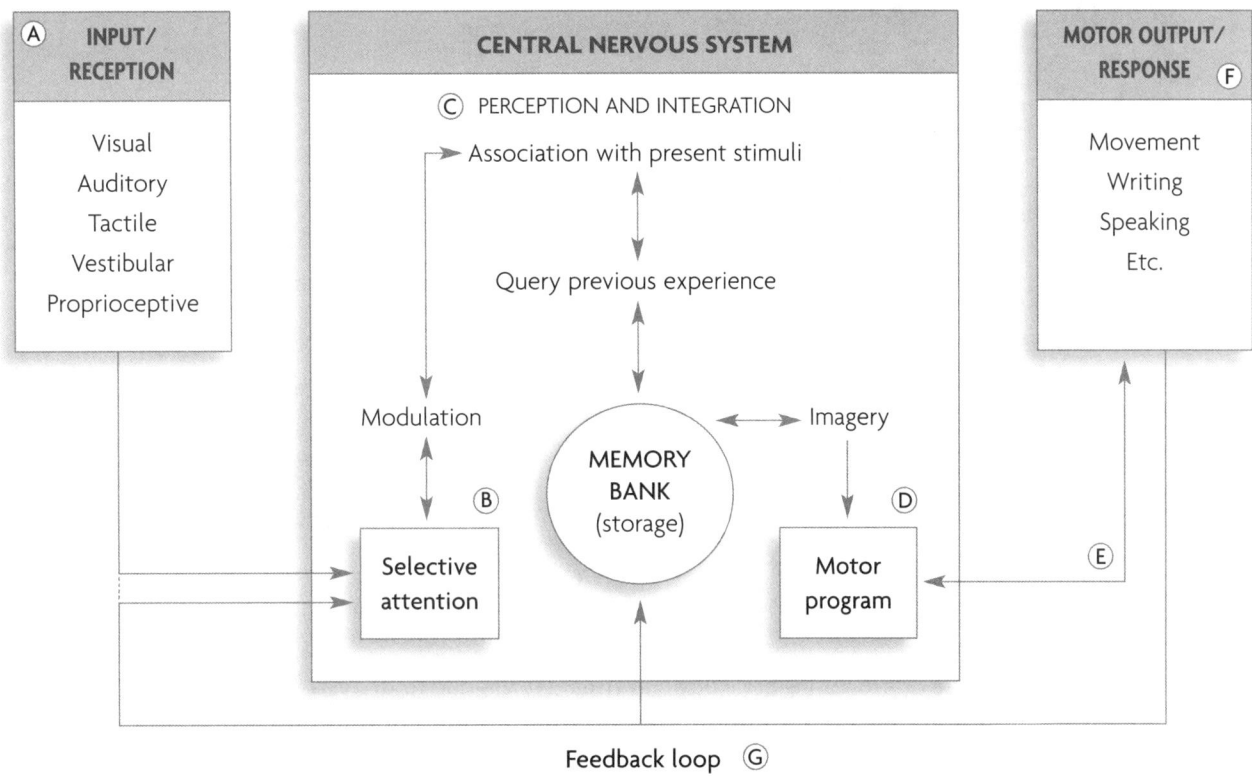

Ⓑ **Selective attention/arousal.** The second source of dysfunction is characterized by a breakdown in the neurological arousal, attention, and selection necessary for central processing. The sensory information is reaching the CNS, but it cannot be effectively processed due to the lack of attentiveness or arousal. Those with responsivity disorders, regardless of specific impairment, may experience difficulty in adequately integrating sensory stimulation for motor output. For those individuals with dysfunction or damage in the CNS areas (e.g., reticular formation, cerebral cortex), the source of atypical motor performance can be traced back to a difficulty in selectively attending to sensory stimulation. This difficulty is frequently found in individuals with mental retardation, a learning disability, traumatic or acquired brain injury, an emotional disorder, or autism. (See also the sections on responsivity located later in this chapter and in Chapter 3.) With this source of dysfunction, it is important that physical education teachers use teaching strategies that assist the students with focusing on the stimuli needed for the desired outcome.

Ⓒ **Perception and integration.** Movement requires the perception and integration of sensory information. If the process of making sense of the sensory information breaks down, the individual will have difficulty interpreting the sensory stimuli or match-

MAKING CONNECTIONS

Processing of Visual Stimuli

Joshua, who is legally blind, has limited sight. What he sees is blurry unless he is very close to the object; therefore, he must rely on auditory and proprioception to move into the proper position. To assume the appropriate position on a weight training machine, Joshua can benefit from verbal feedback and physical prompts from the teacher. In the future, he will need to rely on proprioceptive feedback and reference his memories to guide himself into the appropriate position again.

FIGURE 4.2 — Organic examples of breakdown sites.

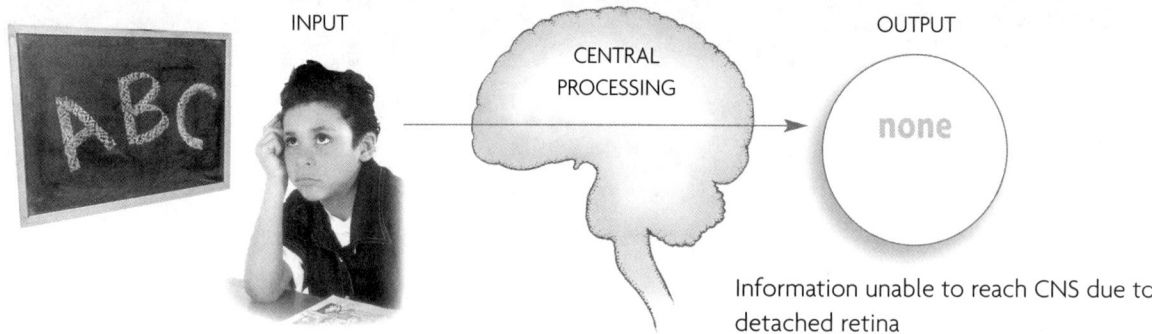

a. Breakdown at A: example of input breakdown of visual system due to detached retina.

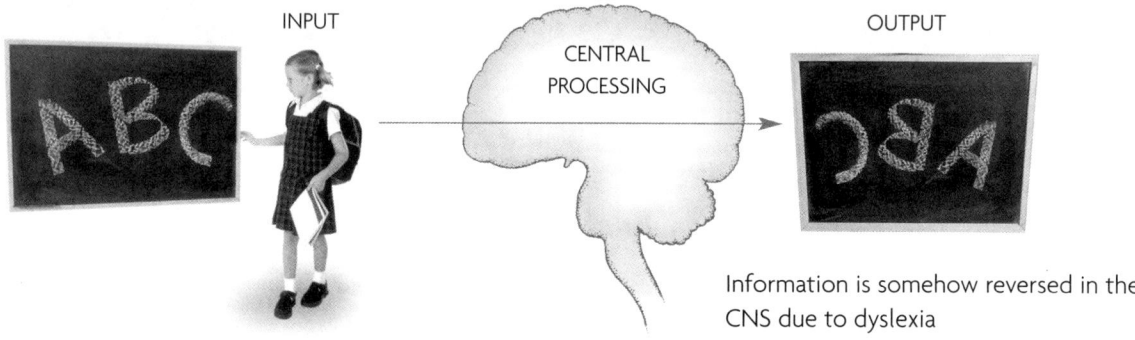

b. Breakdown at C: example of processing breakdown in visual system due to dyslexia.

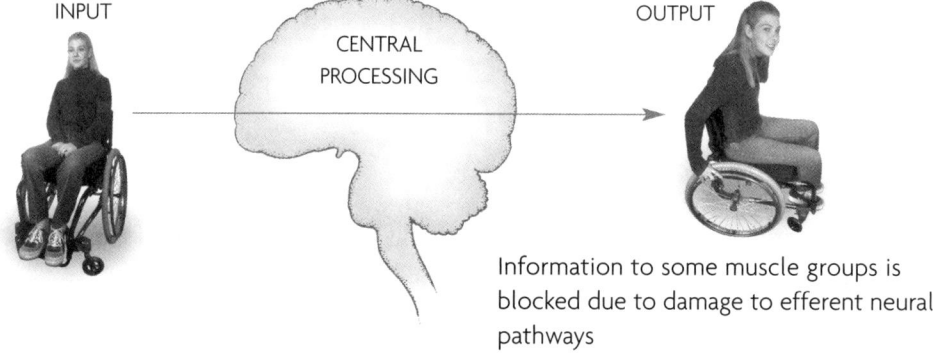

c. Breakdown at E: example of output breakdown of proprioceptive system due to paraplegia.

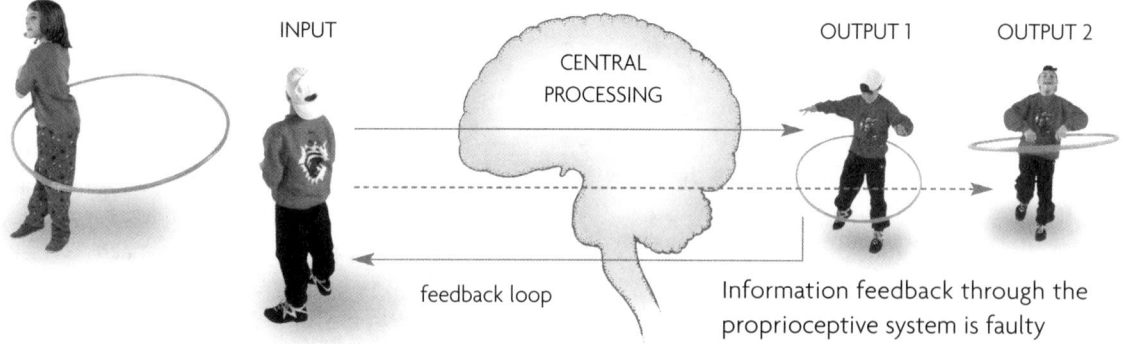

d. Breakdown at G: example of motor program breakdown of proprioceptive system in clumsy child and correction with feedback.

ing the stimuli with memories. The difficulty might arise from having no previous experience (thus, no memory) or having previous experience but limited memory (difficulty in short-term or long-term memory). In addition, one may have difficulty perceiving similarities or differences among stimuli (interpretation). Examples include individuals with an impairment that affects selected areas of the CNS responsible for perception (e.g., learning disability, mental retardation).

Ⓓ **Translation into the motor program.** The adequacy and accuracy of a perception are related to the adequacy of one's ability to translate perception into the motor program. Thus, another source of dysfunction lies with processing perceptions into the motor program. Individuals with damage or dysfunction in the motor areas of the CNS are capable of receiving, attending to, and accurately perceiving the stimuli, but they have difficulty translating the information into a motor program and exercising control over the movement. The source of dysfunction identified here also involves the association areas of the brain, which are responsible for making connections between areas of the brain. For example, individuals with a learning disability or traumatic or acquired brain damage might perceive what is required but have difficulty organizing the sensory information from specific brain centers necessary for planning and executing the desired movements.

Ⓔ **Control of the motor program.** Control of the motor program is the next phase in the SIMSF system, and breakdowns can occur here as well. Individuals with damage to the cerebellum or basal ganglia (primary motor control centers) have difficulty performing tasks, although they are quite capable of processing sensory stimuli to that point. With traumatic brain injury or cerebral palsy, the individual is most likely able to determine the "motor program" for walking on a balance beam but, due to damage to the cerebellum, might have great difficulty controlling the movements necessary to be successful.

Ⓕ **Motor response.** Once the control of the motor program is set, movement (motor response) is initiated. Dysfunctions in this phase can result from damage to the efferent pathways (those going from the brain to the muscles). In this case, even though the individual knows what the task is and how to complete it, the neural transmission is inadequate to stimulate the muscles needed to do the task. This is commonly the case with individuals with a spinal cord injury (e.g., incomplete paraplegia or quadriplegia). Another possibility is that damage to the actual muscles is negatively affecting the motor response. With impairments such as muscular dystrophy, the individual processes information adequately but has limited responses due to the dysfunction in the muscles.

Ⓖ **Feedback loop.** Breakdowns can also occur in the feedback loop. Faulty transmission of feedback results in poor quality and quantity of new input and assuredly decreases the ability of the performer to make progressively more adaptive responses to input. Dysfunction in afferent pathways (those going from the muscles to the brain) among "clumsy" children is an example. Even though all of the anatomical structures needed to perform are intact, these children cannot correct their movement errors. The faulty transmission of proprioceptive information prevents them from "feeling" their body's position in space and making an appropriate adjustment to the position.

MAKING CONNECTIONS

Selective Attention

Mr. Rogers' class is playing a toss and catch practice game. Students are in a scatter formation, and the center player throws the ball up into the air and calls the name of one person in the group. The person whose name is called must catch the ball before it hits the ground. Suzie fails to respond when her name is called because she cannot selectively attend to the center player in her group. She is also hearing the other names called in the groups in close proximity to her group, as well as other extraneous sounds on the playground.

Four strategies that would be helpful for Suzie in this situation are:

- Direct/cue her to look at the person in the middle of her group and concentrate on visually attending to only that person.
- Direct/cue the person in the middle to look at Suzie (and get her visual attention) prior to saying her name and then tossing the ball.
- Direct/cue a peer to tap Suzie on the shoulder before the name is called so that she is prepared.
- Change the game to follow a sequence, such as going around the circle, rather than randomly calling names.

Responsivity Disorders

A process disorder of responsivity may manifest itself in one of three ways: hyperresponsivity, hyporesponsivity, or vacillating responsivity.

Hyperresponsivity. Affected individuals with **hyperresponsivity** tend to be *hyperresponsive to specific types of sensory stimulation* and *demonstrate dramatic reactions to the stimuli*. Children labeled as hyperactive, for example, are often described as "not paying attention," when they might actually be paying too much attention. For example, Paul simultaneously hears the voice of his teacher, the conversation of people in the hall, and the sounds of his classmate shuffling paper. Within the space of a few seconds, Paul may look at his teacher, run to the hallway, and turn to watch his classmate. His CNS is being overloaded with information that it cannot integrate. Just as water must overflow when poured into a bucket that is already full, these children's responses must also "overflow." Many children show this type of response when several forms of stimuli enter the system simultaneously; other children show this reaction only to specific forms of stimuli.

One variation of hyperresponsivity is described as "summating input." With this disorder, the child is able to respond appropriately to normal quantities and qualities of input for a while and therefore function within the limits of homeostasis. Due to intermittent CNS dysfunction, however, after a period of time, the system seems to allow the input to add up or "summate," and the individual is thrown into a state of overload. The reaction to stimuli then becomes hyperresponsive, and behavior is observed to be hyperactive (see Figure 4.3a and Table 4.1).

Hyporesponsivity. **Hyporesponsive** is on the other end of the continuum from hyperresponsive. Selected individuals with a disability often display *little or no response to the stimuli around them*. For example, the severing of afferent peripheral nerves (as may be seen in paraplegia) prevents reception as well as perception, and hence responsivity, because no nerve impulses reach the brain. Individuals with higher lesions in the CNS or with abnormally high thresholds may be capable of receiving stimuli, but they require exceedingly large quantities of stimuli to generate a response. Because their sensory systems are underloaded, they need greater quantities or an improved quality of input to activate neural structures. As opposed to the "full bucket" analogy of the hyperresponsive system, the hyporesponsive system can be compared to a bucket that has a hole in the bottom (see Figure 4.3b and Table 4.1).

Vacillating responsivity. With **vacillating responsivity,** *the individual's CNS seems to vacillate in its ability to mediate, modulate, or integrate sensory information*. This disorder is often seen in individuals with autism spectrum disorders. Their systems seem

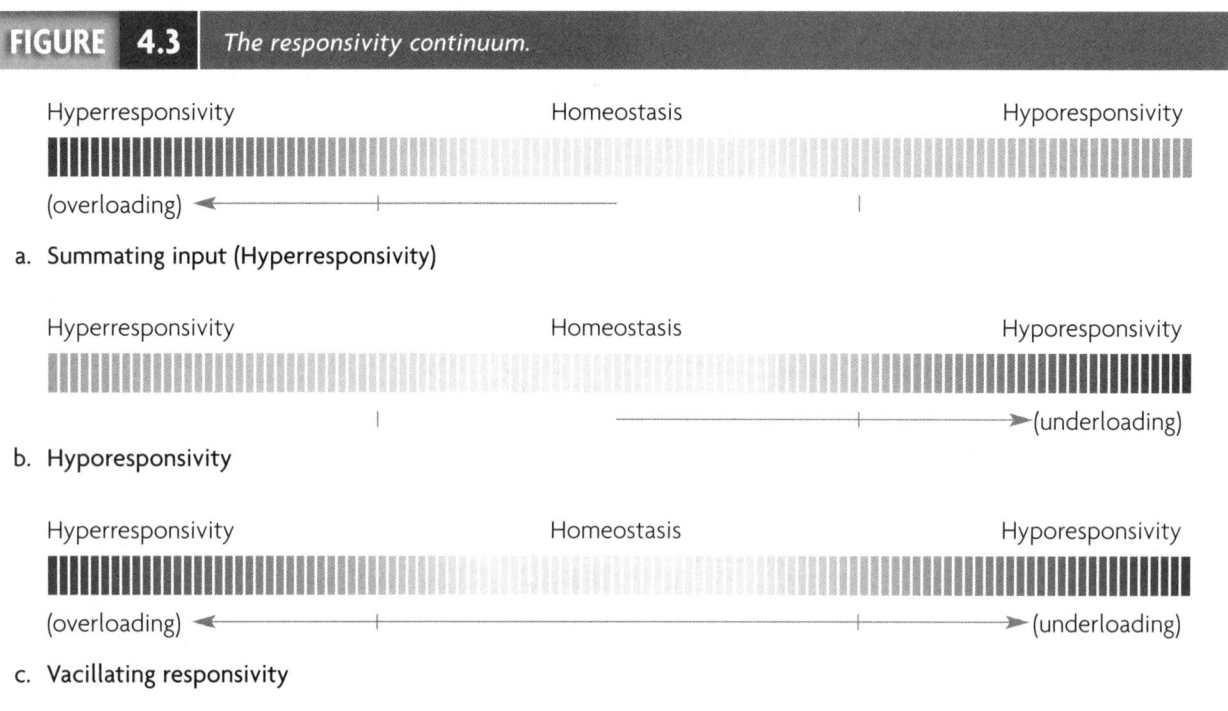

FIGURE 4.3 *The responsivity continuum.*

a. Summating input (Hyperresponsivity)

b. Hyporesponsivity

c. Vacillating responsivity

TABLE 4.1 *Behaviors related to sensory responses.*

STIMULI	EXAMPLES OF SENSORY AVOIDANCE AND/OR LOW TOLERANCE (HYPERSENSITIVITY)	EXAMPLES OF SENSORY SEEKING AND/OR HIGH TOLERANCE (HYPOSENSITIVITY)
Tactile (touch): Body and limbs	<ul><li>wears clothes to cover entire body regardless of weather (resisting unrestricted environmental touch by covering the body)</li><li>wears minimal clothes regardless of weather (resisting touch of garments on body)</li><li>resists physical prompting</li><li>complains excessively of being bumped and poked</li><li>has unusually large personal space</li></ul>	<ul><li>is an older child who touches everything</li><li>frequently rubs, holds, or manipulates objects of a certain texture</li><li>rubs fingers or body parts constantly</li><li>is unaware of substances spilled on body (e.g., glue on hands)</li></ul>
Deep pressure	<ul><li>resists tumbling, contact sports, jumping, bouncing</li><li>appears to lack strength for functional tasks, but on testing has adequate strength</li></ul>	<ul><li>frequently seeks deep-pressure touch such as bear hugs</li><li>will sleep only when wrapped tightly in a sheet or blanket</li><li>frequently bumps into objects and people without apparent reason</li></ul>
Oral/facial	<ul><li>primarily eats one type of food texture</li><li>has extreme resistance to face washing, tooth brushing, and hair brushing and continues to complain when finished</li></ul>	<ul><li>frequently chews or sucks on edibles</li><li>appears unaware of touch to face unless there is visual input</li><li>is often unaware of food on face or drooling</li></ul>
Pain	<ul><li>makes unusual and prolonged complaints of minor incidents of pain</li><li>complains about or interprets minor body sensations as "painful"</li></ul>	<ul><li>is unaware of bleeding or swelling of sustained injury</li><li>has unusual fearlessness of falling on hard surfaces</li><li>does not seem to feel injections</li><li>is unaware of sustained burns or sunburns</li></ul>
Temperature	<ul><li>consistently comments about temperature changes when experienced</li><li>tends to react to and/or label moderate temperature as too hot or too cold</li></ul>	<ul><li>drinks very hot liquids without complaint</li><li>insists on very warm bath water</li></ul>
Auditory (sound)	<ul><li>covers ears frequently</li><li>notices or comments on quiet background noises, such as normal traffic outside, air conditioning fan, or quiet noises in an adjacent room</li><li>consistently seeks quiet areas away from peers on the playground or in classroom</li><li>runs out of room or area in response to sounds</li><li>has irrational fear of small appliances such as blender, vacuum cleaner, or mixer</li><li>hears sirens or oncoming trains before others</li></ul>	<ul><li>does not respond to commands without visual cues</li><li>appears to have poor hearing not verified by hearing tests</li><li>puts ear on speakers</li></ul>

(continued)

TABLE 4.1 Continued.

STIMULI	EXAMPLES OF SENSORY AVOIDANCE AND/OR LOW TOLERANCE (HYPERSENSITIVITY)	EXAMPLES OF SENSORY SEEKING AND/OR HIGH TOLERANCE (HYPOSENSITIVITY)
Visual: Sight and light	<ul><li>turns off regular household lighting for activities such as eating, watching TV, or playing</li><li>covers eyes or squints frequently</li><li>avoids going outdoors on sunny days</li><li>regularly comments when sun goes in and out of clouds</li></ul>	<ul><li>spins brightly colored objects, watches light through leaves</li><li>frequently flicks lights on and off</li><li>watches repetitive movements such as an automatic door opening and closing or flipping pages of a book</li><li>manipulates objects close to face but does not have visual impairment</li></ul>
Movement: Body moving through space	<ul><li>is fearful and/or resistant during team games, such as basketball, softball, chase/tag</li><li>avoids positions and movements that challenge one's balance</li><li>avoids positions where feet are off the ground</li><li>reacts negatively to head being tipped back in space</li></ul>	<ul><li>is not afraid of heights or falling hazards</li><li>excessively seeks tumbling and wrestling activities</li><li>spins or circles excessively</li></ul>
Reactions to movement forces	<ul><li>avoids playground equipment that propels body through space, such as swings, merry-go-rounds, slides, teeter-totters</li><li>gets motion sickness</li><li>is fearful of escalators and/or elevators</li></ul>	<ul><li>seeks spinning activities for prolonged periods</li><li>consistently assumes unusual positions on playground equipment</li><li>craves fast rides at amusement parks</li></ul>
Vibration	<ul><li>is fearful of barber's clippers</li><li>refuses to hold mixer, hair dryer, Dustbuster</li><li>is fearful of electric but not manual toothbrushes</li></ul>	<ul><li>places entire vibrator, or a side of a vibrator appliance, in or near mouth repeatedly</li><li>tolerates vibratory stimuli for extended periods</li></ul>
Smell and taste	<ul><li>primarily eats bland foods</li><li>reacts to or comments on normal odors as though they were irritating</li><li>reacts to or comments on faint odors that go unnoticed by others</li></ul>	<ul><li>fails to notice noxious smells</li><li>seeks highly seasoned foods</li></ul>

Source: Adapted from Wright, D. B., Gurman, H. B., et al. (1998). *Positive Intervention for Serious Behavior Problems* (Rev. ed.). Sacramento: California Department of Education. Used with permission.

to be overloading sometimes and underloading at other times. Children with a disability may demonstrate this vacillation on a day-to-day, minute-to-minute basis or may be hyporesponsive to some forms of stimuli and hyperresponsive to others. There is some speculation that variations in responsivity are the end result of an attempt by the CNS to find homeostasis (see Figure 4.3c).

DEVELOPMENTAL DISORDERS

Every person is born with an innate neural capacity—an inherent capacity that makes possible neurological growth and development. Development takes place even before birth so that one is born adequately programmed to cope with the demands of the environment. This is not to say that each person is born with the same neural capacity. Obviously, differences in neural capacity tend to be evident in individuals with a disability. As stated earlier, developmental disorders are those disorders that result in abnormal reflex behavior; dysfunction in the various sensory systems; and specific deficits in sensorimotor responses, motor patterns, or motor skills. The physical educator should not impose limitations or restrictions on expected performance. Rather, one's innate neural capacity should be accepted as a foundation from which to proceed through the developmental model and to enhance one's functional efficiency and competence in motor performance.

Reflex Activity

Reflex activity is a natural aspect of human development. Some reflexes exist from birth, while other reflexes must develop later. Reflexes are inborn and genetically endowed, and they remain functional or potentially functional throughout life. Although the pioneers in reflex development (Bobath & Bobath, 1971; Fiorentino, 1972) define a great number of reflexes, in this text, we discuss only those reflexes thought to impinge most on motor performance:

1. Spinal reflexes (grasp, startle, crossed extension)
2. Brain stem reflexes (tonic neck, tonic labyrinthine, associated reactions, positive and negative support)
3. Midbrain reflexes and reactions (righting reactions)
4. Automatic movement reactions (protective extension)
5. Cortical-equilibrium reactions (protective reaction in prone and supine)

As discussed in Chapter 3, reflexes emerge and are integrated or inhibited in the same sequence as neurological development. Reflex behavior controlled by the older, lower structure of the CNS (spinal cord) emerges and is integrated or inhibited first. As the development of the CNS proceeds upward toward the cortex, reflexes controlled by those higher, newer structures emerge. Developmental disorders of reflex behavior take one of two forms: interference from dominating reflexes that should have been integrated or inhibited but have not and lack of assistance from reflexes that should have emerged during development but have not.

Interference from Dominating Reflexes

An example of interference from dominating reflexes is the grasp reflex, which is present at birth and becomes integrated at about three to six months of

MAKING CONNECTIONS

Importance of Reflex Integration

Brian demonstrates protective extension, but it is inconsistent and extremely slow. Therefore, he often fails to break a fall. Brian dislikes vigorous physical activities, sits against the wall near the classroom at recess, and often "acts out" in physical education, where the usual form of punishment is to be "benched" (sit out of the game, stand on a dot, go back to class, etc.). He whines and cries when asked to run, step up on a small step or a platform on the playground apparatus, walk on a rough surface such as sand, or participate in a fast-moving activity with peers (e.g., handball, tag).

Brian received adapted physical education services in which improving the speed and consistency of his protective extension response was one of the primary goals. He was released back to general physical education because his performance and behavior had greatly improved. The specialist provided further intervention strategies to use within the larger group setting in case the problem reoccurred.

age (Fiorentino, 1972). Grasping during the earlier stage is involuntary but, when integrated, allows voluntary grasp and release (see Figure 4.4). When this reflex remains dominant beyond six months of age, it interferes with motor responses (e.g., release of an object), with motor patterns (e.g., throwing), and with motor skills of throwing for distance and accuracy (e.g., pitching a softball or throwing a javelin).

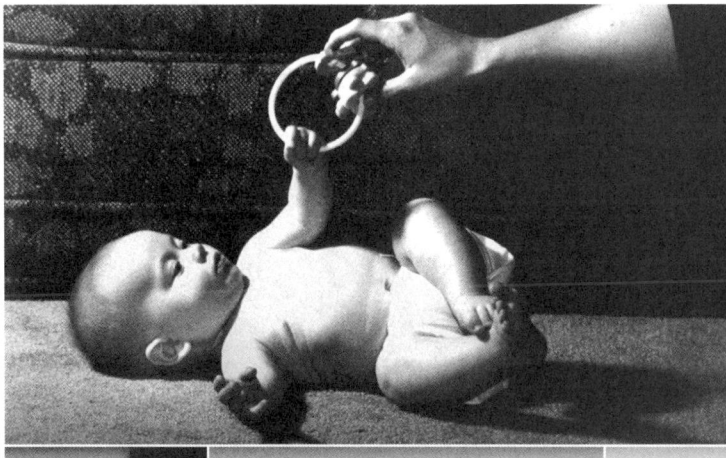

FIGURE 4.4

The grasp reflex is normal in infants to approximately three to six months of age.

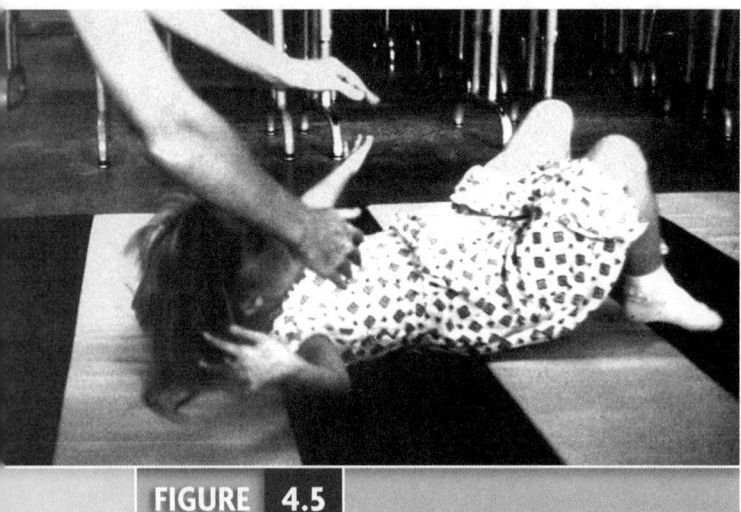

FIGURE 4.5

Interference from the TLR prevents this girl from completing a forward roll in the tucked position.

Another example of interference is from the tonic labyrinthine reflex (TLR). Because the reflex pulls the ends of the body toward the ground, a student who has this problem cannot remain tucked while doing a forward roll (see Figure 4.5).

Lack of assistance from reflexes

The lack of an assistive reflex, such as protective extension, is an example of the second form of disordered reflex behavior. The protective extension reflex emerges at about six to nine months of age (Fiorentino, 1972) and, under typical conditions,

FIGURE 4.6

The protective extension reflex emerges at about six months and remains throughout life.

remains present throughout life. This reflex comes into play to break the fall when one loses balance. Failure of this reflex to emerge during the course of development can have a negative impact on motor performance (see Figure 4.6). Children who do not have assistance from this reflex soon learn that when they play, they fall, and when they fall, they can get hurt. Some children learn the "safe" games to play, and others tend to avoid the very activities that would enhance the course of development of motor patterns, skills, and other forms of movement. In these cases, the lack of assistive reflexes interferes as much, although indirectly, as the direct interference of dominating, residual reflexes.

Sensory Systems

As discussed in Chapter 3, five sensory systems contribute significantly to motor performance. If only one sensory system is negatively affected, development might not be hindered. On the other hand, if more than one sensory system is disordered in development, then the likely impact on motor performance is greater.

Vestibular system

The vestibular system carries out a specific type of proprioception (due to its widespread influence throughout the nervous system, the proprioceptive system is discussed separately). The vestibular system is stimulated whenever an individual moves in response to gravity. Disorders in this system are observable in behavior and motor performance. The many signs and indications of a vestibular disorder include the following:

1. *Atypical muscle tone.* **Muscle tone** refers to *the elasticity of the muscles and fluidity of associated movements.* Some individuals with a disability demonstrate **hypertonicity** *(overly tight tone)* and others, **hypotonicity** *(overly flaccid tone).* If hypertonicity dominates, the individual tends to have limited range of motion, the muscles appear to be stretched (tight), and the movements appear jerky and awkward. On the other hand, if hypotonicity exists, the muscles tend to be flaccid (floppy), with extreme flexibility around the joints. The movements appear labored and lacking precision.

2. *Poor balance and equilibrium responses.*

3. *Poor cocontraction.* Poor cocontraction is demonstrated by the inability simultaneously to contract antagonist muscle groups or to "fixate" two or more body parts around a joint (e.g., the inability

to hold one's outstretched arms in a steady position with the addition of weight or force on the arms).

4. *Postural insecurity.* Postural insecurity is demonstrated by an adverse reaction to sudden movements (e.g., flailing arms upon sudden movement of the body).

5. *Poor eye pursuits.* The inability to track visually the movement of an object, when this can negatively affect motor performance (e.g., catching a ball), demonstrates poor eye pursuits.

6. *Disorders in arousal state (e.g., excitability, lethargy).* Atypical responses to auditory stimuli (e.g., aversive reaction to sound) and visual stimuli may also appear.

7. *Short attention span and distractibility.*

8. *Avoidance of or seeking out swinging, spinning, or twirling activities.* These might include spinning one's body or twirling one's fingers in front of the eyes or active avoidance of these activities (e.g., avoiding merry-go-rounds and swings).

The vestibular system directly affects muscle tone. Consequently, both too much muscle tone (hypertonia) and too little muscle tone (hypotonia, flaccidity) may be related to vestibular dysfunction. Hypotonicity and hypertonicity can, in turn, adversely affect motor development and motor performance. Abnormal muscle tone can affect strength, muscular fitness, flexibility, agility, cardiovascular functions, endurance, perseverance (sustaining a movement), ease of movement, and the ability to perform coordinated movements.

Balance and equilibrium responses can also be affected by a dysfunction of the vestibular system. Signs of this dysfunction are difficulty in achieving and maintaining balance, a decreased ability in regaining balance, an inability to adjust quickly to changes in equilibrium, and an inability to avoid falling. Individuals often assume awkward postures to compensate for the lack of fully functional balance and equilibrium responses. The "clumsy child" and individuals with a disability who exhibit signs of poor balance and equilibrium responses through constantly skinned knees, clumsiness, and disorientation should be assessed for adequate vestibular function (see Chapter 6 for ways to identify vestibular disorders through systematic observation of behavior and specific assessment instruments).

Before humans can respond to stimuli, they must receive the input that neurologically arouses, excites, and prepares them for movement. Often, individuals with disordered vestibular systems do not adequately receive and process the stimuli; as a result, their systems are not in an arousal or readiness state. When the CNS is not aroused, there is little feedback with which to respond further to the demands of the environment. The result is an inappropriate motor response that hinders motor performance. In terms of the computer analogy, there is more feedback, but it is of poor quality; and it is quality of feedback, not quantity, that enhances integration or adequate functioning of the vestibular system.

Proprioceptive system

Disorders in the proprioceptive system are often closely related to vestibular disorders. However, the proprioceptive input deals with stimuli received through the muscles, joints, ligaments, and bones, so there are also specific types of proprioceptive disorders. An understanding of the responsivity continuum is important for an understanding of this system. Too little proprioceptive input fails to activate the system fully and provides little information from which the individual can respond. Sensory overload of the proprioceptive system is possible, but sensory underloading is more common. With a lack of proprioceptive information and inadequate processing of that information, the following signs and indications may be observed:

1. *Atypical muscle tone.* As stated previously, muscle tone refers to the elasticity of the muscles and fluidity of associated movements. Some individuals with a disability demonstrate hypertonicity (overly tight tone) and others, hypotonicity (overly flaccid tone).

2. *Inadequate muscle contraction for maintenance of posture.*

3. *Poor cocontraction.* Poor cocontraction is demonstrated by the inability to contract antagonist muscle groups simultaneously or to "fixate" two or more body parts around a joint.

4. *Lack of body awareness.* Body awareness is demonstrated through the ability to "know" where one's body parts are based upon internal stimuli (without vision). With a lack of body awareness, one's ability to use body parts for movement is limited.

5. *Difficulty in coordinating movement efficiently and effectively.*

6. *Difficulty in moving through space, especially around objects.*

Individuals exhibiting signs of proprioceptive disorders may have difficulty attaining and maintaining certain postures or positions. Performing certain movements or assuming novel positions is difficult for the individual whose proprioceptive system is not providing the necessary input and feedback for successful completion. Other signs include a lack of body part awareness (especially without vision), an inability to push or pull objects, and an inability to maintain the arms in a static position opposing the influence of gravity.

Proprioceptive system disorders adversely affect both static and dynamic balance. Without adequate support through the joints, muscles, and ligaments, the individual's movements appear jerky or aborted. Such an individual has difficulty executing smooth, coordinated movements. Proprioceptive system disorders can be found among individuals with a disability.

Tactile system

The tactile system functions maturely throughout life. It is through this sense (as well as the vestibular and proprioceptive senses) that humans learn about their environment. It provides the feedback through which they can cope with and respond to the demands of their environment. The responsivity continuum is important here also; individuals may show hyporesponsive or hyperresponsive reactions. Disorders in the tactile system may also result from a lack of adequate interpretation, assimilation, and organization of the incoming and outgoing tactile information. The following are common signs and indications of a tactile disorder:

1. *Tactile defensiveness*—demonstrating a negative response to touch or defending oneself from tactile stimuli
2. *Tacile-seeking behaviors*—a strong desire to touch and feel anything and everything
3. *Tactile processing difficulties*—a complete lack of response to touch, the inability to discriminate between different tactile sensations, the inability to locate where one has been touched, or the inability to perceive stimuli simultaneously
4. *Hyperactivity* or *distractibility*
5. *Difficulty in motor planning*—difficulty in planning and executing nonhabitual, purposeful movement

Depending on the type of responsivity to tactile stimulation, characteristics of disordered tactile function, which represent the nervous system's attempt to normalize or reach homeostasis, will vary. Hyperresponsivity to tactile stimulation results in tactile defensiveness. Individuals who are tactilely defensive often show a negative response to touch, a sensitivity to light, and difficulty concentrating. Behaviors such as wearing the same clothes continuously, irritation as a result of close proximity to other individuals, and withdrawal are often misinterpreted, but can be indicative of an overload on the tactile system (see Table 4.1).

Hyporesponsivity generally results in tactile-seeking behaviors. Tactile-seekers may be described as "clinging vines" who are compelled to touch everything and everybody. They often have bruises without knowing where, when, or how they got them. A diminished response to tactile stimulation can be exhibited by not knowing where one has been touched, an inability to distinguish hot and cold stimuli, or an inability to discriminate between textures. These may appear to be behavioral problems at times.

Visual system

The visual system, which develops in stages, demonstrates three basic functions early in life: fixation, accommodation, and convergence. These functions are not established until about the second or third month of postnatal life, long before maturation of the function known as visual perception. Therefore, the distinction between **visual acuity** *(the ability to see clearly)* and **visual perception** *(the capacity to organize and interpret what is seen)* is quite clear. Visual acuity disorders can be identified early because around the third month of life typical observable behaviors include ocular pursuits, holding a rattle and glancing at it, and reaching for dangling objects (see Appendix B). Infants who do not respond (e.g., are hyporesponsive) to visual stimuli are often suspected of having acuity disorders (e.g., visual impairment).

Disorders of visual perception are not easily detectable, and they cannot be detected as early as disorders of other sensory systems; therefore, they present a variety of challenges to the physical educator. All other disorders of the visual system are placed under the broad heading of visual perception (see Table 4.2).

Individuals who have a visual perception disorder, regardless of the amount of useful vision, demonstrate considerably different motor responses from those of individuals without a disorder. Some of these observable signs are:

1. Limited ability to attend to visual stimuli
2. Difficulty following a visual sequence or fixating on a moving object
3. Difficulty discriminating visual objects in the field of vision
4. Difficulty maintaining spatial orientation either at rest or while in motion

TABLE 4.2 Disorders in the visual system.

BEHAVIORS	EXAMPLE	TEACHING STRATEGIES
Poor attending behavior and distractibility for visual stimuli	Difficulty following a demonstration or imitating postures	Supplement instruction with physical guidance
Difficulty following a visual sequence or maintaining eye fixation on a moving object (visual tracking)	Not visually following (tracking) the ball when playing catch with a partner	Change the color (brighter) and size (larger) of the object; exaggerate verbal cues prior to throwing/tossing; shorten distance between partners for more successful response and gradually extend the distance when ready; pair with a peer who will throw accurately
Difficulty discriminating visual objects in the field of vision	Difficulty identifying a specific cone to run to during a shuttle baton pass relay; difficulty identifying the correct target for throwing	Use different color and size of targets; remove or simplify visual objects in background whenever possible
Difficulty maintaining spatial orientation either at rest or while in motion	Difficulty knowing in which direction to move to score a goal in soccer or make a basket in basketball	Enhance visual aspects of goals to differentiate one from the other
Difficulty recalling visual sequences, spatial relations, forms, or other visual features (visual memory)	Difficulty repeating a dance or tumbling sequence from demonstration	Provide verbal rehearsal, visual cues at each stage or sequence, physical guidance, and/or tactile cues when appropriate

5. Difficulty recalling visual sequences, spatial relations, forms, or other visual features

Hyporesponsivity to visual stimuli can appear in students in all educational settings, including the regular classroom. Individuals who are hyporesponsive or unable to make use of visual stimuli are likely to demonstrate inaccurate or inappropriate motor responses to the visual input. Students who are struck by a ball before they have a chance to strike it and students who cannot catch or show delayed reactions to an object moving toward them may be having difficulty following the moving object (visual tracking), fixating on it, or discriminating it from the other stimuli in their field of vision (see Figure 4.7).

Students who seem confused about where they are or are supposed to be on the playing court, who run or throw in the wrong direction, or who cannot replicate a motor pattern they have seen demonstrated may be experiencing quite different disorders. Spatial orientation is needed to know one's placement on a court, and visual

FIGURE 4.7

Some children may avoid climbing this jungle gym because they cannot distinguish which bar to grab to pull up on.

memory is required for recalling and reconstructing a movement sequence that has gone before (see Table 4.2).

Students who show hyperresponsivity to visual stimuli may also be found in any educational setting. Fearful reaction to illumination or changes in illumination, covering the eyes, or running to turn out the lights are behaviors that may indicate visual hyperresponsivity. Individuals with hearing impairment or deafness, some types of visual impairment, and neurologically based disabilities such as autism and brain injury often display this type of atypical processing. Individuals demonstrating hyperactivity, although with more subtle motor responses, may attempt to respond simultaneously to all visual stimuli within their field of vision and hence be unable to attend to a single task. This type of reaction presents challenges to the physical educator for structuring the environment in such a way that learning can take place.

An individual whose visual system seems to vacillate in its need for visual input may demonstrate seeking behaviors such as gazing at a light or bright object, flashing the lights off and on in a room, or hand-flapping in front of the eyes and then masking out all visual stimuli by covering the eyes, hiding in a closet, or in other ways withdrawing from the stimulus. Examples of strategies that may be useful to the physical educator in this situation include:

1. Verbally warning the students prior to changes in illumination
2. Teaching and empowering the students to make their own accommodations, such as turning on more lights, finding an area away from the strong light, adjusting materials to prevent glare, and using sunglasses or a hat or visor

Auditory system

Similar to the visual system, the auditory system is capable of two distinct functions: **auditory acuity** *(hearing)* and **auditory perception** *(audition)*. Hearing disorders, which range from mild hearing loss to total deafness, limit the individual's ability to receive adequate auditory input for use. As hearing losses influence the organization and utilization of this input, or as other disorders intervene in this process, they are said to be disorders in audition—auditory perception.

Students who have a loss of auditory acuity present two major challenges to physical educators: to modify their methods and techniques for communicating information to the learner and to plan appropriate activities for the learner whose hearing loss may be due to damage to parts of the hearing mechanism that also serve the vestibular system.

Individuals who have a disorder of audition are not as easily recognized or understood as those with acuity disorders. Two examples of audition difficulties that may be noted are confusing similar-sounding words (e.g., ball/wall, go/slow) and difficulty discriminating different sounds from one another (e.g., ball bouncing as opposed to someone jumping behind you). The most important signs of auditory perception disorders to be noted by the physical educator are:

1. Difficulty grasping the meaning of words
2. Difficulty using language creatively by conceptualizing the message, associating the appropriate language symbols for use, and sequencing the motor response (expressive language)
3. Inability to recall and use language structures
4. Difficulty discriminating different sounds from one another
5. Difficulty detecting variations in sound, including pitch, volume, direction, and rhythm

Speech and language pathologists have expertise in this area and should be consulted when you suspect a student has this type of difficulty processing auditory information (refer to Chapter 2 for ideas on how to collaborate with other educational personnel).

Motor Sensory Responses

Adequate functioning of the sensory systems, the interrelatedness of these systems, and their relationship to the motor system give rise to sensorimotor responses. The sensorimotor responses reveal the

---

Teaching Tip

STUDENTS WITH HEARING LOSS • Students with a hearing loss in one ear (even a mild loss) often have greater difficulty processing auditory information when background noise is present. This can be particularly challenging in physical activities. Successful physical educators recognize this difficulty and increase the amount and type of accommodations. Examples include: moving closer to the student when speaking, simplifying language, and adding or increasing visual cues.

EXTEND YOUR KNOWLEDGE

Auditory Disorders

Most audition disorders that impinge on motor performance center on the perception of language and musical sounds. Individuals with severe oral language impairment, childhood aphasia, mental retardation, or autism demonstrate a wide variation in their ability to perceive these two sound sources. A lack of response or inappropriate responses to language may stem from the inability to associate language symbols (words) with their meanings. (Although discussion here focuses on the auditory system, the visual system is also very much involved in language detection.)

In other cases, the individual may understand what is said but be unable to organize the words into appropriate linguistic patterns of phrases and sentences, or the individual may not be able to recall the meaningful action components. Examples of inappropriate responses are a student who brings you a ball when you have asked for a bat and a student who does not act at all. Associations with other forms of stimuli, such as the differences in texture and weight between the bat and the ball, are perceptions that must be taught to an individual who seems to be hyporesponsive to auditory input when it takes the form of language. Results of hyporesponsivity to music and rhythmic sounds take the form of arrhythmic motor responses, uncoordinated movements, and general motor clumsiness.

Unless they use proprioceptive stimuli, these individuals have difficulty making use of the feedback from their motor responses, perpetuating inaccurate motor responses. As a result, they tend to have poor muscle tone, reflecting the close relationship between the auditory and proprioceptive systems.

Individuals who are hyperresponsive to auditory input may be identified in the same categorical populations mentioned previously. Attending to all of the auditory input entering the system is characteristic of individuals with hyperactivity who cannot discriminate between the sounds that should have their attention and the sounds that should not. Individuals whose systems cannot modulate or mask unnecessary auditory stimuli appear to be intolerant in their behavior. Individuals with autism or an autism-spectrum disorder are often seen withdrawing from auditory stimuli by covering their ears or hiding. In cases in which the auditory system seems to be vacillating between seeking input and avoiding input, the individual may be observed clapping, pounding, or head-banging—seemingly to create stimuli—then withdrawing, covering the ears, or hiding—seemingly to avoid the input. Often individuals whose behavior suggests that they are seeking auditory stimuli also have a disorder of the vestibular system and demonstrate disequilibrium.

---

early integration of the sensory and motor systems, which results in observable, planned motor behavior. The focal point is the motor response that is based on previous sensorimotor interaction. Deficits in the motor sensory responses can be identified by deficiencies in praxis or motor planning and in integration of both sides of the body.

Praxis

Praxis is *the ability to plan and execute purposeful movement.* Praxis is primarily built on the functioning of the tactile, vestibular, proprioceptive, and visual systems for the necessary input and appropriate motor output. A disorder in praxis implies that an individual will have difficulty in the successful execution of nonhabitual, purposeful movement. A disorder in the sensory systems can interfere with the ability to move efficiently (as discussed earlier). Disorders in interpretation, assimilation, organization, and transmission of sensorimotor information result in some of the following observable signs and characteristics of disordered praxis:

1. Clumsiness
2. Messy handwriting
3. Difficulty imitating movements
4. Lack of body awareness
5. Observable slow, deliberately sequenced (calculated) movements
6. Poor fine motor coordination
7. Poor gross motor coordination
8. Poor eye–hand or eye–foot coordination
9. Uneven or hesitant gait

MAKING CONNECTIONS

Understanding Apraxia

Nine-year-old Michelle was tested for a perceptual–motor program and was asked to sit on a T-stool. She first tried to stand the T-stool up and turn around to sit down. She quickly discovered this would not work. Therefore, her approach to the task was to stand the T-stool up in front of her. She held both sides with each hand, then released one hand and turned halfway around. She then turned her back, reached back to grasp the other side of the stool, and backed up until she could reach the other side of the stool with her other hand. Now, firmly grasping the stool with both hands, she cautiously sat down. This painfully deliberate motor planning took Michelle nearly three minutes to complete. After exhibiting several other signs of apraxia, Michelle was referred for a medical exam. She was diagnosed as having a mild form of cerebral palsy unknown to her parents until this point.

If the sensory input is disordered, difficulty in motor planning results. Disorganization, or lack of integration somewhere in the process of planning and executing movement, also occurs with praxis disorders. This can adversely affect the end product of sensorimotor responses and motor patterns. All motor responses beyond the reflexive level initially require some degree of motor planning. Individuals throughout the range of disabilities may exhibit signs of difficulty with praxis.

The very clumsy student who falls a lot may be exhibiting signs of apraxia (i.e., inability to perform nonhabitual, purposeful movement). In motor performance, the individual may have difficulty with motor sequencing a task such as climbing, going through an obstacle course, or balancing on a one-legged stool (T-stool).

Motor-planning deficits can also appear at higher skill levels, as evidenced by students who have difficulty sequencing a dance routine or karate move, who show an inability to coordinate their bodies sufficiently to run the hurdles successfully, or who have difficulty performing a complex trampoline routine. Learning must always take place prior to and in conjunction with the acquisition of motor patterns and motor skills. Motor planning is a part of that process. When difficulty persists, it is then thought to have implications for disorders in motor planning.

Integration of both sides of the body

Integration of the two sides of the body is both a process and a product. Simply, **integration of both sides of the body** is *the established ability to use both sides of the body together and in opposition*. Developmentally, the use of both sides together develops first, with **reciprocation** (*ability to use the sides of the body in opposition*) following. Both are necessary to further growth in motor development and motor performance. Disorders in integrating both sides of the body are characterized by the following:

1. Difficulty jumping with both feet simultaneously
2. Unequal stance
3. Difficulty crossing the midline of the body (e.g., a child who hesitates as he or she moves a hand to the opposite side of the body or whose eye movements become "jerky" while visually tracking an object across the midline of the body)
4. Poor performance in rhythmic activities
5. Poor coordination of both sides of the body during symmetrical and asymmetrical movements (e.g., difficulty buttoning a shirt or blouse [symmetrical], skipping or galloping [asymmetrical], or jumping up and down)
6. Difficulty isolating one body part for use (e.g., a child who is attempting a task with one hand, whose other hand is moving in response)
7. Slow balance reactions

Individuals who lack integration of both sides of the body demonstrate abnormalities in motor performance and acquisition of skill (see Figures 4.8 and 4.9). For smooth, efficient movement, the individual must be able to respond to the demands of the environment. Integration of both sides of the body requires the following abilities:

1. To use one body part in isolation, without associated reactions in other parts
2. To cross the midline of the body
3. To differentiate between muscles and between movements

Integration also requires communication between the sides of the body for typical motor performance.

FIGURE 4.8

Lack of body integration. This girl cannot yet isolate one body side from the other. Notice the associated reaction in the right arm as she catches with the left.

FIGURE 4.9

This child's right hand is mirroring the left, showing lack of integration (overflow) of the two body sides.

Motor Patterns, Motor Skills, and Culturally Determined Forms of Movement

The emergence of the patterns and skills needed for participation in physical education activities is directly related to age and inversely related to reflex activity. As the individual matures and receives functionally more assistance from later-maturing systems, responses become more complex and skills become increasingly more specific.

Ways in which atypical reflex activity and disorders of earlier- and later-maturing systems and motor responses can adversely affect motor performance have been discussed. The educator should consider these underlying components, integral parts of motor performance, as potential sources of dysfunction in skill acquisition, retention, execution, and refinement. When the supportive functions (e.g., sensory systems and motor sensory responses) are in order, then the focal point for physical education becomes the development and refinement of patterns and skills.

Individuals whose neurological processing support functions (e.g., sensory systems and motor sensory responses) are in order, at least within the scope of their neural capacities, may demonstrate atypical motor patterns or skills for one or more of the following reasons:

- Lack of experience
- Lack of practice
- Lack of motivation to perform
- Emotional difficulties interfering with performance
- Limitations in cognitive function that interfere with the ability to master concepts related to movement
- Lack of fitness or inadequate physiological functioning
- Lack of mechanical efficiency

Individuals who have such physical limitations as loss of sight, limbs, or hearing, or the effective use of these, are usually able to develop motor patterns, skills, and other culturally determined forms of movement to their maximum potential within the scope of the limitations imposed by the disability. Given the opportunity to learn in a sequenced instructional program, children with physical limitations can achieve success.

SOURCES OF DYSFUNCTION AND SPECIFIC IMPAIRMENTS ATTRIBUTABLE TO OTHER FACTORS

As discussed earlier, typical motor behavior is a result of the appropriate functioning of the SIMSF system components:

- Reception of sensory stimulation
- Selective attention/arousal and transmittal of that information to appropriate centers of the CNS for processing
- Integration of that information
- Resultant motor output
- Feedback

Disorders can occur in any portion of this system, resulting in atypical motor performance. In addition, delayed development can result from specific brain damage; specific impairment; and abnormalities in reflex behavior, motor sensory responses, motor patterns, and motor skills. These can cause observable motor deficiency in culturally determined forms of movement.

Many individuals with a disability exhibit atypical motor performance indicative of either process or developmental disorders. In addition, some individuals with a disability exhibit atypical motor performance due to structural (e.g., anatomical, biomechanical) or functional impairment unrelated to either process or developmental disorders. In a general sense, there are impairments that negatively impact neurological functioning (e.g., damage or dysfunction of the CNS) and impairments that do not impact the neurological processes. For the latter, neurological processes are intact, but actual performance is influenced by structure and function (e.g., anatomical, biomechanical, physiological). For example, individuals with limb amputation, arthritis, scoliosis, or certain health conditions (e.g., epilepsy) would not necessarily have process or even developmental disorders, although their motor performance might be considered atypical. See Appendix C for information about specific impairments.

It must also be acknowledged that the use of assistive devices (e.g., canes, crutches, wheelchairs, prostheses) also influences performance. Naturally, this requires an adjustment of the view of typical motor performance. For example, walking must be viewed differently for those with impairments who use assistive devices (e.g., crutches or canes) and for those for whom the anatomical structure of the body varies (e.g., muscular dystrophy, cerebral palsy). For the former, adaptations and modifications become a natural part of the individual's movement repertoire. As already considered and discussed under process disorders, for some individuals (e.g., those with cerebral palsy) the observed motor output initially appears atypical but becomes viewed as natural and typical for the individual. Motor performance in these cases becomes refined and more efficient within the context of the movement repertoire of the particular individual.

SUMMARY

As a vehicle for teaching physical education, the developmental approach provides a myriad of opportunities to teach students who have a dysfunction in innate neural capacity, reflex behavior, the sensory and motor systems, or their interaction. Process disorders result from a breakdown in the SIMSF system, including responsivity to sensory stimulation. Developmental disorders may be seen in abnormal reflex behavior; dysfunction in the various sensory systems; and abnormal motor sensory responses, motor patterns, and motor skills.

To provide meaningful and appropriate physical education programs for individuals with a disability, it is important that physical educators have a complete understanding of the factors underlying movement. Physical educators must understand the role of development in motor skill acquisition and motor performance (i.e., developmental disorders), the neurological processes underlying movement (i.e., process disorders), and other factors influencing motor performance (e.g., anatomical, biomechanical, physiological) in order to identify sources of atypical motor behavior.

CHAPTER 4

Learning Activities

4.1 Observe individuals with a disability in a physical activity setting. Note any difficulty in motor performance. Identify the source of dysfunction as a process disorder, developmental disorder, or both. Share your observations with your classmates and discuss.

4.2 Using the SIMSF system to guide your observation, select one student with a disability and watch his or her motor performance throughout one instructional period. Describe the process (SIMSF) that this student uses to exhibit the desired motor output. Identify the breakdown site(s). Discuss with your classmates specific activities that target the various sources of dysfunction.

4.3 Consider how the responsivity continuum is present in your daily life and how your responsivity to sensory stimuli influences your motor performance. Identify examples of hyperresponsivity and hyporesponsivity.

4.4 For each type of impairment (see Appendix C), identify the probable breakdown sites of process disorders. Do the same with developmental disorders. Using these as the framework, consider the implications for providing physical education programs for individuals with a disability.

REFERENCES

Ayres, A. J. (1972). *Sensory integration and learning disorders.* Los Angeles: Western Psychological Services.

Bobath, B., & Bobath, K. (1971). *Abnormal postural-reflex activity caused by brain lesions.* London: William Heinemann Medical Books.

Caine, G., & Nummela Caine, R. (1994). *Making connections: Teaching and the human brain.* Menlo Park, CA: Addison-Wesley.

Fiorentino, M. R. (1972). *Normal and abnormal development.* Springfield, IL: Thomas.

Howard, P. J. (1994). *The owner's manual for the brain: Everyday applications from mind–brain research.* Austin, TX: Bard.

Jensen, E. P. (2000a). *Brain-based learning.* San Diego, CA: Brain Store.

Jensen, E. P. (2000b). *Learning with the body in mind.* San Diego, CA: Brain Store.

Ornstein, R., & Thompson, R. (1984). *The amazing brain.* Boston: Houghton Mifflin.

Sage, G. H. (1977). *Introduction to motor behavior.* Menlo Park, CA: Addison-Wesley.

Wolfe, P. (2001). *Brain matters: Translating research into classroom practice.* Alexandria, VA: Association for Supervision and Curriculum Development (ASCD).

Wright, D. B., Gurman, H. B., et al. (1998). *Positive intervention for serious behavior problems* (Rev. ed.). Sacramento: California Department of Education.

CHAPTER 5

The Process of Assessment and Evaluation

Guiding Questions

1. What are the differences between testing, measurement, assessment, and evaluation?

2. What are the respective purposes of evaluation and assessment as used by the physical educator?

3. What are the uses of such measurement concepts as central tendency, variability, position in a group, standard scores, and correlation?

4. What are the four levels of measurement?

5. What are the common forms of testing?

You may have had an introductory course in measurement and evaluation in physical education. Few students, however, have had courses in the assessment of motor performance as it pertains to individuals with a disability. Although a basic course in measurement serves as a good foundation for understanding the concepts presented in this chapter, it is not essential. The five basic concepts presented and discussed in this chapter are:

1. Testing
2. Measurement
3. Standards
4. Evaluation
5. Assessment

Each term is graphically represented in its relationship to the others in Figure 5.1.

TESTING

Testing, as used in this text, is *a data-gathering technique that uses tools or specific procedures for systematizing observations.* Testing may take one of two forms: formal or informal.

Formal Testing

Formal testing *is objective and usually involves setting aside a special time, using a preplanned set of procedures (e.g., described in a test manual), using predetermined space and equipment, and recording scores.* In a formal test of aerobic capacity (objective and traditional), the teacher counts the number of laps students complete during a 12-minute run. Besides being traditional, this example also represents objective testing because it is not up to the teacher to judge whether the student has good or poor aerobic capacity. Rather, the precise number of laps is recorded and scored (counted) as an indicator, regardless of who is the examiner. This is also a performance test, although this variable could be measured more directly by capturing expired air in a spirometer and determining oxygen intake.

Informal Testing

Informal or alternative and nontraditional testing *is subjective and may be done at any time and under any conditions. It may not require recording scores.* For example, while watching a seven-year-old on the playground, you notice (subjective and nontraditional) that he climbs the steps to the slide one

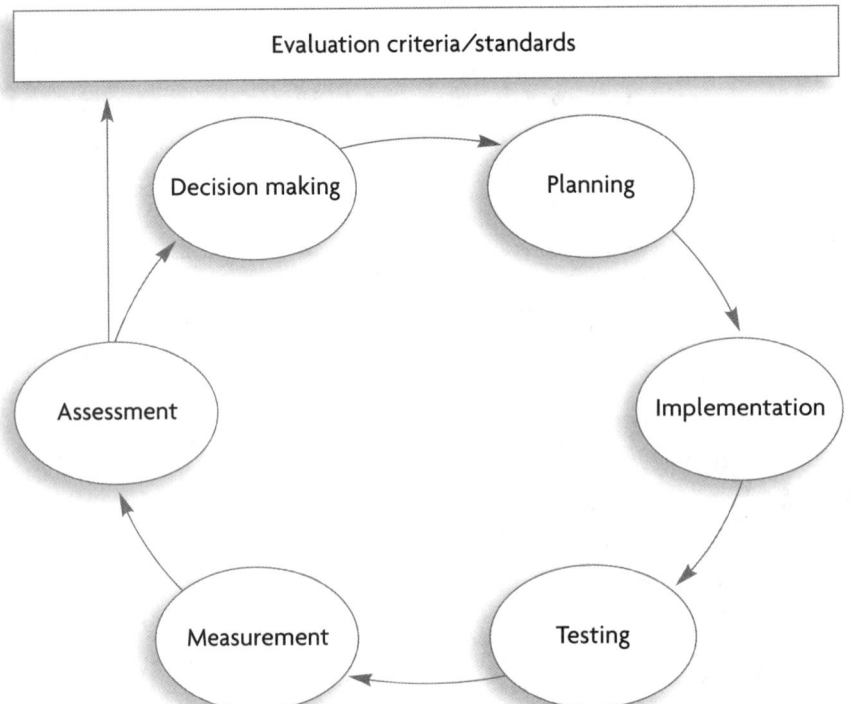

FIGURE 5.1 *The relationship between testing, measurement, standards, assessment, and evaluation.*

at a time, throws the ball while stepping forward on the foot on the same side as the throwing arm (see Figure 5.2), and attempts to catch the ball by rigidly extending his arms forward while turning his head and closing his eyes. Even though there is no score generated or points given or deducted for any element of these skills, it is easy to conclude that this child's skills are immature. Three types of informal assessment are observation, authentic assessment, and functional assessment of behavior.

Observation. Observation relies on a teacher's ability to observe. An informal test of aerobic capacity may take the form of observing that, after three minutes of play in a soccer game, the student appears fatigued and cannot keep up with the other students. She is short of breath and perspiring heavily. The observation that the student appears fatigued is clearly judgmental and is an example of subjective and nontraditional testing. The observation that the student is short of breath and perspiring heavily is further documentation of the teacher's conclusion that the student appears fatigued and gives more credibility to that conclusion.

FIGURE 5.2

What is immature about this throwing pattern?

Authentic assessment. Authentic assessment is simply defined by Baumgartner, Jackson, Mahar, and Rowe (2002) as *"evaluating students in a real-life or authentic setting"* (p. 501). This term is used widely in general physical education literature to mean nontraditional, alternative, subjective testing. Adapted physical educators have been conducting some form of authentic assessment for years. Examples include walking around school with a student to see how he or she negotiates common obstacles such as stairs, curbs, grass, or sand and observing the student's use of playground equipment such as the ladder, swing, slide, or horizontal bars.

Authentic assessment is often necessary when the educator is determining whether a particular student should be referred for formal testing and possible special class placement or when formal testing would not provide a valid measurement for a student's disabilities. Authentic assessment is extremely important in adapted physical activity for the following reasons:

1. To cross-validate that the student can use a skill performed on verbal cue in realistic, practical situations as well.

2. To assess skills the student cannot perform on cue because of language, behavior, sensory, sequencing, or other factors.

3. To determine physical activities, meaningful to the student, that should be targeted for skill development.

Other forms of authentic assessment used in general physical education may be useful with stu-

MAKING CONNECTIONS

Authentic Assessment

Dorothy teaches students with autism in a language-based program that uses concrete positive reinforcers to elicit language. Her students were having difficulty responding to verbal instructions during testing, and Dorothy was having trouble measuring her students' current level of performance in basic motor patterns and skills. She developed a checklist that task-analyzed walking, running, throwing, kicking, and other basic skills. Dorothy was then able to observe students during recess and other activity times and rate their performances according to components of the skills identified in the task analysis. (See the section on Task Analysis in Chapter 10.)

dents with a disability if the students are capable. Game statistics, portfolios, and journals are ways of learning more about students' activity levels and their likes and dislikes, and of acknowledging participation in physical activity outside of school.

Functional assessment of behavior. Functional assessment of behavior, found in IDEA '04, refers to *gathering data to determine which events cause and maintain target behaviors* (Smith, 2004). According to Smith, functional assessment of behavior should be viewed primarily as a means of understanding problem behaviors in order to determine what behavioral supports are necessary. This assessment may take the form of an interview, observations of real-life settings, or observations in settings in which the environment's conditions have been manipulated. Some children may display desirable behavior in physical education but demonstrate problem behavior in the classroom. The physical education environment may be the one to precipitate either desirable or undesirable behaviors and, therefore, would be the context for study.

Fitzsimmons (1998) developed this well-researched system for use with students with severe disabilities, and it has proven effective with all types of students. Besides determining the nature of the problem behavior, the methods lead to the reason for the behavior and conditions under which the behavior does not occur. For example, are a student's temper tantrums a result of his poor performance? Does the behavior diminish when he plays better or wins the game? Does the behavior diminish when he has a closer/lower target or a more easily handled bat/stick?

Here are some steps to follow when conducting a functional assessment:

1. Verify the seriousness of the problem.
2. Define the problem behavior in concrete terms (e.g., tantrums, hitting others, throwing things).
3. Collect data on possible causes of the behavior.
4. Analyze the data.
5. Formulate and test a hypothesis (e.g., lower the basket, give him a fat bat).

Rating Scales and Checklists

Rating scales and checklists may be either formal or informal. A **rating scale** essentially *places a value on the performance observed*, either dichotomously (yes/no, pass/fail, good/poor) or by using criteria for assigning a value, such as 5 for excellent and 1 for unacceptable. **Checklists** *suggest there is no value judgment made other than to determine whether the quality exists or not*. For example, when observing a student's throwing pattern, the physical educator might check off a list of components that account for effective throwing mechanics, such as:

- Turns opposite shoulder toward target as throwing arm moves back
- Steps forward with leg opposite throwing arm
- Transfers weight to forward leg as throwing arm comes forward
- Extends throwing arm and hand in direction of target, rotating trunk to add velocity

Self-Report

Self-report is a *means of collecting data in which students report their own activity levels* by answering questions that reveal their feelings and wishes or demonstrate their accomplishments. This method has two requirements for the students: They must be able to express themselves well enough to make their desires understood, whether verbally or in some other way, and they must be reliable sources of information about their wishes or participation in activities. Self-report is used most frequently with older students and adults.

MEASUREMENT

The technique of testing generates a result known as a **measurement**, which is *information used to make decisions, expressed by associating symbols (i.e., numbers, words, or descriptions of behavior, + or –) with characteristics*. A measurement helps to determine the degree to which a person possesses a defined characteristic or feature (Baumgartner and others, 2002). A distance run test results in a measurement of aerobic capacity in terms of the number of laps completed. The number of minutes a student is able to play soccer results in a measurement of aerobic capacity in terms of physical appearance, regardless of the accuracy of the measurement. The distance run in a given time measures the characteristic of aerobic capacity in a formal, objective, and traditional way. The number of minutes the student is able to play soccer is a measurement obtained in a nontraditional, subjective, informal, and authentic way. A measurement may be in the form of a score, a description of behaviors, or simply symbols such as pluses or minuses. These measurements are compared against the appropriate standard during the evaluation or assessment process, leading to educational decisions.

STANDARDS

The word "standard" is used in many different ways, and the term is proliferating in educational literature and in physical education. Recent years have seen great emphasis on standards for physical education curriculum (NASPE, 1995a), standards for beginning physical education teachers (NASPE, 1995b), and standards for adapted physical educators (Kelly, 2006). A myriad of standards exist for student performance and the degree to which students possess certain characteristics of health-related fitness (e.g., body fat, aerobic capacity, strength). Today, as the "standards movement" sweeps the country, the term is sometimes used to connote excellence rather than a determined competency (Eisner, 1995). According to Lambert (1999), "A *standard* is a defined educational result that guides the development of curriculum and instructional processes leading to high-quality demonstrations of significant learning" (p. 5). Although this is a broad definition, it is adequate for our context as it includes the use of standards that are established through a rigorous process of data gathering and statistical normative procedures.

In the testing and ultimately the evaluation or assessment process, two types of standards are commonly used to compare the measurements that result from the testing: norm-referenced standards and criterion-referenced standards. It is important to understand the difference between them. **Norm-referenced standards** *are determined by gathering data on the performance of a large number of individuals who have specifically defined characteristics (e.g., age and sex).* The data are statistically analyzed, and performance standards called **norms** are constructed based on this analysis. These norms allow for comparing a performance in a hierarchical ordering of individuals; that is, comparing an individual's performance against other similar individuals (e.g., of the same age and sex).

Criterion-referenced standards *describe a task and very often describe the minimum competency.* Any given performance may also be described in terms of the components of the task that are completed, usually on a pass/fail basis—either the criterion is achieved ($x = 1$) or not ($x = 0$). Comparing a performance to the components of the task results in a measurement of the student's approximation to the criterion rather than a comparison of that student's performance to other, similar students as with norm-referenced standards. The criterion may be in the form of a description of the behavior or a score (value) derived from some objective source such as research. Table 5.1 compares criterion-referenced standards with norm-referenced standards.

As the table shows, criterion-referenced standards may take the form of a rating associated with specific criteria, as in the first example of the vertical jump (Los Angeles Unified School District, in press), it may take the form of a description of the expected performance (Ulrich, 2002), or it may take the form of a range of acceptable scores (CIAR, 1993) that are based on research, as in the pull-up example. In contrast, the norm-referenced standards, to the right in Table 5.1, show specific scores that may be compared across age groups. For jumping form, using the criteria on the left, we see that all children are not expected to leave the ground until age 6 (score < 2). By age 9, however, all children are expected to get off the ground, and fewer than 10 percent have poor execution (score <1).

The lateral sliding, norm-referenced by a teacher collecting data over a period of time, could express performances in terms of age norms (e.g., a seven-year-old who is only able to slide to the right 12 feet is functioning at the five-year level on that pattern). Like the single range of scores given as criteria for the modified pull-ups, these sliding scores merely represent an average distance obtained by 105 students of that age. If the student does much better or much worse, the standard provides no way of knowing how far off the norm the student is. Some test makers provide the mean and standard deviation, which allow one to determine, in standard score units (z score), how much the student deviates from the norm.

The last measure, that of strength, shows a range of scores, from the *FITNESSGRAM*, that researchers have concluded is appropriate to achieve in order to derive the health benefits of fitness. In the lower right corner of Table 5.1 (isometric strength), the chart reflects the sum of three handgrip tests completed by adult males and females, showing the scores that place them at various points in the population (i.e., 90th, 75th, 50th, 25th, and 10th percentile of other adults like them).

Witt and colleagues (1997) offer a comparison of norm-referenced and criterion-referenced standards and show how functional assessment relates to standards. They present approaches and identify the advantages and disadvantages of each. Table 5.2 shows these comparisons.

EVALUATION

Adapted physical education specialists and general physical educators have some similar and some different reasons for using measurements. As discussed in Chapter 1, legislation requires the

TABLE 5.1 *A comparison of criterion-referenced standards and norm-referenced standards.*

Criterion-Referenced Standards

FOR JUMPING FORM[1]

4
- Series of jumps over a distance of 6 ft.
- Maintains good bilateral coordination throughout
- Slight forward lean as student jumps
- Preparatory movement of bent knees and ankles
- Body absorbs impact—execution is repetitive

3
- Torso has no forward lean
- Over/underuse of arms to complete jump
- Pattern slightly inconsistent but still effective
- Absorbs contact most of the time

2
- Pattern begins with forward lean and good bilateral coordination but breaks down after three or four jumps
- Movement is labored
- Pattern is inconsistent

1
- Poor execution
- Poor bilateral coordination
- Many inconsistencies to accomplish task

0
- Unable to perform skill

FOR SLIDING[2]

Body is turned sideways to desired direction of travel. A step sideways followed by a slide of the trailing foot to a point next to the lead foot. A short period where both feet are off the floor. Able to slide to the right and left side.

FOR STRENGTH (MODIFIED PULL-UPS)[4]

Age	Male	Female
5	2–7	2–7
6	2–7	2–7
7	3–9	3–9
8	4–11	4–11
9	5–11	4–11
10	5–15	4–13

Norm-Referenced Standards

FOR JUMPING FORM[1]

Percentile	age 5	age 5.5	age 6	age 9
95	3	3	3	3
75	2	2	3	3
50	2	2	2	2
25	1	2	2	2
10	1	1	1	2
5	0	0	1	1

FOR SLIDING[3]

	age 4	age 5	age 6	age 7
right (distance)	6 ft.	12 ft.	17 ft.	22 ft.
left (distance)	4 ft.	10 ft.	12 ft.	17 ft.

FOR ISOMETRIC STRENGTH (SUM OF 3 MEASURES)[5]

Percentile	Weight for Males	Weight for Females
90	536	284
75	479	245
50	414	201
25	361	165
10	301	135

---

[1]From *Adapted Physical Education Assessment Scale II*, Los Angeles Unified School District (in press).
[2]From *Test of Gross Motor Development*, Ulrich (2002).
[3]From teacher-made norms based on 105 children at Franklin Elementary School, Omaha, NE (2001).
[4]From *The Prudential FITNESSGRAM*, CIAR (1993).
[5]From *JAMAR Procedures*, Lafayette, IN, in Baumgartner and Jackson (1999).

TABLE 5.2 *Comparison of types of approaches to the use of standards.*

NORM-REFERENCED STANDARDS

Compare students to a normed group (comparing the number of sit-ups performed with age group norms).

Advantages	Disadvantages
■ Assist in eligibility decisions	■ May be too general for use in classroom
■ Provide information easily communicated to parents	■ A discrepancy may exist between what is tested and what is taught in classroom or a difference may exist in the content of the curriculum and the published tests
■ Are research-based; data information is available	■ May indicate a "problem" with the student rather than focusing on placement, teaching, or curriculum

CRITERION-REFERENCED STANDARDS

Determine if the student can perform the skill related to certain criteria (comparing a throwing pattern with the known standard for mechanical efficiency—opposition of hand/foot, etc.).

Advantages	Disadvantages
■ Identify student skills	■ Determining or describing appropriate criterion
■ Identify student progress	■ Assumption that additional instruction or more exposure will result in passing test
■ Assist in planning next skill to be taught	■ Additional instruction may lead to repeated failures if not the correct type
	■ Potentially, this could be the focus of instruction rather than a sampling (teach to the test, rather than provide variety and depth of instruction)

FUNCTIONAL ASSESSMENT*

Authentic and performance assessment, including play-based assessment (especially used for preschoolers), determine if the student has use of the skill, such as walking up and down stairs using an alternating foot pattern, rather than just standing on one foot for five seconds.

Advantages	Disadvantages
■ Relevant for development of instruction and intervention activities	■ Teacher must be a good detective to select appropriate tasks and make an accurate interpretation of results (no manual to follow)
■ Indicates information about what the students need to learn and how they learn	■ Requires an understanding of content area and proficient training, experience, and knowledge
■ Instructional planning is easily inferred from test data	■ Testing may be influenced by values and biases of assessor
■ Flexibility of use (any time, place, situation, or learning challenge)	■ Not as much supportive research and theory as criterion-referenced or norm-referenced assessment

*Witt uses the term *assessment* in the same way *testing* and *data collection* are used in this text.

Source: Adapted from: Witt, J. C., et al. (1997), *Assessment of At-Risk and Special Needs Children* (2nd ed.). Copyright © The McGraw-Hill Companies, Inc.

adapted physical education specialist to assess each student's current level of performance for the purpose of planning an individualized education program (IEP). The generalist in physical education, on the other hand, most often uses measurement to evaluate students for assigning grades, determining the effectiveness of instruction, and providing motivation. The generalist does not have to use measurements to plan a program because usually a curriculum has already been adopted by the school, district, or state. Even though individualizing instruction in an inclusive setting may mean adapting or modifying the existing curriculum, these different uses of measurements warrant the use of two distinctly different terms. In this text, we make a distinction between the terms *evaluation* and *assessment* and their use.

Evaluation is generally defined as *the process that uses measurements to compare with predetermined standards to facilitate rational decisions.* Baumgartner and others (2002) define evaluation as:

> A decision-making process that involves
>
> (1) the collection of suitable data (measurement);
>
> (2) a judgment of the value of these data against a standard; and
>
> (3) a decision based on these data and standards. (p. 507)

Often, the standards used for evaluation are separate from the needs, capacities, and limitations of the individual student. While they usually are based on the general school population, the adapted physical education specialist could still use them for comparing any variance in performance of students with disabilities.

Tools used in evaluation include rubrics, benchmarks, and norm-referenced criteria.

Rubrics. General physical educators have started using **rubrics** to evaluate students relative to expected outcomes or standards-based curriculum. Wiggins and McTighe (2005) define rubric as: *"a set of criteria used to evaluate a student's performance in a given outcome area.* Rubrics consist of a measurement scale which is graduated to mark varying levels of achievement of an indicator, a list of criteria describing the characteristics of products or performances at each score point, and sample responses (anchors) illustrating each point on the score scale" (p. 39). Although the use of rubrics provides for a more incremental definition of students' abilities along the continuum toward a criterion, many students with a disability are unable to perform at grade or age level. See Figure 5.3 for an example of a rubric.

FIGURE 5.3 | *Skipping rubric.*

4 A rhythmical repetition of the step-hop on alternate feet, foot of nonsupport leg carried near surface during hop, arms alternately moving in opposition to legs at about waist level.

3 A repetition of the step-hop on alternate feet with slight loss of balance from time to time, foot of nonsupport leg carried near surface during hop, arms moving asynchronously about shoulder height.

2 A repetition of the step-hop on one foot with nonsupport leg touching the ground periodically for balance, arms moving asynchronously about shoulder height.

1 An arrythmical repetition of the step-hop on either leg but not alternately, nonsupport leg separates widely for balance, arms held rigidly at the side of the body.

How Would You Respond?

RUBRICS

Sharon is an eight-year-old student with Down syndrome and is motorically functioning at about the four-year-old level. She is just starting to balance on one foot and enjoys games like Statues and Stork Stand. Would she be able to achieve the lowest level of achievement on the rubric for skipping in Figure 5.3?

Benchmarks. **Benchmarks,** which often accompany rubrics, are *grade-level or course-specific expectations for students and mark progress toward achievement of a standard* (FCPS, 2001, p. 1). If we were to write a benchmark for second graders based on what the teacher in Omaha learned about sliding (see Table 5.1), it might look something like this:

> Demonstrate the ability to slide to the right and to the left at least 15 feet in games and rhythmic activities.

If you had a second grader who functioned at the preschool level, however, this benchmark does not allow you to define the degree to which the student approximates the criterion. If the student can slide to the right six feet and to the left four feet, the student has missed reaching the benchmark, but by how far? Rubrics can be helpful in charting a student's course on a day-to-day basis toward achieving a benchmark because they quantify the student's approximation to the ultimate goal.

Norm-referenced criteria. In contrast to benchmarks, **norm-referenced criteria** *usually allow for a number or score for performance to be compared with scores of similar students on a scale.* The most commonly used scales in physical education include percentile ranks, T scores, and z scores. The limitation of norm-referenced criteria is that they do not lend themselves to measuring the quality of movement. Table 5.3 lists sample percentile ranks on a standing balance test for 11-year-olds.

When we know that a particular boy can balance on his left foot with his eyes closed for 15 seconds, Table 5.3 gives a good idea of how he compares with other students like him (i.e., 11-year-old boys), regardless of his mechanics. (He is performing equal to or better than approximately 75 percent of 11-year-old boys.) Norm-referenced criteria are often required to determine **eligibility;** that is, *whether a student should be provided special education services such as adapted physical education* or whether the student is performing well enough relative to his or her peers to return to the general education classroom.

TABLE 5.3

Simple percentile rank norms for standing balance for 11-year-olds—left foot, eyes closed.

PERCENTILE	BOYS # SECONDS	GIRLS # SECONDS
95	30	22
90	23.8	20
80	17.5	10
70	12.8	8
60	9	7
50	8	5
40	6	5
30	4	4
20	3	3
10	3	2
5	1.7	1

Source: Adapted Physical Education Assessment Scale II (in press). Los Angeles Unified School District.

Program Evaluation

Another use of the term evaluation is in **program evaluation**—*determining the overall effectiveness of a program (or service) on the performance of a group of students,* rather than on individuals within the group. This process is becoming increasingly important for making decisions regarding the physical education of students with a disability. More students are being educated in an inclusive environment than before, thus it is necessary to evaluate the program before placing a student. Program evaluation is generally considered to involve three basic considerations: the learning environment, the learners, and the learning taking place.

The learning environment. The learning environment—which includes the quantity and quality of facilities, supplies, and equipment; the teaching staff; and the class size—is exceedingly important to the education of students with a disability. As an example, it may be argued that the availability of a swimming pool does not ensure that students will learn to swim. The absence of a pool, or some substitute, however, will assuredly preclude the students from acquiring those skills. Even with the presence of a swimming pool, some students with a disability are precluded from learning to swim because they also need a wheelchair ramp into the pool, a hydraulic lift, and special flotation devices.

The teaching staff is critical to learning by students with a disability. Whether the available staff possess the necessary training and experience should be considered not only in program evaluation, but also when considering the most appropriate placement for any given student. Seaman (1970) found that class administration and conduct were the most significant factors in students with a disability developing a negative attitude toward physical education. A physical educator who does not have the necessary competencies, knowledge, and understanding of students with a disability can destroy the students' interest in physical activities as well as do harm to the students. For example, a

The Authors Respond

RUBRICS

Sharon would have difficulty demonstrating even the lowest level of the skipping rubric. Because she is just beginning to balance on one foot, it will be a while before she is able to hop on that leg.

teacher who is unprepared to teach students with a language impairment can contribute to their frustration and deter their learning. Teachers who do not have adequate knowledge of certain conditions such as "brittle bones" can aggravate the condition through class conduct or activities or even cause injury to the student.

Class size is also a significant factor. The very existence of special education is based, at least in part, on the demonstration that increased learning occurs among some segments of the population when they are placed in small classes, presumably because this facilitates individual instruction and attention. Class size for physical activity should be optimal, just as for any other curricular area, and is usually determined by state department of education guidelines.

The learners. Evaluation of the learners involves comparing the relative strengths and weaknesses of the students with regard to selected characteristics. Although we do not advocate delivering physical education services to groups of students classified according to traditional disability categories, much can be said for the learning that can take place when students are homogeneously grouped according to their *motor* needs. This is not to imply that students who have low fitness levels should all be grouped into one class, or that students who need to work on ball-handling skills should be placed into another class. Rather, students who have needs at specific levels of the developmental model can more readily have their needs met if grouped according to those developmental levels. Also, the students' style of learning, capacities, and limitations should be among the characteristics considered. A student who has a moderate intellectual disability does not learn in the same way as a typically developing student. Thus, a program evaluation would most likely reveal whether the placement of a student with an intellectual disability into a general education class has brought about the desired learning results. It may be that this student has learning needs so diverse from the group that the program is ineffective. On the other hand, the student's prior experience and motor function may fit right in with a particular class when scores on skill tests and other observational data are brought to bear on the decision.

The learning taking place. There is a nationwide movement to comply with IDEA '04 by including students in general physical education programs. Another movement supports the accountability of educators, with an emphasis on authentic assessment. When considering the placement of a student with a disability into a general education class, you must ensure that the student will continue to learn and grow as a result. An adequate evaluation of the receiving program must be made to determine what supports are necessary to guarantee continued success.

When determining whether a student with a disability should be included in a general physical education program, or when reevaluating inclusion, it may be helpful to use the brief program evaluation checklist offered in Table 5.4. This checklist should not be used to exclude the student if the criteria are not met; rather, it should serve as a means of identifying necessary elements and supports. Program evaluation will be covered in further depth in curriculum development and other teacher preparation courses.

ASSESSMENT

Although the term "assessment" is used differently in general physical education, **assessment** in special education is defined as *the collection of information to identify problems and make educational decisions* (Salvia & Ysseldyke, 2003). Although assessment is the endpoint of data gathering and decision making, it is also an ongoing process of problem solving. You make decisions each time you watch a student perform in class—decisions that lead you to give more instruction in some areas, change a student's understanding of what is expected, or move players to another position in a game where they have more chance for success. In addition to deciding on a student's placement and program plan, you will be problem solving and making decisions about this student's learning the entire time he or she is in your class.

How Would You Respond?

EVALUATING THE LEARNER

Bruce is a six-year-old with Down syndrome. His mother takes him everywhere and includes him in everything. Although somewhat socially immature, Bruce "plays tennis" with his family, bowls, goes picnicking, and participates in Little League baseball. Even though his skills are not at a par with his age-equivalent peers, he learned the functional behaviors to fit right in. If he becomes your student in middle school, what would be your recommendation for physical education placement?

TABLE 5.4 — Checklist for inclusion.

PROGRAM CRITERIA	YES	NO
1. Are the facilities adequate in quantity and quality to provide this student with a variety of movement experiences?	☐	☐
2. Are the facilities accessible?	☐	☐
3. Are the supplies and equipment of appropriate quantity and quality for the unique needs and learning characteristics of *all* students?	☐	☐
4. Is the equipment safe, and is there enough gradation (e.g., large and small balls) of equipment to meet the needs of this student?	☐	☐
5. Are age-appropriate activities being taught in this class? Are they directed toward meeting the national physical education standards?	☐	☐
6. Are the activities appropriate for the developmental age as well as the chronological age of this student?	☐	☐
7. Does the teacher in this class have the necessary competencies, knowledge, and personal qualities to create a successful learning experience for this student?	☐	☐
8. Is the size of the class appropriate for this student's learning?	☐	☐
9. Do the other students in this class have similar learning needs (e.g., in terms of motor, social, cognitive, and language development)?	☐	☐
10. Are the other students making reasonable progress toward the learning goals of the program (e.g., outcomes defined by the school, district, or state)?	☐	☐

For students with a disability, assessment has the following functions and characteristics:

1. It is usually **formative** *(initiated at the beginning of the IEP process)* in nature, although it is considered **summative** when *completed at the end of instruction*—perhaps to consider reentry into the general physical education class.
2. It uses measurements for the purpose of immediate decision making regarding placement, program modification, and individualizing instruction.
3. It involves the synthesis and interpretation of data.
4. It may use norm- or criterion-referenced standards, traditional or nontraditional, and use different materials, equipment, strategies, and techniques over a period of time and in a variety of situations.
5. It helps the teacher identify the strengths and challenges of a student in the learning environment.
6. It is an ongoing process used consistently throughout instruction.
7. It involves a team effort—professionals working collectively to find a solution.
8. It ends with a decision about the least restrictive, most appropriate class placement.

The Authors Respond

EVALUATING THE LEARNER

When Bruce reached middle school, he was included in a general education class most of the time, especially for physical education. As an adult, Bruce now works in a job requiring repetitive tasks and fits in very well socially with the other workers. He is charming, knows all of the current jargon and social behaviors, and lives semi-independently. He continues to be physically active, playing tennis and bicycling.

PURPOSES OF EVALUATION AND ASSESSMENT

Because measurement leads to enhanced decision making for both the physical education generalist and the adapted physical education specialist, it makes sense that some of the purposes of evaluation and assessment overlap. Six widely accepted general purposes have similar value for evaluation and for assessment:

1. Diagnosis
2. Prediction
3. Determining student progress
4. Placement or classification
5. Determining program effectiveness
6. Motivation (Baumgartner and others, 2002)

Two additional purposes of assessment, unique to adapted physical education, are:

7. Individual program planning
8. Determining the need for further testing or related services as part of the ongoing assessment process

Diagnosis

Measurement may be used to identify and diagnose the strengths and challenges of students in both general education and special classes. For the assessment process, this is the heart of planning the IEP. **Diagnosis** is *the result of criterion-referenced assessment in which a label is assigned when the criteria are met.* For example, to receive the diagnosis of weak or poor muscular strength, one must meet the criterion of having little or limited capacity to perform any of the usual tasks requiring strength, such as climbing stairs or meeting daily demands for lifting. However, once the diagnosis is made, it carries with it information about the person in addition to the diagnosis. For example, the adapted physical educator will know that the person is likely to use means to compensate for the limited strength—avoid lifting, rest frequently, or use the elevator. Physical education generalists use measurements to diagnose and classify students according to ability or to identify students who may benefit from being referred to adapted physical education or for whom specific accommodations may be necessary.

Prediction

When adapted physical educators develop goals and objectives for the IEP, they are predicting what the student will learn (be able to perform) after a certain amount and type of instruction. Measurements are critical to making accurate predictions of this type. Assessment employs quantitative as well as qualitative measurements. Norm-referenced standards (usually quantitative) should be used as much as possible when prediction is desired. For example, more predictive value usually comes from knowing that a particular student's vertical jump is equal to or better than 15 percent of her age peers (i.e., norm-referenced) than knowing that she jumped two inches higher today than she did last year (i.e., criterion-referenced) or that she did not meet the second grade standard. Suggestions on how to make predictions when formulating the IEP are provided in Chapter 8 in the section on writing the annual goals.

Determining Student Progress

For educators, one of the most important purposes of evaluation and assessment is to determine whether a student is making progress and has achieved instructional objectives. Whether the educator is using the evaluation process to assign grades or the assessment process to review a student's educational plan, the most important reason to measure is to determine whether any permanent change (learning) has occurred since the last time a measurement was taken. Either criterion-referenced or norm-referenced standards are appropriate.

Placement

One of the purposes of testing and measuring a student with a disability is to provide information to the IEP team so they can make an appropriate determination of class placement for physical education. The IEP team decides whether the student should be placed in a separate adapted physical education class, a general physical education class, or some combination of the two. Both criterion-referenced and norm-referenced standards (as well as medical and other factors) may enter into the determination. Physical educators may also use measurement results to classify or ability-group students within a certain class.

Determining Program Effectiveness

School districts like to use test results, changes in behavior following instruction, and comparison with other programs to measure the effectiveness of the curriculum. Especially in the spring of the year, it is common to hear the results of SAT testing in local high schools; the number or percentage of students in a school who go on to college; and the relative position of a school, school system, or state on various educational measurements that indicate the quality of the programs. Measuring changes in performance (e.g., increased strength, aerobic capacity, flexibility, or decreased body fat) is another way of determining the effectiveness of a program for an individual. In education, we look for permanent changes in behavior or status as indicators of the effectiveness of the learning experience.

Motivation

Assessment and evaluation may also be used to motivate students. Once they achieve important standards, students are often motivated to do more. A knowledge of changes in health-related physical fitness parameters encourages individuals—the hard work they put in is paying off in more strength, less body fat, more flexibility, or whatever variable they are seeking to change.

Individual Program Planning

IEP plans must be made at least yearly for all students with a disability. These plans must be based on the current level of performance and must include a prediction of the student's achievement level at the end of one year or less of instruction. Unlike the traditional method of curriculum development, in which specific units of instruction are provided all students at any given grade level, program planning for students with a disability is based on the results of the assessment process (see Chapter 8, Figure 8.3).

Further Testing and Related Services

Although the primary purpose of motor assessment for the adapted physical educator is seldom to determine a need for further testing for related services, this is very often an outcome. Because the adapted physical educator uses movement as the medium for testing, the results may provide some data that have not been gathered before. For example, atypical muscle tone or residual interfering reflexes may suggest the need for testing for physical or occupational therapy services. These irregularities may become evident through the measurement of motor performance. Either criterion-referenced or norm-referenced standards might produce this information.

Witt, Elliott, Kramer, and Gresham (1994) provide insight into the perceived values or purposes of assessment and evaluation from the viewpoints of the individuals involved: parents, students, teachers, administrators, and policy makers. See Table 5.5 for a summary of these varying purposes.

TABLE 5.5

The many purposes of assessment from the viewpoints of parents, students, teachers, administrators, and policy makers.

Policy makers use assessments to:
- Set standards
- Focus on goals
- Monitor the quality of education
- Reward or sanction various practices
- Formulate policies
- Direct resources, including personnel and money

Administrators use assessments to:
- Monitor program effectiveness
- Identify program strengths and weaknesses
- Designate program priorities
- Assess alternatives
- Plan and improve programs

Teachers and administrators use assessments for:
- Grouping decisions
- Individual diagnosis and prescription
- Monitoring student progress
- Curriculum evaluation and refinement
- Fostering mastery, promotion, grading, and other feedback
- Motivating students
- Grading

Parents and students can use assessments to:
- Gauge student progress
- Assess student strengths and weaknesses
- Evaluate school accountability

Source: Witt, J. C., et al. (1997), *Assessment of At-Risk and Special Needs Children* (2nd Ed.) Copyright © The McGraw-Hill Companies, Inc.

MAKING CONNECTIONS

Further Testing

A nine-year-old girl, Emily, was tested for an after-school perceptual–motor program. Her mother noticed that she was clumsy and preferred to play with younger children. Perceptual–motor testing revealed low muscle tone, difficulty with repetitive movements (dysdyodokokinesia), poor motor planning, and limited motor accuracy. Because Emily lived in a state that did not have physical education specialists in the elementary schools, this was the first time she had been tested by a trained physical educator. It was recommended that Emily visit a physician with the report and a recommendation that she be given neurological tests. This was done, and Emily was diagnosed as having a mild form of cerebral palsy.

USING MEASUREMENT CONCEPTS

The basic concepts involved in the measurement of motor performance are reviewed in Appendix D for students who have previous course work in measurement and statistics. Such course work is not a prerequisite, however, to understanding ways that measurement concepts may be operationalized when teaching students with a disability. The discussion that follows will help you to understand how to use measurement data in adapting a prescribed curriculum to include students of all abilities.

Types of Scores

The two types of scores used primarily in measuring physical performance are continuous and discrete. **Continuous scores,** *those having, potentially, an infinite number of values* (i.e., along a continuum), are used in time and distance measurements. How high students jump, how far they throw, how fast they run are all continuous scores that can be used when grouping according to ability, balancing abilities to make up a team, or assigning grades for physical education. **Discrete scores,** which *have a limited number of specific values,* include repetitions or frequencies of a performance, such as the number of crunches completed or free-throws made. Rubrics use discrete values to quantify approximations to a benchmark or indicator of success.

Ratio, interval, ordinal, and nominal are other ways of classifying scores, and each has a different purpose. **Ratios** *have a common unit of measure between each score and a true zero point* and are the most commonly used when measuring the quantity of performances such as the number of sit-ups, pull-ups, or balls kicked. **Interval scores** are like ratios, but they *do not have a true zero point.* Intelligence or knowledge tests generate interval scores because each score reflects one more question answered correctly than the next lower score, but a zero score does not reflect an absolute lack of intelligence or knowledge. A zero score, in this instance, simply means that no questions were answered correctly. Ratios and interval scores can be added together and manipulated to determine letter grades for a grading period or overall performance on a variety of tasks.

Ordinal scores *define the "order" of things.* When you rank students in a class from the best-skilled student to the poorest-skilled, you are using ordinal scores. They cannot be added or used in any mathematical computations because there is not an equal distance between the *abilities* of each student, even though there are equal distances between the ranks (i.e., 1 is as close to 2 as 2 is to 3, etc.). The student ranked number 1 may be exceedingly more skilled than anyone else in class, yet this rank is as close to number 2 as the second student is to the student ranked number 3. When trying to balance teams for competition at the middle or high school levels, ranking students is one way to create teams of about equal ability. Following are some ways these ranks can be used:

- The top three and lowest three could comprise a volleyball team of six.
- The 1st, 5th, 10th, 15th, 20th, 25th rank could make a team.
- Three students can be randomly drawn from the top half and three from the bottom half of the ranks.

Nominal scores also cannot be hierarchically ordered or mathematically manipulated because they are *names or descriptions of performance or behavior*—one label or name is no better or worse than the next. Male–female and right-handed–left-handed are examples of nominal scores. Labeling is not within the philosophy of this text, but there often is a need to know whether the student is right-handed or left-handed, is subject to seizures or not, or is on any behavior-altering medication. None of these labels or descriptions have any inherent value; they are simply useful information that should help you better prepare to include the student in your class. Rubrics that are designed to provide criteria for achievement on a particular curriculum standard are examples of nominal data. Nominal data are also helpful to describe the behaviors or performances a student has demonstrated. This information is very useful when making referrals for testing for adapted physical education or describing a student's performance to specialists who serve as a resource to the general physical educator. Much more discussion on observation and the description of motor performance is found in Chapter 6.

Organization of Scores

There are times when you may want to organize scores to get a better picture of what the class "looks like" or where you may have to do some extra instruction. A **simple frequency distribution** has *all of the scores listed in order, from best to worst, with the number of students making each score tallied beside the score.* This might be used to assign letter grades on a certain test or assignment. You may want to look at a knowledge test, item by item, to determine which questions the most students missed, in order to review that material. This way of organizing scores may also be used if you need to order team uniforms. Record the various sizes and the number of athletes who wear a particular size, and you have the exact count of each size for ordering. Appendix D provides some examples of frequency tables.

Another simple method of organizing scores is by **graphing;** the graph is referred to as a frequency polygon. This method gives *a schematic picture of the similarities and differences within a group on any given set of scores.* Graphing provides a clear picture of where in the total distribution various students are performing on any measurement. For many human qualities, there is a small number of people (scores) at both the high and low ends of the continuum, with the majority scoring in the middle. Figure 5.4 shows a distribution of scores called a bell-shaped or normal curve. A **normal curve** is a *mathematically defined bilaterally symmetrical curve centered on a point that is simultaneously the mean, median, and mode.* Using this kind of graphing, it is easy to see if a disproportionate number of very high or very low scores was obtained.

Measures of Central Tendency

Whether you are analyzing scores for the purpose of conducting an individual assessment, planning group activities, developing a test, or comparing a group with another similar group, it is important to describe the scores. Although the frequency table and frequency polygon help to characterize the group, other descriptive values are significant when describing specific characteristics or when trying to understand norm-referenced tests. Such descriptive values include measures of central tendency. The **measures of central tendency** define *a score where the scores tend to cluster* and require discrete or interval data. Three of these measures are mean, median, and mode.

The **mean** or *arithmetic average* is influenced by the position and value of each single score in the group. It is the most widely understood measure of central tendency, commonly used in everyday language, and is reported most often in ready-made tests of motor performance. Knowing the average class score on a test, the average number of points scored in a game, or the average number of attempts before a student finds success can be very helpful when teaching and coaching in an inclusive environment.

FIGURE 5.4 | *Normal or bell-shaped curve.*

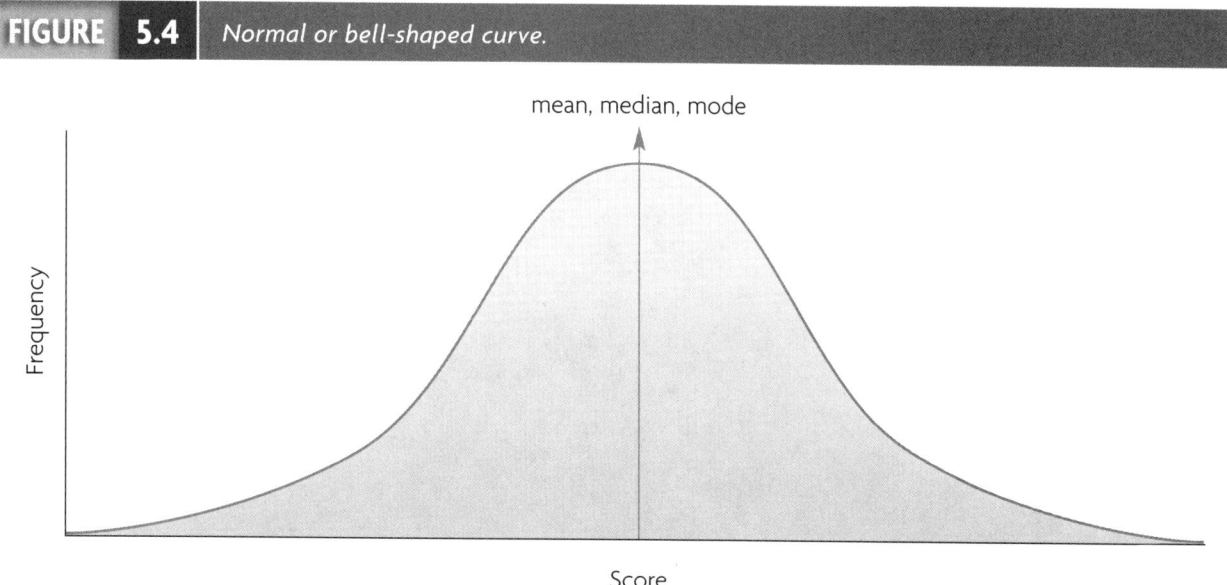

The **median** is *the absolute middle score*—half of the scores fall above this score and half of the scores fall below. If there are extremely high or low scores, using the mean would give a skewed picture of the class, so using the median, which is influenced only by position in the group rather than magnitude of the score, gives a more realistic midpoint of ability or accomplishment.

The **mode** is *the most frequently obtained score* and could serve to identify instructional areas that require extra work. The most frequently missed question on a test or the skill that the most students perform poorly suggests the need for review or further instruction.

Measures of Variability

Another value often used to describe a group of scores is a **measure of variability** or dispersion. Measures of variability indicate *the spread of the scores*—the homogeneity ("alikeness") or heterogeneity ("differentness") of the group. The two measures of variability that are most important to teachers are standard deviation and range.

The **standard deviation,** used with the mean, is the most common measure of variability reported in ready-made tests, describing *the average amount by which all of the scores differ or deviate from the mean.* Figure 5.5 shows the percentage of the population in a normal distribution that deviate one, two, and three standard deviations from the mean.

A large standard deviation describes a wide spread and a rather heterogeneous group of scores; a small one describes a homogeneous group. Students with a disability included in general physical education classes will be most successful if their scores deviate no more than the other students' on measures of motor performance—that is, if their scores are within one or two standard deviations of the mean. This is a reasonable guideline for whether or not a student should be placed in an inclusive class. The standard deviation is very useful when interpreting measurements.

The **range** is the easiest measure of variability to determine, reflecting *the difference between the lowest and highest scores.* It is not a very stable measure, however, because a change in either of the extreme scores can significantly affect the range. It can also be misleading because one score may be exceedingly higher or lower than the rest of the scores, and without it the group might be quite homogeneous. If, on a test of 100 points, your class range is 85 points, you assume you have a much more heterogeneous group than if the range were 40 points. On the other hand, if the highest score is 97 and the lowest is 12, but the next lowest is 57, this group is really more homogenous than the range might suggest. The range points to some very different teaching strategies and class formats depending on whether you have a homogeneous or heterogeneous class.

Position in a Group

A student's score may be more meaningful in the context of the group (rank order). The score takes on further meaning when the mean and standard deviation are also known. Because these values represent the group of which the student is a part, a parent or professional can generally see how the student compares either with a nationally derived group as

FIGURE 5.5 *Percent of population under the curve in a normal distribution.*

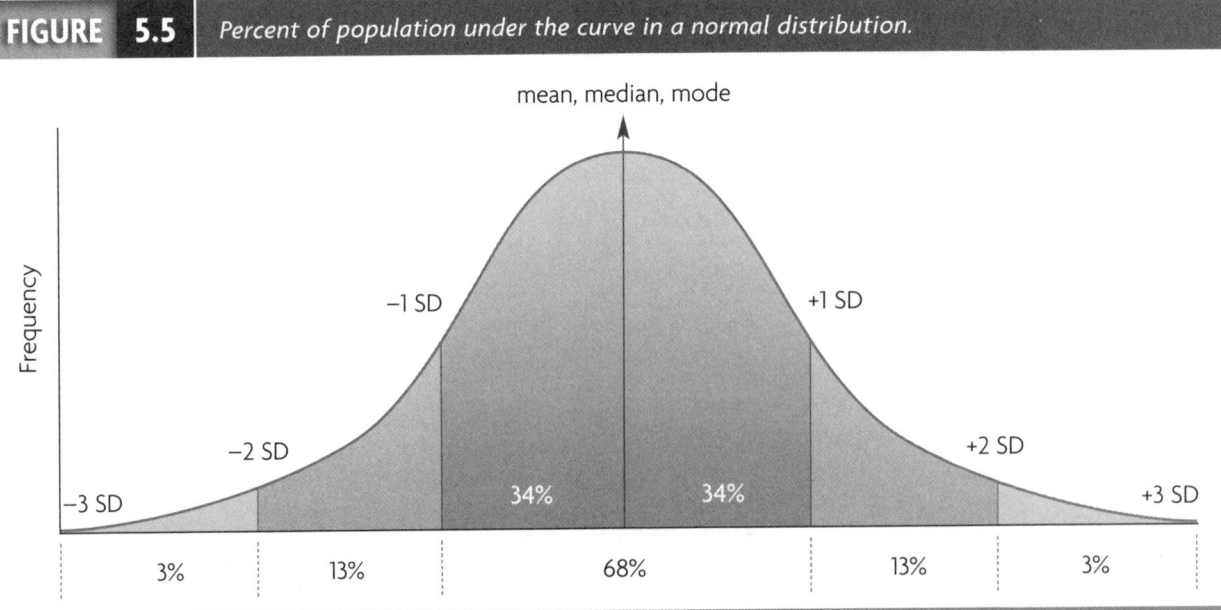

expressed in percentile-ranked norms or with a group of local peers, such as the student's own class. Ready-made tests use more precise methods to explain the position of a certain score, and it is important for the physical educator to be familiar with these methods in order to use them when interpreting a score for making referrals, assigning grades, or just describing to a parent how the student is doing relative to the rest of his or her peers.

Percentile rank. A better indicator of a student's position relative to a group is a percentile rank. Because a **percentile rank** describes *the percentage of the group that scored below a given score*, it tends to be more easily understood. The terms "percentile rank" and "percentile" are used interchangeably. A student who scores at the 75th percentile scores equal to or better than 75 percent of the group. Because a percentile is a point in the distribution, not a segment of the distribution, the score is always reported as being *at* (not in) a certain percentile. Some ready-made fitness test norms and most sport skills and motor development test norms are expressed in percentiles. These are norm-referenced standards.

Many health-related fitness tests use criterion-referenced standards based on research. That is, the score found to be the minimum to describe a "healthy" level of fitness is the only score given for each measurement for students of a specific age and sex. Although these standards are excellent for motivating students to achieve a level so that they derive health benefits from physical activity, they provide little information to the teacher about the student's position in the group. If a referral for adapted physical education or further testing is the reason for testing, it is necessary to know the position in the group. As mentioned earlier, a student who does not score within one or two standard deviations of the mean for his or her age will have difficulty keeping up with the other students. Schools should have clear criteria for determining eligibility for special class placement based on either norm-referenced or criterion-referenced standards.

Standard Scores

The norms on some tests that are appropriate to use with students with a disability are given in the form of standard scores. **Standard scores,** categorically, are *scores produced by "transforming" the raw scores onto a standard scale*. This conversion not only is convenient but also allows one to make comparisons, permits combining scores from unlike units of measure (e.g., a timed event and one that counts repetitions), and offers a great deal of value for interpretation. The standard scores most commonly used in physical education are z scores and T scores. Occasionally, you will encounter stanines, which, unlike z and T scores, use a base of 9 instead of a base of 10. If you have a choice of which standard score to use (some test norms are given in z scores, T scores, and percentile ranks), percentile ranks are by far the easiest to understand and interpret. Figure 5.6 shows the relationship among these three forms of scores.

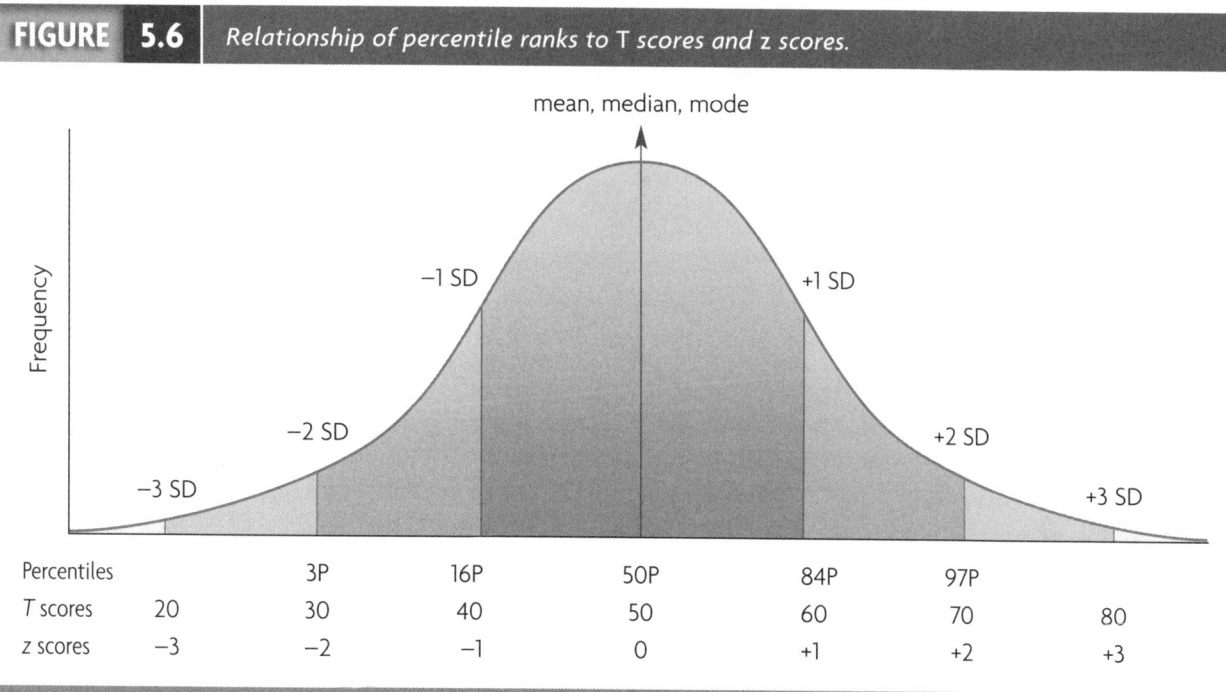

FIGURE 5.6 *Relationship of percentile ranks to T scores and z scores.*

As you can see, if the test provided only z scores, half of them would be less than or equal to zero, because the mean is zero and those scores below the mean are negative numbers. On the T score scale, the mean of 50 is easier to understand, and certainly the 50th percentile, being in the middle of the distribution, is the easiest.

Relationships Between Scores

If you understand the relationships between a student's scores, you can interpret measurements to produce a quality assessment of and make quality decisions for the student. These relationships are used, either formally or informally, for the following purposes:

- To identify the developmental level of the student
- To plan appropriate activities
- To assist with making appropriate decisions

Three different techniques may be used to determine the relationship between scores:

1. Informal
2. Graphing
3. Correlation

Informal. Whether the informal approach is a "technique" or not is debatable; it means merely "eyeballing" the results to see whether relationships exist between scores and whether the relationships make sense. A student with a residual asymmetrical tonic neck reflex (ATNR) who scores poorly on a throwing accuracy test demonstrates two deficits that make sense together. A student who can do very few crunches or curl-ups and cannot get off the ground for a vertical jump demonstrates two deficits that make sense together. When a student who is obese scores poorly on a pull-up test and an aerobic capacity test, your informal interpretation is that there is a relationship between these scores. Relationships between some aspects of motor performance are obvious and do not require more formal or elaborate analyses. Others are not so obvious, and sometimes more formal procedures are needed.

Graphing. Graphing is easier to perform than a mathematically derived correlation and, for many purposes, adequate, but it is not as precise. Graphing requires a coordinate system (as in the frequency polygon), with one measure on the horizontal axis and one on the vertical axis. A dot is placed on the graph above the score on one test and opposite the student's score on the second test. After all of the students' scores are plotted, a trend line (a line showing the trend of the relationship) is drawn connecting them. Some examples of trend lines can be found in Appendix D. A line that goes up to the right indicates a positive relationship; that is, as one score gets larger, the other tends to get larger. This, however, does not necessarily mean better. For example, as body weight increases, so does running time on a 60-yard dash for sixth grade boys. See Figure 5.7. Obviously, a lower, quicker running time is desirable. In this case, there is a positive relationship between body weight and speed—an undesirable relationship.

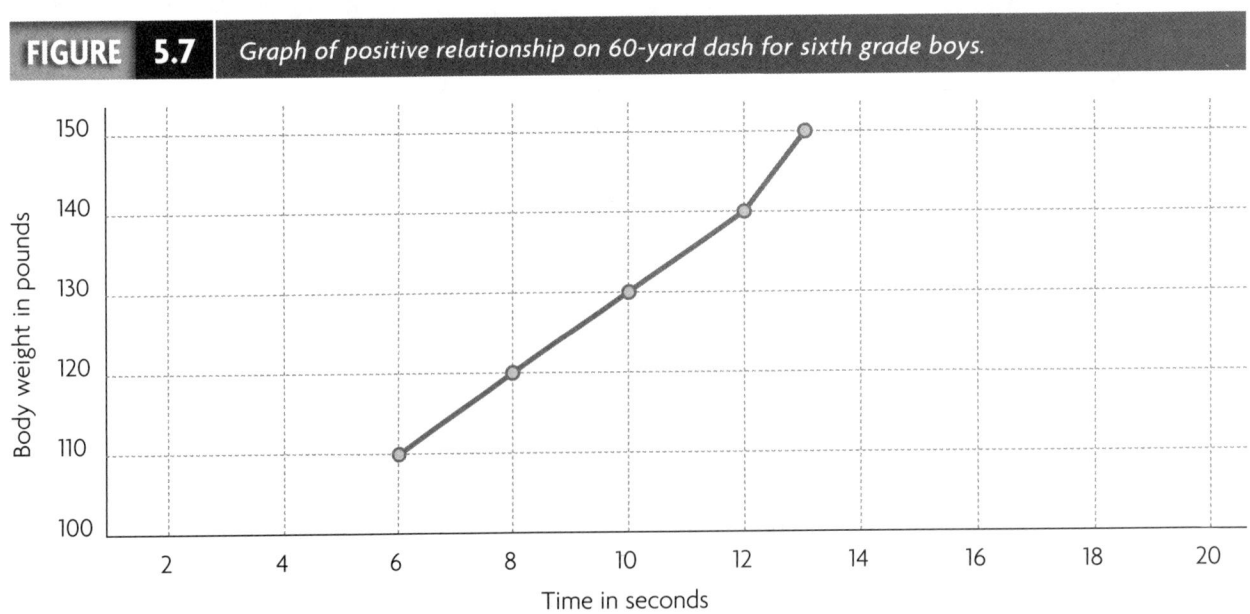

FIGURE 5.7 *Graph of positive relationship on 60-yard dash for sixth grade boys.*

FIGURE 5.8 | Graph of negative relationship on high jump for sixth grade boys.

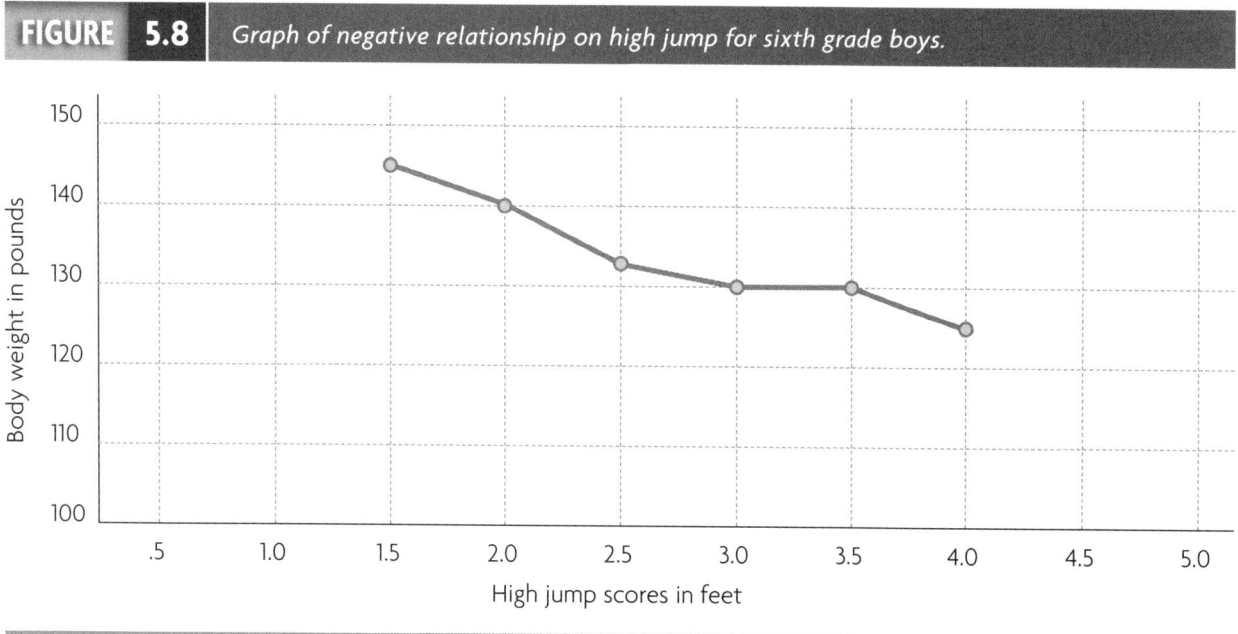

A graph can also show a close relationship that is negative or inverse. In this case, the trend line slopes down from left to right. See Figure 5.8.

If the plotted dots resemble a circle, and no trend line can be drawn through them, a very low or no relationship at all exists (see Appendix D).

Correlation. Correlation is the *mathematical technique for determining the trend or relationship between two measures.* The relationship is expressed as a decimal value between −1.0 and +1.0. A positive number reflects a positive relationship, and a perfect relationship is +1.0 or −1.0. Ready-made tests often report whether a correlation exists between the test items and some real-life application. If a basketball-dribbling test correlates positively with successful basketball play, then that test's predictive value is good and it is a valid way to measure a student's basketball-playing ability.

Test makers use correlations to express the validity and reliability of ready-made tests. The **validity** of a test is *its ability to measure the performances it claims to measure* and is important in real-life situations. The basketball-dribbling test just mentioned is an example of a valid test if it claims to measure playing ability. **Reliability** is *the test's ability to give the same measurement (given the same performance) each time it is used.* A test that relies heavily on a teacher's judgment is not as reliable as one that uses a measuring device such as a stopwatch. If a teacher tells a student that she ran faster today than yesterday, only a stopwatch ensures this to be true. These characteristics of tests are discussed later in this text.

Educators must know about the qualities of ready-made tests and must have a good understanding of correlation in order to select appropriate tools to measure students.

LEGISLATIVE MANDATES

Because adapted physical education is special education, it is subject to the same legal requirements of screening and identifying children suspected to have a disability, referral, assessment, and evaluation that apply to special education. IDEA '04 requires that the student be assessed in all areas related to the suspected disability. It would seem to follow, then, that the areas addressed during the assessment process would parallel the definition of disability—the student could and should be tested in:

- Physical fitness
- Fine and gross motor skills
- Motor development (fundamental motor patterns and skills)
- Sport and recreational skills such as aquatics, dance, and individual and group games

It is also appropriate to test in skill areas related to physical functioning (e.g., safety and mobility) and to test the effect of other disabilities on the ability to learn (e.g., cognitive delays, behavioral difficulties, and emotional disturbances).

The Act also requires a certain amount of credibility in the testing and measurement of educational performance:

- The test must be valid for the student and the purpose for which it was intended.
- The test must measure areas of the student's suspected disability.
- The measurements must not reflect another disability.
- The test must be administered by qualified personnel.

Once the physical educator and the IEP team have the scores, what are the options for physical education? The continuum of services model tends to be used in most school districts and is supported by the "spirit" of the legislation. Essentially, a student can receive instruction in physical education that ranges from full inclusion in a general physical education class with no supports (modifications) to total segregation (i.e., full time in an adapted physical education class), or any combination in between. The California Department of Education (2000) defines four levels of service:

- General physical education
- Modified physical education
- Specially designed physical education
- Adapted physical education

Modified physical education is *participation in a class taught by a general physical educator or classroom teacher with modifications*, such as "no running," "no contact sports," or "no contact with grasses." **Specially designed physical education** is *a special education class with minimal adaptations* and is *taught by the teacher who normally teaches physical education for this population* [Title 5 CCR §3051.5(a)]. For example, if the classroom teacher (special educator) normally teaches physical education, that person is teaching "modified" physical education. If it is the adapted physical educator who normally conducts the class, then he or she is teaching "specially designed" physical education.

Adapted physical education is defined by the profession as *a diversified program of developmental activities, games, sports, and rhythms suited to the interests, capacities, and limitations of students with disabilities who may not safely or successfully engage in unrestricted participation in the vigorous activities of the general physical education program* (AAHPERD, 1952). IDEA '04 defines the program in much the same way, with content parallel to the areas of testing discussed earlier in this chapter.

The federal mandates and most state statutes provide no specific eligibility criteria to use when placing a student in adapted physical education. Some states have aligned selection criteria for adapted physical education with criteria used for other services. California, for example, aligns its recommended criteria with those adopted in many school districts for providing services to students with a speech and language impairment or a specified learning disability. Often, poor performance on motor tasks indicates that the student has some degree of motor "disability." The student is, therefore, tested in this area of "suspected disability." Scores and age-equivalents that school districts commonly use to indicate poor performance include:

- A raw score that falls 1.5 standard deviations below the mean
- A raw score that ranks at the 7th percentile or below
- An age-equivalent that indicates the child is functioning at 30 percent below chronological age

Sometimes, however, children who are identified as having another disability, such as mental retardation, emotional disturbance, or learning disability, score within normal limits on tests of motor performance. Because of the student's limited ability to understand instructions or control behavior in group activities, adapted physical education may be the most appropriate placement. On the other hand, there are students who are clearly limited, such as those who use crutches or a wheelchair or who have cerebral palsy. If they are able to function in general or modified physical education and compensate for their limitations, the IEP team may consider the general physical education class to be the best, most appropriate placement.

Students with a disability should participate in the general physical education curriculum and

MAKING CONNECTIONS

Legislative Mandates

Mr. James uses tests developed for the general population to test his students with moderate mental retardation. He noticed that when testing students on the mile run, many students stopped and rested or waited for their friends to catch up with them. The test was designed with the assumption that students would run "as fast as they could" for the entire distance. Mr. James' students clearly were not running as fast as they could. For Mr. James' students, this test was a better measure of their cognitive abilities and understanding language than it was of motor performance. He realized that, for his students, this test was not valid for measuring aerobic capacity, as required by law.

should be removed and placed in an alternative curriculum only after all other options have been exhausted—only when "supplementary support and services can be demonstrated as benefiting the student" (Yell & Shriner, 1997, p. 7). A local plan should be established at the level of authority governing the school. This entity may be called a school system, county, parish, state, consortium, or something else. The local plan should establish the eligibility criteria for special education, which of course includes physical education. Regardless of the plan or the criteria, "the decision as to whether or not the assessment results demonstrate that the degree of the pupil's impairment requires special education shall be made by the individualized education program team" [Sec. 56341(d) of the California Education Code].

SUMMARY

Testing, measurement, evaluation, and assessment are terms used regularly in the context of providing physical activity programs to individuals with a disability. *Testing* is a data-gathering technique that uses tools or specific procedures for systematizing information. *Measurement*—the association of symbols with the movement aspects being measured—is the result of testing. These symbols may take the form of words, numbers, or graphic symbols. Evaluation and assessment both use measurements for the decision-making process. As used in this text, however, the term *evaluation* denotes the process of comparing measurements with standards that are external to the student or program. *Assessment*, on the other hand, interprets measurements relative to each student's strengths and needs. This interpretation takes into consideration more than just the measurements obtained from testing—it includes information obtained through observation and input from the student, other professionals, and parents.

When measuring a student's current level of performance, the physical educator must consider sampling all levels of the developmental continuum to get a clear picture of the student's functioning. Reflex behavior, sensory system function, development of motor patterns, and the application of those patterns to motor skills should be considered; each level of performance must be sampled with enough information before the data can be considered a true picture of the student's motor performance.

Measurement concepts important to the physical educator include the types of scores and how they are applied, measures and meanings of central tendency and variability, and various types of standard scores for interpreting tables from norm-referenced tests. The relationship between scores is also important for interpretation.

Understanding the relationship between different levels of measurement is important, to ensure that an adequate sampling of motor performance is obtained. Thus, an appropriate IEP is based on complete information. The educator may obtain a profile of a student's development by consulting with other professionals who have gathered data from the language, intellectual, or social perspective. Collectively, this information gives a more complete picture of each student. Ultimately, it is the IEP team that determines the appropriate placement or level of services a student receives. If adapted physical education class is determined to be the most appropriate placement for a student, the measurements obtained during the assessment process provide guidance in planning an appropriate and effective IEP.

CHAPTER 5

Learning Activities

5.1 Visit an adapted physical education class at a time when you can talk with the adapted physical educator. Discuss with him or her whether a criterion-referenced or a norm-referenced test is used to identify students for placement into the class. Based on the reply, ask why that type of test was selected and what the advantages are over the other type. Ask about the advantages and disadvantages of the test. Write up your findings and discuss in class.

5.2 Interview a general physical education teacher and ask what measures are used to assess the students' performance. Ask about formal testing, informal testing, and authentic assessment. Ask how the data from the several sources are used: diagnosis, prediction, determining progress, placement, program effectiveness, motivation? Bring your findings to class and discuss with your classmates. How many different methods are used? How many different purposes are pursued with measurement? Take your findings to the professor who teaches the measurement and evaluation class for physical education majors and discuss your findings with him or her.

5.3 Once you know what kind of measurement is used to assess performance (from question 2), ask to see the school's or district's curriculum or program of studies for the age and grade level you are observing. Write a short paper that describes relationships between the measurements taken by the teacher and the planned curriculum. Would you expect to see a change in performance on the tests as a result of the planned instruction? Is it clear what benchmarks or levels of achievement students must reach in order to be considered as having mastered the skills proposed to be taught? Discuss your findings in class.

REFERENCES

American Alliance for Health, Physical Education, Recreation, and Dance (AAHPERD, 1952). Guiding principles for adapted physical education. *Journal of Health, Physical Education, and Recreation, 23,* 15.

Baumgartner, T. A., Jackson, A. S., Mahar, M. T., & Rowe, D. A. (2002). *Measurement for evaluation in physical education and exercise science* (6th ed.). Boston: WCB/McGraw-Hill.

California Department of Education, Special Education Division (2000). *Adapted physical education guidelines.* Sacramento, CA: Author.

Cooper Institute for Aerobics Research (CIAR, 1993). *FITNESSGRAM.* Champaign, IL: Human Kinetics.

Dunn, L. M., & Dunn, L. M. (1997). *Peabody picture vocabulary test—III.* Circle Pines, MN: American Guidance Service.

Eisner, E. W. (1995). Standards for American schools: Help or hindrance? *Phi Delta Kappan, 76*(10), 758–764.

Fairfax County Public Schools (FCPS, 2001). *On the move: A roadmap to fitness and wellness.* Physical Education Program of Studies: Grades 6–8. Fairfax, VA: Author.

Fiorentino, M. R. (1972). *Normal and abnormal development.* Springfield, IL: Thomas.

Fitzsimmons, M. K. (1998, November). Functional behavior assessment and behavior intervention plans. *ERIC/OSEP Digest.* EDO-EC-98-9. Reston, VA: ERIC Clearinghouse on Disabilities and Gifted Education. Council for Exceptional Children.

Fleming, M. (2001). Average scores on sliding test. Personal correspondence.

Kelly, L. E., Project Director (2006). *Adapted physical education national standards (APENS).* Champaign, IL: Human Kinetics.

Lacy, A. C., & Hastad, D. N. (2003). *Measurement and evaluation in physical education and exercise science* (4th ed.). San Francisco: Benjamin Cummings.

Lambert, L. T. (1999). *Standards-based assessment of student learning: A comprehensive approach.* Reston, VA: NASPE.

Los Angeles Unified School District (in press). *Adapted physical education assessment scale II (APEAS II).* Los Angeles: Author.

NASPE (1995a). *Moving into the future: National standards for physical education.* Reston, VA: Author.

NASPE (1995b). *National standards for beginning physical education teachers.* Reston, VA: Author.

Salvia, J., & Ysseldyke, J. E. (2003). *Assessment: In special education and inclusive education* (7th ed.). Boston: Houghton Mifflin.

Seaman, J. A. (1970). Attitudes of physically handicapped students toward physical education. *The Research Quarterly, 41,* 439–445.

Smith, D. D. (2004). *Introduction to special education: Teaching in an age of opportunity.* Boston: Allyn & Bacon.

Sparrow, S. S., Balla, D. A., & Cicchetti, D. V. (1984). *Vineland adaptive behavior scales.* Circle Pines, MN: American Guidance Service.

Thorndike, R. L., Hagen, E. P., & Sattler, J. M. (1986). *Technical manual, Stanford-Binet intelligence scale* (4th ed.). Chicago: Riverside Press.

Ulrich, D. (2002). *Test of gross motor development (TGMD-2)* (2nd ed.). Austin, TX: Pro-Ed.

Wechsler, D. (1991). *Wechsler intelligence scale for children—Third edition: Manual.* San Antonio, TX: Psychological Corporation.

Wiggins, G., & McTighe, J. (2005). *Understanding by design.* Alexandria, VA: Association for Supervision and Curriculum Development.

Witt, J. C., Elliott, S. N., Kramer, J. J., & Gresham, F. M. (1994). *Assessment of children—Fundamental methods and practices.* Dubuque, IA: Brown & Benchmark.

Witt, J. C., Elliott, S. N., Daly III, E. J., Gresham, F. M., & Kramer, J. J. (1997). *Assessment of at-risk and special needs children* (2nd ed.). Columbus, OH: WCB/McGraw-Hill.

Yell, M. L., & Shriner, J. G. (1997, September). The IDEA amendments of 1997: Implications for special and general education teachers, administrators, and teacher trainers. *Focus on Exceptional Children, 30,* 1–19.

CHAPTER 6

Data Collection

Guiding Questions

1. What are the uses of formal testing and informal techniques?

2. What are the fundamentals of test administration?

3. What are some key elements to generating useful data through the use of informal techniques?

4. What important criteria should be met when selecting an instrument or procedure for measuring the motor performance of students with a disability?

5. What are two tests for measuring each of the following: sensorimotor function, motor patterns, motor skills, and health-related physical fitness? What are two informal techniques for collecting data on these same parameters?

6. Under what circumstances would you choose to use curriculum-embedded testing or curriculum-based measurement?

Students with a disability should have an individualized education program (IEP) based on their current level of performance. Historically, educators have used measurement and evaluation for screening and classifying students, measuring achievement, and grading. Sometimes, measurement has also been used for diagnosing deficiencies. Furthermore, educational programs have traditionally been planned on the basis of categorical, age-related characteristics; predetermined curricular content; or seasonal interests and resources.

Because of this, the content of many adapted, specially designed, or modified physical education programs has mirrored general physical education, with content modifications or omissions suited to the limitations of students in these programs. In contrast, current legislation and social trends call for the identification of the individual strengths and needs of each student and the eventual planning of program content that will enhance those strengths and address those needs.

Chapter 5 defined the process of assessment and evaluation, discussing several methods and techniques for collecting the data or information used to make decisions about an appropriate educational program for students. This chapter addresses specific tools—tests and instrumentation—along with procedures for less formal ways of collecting data (information) for use in planning appropriate programs.

Health-related physical fitness, motor ability, and skill tests have only limited value to the adapted physical educator because they are typically norm-referenced tests standardized on school-age populations that exclude students with a disability. Further, these tests underscore the performances that a student *cannot do* and leave much to the imagination regarding what a student *can do*. Although educators may use norm-referenced tests in the evaluation process when considering the placement or progress of a student in an inclusive classroom, these tests tend to give inadequate quantity and quality of information for individualized program planning.

Although qualitative and diagnostic techniques generate more useful data, they are often impractical for school use because of the time needed to administer them and the level of training needed to become a proficient examiner. Other techniques or methods, however, can be used efficiently in schools to gather the needed data for program planning. These include:

1. Formal testing
2. Measurement at the developmental level
3. Informal testing
4. Self-reporting

MAKING CONNECTIONS

The Limits of Norm-Referenced Tests

On the fitness test given at his school, 11-year-old Jaime scored 4 intervals on the agility run, 10" vertical jump, and 12 laps for the endurance run. The lowest scores on the scale for boys his age were 5 intervals, 12", and 14 laps, each at the 5th percentile. Because Jaime's scores were below the 5th percentile, there is no way to quantify "how much below."

FORMAL TESTING

As discussed in Chapter 5, formal testing is objective and usually involves setting aside a special time, using a preplanned set of procedures, using predetermined space and equipment, and recording scores. In physical education, formal testing can involve the use of performance tests or direct measures. **Performance tests** *measure movement parameters indirectly by having the student perform a motor response, pattern, or skill in a contrived environment.* Both criterion-referenced and norm-referenced performance tests give information about a student in relation to a group of students on whom the norms or criteria are based.

Direct measures quantify known quantities or parameters and have a high degree of credibility. **Direct measures,** in contrast to performance tests, *measure movement parameters directly through the use of instrumentation, which seldom requires the performance of a skill or pattern.* A flexometer for measuring flexibility, a handgrip dynamometer for measuring handgrip strength, and a skin fold caliper for measuring body fatness are examples of direct measures. Performance tests of these same parameters might include a sit and reach (back saver) test for flexibility, a pull-up for strength, and a bathroom scale for measuring body weight. When selecting an appropriate tool for measurement, it is important to identify the specific parameters (movement elements) of interest in order to be certain of selecting the right test.

Criteria for Selecting an Instrument

When selecting an instrument for use, the following factors should be considered:

- validity
- reliability
- objectivity
- appropriateness
- discrimination
- ease of administration
- cost

Validity. A **valid** tool or item is one that *measures what it claims to measure.* Just as a yardstick measures distance and a watch measures time, any motor performance test should measure what it says it measures. Validity is determined by finding the relationship between two measures of a single parameter using a correlation. Usually one tool used to measure the parameter is a well-accepted, often direct measure of that parameter. A **dynamometer,** for example, is an accepted *instrument to measure strength* directly, whereas pull-ups may be used as an indirect measure of upper body strength. The relationship or correlation between those two tests reflects the validity of the pull-up test for measuring strength. The relationship between the two may or may not be strong; hence, the pull-up test may or may not be a valid test of strength. It happens to be, and so you will find pull-ups on most fitness tests as a measure of upper body strength.

Reliability. A test should be **reliable;** that is, the test should *measure the same way each time it is used.* A test of abdominal strength, such as curl-ups, is usually quite reliable; that is, a student will probably be able to do as many curl-ups on one day as on another. In contrast, ratings of gymnastic performance vary—sometimes considerably—not only because the performance varies from one day to the next, but also because the evaluation varies from one judge to the next. Consistency of scoring between judges is called **inter-rater reliability** or **objectivity.** Reliability is determined by finding *a correlation or relationship between two scores on the same performance obtained on different days.* This form is called test–retest reliability. Like interval scores and nominal data, judges' ratings tend to generate scores that are not as reliable as tests generating ratios. Thus, in competition, several judges are used. To improve test–retest reliability, multiple sets of scores are usually gathered with the best or the middle score selected to represent the overall performance.

Objectivity. A test should also be **objective;** that is, *two examiners should be able to obtain the same score for a given performance.* In the earlier examples, the dynamometer, pull-ups, and curl-ups are objective measures because two examiners would obtain approximately the same scores on each measure. Ratings of gymnastic performance are not as objective because judges' ratings often differ from one another.

Validity, reliability, and objectivity can all be greatly influenced by the mere fact that the student being tested is an individual who has special needs. The validity of an endurance run, for example, may be reduced by the fact that a student with a disability does not comprehend what an "all-out" effort means. Therefore, such a test may be as much a measurement of cognitive function as it is of endurance. A student's inability to understand the task or lack of experience may reduce the reliability of performance tests. Any student who has never performed a shuttle-run, a standing broad jump, or a vertical jump may perform significantly better on the second administration than on the first simply because the student has "learned" how the task is to be performed. Many students with a disability have never had the opportunity to use their bodies in the ways required by these tests; hence, familiarity with the task results in improved performance.

Objectivity can be reduced by several factors. Many of the parameters of interest and tests made for use with the population of students with a disability generate **qualitative** rather than **quantitative** data. That is, they define better *"how" the performance is done (qualitative)* rather than *"how many" (quantitative).* These data, therefore, are often interval, ordinal, or nominal. The very nature of this type of data tends to reduce the objectivity of the test. When ratings are used, for example, even though the criteria for a given rating may be extensive, there may still be room for two raters to assign different scores. The interaction or rapport between the examiner and the student can reduce objectivity. One examiner who is skillful and insightful into the problems of individuals with a disability may be able to elicit a much better performance from such a student than an examiner who lacks such qualities.

Most motor performance tests make the following assumptions:

1. The student is already familiar with the performance task or will become familiar with it in a minimum number of practice trials.
2. The student understands the concept of "doing your best."
3. The student is internally motivated or can be externally motivated to "do his or her best."
4. The student is positively reinforced by the knowledge of his or her performance, especially if it compares favorably with earlier performances or the performance of others.

For students who have special needs, these assumptions cannot be made safely because the student's experience, intellectual functioning, associative language, or motivation may not be equal to the task. Therefore, measures of motor performance tend to be confounded or confused by elements of cognition, language, social or emotional development, and achievement. When selecting a ready-made measurement tool, the educator should select an instrument that has elements capable of reducing the impact of disabilities on validity, reliability, and objectivity. These elements are discussed further in the following criteria.

Appropriateness. If the test is norm-referenced, the norming sample or individuals on whom the norms are based should be the same as or include the same type of student as the one who will be tested in terms of age, sex, and disability. The *AAHPERD Youth Fitness Test* (1976) is not an appropriate test for a class of teens who have a moderate intellectual disability, for example, because no individuals with moderate retardation were included in the norming sample. There is sufficient information in the research literature to conclude that individuals with a moderate intellectual disability perform more poorly than their chronological age peers. Using such a test elicits no new information. Norm-referenced tests that exclude individuals with a disability from the norming sample are appropriate for use only when placement is the purpose of testing. If a criterion-referenced instrument is being considered, the tasks should be appropriate to the needs, interests, and capacities of the students with whom the test is to be used.

Discrimination. The test should **discriminate** adequately among a broad range of performances—it must be *able to separate the better performers from the poor performers*. It cannot be too easy for the best performers in the group or too difficult for the poorest performers. For assessment, it serves no useful purpose to find that all students score below the norms; that information has no interpretive value. The educational classification of students seldom considers their motor performance; therefore, it is quite common to find among students in a special education class a range of motor performance, from motor patterns to culturally determined game and sport skills. Thus, a single instrument used to measure performance within such a group must be able to discriminate between the extremes of this range, as well as among students in the middle of the range.

Ease of administration. Regulations for IDEA '04 require that following a parent's consent to an initial evaluation, the child be evaluated within a "reasonable period of time" [IDEA, sec. 300.300(a)(1)(i)]. If it is determined that the student is eligible to receive special education (adapted physical education), a meeting must be conducted to develop an IEP within 60 days [IDEA, sec. 614(a)(1)(D)]. Thus, lengthy, cumbersome diagnostic instruments are not practical for public school use. In addition, as mentioned before, administrative procedures should allow ample practice trials to ensure that a lack of familiarity or learning does not interfere with the validity and reliability of the test. The scoring should be easy to compute and should provide scores that are useful to the examiner. Many norm-referenced tests are scored using discrete, ratio-type data such as time, distance, or number of repetitions. These scores are often converted to percentile ranks. Ratings, when used, usually have no more than five points because it is difficult to distinguish accurately the levels of a performance beyond that number of categories. Criterion-referenced tests often use check marks, pluses, or minuses to designate the capability to complete a task with effort or with ease. Although these scoring methods provide less interpretive value, they do describe the performances the student is and is not able to do. The reader is cautioned to note that the tasks required on the criterion-referenced test must be realistic and meaningful in light of the capabilities of the student; otherwise, the teacher is again left with no useful information for program planning.

Cost. Finally, the test should be economical; that is, cost of materials, time, and personnel should be minimal. A test that requires expensive or elaborate equipment and takes more than 40 to 45 minutes per student is impractical for school use. Because the average adapted physical education specialist may serve 80 to 100 students daily, extensive time spent testing is not possible. Many general physical educators see students only 20 to 30 minutes weekly, making individual testing untenable (Olrich, 2002). A procedure that can be administered in a group setting is desirable.

Test Administration

The administration of performance tests presents unique challenges to the examiner. The following discussion covers some general and specific points relative to data collection to help physical educators address the most common problems associated with this process. These include:

- Use of available resources
- Adequate sampling
- Conditions of testing
- Procedures for testing
- Getting language out of testing

Use of available resources. The educator can streamline the assessment process through the effective use of available resources. A great deal of data that can be used by the adapted physical educator is usually already available. Observational reports from other professionals, test results from other disciplines, and health records often provide valuable information for the decision-making process. Cumulative files maintained by the school district usually include grade or progress reports, anecdotal records, and teacher observations. Sometimes, in this file or in separate files are records of physical examinations; medications used (if any); and a history of various health-related problems such as seizures, visual or hearing losses, childhood diseases, prenatal and perinatal complications, and the like. These data can help the adapted physical educator make decisions regarding instrument selection, selection of parameters to be measured, interpretation of the data collected, and recommendations for program planning and further testing. A more detailed coverage of these methods of data collection is provided later in this chapter.

Adequate sampling. In an educational setting, it is usually only possible (at least initially) to sample motor performance because time does not allow every possible performance to be measured. Rather, a decision must be made about measuring aspects or components of motor performance. A good instrument that samples several aspects of motor performance solves this problem, but few such tools exist in the ready-made test market. A student's diagnosis or the reason for assessment and the physical educator's own observations should lend valuable information regarding possible areas of strengths and needs. Careful planning of assessment procedures and astute observations during both the assessment and the instructional process can minimize the need for one-on-one assessment and help the educator to gather data authentically.

Conditions of testing. In physical education, the term **standardized** is generally used to refer to *tools accompanied by a set of norm- or criterion-referenced standards called "norms."* The norm or standard for performance (e.g., percentage of body fat, acquisition of developmental milestones) is determined through the compilation and analysis of data gathered on a given population and serves as a guide for what to expect from individuals of certain descriptions. Most standardized tests give a description of the **norming sample** or *group of individuals on whom the standards are based*. For example, the Test of Gross Motor Development (TGMD-2) is based on the performances of children 3 to 10 years, 11 months of age and of various ethnic, cultural, and socioeconomic backgrounds keyed to the 2000 census; the Rockport Walk Test is based on adults 20+ years of age; and the Bayley Scales of Motor Development are based on 1,262 typical children from 2 to 30 months of age.

This form of standardization should not be confused with **standardized administration procedures.** Many tools, especially diagnostic tests, *have a specifically described set of physical conditions, equipment, and instructions for the examiner to ensure that the test is administered in precisely the same way each time it is given*. These procedures must be followed accurately to ensure valid results. Although these tools usually have a set of norms accompanying them, some may not.

When administering any test, it is important that the examiner precisely follow the procedures accompanying the test. If the equipment list includes a six-by-six-inch beanbag, a 30-second stopwatch, or an eight-inch ball, then these should be used—with no substitutions. If the procedures require that the examiner give specific instructions to the student, such as, "RAISE THIS FOOT AND BALANCE UNTIL I TELL YOU TO STOP, LIKE THIS" (Los Angeles Unified School District, in press), then these instructions should be used precisely. Any deviation from the prescribed procedures may render the results invalid for the student's performance or for comparison with the test norms. The language used in testing is discussed later in this section.

Be sure the test is appropriate for the students in terms of expected performance and understanding. Considering language and cognitive development can play a major role in obtaining valid results. Tests that do not allow the examiner to demonstrate the required performance are inappropriate for youngsters of some disability groups. The score in these cases often reflects the level of the students' understanding rather than their true performance capabilities.

Be certain the setting in which the test is being administered is not interfering with performance. If the student is easily distracted, the setting should be free from distractions and interruptions. When the test is re-administered (e.g., for an annual review), be certain the setting and conditions are the same as for the earlier administration. This includes being aware of the student's personal environment (e.g., when medication has been taken relative to the testing time; home and school conditions) that may influence performance. All of these factors should be as much the same as possible from one testing session to the next.

Procedures for testing. Besides the specific procedures provided for each test, a few elemental procedures are applicable to all tests. It is important that the examiner be fully aware of the purpose of each test item. Understanding the purpose often gives a clue as to the additional data that can be gathered through observation and may influence the examiner's choice of position during the performance. For example, if the purpose of throwing an item is to measure throwing accuracy, then noting the quality of the throwing pattern and the hand used is incidental, and the examiner should stand behind the thrower in clear view of the target so an accurate score can be obtained. On the other hand, if the item's purpose is to measure qualitatively the development of the throwing pattern, then the examiner should stand in front of and to the side of the thrower to observe the mechanics of the throw. A skilled examiner can obtain both types of information from one position or, if practice trials are allowed, obtain the qualitative data during practice and the quantitative data (accuracy score) during the actual test trials.

Examiners must take their cues from the student. How the student approaches a task often provides as much useful information as the score itself. On a task that produces a permanent product, such as reproducing figures on paper or a chalkboard, the accuracy of the reproduction can be observed after the performance is over. Therefore, the examiner should be in position to observe signs of overflow of movement (e.g., the tongue sticking out of the mouth, opposite hand movements, changing hands at midline). If the student is constantly asking, "Are we almost finished?" or "When can I go back to my room?" a quick check with the classroom teacher should reveal whether this is typical or whether this behavior suggests that the student is having a "bad day." If the behavior is atypical, the testing should perhaps be resumed at another time.

Getting language out of testing. The speech-language pathologist and classroom teacher concern themselves with measuring speech and language parameters, and the pathologist provides speech and language therapy when appropriate. The goal of the physical educator is to circumvent any speech or language disorders so they do not interfere with getting a valid account of a student's motor performance. Certainly, tools that allow the examiner to demonstrate or that provide for testing several children at one time help because the student can see the expected performance even though he or she may not understand the instructions. There is some information, however, that the physical educator can gather through observation or from other professionals that can serve to ensure the validity of motor performance scores.

The questions in "How Would You Respond?" indicate possible signs of speech or language problems that may confront the physical educator. Consider how you would determine and resolve answers to these questions.

The list in "The Authors Respond" offers suggestions for ways in which the physical educator can facilitate learning. This is not an exhaustive list of guidelines or solutions, but is merely intended as a starting point. A speech-language pathologist

---

How Would You Respond?

SIGNS OF SPEECH AND LANGUAGE PROBLEMS

Hearing
1. Do the students hear you?
2. Are the students looking for visual cues?
3. Do the students ask you to repeat instructions?

Auditory processing
1. Can the students discriminate sounds? When you say, "touch your toes," do they touch their nose?
2. Do the students seem to "forget" a sequence of commands? Do they perform only the first or last part of the sequence?
3. Do the students repeat the examiner's command?
4. Do the students wait several seconds before initiating action?

Expressive language
1. Do the students lisp, omit parts of words, misuse sounds, or get words or sounds in the wrong sequence?
2. Do the students speak in simple or complex sentences, speak fast or slowly, use plurals, ask questions, label objects, use words appropriately?

---

should be consulted for advice on specific children and problems.

MEASUREMENT AT THE DEVELOPMENTAL LEVEL

Using the developmental approach requires not only a good understanding of motor development but also a firm grasp of the levels of measurement that are appropriate at each developmental stage. For purposes of assessment, the developmental model has been condensed into five levels:

1. Reflex behavior
2. Sensory systems
3. Motor patterns
4. Motor skills/game and sport skills
5. Physical fitness

The measurement of parameters or variables at each level may be done using a variety of data collection tools or techniques as indicated in the discussion that follows and in subsequent chapters. The graphic of the model in Chapter 3 and Figure 6.1 show

FIGURE 6.1

Types of tests as related to the developmental model.

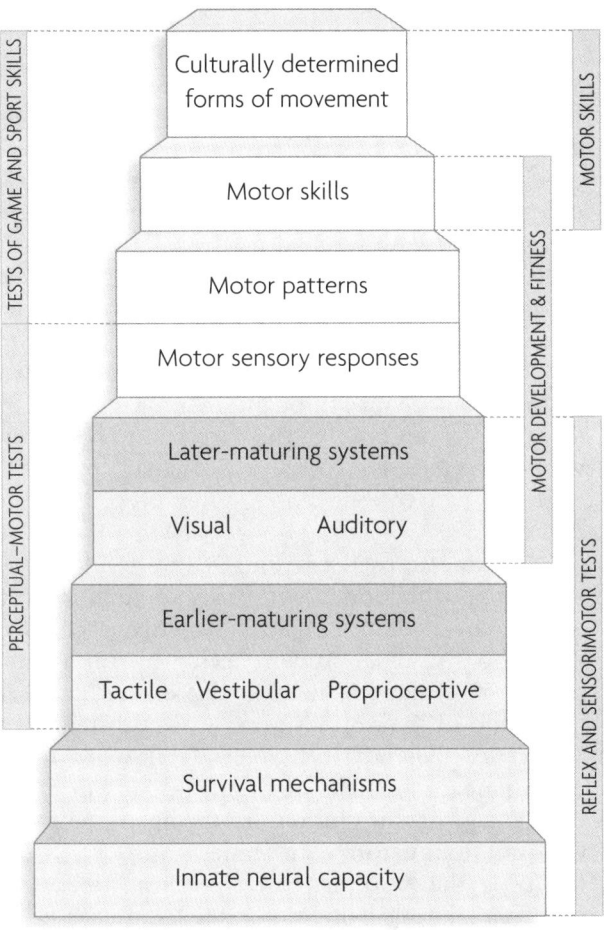

how these levels of tests relate to the developmental pyramid. Although it is not common or expected that physical educators administer tests at all levels of the developmental model, we hope that you will become familiar with some of the names and purposes of the tests used by other professionals. Many of these require motor responses and may fill in pieces of the puzzle, making the interpretation of the physical educator's findings much easier.

Reflex Testing

Reflex testing involves *the sampling of primitive reflex behavior that supports automatic postural and adaptive reactions and makes higher activities possible* (Fiorentino, 1973). The presence of some residual reflex behavior, which should have been inhibited during infancy, interferes with the development of motor patterns and movement skills in school-aged children. Inversely, the absence of some reflex behavior, which should have developed during infancy, can have similar interfering effects on

---

The Authors Respond

SIGNS OF SPEECH AND LANGUAGE PROBLEMS

Hearing

1. Verify students' hearing acuity with the speech-language pathologist or audiologist.
2. Provide visual cues, demonstrations, pictures, or information through other modalities or learning channels.
3. Repeat instructions only after students ask or have had a reasonable period of time to perform. (Students may be "buying time" to process the information. Thus, repeating the instructions too soon may be overloading, and they will have to begin the language processing again.)

Auditory processing

1. Use pictures or demonstrations to clarify the meaning of words that have similar sounds.
2. Reduce the length of the commands or give only one or two commands at a time.
3. If students repeat the command, they are probably experiencing a processing delay or problem with keeping the command in memory. Let them do this.
4. Speed up the command or omit unimportant words to give students less interfering information and more time in which to process it. (For example, the instruction "Step up onto the beam, walk to the other end, and then walk backwards" could be shortened to "Step up, walk beam, walk back.")

Expressive language

1. Take your cues from the way the students speak. Ask them to repeat what they have been asked to do to verify the sequence of the task.
2. Cue off the way students use language. Analyze the level of your language relative to theirs and simplify or change the rate of your command. Use words that have lower semantic content levels (i.e., words that mean the same thing as words commonly used in testing, but that are understood at developmentally earlier ages). If the student seems not to understand the command, try using a lower-level word (see Table 6.1).

TABLE 6.1
Changing words for better understanding.

WORDS COMMONLY FOUND IN MOTOR TESTS	LOWER LEVEL/ ALTERNATE WORDS
like (alike)	same
gently	soft
different	not same
difficult	hard
over	on top of
into	in
on top of	on
first	in front of
last	in back of
left/right	this side/that side (indicate by pointing)
beside	next to
behind	in back of
forward	toward me (examiner stands in front)
as long as	until I say STOP
large	big
small	little

Source: Adapted from C. E. Weiss and H. S. Lillywhite (1976), *Communicative Disorders.* St. Louis, MO: Mosby.

motor behavior. It is clear when looking at the developmental model that if primitive postural reflexes interfere in any way, the child will not develop fully at the subsequent levels of the model. The means available to physical educators to make this determination are discussed later. If the educator suspects there are either residual postural reflexes or reflexes that have not developed, the student should be referred for reflex testing to an occupational or physical therapist.

Although reflex testing is not normally within the purview of the physical educator's responsibilities, every physical educator should be able to recognize when poorly developed motor skills are the result of developmental delays or disabilities or the result of residual interfering reflexes. In the absence of physical or occupational therapy (OT) evaluations, some tools are available to validate your suspicions about residual reflexes (presented later). The various ways in which abnormal reflex behavior interferes with the acquisition of motor skills are discussed in general and should provide enough understanding of abnormal reflex behavior to support a referral to a therapist for in-depth reflex testing.

Spinal reflexes. Residual spinal reflexes *(spinal reflexes that play a role in typical development but do not disappear or become integrated into the system)* that are problematic are the grasp reflex, startle reflex, and crossed extension. For some children, such as those with cerebral palsy, the grasp reflex is **pathological**—that is, the reflex is *present as a result of brain injury or other disruption in the central nervous system* (CNS). As an example, the student grasps an object but cannot let go due to a brain injury, and little will change through physical education or therapy. You can imagine the frustration of children who try to release a ball at a particular point in a throwing pattern, but whose reflex overrides their desire to do so.

The **startle reflex** is equally interfering: every time there is a loud noise, the student jumps or loses balance because *arms and legs abduct and the neck hyperextends.* A student trying to run a competitive race may not make it out of the blocks if the sound of the starter's gun causes this reaction. This reflex is handy to have available when needed to prepare for fight or flight, but it can cause problems when a student is trying to perform. **Crossed extension** contributes to the development of the walking pattern—*when pressure is sensed on the bottom of one foot, the leg extends while the other leg flexes.* When done alternately, the walking pattern begins to emerge. To jump, however, the student must be able to extend both legs simultaneously, so this reflex can interfere with a child's attempt to jump.

Brain stem reflexes. Brain stem reflexes, emanating from a higher, more sophisticated part of the CNS, mainly have to do with the position of the head. The ones discussed here are called tonic neck reflexes (TNR). They are the asymmetrical and symmetrical tonic neck reflexes and the tonic labyrinthine reflex. The presence of these reflexes in infants is considered typical, but they are very often seen in school-aged children with specific learning disabilities and speech or language disabilities. In the case of the **asymmetrical tonic neck reflex (ATNR),** *when the head is turned to the side, the arm on that side extends and the arm on the other side flexes.* Imagine the problems with trying to do a log roll if every time the student turns his or her head to roll, the arm extends, blocking the movement! The **symmetrical tonic neck reflex (STNR)** interferes *when the head is flexed, making the arms flex and the legs extend* (see Figure 3.8). Children in a maze trying to crawl through a tunnel may get stuck or may simply be unable to move forward if they keep their heads down. The **tonic labyrinthine reflex (TLR)** may interfere with students trying to learn a forward roll (see Figure 4.5) or move on a scooter board in prone position. TLR is evident *when in prone—the head flexes, causing the entire body to flex—and when in supine—the head extends and the entire body extends or hyperextends.* This reflex can be seen in infants who are being passed from one person to another. If supported only on the torso—front or back—the infant flexes or extends respectively as a result of this primitive reflex. These reflexes should disappear by the end of a child's first year.

Associated reactions are *sympathetic, bilateral movements also controlled by the brain stem* that become very problematic for children learning skills. When both sides of the body are expected to do the same thing, such as when propelling a scooter board in the prone position, there is no problem. However, as children begin to develop unilateral skills such as throwing or bilateral skills requiring contrasting rather than mirrored use of the body sides, these residual reactions interfere. Even in a bilateral task such as swinging a softball bat, each arm plays a different role, and the student must be able to control that rather than being under the control of these residual reactions.

Midbrain and automatic movement reactions. As discussed in Chapter 3, the higher up into the structures of the brain these reflexes and reactions are controlled, the later they develop and the more mature are the movements. **Midbrain reflexes** and **automatic righting reactions** *contribute to the infant's ability to maintain an upright posture and move against gravity*. Righting reactions, primarily controlled by the midbrain, are considered the basis for developing equilibrium responses. Children who cannot anticipate and regain their balance fall often and find physical activity unappealing. An automatic reaction, also important for these children, is **protective extension** (see Figure 4.6). The *reaction of stepping forward and extending the arms when balance is lost* protects the child from serious injury. Children with skinned chins or elbows may lack full integration of the protective extension reflex and may also have poor righting reactions. If these children fall a lot, they should probably be referred for reflex testing.

Cortical-equilibrium reactions. The cortex controls some more sophisticated reactions to changes in equilibrium. While a person is lying prone or supine, such as on an air-flow mattress or while learning to float supine in the water, subtle *changes in equilibrium cause the arms and legs to extend and abduct*, maintaining position. Hopping in all directions while balancing on one foot is the result of these reactions, which emerge around 15 to 18 months and remain present throughout life.

The following formal test of reflex behavior is appropriate for educators to use with children with a disability:

Milani-Comparetti Test of Reflex Development

Available: Munroe-Meyer Institute, 985450 Nebraska Medical Center, Omaha, NE 68198-5450, 402-559-6402, http://webmedia.unmc.edu/mmi/pdf/Catalog.pdf.

In addition, Table 6.2 identifies some observable signs of abnormal reflex behavior during typical physical education activities. If they are observed, the physical educator should report these observations when making a referral for further testing.

How Would You Respond?

REFLEX DISORDERS

You watch Kimberly playing on the playground and notice that she doesn't climb, she has skinned elbows and knees, and she avoids getting in a position where she will get knocked down. Because her elbows, not her hands, are skinned, what do you have to say about her protective extension reflex?

The Authors Respond

REFLEX DISORDERS

Kimberly's elbows rather than her hands are skinned because her protective extension reflex is not fully developed. In a worst-case scenario her chin or nose would be skinned. More typically, a school-aged child's reflexes are fully developed and she breaks her falls by extending her arms fully. Kimberly is not getting a clue that she's falling (probably because of a dysfunctional vestibular system) and, thus, extends late—being able only to get her arms partially extended. This explains why she avoids heights and risking falling down.

TABLE 6.2 *Signs of abnormal reflex behavior.*

OBSERVED PERFORMANCE	SUSPECTED REFLEX
■ The child's arms collapse when he or she goes through an obstacle course on hands and knees.	Residual STNR or ATNR
■ The child stops crawling toward an object when he or she looks up to see where it is.	Residual STNR
■ The arm on the side where the eyes are facing extends when the child is doing a log roll.	Residual ATNR
■ The child cannot throw accurately toward a target.	Residual ATNR
■ The child's body extends when doing a forward roll.	Residual TLR
■ The child does not remain tucked when attempting a backward roll.	Residual TLR
■ The child rolls over on his or her side to get up from lying on his or her back.	Residual TLR
■ The child often falls and skins elbows and chin.	Undeveloped protective extension and/or poor equilibrium responses
■ The child avoids vigorous activity, running, climbing, jumping, etc.	Undeveloped protective extension and/or poor equilibrium responses
■ The child expresses a fear of heights.	Undeveloped protective extension and/or poor equilibrium responses
■ The child falls off chairs in classroom.	Undeveloped protective extension, poor righting reactions, and/or poor equilibrium responses

Sensorimotor Testing

Sensory system testing should focus on the functioning of those systems that most directly affect motor performance. The five systems of greatest interest to the physical educator are the vestibular, tactile, proprioceptive, visual, and auditory. Only tests that are of primary interest to the physical educator are presented in this section. Although the functioning of the visual and auditory systems is important to program planning for physical educators, these systems are not directly tested by them. These functions are measured indirectly, using instruments presented later in this chapter. Many times, school psychologists and classroom teachers administer tests that measure some sensorimotor functions such as ocular tracking, bilateral control, and fine motor control. You should talk with one of these professionals if you suspect a sensorimotor disorder to learn of any insight or diagnosis that has already been made.

Sensorimotor or perceptual–motor instruments sample (more or less directly) the functioning of the sensory systems as they support or contribute to efficient movement. Because performance tests cannot sample sensory system functioning (at least among the earlier-maturing systems) without movement, it is sometimes difficult to separate the movement of the performance from the manifestation of a sensory system dysfunction. Therefore, it is essential to understand the interplay between the movements of the required tasks in the test and the subservient sensory systems. It is also important to be aware of the potential assistive or interfering influence of abnormal reflex behavior. Finally, when selecting a test for the assessment of sensorimotor function, the physical educator should first know what parameters are to be measured and then select a test that is designed to measure those parameters.

Commonly used performance tests. Sensorimotor or **perceptual–motor testing** *samples the functions of the sensory systems underlying movement through observable motor performance.* Only a list of commonly used tests is provided here. Appendix E con-

FIGURE 6.2

This is a test of visual–motor coordination commonly included in perceptual–motor tests.

tains more information on tests used for measuring sensorimotor or perceptual–motor function.

- MVPT Motor-Free Visual Perception Test, 3rd edition (MVPT-3)
- Quick Neurological Screening Test II, M. Mutti, N. Martin, H. Sterling, N. Spalding
- Developmental Test of Visual Motor Integration (VMI-5), 5th edition, K. Beery, N. Buktenica, N. A. Beery

    Available: Academic Therapy Publications, 20 Commercial Blvd., Novato, CA 94949-6191, 800-422-7249, www.academictherapy.com

- Test of Visual Motor Integration (TVMI)
- Psycho-educational Profile, Revised (PEP-3)

    Available: Pro-Ed, 8700 Shoal Creek Blvd., Austin, TX 78757-6897, www.proedinc.com

Testing Motor Patterns

Motor patterns are *functional units of movement that occur in the normal course of development as a result of sensory feedback.* Testing at this level also involves testing motor responses because they are precursors of motor patterns. Motor patterns include all patterns learned experientially for functional purposes (e.g., rolling, reaching, grasping, and walking). Motor patterns are most commonly measured through motor development profiles, motor ability tests, or comprehensive motor performance tests. Patterns fully developed at this level of the developmental model help support the further development of motor skills.

Motor development profiles. Motor development profiles basically *measure the emergence of motor responses and motor patterns that develop naturally as a result of physical growth, reflex and sensory system function, and the development and interaction of the organism with the environment.* As can be seen in the description of tests included here, many developmental profiles do not distinguish between naturally emerging responses and patterns and the functioning of the sensory systems or the acquisition of skills. When selecting a developmental profile, therefore, it is important for the physical educator to know which responses and patterns emerge naturally and which ones are learned, so as to distinguish between developmental differences and differences or deficits that manifest from lack of experience or learning. Chapter 3 and the motor development schedule in Appendix B document the natural emergence (up to about seven years of age) of motor responses and patterns that would be of interest to the physical educator involved in measuring the motor development of students. The following tests are commonly used in programs for young children up to about seven years.

FIGURE 6.3

Placing pennies in a box measures manual dexterity.

- Denver II
- Prescreening Developmental Questionnaire II (PDQ II)

  Available: Denver Developmental Materials, PO Box 371075, Denver, CO 80237-5075, www.denverii.com

- Guide to Early Movement Skills: A Portage-Based Programme, M. White, C. Bungay, H. Gabriel (two forms: 0–2 years; 1–3 years)

- Bayley Scales of Infant and Toddler Development, 3rd edition (Bayley-III) Screening Test Kit, N. Bayley

  Available: Harcourt Assessment, 19500 Bulverde Road, San Antonio, TX 78259, 800-211-8378, http://harcourtassessment.com

- Peabody Developmental Motor Scales, 2nd edition (PDMS-2), M. R. Folio, R. R. Fewell

- Infant–Toddler Developmental Assessment (IDA), S. Provence, J. Erikson, S. Vater, S. Palermi

  Available: Academic Therapy Publications, 20 Commercial Blvd., Novato, CA 94949-6191, 800-422-7249, www.academictherapy.com

- Battelle Developmental Inventory, 2nd edition (BDI-2), J. Newborg

  Available: Riverside Publishing, 425 Spring Lake Dr., Itasca, IL 60143, 800-323-9540, www.riversidepublishing.com

Motor ability tests. **Motor ability tests** have historically been used in physical education as *predictors of athletic ability*. They tend to include novel tasks, some of which have, more or less, a direct relationship to sports performance, such as high jump, long jump, dashes, and basketball and baseball or softball throws for distance. The distinctive place of motor ability in a developmental hierarchy is not clear, however. Motor ability requires muscular strength, ability to change direction (agility), flexibility, peripheral vision, concentration, timing, rhythm, and adequate functioning at several levels of the developmental model (see Figure 6.1). Tests selected for discussion in this section, therefore, are representative of instruments that sample the broad spectrum of parameters listed above. This particular discussion implies that innate neural capacity, reflex behavior, functioning of the sensory systems, and motor development have progressed to the point of being able to support the performances included in motor ability tests. A discussion of these tests at this point in the chapter does not imply that the student is expected to have had extensive opportunities for learning or experience.

- Test of Gross Motor Development (TGMD-2)

  Available: Pro-Ed, 8700 Shoal Creek Blvd., Austin, TX 78757, 800-897-3202, www.proedinc.com

- Brigance Comprehensive Inventory of Basic Skills-Revised (CIBS-R)

  Available: Curriculum Associates, 153 Rangeway Road, North Billerica, MA 01862-0901, 800-225-0248, www.curriculumassociates.com

Testing motor skills/game and sport skills. Motor skills include all skills learned through modeling (i.e., copying the behavior of others) or formal instruction, the purpose of which is external to the individual's functional needs. **Motor skills tests** include *specific applications of simple and compound motor patterns as well as skills involved in culturally determined forms of movement* (see Figure 6.1). Motor skills include combinations of motor patterns such as skipping (step, hop), hurdling (run, leap), and swimming (overhand, kick). Figure 6.4 shows an example of a skill being tested.

Motor skills are most often measured through the use of game and sports skills tests, but they may also be measured through motor ability and comprehensive motor performance tests. Skills may also be measured authentically by "product of performance" such as the number of free-throws made out

FIGURE 6.4

This test item from TGMD-2 measures the skill of rolling a ball underhand. It involves stepping and underhand throwing, thus it is a skill.

MAKING CONNECTIONS

Understanding the Underlying Concept

A story is told of an adolescent running in the California State Special Olympics games at UCLA. Bruce was 12 years old, and it was his first big competition. He was excited that his friend David was running in the same heat, as they rode the bus to school together. About 15 yards from the finish line of the 220-yard dash, Bruce noticed that David was well behind him. Bruce stopped and waited, and together, arm-in-arm, the two of them crossed the finish line. The concept of an "all-out or best effort" was not within Bruce's or David's cognitive realm. They may have, however, demonstrated one of the primary outcomes of Special Olympics ... to enjoy the event and solidify relationships.

---

of the number of attempts in a basketball game. These forms of authentic assessment should be covered in a regular measurement and evaluation course. Later in this chapter we discuss some alternative methods of data collection.

Because motor skills are learned, the selection of an instrument to measure motor skills should rely heavily on a knowledge of the student's abilities and opportunities for learning and experience. These performance variables are measured quite adequately by the motor ability tests previously discussed and the comprehensive motor performance tests discussed later. Other components of culturally determined forms of movement, such as strength, flexibility, agility, aerobic capacity, and body composition, may be measured directly through the use of physical and health-related fitness tests.

Health-Related Physical Fitness Tests

Testing for health-related physical fitness is, understandably, an area of measurement with which physical educators feel comfortable. The development of appropriate and adequate levels of fitness is a unique contribution to the life of all individuals, especially those with a disability. Although the definition of health-related physical fitness may take many forms in physical education and kinesiology literature, tests designed to measure its parameters, directly or indirectly, tend to have several similarities:

1. They tend to be highly reliable both on a test–retest basis and on scores obtained between two or more examiners.
2. Scoring tends to be objective, usually using ratios expressing time, distance, repetitions, and the like.
3. They tend to use a few items to sample the major parameters or factors that have been documented by research to contribute to overall fitness for a healthy life. These factors are: strength, flexibility, aerobic capacity, body composition, and muscular endurance.
4. They are usually norm- or criterion-referenced on large numbers of typical school-age children (exclusive of the primary grades) ages 10 to 17 years, with the norms expressed in percentile ranks or criterion-referenced standards for age and sex.
5. They tend to be designed for administration to groups, an obvious advantage for physical educators.
6. They tend to require an "all-out or best effort" and assume each student has the ability to understand the meaning of that concept.

Health-related physical fitness testing is quite common in the schools, and many states require the administration of health-related tests. Testing adults on the same variables and having standards available for use has a rather short history, however. It was not until Kenneth Cooper's blockbuster book on aerobics hit the market in 1968 that people started paying attention to the continued value of physical activity and fitness throughout life. Some measures of health-related physical fitness have been commonly used in occupations requiring aerobic and muscular strength and endurance such as the military, law enforcement, fire fighting, and aviation. The health values of aerobic fitness to the general population have been gaining confirmation for the past 40 years. Fitness testing for adults has developed as well over the past 20 years or so, with an expanded scope beyond just aerobic capacity. Today, a variety of field tests can be used to measure the aerobic fitness, body composition, muscular strength, muscular endurance, and flexibility of adults ages 20 and up. Functional fitness tests are also available for people over 60, as interest in the healthy, active living of older adults grows.

Although the measurement of health-related physical fitness represents a unique contribution to the total data-gathering process necessary in appropriate programming for students with a disability, it should not constitute the major focus for decision making. All major health-related physical fitness tests systematically exclude students with identified physical, mental, emotional, and sensory disabilities in their norming samples and in data used as the basis of criterion-referenced standards. The Brockport Physical Fitness test, listed in this section, is the first test measuring a wide range of abilities (see Figure 6.5). Prior to the new millennium, separate tests were used for each different disability.

The selection of a health-related physical fitness test should rely as much on its appropriateness for the group of students being tested as on the parameters measured. Therefore, you are cautioned to consider such factors as physical and organic limitations of performance; innate neural capacity; emotional capacity; the presence of interfering reflexes; and the development or acquisition of prerequisite functions, responses, and skills before interpreting the results of health-related physical fitness performance testing unless students like the one being tested were included in the norming sample.

FIGURE 6.5

Two test items from the Brockport Physical Fitness Test.

Performance tests.

- The Brockport Physical Fitness Test
- FITNESSGRAM
  Available: Human Kinetics Publishing, PO Box 5076, Champaign, IL 68125-5076, 800-747-4457, www.humankinetics.com
- The Rockport Walk Test
  Available: G. M. Kline, et al. (1987). Estimation of VO_2max from a one-mile track walk, gender, age, and body weight. *Medicine and Science in Sports and Exercise, 19,* 253–259
- U of H Nonexercise Test
  Available: A. S. Jackson & R. M. Ross (1997). *Understanding exercise for health and fitness* (3rd ed.). Dubuque, IA: Kendall/Hunt, www.kendallhunt.com

Direct measures.

- Model 01163 Lafayette Manual Muscle Test System (MMT)
- Lafayette Skinfold Caliper II, Model 01128 (see Figure 6.6)
  Available: Lafayette Instrument Company, PO Box 5729, Lafayette, IN 47904, 800-428-7545, www.lafayetteinstrument.com
- Isotonic 1-RM Strength Tests (see Figure 6.7)
  Available: V. Heyward (2002). *Advanced Fitness Assessment & Exercise Prescription* (4th ed.). Champaign, IL: Human Kinetics, 800-747-4457, www.humankinetics.com
- Body Mass Index (BMI)
  Available: A. S. Jackson & R. M. Ross (1997). *Understanding exercise for health and fitness* (3rd ed.). Dubuque, IA: Kendall/Hunt, www.kendallhunt.com

Waist–hip ratio (WHR). A variety of medical conditions including visceral types of obesity create a risk for cardiovascular disease, stroke, and non-insulin dependent diabetes in adults. Central visceral types of obesity are measured by the waist–hip ratio using the following equation:

Waist circumference (waist-C) is measured at the waist horizontally at the umbilicus and divided by the hip circumference (hip-C), which is measured at the largest horizontal circumference around the buttocks. This determines the WHR, the waist–hip ratio.

Research consistently supports the use of BMI to identify overweight individuals when skinfold measurements and other means are impractical. Bray (1993) proposed that both BMI and WHR should be used with obese individuals to define health risk.

| FIGURE | 6.6 | *A skinfold caliper for measuring body fat.* |

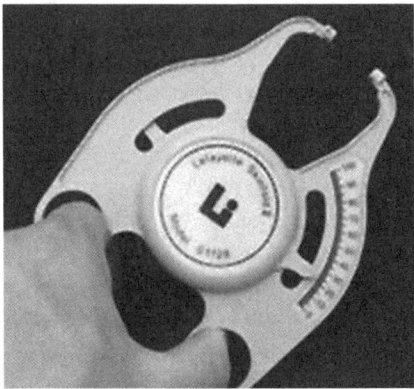 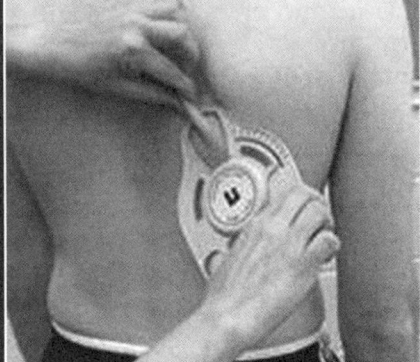 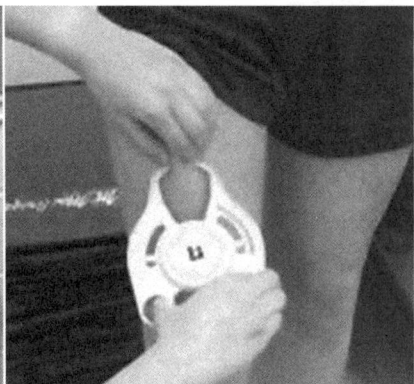

Perceived exertion. The **FIT principles of training** *(frequency, intensity, time)* are as applicable to individuals with a disability as they are to other individuals. To judge the intensity of work for people with a disability, you may find a rating of perceived exertion (RPE) useful. This method relies on the individual to judge on a 15-point scale from 6 to 20 how much exertion is experienced (very, very light; fairly light; somewhat hard; or very, very hard; or somewhere between these). Because some students may not be able to work at a level comparable to students without disabilities, this method allows for individualizing the workload. According to ACSM's *Guidelines for Exercise Testing and Prescription* (2001), 60 percent of maximum heart rate corresponds to a rating of about 12 to 13. A rating of 15 corresponds to about 85 percent of maximum heart rate.

Culturally determined forms of movement. The measurement of a child's ability to perform socially acceptable, age-appropriate, culturally determined game, sport, and other movement skills often serves as the criterion by which students are placed either in the inclusive classroom or in a separate adapted physical education class. Sports skill testing has historically been used in physical education for ability grouping (i.e., classification), determining progress, and grading. Many good sports skill tests are available on the market and referenced in measurement texts in physical education (Baumgartner and others, 2002; Safrit, 1998). These norm-referenced tests are appropriate for students with a disability who have been placed in the inclusive physical education classroom. For students who lack either the skills or the subservient sensory functions, responses, patterns, and fundamental skills to learn the sport skills, criterion-referenced instruments are more useful. As discussed earlier in this chapter, criterion-referenced skill tests can help you identify the skills or components of skills the student *can do*, rather than underscoring performances the student cannot do. Several checklists are included in the "Informal Testing" section on page 127 to give the reader an idea of how game and sport performances can be analyzed to yield effective measurement as well as useful information for program planning.

Comprehensive motor performance tests. Comprehensive motor performance tests are *tests that span several categories of motor performance testing* (previously discussed), and belong in a category by themselves. As discussed earlier, the factors of economy of time and adequate sampling of performance may necessitate obtaining measures of several

| FIGURE | 6.7 |

Photo of adult female doing a 1-RM bench press.

aspects of motor performance not measured by any single tool previously listed. Comprehensive motor performance tests generate data that may indicate areas of dysfunction requiring further testing or that provide adequate information by themselves for making decisions in program planning (see Figures 6.8 and 6.9).

- Adapted Physical Education Assessment Scale II (APEAS II)

  Available: Los Angeles Unified School District, 333 S. Beaudry—16th Floor, Adapted Physical Education, Los Angeles, CA 90017, 213-241-8052

- Bruininks-Oseretsky Test of Motor Proficiency, 2nd edition (BOT-2)

  Available : AGS Publishing, 4201 Woodland Road, Circle Pines, MN 55014-1796, 800-328-2560, www.agsnet.com

Data-based curriculum. As discussed in Chapter 5, the ongoing process of assessment uses criterion-referenced standards to measure a student's progress on a parameter. The criterion may be the student's previous performance on the same parameter or a qualitative or quantitative statement about the performance that is part of a criterion-referenced instrument. The following programs have generated criterion standards and accompanying curricula. Each has a training program for teachers to assure that the test use is valid. You are encouraged to contact the publishers for details on training before embarking on a plan to implement any one of them.

- CARE-R Curriculum, Assessment, Resources, Evaluation

  Available: Los Angeles County Office of Education, Adapted Physical Education Office, Lincoln Annex, 600 E. Grand Ave., San Gabriel, CA 91778, 626-286-6802, E-APE@lacoe.edu

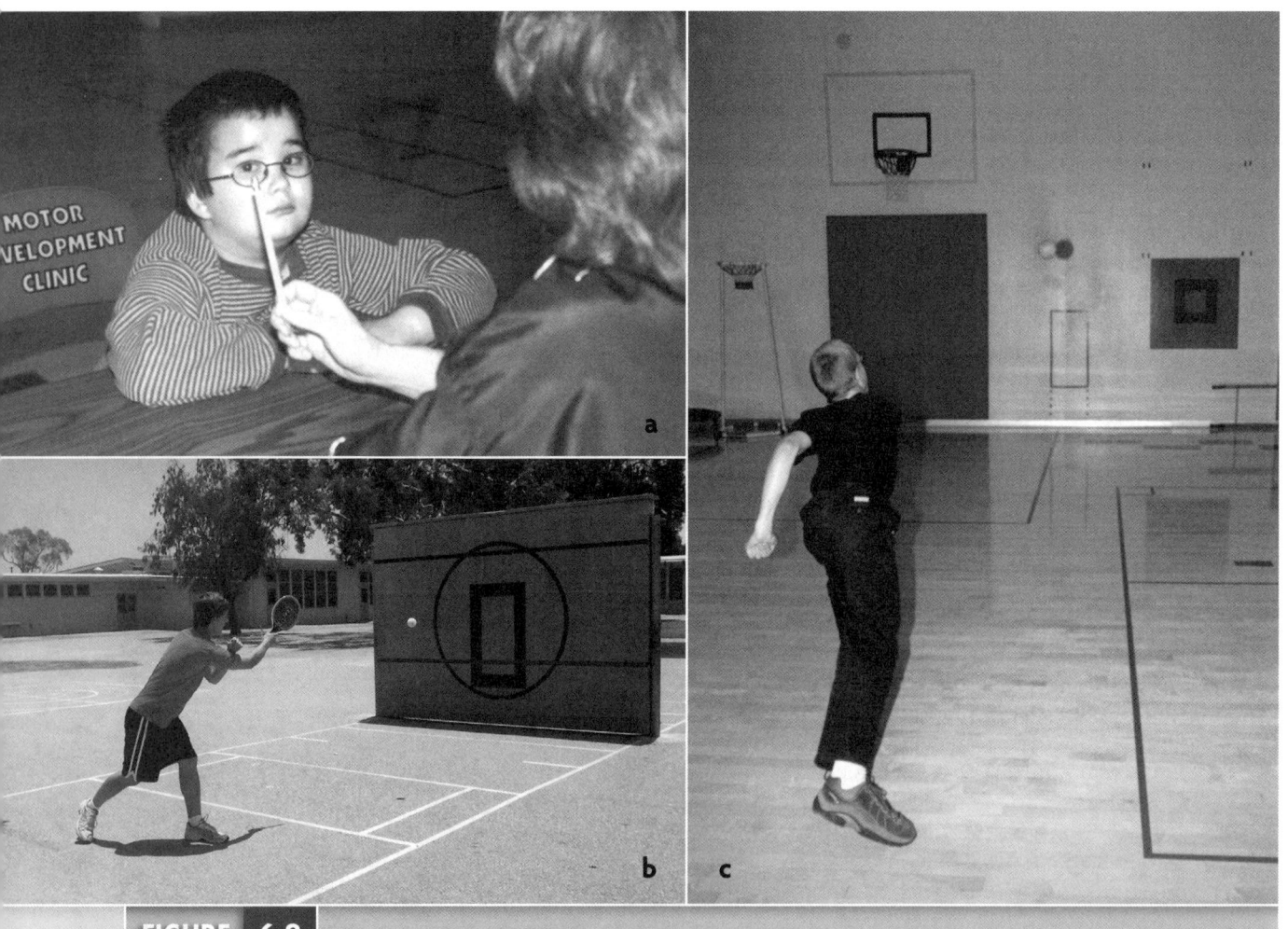

FIGURE 6.8

Three test items from the Adapted Physical Education Assessment Scale: (a) ocular control test; (b) paddle rally; and (c) overhand throwing for accuracy.

- I CAN Primary Skills K–3
  Available: Pro-Ed, 8700 Shoal Creek Blvd., Austin, TX 78757-6897, 800-897-3202, www.proedinc.com

Less formally, special educators use a data collection system called **curriculum-based measurement (CBM),** which could be useful to physical educators as well (sometimes also called curriculum-embedded or curriculum-based testing). Rather than generating a curriculum from the data, *teachers use CBM to generate data from the curriculum.* This method has been thought of as a "self-correcting instructional method" (Reschly, 1999) combined with an evaluation system. The teacher collects data about a student's daily progress on each instructional task. In math, for example, the teacher records daily the number or percentage of problems solved. This method helps the teacher know whether the instructional strategies used are effective. In physical education, a record might be kept of how many or what percentage of times the student caught the ball when thrown, passed to a teammate, or successfully completed a series of square-dance steps.

INFORMAL TESTING

In Chapter 5, we indicated that informal testing techniques are subjective, can be done at any time and under any conditions, and may or may not require recording scores. Thus, alternative methods, sometimes called authentic assessment, are included in this category. Because the assessment process should be ongoing or cyclical, informal testing techniques are a key part of this process. They allow the collection of data and comparison of long-range goals and performance objectives to occur on a continuing basis. The most commonly used tool for implementing this process is a form of informal data collection known as observation.

Observational Techniques

Teachers, merely as a result of their professional training, use authentic measures such as observation regularly. Sometimes, teachers are not aware that they are collecting information as they observe students engaged in activity, but are unknowingly storing it away for future reference. Students know that teachers are watching them. In other words, they know they are being observed, but they may not know the exact timing of or purpose for the observation. Technically, observational techniques are methods of measuring a student's performance or behavior indirectly. For measures of physical activity, the data could provide a record of the frequency and length of time a student plays alone

FIGURE 6.9

The Bruininks-Oseretsky Test of Motor Proficiency also measures running speed, agility, and balance.

during recess or plays with others, or how often the student participates in a walking program before school. Teachers and coaches collect data on a continual basis when they observe performance. The results include corrections to form, suggestions for style, and other "tips" for improving performance. Therefore, teachers are well skilled and well practiced at gathering data in this way—it just may not always be formally planned. Figure 6.10 shows a teacher gathering data on a student playing t-ball.

Valid observational techniques primarily rely on five basic competencies. The observer must have:

1. A solid understanding of the developmental milestones for the performance (parameter) being observed.
2. Knowledge of the elements or movement components of the target performance.
3. The ability to identify variations from the typical performance.
4. The ability to describe the observed performance in performance terms.
5. The ability to make sense out of the relationships among several performances (i.e., interpretation) for the purpose of planning or modifying individual programs (see Figure 7.4).

A good examiner is first a good observer. Knowledge of the typical course of growth and development forms the basis of valid and reliable observations. Knowing the developmental sequence and developmental milestones for skipping, hopping, or throwing a ball with one hand is essential to determine whether a child's motor development and skill acquisition are on schedule. Knowing when a child would typically participate in group games, under-

FIGURE 6.10

This teacher is gathering data on a student playing t-ball.

stand language concepts, or conceptualize spatial relationships is all part of knowing whether a particular child's motor performance varies significantly enough to warrant adapted physical education services or a specially designed program. It is not enough to know that a child would typically sit up unsupported at six months, walk at one year, and go upstairs using alternate feet at three years. In order to teach students with special needs, it is important to have a knowledge of development globally—sensory, language, cognitive, and social development, as well as motor development. A nine-year-old who has age-appropriate motor skills but has a three-year lag in social skills will almost assuredly fail unless the physical educator understands both the implications of the child's social development and the adequacy of the student's motor skills.

How Would You Respond?

DELAYED SOCIAL DEVELOPMENT

Susan, a 13-year-old with learning disabilities, sometimes demonstrated inappropriate social skills in public. While enrolled in a summer recreation program, she was riding a bus as part of a mobility training program so she could travel to the recreation program on public transportation. One day, a man who was missing an arm boarded the bus. She stared at him quite a while and then asked, "What happened to your arm?" Was this appropriate behavior for Susan? What would you do if you were her mobility trainer?

A knowledge of the elements or dimensions of the target performance helps the observer to better understand the quality of the behavior that should be expected. For children seven years of age and older, mature motor patterns should be expected, as well as age-appropriate social, cognitive, and language behaviors. Basic physical education courses in physical growth and development, motor learning, kinesiology, and measurement of motor performance should provide benchmarks for the elements of quality or mature elements of a given performance. What physical education literature lacks, in this regard, are the entry criteria or performances needed at each level of development for any given task and the accompanying language, social, and cognitive skills. This is where the skilled observer uses an "internal yardstick" of development and truly sees what the student is *doing*, rather than seeing only that the student is *not doing* the target performance or expected behaviors.

Once the observer knows what motor performance to expect at any given age and what the criterion is for a mature or good quality performance, the identification of any deviations in the observed performance is easier. Deviations usually take one or more of three forms:

1. Omissions
2. Substitutions
3. Additions

Individuals with motor dysfunction are identified as such based on these irregularities. **Omissions,** wherein *elements of the skill or pattern are omitted* (e.g., no backswing or follow-through in throwing, no flight phase while running, no arm swing while jumping), often lead to inefficient and poor performance. **Substitutions** occur when *one or more elements of a pattern are replaced by elements not typically a part of that pattern* (e.g., running with the arms held overhead, rather than swinging at the side; swinging the arms vigorously while jumping, rather than getting lift from the legs). **Additions,** or *added movement elements*, are often used to compensate for mechanical, perceptual, or muscular deficiencies (e.g., flailing the arms while walking—seen in some individuals with cerebral palsy; thrusting upward onto the toes while walking—sometimes seen in individuals with emotional disturbance).

Once this yardstick for measurement is well in mind, the next most important task for the observer is to describe the observed performance. Any casual observer should be able to conclude that a performance is "awkward," "clumsy," or "funny." It takes a trained observer to describe those patterns or elements of patterns that result in the untrained observer's conclusion of "clumsy." The trained observer should ask, "What do I see the individual *doing* that

The Authors Respond

DELAYED SOCIAL DEVELOPMENT

Although a 13-year-old would be expected to be more discreet in this situation, Susan demonstrated delayed social development in this and other situations. The man she was staring at made the comment, "What's the matter? Haven't you ever seen a man with one arm before?" This broke the ice: the recreation leader told Susan that it was not appropriate simply to blurt out the question, but if she wanted to know to ask the man. He explained the loss to her and she had a good learning experience.

---

results in the label 'awkward'? What is the individual adding, substituting, or omitting in the throwing pattern that results in the statement 'he throws funny'? (See Figure 6.11.) Descriptors such as "poor," "inadequate," or "immature" do not describe performance either. It is far more accurate to describe a performance in performance terms than in qualitative terms (e.g., poor balance, immature throwing pattern, inadequate jumping ability). Knowing that a student can balance only two seconds on one foot, rotates the entire trunk while throwing, or fails to get full body extension while jumping allows the IEP team to address specific, identifiable elements of motor performance. Performance terms also assist with making interpretations and writing objectives. The effort to "make sense out of" or interpret the meaning of several elements or patterns that vary from the typical is probably the most difficult aspect of the assessment process. Herein lies the basis for program planning and program modification, which are covered in detail in Chapter 8 (see "Completing the IEP").

Teacher Rating Scales

Rating scales may be used either with or in place of self-reporting (discussed later in this chapter) for students who are unable to self-report or who are not considered reliable reporters of their own behaviors. For the physical educator, the greatest value in using a rating scale authentically is that data can be gathered on what the student actually *does* relative to physical activity. Rating scales are preferred over dichotomous scores (yes/no, pass/fail—see Appendix D for information on types of scores) when the degree of performance is of interest. That is, rating scales provide scores that are more versatile for use if mathematical calculations are in your plan. Figures 6.12 and 6.13 give examples of ways to record degree of performance.

The rating form in Figure 6.13, although it uses symbols rather than numbers, also allows you to determine degree of the performance being observed.

FIGURE 6.11

What additions is this boy making to the throwing pattern? What is omitted from his mechanics?

How Would You Respond?

DESCRIBING PERFORMANCE

When the physical educator receives the following pieces of information from two classroom teachers, which one provides her with information that she can use in either selecting further data collection procedures or planning a program?

1. Jason is awkward when he throws and catches a ball. He looks like he's afraid of it!
2. When Trent catches a ball, he extends his arms stiffly in front of his body and turns his head to the side with his eyes closed. Once he gets it, to throw it back, he steps forward on the same side as he throws.

FIGURE 6.12 — Rating form—numerical ratings.

OUR SCHOOL, USA

Child's name _Casandra E._   Age _10_   Class _Ms. Blair_

BASIC SKILL	DATE	SCORE	DATE	SCORE
Stair steps—up, both feet	5/1	3		
Down, both feet	5/1	3		
Up, alternating feet	5/1	2		
Down, alternating feet	5/1	1		
Walk over, under, between	5/1	1		

Ratings: Adequate performance = 3   Inadequate performance = 2   Cannot do at all = 1

FIGURE 6.13 — Rating form—symbolic ratings.

Assessment of Student Participation in General Physical Education

Child's name _Sandy Steinberg_   Grade _10_   Teacher _Mr. Hernandez_
Activity _Folk Dance_   Period _4_   No. of students _45_

Instructions: After the student attends the specific general education class for approximately one week, the team reviews all of the skills identified below.

SCORING:
- **+** student consistently performs task during class
- **+/p** performs some of the time but with prompt (verbal–pv or physical–pp)
- **+/−** performs some of the time but not consistently
- **−** student very rarely performs or has never performed
- **NA** item is not appropriate for the student or class on day observed

CLASS ROUTINES AND ACTIVITIES	DATE: 9/15	DATE: 10/15	DATE: 12/12	DATE: 1/20
Dresses out for class and uses locker appropriately	−	+/−	+/p	+
Follows class rules	+/p	+/p	+	+
Shares equipment with peers when appropriate	+/p	+/p	+/p	+
Stays on task for designated period of time	+	+	+	+

Source: Adapted from M. Block & C. Garcia (1995), *Including Students with Disabilities in Regular Physical Education.* Reston, VA: AAHPERD.

The Authors Respond

DESCRIBING PERFORMANCE

The second description gives the physical educator much more information on what the classroom teacher is actually SEEING. Given this information, the physical educator will determine that Trent is demonstrating immature catching and throwing mechanics. The next question should be, "How old is he?"

Checklists

People have used checklists for years to stay "on track." You may use them on a daily basis to mark off tasks to complete, when preparing for a party, or when talking to your mechanic to make sure you have reported all the little "clunks and pings" in the engine of your car. Checklists provide an easy way of collecting information on how far through a sequence of movements a student has progressed. Checklists can be very detailed, and they often are if the student's progress is slow. If progress is likely to come in big chunks or an entire class is being assessed with a checklist, the steps on the list may be larger. Figures 6.14 and 6.15 show two checklists: one rather finite for a single task and the other reflecting more global skills on the playground. Figures 6.16 through 6.19 are checklists for the analysis of game and sport performance.

Game Statistics

A source of data often overlooked, especially once structured play is achieved, is the use of game statistics. When listening to professional sports, you would think that statistics are kept on everything. You can keep track of students' progress in sport

FIGURE 6.14 *Playground observations checklist.*

BEHAVIORS OBSERVED	YES	NO
Asking for a turn to play with a group	☐	☐
Lining up when whistle blows or when the teacher asks	☐	☐
Avoiding obstacles in pathway or people (personal space)	☐	☐
Turn taking: able to take turns or share toys/equipment	☐	☐
Problem solving: asking for help when needed, asking for turn, or finding a new toy to use	☐	☐

Source: Adapted from "Playground Observations," compiled by Jennifer Patel, psychologist, and K. Omoto, adapted physical education specialist, 1996.

FIGURE 6.15 *Detail of playground behaviors checklist.*

BEHAVIORS OBSERVED	YES	NO
Student lines up when whistle blows or when the teacher asks	☐	☐
Student turns head toward whistle or teacher's voice	☐	☐
Student stops activity when whistle is blown or teacher calls	☐	☐
Student moves in direction of area for lining up	☐	☐
Student waits with others for next set of directions	☐	☐

FIGURE 6.16 Roller skating checklist.

NAME	Puts own skates on*	Pushes w/ skates angled	Glides	Reciprocal arm swing	Lowers center of gravity	Stops	Takes own skates off	COMMENTS:

*Check skill components student is able to do independently.

Source: Lou Stewart, adapted physical education specialist, Los Angeles County Superintendent of Schools.

FIGURE 6.17 Swimming skills checklist.

SKILLS	NAMES									
Front crawl with breathing										
Swim underwater (5–8 ft.)										
Jump into deep water and swim 30 feet										
Tread water with arms and legs										
Change direction while swimming										

Enter the names above the columns, then check the skills that students are able to demonstrate.

FIGURE 6.18 | Bowling skills checklist.

Name _____ Age _____ Date _____

Below are listed bowling skill components and two levels of proficiency—"self" and "with help." Please check "self" if the student has learned the skill or component and is able to perform it entirely by himself or herself. Check "with help" if the student can perform the component but needs some assistance in its execution. A brief comment as to the type of assistance needed, such as patterning, prompting, or positioning, should be entered in the "Comments" column.

BALL RELEASE	COMMENTS	SELF	WITH HELP
Pushes ball			
Holds ball with one hand			
Keeps thumb on top of ball			
Swings arm			
Places opposite foot forward at the line			
Follows through (reaches with hand)			

FIGURE 6.19 | Gymnastics checklist.

Name _____ Class _____

SKILL	CAN DO	CANNOT DO
Walk forward on a 4" low balance beam from end to end		
Walk backward on a 4" line on the floor—10 steps		
Walk backward on a 4" low beam from end to end		
Run on 4" low balance beam		

Source: Jean Pyfer, Indiana University.

skills by simply analyzing the statistics that are normally kept in structured sports play. This presents a good opportunity to teach scoring as well—students on the bench or those who are not dressed out for the day can participate by keeping this record. In basketball, the scorer uses symbols to record shots attempted from the field, shots made, free-throws attempted, free-throws made, rebounds, and so forth. Although all of these may not be important in a physical education class, some of these records could be kept, converted to the following statistics, and used to track progress:

- Field goal percentage
- Free-throw percentage
- Number of rebounds
- Number of turnovers

Bowling is a favorite family activity that almost all students can engage in, regardless of ability. Although modern technology has taken the math out of the game, teachers can have their students go back to the paper and pencil scoring method—not only as a means of tracking student progress, but also as a way to teach math across the curriculum. A bowling score can indicate the number of gutter balls, a split (0) in the small box, and a spare or strike, showing accuracy in rolling the ball at the target. Equipment available for use in gymnasiums or activity rooms allows classes to bowl without going out to a public establishment.

SELF-REPORTING

Self-reporting takes many forms. Educators can use it to determine how students feel about physical education in general or what they think about a particular person, activity, piece of equipment, toy, or experience. They can also learn how active students are outside the physical education class, especially after school and on weekends, and what support system they have for being active outside the school environment. Students doing self-reporting must be able to express themselves well enough to make their ideas understood, whether verbally or in some other way. They must be considered reliable sources of information about their wishes or participation in activities. Five forms of self-reporting tools are discussed here:

1. Attitude inventories
2. Self-rating scales
3. Activity preference inventories
4. Portfolios
5. Journals or logs

Attitude Inventories

Attitude inventories measure a person's feelings toward an attitude object, usually a situation, experience, process, group, or value. Attitude objects of interest may include the student's experience with physical education, particular sports, members of a team, or the process of choosing teams in class. If an appropriate tool is not already available to the physical educator, one may be modified or developed. It is wise to try out modifications with a few students of the same age and achievement level as the students to be measured to ensure that the statements are clear and the words are easily understood.

The commonly used Likert Method allows the student to indicate his or her degree of agreement with each statement by responding on the following scale: "strongly agree," "agree," "undecided (neutral)," "disagree, but not strongly," and "strongly disagree." Scoring involves assigning a point value of from one to five depending on the response and whether the statement is favorable or unfavorable (determined in advance).

An example of a statement using the Likert method is: "Physical education provides leadership opportunities for everyone." The individual may respond anywhere on a five-point scale from "strongly agree" (rated as 5) to "strongly disagree" (rated as 1). Positively oriented statements are rated 5, as in this example, and negatively oriented statements are rated 1. These ratings usually are assigned by an objective panel of judges, resulting in a scale that identifies students who are positively disposed to the attitude object receiving the highest scores. Research in this area related to students' attitudes toward physical education can be found in Seaman (1970). See Figure 6.20 for sample statements regarding physical education.

Royeen (1985) developed a method that might be more useful for determining students' preferences for activity or ways of conducting some class procedures. In the model, Royeen asked questions such as, "Does it bother you to play on the carpet?" or "Does it bother you to have your face washed?" Although this inventory was developed to measure tactile defensiveness, it may be equally useful in physical education contexts. This method of asking questions about a specific attitude object and then using the Likert Method may be very useful for gathering the information needed to interpret some behaviors and to develop a program plan with appropriate accommodations.

Self-Rating Scales

Like teachers or parents, students may complete rating scales. The physical educator may use a self-reporting rating scale with students to determine

FIGURE 6.20

Seaman attitude inventory—sample statements.

1. Physical education provides leadership opportunities for everyone.
2. Physical education contributes to the physical development of the students.
3. One who participates in physical education feels healthy.
4. I dislike dressing and undressing for physical education class.
5. It is not possible for everyone to be good at every game, but it is fun to try.
6. Physical education helps to work off emotional tensions.
7. I am afraid of not succeeding in physical education.
8. Playing with others in physical education class is fun.
9. I like to participate in competition between teams.

their interest in class activities. For example, the students may be asked to rate a number of activities on a five-point scale: 5 = my favorite; 4 = I like it a lot; 3 = it's okay; 2 = I don't like it; 1 = I don't like it at all. This scale is useful (especially at the secondary level) for determining the activity units through which individualized goals and objectives can be achieved. Another form of rating scale is to have students rank order their preferences. For example, different ways of forming teams for class participation are listed: (1) using skill test results to balance the teams, (2) teacher chooses, (3) team captains choose, and (4) counting by 4's. The students are then asked to place a 1 on the list in front of the method they like best, a 2 in front of the method they like the next best, and so on. The method that the majority of students prefer is then considered for use.

Activity Preference Inventories

Any of several published scales may be used with adults to determine their preferences for activities. These are used a great deal in the fitness industry and in community programs to determine the level of interest in certain activities for planning class schedules, considering equipment acquisition, and determining the number of offerings needed. You can construct a simple inventory by listing the activities offered in the school's or agency's curriculum and the activities that will best address the student's identified needs or weaknesses. Using Royeen's (1985) technique of simply asking the question, you could ask, either orally or in writing:

- Which activity do you prefer between jogging and line dancing?
- Do you like weight lifting or using the gymnastics apparatus better?
- What team sport do you prefer, touch football or soccer?
- Which method of counting your heart rate do you prefer—two fingers on the jugular for 10 seconds or 30 seconds?
- What type of playground equipment and balls should be available at recess? (This could be divided by grade levels, such as K–2, 3–4, 5–6, etc.)
- Which types of dance classes should be offered as an elective? (modern, jazz, ballroom, etc.)

Depending on your options for developing aerobic capacity, upper body strength, and cooperative play habits, if this information is used to select activities, students can feel that they had an influence on the choices made on their behalf and will recognize that some of the activities are ones they chose.

Portfolios

The portfolio form of assessment is becoming increasingly popular in physical education, providing maximum flexibility for acknowledging individual strengths and differences among students. Portfolios are used to evaluate student progress, challenges, and sometimes opportunities for creativity, as well as types of effective accommodations. They provide a holistic view of the student's work, which may contain test scores, permanent products, and various work samples. Some examples of products that can be included in a portfolio assessing the frequency, duration, and context of physical activity for students with a disability are:

- Drawings by the student of an activity, favorite game or sport, or preferred equipment.
- Awards such as certificates, ribbons, or medals from Special Olympics or other extracurricular competitions.
- Log of daily physical activity after school, daily or weekly progress toward goals, and activities of special interest on weekends and holidays.
- Test scores on fitness and motor or sports skills tests.

- Photographs of the student engaged in an activity, participating with family or friends, or in competition.
- Records of the student's participation in physical activity with family or friends, such as bowling score sheets, used ski lift tickets, and receipts from skating rink.
- Journal entries such as daily writing (diary), papers on activity topics, newspaper articles, and cartoons.

This type of assessment makes a great display for "Back to School" night or some other occasion that brings parents and other members of the community to school. In addition to demonstrations or family participation, which are common ways to show off the array of activities offered in physical education, having portfolios available for parents to view will help broaden their understanding of the scope of a comprehensive physical education program and the value of physical activity outside the school program. Portfolios are usually easily understood by students and therefore can improve motivation. In addition, they provide concrete evidence of activity (behavior) for students who have difficulty with abstract thinking.

Journals

Having students keep a journal or log of activity can be very useful for tracking their frequency and context of activity. It is difficult to achieve the health benefits from physical activity if the student is active for only 40 minutes two to three times per week, which is about the median for American youth in grades K–12 (NASPE, 2002). Among college students who were consciously trying to effect changes in body composition, strength, flexibility, or aerobic capacity, less than 10 percent were able to make any measurable gains in a 10-week class meeting two times per week (Seaman, 1993). Students in these classes found they had to add at least one additional exercise session to their schedule in order to achieve measurable changes. A journal or log could be used to help students follow their progress by recording the amount of exercise they get and then recording some kind of health-related reflection, such as how they felt, how they slept, what their food intake was, and so on. These entries can also reflect learning across the curriculum—students have the opportunity to bring nutrition, biology, current events, decision making, math, or conflict resolution into their logs.

Journals, logs, and self-recording can be used effectively to track work in physical education classes as well. For example, in a weight training class, students may record stations used, number of repetitions, and amount of weight lifted at each station (or each week). Other devices, such as pedometers and heart rate monitors, can also provide useful measurements. These techniques help the teacher manage data collection for assessment while increasing student involvement in goal setting, practicing, and taking responsibility for their own exercise program.

USING TECHNOLOGY

Various forms of technology are becoming increasingly available in schools. These should be used as often as possible to supplement the physical education curriculum. Students are coming to expect to use technology in the learning process, and physical education should be no different. Elaborate hardware and software that perform wellness screening, including body fat measurements, nutritional analysis, and activity preferences, are available. Many schools have purchased class sets of heart rate monitors and pedometers. In other areas, students come to school with their own such equipment. A number of websites provide support for the active lifestyle. Teachers must become versatile in the use of such technology to remain current.

Pedometers are relatively inexpensive devices that students can easily obtain through local sporting goods suppliers or as premiums at wellness fairs and the like. Although they are not considered highly reliable measures for scientific work, they can allow students to assess their own activity levels. The device should be able to be set to the stride length of the person wearing it and should be able to be worn so the face is perpendicular to the ground. Cuddihy, Pangrazi, and Tomson (2005) provide a protocol for finding the best place to wear the device. The promotional "message" of manufacturers is, "Did you get your 10,000 steps in today?" This is the recommended number, assuming a 2.5-foot stride length, and would take the person five miles—a standard most often referenced for cardiovascular disease prevention. The recommended standard for children is 11,000 steps for girls and 13,000 for boys (Cuddihy and others, 2005). Pedometers are useful for establishing an activity baseline, showing progress, setting goals, and motivating students to be more active on a daily basis, not just during physical education class.

A heart rate monitor can be used to monitor intensity rather than duration of exercise, as it monitors the heart rate of the person wearing it. Many schools have purchased class sets of these for use in class or for a defined time period on a "check-out" basis. The accuracy of this device corresponds at a level of about 99 percent with EKG readings, so it can be used, and has been, for research as well as supplementing the physical education curriculum. A common use for the heart rate monitor is to identify when the heart rate is in the target heart rate zone (THR). This is the level at which individuals realize health-related benefits from exercise. Some devices have a sounding device that lets wearers know when they are in (or out of) the zone, so they can increase activity if it is not vigorous enough. Monitors may also record the amount of time the heart rate was in the zone, to give the student and the teacher information about how long the wearer was receiving health-related benefits. Software created by the manufacturers of heart rate monitors allows the teacher to download the information from many models for assessment purposes, permanent student records, class comparison, charting for motivation and reward systems, and to follow progress as students become more physically fit.

ASSESSING THE WHOLE CHILD

To use the developmental approach effectively, the educator should bring as much information as possible to bear on the decision-making process. Granted, it is not possible to assess a student in all areas affecting motor performance. The physical educator, therefore, must make some decisions regarding the assessment process. By answering the following questions, the physical education specialist can narrow the focus of the assessment plan for each student, based on that student's unique characteristics.

1. Do you have access to reports from other professionals, such as occupational or physical therapists, psychologists, speech and language pathologists, or audiologists?
2. Is there a medical report, and did it involve a neurological examination, including sensory system function? If not, is there any reason to suspect that one might be needed?
3. Is there a history of developmental milestones, or can you get one from school records or the parent?
4. If this student was referred by another professional, what were the reasons for the referral?
5. What other special services, if any, is the student receiving (e.g., psychological, counseling, speech, or occupational or physical therapy)?
6. How does the student learn, process, and respond to information in class?
7. What are the student's and parents' interests in terms of physical activity?

While you are making an effort to provide appropriate physical activities for the students in your class who have a disability, other professionals who teach and work with the child are also trying to create the best learning situation. Usually a large amount of information is available among the various professionals who see each child, some of which could be useful to you as a physical educator. Measures of intelligence, adaptive behavior, language, visual perception, auditory ability, and perceptual abilities may exist in each student's file and could help you make sense of some of the behaviors and performances you are seeing during physical activity. A few of the more commonly used instruments are discussed next with reference to how they relate to physical activity.

Measures of Intelligence

Intelligence is a general concept of *an individual's ability to function effectively within various settings.* It is assessed by intelligence tests that usually express the results in the form of IQ, intelligence quotient. The average is 100, and the standard deviation on most tests is between 15 and 20 points. Although the IQ does not reflect a global summation of the brain's capabilities (Kaufman & Kaufman, 2004), it does effectively predict school achievement. Adaptive behavior, social skills, and language development also play a major role in a child's ability to be successful in school.

The Wechsler Intelligence Scale for Children, 4th edition (WISC-IV) (Wechsler, 2006), is composed of two separate tests—verbal and performance. Even though verbal expression is also a motor act, this subtest measures general information thought to be common knowledge among school-aged children. It is presented orally, and the student responds orally. The performance subtests contain many timed manipulative tasks. Students with a motor impairment such as cerebral palsy, muscular dystrophy, poor eye–hand coordination, or other perceptual–motor difficulties could be adversely affected and render an invalid score. There is also an adult version of this test: the Wechsler Adult Intelligence Scale, 3rd edition (WAIS-III). Both Wechsler scales have a mean of 100 and a standard deviation of 15.

The Woodcock-Johnson—III (WJ–III) achievement battery (Woodcock et al., 2006) consists of seven subtests in the standard battery and eight in the cognitive battery. The test is designed to allow comparisons between aptitude and achievement and is very useful in identifying children with a learning disability. There are a few performance tasks involving motor output, but problems with visual and auditory perception would also be revealed and may show up in physical education activities, as well.

One of the first tests used for the purpose of identifying students with an intellectual disability is the Stanford-Binet Intelligence Scale (Roid & Barram, 2004). This test, now in its 5th edition (Stanford-Binet V), has been significantly revised since its inception. The test has three levels: the first level measures general ability, the second level measures crystallized abilities, and the third level measures content-specific areas including abstract reasoning. It has uses for students as young as two years, but it does involve some performance items such as copying, paper folding, and cutting with scissors. This test has a mean of 100 and a standard deviation of 16. Other intelligence tests with fewer motor requirements may be more appropriate for individuals with a disability affecting their voluntary movement.

Another popular test, used frequently for preschoolers, is the Kaufman Assessment Battery for Children (K–ABC). It contains both achievement and intelligence measures for children ranging in age from 2.5 to 12.5 years. This test includes some manipulative items, but it is particularly sensitive to the needs of preschoolers, minority groups, and students with a disability. There is also a Spanish version and a version with Spanish instructions for children who speak some English. The mean is 100 and the standard deviation is 15.

For more discussion of cognitive development, see the "Extend Your Knowledge" box in Chapter 11.

Assessing Adaptive Behavior

When testing a student's intelligence for the purpose of diagnosing an intellectual disability, it should be remembered that the measure of intelligence is only one component. Besides subaverage intellectual functioning, the federal law also requires an assessment of **adaptive behavior**—*one's ability to function in various environments.* Adaptive behavior scales are usually instruments that are answered by a parent, teacher, or some other person about the student's functioning level both in and outside of school. Many of the items measure self-help skills and independence. The Vineland Adaptive Behavior Scales, the AAMR Adaptive Behavior Scale—School (2nd ed.), and the Adaptive Behavior Inventory are tools commonly used in the schools. Although most of these instruments are quite time-consuming to administer, they can provide important information and insight into the self-care, communication, social, academic, and occupational skills the student brings to the learning situation.

The results from these tests also reveal whether a student has social skills commensurate with his or her chronological or mental age. Variances suggest that although the student may be old enough for certain activities, such as team sports, he or she may not be cognitively capable of grasping the concepts, taking the other person's point of view, and functioning maturely enough to be part of a team.

Assessing Language

While speech is a motor act, language represents the verbal concepts and understanding of ideas that are articulated through speech. Very often, children with a speech disorder also have other motor disorders of concern to physical educators because both require some degree of fine muscle control. Language assessment usually measures concepts and an understanding of receptive, expressive, and written language. A few of the commonly used tests are mentioned here.

The PPVT-III (Peabody Picture Vocabulary Test, 3rd ed.; Dunn & Dunn, 1997) uses pictures to measure a student's ability to understand verbal language—the child points to the picture named, an obvious challenge for students with motor impairments such as cerebral palsy. Students who speak English as a second language may also have difficulty scoring well on this test if their vocabulary is limited.

Tests of Language Development (TOLD; Newcomer & Hammill, 1996) is available for use with students age four years to adult. The range of tests measures a student's ability to understand spoken language and to speak using correct semantics, syntax, and phonology—in other words, to use correct pronunciation and to put words in the proper sequence according to the conventions of the student's primary language. In a physical education class, children with problems in these areas are likely to have difficulty following directions, getting the right piece of equipment, and keeping pace with the class. They are likely to take their cues from other students by looking around or watching what the others are doing before they act.

A student who is suspected of having auditory difficulty should first be referred for a test of hearing acuity. If no hearing loss is detected, then the student should be tested for auditory perception problems. Several tests previously discussed have subtests that measure short-term auditory memory and auditory discrimination—the ability to differentiate between auditory stimuli.

A commonly used test for auditory discrimination is the Test of Auditory Discrimination (Goldman, Fristoe, & Woodcock, 1970). The words used are similar in sound, and students are assessed on their ability to discriminate between them when the background environment is either quiet or noisy. Students who have difficulty on this test may also have difficulty on the playground or the playing field during physical education. As with students who have hearing problems, these students should be moved to the front of the class, where they can more readily hear the teacher. The educator can use gestures and demonstrations to augment verbal instructions. Visual signals should be used among players on a team so students with auditory discrimination problems can get the message without having to discriminate between sounds with a noisy background.

SUMMARY

Students with a disability should have an IEP based on their current level of performance. Several procedures are available for collecting motor performance data on these students, including formal and informal testing. Skillful observation is the foundation on which all other forms of data collection are based. The observer must have a solid understanding of developmental milestones, a knowledge of the dimensions of the target performance, the ability to identify deviations from the performance norm or standard, the ability to describe the observed performance, and the ability to make sense of the relationships among performances (interpret) for the purpose of program planning. The educator must consider the student's level of language and cognitive development and the presence of interfering reflexes when judging the validity of data and planning a program.

Formal testing and direct measures require not only the skill to administer the test validly and reliably, but also the ability to select an appropriate tool that will generate useful information. Qualities of a useful instrument include validity; reliability; age-appropriateness to the student and performances measured; discriminating ability; and administrative ease and economy in terms of time, equipment, and personnel needed.

Some data collected by individuals other than the physical educator can be useful in test administration and interpretation. Although physical educators can usually rely on other professionals to provide needed information, to make the best use of this information they should have a working knowledge of the elements involved and the limitations imposed by abnormal reflex behavior.

Numerous tools are available for measuring the motor performance of students with a disability. These are categorized according to their titles or the parameters measured. The categories of tests discussed in this chapter are: sensorimotor; motor development; motor and game and sport skills; physical fitness; comprehensive motor performance; and curriculum-based. More detail on the validity, reliability, and types of standards found in each test listed in this chapter is found in Appendix E.

CHAPTER 6
Learning Activities

6.1 With a classmate, observe a class of students with disabilities, preferably students likely to have residual postural reflexes. With the help of the teacher or therapist, identify one student to observe during activity. Using the tally sheet below, tally the number of times you see signs of the reflexes listed. Compare your notes with your classmate and discuss the amount of agreement and disagreement between your tallies.

REFLEX OBSERVED	NUMBER OF OBSERVATIONS
Residual symmetrical tonic neck reflex	
Residual asymmetrical tonic neck reflex	
Residual tonic labyrinthine reflex	
Undeveloped protective extension	

6.2 Using the checklists in Figures 6.14 through 6.19, measure a student's or classmate's performance on one or more of the skill sets.

6.3 If possible, administer at least one formal test to a student with a disability. These tests are often available in testing materials centers at universities or school districts; school psychologists or classroom teachers may have them, or adapted physical educators may have access to one or more of them. Write a three-page paper on your experience, including a discussion of the student's abilities, limitations, and behavior during testing; comments (if any) made to you about the testing; your level of comfort with the testing; and anything that surprised you or was unique about the experience.

6.4 Go to a school or playground where there are children with cerebral palsy. Observe the omissions that occur in patterns or skills they are using. What movements do they substitute in order to maintain balance or execute a skill? What movements do these children add in order to maintain balance, execute a skill, or apply force to their movements?

6.5 Spend some time with an adapted physical education teacher while he or she is testing students for placement considerations. Discuss the test used, why that particular one was selected, what parameters are measured with it, and how much other data the teacher already knows or will gather from other sources before scoring and interpreting the data. Discuss your information in class, especially if your classmates had an opportunity to visit different schools or different school districts. Compare and contrast the processes used. Discuss the processes with regard to the mandates of the law.

REFERENCES

AAHPERD (1976). *Youth Fitness Test.* Washington, DC: Author.

ACSM. (2001). *ACSM's resource manual: Guidelines for exercise testing and prescription* (4th ed.). Baltimore: Lippincott Williams & Wilkins.

Ayres, A. J. (1979). *Sensory integration and the child.* Los Angeles: Western Psychological Services.

Baumgartner, T. A., Jackson, A. S., Mahar, M. T., & Rowe, D. A. (2002). *Measurement for evaluation in physical education and exercise science* (6th ed.). Boston: WCB/McGraw-Hill.

Block, M., Connor-Kuntz, F., Pyfer, J., & Huettig, C. (1999, April). *Authentic assessment.* Paper presented at the AAHPERD National Convention & Exposition, Boston.

Block, M., & Garcia, C. (1995). *Including students with disabilities in regular physical education.* Reston, VA: American Alliance for Health, Physical Education, Recreation, and Dance.

Bobath, B., & Bobath, K. (1975). *Motor development in the different types of cerebral palsy.* London: International Ideas.

Bray, G. A. (1993). Fat distribution and body weight. *Obesity Research, 1,* 203–205.

Brown, L., & Leigh, J. E. (1986). *Adaptive behavior inventory.* Austin, TX: Pro-Ed.

Cuddihy, T. F., Pangrazi, R. P., & Tomson, L. M. (2005). Pedometers: Answers to FAQs from teachers. *JOPERD 76*(2), 36–40, 55.

Dunn, L. M., & Dunn, L. M. (1997). *Peabody picture vocabulary test—III.* Circle Pines, MN: American Guidance Service.

Fiorentino, M. R. (1973). *Reflex testing methods for evaluating CNS development.* Springfield, IL: Charles C. Thomas.

Fiorentino, M. R. (1981). *A basis for sensorimotor development—normal and abnormal: The influence of primitive, postural reflexes on the development and distribution of tone.* Springfield, IL: Charles C. Thomas.

Goldman, R., Fristoe, M., & Woodcock, R. (1970). *Test of auditory discrimination.* Circle Pines, MN: American Guidance Service.

Hodges, P. B. (1978). *A comprehensive guide to sport skills tests and measurements.* Springfield, IL: Charles C. Thomas.

Huettig, C., & Roth, K. (2002). Maximizing the use of APE consultants: What the general physical educator has the right to expect. *JOPERD 73*(1), 32–35, 53.

Kaufman, A. S., & Kaufman, N. L. (2004). *KABC-II Kaufman assessment battery for children* (2nd ed.). Circle Pines, MN: American Guidance Service.

Kaufman, A. S., & Kaufman, N. L. (2004). *KTEA-II Kaufman test of educational achievement.* Circle Pines, MN: American Guidance Service.

Kelly, L. E., & Gansneder, B. M. (1998). Preparation and job demographics of adapted physical educators in the United States. *Adapted Physical Activity Quarterly, 15,* 141–154.

Lambert, N., Henry, L., & Nihira, K. (1993). *AAMR adaptive behavior scales—schools (ABS-S:2).* Austin, TX: Pro-Ed.

Likert, R. (1932). A technique for the measurement of attitudes. In N. R. S. Woodworth (Ed.), *Archives of Psychology* (Vol. 22, pp. 140–146). New York: Columbia University Press.

Los Angeles Unified School District. (in press). *Adapted Physical Education Assessment Scale II.* Los Angeles: Author.

Melograno, V. J. (1998). *Professional and student portfolios for physical education.* Champaign, IL: Human Kinetics.

National Association for Sport and Physical Education (2002). *2001 Shape of the Nation Report.* Reston, VA: Author.

Newcomer, P., & Hammill, D. (1996). *Test of Language Development—Primary (TOLD-P:3)*. Austin, TX: Pro-Ed.

Nihira, K., Leland, H., & Lambert, N. (1993). *AAMR adaptive behavior scales—residential and community (ABS-RC:2)*. Austin, TX: Pro-Ed.

Olrich, T. W. (2002). Assessing fundamental motor skills in the elementary school setting. *JOPERD 73*(7), 26–28, 34.

Osness, W. (Ed.). (1996). *Functional fitness assessment for adults over 60 years*. Dubuque, IA: Kendall Hunt.

Patel, J., & Omoto, K. (1996). *Playground observations checklist*. Las Vegas, NV: Unpublished.

Pyfer, J. (n.d.). *Gymnastics checklist*. Bloomington, IN: Unpublished.

Reschly, D. (1999). *Curriculum based measurement: A self-correcting method*. Presentation made at the Alliance Project Seminar on Placement of Students of Color in Special Education, Marina del Rey, California.

Rikli, R. E., & Jones, J. (2001). *Senior fitness test manual*. Champaign, IL: Human Kinetics.

Roid, G., & Barram, R. A. (2004). *Essentials of Stanford-Binet Intelligence Scales (SB5) assessment*. Hoboken, NJ: Wiley Publishing.

Royeen, C. B. (1985). The development of a touch scale for measuring tactile defensiveness in children. *The American Journal of Occupational Therapy, 40*, 414–419.

Safrit, M. J. (1998). *Introduction to measurement in physical education and exercise science*. Columbus, OH: McGraw-Hill.

Seaman, J. A. (1970, October). Attitudes of physically handicapped children toward physical education. *The Research Quarterly, 41*, 439–445.

Seaman, J. A. (1972). The effects of a bowling program on number concepts and social self-esteem of mentally retarded children. Unpublished doctoral thesis, Indiana University, Bloomington.

Seaman, J. A. (1979). *Adapted physical education assessment scale (APEAS)*. Los Angeles: Los Angeles Unified School District.

Seaman, J. A. (1993, March). *Effective changes in health-related measures in a 10-week college course*. Paper presented at CAHPERD conference, San Diego, California.

Stewart, L. (n.d.). *Roller skating checklist*. Los Angeles: Unpublished.

Strand, B. N., & Wilson, R. (1992). *Assessing sport skills*. Champaign, IL: Human Kinetics.

Tripp, A., & Zhu, W. (2005). Assessment of students with disabilities in physical education: Legal perspectives and practices. *JOPERD 76*(2), 41–47.

VanderLinden, D. (2000). Ability of the Milani-Comparetti developmental examination to predict motor outcome. *Physical and Occupational Therapy in Pediatrics, 5*(1), 27–39.

Webb, E., Campbell, D., Schwartz, R., & Sechrest, L. (1999). *Unobtrusive measures*. Thousand Oaks, CA: Sage Publications, Inc.

Wechsler, D. (2006). Wechsler Intelligence Scale for Children (4th ed.), Integrated. San Antonio, TX: Harcourt Assessment.

Wessel, J. A., & Zittel, L. L. (1998). *I CAN, primary skills, K–3*. Austin, TX: Pro-Ed.

Woodcock, R. W., McGrew, K. S., & Mather, N. (2006). Woodcock Johnson III Complete. Ithaca, IL: Riverside.

CHAPTER 7
Completing the Assessment Process

Guiding Questions

1. When are formal and informal data collection used?

2. How do test validity and reliability influence how you interpret the data you have collected on a student?

3. How can test results be used to identify functionality and to find relationships among areas of weakness to identify dysfunctionality?

4. What are the six concepts necessary for interpretation?

5. What are some of the relationships among reflex behavior, sensorimotor function, motor development, motor ability, motor skills, and health-related physical fitness that are meaningful when interpreting collected data?

6. How does the model for interpretation of data relate to the developmental model on which this text is based?

7. What three types of statements should be made when reporting the results of data collection?

INTERPRETATION OF DATA

The interpretation of data gathered on a student is the point in the assessment process at which decisions are made about a student's educational program. It is probably the most challenging aspect of the process. It requires skills that most physical educators have not been taught or previously been required to demonstrate, such as analyzing measurements and determining relationships among them.

In states that do not have adapted physical education specialists, the general physical educator may have to gather and interpret data for the individualized education program (IEP) team with limited support. Certainly, the more sources of data you have used for collaborating information, the more confident you, as a generalist, can be when reporting your results and making recommendations. An adapted physical education specialist may adopt a model for interpretation "to make sense of a student's performance" because many useful tools do not provide interpretive information. Because the adapted physical educator may use a combination of data-gathering methods to get a broad picture of a student's performance, it is important to have a comprehensive model that allows the educator to determine the relationships among information from sources including tests, observation, and medical records.

Under IDEA '04, assessment is required before planning an IEP for students with a disability. The purpose of the assessment process is to make the following decisions:

1. To determine the student's current level of performance
2. To determine whether that level of performance is such that the student could benefit from special education services—that is, what would be the least restrictive environment (placement): the general physical education class, adapted physical education, or some combination?
3. To gain information for selecting and prioritizing possible goals and objectives, adaptations, and other program strategies

> ## Teaching Tip
>
> **BALANCING TEAMS** • One method of balancing teams for in-class competition is to rate the students on their skill in an activity (such as excellent, good, average, below average, poor) or to rank order them, starting with 1 for the best-skilled student. Then, either select a student from each of the categories or pair students up, taking one from the top and one from the bottom until the teams are populated.

Using measurements to determine appropriate placement is not really new to physical educators; testing for the purpose of classification is common and is mentioned by most measurement textbook authors (e.g., Baumgartner & others, 2002; Vincent, 2005). These authors, however, are referring to the process of classification or placement of students into homogeneous ability groups or grading categories or to partitioning students out to meet a group need or the instructor's needs. Herein lies a major difference between general and adapted physical education: adapted physical education recognizes that the placement of students into or out of groupings or programs should be based on the student's needs, not on any external criterion such as the number needed to make up a team.

Educators should use **evaluation**—referring to *the use of norm-referenced tests, benchmarks, standards, or rubrics*—when making placement decisions because consideration must be given to whether the student "measures up" to the expectations for the general physical education class. The guidelines in Table 7.1 should be useful.

When an assessment is performed for the purpose of program planning or continued programming, criterion-referenced tools, observations, consultation with parents and teachers, self-reporting methods, and other unobtrusive measures may—and perhaps should—be used. Even a stu-

TABLE 7.1 *Guidelines for making placement decisions.*

■ Student performs within range of GE students.	■ General PE class is least restrictive environment.
■ Student performs well off the norm of GE students.	■ Adapted PE class is least restrictive environment.
■ Student in APE performs within range of GE students.	■ Student re-enters general PE class, and it is now the least restrictive environment.

dent's annual goal and short-term performance objectives, if written in measurable terms and based on the student's current level of performance at the time they were written, can serve as the criteria against which a given performance may be compared. Additionally, if programming in adapted physical education is going to be continued, criterion-referenced tools often provide more useful information regarding program content and the sequencing of learning experiences than the typical norm-referenced instrument or curriculum benchmarks. When making placement decisions, the educator should consider the use of adaptations, accommodations, and modifications in addition to the data, to facilitate placement in the least restrictive environment.

CONCEPTS NECESSARY FOR INTERPRETATION

he six general concepts necessary for the interpretation of data are:

1. Performance sampling
2. Test validity
3. Test reliability
4. Test specificity
5. Tests as indicators
6. Test relationships

Performance Sampling

Human qualities are composed of many intricately woven factors, and motor performance is no exception. Because many factors contribute uniquely, or in combination, to make up a given quality, it is virtually impossible to measure all of them. Thus, the typical approach to measurement is sampling the factors to draw conclusions about the presence or absence of the quality. Consider the parameter known as "strength" (the word **parameter** here refers to *one of the qualities of motor performance*; in this case, strength) as an example. Some of the strength factors that make unique or collective contributions to the quality can be readily measured (see Figure 7.1).

In Figure 7.1, the entire area within the circle defining strength is not covered or sampled by the factors indicated. Some contributions to strength (labeled "Other") cannot be reasonably measured, such as oxygen transport efficiency, the student's motivation to perform, and competitiveness. Furthermore, some factors that contribute to strength either are not yet fully understood or are so variable that they cannot be consistently measured (e.g., the

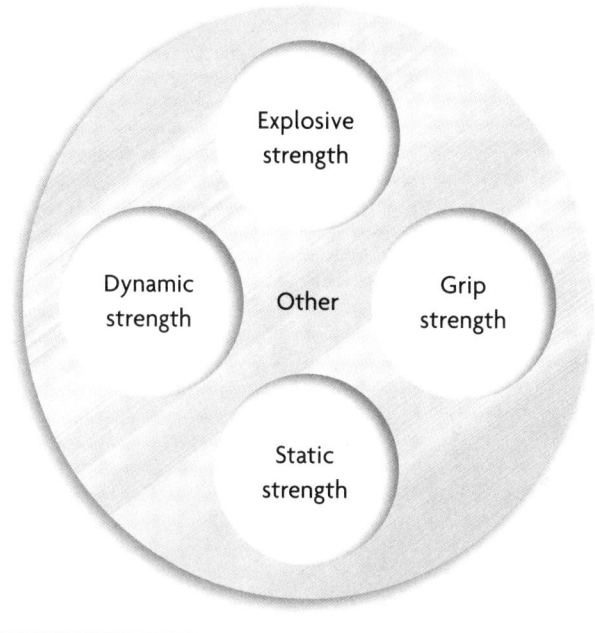

FIGURE 7.1

Factors that contribute to strength.

contributions of hormones, adrenaline, and emotions such as fear). Therefore, the aspects of strength that can reasonably be measured are used as a sampling of strength to draw conclusions about the overall strength of the performer.

Likewise, we measure the larger parameter of health-related physical fitness by sampling some of the contributing factors (see Figure 7.2). As in the previous example, all of the factors cannot be reasonably measured, nor are all of the contributing factors truly known, understood, or agreed upon. Furthermore, all factors do not make equal contributions, and they do not make contributions of the same importance in all situations. Therefore, most health-related physical fitness tests sample the larger parameter of health-related physical fitness by measuring those parameters that are known to contribute consistently to health-related physical fitness, so that a conclusion can be made regarding the "presence or absence" of physical fitness in a given individual. In order to have an adequate sampling of the overall quality or parameter known as fitness, all items on a particular fitness test must be administered. At best, only a sampling of each parameter can be made anyway, so to leave out an item or section of the test (test item) gives less than a complete picture. Understanding this process of sampling performance is important in interpretation.

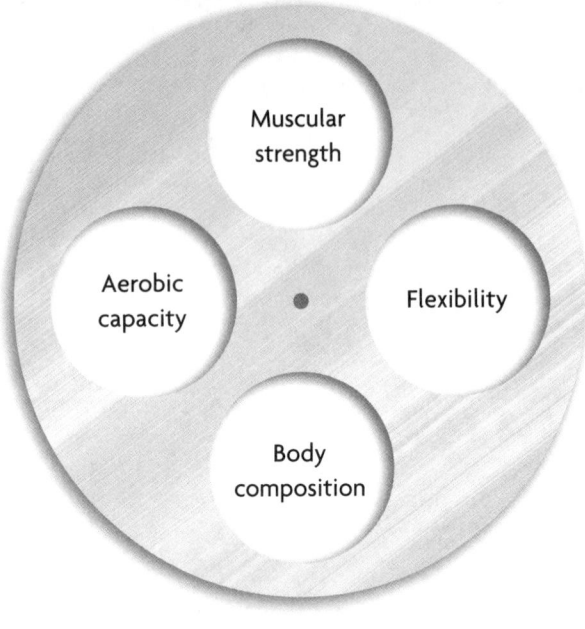

FIGURE 7.2 Factors that contribute to health-related physical fitness.

Test Validity

As discussed in Chapter 6, the physical educator must know what a test is intended to measure and should analyze each test item to validate that it does indeed measure that parameter. For example, the APEAS II (Los Angeles Unified School District, in press) test of static balance gives this instruction:

PROCEDURE: Student should be wearing tennis shoes or appropriate rubber-soled shoes.

- Student folds arms (with hands grasping opposite elbows) and holds close against the chest.
- Examiner touches the student's right leg and says: "RAISE THIS FOOT AND BALANCE UNTIL I TELL YOU TO STOP, LIKE THIS."
- Examiner demonstrates the standing posture with arms folded as described and right foot off the ground approximately 6" without legs touching.
- Examiner says: "NOW YOU DO IT."
- If student has difficulty balancing within the first five seconds he/she may begin that trial again.
- The watch is started as soon as the right foot leaves the ground and continues until the command "STOP" is given.

Another test of static balance, however, may give a somewhat different instruction:

Examiner stands facing the student and says: "Fold your arms, raise your right leg, and balance as long as you can."

The physical educator who is comparing these two tests for validity should recognize that students with a temporal or timing relationship difficulty (those with a language disorder or other cognitive disorder) would have trouble with the second set of instructions when deciding how long "as long as you can" is. On one day, they may feel like trying to stand there all class period; on another day, they may not feel like they can do much of anything. The first instruction allows the student to understand the task by watching the examiner perform, eliminating the need to process language and temporal concepts. It also has a definite beginning—"Raise this leg"—and a definite ending—"Stop"—that further eliminate the need to process information such as "Which is the right leg? How long is 'as long as I can'? How many things do I have to do and in what order?" For some students, instructions like the second example can be as much a measure of language and cognitive function as of balance. For general education students, those instructions may render a perfectly valid performance.

Analyzing a test in this way yields **face or content validity** because *it appears to be valid,* yet the test does not necessarily clearly measure what it claims to measure. Sometimes, test makers report **external validity.** External validity shows *the relationship between performance on a particular test and some external criterion,* such as laboratory measures or performance in a game (an authentic assessment).

As an example of validity, consider a basketball dribble skill test that requires the student to dribble a basketball the length of the court around three traffic cones, keeping the ball on the side away from

MAKING CONNECTIONS

How Valid Can a Test Be?

Darrell, a student with autism, was very often in his "own little world." One day in the pool, he used two kick boards stacked on top of one another to buoy himself up more than usual, as it was a cool day. This behavior indicated he had much more grasp of the concept of buoyancy than one might expect from his response on other occasions. You may question the validity of his measured IQ of 15!

the cones, and back to the other end of the court. It seems to have face validity in that it does require dribbling the basketball and changing hands as though a defensive player was there. A criterion for external validity might be the number of turnovers while dribbling that occurred during a game. The *relationship between the two scores* can be found by using a **correlation coefficient.** If you are not sure whether other factors, such as language and cognition, are affecting the validity of the performance, this possibility should be considered and mentioned when you report the results. An IEP team meeting will probably include a specialist such as a speech pathologist or parent whose input could be very helpful.

Test Reliability

The **reliability** or *consistency with which a test measures performance*—as well as the magnitude of the measurement error—is important. A great deal of inconsistency could mean the difference between recommending a student for placement in adapted physical education based on testing one day, and *not* recommending placement based on testing on another day. Tests that require multiple trials or practice trials to mitigate learning effects and tests that include several items sampling a given parameter tend to be more reliable than tests that do not have these features. Even test items that are known to be fairly reliable often result in slightly different scores each time students take the test. Because younger children and students who have a disability tend to be less consistent in performance, the factors that affect validity also influence reliability. Thus, the variance in some performances is inherent in the performer and not due to the measurement device. The physical educator must be alert to the student's mood and nonverbal cues in order to determine both the validity and reliability of the performance.

MAKING CONNECTIONS

Importance of Test Reliability

When Miko tests fifth graders who are referred for adapted physical education, she is always certain to use an instrument that has established reliability. The students will be transferring to a middle school next year and it is important for the receiving teachers to be able to obtain scores that are consistent with the assessment results provided when Miko tests them in the fifth grade.

> ### *Teaching Tip*
> **ESTABLISHING RAPPORT** • Take steps to establish rapport with the student before starting testing. Simple rapport-building techniques include:
> - Smile
> - Interact pleasantly
> - Avoid correcting the student unnecessarily
> - Give simple choices (e.g., What do you want to do first? Do you want to use a red ball or a yellow ball?)
> - Praise, compliment, or use other comments that show positive regard for the student
> - Be a good listener

The examiner must watch for signs of boredom, lack of motivation, or statements such as "Can I go back to my room now?" and "How many more do I have to do?" Obviously, a student who cries through the entire testing session, throws a tantrum, or hides under the table is likely to perform better under different conditions on another day! When these situations occur, it is best to report them when interpreting results and perhaps even to recommend retesting once a better rapport is established between teacher and student.

Test Specificity

Because test items are fairly **specific**—that is, they *measure a specific variable usually to the exclusion of others*—three- or four-item tests have obvious limitations unless research has demonstrated that those items have excellent predictive value for the parameter they are measuring. With health-related physical fitness tests, for example, the more samples of motor performance that can be obtained for a student, the more accurate the picture of motor ability (see Figure 7.3). If it were possible to obtain scores on all factors, then a complete picture of true ability could be drawn. However, such a task requires an enormous series of tests that is neither practical nor possible. An unnecessarily lengthy test may be as inappropriate as too short a test. An appropriate test should have enough items to yield valid information for interpretation, yet be short enough so that fatigue and boredom do not interfere with the reliability of performance. Generally, the expected attention span for the age and disability of the students being tested should determine the length of the test. A test that exceeds this time span can be partially admin-

FIGURE 7.3
All factors of motor performance.

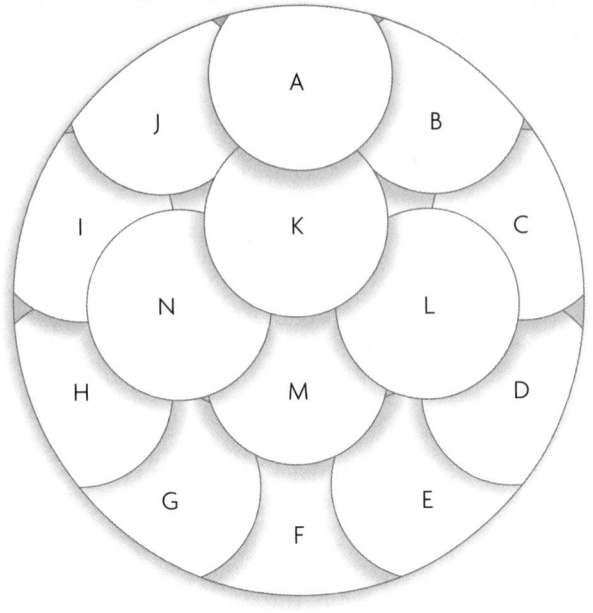

istered on one day and continued on another day. This break in test administration should be considered during interpretation, and the test's manual or other technical report should be reviewed to ensure that this time delay will not affect the validity or reliability of the test.

Some tests are developed in such a way that an **order effect** is present. This means that *all the normative data are gathered at one time, with test items given in a specified order.* Thus, performance on item 2 is influenced by the student's performance on item 1 just before, and item 2 may influence the performance on item 3. If there is an order effect, it is reflected in the norms. Therefore, if the teacher stops testing a student after item 8 and begins fresh with item 9 on another day, the student's performance is likely to be different—probably better—than if it had occurred right after the eight other items. This break in administration should be reported (and usually should be avoided), and if the fresh testing session yields considerably different scores than expected, the measurements should be interpreted accordingly. Some tests are developed in such a way as to avoid an order effect. Look for information on order effect in the test manual or other technical information before testing.

Tests as Indicators

Test items on which the student scores poorly indicate areas of weakness. Thus, a student who does poorly on the flexed arm hang can be described at least as having poor arm strength, and possibly poor overall body strength. Other information, including observation, muscle testing reports from a physical therapist, or classroom teacher reports of the student "not being able to keep up" with the other students, would validate this conclusion. Health-related physical fitness tests have been analyzed statistically to identify the items included in each test that tend to be the best indicators of specific parameters.

It is usually necessary for the adapted physical educator to discover the commonalities among test items to determine strengths and areas of need. For example, balancing on one foot, vertical jump, and curl-ups are common performances found on tests used in physical education. Balancing on one foot is often found on perceptual–motor, motor development, and motor ability tests; vertical jump is usually seen as a motor ability, physical fitness, or developmental item; and curl-ups are usually found on health-related fitness tests. It is very likely that data from these three items will be obtained through the use of more than one tool or data-gathering method. Therefore, the physical educator must find the commonality or commonalities among these three items in order to interpret the measurements, especially if the data have come from three different sources. If left to the examiner, this becomes a question of face or content validity.

The challenge of interpreting inadequate performances is becoming more difficult because many states have adopted Standards of Learning (SOL) or have curricula with benchmarks and rubrics provided. Although these standards and benchmarks provide criteria against which typical students can be compared, they provide little help with deciding whether a particular student could learn best in a general, specially designed, or adapted class or deciding what the curriculum content

Teaching Tip

FITNESSGRAM • The FITNESSGRAM includes the flexed arm hang to measure upper body strength, but some other tests use the push-up, pull-up, or bench press. Authors of the FITNESSGRAM found data indicating that the flexed arm hang is the best indicator of strength, so that item is included in the test.

MAKING CONNECTIONS

Tests as Indicators

Ms. Johnson uses several tests to measure upper body strength in her fitness testing program. While taking a graduate class, she learned that factor analysis, used in test construction, identifies test items that "cluster" on one variable. Ms. Johnson noted that students who performed well on the bench press also scored well on push-ups, flexed arm hang, and pull-ups. She further found that the developers of FITNESSGRAM, a criterion-referenced physical fitness test, made the same observation and statistically determined that the flexed arm hang by itself was just as good an indicator of upper body strength as giving all four tests. Most fitness tests use one test item as an indicator of the level of fitness on each of the four parameters that describe physical fitness.

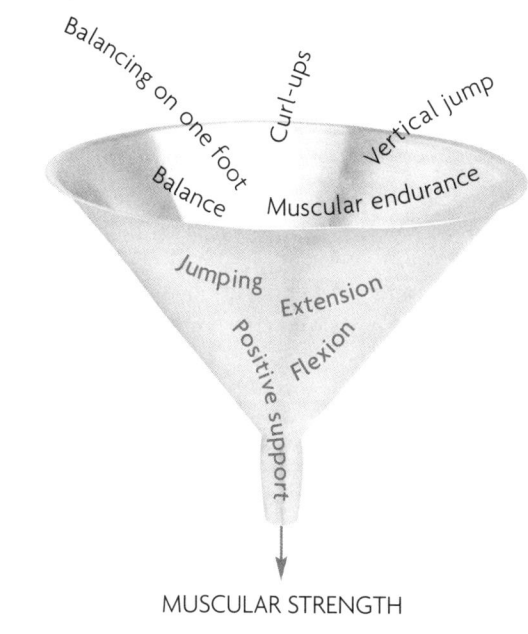

FIGURE 7.4

Determining commonalities in test item performance.

should focus on for this student. The question must be asked, "Besides balance, the jumping pattern or jumping ability, and muscular power, what other element, parameter, or entity is entering into these performances?" The educator answers this question by logically examining the three performances and finding the common element or elements that resulted in these three items clustering together—the factor that is present or absent in all three test items, causing substandard performance on all items (see Figure 7.4). The factor in this instance is muscular strength, but only direct or performance measures could verify this, and only norm-referenced tests can determine how far from the standard the performance is. The teacher must then decide what should be done to bring the student up to the standard.

Test Relationships

Although part of the interpretation process involves finding commonalities to explain a cluster or group of performances, some variables simply have nothing in common with one another. Relationships found in such cases are nevertheless true relationships. For example, the amount of education and income of a person, age and hairstyle worn, and gender and life expectancy are all relationships that tend to exist at a fairly predictable level. Thus, information that is available for one parameter could be used to interpret or explain scores on the other, even though they seem to lack a common entity.

STEPS IN INTERPRETATION

Once the general concepts for interpretation described above are well in mind, six procedural steps should be followed to identify the underlying sources of movement deficiencies:

1. Analyze the demands.
2. Order developmentally.
3. Determine the commonalities.
4. Cluster by commonalities.
5. Describe performance.
6. Draw conclusions.

To draw valid conclusions and make confident recommendations, the interpreter must follow these steps in sequence.

Analyze the Demands

Analyze the sensory and motor demands of the task(s) for each test item. Using the developmental model and Appendix B, determine which reflexes have to be present or inhibited; which sensory systems have to be functioning normally (or on which sensory systems the task places demands); and which motor responses, patterns, or skills are required for

MAKING CONNECTIONS

Interpreting the Results

Students in Mr. Carpenter's class just finished an instructional unit in track and field. In the spring, Mr. Carpenter is required by state mandate to administer a fitness test. He noticed that one of his students, Jamal, did not run very fast, could not long jump more than four feet, and during the fitness test scored sub-average on the flexed arm hang. Mr. Carpenter's conclusion was that Jamal lacked overall body strength. What Mr. Carpenter did not know at the time was that Jamal has a rare form of muscular dystrophy. This information certainly changed Mr. Carpenter's interpretation of the test results and his recommendations for Jamal's program.

The Authors Respond

ANALYZING DEMANDS

Although Jason is six years old, his premature birth and perhaps other factors delayed development of his vestibular system, protective extension, and social skills. Given more specific correction for behavior and a variety of movement experiences, he should "catch up" with his peers.

---

the student to complete the task successfully. Consider also at what age each of these should have been developed. Figure 6.1 will help you identify the types of tests that measure parameters at the various levels of the developmental model.

This analysis will help you identify the commonalities among the various performances or parameters. For example, standing on one foot is commonly used as a measure of balance. Without proprioception, vestibular function, equilibrium responses, and vision, the performance will be poor. In the log roll—a commonly used developmental item—interference from the asymmetrical tonic neck reflex (ATNR), an inability to isolate body segments due to poor proprioception, or an inability to keep the body extended due to overriding flexor tone will certainly result in poor performance, if not in an unsuccessful attempt. Finally, kicking a rolling ball relies on standing balance and equilibrium responses, proprioception, kicking pattern, ocular control (tracking), convergence, eye–foot coordination, and a certain amount of strength. If many of these are dysfunctional, the performance will be less than satisfactory.

The language demands of the test and the concepts represented in the language must also be analyzed:

- Did the test require the student to sequence several commands before performing?
- Did the administration procedure allow the student to get a demonstration in addition to the verbal command from the examiner?
- Did the performance require good auditory discrimination (e.g., when the child was asked to touch his toes, did he touch his nose)?
- Did the student seem to understand the meaning of the words that were used?
- Did the test require an understanding of words expressing time, space, and directional relationships?

These and other language and cognitive demands must be considered in the analysis to determine the underlying source or sources of motor deficits before any logical course can be taken toward interpretation.

The 1-mile run or 12-minute run is used to measure aerobic capacity on a number of health-related fitness tests (e.g., FITNESSGRAM, Rockport Walk Test, Brockport Physical Fitness Test). The limitations imposed by intellectual disabilities and other cognitive disorders may rule out a valid performance. If students are not motivated, do not understand the concept of an "all-out effort," or lack the proprioceptive and tactile feedback to "pace" the rate at which they run, this test item may be a better measure of cognitive or intellectual function than of cardiorespiratory endurance. In your analysis, ask yourself the question, "How do the attributes or characteristics of this student's disability affect his or her performance on this test?" (See Appendix C.)

Many students with a physical disability are limited in their ability to meet the motor demands of many tasks, or they have to approach the task differently than students without a disability. For example, a girl with paraplegia in a wheelchair is

---

How Would You Respond?

ANALYZING DEMANDS

Jason, age six, is unable to balance on one foot, stumbles and falls a great deal, and is always getting out of line when it is time to get ready to leave the classroom. His mother reports he was born prematurely. What do you suppose is going on with him?

limited in meeting the motor demand of standing on one foot as a measure of balance, but this does not mean that she does not have adequate balance within the limits of her disability—that which is typical *for her*. Measures of balance for her more appropriately center on sitting upright in her chair; maintaining balance and equilibrium when transferring from her wheelchair to the floor, a desk chair, or a bus or car seat; or performing independent self-help skills in the bathroom. Students with a deficit in proprioception, vestibular, or tactile functions may also be unable to balance successfully on one foot. It is the physical educator's challenge in interpretation to identify *which source or combination of sources* is contributing to substandard performance on a balance task.

Order Developmentally

The items tested should be ordered according to the developmental model (see Figure 6.1). Because each level of function in the developmental model relies on adequate function at the lower levels, programming and interpretation should address the basic or lower-level functions first. This is not to say that the sensory systems, responses, or patterns at higher levels are not involved in a given test item, but the selection of a given activity for the IEP should be based on the most fundamental needs of the student that can be identified through data collection. Many times, once the fundamental difficulty is resolved, the rest of the functions fall into place.

The ultimate goal in all physical education programs is to give each student the functions, responses, and patterns necessary for learning the activities included in a physical education curriculum. An analysis of the task and developmental ordering can help you better identify the basis of successful motor performance and plan appropriate programs for each individual.

Teaching Tip

MOVING DOWN THE DEVELOPMENTAL MODEL •
Signs that you may need to address an activity at a lower point on the developmental model:

- Student is frequently frustrated.
- Performance is not improving at the expected rate.
- Student avoids certain tasks.
- Student makes negative comments such as, "When will we be finished?" or "Do I have to do this?"

MAKING CONNECTIONS

Developmental Order

The clinicians at a university's motor clinic learned to use the developmental model when interpreting test results and analyzing students' weaknesses. Children worked on proprioception and body awareness before learning tumbling skills. Students who needed more work on integrating the two sides of the body (a sensory integrative requirement) practiced striking by swinging a stick at a suspended ball.

Determine the Commonalities

Once the demands of each task have been analyzed and developmentally ordered, the commonalities of performance from the lower levels of the developmental model should be apparent. Items that share no common factor with the other items should be separated out and considered as independent variables or parameters. Do these seemingly unrelated items share some other factor, such as language or cognition? Do they involve variables on which the desired performance depends, such as body weight, body type, or even cultural factors? (For example, some Native American communities have a concept of time that differs from our traditional view of time, and some other nations have no equivalent for competition against another person.)

Some relationships will be found in this way, and clusters will form among these items. If items remain for which no mutual factors can be found, they should be set aside. Such items may represent totally independent parameters that require a separate interpretation.

Cluster by Commonalities

Substandard performances should be grouped according to clusters of common factors and kept in order developmentally. At this point, the profile of the student's performance should begin to take shape, and the factors underlying poor performance should begin to emerge. The developmentally lowest factor or problem area should be the first priority for program planning. The remaining factors should be ordered developmentally and according to the frequency with which they appear in poor performance. Because each level of function depends on adequate functioning at lower levels, this hierarchy should be followed in interpretation and subsequent program planning.

MAKING CONNECTIONS

Finding Commonalities

When Mrs. McMasters looked at test results of one of her students, she had to spend some extra time finding what the tests had in common. One of her students, Caleb, scored at the 10th percentile on one-foot balancing, the 5th percentile on running form, and the 5th percentile on alternate hopping. His classroom teacher reported that he falls a lot, and his mother reported that when they go to the park, all he wants to do is swing and not play with the other children. Mrs. McMasters recognized that the vestibular system plays a major role in all these tests and activities. She decided to design Caleb's program to include many vestibular-stimulating activities and to measure his performance again at the end of the year.

Describe Performance

At this point, the actual reporting begins, either in written or verbal form. If information from other sources is not needed (discussed in Chapter 6), the report should begin with a description of the positive attributes of the student's performance—what the student was able to do and how the performance was executed (see Chapter 8). Many IEP forms are designed this way, with a report of the student's strengths, areas of need, then a description of how the areas of need (weaknesses) impact the student's participation and progress in a general education curriculum. This protocol should be followed in both the verbal report and the written report or IEP.

The written report form may not provide enough space for detailed documentation supporting your conclusions. You should be prepared to report what the student was not able to do and how the student approximated the desired performance. The report of performance should consist of only what was seen when the student was asked to perform a certain task. Describe the performance as accurately as possible, using movement terminology such as, "Joey raised his arms above his head when walking the balance beam" or "When Carolyn threw the beanbag, both arms described the throwing pattern, mirroring one another." The names of the tests, scores, percentile ranks, and other objective information should be reported along with the description. We recommend that the adapted physical educator write a detailed assessment report, including interpretation and conclusions, for each initial and subsequent IEP meeting.

Draw Conclusions

If the test maker has already statistically analyzed the test items for you, this step will be much easier. The language of the test maker should be used to define the areas of dysfunction. For example, if the test maker calls an area of performance "balance and equilibrium responses," then based on atypical performances on that section of the test, you should conclude that the student has poor balance and equilibrium responses. If the test maker defines a grouping of test items as measuring "fine motor control," low scores on those items require you to report that the student has poor fine motor control. Ultimately, you will be able to relate these performances to the levels of the developmental model once the data are fully reported and interpreted.

The statistical analysis mentioned earlier may not be readily available, or the test maker may not have reported it. In this case, you should refer to the basic clusters of common factors in the developmental model and the interpretation model (Figure 7.5, discussed later in the chapter) to label the areas of weakness. Be specific without drawing conclusions that cannot be supported by observed performance. If the interpretation is reported verbally in the IEP team meeting, the data are frequently supported or verified by data gathered by other professionals. This is why the team assessment process is so helpful and efficient. One of the benefits of the team is that these discussions and observations of the many and varied aspects of the child from different points of view can assist the team in preparing the multidisciplinary team report and drawing conclusions.

Very often in a team meeting, a professional will bring up something for speculation. This is the time to raise questions, opinions, or inferences—"I wonder if Johnny should be given a postural reflex test by a therapist" or "I also noticed that he had

---

EXTEND YOUR KNOWLEDGE

Reporting Commonalities

Specialists should be able to elaborate on test results by discussing performances in clusters according to the common factors of performance identified earlier. The commonalities should not be discussed until the conclusions have been reported. Commonalities should be reported later, after all the data have been presented.

some problems with tasks requiring visual figure–ground discrimination" or "He acted like he was not hearing everything I said to him because he would...." This cross-validation with other professionals may help to make sense of those seemingly unrelated performances mentioned earlier. Speculation should not go beyond the limits of the data. The general physical educator or adapted specialist should interpret only what is certain, maintaining a policy of silence as matters get further away from documentable information.

In the best case, all the necessary information can be gathered before the final conclusion is drawn. Sometimes, this information is not known prior to the meeting because other professionals may be collecting data during the same time period. Therefore, the physical educator must be alert and ready to analyze and interpret new information as it is added during the team's discussion. This is one reason why goals and objectives must be formally written at the IEP meeting, although it is still a good idea to go to the meeting prepared with a draft of proposed goals and objectives.

RELATIONSHIPS FOR TEST INTERPRETATION

When a student is referred to the adapted physical educator for assessment, the data-gathering process has already begun. A student who is continually falling and skinning his or her chin, an individual who misses the ball every time it is thrown, or a student who can complete only five laps on the FITNESSGRAM Pacer test is bringing data to the testing situation that lends itself to and requires interpretation. Each of these pieces of information not only suggests some specific areas of dysfunction that can be used to plan the testing program, but also adds extra information to the formal and informal test results that can validate and support the reason for the referral. For example, a student who is referred for testing on the basis of poor vitality and low fitness should be tested on parameters measured by a fitness test—strength, flexibility, body composition, and endurance. A test of motor ability not only is likely to miss identifying the sources of poor vitality, but it also may not generate data that can validate or support the initial referral. The student who falls often and skins his or her chin should be tested for protective extension reflex, balance and equilibrium responses, body awareness, motor patterns, and sensory responses including proprioception and vestibular function. Formal test results, then, can be combined with informal observation and referral information for interpretation.

The strength of formal data gathering should be obvious—it provides quantifiable, documentable evidence of how the student performed during testing. It helps teachers justify their recommendations. The drawback, as discussed earlier in this chapter, is that the validity of formalized tests is often questionable when they are used with students with a disability. Teacher-made tests raise even more red flags as to their validity. Additionally, factors contributing to motor performance are neither fully understood nor measurable to the extent that full confidence can be placed in conclusions drawn exclusively from formal test results. Informally gathered data has grown in popularity in recent years and can lend credibility and logic to formally gathered data, completing the picture of a student's motor dysfunction. Furthermore, some students' dysfunctions are exceedingly complex and severe, making it most difficult to use formal data-gathering procedures.

The physical educator must clearly understand the relationships among the various levels of the developmental model, as well as the "real life" manifestations of dysfunction at each level of the model, to make maximum use of the information available. The educator should strive to obtain information that is as concrete, as objective, and as defensible as possible when considering special class placement. (See Figure 8.2 for a pre-referral checklist.)

Reflex Behavior

If a student referred for testing is known to have brain damage from traumatic brain injury, cerebral palsy, or another known condition, abnormal reflex behavior should always be suspected. If a student referred for testing is not thought to have brain damage, abnormal reflex behavior should not be ruled out. In other words, the adapted physical educator should start looking for deficits at the lowest level of the developmental model and then work up. Even if a therapist is available to do reflex testing, the specialist should still watch for abnormal reflex behavior as it manifests itself in motor performance, which can be further validated through formal testing by a therapist or physician (refer back to Table 6.2 for a list of observable signs of abnormal reflex behavior and corresponding reflexes to suspect).

Although the list provided in Table 6.2 is not exhaustive, it should give some idea of how the relationship between referral information and observed behavior can be used to plan the testing program, interpret and validate measurements, and form the basis for referrals.

Sensorimotor Measurement

Sensorimotor tests have historically focused on the later-maturing systems and their interaction with movement—vision and audition—perhaps because many of the early tests were designed by psychologists such as Kephart and Frostig, whose major interest was classroom performance, not motor performance. A child's development, however, does not begin with visual and auditory function and the motor responses of eye–hand coordination, bilateral use of the two body sides, or reaching and grasping. Thus, the interpretation of sensorimotor measurements should include an analysis of the processing and integration of all sensory input, regardless of whether the test measures them directly. Sensorimotor functioning is inherent in all motor performance: throwing an object cannot be done without "feeling" the object in the hand through the tactile system; striking a ball with a bat cannot be done with the eyes alone—sensorimotor functioning assists the proprioceptive system with getting the hands and arms in position to swing the bat. Although novel tasks are often used to measure sensorimotor parameters (see Figures 6.2 and 6.3, p. 121). The influence of these parameters cannot be truly separated from all other elements or parameters of motor performance, any more than the influence of muscular strength can be separated from cardiovascular functioning in a mile run.

The three principles for the interpretation of sensorimotor measurements are:

1. Hierarchical sequence of influence
2. Intrasensory influence
3. Structural interdependence

Like the parameters they deal with, these principles cannot be considered apart from the previous discussion of reflexes or the discussion following this section regarding other types of measurements.

The hierarchical sequence of influence follows the same route as motor development—the higher levels of development, such as motor skills, rely on the adequate development of the lower levels, such as motor patterns. These in turn rely on the typical development of even lower levels, such as the integration and emergence of key postural reflexes. There is also influence across the sensory systems. For example, the visual system is strongly influenced by the vestibular system and vice versa. The fact that we may get dizzy when watching fast-moving action on a wide movie screen even though we are not moving is an example of intrasensory influence. Structural interdependence, both vertically and laterally, can be seen when simultaneous tasks are being performed. The cortex is basically a "one-way path" to directing motor activity. A novel task such as patting your head and rubbing your stomach takes some time to master, although the brain stem is perfectly capable of overseeing the head patting by itself. Rubbing the stomach adds an additional challenge, so initially the cortex must pay attention to that task and cannot "allow" the brain stem to do its job. Lateral influence is obvious in the case of people with cerebral palsy—the cerebellum cannot smooth out movement because it is damaged, even though the motor cortex is perfectly capable of initiating movement. Thus, the influence is obvious in the jerky, uncoordinated movements of a person with this disability.

Motor Development Measurement

Tests designed to gather data on motor development often include other aspects of human development as well. Because movement is the first apparent way of showing cognitive, social, and language development, motor tasks are commonly used to measure these parameters. Thus, tests like building with blocks, stringing beads, or pointing to pictures of animals and other things are used to test language and cognition, even though movement is required to carry out the tasks. The developmental schedule in Appendix B can be used to separate out (as much as is possible) the expected motor output from the other parameters at any given level of development.

Measurements of motor development are usually reported on tables in terms of months or years of developmental lag or in terms of the age of actual functioning. A nine-month-old infant who cannot sit upright unsupported is said to be developmentally at approximately the six-month-old level or showing at least a three-month lag in motor development, because most children accomplish that milestone by the sixth month of life (see Appendix B). Understanding and applying the principles discussed in the previous section are important here because the interference of undeveloped reflexes may be contributing to lack of "performance" on the independent sitting task. Development, although sequential, may have gaps, and individuals may be capable of performing some tasks at one level and incapable of performing tasks at an earlier level. Any physical impairment will interfere with the accomplishment of some developmental milestones. The presence of cerebral palsy, clubfoot, or other lower limb conditions obviously interferes with weight bearing and upright posture. Motor development measurements should be reported in terms of these physical restrictions.

Data gathered through observation can help the educator piece together the developmental puzzle for some children. Children with **dyspraxia**, who have *difficulty sequencing motor tasks,* sometimes demonstrate performances in play that the tester cannot elicit in a formal testing situation. A keen observer and

EXTEND YOUR KNOWLEDGE

Hierarchical Sequence of Influence

Because there is a hierarchical sequence of influence upward through the developmental model, *systems and functions that mature later are related to and interdependent on earlier-maturing systems and functions.* The motor response of balance, for example, is often used as an indirect measure of vestibular function. In addition, the ability to stand on one foot relies heavily on righting responses as well as the motor response of contralateral body side use. Body awareness is measured by several sensorimotor tools, which usually require postural and equilibrium responses to remain upright, proprioception to know where the body parts are in space, and, in some instances, auditory perception to understand the instructions of the task. Tasks measuring spatial orientation, directionality, and spatial awareness typically rely on vestibulo-ocular interaction to process and plan movement of the body through space; righting reactions; proprioception; and patterns such as walking, running, stepping, hopping, and jumping. Therefore, interpretation of inadequate performance on tasks measuring each of these parameters should be based on the hierarchical sequence of influence inherent in human development.

Intrasensory influence. Intrasensory influence means that *one sensory system influences the functioning of another.* For example, because vestibular stimuli have a profound influence on visual and auditory processing, performance on visual tasks that involve movement is likely to be enhanced by the vestibular influence derived from the movement. Moving through an obstacle course requires visual processing and planning as well as the motor output demands relative to body awareness. Mere movement may assist with the solution of the visual problem in the obstacle course, which may not have seemed possible based on a given student's performance on strict visual tasks. Proprioceptive influence from the muscles of the neck, along with the vestibular influence from head position, enhances visual function. Tilting the head forward to write at a desk sends continuous bombarding proprioceptive and vestibular stimuli to the central nervous system (CNS) and enhances visual function. Writing on a white board allows righting responses to control the head position automatically, thus providing less proprioceptive influence and negligible vestibular activity. Thus, performance on visual perception tasks is likely to be better when the tasks are performed at a desk or table as opposed to on the white board.

Structural interdependence. Structural interdependence, *the ability of one brain structure to rely on or compensate for the dysfunction of another structure,* may enhance or deter motor performance. The following example demonstrates the vertical structural interdependence of the CNS.

When the brain stem—the master control area for muscular activity—is performing its function adequately, performance on tasks such as moving through an obstacle course is controlled automatically, and the attention of the cortex can be directed to the planning, processing, and adapting required to complete the obstacle course successfully. If the brain stem is not doing its job, then the cortex or the conscious attention must be focused on the muscular activity rather than on planning how to get through the obstacle course, thus deterring or interfering with motor performance.

There is also a **lateral interdependence**, that is, *interdependence between the hemispheres of the brain and the related structures,* which is also significant in motor performance. On a bilateral, contralateral, or ipsilateral task found in many tests (e.g., APEAS II, Bruininks-Oseretsky), the global meaning of the task must be interpreted and processed in one hemisphere of the brain; that information is communicated to the other hemisphere of the brain for control of the motor output.

This is not to imply that only one hemisphere processes a specific type of information. In fact, both hemispheres are involved, but some tasks are handled more efficiently by one hemisphere or the other. For example, a task such as "Angels-in-the-Snow," found in the Purdue test, requires the examiner to point to the right arm and say, "Move that arm." The auditory and visual stimuli enter both ears and eyes at the same time. While the left hemisphere is discriminating the sounds of the words, the right hemisphere is interpreting the meaning of the words. This information is passed through the corpus callosum and brain stem to the left hemisphere, which integrates, plans, and then controls the motor output or movement of the right limb. Simultaneously and similarly, the visual stimuli (pointing) are being interpreted and associated with the language (auditory). Without this interhemispheric communication, neither the global concept of the task nor the meaning of the command could be brought to bear on the motor output. (When the left limb is moved, the problems of executing the movement are reversed.)

Observational data, too, can lend insight into the way a student processes sensorimotor information. A student who pulls away from your touch, or touches everything and everyone in sight, may be displaying a disorder in the tactile system. Avoiding swings and slides, or constantly running to these pieces of equipment, may indicate a vestibular disorder. Constantly jumping, pushing, or pulling may be proprioceptive-seeking behavior. These observations should be considered along with formal measurements. A behavioral checklist is useful for gathering observational data on suspicious sensory system function (refer back to Table 6.2).

good teacher will store this information away for use when it comes time to interpret formal test results.

Motor Ability Measurement

Motor ability tests typically measure novel tasks that have some ability to predict success in game and sport skills. Historically, they make the assumption that there are basic innate abilities that cut across many different physical activities. In terms of the developmental model, motor ability tests tend to measure at the sensorimotor responses and motor patterns levels. Common motor ability items, such as striking a stationary ball, stationary dribble, and overhand and underhand throw, measure patterns and learned skills more or less directly. The Test of Gross Motor Development 2 (TGMD-2) is one of the few tests available that measures these parameters; it is used extensively to identify students for adapted physical education. To interpret scores on this test, the examiner must be able to analyze the required tasks relative to:

- Reflexes that can interfere with performance
- Sensory systems that are involved
- Systems on which demands are being placed

For example, to throw a ball accurately overhand, a student must have an integrated ATNR and adequate tactile, proprioceptive, and visual system functions, as well as the motor responses of contrasting body side use and the pattern of throwing. If the ATNR is present, the head position interferes with full extension of the throwing arm; poor tactile discrimination diminishes the ability to know where the ball is in the hand; lack of accurate proprioceptive information limits the ability to know where the body parts are in space; and the visual system is the key to discriminating the target from other things in the visual field. Obviously, without the ability to use the two body sides in contrast, the task will not be well executed.

Together, these support systems, when they function well, generate a coordinated performance. Without them, the result is motor *inability* or motor dysfunction. When analyzed, motor ability test items tend to cluster together based on deficits in the supporting systems or functions, such as proprioceptive, tactile, or postural reflexes.

Motor Skills Measurement

Motor skills tests typically measure specific applications of motor patterns and combinations of motor patterns. Many instruments in this category also include motor responses and fine motor control. Because tasks required by these tests tend to rely heavily on learning and experience, a student's innate neural capacity, cognition, and educational opportunities strongly affect the ability to perform reliably. Motor skills are so specialized and tend so often to take the form of sport or recreational activity skills that they are usually measured with a teacher-made test or rating scale or are authentically embedded into the context of an activity. Several tests exist, including the Basketball Skills Test (1984), Gymnastics Skills Tests for College Women (1973), Golf Skill Test Battery for College Males and Females (1987), and A Racquetball Skills Test (1979), but most are either out of print or were published in a research journal, making them inaccessible to the practitioner. The common approach is to use rating scales (Baumgartner & others, 2002) or user-developed instruments, whose reliability and validity are questionable (Burton & Miller, 1998).

Regardless of the method used to identify deficit areas, disorders should be approached developmentally, with programming beginning at the lowest identifiable developmental level of dysfunction, rather than working on the specific skills.

Health-Related Physical Fitness Measurement

Fitness tests are probably the easiest tools for physical educators to interpret because these tests have been refined through factor analysis, reducing them to four to five test items that each measure distinctly separate variables. Thus, when a student scores below standard on a test item measuring strength, such as pull-ups, the only possible interpretation is that the student is weak in the upper body. One challenge is to ensure that each test item is truly measuring the fitness variable and not the student's

MAKING CONNECTIONS

Improving Motor Skills

In a parent meeting explaining what activities were done in physical education, Mrs. Benedict said, "Bruce finally stayed up on his inline skates, for the first time, this week. We are so excited!" Ms. Marks, Bruce's teacher, explained, "We have been doing activities that stimulate and develop the vestibular system, and that system has helped Bruce have better balance." Activities such as swinging, twirling, and balancing on T-stools and balance boards challenged Bruce's vestibular system, developing the system to better support balance activities. Bruce's improvement in balance was measured by his ability to stay up on his inline skates!

Teaching Tip

TESTING CHILDREN WITH A DISABILITY • Familiarity with the test items tends to increase both the reliability and validity of performances for many students with a disability, especially in fitness testing. It is important that the student with a disability be familiar with the equipment and language used for each of the fitness test items. Stretching exercises and reaching for the toes in an "L" sit facing a wall or a "V" sit on the floor require movements that are similar to those used in flexibility tests (e.g., Back Saver on FITNESSGRAM, the "V" sit or sit and reach on President's Challenge). Making the target concrete for students with a learning disability or mental retardation conveys the concept of how far to stretch. Visual aids such as strips of tape on the floor in front of the legs are useful in getting the concept across. As the student improves, the next strip farther away is the target. Any opportunity to provide practice or simulation of fitness test items will help ensure that the student's score is a valid measure of his or her health-related physical fitness and not a measure of intellect or language comprehension.

How Would You Respond?

DETERMINING COMMONALITIES

Natashia, a fourth grade student, is referred for testing. She continually bumps into people and things; swings a bat long after the ball has gone by; and even when she does hit the ball, hesitates before running, sometimes running toward the wrong base. She is observed to have difficulty identifying body parts, imitating postures, tracking objects visually, and reproducing forms drawn on the chalkboard. Figure 7.5 helps identify what these difficulties have in common: directionality, body image, ocular control, midline crossing, bilateral limb use, and fine motor control. What is the underlying sensory system that all these functions share?

---

ability to understand instructions or grasp the concepts involved. Another challenge is to differentiate between deficits in the parameters that the fitness test is measuring and deficits in the numerous other systems that support the fitness performance (e.g., proprioceptive, tactile, and vestibular function). For example, the flexed arm hang is used in many fitness tests as a measure of upper body strength. When a student fails to perform well on this item, the interpretation is typically that the student is weak in upper body strength. The examiner must be aware that tactile function (for contact with the bar), proprioception (for identifying which muscles to contract), head and ocular righting reflexes, and understanding the concept of a sustained effort must *precede* the performance of a flexed arm hang. With regard to many parameters, fitness test results can be validated by direct measures or other performance measures (e.g., handgrip dynamometer, the student's stamina in class activities, helping with lifting and carrying at home).

A MODEL FOR INTERPRETATION

A generic developmental model for the interpretation of measurements can, at least, stimulate ideas and guide analysis of test performances from a developmental point of view. Some test makers, such as Bruininks and Ulrich, include information for use in the interpretation of measurements gathered using these instruments. As has been stated previously, however, most tests available to the adapted physical educator are not factor analyzed, nor are guidelines for their interpretation provided. (See Figure 7.5 for an analysis of the sensory demands of many parameters commonly used in the types of tests discussed in Chapter 6.)

The test items or tasks used to sample each of the parameters in Figure 7.5 require the functioning of or place demands on the sensory system(s) indicated at the top of the column(s) in which the parameter appears. The type of test and the variety of parameters each type usually measures are framed in the corresponding box. For example, because static balance is commonly found in sensorimotor and motor development tests, it is framed by those two boxes. Tasks usually used to measure static balance include standing on one foot with eyes open or closed. Static balance may also be measured in developmental profiles in the form of balancing while sitting independently or standing on two feet. Authentically, the educator may measure static balance by observing a student waiting in line, standing on a designated spot, or holding a pose in a game. Static balance requires proprioception and vestibular function; if the eyes are open, the visual system is also used. Therefore, this parameter appears in the three columns headed by each of those three sensory systems. Of course, static balance also requires some typically developed reflex activity such as positive support, equilibrium, and righting reactions, which do not appear in the model.

FIGURE 7.5 A developmental model for test interpretation.

TEST		PROPRIOCEPTION	VESTIBULAR	TACTILE	VISUAL	AUDITORY
FITNESS		Endurance	Endurance			
		Flexibility		Flexibility		
		Strength		Strength		
MOTOR DEVELOPMENT	**MOTOR ABILITY/SKILLS**	Agility	Agility		Agility	
		Dynamic balance	Dynamic balance		Dynamic balance	
		Eye–hand/foot coordination		Eye–hand/foot coordination	Eye–hand/foot coordination	
		Gross motor control	Gross motor control			
		Fine motor control		Fine motor control		Fine motor control
	SENSORIMOTOR	Motor sequencing			Motor sequencing	Motor sequencing
		Static balance	Static balance		Static balance	
					Figure–ground discrimination	
		Postural mechanisms	Postural mechanisms		Position in space	
			Spatial relations		Spatial relations	
		Laterality			Form constancy	
		Bilateral limb use	Bilateral limb use		Bilateral limb use	
		Midline crossing		Tactile discrimination		
		Ocular control		Tactile function	Ocular control	
		Body image	Body image			
		Directionality	Vestibular function		Directionality	

Although this model is presented as a springboard for thought, it also graphically describes how a task can be analyzed to identify the underlying sensory system commonalities. If, for example, the motor skill of forward roll is observed in a tumbling unit and you determine that body image, bilateral body side use, balance, flexibility, spatial relations, and postural mechanisms are some of the functions required to complete the forward roll successfully, the single commonality found among these functions is adequate function of the vestibular system. There are some direct or clinical measures of vestibular function, such as a test of postrotary nystagmus, but physical educators are not usually trained to use them. On the other hand, performance tests requiring vestibular system function can be administered (e.g., standing one-foot balance, balance beam walking, or heel-to-toe walking a line). Further information can be gathered from the student or the student's parents, classroom teacher, and others to determine whether the student has ever had the opportunity to learn the forward roll, has any interfering condition such as atlanto-axial instability, or has any postural reflexes or language or cognitive disorders that would interfere with performing the skill. If clinical test data are available, naturally those are useful to have as well.

REPORTING ASSESSMENT RESULTS

Within the mandates of IDEA '04, assessment reporting takes place in a formal meeting of multidisciplinary personnel comprising the IEP team. Some education agencies may refer to this

The Authors Respond

DETERMINING COMMONALITIES

In Natashia's case, the support system common to all of these parameters is proprioception. Vision, while certainly a factor, is reliant on proprioception and the vestibular system for optimal function.

The dysfunction, therefore, should be considered grounded in the proprioceptive system, and activities designed to enhance proprioception should be planned for her program.

---

group using different terminology (e.g., Evaluation and Planning Team, Eligibility Review Team, Child Study, or the School Appraisal [Review] Team). The participants must include:

1. The parents of the child
2. At least one general education teacher (if the student is participating in general education)
3. At least one special education teacher or related service provider
4. A representative of the local education agency (LEA) who is:
   a. Qualified to provide specially designed instruction
   b. Knowledgeable about the general curriculum
   c. Knowledgeable about the availability of LEA resources
5. The child whenever appropriate
6. An individual who can interpret instructional implications of the evaluation results
7. Other individuals who have knowledge or special expertise regarding the child—at the parents' or agency's discretion [IDEA, sec. 300.320(a)(1)].

IDEA '04 allows for reevaluation to occur at least once every three years unless conditions warrant or the student's teacher or parent requests it sooner.

Legal Requirements

IDEA '04 continues to place the generalist in physical education in an active role in the IEP process. Besides the fact that the adapted physical educator may not be school-based (that is, he or she may be itinerant, serving several schools) and may not be on campus when the IEP team meeting is scheduled, the Act calls for a professional who is "knowledgeable about the general education curriculum" [IDEA, sec. 300.320(a)(1)(i)]. The discussion about the appropriate placement and the least restrictive environment is likely to focus on whether or not the student being reviewed can meet the demands of the general curriculum in physical education. Therefore, each physical educator must be familiar with the curriculum and perhaps more familiar with the IEP process than one might expect.

Reporting assessment results requires a good understanding of the assessment process as well as well-practiced interdisciplinary communication skills. In addition, the parent will often be present, requiring the teacher to have the ability to communicate technical information in nontechnical language, without jargon. If the adapted physical educator is not present, the general physical educator should be adequately familiar with the assessment process to answer any questions. Chapter 8 provides more detail on using the assessment results to develop the IEP, establishing goals and objectives, and recommending related services.

There are three levels of reporting assessment findings to keep in mind to ensure credibility, communicate clearly, and remain in compliance with current legislation. These levels are factual, probable, and inferential.

A **factual statement** must be *based on something that is known, that can be observed, and that comes as close as possible to certainty.* Thus, a statement of fact can come only after an observed performance. For example, "Sam has 30 degrees of extension in the right arm" is a statement of fact. It is observable; it is being made after testing; and it is as close to certainty as anyone can come. "The student cannot throw a ball" is not a statement of fact because it goes beyond what can be observed. It may "become" a fact, after Sam is given a throwing test, but without an attempt at performance the second statement is not factual.

Statements of **probability,** on the other hand, go beyond what can be observed. They *describe performances that are very likely based on what has been observed and on theoretical foundations* established as part of the specialized training of the adapted physical educator. They should include such phrases as "It is likely," "It is very possible," or "It is highly probable," to differentiate them from statements of fact. Using the previous example, "Sam has 30 degrees of extension in the right arm, and it is very possible that he cannot throw a ball," is a valid use of a statement of probability because it is supported by a statement of fact.

The final level of assessment reporting is **inference.** As with statements of probability, inferences go beyond what can be observed. They actually *are degrees of probability and, when possible, should be supported by statements of fact.* They can be made at any time relative to the performance and are often characterized by the use of such terms as "theoretically," "presumably," "possibly," "wondering," "assuming," and "thought." Statements of inference are assumptions or projections based on previous, similar circumstances. To elaborate on the ball-throwing example, the information is added that Sam—the student with limited range of motion who probably cannot throw a ball—is a 15-year-old student with cerebral palsy. An appropriate inferential statement, added to the factual and probability statements already made, might be, "I assume that because of his age he will not ever be able to gain enough extension in the elbow to throw a ball with any degree of accuracy." Based on the teacher's experience, what he or she knows about cerebral palsy, and the fact that this adolescent has gone so many years with limited extension in the arm, it is very unlikely that extension can be developed at this late date, and the inference is probably valid. This is not to imply that the teacher should stop working with Sam to maintain whatever range of motion he has, nor should he stop trying to throw a ball using different mechanics that work for him. The teacher has simply stated that the mechanics of an efficient throwing pattern are probably beyond the realm of possibility for this student.

CONSIDERATIONS FOR PLACEMENT

Depending on whether the purpose of assessment is to place the student into a regular or separate class or to measure progress toward the goals of an IEP (triennial review), the methods or tools selected may vary. For placement purposes, tools that are norm-referenced on the general school population should serve as the criteria against which students with a disability are compared. This is becoming increasingly difficult, however, because the trend in fitness test development is toward tools that are criterion-referenced, not norm-referenced. Several tests of motor performance and skill acquisition still report norm-referenced standards in percentiles as well as other forms of standard scores. Alternative methods of data collection can be coupled with data gathered with criterion-referenced tools to get a more complete overview of the student's ability, so that the IEP team can decide whether special class placement (adapted, modified, or specially designed physical education) is the most appropriate for this student. We concur with the California Department of Education (2001) that "Before identifying adapted physical education service for that child, the adapted physical education specialist must also ensure that the assessment results indicate that performance in physical education has been adversely affected and that the child needs the special education service of adapted physical education."

Somewhat different recommendations are offered when the purpose is to measure progress toward educational goals among students in separate adapted physical education classes (annual or triennial reviews). Criterion-referenced, rather than norm-referenced, tools may be more appropriate in some instances, particularly if change in performance is slow. Developmental scales may provide more useful information when used with young children (birth to 48 months) or students with very limited ability because they contain a sequence of developmental tasks that can be used to develop performance objectives. Rubrics that reflect steps along the continuum of acquisition of desirable behaviors are also useful in measuring progress.

The most comprehensive approach to the assessment process is the development of an instrument such as the Adapted Physical Education Assessment Scale II (APEAS II) used by the Los Angeles Unified School District. APEAS II meets most of the criteria for test selection and measures a broad spectrum of motor performance. APEAS II is appropriate for all students from 5 to 18 years, and the norming sample includes representative samples of students with a disability. A future goal for tests measuring a more narrow spectrum of parameters is to include students who have a disability in the norming sample. Including these students results in a set of norms that is truly representative of the general population. Combining data from a test such as this with alternative methods (e.g., parent report, student portfolios, and reports of other teachers) gives a broader picture of whether or not the student is likely to be successful in a general physical education class.

Eligibility Criteria for Adapted Physical Education

According to the California Department of Education (2001), "Assessment results are used to determine if placement in adapted physical education is appropriate" (p. 21). Because no specific placement or eligibility criteria are established in federal statutes, states and LEAs have been left on their own to determine these criteria. Many LEAs have adopted guidelines that identify normative scores. Developmental scales can produce scores in years or percentage below chronological age to qualify students. Other agencies use a more subjective measure of when the student is "having trouble" in a general physical education class. It is desirable to use a combination of these measures depending on the student's needs, age level, and learning environment.

With the trend in fitness testing moving toward criterion-referenced health-related fitness tests and physical education moving toward rubrics using curriculum-embedded measures (Block, Connor-Kuntz, Pyfer, & Huettig, 1999), the process for identifying students for special class placement is changing. According to Huettig & Roth (2002), "While this may be expedient, and is perhaps appropriate at the middle school or high school level, it fails to fully address young students' physical education needs." When norm-referenced tests are used, it is easy to identify how a student relates to others in the norming sample. If the decision is to consider taking the student out of general physical education and placing him or her into an adapted or specially designed class, a test standardized on students representing the general population is usually appropriate. Therefore, if the student scores at the 5th percentile (or first stanine, a z score of -3, or a T score under 10), it is clear that the student will have difficulty keeping up with the students in the regular class. When a criterion-referenced test is used for this purpose, the only information available is that the student did not meet the criteria—with no further information on how significant the shortfall is. Further, it gives little help in identifying what should be included in the instructional program.

Although rubrics and benchmarks are becoming commonplace in physical education curricula along with standards-based instruction, they provide little help in determining a student's eligibility for special class placement. The rubrics written by teachers or curriculum specialists may "seem" appropriate for grade level and gender, but they are merely unvalidated criteria—not based on data gathered from students of that age and gender, but on experience and a sequence of learning. Not only do rubrics and benchmarks make it impossible to quantify or determine a "cut-off" point for qualifying students for special services, they also provide little information for developing an IEP. The Special Education Division of the California Department of Education (2001) recommends that the physical educator consult the local plan or guidelines for suggested eligibility and placement criteria, which include functioning levels and use of statistical scores.

We recommend that a set of eligibility criteria be determined by a school district committee, service area, or similar authority responsible for special education, including physical education. Using reference points for various types of tests—"two years below age level" in motor development, "at or below the 5th percentile on a test of motor skills," "below the criteria on two of the four test items of a health-related physical fitness test"—aids educators in determining objectively what scores will be used as the eligibility cut-off. These criteria would identify only 5 percent of the students, and data presented earlier indicate that as many as 10 to 12 percent of the student body might be identified as eligible for special education services. This is not to say that other factors should not be considered—the student's ability to grasp concepts taught in the general class, his or her ability to work cooperatively with others in a team, and other class interactions. This committee should reach an agreement before individual students' cases are considered by IEP teams across the district. This will enhance objectivity and streamline teams' decision making because they will know exactly what they are looking for in each report. This process should be followed for each special education and related service. (Review Chapter 2 for more detail on the functioning of an effective multidisciplinary team.) In the end, the IEP team has the final decision regarding placement decisions.

SUMMARY

The interpretation of measurements is one of the most challenging of all aspects of teaching students with a disability. Understanding the significance of test results requires an analysis of the parameters measured by a given tool or procedure, as well as an analysis of the demands of each task. Ordering items developmentally, determining commonalities among inadequate performances, and describing the deficits identified assist with interpretation. General physical educators are becoming more involved in the IEP process and should maintain regular communication with the adapted physical educator regarding the assessment process and the eligibility criteria used to identify students for special services. The general physical educator is also familiar with the general curriculum in physical education, making them better prepared to respond to questions about a student's ability to participate safely and successfully in general physical education.

Distinguishing between statements of fact and inferences based on described deficits is an important skill for reporting and interpreting assessment results. The IEP team meeting provides an invaluable forum for validating and piecing together bits of information that may not make sense alone. The adapted physical educator should utilize the team's rich resources as much as possible to get the full picture of each student's motor performance profile in order to implement the most appropriate physical education program possible.

Once it is time to use the data collected to make decisions about a student's physical education program and placement, the LEA should have available objective eligibility and placement criteria for making these decisions. We recommend that norm-referenced or criterion-referenced standards be used as much as possible as the foundation for putting students' performance into a context. Additional, alternative data also are important to consider so that the "big picture"—whether or not the student can function successfully in a general physical education class—is clear.

CHAPTER 7
Learning Activities

7.1 Visit an elementary or middle school and, with the help of the classroom or physical education teacher, identify one or two students who scored poorly on tests of physical fitness in strength, flexibility, or aerobic capacity. Observe those students during activity—physical education class, an after-school activity, or at recess—and write a one-page description of how these low fitness test performances manifest in regular activity. Remember to describe what the student is *doing!*

7.2 Visit a preschool and observe two students on the playground. Make notes on what you observe in terms of their motor development. Using your interpretive skills and Appendix B, write down your guesses as to the students' ages and seal them in an envelope. Ask the teacher to write down the students' dates of birth and place in another sealed envelope. In class, discuss your observations with your classmates, then open the two envelopes and see how close you were to guessing the children's ages.

7.3 Observe any class of students that includes a student with a disability. Write a one-page description of what you observe the student to be *capable of doing*, followed by a one-page description of the challenges the student might have in physical education. In class, discuss these and identify two or three ways you might accommodate this student if he or she were in a class you were teaching.

REFERENCES

AAHPERD (1984). *Basketball skills test manual for boys and girls.* Reston, VA: Author.

Baumgartner, T. A., Jackson, A. S., Mahar, M. T., & Rowe, D. A. (2002). *Measurement for evaluation in physical education and exercise science* (6th ed.). Boston: WCB/McGraw-Hill.

Block, M., Connor-Kuntz, F., Pyfer, J., & Huettig, C. (1999, April). *Authentic assessment.* Paper presented at the AAHPERD National Convention & Exposition, Boston.

Bruininks, R. H., & Bruininks, B. D. (2005). *Bruininks-Oseretsky test of motor proficiency* (2nd ed.). Circle Pines, MN: American Guidance Service. www.agsnet.com

Burton, A. W. (1990). Applying principles of coordination in adapted physical education. *Adapted Physical Activity Quarterly, 7,* 126–142.

Burton, A. W., Greer, N. L., & Wiese-Bjornstal, D. M. (1993). Variations in grasping and throwing patterns as a function of ball size. *Pediatric Exercise Science, 5,* 25–41.

Burton, A. W., & Miller, D. E. (1998). *Movement skill assessment.* Champaign, IL: Human Kinetics.

California Department of Education (2001). *Adapted physical education guidelines in California schools.* Sacramento, CA: Author.

Cooper Institute (1993). *FITNESSGRAM.* Champaign, IL: Human Kinetics.

Department of Education (June 21, 2005). *Individuals with Disabilities Education Act Amendments of 2004.* Volume 70, Number 118. 34 CFR Parts 300, 301 and 304. Washington, D.C.: Author.

Ellenbrand, D. A. (1973). *Gymnastics skills tests for college women.* Master's thesis, Indiana University, Bloomington, IN.

Green, K. N., East, W. B., & Hensley, L. D. (1987). A golf skill test battery for college males and females. *Research Quarterly for Exercise and Sport, 58,* 72–76.

Hensley, L. W., East, W. B., & Stillwell, J. (1979). A racquetball skills test. *Research Quarterly for Exercise and Sport, 50,* 114–118.

Huettig, C., & Roth, K. (2002). Maximizing the use of APE consultants: What the general physical educator has the right to expect. *JOPERD, 73*(1), 32–35, 53.

Los Angeles Unified School District (in press). *Adapted physical education assessment scale—II (APEAS II).* Los Angeles: Author.

Morrow, Jr., J. R. (2005). *Measurement and Evaluation in Human Performance.* Champaign, IL: Human Kinetics.

Ulrich, D. (2000). *Test of gross motor development (TGMD-2).* Austin, TX: Pro-Ed.

Vincent, W. J. (2005). *Statistics in kinesiology* (3rd ed.). Champaign, IL: Human Kinetics.

CHAPTER 8

Preparing the Individualized Education Program

Guiding Questions

1. What are some of the elements of an individualized education program (IEP)?

2. What are some of the procedural elements in the assessment process that are identified in federal legislation and are important to the physical educator?

3. What are the three necessary components of a performance objective?

4. What are some purposes of performance objectives?

5. What are some ways in which realistic criteria for annual goals may be set?

6. What are the steps to take in preparing for an IEP meeting?

The primary topics of this chapter are the fundamental concepts of the IEP, along with basic procedures and strategies the physical educator can use to participate in the IEP process. It is important to understand how program planning for physical education (discussed in Chapter 9) serves as a framework for the IEP. This chapter provides an overview of the two federal Acts that drive educational services for individuals with a disability in order to facilitate your understanding of the IEP process and how it relates to program planning for all students.

THE SIGNIFICANCE OF THE INDIVIDUALIZED EDUCATION PROGRAM

The IEP document is the blueprint for the significant educational process of identifying a student's strengths and supports needed and for evaluating progress. Because the IEP procedures require readjusting goals in a timely manner throughout the student's education, it is an ongoing process. It is important to focus on how the team works together, before, during, and after the IEP meeting day, to set accurate priorities and document them in the written IEP. The written IEP serves as an accountability tool for teachers, parents, and school administrators as they conduct a program of learning for the student. Therefore, effective teamwork that results in a thorough and accurate written IEP is critical.

Once the IEP is developed, it becomes the blueprint for the student's education for the current school year. For the student, this means that a clear and specific direction has been set by those who have the most intimate knowledge of his or her educational strengths and challenges.

For parents, the IEP provides some assurance that a specific curriculum and set of behaviors for their child will be pursued. In recent years, parents have initiated litigation against school districts for not having taught their children to read, write, or calculate as described by the IEP. In addition, a failure to implement the IEP can in some instances be grounds for a federal civil rights complaint. Although the IEP is not a binding contract, it does provide students and parents some level of commitment that the program will focus on specified objectives and accommodations. The IEP does help facilitate accountability between the home and school, the teacher and parents, and the student and school staff. If the parents are not satisfied with the process or the program outlined in the IEP, they have legal rights and privileges that allow for the resolution of the problem as provided by the law. The

MAKING CONNECTIONS

Accommodations in General Physical Education

At an IEP meeting for Shea, a middle school student with a disability, Shea's mother, Mrs. Hain, requests adapted physical education. The main reason Mrs. Hain cites is Shea's low level of arm strength, which interferes with her participation in ball games. The adapted physical education specialist describes his use of foam balls, beach balls, and other light balls to enhance participation in ball games. The general physical education teacher suggests that Shea be placed in general physical education for ball sport units in volleyball, basketball, and soccer and given a choice of the types of light and bouncy balls to use. She describes her use of this strategy for many of her students who, for a variety of reasons, are not successful using regular balls for these sports. The adapted physical education specialist offers to consult with the general physical education teacher monthly on this and other accommodations. Mrs. Hain relates that she is particularly pleased Shea will have the opportunity to participate and socialize with general education peers during physical education. The student's counselor cites the ways in which this may support Shea's socialization goals.

team approach assists the school staff in meeting the full requirements of the IEP for each student, helping to avoid legal intervention.

A thorough and well-written IEP should address all areas required by law and should be developed by the whole team. Although some may find it time-consuming and tedious to do this for all IEPs, the time spent in the development phase minimizes the potential need for remedial education and avoids litigation. By law, the IEP team includes the parents (or guardians). In practice, including parents as genuine, collaborative partners on the IEP team almost always results in greater satisfaction with the program and the best progress for the student.

A parent once said to an adapted physical education specialist, "My son needs so much, no matter what you do, it has to help him." There are many students in adapted physical education about whom this statement could be made. Thus, the IEP assists the physical educator in maintaining a focus on the behaviors that are considered of greatest importance at any given point in time. It is a record of the specific priorities that the IEP team has agreed upon. Dedicated professionals, especially when working with individuals with severe or multiple disabilities, often feel that there are many things that can be done to enhance growth and development. The IEP helps to narrow the scope of the behaviors being addressed within a realistic framework. The IEP not only sets the direction for the educator and provides assurances for the parent, but it also facilitates the most important goal: learning for the student.

Types of IEPs

The general IEP is the most prevalent type of IEP and was the first to be described in the federal legislation. However, as special education has evolved, it has become apparent that both very young and older students required some special provisions in the IEP. Two other types of IEPs are now described in IDEA '04: the individualized family service plan (IFSP) and the individualized transition plan (ITP). Some of their differences are outlined in Table 8.1.

TABLE 8.1 The IFSP and ITP.

IFSP (INDIVIDUALIZED FAMILY SERVICE PLAN)	ITP (INDIVIDUALIZED TRANSITION PLAN)
■ This is the name of an IEP written for an infant or toddler (child under three years of age). Services are provided to families as well as to the infant or toddler, because the law recognizes that infants and toddlers are provided services in a variety of settings including the home. ■ Legal provisions emphasize a multidisciplinary team assessment and provision of educational service in "... natural environments in which children without disabilities participate" (Sec. 632(4)(G)) "... to the maximum extent appropriate" (Sec. 635(a)(16)(A)). ■ The program is often referred to as "Early Intervention" and is described in Part C—Infants and Toddlers with Disabilities. ■ Federal law requires that special education apply to all preschool-age children. Special education is usually interpreted to include designated instruction and services such as adapted physical education.	■ This is the name of an IEP that must be written for a student not later than the first IEP to be in effect when the child is 16 years old. There is recognition that plans must be made to transition from school to post-school activities, including measurable post-secondary goals related to training, education, employment, and, where appropriate, independent living skills.
Key Features of the Targeted Developmental Level	
■ The child is just beginning to learn to respond to people other than close family members. ■ Stranger anxiety may affect the educational process. ■ The child has a very short attention span. ■ Basic learning skills are not present or are just beginning to emerge (e.g., following routines, listening then doing, inhibiting movement and other impulses). ■ The period of language learning is just beginning. ■ The child learns best through doing and experiencing events. ■ The child achieves mastery through repetition. ■ Motor learning focuses on basic body control for mobility, self-care, regulating sensory input, and manipulating simple common objects.	■ The focus is to develop independence. ■ Strengths, challenges, and interests are often well established by this time. ■ Motor development focuses on culturally determined forms of movement. ■ Social interests often are at a peak. ■ Applying learned skills to meaningful tasks is most critical in this time period.

(continued)

TABLE 8.1 Continued.

IFSP (INDIVIDUALIZED FAMILY SERVICE PLAN)	ITP (INDIVIDUALIZED TRANSITION PLAN)
Key Elements of Assessment	
■ Standardized tests and group assessments are not appropriate. ■ Family input and participation in assessment are essential because of the recognition that services to families as well as the child are important. ■ Performance is usually enhanced in familiar, natural settings with familiar people. ■ Use of a transdisciplinary play-based assessment model is the best practice. ■ Observation and interview are key assessment tools. ■ Assessment of and consultation with the family and other service providers (rather than direct instruction) may be the primary service an adapted physical educator provides.	■ Assessment should include the student's ability to apply learned motor skills to accessible activities. What support is needed for the student to participate in motor activities in the community, in the workplace, or at home? ■ Observe in environments that the student can access regularly. ■ Determine skills needed to maintain participation in fitness and physical recreation activities outside of a school environment (e.g., in postsecondary education, in the community, at home). ■ Assess physical skills and adaptations needed for employment.
Focus of Goals and Teaching Methods	
■ Set programs that can be implemented by the family (e.g., activities that can be done at home with or without help and consultation from professionals, and therapies that include family participation). ■ Developmental model is likely to be most appropriate at young ages. ■ Use play-based and/or activity-based assessment and instruction. ■ Family preferences are important when setting goals and selecting activities. ■ Developmental motor needs of infants and toddlers with a disability are often addressed through occupational and physical therapy. ■ Teaching students to apply motor skills to play and interaction with others is often a key contribution of adapted physical education.	■ The functional skills model is likely to be most appropriate at older ages. ■ Goals are based on age-appropriate transition assessments. ■ Student preferences are important when setting goals and selecting activities. ■ The plan should capitalize on peer support and involvement. ■ Adapted physical education services may have to take place, at least partially, in community settings.

LEGAL FRAMEWORK FOR THE INDIVIDUALIZED EDUCATION PROGRAM

One of the important elements written into IDEA '97 was the strengthening of the requirements to include children with a disability in the general education program, and this was reaffirmed in IDEA '04. This had several implications for general physical education including:

- General physical educators included a greater number of students with a disability.
- General physical educators had greater involvement in implementing IEP provisions.
- General physical educators benefited from knowing how to access available supports (contact and consult with special educators, review IEP, etc.) and services to help them successfully teach students with a disability.

- General physical educators needed to attend some IEP meetings.
- It became more important than ever for general and adapted physical educators to work collaboratively.

Another federal law, Section 504 of the Rehabilitation Act of 1973, affects the education (and therefore physical education) of individuals with a disability. It requires equal access to education for all individuals with a disability. Although this Act has been on the books for nearly 30 years, its impact on education has come to the fore only during the last 10 years.

In general, the physical educator can expect to see individuals with relatively mild disabilities receiving accommodations under the provisions of and case law interpreting Section 504. In some states, there is a growing trend to provide educational services based on this Act. The written document required under Section 504 is usually referred to as a "504 Plan," "Accommodation Plan," or "504 Accommodation Plan." Because the effect of this Act on education derives primarily from case law, there are likely to be more differences in its practical implementation from state to state than are seen under IDEA '04. In addition, new case law may bring changes at any time. Therefore, the physical educator should consult local administrators to address any questions regarding local implementation of Section 504.

The professional's goal of and purpose for assessment is to determine the student's strengths and challenges and plan a program to help the student reach his or her maximum potential. This may or may not involve the development of an IEP, depending on whether or not the student has one of the disabilities listed in IDEA '04. Because many students with a disability do qualify for special education services, this chapter discusses the legal and practical issues related to the development of an IEP.

As discussed in Chapter 5, assessment involves gathering data through testing, taking measurements, obtaining information from interviews and prior records, and observing a student's performance. This process is referred to as *determining the current level of performance*. This information is then interpreted for the purpose of program planning. The physical educator should be familiar with some of the procedural elements necessary to achieve this goal, and the adapted physical educator should follow most or all of the steps listed above. Data gathered on all aspects of motor performance, including physical and motor fitness, fundamental motor skills and patterns, culturally determined forms of movement, sensory function, and reflex behavior, should be analyzed. In addition, other factors that influence motor performance within the general education setting should be considered, such as social and behavioral interaction, attention, participation within the large group, and student preferences. The educator may also wish to investigate the effects of any prior interventions (e.g., occupational therapy, peer tutoring, or special instructional strategies) on motor performance.

Legal Requirements of the IEP Related to Assessment

The IEP must meet legal requirements related to the assessment process in the following areas: (1) informed consent, (2) time period, (3) native language, (4) validity and specificity, (5) placement based on evaluation, and (6) independent evaluation.

1. Informed consent. *Before an assessment is conducted, parents or guardians must be fully informed of and give consent to the selective testing and measurement of their child.* This process—known as **informed consent**—must be carried out if a student is singled out for testing or observation. Because one of the primary functions of testing in physical education has always been to measure achievement, many schools carry on a regular program of skills and fitness testing of all students throughout the year. Thus, if a student's poor performance is first identified through a mass testing program that is normally carried out as part of the physical education curriculum, informed consent is not necessary. Through regular testing, many students are identified who require further testing and assessment to determine the need for special services such as adapted physical education. In these cases, further testing requires informed consent, and the testing is almost always conducted by the adapted physical education specialist.

2. 60-day time period. *The initial assessment procedure must be completed within 60 days after the parents submit their written consent.* In addition, a meeting date must be set to discuss the results of the assessment and determine the need for and scope of an IEP. Sixty days may seem like an adequate length of time to complete the assessment procedure; however, it is important to act on assessment requests as soon as consent is received because many variables impinge on the 60-day assessment period. Consideration must be given to the possibility of time lost due to the student's absences from school, school assemblies, and other demands on the student's time such as speech therapy, physical therapy, and special reading groups. Demands on the adapted physical educator's time for instruction, attending meetings, and the assessment of other students must also be considered. In addition, it is best to schedule observation during the student's physical education class time because it is a realistic setting with many natural cues, supports, and distractions (e.g., peer interaction) and a familiar structure. Most adapted physical educators find it essential to schedule regular time periods (e.g., weekly or monthly) during which direct testing can be carried out. This helps to avoid some of the last-minute pressure often created by circumstances beyond the adapted physical educator's control.

3. Native language. By law, *testing and measurement materials and procedures must be presented either in the native language of the pupil or in the student's usual mode of communication.* In addition, as with all educational materials, the assessment procedure should not in other ways be racially or culturally biased. This means that if a student has a sensory, physical, mental, or language impairment, the test must accurately reflect motor performance rather than a manifestation of the impairment (this relates to validity). Therefore, it is vitally important that measurement tools be analyzed and selected with this in mind so a true measure of the student's abilities results, not a measure of his or her disability.

4. Validity and specificity. A fourth legal element mandates that assessment procedures be technically sound. *They should be valid* for the specific purpose for which they are being used. Furthermore, *the procedures must be designed to measure performance specific to the pupil's educational needs.* Two parts of this element require discussion. First, the tool selected for measuring motor performance must have validity: it must actually measure motor performance, not the student's language, or any mental ability or other interfering variable. For example, some standardized tests laden with complex directions may not measure the motor performance of a student with low receptive language ability. The test results in this situation may be more reflective of the student's language ability, not motor ability. (Refer to Chapters 5 and 6 for more information regarding validity.)

The physical educator must analyze the tool relative to each student being assessed in order to determine its validity. The statistical question of validity may already have been answered by the test maker, and some test makers use additional, commonly accepted measures against which to compare performances on their tests, to assure external validity. Although external validity is different from the first question of validity, this information can serve to instill confidence in the tool and the results the tool generates, as well as contribute to the determination of its validity for use with a particular student.

The second part of this element refers to the measurement of performance specific to the pupil's educational needs. This particular issue requires careful consideration and is slightly different from the IEP determination of services provided to meet the student's educational needs. As related to assessment, this requirement helps focus the assessment on educational needs and prevents excessive testing in areas that will not contribute to IEP development. For example, a student with a heart condition may need alternative fitness testing to determine an appropriate physical fitness program but may not need extensive motor skill and coordination testing. A student with a visual impairment may need motor skill testing with a view toward identifying the types of equipment adaptations or types of supports necessary for successful participation within the general physical education curriculum.

Because early physical educators were medical doctors, the philosophy and rationale underlying the contribution of physical education to the growth and development of students with a disability historically have been based on the medical model. Occasionally, this causes confusion in planning assessments and determining service needs. As discussed in Chapter 1, the medical model typically suggests a diagnosis of the impairment, treatment, and an evaluation of the results, which are expected to show some form of cure or remediation. Under IDEA '04 and modern educational philosophy, however, the educational model requires that professional educators identify and address a student's educational, not medical, needs. For example, a boy who is diagnosed and treated medically for epilepsy may or may not have special educational needs. If his seizures are under control through medication, there is usually no reason to separate this youngster from his peers for physical education. In contrast, a student who is diagnosed as having moderate scoliosis and who also has a limited range of motion and poor performance on other physical measures is a very likely candidate for adapted physical education services. Thus, a pathological condition *alone* is not reason enough to separate students from their peers for physical education. The assessment should, among other things, collect data that will assist in making this decision. Medical data may be—and, when available, should be—brought to bear on the decision-making process. The effect of any existing pathology on the motor performance, and hence on the educational needs, of the student must be the primary focus in the physical education assessment process.

5. Placement based on evaluation. The fifth element is that *the decision for placement and the planning for the IEP must be made by the multidisciplinary IEP* *team based on an evaluation.* In a statement of clarification and interpretation published in 1980, the U. S. Office of Education identified four levels of physical education for students with special needs: (1) a general physical education class, (2) a general physical education class with modifications, (3) a separate class such as adapted physical education, and (4) a physical education class in a separate facility such as a school for students with a disability. (In some states or areas, classes are called "specially designed physical education" when students who need modifications but are not eligible for adapted physical education are grouped together in the same class.) Usually, the placement in either a regular school or a special school is made prior to the physical educator's involvement. Placement in a separate adapted physical education class, however, has sometimes mistakenly been based on a student's placement in a separate special education classroom. This decision for placement is often invalid. Placement into a separate adapted physical education class must be made by the student's IEP team and must be based on an assessment of educational need, not on the classroom placement of the student. When a student who is eligible for special education is placed in a general physical education class without adaptations, the IEP only needs to indicate participation in general physical education. When an eligible student is placed in adapted physical education, the IEP should indicate the frequency, location, and duration of the service; present level of motor performance; annual goals and objectives; and any accommodations or modifications. When the student is placed in general physical education with modifications, the IEP should include the specific modifications and/or accommodations.

6. Independent evaluation. The final element provides that *the parents or guardians have a right to obtain an independent evaluation of their child by a qualified examiner who is not employed by the educational agency.* This mandate alone could have grave impact on professionals who are not thorough in their assessment. It is imperative that the physical educator follow the procedures outlined in Chapters 6 and 7 and throughout this chapter to identify all of the possible sources of motor difficulty. This is where the developmental model has special significance as a framework for conducting a thorough assessment and analysis. Although physical educators in private practice are not plentiful, there are other qualified examiners who may be able to measure the parameters that impinge on motor performance, including psychologists, educational and movement therapists, physical and occupational therapists, orientation and mobility specialists, and medical personnel. Thus, it is incumbent on the physical educator to identify possible sources of motor difficulty by using the developmental model and to interpret them or make referrals for further assessment to professionals in related areas. This concept is discussed more fully later in this chapter.

Although these procedures may seem cumbersome at first, they do provide guidelines for educators and assurances for parents and students that each student's educational needs will be systematically addressed. Further discussion of the significance of these procedures and the IEP for the student, the parents, and the educator appears in Chapter 9.

Legally Mandated Components of the IEP

In addition to the above requirements for assessment, the legal mandates of IDEA '04 require that several components be included in the IEP:

1. Present levels of performance
2. Measurable annual goal(s)
3. Titles of persons responsible for monitoring progress toward each goal (e.g., adapted physical education specialist, speech-language pathologist, occupational therapist)
4. Strategies or materials to be used to achieve goals
5. Related services needed for the student to benefit from special education
6. The frequency, duration, and location of those services, and the projected dates for beginning and ending the services and accommodations
7. An explanation of the extent, if any, to which the student will not participate with children without disabilities in the general class and activities
8. Modifications and accommodations that will be provided, including supplementary aids and services
9. That the provision of assistive technology has been considered
10. Beginning at age 16, a statement of transition services needed for the student to meet his or her post-secondary goals
11. How the student's progress will be measured, how regularly the parents will be informed, and the extent to which the progress is sufficient to enable the child to achieve the goals by the end of the year

Although states can have additional requirements, they cannot eliminate any requirements or they may risk losing federal funding.

PREPARING FOR THE INDIVIDUALIZED EDUCATION PROGRAM MEETING

Preparation for the IEP process begins with the referral and ends with the IEP meeting. Figure 8.1 suggests a graphic analogy for understanding the referral and IEP process. This analogy conveys the idea of a "growing" process that is based on strong roots and develops into a mature tree with many branches and leaves—the many elements of the program for each student. This process is one of planting, growing and developing, changing, and "re-seeding." The model is offered to help you keep in mind the whole process because sometimes it can seem overwhelming. This IEP process does not necessarily follow a linear pathway—hence, the tree analogy may help you to visualize something that is continually adapting and changing according to the conditions (or circumstances), time, and people involved.

Sometimes, a "draft" of the IEP can be prepared prior to the meeting date and presented at the IEP meeting for review and revision as needed. This not only saves time, but it also allows the parent and other team members to make suggestions and changes as needed. Once the IEP has been completed, there is still more work that must be documented, such as the progress on goals and benchmarks, other types of assessment, or the implementation of a behavior plan. These often involve further collaboration and communication with team members, which leads to another IEP meeting; thus, the cycle of growth continues.

The adapted and general physical educators will not always be required to attend the IEP meet-

FIGURE 8.1 Growth of the IEP process.

The tree is an example of a growing process that is analogous to the IEP process. The roots begin the growth of the tree. There are several ways in which a referral can be made, beginning the growth of the IEP process. The information in the referral and the initial actions of the person receiving the referral provide nourishment, just as water and soil provide nourishment to the roots of a tree. The plants, grass, and flowers around the tree provide support for the soil to hold the water; throughout their life cycle, they provide food to nourish the roots, just as the people making the referral provide support for the initial stage of the IEP process. Although IDEA '04 clearly calls for specific people to serve on the IEP team, other people involved at this level may include, but are not limited to, the child's occupational therapist (OT), physical therapist (PT), doctor, nurse, psychologist, principal, orientation and mobility instructor (O&M), social worker, or rehabilitation services personnel.

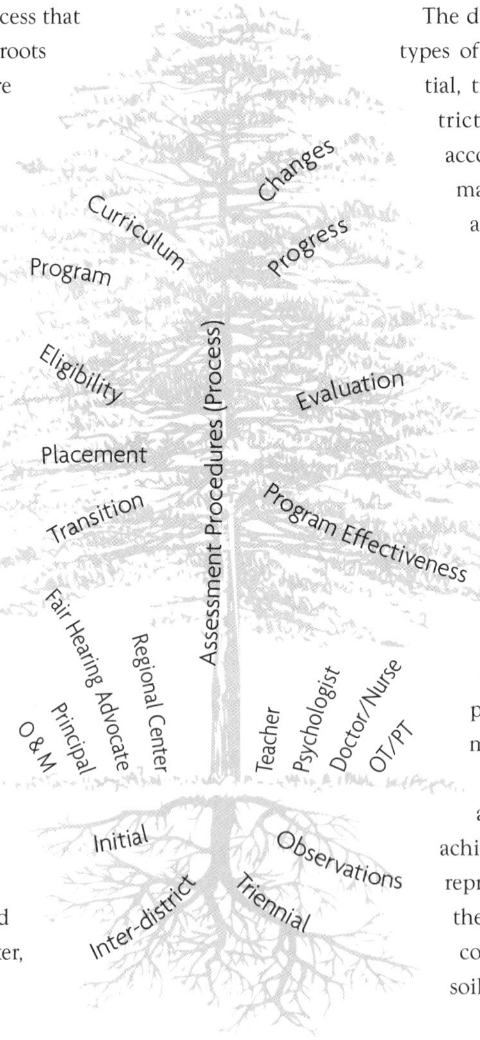

The different roots of the tree represent the types of referrals that can be made (e.g., initial, triennial review, an inter- or intra-district referral, or needed supports or accommodations). The type of referral made leads to the specific reasons why an assessment is conducted. The trunk is the base of the tree and represents the assessment and information-gathering process, which is the base of the IEP process. The trunk (or base), which carries and organizes the nourishment contributing to the growth and development of the tree and branches, represents the timelines and procedures involved in the assessment.

The branches represent each of the specific areas that the IEP process must address (e.g., the placement, how to determine and document progress, supports needed, and the evaluation procedures). The achievement of goals and objectives is represented by the "fruit" produced by the tree. The fruit (the achievements) contain seeds that fall and "re-seed" the soil to begin the process of growth again.

ing. Someone familiar with the assessment is required to attend, and IDEA '04 provides for written input to the meeting to be made by individuals other than the core team members. It will usually be very helpful—to you and to the education of the student—to attend an initial and triennial IEP meeting, and attending annual IEP meetings is often helpful as well. Sometimes scheduling and other circumstances make it almost impossible for all team members to attend, and state and local rules may also affect your attendance. Written input to the IEP should be prepared carefully, as you will need to be clear and concise to facilitate accurate and productive development of the physical education portion of the IEP document. Preparation prior to the IEP meeting is an important and efficient way to participate in the IEP process, especially when you are unable to attend the meeting. By communicating with the parents and other team members prior to the meeting, you may be able to identify areas of discussion that might come up or answer questions that the parents may have regarding services. In addition, when other team members are familiar with the general or adapted physical education report or goals, objectives, and accommodations, they are able to present the information in your absence in a more concise and efficient manner.

Another strategy that is sometimes effective is to leave a contact number with the IEP team so that the team facilitator will be able to contact you during the IEP meeting if there is an urgent need to clarify something. Often, team members who are representing another member find it helpful to have a checklist of items to cover. These individuals may also take responsibility for sharing with you any information discussed at the meeting, as well as obtaining a copy of the IEP for you.

As part of the preparation process for IEP meetings at each school, the adapted physical education specialist should make sure to be invited to the IEP meetings for students on their caseload. Giving a list of your students to the case manager or facilitator is often a good way to ensure that you receive a notification for the IEP meeting.

Referrals

Referrals may come from many sources. They can be generated by different people involved in the student's life and can be of several types:

1. Initial referrals, often based on medical information, observed motor delay, parent request, and/or need to transition (e.g., elementary to middle school, high school to adult programs).
2. Inter-district or intra-district referrals, referrals made between agencies in a city, county, state, or country.
3. Triennial or annual assessments, parent updates, and requests.
4. Observation or resource requests.
5. Referral from the SST (student study team) process (sometimes called the student improvement plan or student intervention team).

The last type of referral will usually include documentation of prior intervention attempts. Figure 8.2 provides a checklist for referrals to adapted physical education, for use by a classroom teacher or general physical education teacher making a referral.

Assessment

As discussed in Chapter 5, the process of assessment involves much more than just gathering data. The physical educator should review the type and validity of all data and any information available from as many sources as possible.

Following certain procedures and timelines during the assessment process assures that the following five purposes of assessment (Vetter, 1998) are fulfilled:

1. Determining eligibility for placement in special education and the type of physical education services to be provided for the student.
2. Program planning and curriculum (guided by the goals and benchmarks, and the yearly, monthly, weekly, and daily lesson plans).
3. Student progress (based on the goals and benchmarks and decisions needed for formal and informal documentation for revisions).
4. Ensuring program effectiveness (setting standards and evaluation procedures, for both the students and the program, to be used throughout the year).
5. Evaluation of procedures and accountability (all teachers have a professional responsibility to make decisions and to discover ways to evaluate themselves, in order to develop programs that evolve to meet the needs of all students).

Some students' performances can be documented only through informal testing or observation (see Chapter 6). When referring to their notes, physical educators should be certain that the description of a student's performance is clear, objective, and focused on what the student was *doing* when asked to perform a specific movement. Although omissions, substitutions, and additions by the student should be noted, they should not take the place of a clear description of what the student did. Any

> **FIGURE 8.2** | *A checklist for identifying students who may need adapted physical education assessment.*

ADAPTED PHYSICAL EDUCATION PRE-REFERRAL CHECKLIST

Dear Teacher:

The following motor performances and play behaviors may indicate the need for further intervention if they interfere with safe, appropriate, successful interaction with peers. Please complete this form and return to the adapted physical education specialist at your school.

Thank you,

Student _____ Age _____ School _____

P.E. Days _____ Times _____ Teacher _____

	ABLE	ABLE MOST OF THE TIME	IS RARELY ABLE	IS UNABLE
Rate the following motor performances:				
Stands on one foot (2 seconds minimum)	☐	☐	☐	☐
Hops on one foot three times	☐	☐	☐	☐
Jumps in place (5 consecutive times—two-foot take-off and two-foot landing)	☐	☐	☐	☐
Skips 20 feet or more	☐	☐	☐	☐
Kicks a stationary ball	☐	☐	☐	☐
Throws overhand 15 feet	☐	☐	☐	☐
Hits a ball off a batting tee	☐	☐	☐	☐
Bounces and catches to self (8½″ or tennis ball)	☐	☐	☐	☐
Jumps rope turned by others (5 consecutive jumps)	☐	☐	☐	☐
Turns own jump rope (5 consecutive jumps)	☐	☐	☐	☐
Climbs 3-rung ladder up and down	☐	☐	☐	☐
Uses a slide independently	☐	☐	☐	☐
Writes legibly for age	☐	☐	☐	☐
Takes care of personal items and hygiene adequately for age	☐	☐	☐	☐
Follows directions	☐	☐	☐	☐
Uses free time for active play	☐	☐	☐	☐

(continued)

FIGURE 8.2 Continued.

Rate the following behaviors:	DOES NOT INTERFERE WITH LEARNING	DOES NOT INTERFERE WITH LEARNING MOST OF THE TIME	USUALLY INTERFERES WITH LEARNING	ALMOST ALWAYS INTERFERES WITH LEARNING
Touches many things in room when coming and going	☐	☐	☐	☐
Touches or pokes classmates	☐	☐	☐	☐
Falls excessively	☐	☐	☐	☐
Is awkward and clumsy when moving	☐	☐	☐	☐
Is easily distracted	☐	☐	☐	☐
Distracts others	☐	☐	☐	☐
Performs tasks more slowly than others	☐	☐	☐	☐
Prefers solo play	☐	☐	☐	☐
Indicates a dislike for physical education/activity	☐	☐	☐	☐

Source: Adapted from format created by Jacquelyn S. Brougher, Corona-Norco Unified School District (1982).

apparent cognitive or language difficulties, confusion, or student verbalizations related to the task (e.g., "I can't" or "This is too hard") should be noted, as well as the setting (e.g., large group, unstructured play, general physical education class). Behavioral, social, language, attention, student preference, and motor behavior observations should be similarly documented even for students who can participate in formal or structured testing.

When done by a skilled physical educator, informal or structured observation is just as valid as any formal or direct-measure protocol. Statements that are factual should precede any statements of probability or inference, and the delineation among the three should be clear. The physical educator must try not to feel threatened if a member of the IEP team challenges his or her report, as long as the report is factual and any comments beyond fact are qualified. This is a report of a student's performance at one point in time, and it is entirely possible for the student to perform differently on another occasion or with even minor differences in setting.

The physical educator is responsible for gathering information from other professionals, school records, and parents, if possible, to make sense of the findings. It is most important to gather information from the general physical educator and the parents whenever possible. Discussion, observation checklists, and comments from these team members provide valuable information in the IEP process. If a large discrepancy exists between the reported motor performance and other team members' impressions of what the child can do, simply offer to retest or gather additional data. The goal is to provide the most appropriate placement and program available for the student, not to feed the ego of any professional. Once a level of credibility is established among professionals, peer support will be forthcoming.

Report of teacher assessment

The Report of Teacher Assessment is prepared by the person(s) conducting the assessment and presented at the IEP meeting by that person or someone else who is familiar with the assessment. It should be legible, clear, concise, professionally prepared, and parent friendly. That is, professional jargon and acronyms should be avoided or clearly explained. The parent reading the report should be able to understand the who, what, why, where, and how of the assessment, as well as how the interpretation leads to the recommendations, which can be presented orally

> ## Teaching Tip
>
> **USING A DEFICIT OR A STRENGTH MODEL** • Either the deficit or strength model can be effective if professionals are careful to avoid inherent pitfalls. This often involves a blending of the two approaches. If focusing on the remediation of deficits, it is important to look to the student's strengths in order to compensate, accommodate, and adapt tasks. If primarily looking at building on strengths, it is important not to overlook deficits that can be remediated or at least improved.

> ## Teaching Tip
>
> **DRAFTING AN IEP** • Before the IEP meeting, prepare a draft containing the following information, but be prepared to change it based on information presented at the meeting:
>
> - Present level of performance
> - Goals and objectives that you may be responsible for monitoring
> - Frequency, duration, and location of services that you may recommend, as well as the starting date
> - A list of accommodations or modifications you think the student will need

or in writing. Figure 8.3 provides specific guidelines for preparing the Report of Teacher Assessment.

IEP Content

District IEP forms vary, but they all include the same general information and the following IEP components (essential components that the adapted physical educator should carefully consider prior to the meeting):

1. Statement of current level of functioning
2. Statement of measurable goals
3. Frequency, duration, and location of special education and related services, as well as the extent of general education participation
4. Starting and review dates
5. Objective criteria and evaluation procedures, as well as the person (by title) responsible for monitoring the progress toward the achievement of each goal
6. Private school responsibilities, if applicable
7. Transition services information (beginning by age 16) that includes: (a) post-school activities, (b) a coordinated set of activities, (c) the outcome-oriented process, and (d) areas of transition activities. The IEP (or ITP) meeting will include a discussion about what services will be provided and when; a determination of who will provide the services and where; and the role of parents, educators, and other professionals. The curriculum areas include instruction, community, and employment.
8. IEP accountability and follow-through (conduct your program so that you meet the dates stated)
9. Statement indicating the need for assistive technology has been considered

FIGURE 8.3 *Guidelines for preparing the Report of Teacher Assessment.*

Interpreting Assessment Results

(analyzing your assessment results and observations)

1. Look for item scores or data that cluster or are similar. Scores cluster for the following reasons:
   - They are related to each other.
   - They test the same thing.
   - They confirm/support other tests presented to the child.
2. Analyze the perceptual, language, cognitive, and motor demands of the tasks (e.g., did the student have a low shuttle run score because of complex language that resulted in poor understanding of the task, or was it really poor agility?).
3. Compare the subtest items and other data to determine strengths and weaknesses.
   - The deficit model looks at skills or abilities the child is missing as a method for identifying needed interventions. However, this is sometimes thought to be a negative approach that fails to build adequately on the student's strengths.
   - A model that focuses on building upon the child's strengths is often thought to be more positive and to lead educators to work in areas

(continued)

FIGURE 8.3 Continued.

in which the child is most likely to achieve success.

4. Determine whether to teach within a developmental or functional skill model, or a combination of the two.
   a. Order deficits developmentally so they can be addressed sequentially when using a developmental model.
   b. The functional model looks at how the student uses the skill in realistic settings and frequently available activities. A fundamental concept is the premise that all developmental skills do not need to be mastered, especially when adaptations, accommodations, and modifications can be made. When using this approach, identify skills in the order in which they are most critical to increasing the child's independence.
      - *Example in the area of walking.* The student may have achieved a functional walking gait, although it is not rhythmical and symmetrical. Using a functional skills approach, you would not continue to work on an even gait. You would focus instead on skills such as stepping up on a curb, using stairs, using elevators and escalators, and moving around environmental obstacles (furniture, crowds of people, playground equipment, surface changes, displays in school building or office or store aisles, etc.).
      - *Example in the area of bicycle riding.* Although riding a bicycle may be a skill usually achieved at the child's current developmental level, if the child is not interested in it or motivated to work on it, a more meaningful skill should be selected and addressed (riding a scooter, fitness walking, riding a bicycle ergometer while listening to music, etc.).
      - *Example for a student who is deaf and has difficulty participating in playground games.* The most salient reason for the difficulty must be identified and addressed. Reduced balance, which is often present in individuals who are deaf, may be an interfering variable. However, if the most salient feature is reduced social skills, then working on improving or using accommodations for balance difficulties is not likely to result in increased participation in playground games.

Reporting Assessment Results

1. Select a *format or method* for organizing points of data.
2. Use *declarative statements* (statements of fact). Declarative statements can be made only after something happens, and they state information that was observed.
   - "Tell" the reader in a believable way (e.g., throws ball 15 feet with right hand).
   - Describe an event and behavior with a statement. For example, "demonstrates ability to . . ." and state the specific skill(s). This does not mean the child does it all of the time, only that he or she does demonstrate the skill. Including known information about the frequency with which the skill is demonstrated (e.g., two out of three trials) may be helpful.
3. Use *statements of probability* (statements that make an assumption) to describe interpretations of data. An assumption goes beyond what is observed—it is based on other observations and knowledge.
   - For example, "This may indicate there is . . ." Or, "Judy may have tactile discrimination difficulty because she only wears long sleeves and does not like to touch sand, Play-Doh, or beanbags."
   - Identify statements of probability by using descriptive words and phrases such as *may indicate, could be considered to, is likely to,* and so forth.
4. Use *statements of inference* to describe the likelihood of something happening, based on similar circumstances. Similar circumstances may include the same child's behavior or response in a similar circumstance, or the behavior, response, or result of other similar children in the same circumstance. Statements of inference should follow factual and probability statements. For example, the following statements describe a student who is three years old: *He saw me put the ball away in a bag behind the barrel one time. He remembered where to get the ball at recess time. Most three-year-olds cannot find the ball without verbal cues or more practice.* (These are the factual statements.) *He is likely to have good visual memory.* (This is the statement of probability.) *Using ample amounts of visual cues and materials is likely to be an effective teaching strategy for this child.* (This is the statement of inference.)

> ## Teaching Tip
>
> **PRIORITIZE CURRENT LEVEL OF PERFORMANCE** • When writing about the child's current level of performance, it is helpful to prioritize what will be important to the child. It is occasionally acceptable to "teach to the test" or write goals or objectives based on test criteria. For example, if physical fitness or physical development is identified as an area of need for the child, then write objectives for abdominal strength or running with correct body mechanics that are based on the age of the student, grade level, and physical education standards or curriculum.
>
> When a student has difficulty with ball skills, ask yourself why you want to improve the ball skills. The student may not be able to generalize the skills because ball skills in a playground game are different from the ball skills used on the test. The objectives or benchmarks should lead the student to measurable behaviors that he or she can use in realistic situations.

COMPLETING THE INDIVIDUALIZED EDUCATION PROGRAM

Based on your decision making, the results of the assessment, and the contents of the IEPs for children in your classes, you can now design an appropriate physical education program plan. Program planning is discussed in Chapter 9. Below we discuss writing the IEP in detail (completing the IEP template and writing goals and objectives). Because of time constraints, it is often helpful to draft the IEP prior to the meeting (with input from other team members, especially the parents). The process may stop and start several times in order to address certain areas in more depth, gain additional information, and so on. However, there is a linear thread, or progression, that goes through any IEP process and that includes evaluating the current level of functioning, writing goals, collaborating with team members, rewriting portions of the IEP document, and discussing the contents of the IEP. Although IDEA '04 does not specifically require short-term objectives for most students, it may be a good idea to write them. Even if they are not formally part of the IEP, short-term objectives will help to focus instruction as well as communicate projected progress to the rest of the IEP team. State and local policy will determine whether or not short-term objectives will be included in the IEP document. Examples in this book will include objectives.

The information from the multidisciplinary team assessment report is vital to an individually planned, well-organized, effective physical education program. For example, the levels of cognitive language and social development greatly affect the teaching methods selected. Knowing the student's preferred modality for learning is important so that the teacher can select appropriate activities. Knowing techniques for supporting positive behavior assists the teacher with maintaining class control, enhancing motivation, and providing the best learning environment for all students.

Preparing an IEP

Now consider, as an example, preparing an IEP for Carol Jean Smith. Carol is a second grader referred by her special education classroom teacher for assessment in a number of areas, one of which is motor performance. You are the physical educator. After receiving the referral notice, you look into Carol's cumulative record file and find a physician's report indicating that Carol has cerebral palsy with mild right-side involvement. You know she speaks English, and because of her diagnosis of moderate mental retardation, you predict she will be slow to grasp concepts.

Once parental consent is obtained for testing, you arrange with the classroom teacher to observe Carol on the playground. Information about the kinds of activities Carol seeks, those she avoids, and how she moves provides insight into her movement profile and helps you make sense of your findings. Later, it will help you to recommend a program. You note that she was knocked down twice during the play period and caught herself with her elbows. She participated primarily in climbing and stayed on the swing when the other children started playing a ball game.

During Carol's formal testing, you give verbal instructions in short, simple commands and demonstrate the tasks she is to do. You note that she is eager to please, but she giggles and runs around the room after attempting a task that is difficult for her. Your profile reveals that she is three years below age level in acquiring developmental milestones, scoring above the 10th percentile only on physical fitness test items. The other areas measured, including perceptual motor object control and locomotor skills, show Carol's performance to be below the 5th percentile of her age mates.

A discussion with the classroom teacher validates your observation of her giggling—which you both conclude is an attempt to escape further failure and challenging tasks—her poor balance, and her reluctance to play ball games. These observations have been further validated by her poor performance on balance, ocular control, object control, and locomotor skills scores. Therefore, you are prepared to report the following:

1. Carol's physical fitness is her strongest area, with scores ranging from the 10th to the 15th percentile.
2. Carol's motor development is just under that for four years of age, indicating she is about three years behind her chronological-age peers in achieving developmental milestones.
3. Her perceptual motor development is equal to or below the 5th percentile of the norming group on balance, imitation of postures, and ocular control.
4. She has learned object control and locomotor skills that fall within the lowest 5 percent of the norming group.
5. She seems to avoid failure and difficult tasks by giggling and running away or otherwise not participating.
6. You wonder about her safety on the playground because she seems to have a lag in her ability to keep herself from falling all the way to the ground and does not show a good protective extension response when she does fall.

Carol's academic achievement shows a flat profile at four years, her speech and language scores range from three and one half to four years, and the school psychologist reports that she has moderate mental retardation. You are equipped with statements of fact (motor profile test results and description of the observation), probability (apparent escape behavior), and inference from undeveloped reflexes (poor protective extension). Your data fit Carol's profile, and with this added information on cognition and language, you can better plan the teaching strategies you will use in implementing her program.

An Example of an IEP Document

Figure 8.4 shows selected pages of a completed IEP. The physical educator can use its medical information, intellectual achievement, social and language development, and motor performance information to plan an effective program and select appropriate teaching strategies. Since Carol Jean Smith is slow to grasp concepts, is functioning intellectually at about the four-year-old level, and is rather passive in her social interactions, she might function better in a small group. The physical educator should consider using strategies such as demonstrating; making concepts concrete; using multisenses; and providing structure, routine, and perhaps patterning, positioning, and prompting to assist learning (see Chapter 10 for an explanation of these strategies). Carol would probably learn best in a small group or at teaching stations where she will get a lot of individual attention.

The development of skills in the object control, locomotor, and physical fitness areas should progress from simple to complex, emphasizing first Carol's strong left side and maximizing function in her right side. The mechanical principles of catching may have to be modified to accommodate her right-side hemiplegia. For example, she may need to learn to catch a large ball with her noninvolved left hand stabilized by the right hand. Then, the progression should proceed to a smaller ball. Carol can enjoy activities appropriate for four- to five-year-olds, such as "hot potato," "over-and-under," and modified four-square. Activities requiring balance can supplement Carol's academic objectives being targeted in the classroom; for example, have Carol identify and balance on colors or painted letters and numbers on the playground. She might also be asked to repeat simple motor performance commands while accurately reproducing the sounds the speech pathologist is currently focusing on with her.

Other students in Carol's class are likely to have similar needs for cognitive, speech, or language development. Therefore, involving other students in the activities outlined for Carol might be appropriate, but with individual sets of expectations for each student. For example, other students may work on identifying different letters or numbers or articulating different sounds. The activity might be the same, but the levels of expectation for motor, cognitive, and speech behavior are individualized. Individualizing doesn't necessarily mean one-to-one instruction; it does mean focusing on each individual's goals and levels of performance within the lesson. It is imperative for anyone directing instruction related to an IEP to understand fully the concept of individualized instruction.

FIGURE 8.4 — Example of an IEP for Carol Jean Smith.

PRESENT LEVELS OF PERFORMANCE
(including results of most recent evaluation)

Student: Carol Jean Smith
Date: January 28, 2007

Strengths/interests/learning preference:

Carol is eager to please adults, cooperative with direct requests and instruction, and attempted all tasks presented during assessment and observation.

She enjoys physical activities and readily explored equipment in the motor assessment area.

Her family reports that they enjoy weekly bicycle riding in the local park or along the bike path at the beach and swimming in a pool as well as the ocean during the warm weather months.

PREACADEMIC/ACADEMIC/FUNCTIONAL SKILLS

Communication development:

Speech and language scores are at the three and one half to four year level—comensurate with cognition.

Motor development (summarized from Report of Teacher Assessment):

Gross Motor:

Adapted Physical Education Assessment Scale (APEAS):

- Perceptual Motor below 5th percentile
- Object Control below 5th percentile
- Locomotor Skills below 5th percentile
- Physical Fitness: 10th—15th percentile

Revised Diagnostic Brigance Inventory of Early Development (gross motor portion): demonstrates all milestones up to four years of age.

Teacher observations:
- falls often and lands on elbows (incomplete arm extension)
- selects individual activities of climbing and swinging rather than choosing a ball game with peers
- giggles as a response when invited by a peer to play a ball game; frequently engages in run/chase games with younger children

Social/emotional development:

Classroom teacher reports that giggling and silly behavior often interfere with her participation with partner or small group activities in the classroom.

Health:

Mild cerebral palsy—right hemiplegia

Prevocational skills:

Self-help:

She doesn't maintain an adequate personal space (she was knocked down twice by peers on the playground during recess observation).

Source: Adapted from California Dept. of Education, Division of Special Education. Used with permission.

FIGURE 8.4 *Continued.*

Student: Carol Jean Smith   Date: January 28, 2007

Areas of educational need to be addressed in goals/objectives:

- balance and protective extension
- safe participation on the playground
- peer interaction during physical activities

SPECIAL FACTORS

Concerns of parent relevant to education progress:

Parents would like Carol to play independently with small groups of siblings and extended family, as well as with other children at the park and beach.

How disability affects involvement and progress in general curriculum (or for preschoolers, participation in appropriate activities):

She will need accommodations to ensure her safety and an understanding of movement and game concepts, rules of play, sharing, etc. with peers; and to her right hemiplegia.

Student will participate with children without disabilities in the general education environment for:

Selected physical education activities with typical peers and recess, including special events such as P.E. and Sport Week activities, ACES, field day, Jump Rope for Heart, jog/walk-a-thon, etc.

Will all special education services be provided at student's school of residence?   ☒ YES   ☐ NO (rationale)

Specify supplemental aids and services to be provided to or on behalf of the student and/or program modifications or supports for school personnel:

Adapted physical education specialist will consult twice per month with the classroom teacher and paraeducators who teach specially designed physical education.

Does student require assistive technology devices and services or low incidence services, equipment, and materials to meet educational goals and objectives?   ☐ YES   ☒ NO (specify)

Parents will be informed of progress: ☒ Quarterly   ☐ Trimester   ☐ Semester   ☐ Other (specify)

How?   ☐ Annotated Goals/Objectives   ☒ Progress Summary Report   ☐ Other (specify)

If student is blind or visually impaired, instruction in Braille and in the use of Braille will be provided:
☐ YES   ☒ NO (explain)

FIGURE 8.4 Continued.

Page 3 of 6

Student: Carol Jean Smith   Date: January 28, 2007

COMMUNICATION

If Limited English Proficient, specify how student's level of English proficiency, related to the IEP, will be addressed:

If student is Deaf or Hard of Hearing:

a.) Are specialized communication strategies required: ☐ YES ☒ NO (describe)

Describe opportunities for direct instruction and communication with peers and adults in the student's language and mode of communication:

BEHAVIOR

Does student's behavior impede learning? ☒ YES ☐ NO (describe)

Socially immature behaviors interfere with peer interaction during group games and physical activities, especially on the playground but also during structured motor activities.

a.) Specify positive behavior interventions, strategies, and supports to address the behaviors:

Instruction in appropriate peer interaction, including initiation, turn taking, and sharing equipment during planned group motor activities. Reinforce target behaviors with praise and by sharing information with classroom teacher so it can be included with the classroom reinforcement system. Conduct brief meeting with classroom teacher and paraeducator twice a month in order to apply other behavior intervention strategies consistently as appropriate.

b.) Positive Behavior Intervention Plan: ☒ Not required ☐ Attached

TRANSITION

For students at age 16, or younger as appropriate, describe transition service needs of student related to courses of study:

See attached Individual Transition Plan (ITP) dated _____

On or before the student's 17th birthday, he/she has been advised of rights at age of majority (age 18). Advised:

Date _____   By Whom _____

FIGURE 8.4 Continued.

IEP TEAM MEETING NOTES

Page 4 of 6

Student: Carol Jean Smith   Date: January 28, 2007

Addendum to IEP   ☐ No   ☒ Yes   ☐ To be attached to IEP dated   Dec. 5, 2006

Purpose of the meeting:
To review adapted physical education assessment and consider appropriate placement options for physical education.

Comments:
Parents request emphasis on leisure/recreational skills within the school program. Team agrees that adapted physical education specialist will provide referrals to recreational programs and provide telephone consultation with parents to assist them in accessing appropriate recreational programs.

Parents agree to respond to recreation/leisure survey that was given at this meeting to expand the information gathered regarding preferences and interest areas for Carol to assist adapted physical education specialist in selecting appropriate referral program options (e.g., VIP, Challenger, Special Olympics, therapeutic horseback riding, ARC, Easter Seals).

Informal collaborative meetings with classroom teacher and paraeducator will include suggestions for other physical education activities that can be provided by other school staff (e.g., general physical education teacher, paraeducator, parent volunteer, playground assistant).

Parents were encouraged to volunteer and participate in the schoolwide special events such as the Physical Education Sport Week and ACES program, and Jump Rope for Heart activities.

Parent/Guardian/Surrogate	Date	Parent/Guardian/Surrogate	Date
Special Education Teacher/Provider	Date	General Education Teacher	Date
Student (when appropriate)	Date	Administrator or designee	Date
Additional Participant/Title	Date	Additional Participant/Title	Date
Additional Participant/Title	Date	Additional Participant/Title	Date

FIGURE 8.4 Continued.

ANNUAL GOALS AND BENCHMARKS/SHORT-TERM OBJECTIVES

Student: Carol Jean Smith   Date: January 28, 2007

Area of need:	Measurable Annual Goal:	Annual Goal Review:
Balance and protective extension Baseline: Falls on elbows	Goal #1: When participating in stunts and tumbling tasks on a mat, Carol will demonstrate increased balance and protective extension by successfully supporting her body weight and maintaining balance when doing animal walks, sustaining each position or movement for 10 secs. without collapsing her body on 4 out of 5 trials.	Date: ☐ 1. No progress ☐ 2. Partial progress (1%–49% of goal met) ☐ 3. Substantial progress (50%–99% of goal met) ☐ 4. Goal met or exceeded

Person(s) Responsible: Adapted & General Physical Education Teachers

☐ Enables student to be involved/progress in general curriculum and/or   ☒ Addresses other educational needs resulting from the disability.

Present level of performance	Benchmark/Short-Term Objective:	Review:
2–3 secs.	#1.a: Carol will be able to hold hand/knee position and lift right arm (and then left arm) in extended position in front of her at shoulder height and maintain balanced position for 10 secs. when given a verbal instruction in 4 out of 5 trials, by end of 1st grading period.	Date: ☐ 1. No progress ☐ 2. Partial progress ☐ 3. Substantial progress ☐ 4. Goal met or exceeded

Person(s) Responsible: Adapted & General Physical Education Teachers

Present level of performance	Benchmark/Short-Term Objective:	Review:
Assumes bear walk position for 5 secs. in place, but does not "walk"	#1.b: Carol will be able to bear walk in forward and sideways directions for 10 secs. directed by her partner, 4 out of 5 trials, by end of 2nd grading period.	Date: ☐ 1. No progress ☐ 2. Partial progress ☐ 3. Substantial progress ☐ 4. Goal met or exceeded

Person(s) Responsible: Adapted & General Physical Education Teachers

Present level of performance	Benchmark/Short-Term Objective:	Review:
Lifts feet off ground one at a time	#1.c: Carol will be able to perform at least 3 consecutive donkey kicks, while maintaining an extended arm position and landing on her feet on 4 out of 5 trials, by end of 3rd grading period.	Date: ☐ 1. No progress ☐ 2. Partial progress ☐ 3. Substantial progress ☐ 4. Goal met or exceeded

Person(s) Responsible: Adapted & General Physical Education Teachers

FIGURE 8.4 *Continued.*

Student: Carol Jean Smith
Date: January 28, 2007
Page 6 of 6

Area of need:	Measurable Annual Goal:	Annual Goal Review:
Safe participation on the playground Baseline: Is bumped by others around her	Goal #2: When participating with a large group in directed movement exploration activities involving moving within specified boundaries of play (spatial awareness during movement in general space), Carol will maintain her own personal space to safely perform locomotor patterns, including starting, stopping, and turning, on 3 out of 5 days of practice.	Date: ☐ 1. No progress ☐ 2. Partial progress (1%–49% of goal met) ☐ 3. Substantial progress (50%–99% of goal met) ☐ 4. Goal met or exceeded

Person(s) Responsible: Adapted & General Physical Education Teachers

☐ Enables student to be involved/progress in general curriculum and/or ☒ Addresses other educational needs resulting from the disability.

Present level of performance	Benchmark/Short-Term Objective:	Review:
Moves close to others, drops arms and hoop	#2.a: Carol will play the scatter formation game "Cars and Motorcycles," and maintain her own personal space by holding her hula hoop (the car) at waist height and moving around the space without touching another "car," given 5 or fewer verbal prompts, during 5 minutes of play, on 4 out of 5 sessions of play by the end of the 1st grading period.	Date: ☐ 1. No progress ☐ 2. Partial progress ☐ 3. Substantial progress ☐ 4. Goal met or exceeded

Person(s) Responsible: Adapted & General Physical Education Teachers

Present level of performance	Benchmark/Short-Term Objective:	Review:
Difficulty moving and changing directions, tagged often	#2.b: Carol will be able to avoid being tagged during a flee/chase game of tag by changing directions and moving away from the "chaser" 1 out of 3 times during 5 minutes of play without verbal prompts by the end of the 2nd grading period.	Date: ☐ 1. No progress ☐ 2. Partial progress ☐ 3. Substantial progress ☐ 4. Goal met or exceeded

Person(s) Responsible: Adapted & General Physical Education Teachers

Present level of performance	Benchmark/Short-Term Objective:	Review:
Does not stay in playing area or move to corner	#2.c: Carol will be able to avoid being tagged in the Four Corners tag game with peers by standing on the corner, moving when signal is given, and safely negotiating other players to move to next corner before getting tagged, during 5 minutes of play by the end of the 3rd grading period.	Date: ☐ 1. No progress ☐ 2. Partial progress ☐ 3. Substantial progress ☐ 4. Goal met or exceeded

Person(s) Responsible: Adapted & General Physical Education Teachers

WRITING THE ANNUAL GOALS AND PERFORMANCE OBJECTIVES

Writing specific individual goals and objectives for the IEP, and also writing those for the physical education program, involves defining what each student needs and how to incorporate specific individual needs into the program plan. Assessment is used to determine the current level of functioning for an individual with a disability, which leads to appropriate goals and objectives for the IEP. In addition, assessment can assist with determining goals and objectives for an exemplary physical education program plan. Following is a description of goals and objectives, how to compose and prioritize them for the IEP, and how to implement them within the physical education program.

Goals are *statements that indicate the broad, general outcomes desired for the student.* Because goals, by definition, are to be achieved in the future, some students with a disability may not attain a stated goal within the year for which it has been set. However, because IDEA '04 refers to annual goals, every effort should be made to set goals that the student is likely to achieve within one year. It is not usually helpful, in terms of educational planning, to set goals for which the timeline for achievement is longer. On the other hand, goals can be sufficiently broad to be achieved in one year, then set again for the next year. For example, if the goal is to improve ball-handling skills, the student could add several skills one year and several more skills the next year.

Once the current level of performance has been determined and the student's strengths and needed supports have been identified, the goals and benchmarks that set a direction for programming must be established. Physical education goals for individuals with a disability should draw from the areas of physical and motor fitness; fundamental motor skills and patterns; and skills in aquatics, dance, and individual and group games and sports. This definition implies that other behaviors accompanying motor performance in an intramural or lifetime sports context (leisure time) are within the purview of physical education. For some students, it is of far more developmental value to be able to miss a point in a game without engaging in a fight than to learn a new basketball skill. Thus, the behavioral goal should be considered at least equal in value to a goal related to learning the sport skill. Teachers are, therefore, encouraged to consider the student's total needs when planning effective programs of physical education and physical activity.

Examples of typical goals in physical education include improving:

1. Cardiovascular endurance
2. Eye–hand coordination
3. The ability to play cooperatively with peers

These are rather traditionally stated goals, and some school districts would accept them in this form. Most school districts, however, require that the annual goals stated in the IEP be measurable. That is, the statement must include a specific, observable behavior that can be used to measure whether the goal has been met, especially as the behavior is related to the stated curriculum outcomes. Given this criterion, the typical goals in physical education listed above may be rewritten as follows:

1. To improve cardiovascular endurance by scoring at least at the 10th percentile on the APEAS II endurance subtest.
2. To improve eye–hand coordination by catching the ball at least half the time in a softball game.
3. To improve the ability to play cooperatively with peers by participating in a handball or tetherball game daily, taking turns appropriately, following the rules, and demonstrating good sportsmanship.

Objectives, on the other hand, are *short term, are more specific, and are based on the student's present level of performance.* They are "stepping stones" to the goals and are written in such a way that they can be achieved within one year's time or less. An objective generally divides the skills described in the goal into specific (discrete) components (steps). These components are determined through a task analysis procedure and should guide the student through a step-by-step process to accomplish the objective. (See Chapter 10 for a discussion of task analysis.) The components of a performance objective are discussed more fully later in this chapter. In some school districts, the term *benchmark* is used to describe this type of performance objective. Usually, a **benchmark** is defined as *a specific expectation for a student that is based on grade level or specific course curriculum and indicates progress toward achievement of a standard or goal.*

Measurable annual goals (and objectives when included) must contain dates that estimate when the student would reasonably be expected to execute the performance under the stated conditions for the specified criteria.

Several terms used in educational literature are useful in writing goals and objectives and implementing the IEP.

1. **"Behavior"** refers to any visible activity displayed by the student. The word *performance* is

commonly substituted for *behavior*; they are used interchangeably in this text.
2. **"Terminal behavior"** refers to the behavior the student should demonstrate at the end of the period specified by the IEP.
3. **"Standards"** usually refers to what students should know and be able to do. In effect, standards involve "the knowledge and skills essential to a discipline that students are expected to learn" (NASPE, 2004, p. 1).

Purposes for Writing Measurable Goals and Objectives

Measurable goals and objectives serve several purposes. First, they tell the teacher what must be taught. Sometimes, students with a disability have a number of areas of deficit in motor performance, and it can become difficult to know how they are interrelated and should be prioritized. The goals and objectives or benchmarks include the behaviors to be learned and a schedule (or timetable) of estimated accomplishment, helping the teacher to focus on those parameters of performance that are most important at a given point in time.

Second, goals and objectives are written to communicate the order or sequence in which skills must be taught. Because goals are long range, usually addressing more global performances such as improved physical fitness, eye–hand coordination, or playing cooperatively, the teacher must use objectives to sequence the behaviors to be learned. Consider an example from the construction industry: The goal is to build a house, but in working to attain that goal many short-term objectives have to be reached first. The foundation must be laid, the frame erected, the electricity and plumbing installed, and the siding applied. The steps to building the house must be done in a specific sequence, and the accomplishment of any one step alone does not attain the goal of a completed house.

The ability to analyze performance in terms of its component parts and order the parts developmentally is essential for writing performance objectives. Once the objectives are defined, the sequence of instruction is obvious as an integrated whole.

Third, goals and objectives state observable behaviors that indicate what the student has *learned*. Generally, anyone observing the student—parent, teacher, or administrator—can read the goal or objective and conclude through observation whether the student has learned what he or she was supposed to learn. Well-written performance objectives are stated in terms of student behavior and should always begin with the student's name or, when referring to a member of a group, should begin with the phrase, "The student will. . . ."

Parts of Measurable Goals and Objectives

Measurable goals and objectives include three components (Mager, 1997): performance, conditions, and criteria.

Performance. The performance stated in the goal or objective is the observable behavior that proves the student has achieved the goal or objective and learned what was being taught. Physical education should be the easiest area of instruction for writing measurable goals and objectives because most involve observable movement performances. Even in a general physical education class, the vast majority of material taught results in the students' demonstration of learned responses, patterns, or skills. Observable behaviors or performances commonly sought in physical education instruction include: run, jump, leap, skip, hop, somersault, throw, swim, skate, ski, dive, and pitch. Additional performance terms describing motor responses and patterns that are often the focus for developmentally younger individuals include: reach, grasp, roll, bend, push, pull, float, walk, stand, stretch, climb, and kick.

Conditions. The second component found in well-written goals and objectives is a description of the conditions under which the performance will take place. For example, the performance of running can be done under a number of conditions—on the track, with help, without stopping, and so on. The conditions for running are determined by various factors, including the student's needs; the physical environment in which the student is being taught; the student's limitations as a result of a disability; or movement elements such as speed, force, or direction. For example, the performance objective "Johnny will be able to run . . . " could be completed with the following conditions: ". . . without verbal coaxing" (student's needs); ". . . on the grass" (physical environment); ". . . with the use of canes" (student's limitations); and ". . . toward the teacher's voice" (movement element). Thus, it can be seen that performances vary based on what is to be learned and the conditions under which the performance is to occur. The conditions can be changed according to various circumstances.

Criteria. The final element in a well-written goal or objective is the criteria used to determine whether the student has performed at an acceptable level. This element describes the extent or accuracy of the performance, helping the teacher know whether the student has learned enough to go on to the next learning task. For example, the teacher finds that, for Olivia's age group, unless she can run 400 meters on the track in 90 seconds or less, she will not have an adequate opportunity for success in her after-school activity with Special Olympics. Thus, the performance objective of running, with the condition of 400 meters on the track, must meet the criterion of 90 seconds or less to show improved performance and the ability to compete. The criteria, like performance and conditions, can be varied to place greater and greater demands on the student. A variation in the criterion for this particular objective might include gradually reducing the amount of time in which the performance is to be completed. Thus, a series of performance objectives can direct the learning process closer and closer to the goal of improved cardiovascular efficiency.

A decision to place a student into the general physical education class might be based on setting the criteria for performance at a level that represents what age-appropriate peers (general education students) are capable of doing. For example, for a 12-year-old boy, the number of curl-ups to complete within the FITNESSGRAM healthy fitness zone is 18 to 36. The goal statement for a 12-year-old boy might be: "To improve abdominal strength, Michael will increase the number of completed curl-ups to within the healthy fitness zone based on the FITNESSGRAM." Michael's current level of performance indicates that he is able to do eight curl-ups, which puts him below the healthy fitness zone for his age. To help Michael reach his goal, a series of performance objectives, such as the following, can be developed to guide instruction for the coming year:

1. Michael will be able to assume the bent-knee curl-up position with arms extended and hands flat on floor; raise himself 10 or more times without stopping to a slow cadence count of "up, 2, 3, 4"; and lower himself 10 or more times without collapsing, by the end of the 1st grading period (slow cadence of 1001, 1002, 1003, 1004, etc.).

2. Michael will be able to assume the bent-knee curl-up position with arms extended and hands flat on floor; raise himself 12 or more times without stopping to a slow cadence count of "up, 2, 3, 4"; and lower himself 12 or more times without collapsing, by the end of the 2nd grading period (slow cadence of 1001, 1002, 1003, 1004, etc.).

3. Michael will be able to assume the bent-knee curl-up position with arms extended and hands flat on floor; raise himself 16 or more times without stopping to a slow cadence count of "up, 2, 3, 4"; and lower himself 16 or more times to the same cadence count without collapsing, by the end of the 3rd grading period (slow cadence of 1001, 1002, 1003, 1004, etc.).

4. Michael will be able to assume the bent-knee curl-up position with arms extended and hands flat on floor and raise and lower himself 18 or more times without stopping to a slow cadence count of "up, 2, 3, 4," by the end of the 4th grading period (slow cadence of 1001, 1002, 1003, 1004, etc.).

Considering the content and performance standards written by NASPE, the general physical educator and the adapted physical education specialist should work together to plan the program and to write the goals and objectives (benchmarks) for the students. Assessment of the performances of all students should be an ongoing process throughout the school year, but specific criteria and procedures are followed for the IEP process. The examples presented in Table 8.2 use the NASPE standards. Two examples are given for each standard, addressing the needs of a younger student and an older student who could be considered for inclusion in an IEP.

Remember that the examples shown in Table 8.2 are only suggestions. The professional should always write specific and individualized goals and objectives based on the assessment, current level of performance, and needs of the particular student.

Prioritizing Goals and Objectives

Progress may be slow with some students, and change may be difficult to assess. According to Mager (1962, p. 18), "The more objectives you include, the more successfully you will communicate your intent." Thus, by writing several incremental objectives, the educator can make change more easily seen. For example, the following broad objective might be written for a child who is just learning to balance on one foot: "Mario will balance on one foot for five seconds when asked to do so." Because Mario is a five-year-old child with Down syndrome, however, it may be months before he can achieve this objective. An appropriate series of objectives might be:

1. Mario will shift his weight to one foot when given a verbal and visual cue three out of five times.
2. Mario will raise one foot off the ground three out of five times after shifting his weight to the opposite foot.
3. Mario will raise one foot off the ground and balance on the opposite foot for one second, three out of five times, when asked to do so.

TABLE 8.2

Examples of one elementary and one secondary goal and the related goal components based on the NASPE standards.

GOAL	*Content standard #1: Demonstrates competency in motor skills and movement patterns needed to perform a variety of physical activities.*
Conditions:	Given five hula hoops placed next to each other,
Performance:	the student will be able to jump with both feet off the ground at the same time, in a forward direction, using arm swing to propel forward, and maintain a stable landing position;
Criteria:	for 5 or more consecutive jumps on 3 out of 5 trials as observed and recorded by the general and adapted physical education teachers.
GOAL	*Content standard #1: Demonstrates competency in motor skills and movement patterns needed to perform a variety of physical activities*
Conditions:	Given a 50-meter pool,
Performance:	the student will be able to demonstrate 2 swimming strokes with efficiency and smooth movement, using correct mechanics for arm stroke, kicking pattern, and breathing techniques, for one complete lap of the pool, for each stroke;
Criteria:	on 3 out of 5 trials as observed and recorded by the general and adapted physical education teachers.
GOAL	*Content standard #2: Demonstrates understanding of movement concepts, principles, strategies, and tactics as they apply to the learning and performance of physical activities*
Conditions:	When accurately tossing a beanbag to a partner over a 10- to 12-foot distance,
Performance:	the student will be able to identify and demonstrate at least 2 characteristics of a mature underhand throwing pattern (opposition of hand/foot, arm swing, follow-through, position of hand on release, etc.),
Criteria:	for 5 or more exchanges on 3 out of 5 observations/trials as observed and recorded by the general and adapted physical education teachers.
GOAL	*Content standard #2: Demonstrates understanding of movement concepts, principles, strategies, and tactics as they apply to the learning and performance of physical activities*
Conditions:	When asked to rebound the ball against a backboard or wall 3 or more times in succession to increase the number of hits,
Performance:	the student will be able to demonstrate and/or explain a forehand volley for paddle tennis (e.g. move more quickly, return to ready position, amount of force),
Criteria:	when requested by teacher and as indicated by completed task sheet checklist on 2 out of 3 practice trials.
GOAL	*Content standard #3: Participates regularly in physical activity*
Conditions:	Given a physical education homework chart listing days of the week and activity (e.g. flee/chase game or manipulation of objects, such as kicking a soccer ball around the yard or bouncing a tennis ball, walking, swimming),

(continued)

TABLE 8.2 Continued.

Performance:	the student will be able to describe the activity (in written or picture format), participate, and then chart the amount the time completed during each movement opportunity,
Criteria:	for 3 out of 5 days of play activities outside of school hours.
GOAL	**Content standard #3: Participates regularly in physical activity**
Conditions:	Given a pedometer and physical activity log (in written or picture format),
Performance:	the student will set personal goal to increase aerobic fitness by accumulating a specified number of steps during the day, and work on achieving the goal,
Criteria:	for 3 out of 5 days for 3 consecutive weeks.
GOAL	**Content standard #4: Achieves and maintains a health-enhancing level of physical fitness**
Conditions:	When performing tumbling stunts and rolls on a mat,
Performance:	the student will be able to demonstrate support of body weight, by safely and successfully completing a forward roll from straddle position and a frog stand for a minimum of 10 seconds,
Criteria:	on 3 out of 5 observations.
GOAL	**Content standard #4: Achieves and maintains a health-enhancing level of physical fitness**
Conditions:	When provided with access and instruction within the school fitness center,
Performance:	the student will show improved muscular strength and endurance as indicated by an increased number of curl-ups and increased number of seconds for straight arm hang using overhand grasp,
Criteria:	as recorded on individual testing records for pre- and post-testing during October and May.
GOAL	**Content standard #5: Exhibits responsible personal and social behavior that respects self and others in physical activity settings**
Conditions:	Given a recess game or class practice activity,
Performance:	the student will demonstrate the ability to play four-square successfully and interact positively with peers, by rotating appropriately, serving accurately, and leaving a square without argument or yelling and returning to line to repeat task with others,
Criteria:	for 10 minutes or more of play on 3 out of 5 observations.
GOAL	**Content standard #5: Exhibits responsible personal and social behavior that respects self and others in physical activity settings**
Conditions:	During instructional lesson with a large group,
Performance:	the student will use appropriate strategies for effecting behavior change by fully participating without delaying the group process and by contributing to the group,
Criteria:	for 20 minutes of active play on 2 out of 3 days observed.

(continued)

TABLE 8.2 Continued.

GOAL	*Content standard #6: Values physical activity for health, enjoyment, challenge, self-expression, and/or social interaction*
Conditions:	When provided with a new task during class instruction on the playground (climbing) apparatus,
Performance:	the student will approach and attempt the task and be able to maintain appropriate behaviors (i.e. attending, voice tone, composure, sharing turns) while completing task 2 or more times (or for 10 minutes with peers),
Criteria:	on 2 out of 3 days as observed/recorded by the general and adapted physical education teachers.
GOAL	*Content standard #6: Values physical activity for health, enjoyment, challenge, self-expression, and/or social interaction*
Conditions:	When provided with a social dance activity (square or line dance),
Performance:	the student will be able to use his or her wheelchair safely and successfully and maintain pace with partner and group, maintain personal and social space, and indicate to partner (or group) individual needs for assistance,
Criteria:	on 3 out of 5 days of dance practice activities.

4. Mario will balance on one foot for three seconds when asked to do so.
5. Mario will balance on one foot for five seconds when asked to do so.

Physical performance is probably the easiest area for which to write objectives because the behavior is almost always observable. Writing performance objectives for something that is seemingly not observable—for example, understanding, appreciating, knowing, enjoying, or believing—is a bit more challenging. In these instances, students must demonstrate knowledge or appreciation by *doing* something. They may write, recite, identify, explain, construct, list, compare, or contrast. These are observable behaviors that can be compared with the objective. For example, to teach students to appreciate the game of soccer, the educator might use the following objective: "The students will demonstrate an appreciation of soccer by attending at least two soccer games during the fall semester." For this objective, the three components are as follows:

Performance: attending a soccer game (an activity that can be observed)

Condition: during the fall semester

Criterion: two times

One can only assume, based on psychological and educational research, that individuals acquire appreciation through experience, and that the more the students "experience" the game of soccer, the greater their appreciation will be.

Determining Achievement Dates

The inclusion of dates for achieving performance objectives should show progression throughout the school year; that is, the benchmarks should be written in a sequence such that one or more can be achieved every two to three months. To illustrate this sequence, here are some benchmarks that might be appropriate for Olivia, a student who is making a transition into the middle school physical education program.

PERFORMANCE GOAL #4:

Locker-room skills. Given instruction and an opportunity to practice skills, Olivia will be able to demonstrate appropriate locker-room skills on five out of five days as observed and recorded by adapted physical education specialist.

BENCHMARK OR SHORT-TERM OBJECTIVES:

#4.1: Olivia will be able to "dress out" at the beginning of her physical education class by exchanging street clothes for physical education clothing (and reverse the process at the end of class) and maintain possession of her own clothing each day by November 2007.

#4.2: Olivia will be able to use the combination lock or alternative (e.g., key lock, punch lock) and secure her own locker when dressing out each day before class and at the end of class in a timely manner by the end of November 2007 or early December 2007.

#4.3: Olivia will be able to complete the locker-room skills and get to the squad line or the location of class instruction promptly and in the correct position with peers by January 2008.

#4.4: Olivia will be able to maintain a clean physical education uniform and bring clothing home for laundry over the weekend and return it to school on Monday each week by January 2008.

Sometimes specific dates are used instead of terminology such as "by the 1st reporting period" or "by the 2nd grading period." Timelines for the achievement of objectives are very difficult for the beginning teacher to determine. The experienced teacher, who presumably has taught many students similar to the student currently being assessed, has a point of reference from which to predict approximately how rapidly a particular student will progress. A little more effort may be required of the beginning teacher to determine the amount of progress to expect from a student in any given period of time. It may be necessary to locate test norms, preferably ones based on the population that includes this student.

If, for example, Olivia is a student with moderate retardation, her current level of performance could be found on a table of norms based on this population and used in deciding on goals and benchmarks for improving Olivia's physical fitness. The teacher can use the norms by finding Olivia's current raw scores (according to her age) and then moving to the next year's age-level table of raw scores to determine what the next realistic target scores or performances would be.

The term *benchmark* is being used increasingly to describe this type of performance objective. One reason why this system for setting achievement dates is popular is that it is highly compatible with task analysis and facilitates the reporting of progress at the end of scheduled grading periods for the whole school. For example, the elements of a mature, overhand throwing pattern (step forward with opposite foot, full swing of arm, rotation of body, release, and follow-through) might be broken down into four performance objectives, scheduled to be taught and achieved in sequence by the end of each grading period. The annual goals should be based on the curriculum standards for the student's school district and state in the area of physical education.

Consider one more example of developing performance objectives based on test data. Alicia is a 13-year-old student who is blind and scored at the 10th percentile on the standing broad jump. According to the norms provided in Table 8.3 (Winnick & Short, 1985, p. 123), Alicia jumped 18 inches (10P = 18). To project what Alicia would be expected to jump in one year, look at the norms for 14-year-old girls, because she will be another year older at her annual review next year. Even if Alicia makes no progress relative to the norming sample, she would be expected to jump 31 inches. This would place her at the 10th percentile for 14-year-olds. Given instruction suited to her needs, capacities, and limitations, she should be expected to improve at least 5 percentile points (or surpass another 5 percent of the population with visual impairments). In this case, she would be expected to jump 35 inches. With additional extraordinary work on leg power, she may even improve more than this. It is easy to see that a criterion of 24 inches (25th percentile for 13-year-olds) would probably not be challenging for her because it compares her with 13-year-olds when, in fact, she will be a year older. Of course, personal factors must be considered as well. For example, if Alicia is significantly overweight her predicted success might be different.

A series of objectives can be written for three- to four-month intervals, leading to the terminal objective for next year. Thus, Alicia's objectives related to leg power might read as follows on the next page.

TABLE 8.3

Standing broad jump (inches): Percentile table for boys and girls who are blind.

	AGE			
	M	F	M	F
	10–13	10–13	14–17	14–17
PERCENTILE	(N = 23)	(N = 32)	(N = 57)	(N = 41)
45	43	34	61	46
40	43	33	61	45
35	42	30	60	42
30	41	30	57	41
25	38	28	53	40
20	38	24	51	39
15	36	24	49	35
10	36	18	41	31
5	15	12	40	31

Source: Adapted from Winnick, J. P., and Short, F. X. (1985), *Physical Fitness Testing of the Disabled.* Champaign, IL: Human Kinetics.

Alicia will be able to long jump 22 inches on the mat. (dated three months in the future)

Alicia will be able to long jump 26 inches on the mat. (dated six months in the future)

Alicia will be able to long jump 31 inches on the mat. (dated nine months in the future)

Alicia will be able to long jump 35 inches on the mat. (terminal objective defined as the date of the annual review)

When objectives are based on data obtained from criterion-referenced instruments, the change will likely appear to be more linear. Age is a factor that is already accommodated; thus, the next task (or series of tasks) on the instrument is targeted in the performance objective. Table 8.4 presents a sequence of tasks taken from CARE–R (*Curriculum, Assessment, Resources, and Evaluation—Revised*) from the Adapted Physical Education Curriculum of the Division of Special Education, Los Angeles County Office of Education (1998).

The first behavior described in Table 8.4 occurs around 4 months of normal growth and development, the second within 6 to 8 months, the third within 8 to 10 months, and the fourth within 12 to 15 months. It seems appropriate to use these developmental milestones as the performance element in a series of objectives for students who are functioning at that level. What is uncertain is when the milestones will be achieved. It is unlikely that they will be acquired at three-month intervals, as they are by a person who has been following a typical schedule of development. As stated in Chapter 5, however, the student's level of development compared to chronological age can be used as a guideline for how long it may take for each milestone to be developed. For example, a six-year-old function-

TABLE 8.4 CARE–R sequence of tasks.

CURRICULUM ITEM/BEHAVIORAL STATEMENT	LEVEL OF SUPPORT	RUDIMENTARY	EMERGING	FUNCTIONAL	MASTERY
(10.12) Raises trunk with elbow extension and maintains head control (3–5 sec.). (Student will raise trunk from a prone position by bearing weight on hands with elbows extended and head held in midline for three seconds on three out of five trials.)					
(10.17) Demonstrates protective extension. (Student will demonstrate protective extension when placed in a safe falling position [e.g., prone position with chest over bolster, then roll student and bolster forward] by extending arms toward floor on three out of five trials.)					
(10.29) Recovers balance forward, backward, and laterally while in seated position. (Student will recover balance while seated on floor and gently pushed/tilted off balance in each direction—forward, backward, left, and right—on three out of five trials.)					
(10.44) Creeps or hitches up a few stairs (3–5 stairs). (Student will creep up or hitch up [scoot backward up stairs on bottom] three steps on three out of five trials.)					

Source: Los Angeles County Office of Education (1998). *CARE–R: Curriculum, assessment, resources, and evaluation—revised.*

MAKING CONNECTIONS

Example Goals and Corresponding Objectives

For a student with visual impairment who is transitioning to increased inclusion time with peers, with decreasing support from the adapted physical education specialist, the IEP might include the following goal and corresponding objectives in object control skills:

Goal: By June 2007, given instruction and an opportunity to play and practice skills, Billy will be able to demonstrate 3 object control skills (reception/propulsion) within a practice or modified game activity with peers on 3 out of 5 days as observed by general and adapted physical education teachers.

Objective #1: Billy will be able to roll the 8½" playground ball (or alternative) using underhand rolling pattern (back arm swing, bend of knees, release low to ground) and: (a) accurately hit target or partner from 20 to 25 feet away, (b) receive rolling ball from partner when provided with verbal cues to retrieve object coming to him using both hands without passing by him, and (c) demonstrate opposition of hand/foot pattern consistently during play activity or instructional lesson, by March 2007.

Objective #2: Billy will be able to strike or bounce the 13" playground ball with both hands and maintain control and placement of the ball by pushing ball in forward direction over the line and (a) explain necessary accommodation (i.e., calling his name first, etc.), (b) make correct rotation during the game, and (c) be able to exchange ball more than 2 times during a modified four-square game with peers, by April 2007.

Objective #3: Billy will be able to participate in a team game with peers by: (a) throwing soft foam ball over midline more than 12 feet to target person or cone, (b) kicking the rolling ball when pitched to him slowly and running to the correct base position, (c) retrieving objects as they are rolled or softly tossed to him, and (d) explain necessary accommodations to peers when catching objects for safe participation during practice game or instructional lesson with peers, by May 2007.

---

ing at the three-year level of development could be expected to learn at roughly half the rate of a typically developing child because three is one half of six; a six-year-old functioning at the two-year level, at about one third the rate; and so on. The previous learning rate of the child, if known, can be an accurate predictor of the rate of learning and the amount of progress to be achieved. It should be remembered that children do not necessarily learn at the same rate throughout their lives. Furthermore, some areas of learning may be more difficult than others because of the disability. For those children functioning at a very young age of development and predicted to learn in small increments each year, it may be very difficult to determine what skill would represent the next milestone. Task analysis may be used to break the learning steps down further when the increments on a developmental schedule, curriculum, or scale are too big.

Note that these performance guidelines are not scientifically based; rather, they are based on the experience of the authors, research, and a quantification of logical thought. Each child is unique and brings a unique set of capacities and limitations to the learning experience. In the absence of any more systematic or scientifically based guidelines, those suggested here provide a beginning. Some other factors that are likely to be very important and helpful to the educator projecting a learning rate include:

- A knowledge and understanding of the physical education standards (national, state, local) because they may help determine other fundamental skills the student may have.
- Prior rate of motor learning.
- Prior experience or training the student has had in related areas and the progress made (e.g., if Lois has worked on protective extension for two months and made rapid progress, that might affect the projected achievement rate).
- Physical development and health status (e.g., a student has recently been hospitalized, takes various medications, or has been malnourished).
- Motivational and emotional factors (e.g., a student with mental retardation has many variables to consider, such as strength, social skills, language, and comprehension).
- The uneven rate of development for children with autism spectrum disorders.
- Determination of the level and types of support needed for successful performance (e.g., FP = full physical prompt or complete physical support, through a continuum of supports/prompts to I = independence).

MAKING CONNECTIONS

Targeting Appropriate Goals

Jimmy is 12 years old but is developmentally functioning at the 4-year-old level. We do not expect him to start using the skills for Little League participation, as would other 12-year-olds, but we do expect him to begin trying to shift his weight from one foot to the other while swinging an implement across his midline. He might be estimated to make four months' progress in one year because four months is one third of a year, and he is functioning at about one third of his chronological age. Therefore, an appropriate goal for him for a year from now is the next instructional target—shifting his weight while swinging an implement, not fielding ground balls!

The teacher must remember that learning and development do not always progress at a steady rate. Usually, when dealing with physical parameters that require a strictly physiological response to conditioning, the changes in observable performance appear to be steadier. But where cognitive learning is involved, research indicates that observable performance shows rapid gains early in an instructional program, followed by a leveling off or plateau with little or no observable change. Later in the program, an increase in performance is again observable. Thus, it is important for the adapted physical educator to be a good observer of the way a student approaches a new learning task in order to determine whether progress is likely to be rapid or slow at the beginning of instruction. If the student approaches the new task with all of the prerequisite behaviors (e.g., patterns, skills, balance, and strength) and must merely use them in a new and unique way, progress is likely to be rapid. If the entry-level or prerequisite behaviors must be developed, then progress is likely to take more time.

Evaluation of Goals and Objectives

When writing goals and objectives, use vocabulary that defines an observable performance (*demonstrates, shows, performs, lists, describes, identifies, labels, names, selects, explains, writes, tells,* etc.). Motor skills are physical acts that are almost always clearly observable. It is important to remember that goals and objectives related to the other domains of learning (cognitive, communicative, affective, etc.) can only be measured through observable behaviors as well. The following terms do not describe an observable behavior and should be avoided when writing objectives: *understands, knows, appreciates, enjoys, grasps the significance of, believes, has faith in,* and *feels*. Unless terms describing observable behaviors can be associated with these words to demonstrate that these qualities have been acquired, there is virtually no way of measuring whether the objectives have been attained. Figure 8.5 provides a checklist against which written goals and objectives can be compared. Once the educator becomes skilled at writing IEPs, such an aid will not be necessary.

Framework for Goals and Objectives

When writing an IEP, you must keep the "big picture" in mind. One way to do this is to use the framework for the Ecological Model of Student Performance (EMSP; Dunn, Brown, & McGuigan, 1994). The EMSP is a useful team model, especially when working with younger children. The transdisciplinary team is able to work together and meet the challenges of the student. This allows you to view the interaction of the environment (including social environment), student roles and expectations (learning expectations, behavioral expectations, etc.), and curriculum (tasks or skills). Figure 8.6 represents this pictorially. Viewing the goals and objectives for the student in terms of an ecological model can ensure that you write goals and objectives that are accessible, meaningful, and appropriate for the indi-

FIGURE 8.5

Checklist for evaluation of goals and objectives.

1. Do the goal statements refer to target areas of skill development?
2. Given the assessment data, is it probable that these goals could be achieved in a year (i.e., annual period for the IEP)?
3. Do the goals contain observable performances?
4. Do the objectives describe a subskill of the goal?
5. Are the objectives presented in a sequential order that leads to the goal?
6. Do the objectives contain appropriately stated conditions?
7. Do the objectives contain appropriately stated performance criteria that can be measured or observed?

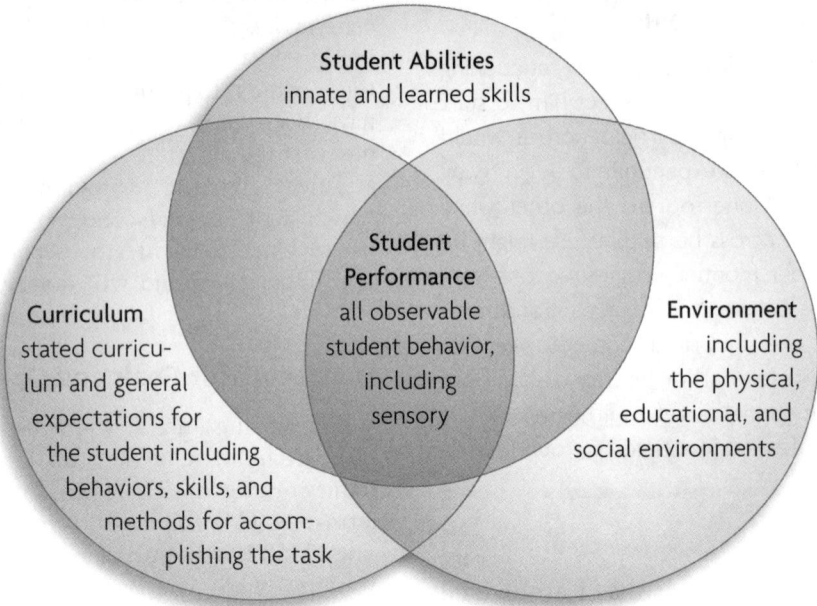

FIGURE 8.6 *Ecological model of student performance.*

Source: Dunn, W., Brown, C., & McGuigan, A. (1994). The ecology of human performance: A framework for considering the effect of context. *American Journal of Occupational Therapy,* 48, 595–607. Copyright © 1994 by the American Occupational Therapy Association, Inc. Reprinted with permission.

vidual student. The following are assumptions to remember when using the ecological model:

1. There is an interaction between student and environment that affects student performance (often referred to as the ecology of the learning environment).
2. Performance is best viewed within the context of daily activities and school routines (look at all of the environments where the student spends time).
3. The environment may support or hinder the student's abilities, especially as it pertains to changes in social abilities and attitudes of the student, staff, and peers.

This global view will help you integrate each IEP within your physical education program plan. Keep this information in mind as you read Chapter 9, Developing and Implementing the Program.

DETERMINING RELATED SERVICES

Another contribution the physical educator may make to the IEP is to help determine any necessary related services. The physical educator usually sees students in a different context than do many of the other professionals who work with them. Furthermore, the physical educator sees students perform in more of a total body effort than most other professionals. It is possible, then, that a student will display behaviors not observed by other members of the multidisciplinary team. It is extremely important that the physical educator be a good observer—of motor performance in particular—in order to recognize significant deviations that may require related services.

The physical educator must have a good understanding of the various roles of the members on the multidisciplinary team and which of those potential team members are available to deliver services to the student. Remember that related services are defined by law as those "services . . . as may be required to assist a child with a disability to benefit from special education" [20 USC 1401 Sec. 602 (26)(A)]. In addition, it is important that you be aware of all state regulations and the policies and procedures of local education agencies and school districts, particularly those addressing referral procedures for related services.

SUMMARY

The primary purpose of a systematic assessment process is to plan an appropriate physical education program for each student who has a disability. Understanding the legal mandates and the procedures for appropriately placing students so they can receive services is the responsibility of the adapted physical educator.

Once a student with a disability is appropriately placed, annual goals, performance objectives (benchmarks), teaching strategies, related services, and the extent to which the student participates in the general physical education program must be identified to complete each student's IEP. Preparing for the IEP meeting requires an extended effort beyond simply gathering motor performance data on the student. With practice, the adapted physical educator will prepare with ease and become an integral part of the IEP team.

Writing appropriate and realistic goals and objectives (benchmarks) is a systematic procedure to be performed by the adapted physical education specialist.

CHAPTER 8 Learning Activities

8.1 Within a small group, discuss the legal requirements of the IEP process. Use a large white board or easel paper to problem solve the ways that the adapted physical educator can meet each of the elements required by law. For example, one element requires that testing and measurement materials and procedures be presented either in the native language of the pupil or in the student's usual mode of communication. How might the adapted physical educator ensure that the student is tested in the appropriate language or mode of communication? Be sure to give examples for each element required by the law.

8.2 Use real data generated from assessment experiences. Determine the age of a student (from the assessment data) and list three possible annual goals and three performance objectives (benchmarks) for each goal that will facilitate meeting the goal within one year. Indicate how you would determine (estimate) achievement dates. List two possible activities that could be used to achieve each of the three goals. Discuss with a classmate the components of performance objectives, or benchmarks, and determine if all are included in those written. Revise the program, if needed, based on the measurement criteria.

8.3 Interview an adapted physical education specialist and gather the following information:

a. The related services available and provided for students within the school district

b. The procedures for making referrals for assessment, especially for those students with motor needs (include any differences within the various age levels: infant, toddler and preschool, high school, etc.)

c. The types and sources of funding for services provided within the school district

d. Tips and suggestions for future physical educators and adapted physical educators

REFERENCES

Block, M. E. (2000). *A teacher's guide to including students with disabilities in regular physical education* (2nd ed.). Baltimore: Brookes.

California Department of Education, Division of Special Education (2002). Individualized Education Program Form. Sacramento, CA: Author. www.cde.ca.gov.

Conatser, P., & Summar, C. (September/October 2004). Individual education programs for adapted physical educators. *Strategies*, 18(1), 35.

Cooper Institute for Aerobics Research, (1994). *FITNESSGRAM Test Administration Manual.* Champaign, IL: Human Kinetics.

Dunn, W., Brown, C., & McGuigan, A. (1994). The ecology of human performance: A framework for considering the effect of context. *American Journal of Occupational Therapy*, 48(7), 595–607.

Los Angeles County Office of Education (1998). *CARE—R: Curriculum, assessment, resources, and evaluation—Revised.* Los Angeles: Author.

Los Angeles Unified School District (in press). *Adapted physical education assessment scale—II (APEAS II).* Los Angeles: Author.

Mach, M. (November/December 2000). Using assistants for physical education. *Strategies*, 14(2), 8.

Mager, R. F. (1997). *Preparing instructional objectives: A critical tool in the development of effective instruction* (3rd ed.). Atlanta, GA: The Center for Effective Performance.

National Association for Sport and Physical Education (NASPE) (2004). *Moving into the future—National standards for physical education* (2nd ed.). St. Louis, MO: Mosby.

National Association for Sport and Physical Education (2005a). *Physical best activity guide: Elementary level* (2nd ed). Champaign, IL: Human Kinetics.

National Association for Sport and Physical Education (2005b). *Physical best activity guide: Middle and high school levels* (2nd ed.). Champaign, IL: Human Kinetics.

Piletic, C., Davis, R., & Aschemeier, A. (May/June 2005). Paraeducators in physical education. *Journal of Physical Education, Recreation, and Dance,* 76(5), 47.

U. S. Education Department (1980). *Individualized education programs (IEPs) OSE policy paper.* Washington, DC: U. S. Government Printing Office.

Vetter, P. (1998). Modified from lecture notes for KIN 401: *Motor assessment for the exceptional individual,* California State Polytechnic University, Pomona.

Waugh, L. M. (September 2004). Digital cameras in elementary adapted physical education. *Teaching Elementary Physical Education,* 15(5), 38.

Winnick, J. P., & Short, F. X. (1985). *Physical fitness testing of the disabled.* Champaign, IL: Human Kinetics.

Winnick, J. P., & Short, F. X. (1999). *The Brockport physical fitness test manual—A health-related test for youths with physical and mental disabilities.* Champaign, IL: Human Kinetics.

CHAPTER 9

Developing and Implementing the Program

Guiding Questions

1. What are some specific methods of organizing a framework for the physical education program plan?

2. How are goals, benchmarks, and objectives from an individualized education program (IEP) incorporated into the physical education program plan?

3. What are some of the necessary components of an effectively implemented program?

4. What are some of the barriers to successful inclusion that relate to the parent, the general physical educator, and the adapted physical education specialist, and how can they be addressed?

5. How does a physical educator appropriately select and adapt activities to meet the ability and needs of each student and for a group of individuals in class at the same time?

6. How can the program adaptations be used to enhance learning for all students in physical education?

Although an IEP is the framework for an individual's education program, each physical educator also must prepare the overall physical education program plan in order to meet the educational needs of all students in the class. A well thought out program plan is a blueprint that encompasses the educational philosophy, curriculum, and activities that enable you to meet the specific needs of each individual. In this chapter, we discuss the various levels or components of the program plan, as well as provide suggestions on how to include individuals with a disability within the general physical education program.

DETERMINING AN APPROPRIATE AND MEANINGFUL PROGRAM

Everything that a professional does within the educational setting relates to curriculum and instruction (i.e., methodology, or how to deliver the content). An important task for physical educators is to think through the process of program planning so that the result is an effective and ever-changing process of facilitating the student's learning.

Sometimes, it is easier to work from a framework, just as the construction worker works from a blueprint. A framework for curriculum and instruction helps guide our thinking and provides a roadmap for effective teaching. The physical educator must think about a series of issues that require decisions. All teachers make similar decisions about the same things no matter what level of ability or age is involved. Each professional must strive to make decisions that are effective and appropriate for each class, and using a framework helps to make these critical decisions. As a physical education teacher, you may choose from a variety of frameworks, or you may be directed by your employer (e.g., school, district, state) to use certain frameworks. The decision-making process is much easier if you identify the framework you will use and learn to use it proficiently to make daily educational decisions.

Physical educators deliver a program every day via movement and physical education activities. The specific activities used are in the curriculum—one part of the framework for making educational decisions. However, beyond that, it is the responsibility of the teacher to make decisions about developmentally appropriate activities, appropriate timing, the use of teachable moments, and the use of appropriate teaching strategies for all students. For example, are you searching for an activity to fill the hour, or are you planning the activities based on the goals of your program? The goals of the program are another component of a framework for decision making. The physical educator should ask him- or herself, "Why am I doing this?" and "What do my students need?" in order to facilitate effective educational planning.

In the program planning process, interwoven components of the framework involve considering the program's time element in conjunction with the curricular direction based on the needs of the students. With regard to the time element, there are many types of planning:

1. The yearly plan
2. The monthly plan
3. The weekly plan
4. The daily plan

Other types may include thematic approaches (e.g., Peace Week, Multicultural Week, Physical Education and Sport Week, Jump Rope for Heart) and unit planning.

Philosophy, Beliefs, and Program Goals

The philosophy, beliefs, and program goals form the foundation of the framework. They provide an anchoring force when the physical educator makes program planning decisions. Planning the curriculum for the program is usually influenced by the following:

1. Mission of the school district
2. School district curriculum focus
3. Physical education curriculum (for school, district, or state, etc.)
4. Teacher's philosophy and goals for the program
5. Students' strengths and areas of need
6. Evaluation procedures (e.g. for program effectiveness, student progress)

The teacher's philosophy (your set of beliefs) should focus on:

1. The role and responsibility of education, including what you believe about the delivery of services for each age group (infant, preschool, elementary, secondary, and throughout the life span).
2. The role and responsibility of physical education, including what you believe students are capable of learning in the physical education setting.
3. The role and responsibility of adapted physical education and the adapted physical educa-

tion specialist, including what you want the student to learn from class instruction and participation.
4. The role and responsibility of the students, including how you want them to learn and how you expect them to perform and behave.

Once you have identified your beliefs (philosophy), the goals of your program easily evolve. For example, "I believe in the enjoyment of play activities" or "I believe in the developmental approach" or "I believe all children can learn." Having goals will enhance your teaching and help you select activities.

Based on the program goals, the teacher makes decisions about the activities and the methods (teaching strategies) to be used to meet them. It is important to become acquainted with a variety of possible activities and teaching methods (e.g., the curriculum areas for physical education and the different teaching styles).

As the professionals gain new information, they continually refine their philosophy and beliefs—it is a step-by-step pattern of growth and change. To become the best teacher that you can be requires learning and change. After you have taught for 10 years, you are a teacher who has 10 years of experience, not a teacher with one year repeated 10 times—if you have constantly learned from your experience. To become an effective teacher, you must be willing to learn and discover new methods, as well as be available to learn more about your students, how they learn, what they already know, and what areas of need should be addressed.

Curriculum

There are various ways of organizing the physical education curricular areas for use with different teaching styles and different student ages. Many school districts or schools provide the teachers with a written curriculum for physical education, and some districts or schools have done the same for adapted physical education. However, some provide neither. Whether your district or school has a formal curriculum or not, it is helpful to understand that there are a variety of models for developing a curriculum. Figures 9.1 through 9.5 are examples of curriculum models.

Physical educators often choose the philosophical model and the teaching styles that reflect the type and amount of instruction that was provided to them during their own educational process. However, by exploring and becoming familiar with a broad base of knowledge, the teacher gains greater

FIGURE 9.1

National Association for Sport and Physical Education (NASPE) standards.

NASPE has developed physical education content standards with guidelines for assessment that are an excellent starting point for professionals thinking about philosophy, program planning, curriculum, goals, and objectives. *Moving Into the Future—National Standards for Physical Education, Second Edition* (2004) describes the six characteristics of a "physically educated person" that result from an appropriately designed and implemented physical education program. The standards also identify the competencies at specific grade levels that guide a student's progress toward achieving the goal of becoming a physically educated person.

A physically educated person:

1. Demonstrates competency in motor skills and movement patterns needed to perform a variety of physical activities.
2. Demonstrates understanding of movement concepts, principles, strategies, and tactics as they apply to the learning and performance of physical activities.
3. Participates regularly in physical activity.
4. Achieves and maintains a health-enhancing level of physical fitness.
5. Exhibits responsible personal and social behavior that respects self and others in physical activity settings.
6. Values physical activity for health, enjoyment, challenge, self-expression, and/or social interaction. (NASPE, 2004, p. 11)

These standards apply to all students and can guide the goals and benchmarks written from the curriculum within each school. Programming ideas using the NASPE standards are discussed in Chapters 12 and 13.

resources and options that can be incorporated into the program plan, benchmarks, and lessons. It is important to remember that there is not just one method of teaching or one discipline to focus on, because we are teaching and interacting with the whole child. The training and experiences of each professional do influence, but should not dictate, the approach used.

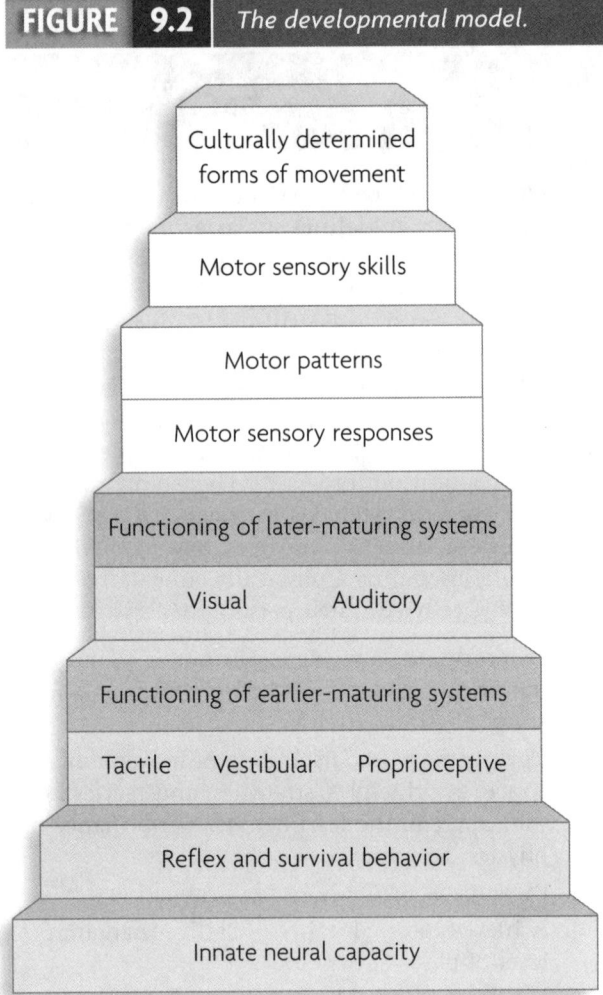

FIGURE 9.2 | The developmental model.

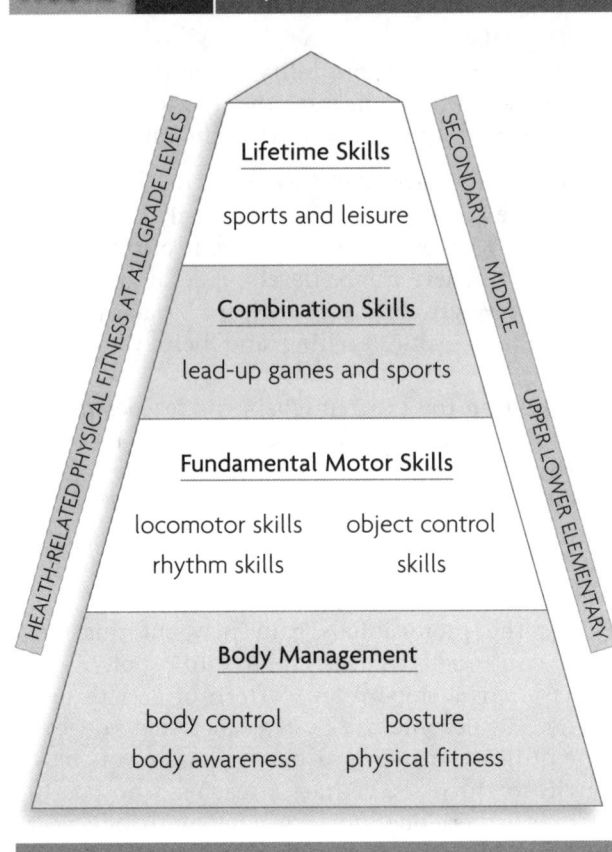

FIGURE 9.3 | Top-down curriculum model.

Source: Adapted from Kelly, L. E. (1991), *Achievement based curriculum: Teaching manual.* Charlottesville: University of Virginia. Used with permission.

The developmental model provides a framework for understanding development that can also be used for developing a curriculum of developmentally appropriate activities.

Program Planning for Inclusion

Before planning specific activities to include individuals with a disability within a general physical education program, the physical educator must develop the general program plan for all students in the class. When planning an effective program for students with a disability, both the general physical education teacher and the adapted physical education specialist must do the following:

1. Gather valid and reliable data on the students' current level of performance.
2. Interpret that data to identify the students' strengths and challenges.
3. Identify goals that are developmentally appropriate, meaningful, and accessible to the students.
4. Determine objectives that will contribute to the students' accomplishment of the goals.
5. Select teaching strategies appropriate to the students' strengths and challenges.
6. Identify, plan, and implement activities that are meaningful and fun, and that contribute to the students' growth, development, and pursuit of an active lifestyle.

The publication *Adapted Physical Education National Standards* (APENS) details specific skills related to these six areas of competency (Kelly, 2006). All adapted physical educators are encouraged to study and learn the components, subcomponents, and content knowledge offered in APENS. Although APENS uses a different organizational format, its standards 8 (Assessment), 9 (Instructional Design and Planning), and 10 (Teaching) are closely related to this section. These skills are important to the planning process for the whole class as well as

FIGURE 9.4 | Activity model.

There are several types of curriculum implementation models for elementary school physical education. Those that are familiar are the traditional curriculum model, which is activity-centered; the unit curriculum model, which focuses on presenting many separate activity units during the school year; the integrated curriculum model, which teaches the relationships between what is learned about movement, motor skills, and performance in various physical education activities; and the movement model, where the emphasis is on movement experiences that result in motor skill development. Common types of activities, such as those listed below, are found in many of these curriculum models:

- Body awareness (e.g., management, balance)
- Locomotor skills
- Continuous movement and physical fitness
- Rhythms and dance
- Stunts and tumbling
- Object control
- Games (e.g., playground, flee/chase, team, cooperative)
- Individual and dual sports
- Team sports
- Health and safety concepts
- Aquatics
- Outdoor education (e.g., adventure courses, community programs)
- Combatives (e.g., self-defense, fencing)

FIGURE 9.5 | Philosophical or theoretical model.

A philosophical or theoretical model organizes the types of movement activities by specific conceptual goals such as those used in the *Physical Education Framework for California Public Schools—Kindergarten through Grade Twelve*. This framework emphasizes three major goals for the physical education curriculum. Supporting and reinforcing each of these goals are underlying disciplines.

Goal: Movement Skills and Movement Knowledge. Students need to develop effective motor skills and to understand the fundamentals of movement by practicing and analyzing purposeful movement.

Disciplines:
1. Motor learning
2. Biomechanics
3. Exercise physiology and health-related physical fitness

Goal: Self-Image and Personal Development. Students need to develop and maintain a positive self-image and strive to become the best that they can be through planned physical activities.

Disciplines:
1. Human growth and development
2. Psychology
3. Aesthetics

Goal: Social Development. Students develop appropriate social behaviors by working independently and with others during planned physical activity.

Disciplines:
1. Sociology
2. Historical perspectives

Source: California State Board of Education (1994), *Physical education framework for California public schools: Kindergarten through grade twelve*. California Department of Education, Sacramento, CA (pp. 16–22). Reprinted with permission.

---

for each individual student and can help you develop an appropriate, effective, and meaningful program for all students.

The program plan for physical education encompasses the general areas of concentration including physical and motor fitness, developmental activities, games and sports, and lifetime sports and activities. The developmental model identifies (in greater detail, but in a somewhat different manner) aspects or levels of activities appropriate in physical education programming. In addition, the program plan includes individualized elements (e.g., supplementary activities, adaptations) for each person with a disability in the class. The best way to determine the physical education program content is to gather documents from the school, district, state, and national levels regarding the framework for physical education, adopted or suggested curriculum, and other guidelines.

The program plan should serve as a guide for implementing physical education activities for individuals with a disability. Each individual should be taught, as needed, to achieve the specific goal or objectives. As much as possible, the class should be taught in groups, with one-to-one instruction occurring briefly or infrequently.

The intent of IDEA '04 is for the student to participate within the general education program as soon and as much as possible—this intent should always be in the mind of the physical educator. For example:

- A preschool student with a hearing impairment may learn best from age-appropriate peers in a structured play activity.

- An elementary student with autism may learn best from participating in selected small group activities and gradually increasing the amount of time with the large group as skills (language, social, and motor) develop.

- A middle school student with cerebral palsy may learn best from a program of selected activities that enhance exposure to interest areas and to recreation and leisure skills, and that develop physical fitness for functional and daily living tasks. For example, two units of volleyball instead of one unit of volleyball and one unit of football; or a full year of conditioning and dance activities to develop strength, endurance, and flexibility.

- A high school student with an emotional disturbance may learn best from a program of individual sports activities or from community programs for bowling, swimming, weight training, or bicycling, when given help to access them.

MAKING CONNECTIONS

Access to the General Physical Education Curriculum

William is a student participating in the general middle school physical education class with his peers. He has weak upper body strength and difficulty grasping and holding on to objects for extended periods of time. He has recently learned how to hold the tennis racquet using his preferred hand and to perform the forward volley while maintaining his grasp after making contact with the ball. He is able to drop the ball with his nonpreferred hand, strike the ball by swinging the racquet, and propel the ball toward the backboard. He is also beginning to practice rebounding the ball off the wall. While the other students in class are attempting to serve and volley the ball to each other, William and another student, who is also practicing rebounding, gain quality skill practice by alternating turns. William is able to practice rebounding and his friend provides some verbal cues while also retrieving the balls William misses.

All children should have access to the general physical education curriculum, but what does "access" mean? Some have interpreted it to mean teaching the general physical education curriculum using any necessary supports and services regardless of the child's developmental level or prerequisite skills, or regardless of the program's meaningfulness or appropriateness. The courts have indicated that equal access does not necessarily mean teaching the general physical education curriculum that is being used at the student's chronological age or grade level. In other words, equal access to the general physical education curriculum requires teaching the skills from a lower grade or developmental level when necessary; for example, teaching basic ball-handling skills (object control) in the racquetball unit instead of the game itself.

Determining the Appropriate Level of Programming

The level of physical education programming for individuals with a disability generally runs the gamut of the developmental model, depending on the individual's age, level of development, strengths, and challenges. For young children, more emphasis can and should be placed on the lower levels of the model to foster their further growth and development. As the student grows older, the physical educator should provide a shift in activities so greater emphasis is placed on those age-appropriate activities found near the top levels of the model. At a younger age, emphasis is more developmental than adapted; for the older student, more emphasis is placed on the adaptation of activity than on developmental patterns.

Activity analysis

As used in this text, **activity analysis** is *a technique for (a) analyzing the sensory, motor, social, and integrative (motor–sensory, perceptual–cognitive) demands of a given activity, or for (b) determining appropriate activities based on the identifiable needs of individuals in a class.* (Figures 9.6 through 9.8 present examples of activity analysis.) By identifying the demands of a given activity, the physical educator is able to:

1. Determine the source of difficulty for the student. This enables the physical educator to select specific remediation activities and determine appropriate adaptations for successful participation in that activity.

2. Determine appropriate activities that can be employed to the benefit of the individuals in the class, as well as the class as a whole. This process facilitates overall program planning.

Activity analysis is similar to task analysis (discussed in Chapter 10), but it looks at a set of tasks (e.g., a game) and a group of individuals (e.g., a class) participating in the tasks.

IMPLEMENTING THE PROGRAM PLAN

After developing the program plan for physical education, participating in the IEP meeting, and prioritizing the goals and objectives for each student, the next task is for you to include the student successfully in the class activities. When implementing the IEP (and your physical education program plan), the main task is to compile and organize your resources effectively.

FIGURE 9.6 Activity analysis 1 (kickball).

MOTOR DEMANDS	SENSORY DEMANDS	SOCIAL DEMANDS	INTEGRATIVE DEMANDS
■ Kicking ■ Running ■ Catching	■ Visual (e.g., tracking object) ■ Proprioceptive (e.g., integrating feedback from contact with moving object) ■ Vestibular (e.g., balance when running, changing direction) ■ Tactile (e.g., integrating feedback from tactile stimuli when catching the ball) ■ Auditory (e.g., locating the sound of the ball bouncing off the ground or the kicker's foot)	■ Turn taking (e.g., waiting for turn) ■ Team participation (e.g., position of player on team) ■ Rules (e.g., understanding strategies, rules, scoring) ■ Competition and cooperation (e.g., working together, fair play)	■ Motor planning ■ Eye–foot coordination ■ Eye–hand coordination ■ Balance ■ Ocular tracking ■ Position in space ■ Timing skills

FIGURE 9.7 Activity analysis 2.

IDENTIFIED NEEDS OF INDIVIDUALS IN CLASS	POSSIBLE PHYSICAL EDUCATION ACTIVITIES
■ Basic motor pattern development (e.g., running, walking) ■ Motor planning ability ■ Visual perception	■ Obstacle courses ■ Follow-the-leader type activities and games ■ Games using playground markings ■ Kickball (see Figure 9.6)

FIGURE 9.8 Activity analysis 3.

IDENTIFIED NEEDS OF CLASS	POSSIBLE GAMES AND SPORTS ACTIVITIES
■ Motor skills of running, throwing, and catching ■ Figure–ground discrimination ■ Visual tracking ■ Balance ■ Eye–hand coordination	■ Line and circle games ■ Tetherball ■ Kickball (lead-up games and activities) ■ Softball (lead-up games and activities) ■ Basketball (lead-up games and activities)

Components of an Effective Program Plan

Some of the necessary components of an effectively implemented program are:

1. *Communication:* Educators must collaborate to determine and implement the types of adaptations and modifications needed within the lessons. Communication between the physical educator and adapted physical educator is important for sharing strategies and problem solving to meet the needs of each student. (Refer to Chapter 2 for a review of techniques for working with other professionals.)
2. *Learning environment:* Determine the space and facilities needed for safe and successful participation. This subject is discussed in Chapters 11 through 13.
3. *Administrative support:* Determine the types of administrative support needed, especially for time to collaborate, schedule classes, and possibly budget for specific materials and equipment needed.
4. *Team interaction:* Determine the amount and types of support needed from other staff members. This is usually designated at the IEP meeting, but now it is time to determine how staff members will function within the lesson and how much time will be spent with the student during the activity. In addition, it is important to set up procedures for requesting resources and support or collaborating with other specialists for assistance when needed, such as working with the speech-language pathologist on specific strategies for giving verbal instructions or using sign language and gestures.
5. *Reporting mechanism:* Determine the types and methods of reporting progress (refer to the appropriate forms from the IEP meetings).
6. *Continuing education:* Determine the staff development needs; request support from school personnel; and make arrangements to attend or use workshops, conferences, and other materials (journals, websites, etc.).

Sequencing Activities

Activities used to achieve the goals and objectives of the program, as well as the IEP, must be sequenced according to logical considerations, including seasonal appropriateness, degree of complexity, and the developmental model.

Seasonal and regional appropriateness. First, at the secondary and upper elementary levels, some consideration must be given to appropriate seasonal activities or instructional units being taught in general physical education. For example, if soccer is a typical seasonal activity in the general physical education classes in the fall, it is appropriate to work on achieving individual performance objectives using soccer and soccer-like activities in adapted physical education, or with adapted physical education support in the general class. These activities may include dribbling the ball with the feet, running, and kicking a stationary or rolling ball. Each of these represents a skill used in soccer that can serve as part of the lead-up sequence for more fully including students with a disability in general physical education classes.

Some activities are included in the physical education curriculum based on the region of the country in which the school is located as well as the season of the school year. Different climates and geographical features facilitate some specialized activities. In addition, some subtle cultural differences are present in various parts of the country. In Southern California, for example, surfing is taught in some schools located near the ocean. Schools in mountain areas often include skiing in the curriculum. Canoeing, fishing, kayaking, rock climbing, and orienteering are taught in many areas near lakes and rivers. It is appropriate for adapted physical education instruction to conform to seasonal and regional differences.

Degree of complexity. A second consideration in sequencing activities is the complexity of the activities. The teacher should start with the simple and progress to the compound and complex motor activities. A student whose current level of performance in kicking a stationary ball is at the 5th percentile on a soccer skills test is certainly not ready to run, intercept, and kick a rolling ball at the goal, as is required in a game of soccer. However, a sequence of activities may be used to shape these game skills:

- Kick a stationary ball while standing.
- Run up to and kick a stationary ball.
- Kick a rolling ball while standing.
- Run up to and kick a rolling ball.
- Run up to, trap, and kick a soccer ball.

In this example, activities are sequenced from the simple to the complex.

Developmental level. The third consideration, fundamental to the other two, is the developmental sequence of activities. For example, a student whose goal is to improve eye–hand and eye–foot coordination should have developmentally sequenced tasks leading from simple to complex within a unit-appropriate context. Thus, a 12-year-old who cannot catch an 8-inch ball cannot be expected to catch and kick a football from a 20-foot distance, even though the unit is being taught in general physical education. Learning to catch and drop-kick a soccer ball or other alternative for the football is just as seasonally appropriate, but it requires developmentally lower-level skills because the ball is larger and round and, therefore, easier to handle.

Students with a disability are most easily supported and integrated within the general physical education program when developmentally appropriate activities and a variety of teaching styles are used. Most physical education curricula and achievement standards are based on a developmental model. Therefore, these can be used to select and write goals and objectives related to the student's educational needs as written in the IEP, as well as for the physical education program plan.

The Importance of Pivotal Skills

One important key to successful inclusion in general physical education is the development of **pivotal skills,** *those skills necessary in order to perform many other skills.* Examples of pivotal skills include pointing, making a choice, following a simple routine, or using a picture schedule. Not only are there social and emotional skills to consider, but it is also appropriate to teach motor patterns and skills that can be applied to participation in the general physical education class. Examples of pivotal motor skills are listed in Table 9.1. Targeting pivotal motor skills through goals and benchmarks may enable a student to access a greater variety of activities and have more successful experiences with peers in the general education class setting.

SUCCESSFUL INCLUSION IN GENERAL PHYSICAL EDUCATION

Inclusion represents one alternative in the continuum of services required by the least restrictive environment mandate contained in IDEA '04. Safely and successfully including students with a disability in the general physical education program can be a positive experience for all participants (teachers and students). A brief discussion of inclusion and tips for its success follow.

Defining Inclusion

Although currently a major focus in education, the term *inclusion* is sometimes misunderstood and misused. **Inclusion** can be described as *an educational procedure and process for children with a disability based on the ethical and legal requirements that each child be educated in the least restrictive environment in which the child's education and related needs can be satisfactorily provided.* The term connotes the following:

- Providing a free, appropriate, public education in the least restrictive environment.
- Embracing the concept of educating all children in the least restrictive environment regardless of clinical or diagnostic labels.
- Creating alternatives that will help general educators address the learning and adjustment problems of children within the regular education setting.
- Uniting the skills of general education and special education so that all children have

TABLE 9.1 *Targeting pivotal motor skills.*

PIVOTAL SKILL EXAMPLES	OTHER SKILLS RELYING ON THE PIVOTAL SKILL
Standing	Walking, running, transfers (e.g., from chair to mat on floor, chair to chair, chair to restroom)
Running	Soccer, long jump, fitness games, fast-moving activities
Two-handed catch	Catching a kickball, softball, or beanbag; playing basketball, baseball
Lower back flexibility	Bending to retrieve an object from the floor, jumping, moving from sit to stand, getting up from the floor
One-foot balance for 3–5 seconds	Kicking a ball, stepping up on a stair or curb, dancing, hopping
Pushing with arms (by extending elbows)	Using doors (especially the emergency exit); some weight-lifting exercises; getting up from the floor; volleyball; some forms of gymnastics, dance, and martial arts

access to the general education curriculum with appropriate supports and services.

Some misuses of inclusion are as follows:

- Wholesale return of all children with a disability to general education classes.
- Permitting children with a disability to remain in general education classes without the needed supports and services.
- Ignoring the needs of some children for the needs of others.
- Using inclusion as a cost-cutting strategy.

When making inclusion decisions, the physical educator should have input regarding the amount and type of support or services needed. All personnel who will work with an individual with a disability, including the physical education generalist and adapted physical education specialist, should be involved in planning and evaluating the student's program. More specifically, the physical educator must obtain data at least yearly to evaluate the student's progress in physical education and the effectiveness of the program. The annual physical education evaluation for an individual with a disability should be shared with those involved in the process of planning, implementing, and evaluating the education program in order to continue and improve services.

The law requires that a determination and explanation be made of the extent to which the student is not educated with students without a disability. In physical education, inclusion may range in frequency from daily (with special services provided in addition to the general physical education program) to very little, or even none at all if, for example, the student is enrolled in a separate school or facility. Depending on the extent of the disability, the student may be able to participate in the regular program for most activities and have accommodations or modifications for other activities. At the secondary level, it may be possible for a student to participate with one class during some units of instruction and another class (or teaching station) for other units. For example, a student who uses a wheelchair may do some field events in a track and field unit but participate in the swimming unit with another instructor in lieu of the running events. Another option is for the student to work on developmental activities with the adapted physical educator, then rejoin his or her class when it moves to an activity in which the student can participate independently.

The extent and frequency of participation with the general education class, like the rest of the IEP, depends on the needs of the student. Therefore, it takes a concerted effort of the physical educator and the interdisciplinary team to explore all opportunities available to best meet the needs of each student. This is one reason why it is important for the physical educator and adapted physical educator to embrace the collaborative consultation model described in Chapter 2.

Every person involved in the process of inclusion contributes to its success. It is helpful to remember that the inclusion of students with a disability, sometimes referred to as "inclusive physical education," is more about an attitude than the placement. The following are tips specific to the physical education teacher:

1. Learn about different disabilities and the characteristics frequently displayed by an individual with a specific disability.
2. Discuss with students without a disability the process and purpose of including individuals with a disability in the general physical education program.
3. Select peers as companion guides and for modeling as necessary for each new activity unit.
4. Constantly reevaluate the effectiveness of the program.
5. Relax and have fun when teaching and interacting with each student with a disability (see Figure 9.9). Help the other students to do the same. (Remember, they are people first and "have" a disability. Person-first language and your "thinking" and perceptions go together.)
6. Keep your perspective. Focus on the whole person, not the disability.
7. Ask the person with a disability about his or her strengths, challenges, areas of need, sugges-

FIGURE 9.9

Relaxing, being enthusiastic, and having fun are fundamental qualities for teachers.

tions for participation and inclusion, preferences or interests, desires, and so on.
8. Let common sense, respect, and consideration be your guide.
9. Be empathetic, compassionate, kind, and friendly to all students.

Barriers to Inclusion

It is an exciting and thrilling experience to see what can happen when people collaborate and take a proactive stance to make positive changes that support an inclusive learning experience. The potential barriers to successful inclusion in physical education can be easily negotiated with effective problem solving and communication between team members. Some of the barriers that might be encountered include:

1. Legal requirements. Implementing the IEP in the general physical education class setting may require more individualized instruction than has usually been presented in class. The responsibility for following the IEP shifts to the general physical educator.

2. Accessibility. Although this is already a legal requirement, some schools have not had the need to modify their facility to accommodate students with a disability (e.g., ramps as alternatives to stairs, Braille signs). A careful analysis of the potential physical barriers prior to the arrival of a student with a disability at a school site can facilitate a smooth and successful transition.

3. Confidentiality (privacy rights). Consideration must be given to protecting confidential information regarding the parents and the student. For the student with a disability, privacy rights protection may even be more rigorous. All personnel should be trained in order to ensure that confidentiality is not breached. It is important to provide information to the class to facilitate the transition of a student with a disability; however, caution should be used when determining what information is shared with other students, parents, and volunteers. Parents of the student with a disability should be encouraged to discuss issues of confidentiality with staff prior to placement.

4. Class size. Although class size is often a "hot" topic of discussion in the educational environment, it is definitely a strong consideration when providing an appropriate program plan. Class size needs (or, more specifically, student to staff ratio) are affected by safety, the type of activity, and the ability of the students to support and help each other, including providing assistance to the student with a disability. Of course, various community, school, and district factors influence class size, including finances, space, educational philosophy, and curriculum. Examples of strategies that may help compensate for a large class size include peer buddy programs, team teaching, volunteer programs, strategic assignment of instructional assistants (i.e., paraeducators), and careful scheduling of collaboration time between adapted and general physical educators.

5. Attitudes. Sometimes, a variety of attitudes exist toward the inclusion of students with a disability in the general physical education setting. The attitudes of the physical educator, general education students, special educators, parents, and administrators can all influence the experience. If the program plan is to be implemented successfully, all participants must perceive the inclusion of the student with a disability in a positive way. This might mean a change in how grades are assigned, progress is indicated, and the social environment is prepared. A range of disability awareness activities can be very helpful to support positive attitudes among both students and adults.

In addition, specific barriers may arise when the parents, special educator, and general education teacher experience change. It is important to use a problem-solving approach to address these concerns in developing the program. In-service training and collaboration are important channels for sharing information and creating options.

Some of the barriers to successful inclusion may be voiced in the lunch room or on the field during activities. These should be addressed in the IEP meetings, as well as during transition planning meetings, collaborative planning meetings, and problem-solving sessions. For example, the adapted physical educator may have a deep commitment to the progress and success of a student he or she serves and, therefore, may have difficulty "sharing" the interaction, information, and responsibility for the educational program with other staff in the general education setting. This attitude may be reflected by such comments as:

- "The physical education teacher may not have the expertise to work with a student with traumatic brain injury."
- "It is difficult to implement the IEP within the general education setting."
- "My students will not get as much individual attention in the larger group."
- "My students may become isolated from their peers."

- "There might not be enough supervision to meet the student's needs."

The general physical education teacher may lack knowledge or understanding of a disability. This may create concerns that are reflected in such statements as:

- "I don't know how to work with a student with a disability."
- "No one notified me that this student was coming to my class."
- "The student may need more assistance than I am able to provide."
- "The student might take too much time away from the other students."
- "I don't know how to address the goals and objectives in the large group."
- "I am afraid that she will be teased or become a scapegoat."
- "I am not sure how the other parents will react or what they will say."
- "Will the parent of the student with a disability be more demanding of my time?"
- "What kinds of support and assistance will be provided?"

The parents' concerns are often similar to those of both the general and adapted physical educators. Statements heard often include:

- "I am not sure that the physical education teacher will have the expertise or time necessary to meet my child's needs."
- "I am worried about my child's self-esteem and acceptance within the larger group activities."
- "Will my child be safe?"
- "Will less instruction or attention be provided?"
- "I want my child to have the opportunity to be with his peers—he has that right!"
- "I want one-on-one supervision of my child within the group."
- "How will you communicate progress to me?" Or, "I would like to have a daily note indicating what my child is doing in class."

These are all valid ideas and concerns that school professionals, parents, and students must address in order to develop and implement an effective program for all students.

The inclusion of a student with a disability in the general education program is not just a legal right, but also a social and ethical right. The benefits outweigh the challenges (barriers) because more positive attitudes are developed in an environment of accepting change and valuing differences. Other benefits include improved social skills and cooperation, enhanced communication skills, improved accessibility to curriculum and facilities, and increased sharing. The best approach to providing a successful program that includes the student with a disability and meets the needs of all students in the class is to use a team approach and collaboration (see Chapter 2).

TEACHING STRATEGIES FOR ALL STUDENTS

Before we discuss some teaching suggestions and strategies to use in the physical education program, two words must be defined and described. First, **accommodations** are *those instructional strategies (e.g., materials, modality of presentation, grouping) or learning environment elements (e.g., position in class structure) that are adapted for students with a disability.* The instructional strategies and learning environments may be the same for all classes or activities in the school day for a particular student, but several specific strategies apply to physical education. Second, **modifications** are *those changes in the program and curriculum that are required when the accommodations will not effectively allow the participation of the student with a disability in the general education program.* Modifications are usually extensive changes that are based on the student's needs and involve adjusting the content of the curriculum. Modifications, therefore, should be used only after all possible accommodations have been considered and determined ineffective.

Appropriate adaptations in the general physical education program should be determined by the teacher, often with the assistance of the adapted physical education specialist. Parents and other specialists may need to be consulted as well. Once identified, these adaptations may be implemented by the general physical education teacher, a teaching assistant, the adapted physical education specialist, or any other person (e.g., peer tutor) who participates in the activities. The list in Table 9.2 was compiled from a variety of sources, including the suggested list developed by AAHPERD (1976a), regular program adaptations from the Riverside Unified School District Adapted Physical Education program, and personal experience of the authors. Educators should review the list frequently and use it as a guide for designing adaptations that enhance learning by all students in the inclusive setting.

When implementing the lesson, the teacher may use several adaptation categories to provide successful experiences to all students participating in the activities. These categories should be considered as continuums when planning all parts of the lesson: warm-up exercises, cool-down activities, skill

TABLE 9.2 *Program adaptations for general physical education and examples.*

Formation	*Space to be used, boundaries of play, placement or positioning of students within the large group*

- Permit the substitution or interchange of game or activity duties by analyzing and assigning positions in games. For example, rotate one person with another or use two players for one position.
- Modify facilities by limiting the play area to increase the level of participation.
- Provide environmental markers, such as poly spots, cones, ropes, and starting and ending points, to identify boundaries.

Equipment	*Type, size, and number to be used*

- Modify the size, shape, and weight of the equipment to vary speed and performance standards; for example, more air for better bounce, less air for kicking practice.
- Use colored balls, beeper balls, nerf balls, longer or shorter striking implements, lowered targets, and lightweight objects.
- Supply one piece of equipment for each student when the instruction is on object-control skills or manipulative tasks.
- Use pedometers, computers, textbooks, or reading books.

Number of Players	*Number of students, groupings, number of stations and participants at each station*

- The division of students into groups is based on equity and opportunity to participate.
- Use a variety of grouping strategies, such as 2 groups of 25 students or 25 groups of 2 students, 10 groups of 5 students or 5 groups of 10 students.
- The number of stations depends on lesson focus (intent) as well as the practice necessary for participants.

Rules	*Simple to complex, changing rules (including class rules) as needed with the number of rules appropriate to the skills of the group (as many as the students can reliably remember)*

- All changes in rules should include, not exclude, students. For example, in a game of softball, fielders must toss ball to three or four teammates prior to throwing to a base when a student with a physical disability is at bat, or each person on the team has a turn at bat before changing runners and fielders.
- All changes in rules must emphasize cooperation.
- All changes in rules must ensure the safety of all participants.

Objectives	*Skill levels to be taught, lesson focus (affective, cognitive, social, motor, etc.)*

- Provide successful learning for all students by having different objectives for various students in the same activity.
- Allow students to set their own goals.
- Allow skill adaptations (e.g., catching ball after one bounce instead of catching it in flight), monitor heart rate.

(continued)

TABLE 9.2 Continued.

Environment	Social environment, facilities, sensory environment, additional supplies or materials to be used

- Use peer tutors as student assistants (e.g., to work on individual skills or for assistance in locker room).
- Reverse adaptations by having the general education student assume a specific disability (e.g., use a wheelchair or a blindfold, or use sign language to give directions).
- Motivate the students (e.g., with tangible reinforcers or with verbal praise, encouragement, and feedback provided from the teacher to students and from student to student such as "high fives," thumbs-up, or behavioral momentum).
- Vary the team selection procedures and group size to encourage interaction and initiation.
- Make allowances for rule changes during extreme weather or varying facility conditions (e.g., temperature and clothing worn, using indoor space for an outdoor game).

Language	Directions given, concepts required, problem solving required, different languages used, including the type of responses that students make to each other and to the adults in class

- Use clear, specific, and age-appropriate instructions.
- Use positive, enthusiastic, calm, and patient emotional content.
- Use gestures, demonstrations, sign language, or pictures to enhance understanding of directions and concepts.

---

instruction, practice activity, game, and so on. For example, when considering formation, it can be from small to large, wide to narrow, or in an open or closed space. When considering equipment, it can be small to large sizes, light to dark colors, heavy to light weights, or smooth to rough textures. Asking students to identify the numerous changes that can be made can make this a fun learning experience for students as well.

The following suggestions for pacing the lesson and teaching strategies facilitate the inclusion of students in the activity.

1. Allow for a variation in time scheduling and lesson pacing to:
   a. Provide extra practice time and practice repetitions.
   b. Permit students to rest at their own discretion; space rest intervals for students with limited endurance or a short attention span.
   c. Divide the student's physical education experiences between general physical education and adapted physical education as appropriate.
   d. Accommodate the attention and interest levels of all students.
   e. Provide a balance between vigorous and less demanding activities.
   f. Allow for flexible scheduling when participating in units of activity, such as two units of tennis rather than one tennis and one wrestling; the decision should be based on the appropriateness of the activity, accessibility, and student interests.
2. Use teaching strategies that allow different responses such as:
   a. Using experiences that allow all students to have the maximum time on the task.
   b. Using activities in which contact is made and maintained with a partner, small group, or object. This is especially useful for students with a visual impairment.
   c. Avoiding or modifying elimination-type games and activities.
   d. Varying the teaching modes by using peer models, repeating directions, or using demonstrations. This is especially useful for students with a speech, language, or communication disability.
   e. Dividing large groups into smaller groups. This is especially useful for students with autism.

f. Progressing slowly and building new concepts and skills on familiar learning experiences.

At this point, there is great temptation to look at specific disabilities and learn about teaching strategies that apply to individuals with each particular disability. Although it is true that the adapted physical educator should consider certain strategies based on a student's disability, it is imperative that the teacher remember that each student is an individual. Therefore, the selection of specific teaching strategies, adaptations, and accommodations should be made on the basis of the individual student's profile of strengths and challenges (see Chapters 3 and 4), and not merely on the disability.

There is variability within the disability, variability within the activity, and variability within each individual. For example, not all children who are blind need a sighted guide for running the track, and those who need a guide for track may not need a guide for other activities. Not all children with severe mental retardation need physical prompting to initiate movement. Not all children with asthma have to limit their cardiovascular endurance activities. Table 9.3 is offered as a guideline to help the teacher begin the process of selecting interventions for individual students. Although the adaptations are listed by disability category, they can cross categories and can be used for all students as needed, including those who do not have an identified disability.

Effective teachers continually collect a library of information, ideas, and resources so that they can modify their program plan each year to best meet the needs of individuals enrolled in their classes. The remaining chapters offer a myriad of teaching strategies, adaptations, resources, and activity ideas that will assist the practitioner to enrich and broaden the program plan.

> ## Teaching Tip
>
> **IS EYE CONTACT IMPORTANT?** • When working with children with autism, it may be important to give a specific direction that elicits a motor response instead of trying to force eye contact. Because each student has individual needs, consider your intent and reason for wanting eye contact before requiring it from a child. In general, eye contact is a facial expression that communicates attention to the speaker or task. However, children with autism often have difficulty connecting facial expression with communicative intent and may use their peripheral vision instead of their central vision. Therefore, eye contact may be unrelated to whether a child with autism is actually attending or not.

TABLE 9.3 Adaptations commonly needed for children with a specific disability.

Listed below are suggested adaptations (sometimes referred to as interventions) that can be used with students with a disability to facilitate safe and successful participation. *It cannot be stated strongly enough that there is no substitute for getting to know each student as an individual.* Furthermore, it is the professional's responsibility to individualize the programming for each student. Thus, these are only offered as suggestions to get you started in identifying your own successful adaptations for students within your class. (For additional information on specific disabilities and movement attributes, refer to Appendix C.)

CATEGORY	SUCCESSFUL ADAPTATIONS
Considerations for all students	■ Ideal: collaborate with OT, PT, SLP, classroom teacher, and other team members. The team approach is used to facilitate students' increased participation, language development, independence, and social interaction.
	■ Questions for the specialist: (1) Why am I doing this activity? (i.e., focus on the meaningfulness of the activity for each learner) (2) What supports does the student need in order to participate safely and successfully in the activity?
	■ Consider equipment selection: color, size, type, shape, texture, weight, etc.
	■ Consider safety and protection needed, as well as behavioral support and expectations.

(continued)

TABLE 9.3 *Continued.*

CATEGORY	SUCCESSFUL ADAPTATIONS
Student with autism Common strengths: visual learners; learn and follow routines	■ Provide behavior support and expectations, such as structure; routine; consistency; behavioral momentum; and specific, frequent positive reinforcement that is meaningful. ■ Use visual cues, demonstrations, modeling, auditory cues, environmental markers (e.g., picture communication, clearly marked boundaries, target areas for start/stop). ■ Consider sensory needs (e.g., accommodate noise responses, tactile sensitivity, and proprioceptive needs to calm or vestibular needs to alert).
Student with cerebral palsy (ambulatory) Common strength: socially engaged	■ Consider safety and balance (agility) (e.g., positioning or placement in a group and the need for environmental supports). ■ Modify pacing and distances (e.g., shorter distances, variable pacing of the lesson, need for rest). ■ Consider equipment selection (e.g., lighter weight equipment, suspended objects for striking). ■ Contraindications: the student may need protection from falling because of poor protective extension responses and balance; jumping should be on soft surfaces; and students should be guided in their efforts until good patterns are established so that they can become familiar with their own correct performances.
Student using a wheelchair Common strength: socially engaged	■ Consider comfort, fatigue, and pain management (e.g., comfortable, soft seating; positioning for subluxations or contractures). ■ Provide for surface changes, transitions, and inclement weather (e.g., transition from grass to blacktop, indoors to outdoors; avoid extreme weather conditions), especially for students using a manual wheelchair. ■ Consider alternative activities (e.g., small group, parallel activity). ■ Collaborate with general physical education teacher, occupational and/or physical therapist, or others for activity and location planning prior to lesson presentation for full and successful participation. ■ Facilitate advocacy and assertiveness (e.g., asking for assistance when needed, changing rules of play).
Student with deafness and/or blindness Common strengths: tactile, vestibular, proprioceptive learners	■ Communication should provide tactile or sign cues, be simple and concrete, and be specific and consistent. For example, use objects for transition, such as a rope or chain link to represent the swings. ■ Activities should be structured, routine, developmental, and with clearly defined boundaries of play. For example, set up a pathway of travel (e.g., straight line, circle, square) or a rope leading to each task. ■ Place emphasis on age-appropriate, meaningful, functional, and leisure time activities that can be practiced in a variety of settings.
Student with emotional disturbance Common strength: physical capacity	■ Learning environment should provide structure, routine, and consistency; firm and fair procedures; clear consequences; and calm interactions. ■ Spend maximum time on task activities and in smaller groups; minimize lining up or waiting in line; use noncompetitive games and activities. ■ Emphasize the importance of participation and fun, reinforce attempts, reduce distractions, provide choices, and plan for supervision (when needed).

(continued)

TABLE 9.3 Continued.

CATEGORY	SUCCESSFUL ADAPTATIONS
Student with hearing impairment Common strengths: visual learners, socially engaged	■ Use total communication, sign language, demonstrations, and gestures to give instructions and provide feedback; use experiential instruction for language concepts. It is especially important to understand the differences between sign language and lip reading (e.g., not exaggerating volume, pitch, pronunciations, or movement of the face or hands). ■ Change the task to accommodate balance difficulties. ■ Be aware of students using cochlear implants and the necessity to avoid static electricity for safety and care of the implant. ■ Strategies for group interaction: position the student near the speaker, ask student to follow the example of classmates, instruct classmates to establish eye contact before propelling objects, and use signals for team interaction.
Student with mental retardation, including Down syndrome Common strength: multimodal learners	■ Provide simple, concrete, one-step directions that are consistent and matched with the student's language level. ■ Use firm, consistent, and routine behavior support techniques to foster independence. ■ Allow for delayed responses, structured choice making, and self-help skills for independence; facilitate age-appropriate social skills within the group setting. ■ Use peer buddies to facilitate participation without "doing for" the student. ■ Use caution with inverted positions, e.g., Atlanto-Axial Instability (AAI) release for tumbling and sports participation, diving, and soccer, for students with Down syndrome.
Student with multiple disabilities Common strengths: depend on specific configuration of disabilities	■ Seek out medical information for specific or rare syndromes and their characteristics and contraindications (e.g., rare condition, spinal abnormality). ■ For neurological disability, learn about seizure control and management. ■ Use the learning, teaching, and activity strategies suggested for students with mental retardation, visual impairment, and specific learning disability.
Student with other health impairment Common strengths: cognitive and language abilities are often intact	■ Be aware of the student's medical status: current information, contraindications, and procedures to be used in the physical activity setting (e.g., using the inhaler prior to physical education class). ■ Pace activities and lessons to provide for active and rest intervals that are appropriate. ■ Consult and collaborate with nurse and parents for medications and physician information, and update as needed (e.g., sugar level check before activity, amount of time needed before participating after treatment, amount and intensity of exercise after radiation treatment). ■ Provide "germ-free" environment for play (e.g., not sitting on floor, providing individual equipment, limiting exposure to children who have a virus or cold). ■ Share updated medical information with general physical educator and paraprofessionals.
Student with intracranial shunt Common strengths: ambulatory, socially engaged	■ Use caution with inverted positions (e.g., tumbling, playground apparatus, "cherry-pickers" exercise) and backward movements (e.g., locomotor patterns, use of scooterboards). ■ In ball-handling activities, change game rules, use small groups, use adaptive equipment. ■ In large group activities, control roughness and flying objects, use a safe position within the group, and appropriately pace activities.

(continued)

TABLE 9.3	*Continued.*
CATEGORY	**SUCCESSFUL ADAPTATIONS**
	■ Use caution with jumping or jarring movements, especially on blacktop (e.g., jump rope, jumping, hopping); protect from blows to head.
Student with specific learning disability Common strength: active learners (learn by doing)	■ Use familiar words; use a variety of words (vocabulary) to describe the same movement (e.g., labels, categories, descriptions). ■ Provide directions that are simple and concrete; provide one-step instructions unless student can process more than one at a time. ■ Allow for uneven and unpredictable performances and behaviors; provide highly structured activities, clear expectations, and flexibility in class procedures as needed. ■ Provide time for delayed responses (e.g., to process instruction and then initiate movement); provide time for verbal rehearsal (e.g., to practice "what is to be performed" or "what was just performed"); provide opportunities for successful experiences and positive support for appropriate social skills.
Student with speech-language impairment Common strength: physical capacity	■ Use familiar words and supplement with visual cues (e.g., gestures, objects, demonstrations); use a variety of words (vocabulary) to describe the same movements if needed (e.g., labels, categories, descriptions). ■ Provide directions that are simple and concrete. ■ Provide time for delayed responses (e.g., to process instruction and then initiate movement); provide time for verbal rehearsal (e.g., to practice "what is to be performed" or "what was just performed"); encourage and allow student to point, gesture, or use explanations and similar words to increase the listener's understanding of expressive language.
Student with traumatic brain injury Common strengths: depend on type of injury	■ For student with impaired balance, provide safe positioning of student within the large group setting, appropriate pacing of activity, and identification of environmental obstacles (e.g., changes in surface, obstacles, playground apparatus). ■ For student with impaired processing, use specific language for direction and instruction, and appropriate modality choice for teaching (e.g., visual, auditory, kinesthetic, or a combination). ■ Accommodate for time delays, variable responses, and changes in fitness or emotional levels and stamina. ■ Emphasize task analysis. ■ Consider safety and protection precautions (e.g., helmet, if necessary), type of equipment used (e.g., lightweight and soft, size, color), visual cues for boundaries of play, and the possibility of student's poor judgment of own abilities.
Student with visual impairment Common strength: auditory and tactile learners	■ Use sound cues; bell ball; size, texture, and distance changes; bright colors. See Figure 9.10. ■ Consider selection of specific words for location or position in space and "anchoring" student in relation to the group. ■ Use prompts, such as peer buddy or physical prompts, to help student initially learn skill; consider use of sighted guide techniques. ■ Consider safety precautions for potentially dangerous situations that may cause additional eye damage, including appropriate lighting and protection from glare, environmental obstacles, or hazards.

FIGURE 9.10 For students with a visual impairment, using a large ball can assist in developing eye–hand coordination.

PARAEDUCATORS

The use of paraeducators requires some extra effort on the part of the physical educator but can serve to enhance the physical education program. Therefore, the physical educator should make the paraeducators who are part of their physical education program feel as though what they are doing is important (see Figure 9.11).

Guidelines for Using Paraeducators in Physical Education

The following five guidelines for the use of paraeducators are important considerations for teachers.

1. Assign paraeducators to important, significant tasks. Certainly, some necessary tasks are not the most desirable chores to delegate to paraeducators, including taking roll and transporting equipment to and from the activity area. The key in assigning paraeducators to these sorts of tasks is that the physical educator should also be seen doing the same tasks. Physical educators should ask themselves, "Would I be willing to do the job I have asked the paraeducator to do?" If the answer is yes, more than likely you are assigning appropriate, needed, and meaningful tasks that will enhance their performance of duties.

Paraeducators are usually most helpful when given a well-defined job that is within their capabilities. Therefore, the individual skills and abilities of the particular paraeducator should be considered. For example, before asking a paraeducator to help move equipment, it is wise to make sure that the person has an adequate level of strength and endurance to do the job.

2. Provide regular in-service education. Sessions held at the beginning of each semester, school year, or instructional unit may include information on program and class procedures, general goals, and the assignment of specific tasks. As the instructor and director of the program, whether it is the instructional program or an extracurricular activity such as Special Olympics or Unified Sports, it is the physical educator's responsibility to analyze what the paraeducators need to know, what knowledge they bring to the experience, and what the paraeducators will do with the information that is given them. Then, the in-service education program can be planned accordingly.

3. Assign specific tasks. Assigning a specific task such as, "Line up the class in two lines, have them practice the bounce-pass back and forth in partners for five minutes, then divide them into four groups and run the bounce-pass relay that we did last week" is an example of a specific task. This is far more clear to any paraeducator than merely saying, "Drill the students on the bounce-pass." Obviously, the second, more general request assumes that the paraeducator knows what a drill is and how to set one up. Providing more specific information for the paraeducator is even better. For example, the physical educator might add to the assigned task for the bounce-pass drill, "Remind Johnny to step forward with his left foot, and keep trying to get Susie to use her stump to support the ball."

4. Clearly state the expected student performance. The physical educator must make clear to the paraeducator the performance that is expected from the students. The physical educator may have noted in the previous class period that Johnny could step forward with his left foot but needed to be reminded to do it consistently. So that Johnny does not regress while the paraeducator is directing the drill, the paraeducator must be given infor-

FIGURE 9.11

Paraeducators at schools and programs such as the Special Olympics and Wheelchair Games give hundreds of hours of their time to make these programs successful.

mation as to what to expect from Johnny. Some paraeducators are more capable, more observant, and better trained than others. The amount and type of input from the physical educator must be based on these qualities.

5. Keep records of each paraeducator's work. It is always best to document the work of paraeducators just as one would document the progress of students. There are numerous reasons why this should be done, the most important of which is so that the physical educator can give periodic and appropriate recognition. Another reason is to provide employers or other agencies with information about the nature and quality of the service delivered by the paraeducator. Information that should be kept includes a running record of the number of hours worked in the physical education program, a log of the type and quality of the work being done by the paraeducator, and notes on reliability and dependability.

Clearly, paraeducators come with a variety of skills, personal qualities, experiences, and backgrounds. The skillful educator will match each paraeducator to appropriate tasks to enhance the quality of the program for students.

Helping Paraeducators Assist with Physical Activity

The following pointers can be passed on to paraeducators to help them to be more effective when assisting students with a disability in physical activity:

1. Think about how the body works. To help students learn a new skill or pattern, it is important to know how the body works. Think about how the limbs and trunk move; better yet, go through the movement yourself and pay particular attention to what your body does. Then, assist the student by moving the body parts in the same order and through the same motion.

2. Break the skill into parts. Most of us do not learn an entire skill all at one time. Teach each small segment of the skill in order and, as they are learned, put the segments together. This is very much like learning the words to a new song. You learn the first verse, then the chorus; then, you practice those two parts together before going on to the second verse.

3. Teach movement parts in order. The sequence of movement parts can be very critical in some activities. For example, a child cannot do the hopping part of a skip before stepping and shifting the body weight to one foot. In other activities, one component can be learned before others that ordinarily come in a different order in the game. For example, a child can learn to shoot the basketball at the hoop before learning to dribble or pass the ball.

4. Be the model. Let the student imitate the movements of another student or yourself. Some students learn best this way, and there is no need to confuse the issue with a lot of verbal directions. Start by saying, "Watch me." Demonstrate, then say, "Now you do it."

5. Move with the student. Many concepts of movement can be taught by moving with the students while they are learning. The concept of running "fast," for example, may be "felt" only if someone runs with the student, holding on to his or her hand and moving along at a fast pace. Exaggerate arm movements and facial expressions, if necessary, to get the point across.

6. Use cues. Often, single-word cues can be used to remind the student what to do. This technique is used in coaching all the time. Words like *back*, *down*, and *up*, as well as phrases such as *hands up*, *thumbs up*, and *roll over*, can provide a means of assisting a student who is learning a movement sequence.

7. Keep the instructional periods short. Look for signs of fatigue and boredom. All of us get tired of doing the same thing eventually, no matter how motivated we might have been at the beginning. Students with a disability are no different. In about 15 to 20 minutes, most young children tire of a structured activity. Thirty to 45 minutes is about enough, even for older students. If instructional periods are controlled by the school schedule, break up the available time into two or three parts.

8. Make it fun. At first, learning a new skill may not seem like fun. Make the instructional time as much fun as possible, and reinforce the notion that being successful is fun even though the effort was a repetitious drill. Reward the student for every attempt, even if unsuccessful, with a "nice try" or something like, "You are really doing a good job of stepping forward when you pass the ball, Johnny!" Eventually, students will develop their own measures of success and the external rewards will not be necessary. Physical or gestural praise such as high fives, thumbs-up, or clapping may be used, especially with students who have difficulty processing language.

9. Provide as much success as possible. Do everything you can to help the student feel successful. This is especially important during the early stages of learning new skills. The student will, however, have periodic opportunities to experience mild failure if the level of challenge is appropriate. Put the student in situations in which success is most likely, such as near the net in volleyball or right in front of the basket in basketball, or shorten the basepaths in softball and kickball. Once skills are learned and success is consistent, change these variables so the students with a disability are playing more like other students.

SUMMARY

The physical educator who effectively includes individuals with a disability in physical education programs must not only be able to plan specific activities to accomplish the goals and objectives of a particular student's IEP, but must do so within the general program plan for all students in the class. This requires an activity analysis, selection of the appropriate level of activity, development of the program plan, and use of appropriate accommodations and supports. To accomplish these purposes, the physical educator should focus on ability instead of disability, ensure safety but not overprotection in the activities, and provide challenges for all students. The process of collaboration, especially with paraeducators, and the use of carefully selected adaptations will result in an effective and successful program of activities for all children.

CHAPTER 9

Learning Activities

9.1 Research and identify basic beliefs and philosophies regarding physical education and curriculum development. Present the basic components of a philosophy to a group. Include how it might be incorporated into a physical education program plan.

9.2 Select one specific philosophical model to follow and one NASPE standard to incorporate in a program plan, and prepare a three-week unit of instruction, including the specific age levels and the types of accommodations provided for specific disabilities within the class. Include a discussion of how the philosophical model matches the curriculum plan presented. Do this activity as a small group or as a whole class.

9.3 With a group, use a physical education program plan (yearly, monthly, weekly, or daily) and incorporate the program adaptations for general physical education into the plan (Table 9.2). Specifically, each group should discuss, design, and implement (role-play or demonstrate to the class) how the adaptations can be applied to a specific movement activity.

9.4 Discuss the legal, social, and ethical rights of a student with a disability to participate in the general physical education program. Choose one possible barrier and brainstorm solutions. Role-play the situation for the whole class.

REFERENCES

American Alliance for Health, Physical Education, Recreation, and Dance (AAHPERD, 1976a). *Physical activities for impaired, disabled, and handicapped individuals.* Reston, VA: Author.

American Alliance for Health, Physical Education, Recreation, and Dance (AAHPERD, 1976b). *Physical education, recreation, and related programs for autistic and emotionally disturbed children.* Reston, VA: Author.

Ashworth, S. (1992). The spectrum and teacher education. *Journal of Health, Physical Education, Recreation, and Dance, 63*(1), 32–35.

Block, M. E. (1994). *A teacher's guide to including students with disabilities in regular physical education.* Baltimore: Brookes.

California State Board of Education (1994). *Physical education framework for California public schools—kindergarten through grade twelve.* Sacramento, CA: Author

Coleman, M. (July/August 2003). Let's really make the curriculum K–12. *Strategies, 16*(6), 15.

Driver, S., Harmon, M., & Block, M. (September 2003). Devising a safe and successful physical education program for children with a brain injury. *Journal of Physical Education, Recreation, and Dance, 74*(7), 41.

Hilgenbrinck, L. C., Pyfer, J., & Castle, N. (April 2004). Students with cochlear implants: Teaching considerations for physical education. *Journal of Physical Education, Recreation, and Dance, 75*(4), 28.

Jones, K. J., & Block, M. E. (March/April 2006). Including an autistic middle school child in general physical education: A case study. *Strategies, 19*(4), 13.

Kelly, L. E. (1991). *Achievement-based curriculum: Teaching manual.* Charlottesville, VA: University of Virginia.

Kelly, L. E. (2006). *Adapted physical education national standards (APENS).* Champaign, IL: Human Kinetics.

Lieberman, L., Lytle, R., & Irwin, G. (November/December 2003). Ideas for including a student with quadriplegia into physical education. *Strategies, 17*(2), 21.

Mager, R. F. (1997). *Preparing instructional objectives: A critical tool in the development of effective instruction* (3rd ed.). Atlanta, GA: The Center for Effective Performance.

Mitchell, M. (September/October 2003). The ABC's of teaching in physical education. *Strategies, 17*(1), 36.

Mosston, M. (1992). Tug-o-war, no more: Meeting teaching-learning objectives using the spectrum of teacher styles. *Journal of Health, Physical Education, Recreation, and Dance, 63*(1), 27–31.

Mosston, M., & Ashworth, S. (1994). *Teaching physical education* (4th ed.). New York: Merrill.

National Association for Sport and Physical Education (NASPE, 2004). *Moving into the future—National standards for physical education, second edition.* Oxon Hill, MD: AAHPERD Publications.

Sanders, S. W. (1992). *Designing preschool movement programs.* Champaign, IL: Human Kinetics.

Seaman, J. A., & DePauw, K. P. (1989). *The new adapted physical education: A developmental approach* (2nd ed.). Mountain View, CA: Mayfield.

CHAPTER 10
Strategies for Meeting Individual Needs

Guiding Questions

1. What are the factors that affect learning, and how do they apply to students with a disability?

2. What are some of the methods of individualized instruction?

3. What are three behavior modification techniques, and how are they applied in the general and special education settings?

4. What is the purpose of task analysis?

5. Why must, and how can, behavior support techniques be used successfully in physical education?

6. What are some of the influences of sensory responsiveness on behavior?

To plan, implement, and evaluate effective physical education programs for individuals with a disability, you must master a variety of teaching strategies. The physical educator must understand (1) the process of learning, including the factors that affect learning, (2) individualized instruction, (3) adaptation techniques, (4) task analysis, (5) creating a positive environment, and (6) positive behavior support. The physical educator must rely on and be able to use a variety of creative strategies based on the developmental approach to support the differing needs of individuals with a disability.

THE PROCESS OF LEARNING

Learning, which is *a relatively permanent change in behavior that results from experience and training*, is the outcome of the successful interaction between the individual and the environment. It is a process of adaptation to the environment and a progression from simple to complex adjustments (Lawther, 1978).

Laws of Learning

E. L. Thorndike (Thorndike, Bregman, Tilton, & Woodyard, 1928), a pioneer in learning theory, identified three laws of learning: (1) the law of effect, (2) the law of frequency, and (3) the law of readiness. The *law of effect* refers to the sense of accomplishment and feeling of satisfaction that aid the learning process. Knowing that one has learned and has made progress enhances subsequent learning. The *law of frequency* refers to how often time is spent learning. Repetition is necessary for the attainment of particular levels of learning. The *law of readiness* means that, for optimal learning to take place, the learner must be prepared to absorb the material presented. Very little learning occurs when a person is not receptive and interested.

Factors That Affect Learning

Both the teacher and the learner bring factors that affect learning to the learning situation. The mental conditions (e.g., preconceived ideas, distractions, shyness, boredom, mental block, and fear) and physical conditions (e.g., fatigue, illness, and discomfort) of both teacher and student can negatively or positively influence learning. The teacher's approach, physical mannerisms, speech quality, patience, relationship to class, and levels of expectation are examples of conditions that the teacher can control to influence the learning process positively. An awareness of the presence and effect of these conditions is the first step in meeting students' individual needs and selecting appropriate strategies.

The literature on motor learning describes other factors that influence the learning process, particularly for individuals with a disability but also for those without a disability.

1. **Amount and type of practice** refers to *whether practice is concentrated into one large unit (massed) or done at intervals (distributed)*. Students generally learn motor activities more readily if practice (exposure or experience) is distributed. Practice distributed over time is better for some individuals with a disability. Daily physical education and continuous practice of a specific motor activity will enhance the progress and ability levels of students. If the student is distractible or hyperactive or has a short attention span, shorter periods of practice with breaks are definitely more beneficial.

2. **Methods of learning** refers to *learning material as a whole or breaking it down into parts*. The "part" method is better for learning and practicing unfamiliar motor activities. The "whole" method is better used with familiar activities and is more effective for the more intelligent learner. Both methods are discussed as instructional techniques later in the chapter. Physical educators should consider the range of whole and part methods as viable options for instructing individuals with a disability depending on the nature of the material and the conditions impinging on the learning process.

3. **Meaningfulness of activity** refers to *how meaningful the material is to the learner*. The familiar tends to be more meaningful; teaching from known activities to the unknown enhances the learning process. As with individuals without a disability, the meaningfulness of the activity is important to learning for the student with a disability. If an activity is not meaningful, a learner may not readily understand it. You may think that some individuals with a disability, such as those with emotional disturbance, severe mental retardation, or multiple disabilities, may find no meaning in the activity except that imposed by a teacher. However, these students often find meaning in those activities in which they:

- Can see closure; for example, filling a bucket with balls instead of counting the number of throws for throwing practice
- Receive immediate reinforcement; for example, running a lap and receiving a hug
- Engage in simple social interaction; for example, running next to a peer

4. **Activity versus passivity** refers to *the level of involvement with the material by the learner.* Learners who are more actively involved in the process tend to learn faster.

5. **Knowledge of results** occurs *when learners actually know what they have done.* Knowledge of results refers to verbal or nonverbal feedback. Providing reinforcement as a form of knowledge of results through verbal, nonverbal, and even tangible or activity reinforcers when students have done well may be even more important for those with limited cognitive ability.

6. **Transfer of learning (generalization)** refers to *the effect that previous learning or experience has on the learning of a subsequent task.* **Positive transfer** means that *the previous experience (usually of a similar nature) enhances the learning of subsequent tasks*; **negative transfer** means that *a previous experience interferes with subsequent learning.* Transfer of learning is variable among students with a disability. Generally, the type of transfer of learning (positive or negative) is closely related to the innate neural capacity and intellectual capabilities of the person. You should not assume with students with a severe disability that any transfer has taken place. Some particular disabilities, such as autism, create additional difficulties with transfer of learning regardless of the level of cognition. Instructional planning may have to include specific activities to teach transfer of learning (generalization). For example, once a student learns to catch and throw accurately, he or she may require instruction to apply those skills to different types of balls, different games, different settings (e.g., school, park), and playing with a variety of partners (e.g., peers, family members, recreation leaders).

7. **Plateaus in learning** is the name for *the "leveling off" or the temporary stoppage of learning at a given ability level that tends to occur normally in the process of learning.* Plateaus in learning are more common among individuals with a disability than in the general population, both in frequency and duration. However, predicting the occurrence or duration of plateaus is difficult, and some disabilities, such as autism spectrum disorders, are associated with uneven development in general.

8. **Retention** is *the degree of persistence of learning over periods of no practice* (Lawther, 1978). Retention, or memory, is better with meaningful, active learning in which the learners have knowledge of their progress. Overlearning can contribute to better retention, unless the activity becomes boring or uninteresting to the student. Retention, or memory, is variable among individuals with a disability. Those with retardation or a processing dysfunction (i.e., lack of integration) may not retain a given level of motor ability over a period of time without practice. Allowing time and experience for overlearning for individuals with mental retardation, severe or multiple disabilities, or a learning disability is considered appropriate programming. In addition, teaching skills that these students can regularly access in order to aid retention is appropriate. These skills tend to have meaning for them, which further reinforces retention.

9. **Motivation** refers to *being aroused to action.* Psychological alertness and interest in a particular task tend to enhance learning. Often, students with a disability such as autism, mental retardation, multiple disabilities, and learning disabilities require extrinsic sources of motivation when other students are intrinsically motivated. The principle remains the same with *all* students—the greater the motivation, the better the chance for improved learning and performance. (Motivation is discussed in relation to behavior support later in this chapter.)

10. **Feedback** refers to *information that arrives constantly during an activity as a consequence of one's own response or as new information input from external sources* (Robb, 1972). It is used to compare present

> ## *Teaching Tip*
> **EXTRINSIC MOTIVATION** • Learning is difficult for many students with a disability. They do not experience the intrinsic motivation of self-satisfaction and success in learning activities as often as individuals without a disability. Providing extrinsic motivation is often a key factor in boosting learning rates.

MAKING CONNECTIONS

Bicycle Riding: Meaningful or Not?

James is a seven-year-old boy with mental retardation and a high interest in mechanical objects. He rides his tricycle on family bike rides several times a week and helps his dad maintain and repair the family bikes. Learning to ride a two-wheeled bike at school is meaningful to him, as well as easily accessible.

Mark is a seven-year-old boy with mental retardation. He loves ball games and plays soccer regularly at a local park. He lives in an apartment and few people he knows ride bikes. Learning to ride a two-wheeled bike at school is not meaningful or accessible to him.

behavior to a reference response. Feedback is necessary to motor function and is associated with information fed back into the central nervous system (CNS) via the sensory systems. Appropriate, high-quality feedback is of utmost importance to individuals with a disability. Many disabilities involve a neurological impairment that alters sensory feedback. Individuals with a physical disability may have a reduction in the amount of sensory feedback they receive because of dysfunction in some body parts. These are two examples of individuals with a disability who may have to be provided with more, less, or different types of feedback than other students in order to optimize learning.

INDIVIDUALIZED INSTRUCTION

Developing instruction intended to meet individual needs may seem like a challenging task to the physical education teacher. Individualized instruction is not synonymous with one-to-one instruction, although that is considered one of the appropriate contexts. Designing instruction to meet individual needs involves understanding the individual students; knowing their needs, limitations, and capacities; and developing appropriate strategies for working with them. An entire class may be engaged in one activity, but a teacher may vary the levels of expectation, the quality and type of communication he or she uses, and the particular performances he or she emphasizes for each student. (For further information on the individualized education program [IEP], see Chapters 8 and 9.)

Styles, techniques, and methods of instruction are many and varied. Although each teacher usually develops a personal teaching style, it is important that every teacher be aware of and be able to use a variety of methods and techniques.

The term **strategy** is used to refer to *the myriad styles, techniques, and methods used in concert at any given time by any given teacher.* The strategies used may vary from one activity to another and from one student to another. The variability among individuals with a disability makes it imperative that the physical educator have a variety of strategies available. The remainder of this section discusses selected strategies and techniques that can be used to individualize instruction.

Part and Whole Methods

In the true **part method,** *the parts of an activity are learned and practiced as parts.* After all of the parts have been learned, they are put together into the whole activity. An example of using this method is teaching the skills of dribbling, shooting, and passing before presenting the experience of the entire basketball game. For a gymnastics routine, the part method of instruction involves learning and practicing each of the stunts independently, adding transitions between each stunt, and then putting them together into the whole routine.

The true **whole method** refers to *practicing only the whole activity.* This method involves practicing the entire task with as many repetitions as needed to reach criteria. This method has value for instructing individuals with a disability depending on the size of the task and the severity of the disabling condition. In general, the greater the degree of impairment, the smaller the whole task must be for this method to be effective. Students with autism or severe retardation often have to learn and practice a particular task (e.g., throwing) as a whole. Breaking the pattern into parts is unlikely to benefit students who have severe processing deficits or mental retardation. The whole method allows individuals with a disability to make their own modifications and adaptations or point out problem areas so the teacher can help them make modifications and adaptations. The whole method may also be beneficial to those who have normal or above normal intelligence.

The **whole-to-part-to-whole method** is *a commonly used variation of the part and whole methods in which the whole task is presented, then the parts are taught and put back into the whole.* Teaching the javelin throw using this method involves presenting the entire skill and having the student attempt it; teaching the approach, release, and follow-through or a combination of these; allowing the student to practice each part separately; and then practicing the whole skill again. For jumping, the motor pattern is experienced as a whole; then the arm swing, forward body lean, two-footed take-off, and landing are taught and practiced; and finally, jumping as a whole is practiced. Most individuals with a disability could benefit from this or a slightly modified whole-part-whole approach. The smaller the steps, the greater the chance that students with severe disabilities can attain success. The rate of instruction and the amount of repetition and reinforcement are inversely related to the progress that can be made by individuals with a disability. The slower the pace of instruction and the greater the repetition, the better the progress the person with a disability is likely to make.

In the **progressive part method,** *the parts are taught sequentially and then put together progressively.* For example, part one and part two are taught separately, then combined and refined; part three is taught and subsequently combined with the previously learned parts one and two. This pattern continues until the whole skill or task is taught. The progressive part method is commonly used to teach the steps in a folk dance. This technique is especially good for those students who have difficulty processing, sequencing, or integrating information (e.g., those with mental retardation or emotional disturbance). For example, a student can be taught the appropriate stance for jumping (part one) and the proper arm swing (part two) in combination; then the two-footed take-off and landing (part three). By progressing at the child's own rate and teaching the parts along the way, teachers can help a student who has not developed it naturally to learn the jumping pattern. The progressive part method is similar to chaining strategies, discussed later in this chapter.

Explanation and Demonstration

Explanation and demonstration (Mosston, 1989) are commonly used in physical education programs. The key for this method's use is combining and focusing on explanation (verbal, written, or manual communication) and actual demonstration. For example, teachers can describe an overhand throw orally, in writing, or using a pictorial form, and then demonstrate it themselves or have a student demonstrate it. (A slight variation includes an explanation during the demonstration.) Explanation and demonstration serve to reinforce learning, and most students can profit from this instructional technique. For some individuals, such as those with a language, hearing, or mental disability, the explanation might have limited effectiveness, but the demonstration might help them put the pieces together. Conversely, students with a visual impairment or those with visual perception disorders may derive more meaning from the explanation than the demonstration. Still others, such as those with an emotional disturbance, deafness/blindness, severe mental retardation, or multiple disabilities may require additional assistance or adaptation of instruction (e.g., physical guidance, tactile input, or anchoring).

Guided Discovery (Movement Exploration)

In the **guided discovery** approach to teaching, *the teacher takes the learner through small, sequential discoveries until the ultimate focus or selected goal is reached* (Mosston, 1989). Teachers can use guided discovery effectively when the entire class determines the best way to modify a game for fair and equal participation. Because guided discovery involves cognitive processing, it can be used both as an approach to instruction and as a means to encourage the processing of information. Students with a mild disability might find this approach most interesting for

FIGURE 10.1

A slanted rope is presented to a child to help him learn how high to jump (guided discovery and problem solving).

discovering the best methods of moving or adapting within their physical environment (see Figure 10.1).

Students who use a wheelchair and have limited movement may also present an excellent challenge to the class as a whole in discovering new and innovative ways to move or problem solve. For example, the class could experiment with how to accommodate limited movements such as low strength for propelling an object (e.g., muscular dystrophy) or consider how to explore and continue to change the rules of play to accommodate a slower pace of movement (e.g., negotiating a wheelchair around the play space).

Problem Solving

Problem solving is *a specific method that allows students the freedom to investigate various ways of moving and using their bodies*. The teacher tells the students what to do, but not how to do it. The "how" of the activity is the invention of the student. For example, the teacher tells the students to balance on five different body parts. Each student then discovers how many different ways he or she can balance on five body parts (see Figure 10.2). Or the teacher tells a student to throw a basketball to a classmate in as many ways as possible, prompting the student to explore the multitude of choices. The problem-solving approach is often used in movement exploration and movement education curricula.

Problem solving is a good strategy to use when teaching a class in which most students have a dis-

FIGURE 10.2

These children are responding to the command "balance on two body parts" as part of a movement exploration exercise.

ability. Generally, students who can benefit the most include those with a perceptual–motor deficit, short attention span, poor body image, low retention, poor self-esteem and self-identity, low tolerance for competitive activities, emotional or behavioral disorders, and learning disability. Problem solving provides the opportunity for success-oriented, failure-free motor activity and can be used to reinforce or help develop cognitive or perceptual processing ability. Problem solving can also help students develop a tolerance for diversity within the group. To assist students with tolerating diversity, the teacher should point out that students have found more than one way to "solve the problem" or "do the task." The activity "People to People" (Figure 10.3) is a very flexible way to present different movement challenges for children to solve together. In "People to People," the introduction of language concepts as they relate to movement and position in space, as well as how each individual moves, is a fun experience for all children.

ADAPTATION TECHNIQUES

To develop appropriate strategies to meet the needs of individual students, the physical educator must consider adapting methods of instruction, the learning environment, and the physical activity.

Techniques for Adapting Instruction

To meet the needs of students with a disability in physical education, instructors often find it necessary to modify or adapt specific behaviors. The degree and type of adaptation vary with the needs, limitations, and capacities of the student with a disability and with the educational setting. The ability to adapt and modify any of the methods of instruction described previously, and to make a careful selection among the techniques discussed in this section, will prove to be a valuable asset.

Although closely related to the instruction methods, techniques for the adaptation of instruction often escape notice. When performed skillfully, these techniques do not require additional teacher effort and do enhance learning. The following six instructional adaptations increase communication to the learner:

1. Adapting language
2. Making concepts concrete
3. Sequencing tasks
4. Allowing time for learning
5. Using multisenses
6. Using creative teaching techniques

Adapting language

Language provides the basis for communication. Before learning can occur, the student's understanding must take place. This understanding is founded in communication between the instructor and the learner. Therefore, adaptation of language may be necessary for a student to understand fully the instruction given. The teacher must remember that language can be verbal, nonverbal, or para-verbal (i.e., pitch, cadence, and tone).

Individuals with a language impairment are not the only ones for whom adaptation of language is necessary. Students who are very young or functioning at a young age level, who have processing or behavioral disorders, or who have mental, sensory, or minor language disabilities all require that attention be given to the instructor's use of language.

The seemingly simple sentence "I want you to run to the fence and run back" can cause a great deal of confusion to students who have some language difficulty. Some can process only the first few words, and the first part of the command blocks out the last (retroactive inhibition). Others can process only the last few words, and the last part of the command blocks out the first (proactive inhibition). Many students may follow what the rest of the class does without understanding the task; some simply may not respond at all.

Some students will hear and understand "run" or "run to the fence," and they will probably run somewhere, but they might not run back. Fortunately, many of the students will process the entire sentence or at least pick up the key words ("run," "fence," and "run back") and complete the task appropriately.

FIGURE 10.3 "People to People."

1. **Purpose/objective(s):** to connect with a partner according to a signal given by the "director."
   a. Listen for verbal cue and direction to change positions
   b. Change partners
   c. Practice locomotor patterns
   d. Identify body parts
   e. Participate in a cooperative activity with others
   f. Encourage interaction with others in class
2. **Supplies/equipment:** none needed
3. **Playing area/formation:** playground, gymnasium, or classroom with children in scattered formation
4. **Number of players:** entire class/group
5. **Rules:**
   a. With all the children in a scattered formation around the play space, each child should be standing "back to back" or "elbow to elbow" or "toe to toe" with a partner to begin the game.
   b. The number of children should be uneven. If the number is even, then the teacher can be another player.
   c. One child will be without a partner and is designated the "director." This child gives a verbal cue of the body position and/or body part to connect as the signal for everyone to change partners, with the extra player seeking a partner also. The director says "people to people" to indicate when everyone should begin moving.
   d. Everyone moves around the space quickly, locating a new partner and making contact with the partner as directed (touching knees, toes, elbows, etc.).
   e. The person who does not have a partner can then become the director, giving the next signal to the group.
   f. The game continues with changes provided, such as the type of locomotor pattern used to move around the space, different body parts and/or positions for the partners to connect, or different ending positions (e.g., sitting, standing, kneeling, etc.).
6. **Suggestions to incorporate language concept instruction:**
   a. Encourage children to use different body parts, such as "shoulder to shoulder," "calf to calf," "ankle to ankle," "knee to knee," etc.
   b. Encourage children to use left/right sides of the body, such as "right hand to right hand," "left elbow to left knee," etc.
   c. Encourage children to use social greetings when meeting a new person, such as "hello" and shaking hands or introducing themselves and asking the partner's name.
   d. Encourage children to share their favorite color, food, or game, or the name of their pet as they meet a new partner.
7. **Suggestions for other adaptations of lesson focus:**
   a. Encourage children to use different speeds, such as fast, slow, etc.
   b. Encourage children to use different levels, such as high, medium, low.
   c. Encourage children to use different directions, such as forward, backward, sideways, etc.
   d. Encourage children to use different pathways, such as straight, zigzag, curved, etc.
   e. Other commands can be given, such as "walk like an elephant," "slide like you are on ice skates," etc. (Academic instructional themes can be incorporated as well, such as seasons, animals, transportation, insects, dinosaurs, etc.)
   f. This activity is very useful to promote disability awareness because the children get to know others in class and practice solving suggested challenges such as the following:
      1. How can you move around the space with one hand behind your back and touch shoulder to shoulder with a partner?
      2. How can we move around the space and connect "People to People" when some of us can't hear the words?
      3. How can we move around the space and connect "People to People" when many of us cannot see? (How would we do that safely?)
      4. How can we move around the space and connect "People to People" when many of us are using wheelchairs? walkers? crutches?

Source: K. Omoto (1985). *People to People,* Unpublished.

You can adapt language in many ways, but the first step is always to be aware of the language you use and to observe your students' responses to language. In addition, gathering information from school records or other adults who know the students is often helpful. You may find it necessary to make appropriate language adjustments, such as shortening your sentences or statements. You could easily shorten a sentence such as the one mentioned earlier to "Run to the fence and run back." Students with a severe language impairment (this is not intended as a category but as a descriptor of individuals with a disability in any category) may benefit most from the abbreviated phrase "run fence, run back." Other modifications to simplify language include the following:

- Simplify the words used (e.g., "next to" rather than "beside," "in back of" rather than "behind," "same or not same" rather than "alike or different").
- Use single-meaning words, especially action words (e.g., "run to first base" rather than "go to first base," "step back" rather than "get back").
- Give only one command at a time or as many pieces of information as the child can process at once.
- Say the command and demonstrate the task, unless the demonstration inhibits (blocks out) the command.
- Use the "explore–listen–do" approach. First, let the students explore the area or equipment, then ask them to stand or sit quietly away from the equipment or play area while you give verbal instructions. Finally, have the students do the instructed task. (This approach is often effective for students with attention difficulties, sensory impairments, or sensory-seeking behaviors.)
- Give the command and participate with the students in the task. For example, say, "up" while holding and lifting a parachute with the class; say, "ready, set, run," then begin running around the track.
- Ask the student to repeat the command before performing (verbal rehearsal). This serves as a check of what the student has processed, reinforcement for language development, encouragement of language use, and verbal practice of what is to be physically performed.
- Have the student verbally repeat what he or she performed when the task is completed to provide more practice of the "verbal rehearsal."
- Provide language-processing time after each short sentence by waiting for a response. Teach-

MAKING CONNECTIONS

Explore–Listen–Do

Ms. Sims is working on throwing skills with her first grade adapted physical education class of 10 students with such disabilities as autism, mental retardation, and language disability. She is using animal-shaped beanbags for the lesson. At the beginning of class, the students sit in a circle. Ms. Sims walks around the circle one time, giving one beanbag to each student to hold. She immediately goes around the circle again, asking the students to put their beanbags in the bucket she is holding (this is the "explore" portion of the strategy). Next, she demonstrates throwing a beanbag at a target, stepping over a line to practice weight shifting (this is the "listen" portion of the strategy). Finally, the students line up horizontally and are given several beanbags each to practice throwing (this is the "do" portion of the strategy).

ers may want to train themselves to do this by silently counting off seconds to themselves before speaking or expecting a response. Ten seconds is usually a good place to start, then change the amount of "wait time" as needed.

- Combine verbal instruction with visual cues. As previously mentioned, demonstration is one type of visual cue. In addition, it may be helpful to display equipment while telling students what to do with it or to point to an area to be used. The use of pictures, icons, and even photos as visual cues to augment verbal communication is often very effective, particularly if a sequence of steps is involved or students must move from station to station. Some examples of using visual cues to augment verbal communication include:

  a. Gesture: "Run to the fence (point to fence) and run back (point to or touch the poly spot on which a student is standing)."

  b. Sign language: "Run (sign the word *run*) to the fence (sign the word *fence*) and run (sign the word *run*) back (sign word for *back/return*)."

  c. Picture or icon: Show students the three pictures "run," "fence," and "bench," which are placed in left to right sequence. Point to each as you say, "Run to the fence and back."

  d. Use the Picture Exchange Communication System (PECS), as depicted in Figure 10.4.

Making concepts concrete

Making concepts concrete goes hand in hand with the appropriate use of language. The focus is on making the task or activity as clear and meaningful as possible. For example, the teacher might ask, "How many ways can you make a circle? Can you *draw* one on paper, *form* one with your hands, *bend* your body into the shape of a circle, *join hands* with the rest of the class in the shape of a circle, *form* the shape with a rope individually or with a partner, and so on?" Each requires action, yet there is no specific action word in the question. This provides students with multiple concrete opportunities to practice the concept "circle" by doing, seeing, and hearing it.

The physical educator can communicate precisely what is desired by choosing the most appropriate action words, then teach the concept of "circle" through demonstration and cues. Using lines painted or drawn on the ground is an example of providing a cue to make the concepts of "lining up" or "making a circle" more concrete. For students who have limited mental ability or those with a high need for structure and routine (e.g., individuals with autism, emotional disturbance, severe mental retardation), using the same words consistently to denote an activity or convey a specific meaning is often necessary. In other words, for some students the concept is associated with one word or cue.

Using simple visual imagery is another way to make concepts concrete. For example, suggest a comparative object for the concept by saying, "Make a circle like this hoop," "Make your body round like a ball," or "Roll with your body straight like a pencil." If you combine this strategy with the use of visual cues (described in the previous section) by showing students the object mentioned, you may further increase instructional effectiveness.

Finally, relying on common patterns (e.g., left to right, top to bottom), common words, and natural boundaries or landmarks (e.g., edge of grass, sidewalk, fence) will help to make concepts concrete for many students. In addition, it may aid in the generalization of skills and in teaching pivotal skills (see Chapter 9, Table 9.1 for examples).

FIGURE 10.4

The adapted physical educator collaborates with this student's classroom teacher and the speech-language pathologist to make pictures related to specific physical activities available from the Picture Exchange Communication System (PECS; Frost & Bondy, 1994) book.

Sequencing tasks

To sequence a task, the learner must have the ability to understand and perform the movements in a prerequisite order. The command, "Walk to the door" given to a seated individual requires the individual to take many steps prior to actually walking to the door: the person must hear, process, and prepare to respond; adjust the body in preparation for standing; stand up; and walk. If a student is having difficulty with a sequence of events, accomplishing the task may be a major challenge. You must be aware of this and assist either verbally or manually at any given step in the sequence. For example, you ask a student with a language impairment or autism to do a forward roll. You may find it necessary to instruct the student in each step of the forward roll: "Stand on the mat, bend your knees (squat down), place your hands on the mat, lean forward, tuck your head," and so on. For many students with a disability, you should not make the assumption that they have fully processed and understood the steps to be taken to complete the task.

Teaching Tip

CONCRETE CONCEPTS • Many ideas for making concepts concrete can be found in curriculum guides and learning activities for young children (i.e., preschool and kindergarten). These may be adapted for different age groups as necessary. For example, the teacher might use a milk carton scoop to teach the concept of release when throwing. To teach the concept of running across a distance to a landmark, the teacher might roll a large ball and ask the child to chase it.

Sequencing tasks involves **sequential memory**—*the ability of the learner to process and respond to a series of commands in sequence.* An awareness of the student's level of sequencing ability helps the physical educator to know the number of tasks or directions that can be given and understood in sequence. This information can be obtained from the classroom teacher, speech therapist, or psychologist (or their reports). The physical education teacher should start with simple commands, directions, or tasks and progress through compound to complex tasks. Task cards (or sequence cards, picture cues, or charts) are helpful in encouraging student participation in each of the tasks requested. Task cards are particularly effective tools to use with tumbling, jump rope, physical fitness, and object control activities.

Students who have difficulty with **motor planning**—*the ability to select, sequence, and perform movements, especially those that are novel*—may require a significant amount of instructional modification to learn the sequences of motor tasks. (Difficulty with motor planning is also referred to as *apraxia* or *dyspraxia*.) It is important not to misinterpret students' performances as misbehavior. They may be able to perform a motor task within the context of a game or self-care activity but unable to do it when directed by another person.

Motor planning difficulty may also appear as:

- The ability to explain how to do a motor sequence, but the inability to demonstrate it physically.
- Inaccurate imitation.
- Inconsistent errors when performing the same skill.
- Poor judgment of visual–spatial relationships, particularly when new skills or tasks are presented.
- Difficulty performing a motor skill in different contexts (e.g., performing the skill of jumping during jump rope, but not during other games, obstacle courses, or tumbling activities).
- Performing some complex motor skills using mature motor patterns, but being unable to perform more simple motor skills until large amounts of guided practice have occurred.

Allowing time for learning

The amount of time to allow for learning or even processing certain information requires consideration when working with individuals with a disability. Many individuals require only the average amount of time for learning, but others need more time to process information and to learn a particular motor skill. Overlearning is sometimes necessary for the student with a more severe disability. Providing practice time for known skills not only results in overlearning, but also serves as its own reward for students who may seldom experience success while moving. The need for extra time for learning is one reason to target skills that are functional and meaningful for the student and that can be applied to activities throughout the student's lifespan. Some motor skills, such as skipping, are considered developmental because they are useful during a short period of childhood. However, the time it takes to teach them may take up valuable learning time that could be devoted to teaching skills with more longevity, such as negotiating stairs, walking on a variety of surfaces, fitness activities, and skills directly related to games and physical activities of interest to the particular student.

Using multisenses

Physical educators often use techniques that stimulate more than one sensory system at a time, but they do not always use these techniques systematically. Many children learn more easily when one sensory system is used as a cue or reinforcement for another—a multisensory approach. A few examples include the following:

1. Verbally describing and demonstrating the performance.
2. Touching the body part to be moved while describing the movement.
3. Having the student describe or give verbal cues at the same time he or she is performing.
4. Pointing out to the learner how the performance "feels" while the student's eyes are closed and the teacher is physically guiding a body part through a movement.

One individual might need combined sensory stimulation to process what another individual can get through the stimulation of only one sense. Keep in mind that some individuals with a disability (e.g., those with hyperactivity, distractibility, or a learning disability, or who have a short attention span) may become confused with too much stimulation from one or more sensory systems. If the student is not learning with multisensory stimuli, reduce the input to just one modality and use that to teach. Then, gradually introduce another form, using the first to reinforce it (see Figure 10.5).

The key to the multisensory approach, and any of the other techniques discussed, lies in the teacher's ability to observe the behaviors and motor responses of the students. If the desired performance is not occurring, the physical educator should analyze what is happening and adjust the technique quickly. There is great variation in abilities among students with a disability, and each individual's degree of performance consistency demands much of the physical educator.

Using creative teaching techniques

Many teaching techniques evolve from teacher creativity, while others are tried and true. An example of a tried and true program that facilitates teacher creativity is the "6P" program. This program, developed by Seaman (1973), comprises the following six categories of teaching techniques: (1) patterning, (2) positioning, (3) progression, (4) perception, (5) prompting, and (6) principles. The techniques of patterning, positioning, perception, and prompting are discussed here. Although originally implemented with students with mental retardation, the applicability of these techniques to individual needs should be evident.

Patterning, sometimes called "motoring" or "physical guidance," refers to *the manipulation of a body part through a range of motion* (see Figure 10.6). This process provides the student with kinesthetic and proprioceptive feedback. The information received through this manual assistance helps guide the student's movement later, when she attempts it unassisted. Having "felt" the correct motor response, the student can store the information in memory for retrieval at a later time.

Positioning the body limbs is often necessary to provide accurate proprioceptive feedback. For example, a child may not understand the simple command "bend your knees." If you position the child in the bent knee position, however, he can make the association between the command and the feedback. Again, the storage of this information for later use is more likely to occur because positioning the body has enhanced the quality of the child's internal environment (feedback).

Perception refers to *the reception and integration of sensory stimulation, which adds to the student's pool of information* and enhances learning. Using sensory stimuli in the environment can assist the child with processing information. Pairing a visual or tactile cue with a verbal cue can also be helpful.

Prompting, *through verbal, visual, or manual assistance, helps the child retrieve the task or sequence from memory.* You can eliminate prompting once the student is able to make the associations without it. It is important not to wait too long to decrease or eliminate prompting. When students are prompted too much, they may become overly dependent on prompts. Sometimes, students with a severe disability become so dependent on prompting that they are unable to initiate the skill without a specific prompt. Physical educators who work with instructional aides and peer tutors should be aware of the amount of prompting being used and provide guidance to the aide or tutor as necessary. Refer to Table 10.1 for further explanation of the prompting hierarchy.

FIGURE 10.5

Incorporating multisenses, children search through ball pit for textured beanbags, and then they practice locomotor patterns while taking beanbags to their own bucket.

FIGURE 10.6

When teaching hockey skills, the teacher provides physical guidance for a student who is striking the puck.

| TABLE 10.1 | *Prompting hierarchy.* |

The **prompting hierarchy** *is a range of instruction stimuli that may be provided to direct an individual toward the performance of a desired response.* Prompts are listed in order from the least to the most intrusive. The amount of assistance increases with each level in the hierarchy. Use the least intrusive prompt that will elicit the desired response.

1. Natural cue	Behavior independently occurs as a result of a natural cue to a stimulus in the environment. The individual performs the behavior without any assistance.
	Example: John runs when he sees the rest of the class begin to run.
2. Gestural cue	Physical gestures may include pointing, beckoning, or nodding or shaking one's head to indicate approval or disapproval.
	Example: Ms. Smith drops a raised arm to signal students to start running.
3. Indirect verbal prompt	The instructor uses a question format to imply that some behavior needs to occur.
	Example: Jimmy is bouncing the ball while the teacher is giving verbal instructions. The teacher says, "Jimmy, what do you need to do?" Jimmy stops bouncing the ball.
4. Modeling	By performing the desired behavior, the teacher, other adult, or peer encourages the student to initiate that behavior.
	Example: Teacher or peer stands near student and performs the forward lunge with correct knee bend and upright body posture to cue the student to perform the lunge correctly.
5. Symbolic prompt (pictorial or written)	Symbols (pictures or words) are presented to guide behavior. Often, an array of pictures or a list of words is used, combined with the gestural prompt of pointing to the symbol of the behavior appropriate at that time.
	Example: Teacher posts (or provides) task cards with pictures of the four elements of performing a forward roll: squat, tuck, roll, stand.
6. Direct verbal prompt	The instructor explicitly states the behavior that needs to occur.
	Example: "Boys and girls, please get into a circle now."
7. Minimal physical prompt	Slight physical contact guides the individual toward the behavior.
	Example: Teacher stands near student, modeling the forward lunge with correct knee bend, and provides a slight touch to the back of the student's knee to prompt forward knee bend.
8. Partial physical prompt	The instructor physically starts the individual on the desired behavior, then ceases the physical assistance so the individual may complete the behavior independently.
	Example: To help the student perform a curl-up movement, teacher lightly touches the back of the shoulders and pushes until the student moves through the beginning portion of the curl-up movement.
9. Full physical prompt	The instructor physically guides the individual through the entire behavior.
	Example: When a student is unable to attempt an overhand throw (consistently performing the underhand pattern), Mr. Wilson physically moves the student's arm into the correct position above the shoulder for the overhand pattern.

Techniques for Adapting the Learning Environment

At the very basis of the educational deficit for some students is a difficulty learning in the general education setting. To enhance learning in physical education, it may be necessary to change the setting or learning environment to better meet the educational needs of these students.

Techniques for adapting the environment of each student, to achieve the setting that is most conducive to learning, include the following. These can be used as the students' needs demand and the educational environment permits.

1. Adapting the facilities
2. Using space creatively
3. Eliminating distractions and focusing attention
4. Providing structure and routine
5. Varying class format

Adapting the facilities

Making structural adaptations to existing facilities or providing new facilities might be necessary to provide adequate physical education programming for students with a disability. The physical education teacher should be aware of architectural standards for accessibility, barrier-free construction, and fixtures to assist individuals with a disability and should make suggestions for appropriate modifications.

Until, and even after, adaptations of facilities occur, the physical educator may have to make some minor alterations. Adaptations a teacher can implement include:

1. Painting, chalking, or taping lines and boundaries
2. Devising "temporary" ramps for wheelchair accessibility
3. Painting or taping a trailing path for the student with visual impairments
4. Constructing movable basketball goals
5. Devising creative ways for storage
6. Using existing playground equipment creatively
7. Using existing landmarks for boundaries, bases, goals, etc.

See Chapter 13 for further discussion of facility adaptations.

Using space creatively

If at all possible, a teacher should obtain both indoor and outdoor space for use in physical education. A space that is too small or too large can be a deterrent to a good physical education program; however, there are ways of working with almost any space available to make it an appropriate learning environment.

Whether indoors or outdoors, it is helpful to use any existing markings or landmarks as boundaries or dividers. A large, fenced playground can be made smaller simply by using one corner of it. To control students with hyperactivity or distractibility, place the students' backs toward the corner of the playground and stand in front of the class to limit their movement area (see Figure 10.7). For a student who may leave the group, the visual stimulus of seeing the wide open spaces (the field) may be enticing or trigger a fleeing or running away behavior. Therefore, the formation of students facing the corner of the fence, or directing the activity toward a corner, may decrease the fleeing behaviors. This use of space enables the teacher to stop any student who is inclined to run away from the group. However, this format may not help to focus the students' attention if a lot of activity is taking place on the playground behind the teacher.

Various pieces of small equipment make excellent space dividers—hula hoops, bicycle tires, carpet squares, poly spots, chalk (for use on blacktop), and Velcro strips (for use on carpet). You can use them to define each student's own personal space while sitting, standing, or moving. You can also use them ini-

FIGURE 10.7

Adaptation of play space. The students stand with their backs toward the corner of the playground, and the teacher stands in front of the class.

FIGURE 10.8

By defining spatial limits, poly spots help students learn to stay in their own space.

tially for class organization and warm-up exercises, as well as for activities involving movement exploration and guided discovery methods (see Figure 10.8).

Eliminating distractions and focusing attention

Distractions should be eliminated or at least reduced as much as possible. Distractions may include the following:

1. Extraneous noises and sounds
2. Other people within the visual field
3. Obstacles and objects in close proximity to the working area
4. A busy environment (e.g., too much stimuli on bulletin boards or a lot of equipment stored in and around the instructional area)
5. Too much talking by the teacher
6. Extraneous movement or gestures by the teacher

Especially for those individuals who are distractible or hyperactive or who have a short attention span, you should view these items as potential distracters; the same factors may not be distractions to other students with a disability. It may be necessary to remove or eliminate any and all distractions to allow all students to focus attention on the task. It may also be necessary to use class time to teach planned transitions. Teaching students where to focus their attention during outdoor activities can increase participation time and encourage appropriate, on-task behaviors. To redirect or focus attention on the task, consider the following tactics:

1. Have students spend more time in active participation.
2. Provide organized, smooth-running, and adequately paced instruction.
3. Support behavior appropriately.
4. Teach class routines and transition procedures.
5. Use a class organization format appropriate to students' needs.
6. Be enthusiastic.

Providing structure and routine

Young children and most students with a disability need relatively high levels of structure and routine. Those individuals who do not have a processing, cognitive, or emotional disability can often function within the usual class structure, and routine modifications may be minimal. Students who do have a processing, cognitive, sensory, or emotional disability usually require more structure and a more regular routine than students without a disability. Keep in mind that cognitive, mental, social, and emotional disabilities can cut across all categories of disabling conditions.

Students who have only a sensory impairment (e.g., deafness, hard of hearing, or visual impairment) need some structure and routine to help them cope with the environment. Inconsistency or a lack of continuity in the class structure and routine can be upsetting and confusing to the student with an emotional disturbance, behavior disorder, autism, learning disability, or mental retardation. Students with a more severe disability need more structure and routine for learning to take place and to lessen their frustration and confusion.

Adaptations in structure and routine should not be overused. For persons with a disability, learning to adapt to change is part of their education, but change should be introduced gradually. Teachers should not allow students to become bored. Structure and routine can enhance learning and development for students with a disability, but they should not be allowed to inhibit learning and independence.

Varying class format

The formats used for class organization in adapted physical education often are unique. They may vary from (seemingly) no organization at all to highly structured organization. The following are typically used types of class organizational formats, listed in order from highly structured to the least structured:

1. *One-to-one instruction*—a ratio of one teacher to one student. Teaching aides, assistants, or classroom teachers could be employed to work one-to-one with a student during physical education. One-to-one instruction is not synonymous with individualized instruction. It can be used in conjunction with any other class format and may be necessary for the maximum development of children with a severe disability.
2. *Small group*—three to four students working together with the teacher or aide. The entire class may consist of only these three or four students, or it may be composed of several small groups. Small groups are often beneficial to the students. They are more commonly found in adapted physical education, but are helpful to all children and can be an effective teaching strategy in most physical education class activities (see Figure 10.9).
3. *Large group*—the entire class participating together as one large unit.
4. *Mixed groups*—the use of varying group organizations within a class period. One possibility is to start with the large group, go to small group activity, then return to the large group at the end of the period.
5. *Peer teaching*—having general education classmates or students from other classes assist students with a disability.
6. *Teaching stations*—setting up several locations around the activity area and requiring different performances at each. In this manner, students can gain practice in or exposure to several skills or abilities during one physical education instructional period (see Figure 10.10).
7. *Self-paced independent work*—individually planned instruction pursued by each student at the student's own pace. Students may work randomly on each aspect of their program and have the teacher check them against criterion-referenced performances when they are ready.

These various class formats can be used in almost any educational setting, from the general to the special education class. The physical education teacher can select a format based on the individuals involved and the specific goals and objectives to be met. Consideration should be given to structuring an appropriate and smooth transition from one activity to another or one type of format to another. Examples are included in Chapter 13.

The following general comments should help guide the decision-making process when you are choosing an appropriate class format:

FIGURE 10.9

Small group instruction is used to teach students to shoot a basketball.

- Varying the group organization helps to hold interest and attention; however, a teacher should not use it so much that it distracts or confuses students.
- The physical education teacher must carefully plan the transition between group formats.
- The transition itself can be particularly difficult for some students with a disability.
- Providing a variety of combinations of class formats facilitates access to general education routines.

FIGURE 10.10

Using stations for different activities—such as this curl-up station—allows students to progress at their own pace.

Techniques for Adapting the Activity

Any physical activity can be modified or adapted. Adaptations of the activity in physical education should be done with the participation and learning experience of all students in mind. That is, the adaptations should be made for the purposes of inclusion and equal participation by individuals with a disability, but not to the exclusion or limitation of participation by students without a disability. Following are seven ways in which physical education activities may be modified:

1. Placement of the individual in the activity
2. Adaptation of the time of participation
3. Use of substitutions
4. Adaptation of a skill
5. Adaptation of equipment
6. Adaptation of rules
7. Simplification of the language used

These may be used in a class in which all students have a disability, as well as in inclusive classes.

Placement of the individual in the activity

Most team sports include active and less active positions. Providing a less active role for a student with limited mobility may be the only adaptation needed. In a softball game, for example, a student who uses a wheelchair could probably play the pitcher position. She may also be able to play right field, first base, or catcher with minimal adjustments. When determining the adaptation, you must consider safety factors, as well as equality for individuals with and without a disability. In most cases there are no "right" or "wrong" adaptations, only degrees of appropriateness.

Placing a student with visual or hearing impairment close to you during instruction and near other students during activity is appropriate. Students with hyperactivity or distractibility probably should be located near the teacher for behavior control and on-task monitoring. However, in some situations, it is very distracting for the student to be near the teacher because of the extra conversation and activity that occur. Once again, you should base the decision on individual student needs.

Adaptation of the time of participation

Limiting or altering the amount of time a student participates may be necessary for those who have a health impairment, either as their sole disabling condition or coexisting with other conditions. Limiting the time (i.e., shortening the time) may also be recommended for the very young and those with a short attention span. Additionally, a teacher must consider the student's level of endurance and strength when determining the time of participation. Students who have prostheses and assistive devices, as well as students who are sedentary or obese, usually become fatigued quickly and may have limited strength, flexibility, and endurance. Students with cardiac conditions, asthma, hemophilia, sickle cell disease, cancer, or other health impairments may need their time of participation limited, depending on the severity of the condition. Spacing rest intervals or varying the pace of the activity (e.g., alternating vigorous activity with quiet activity) are additional ways to modify the time of participation. Physical educators should be aware that the endurance of students with a health impairment may vary from day to day or week to week, depending on a variety of life factors (e.g., nutrition, medications, stress, other activities of daily living). Therefore, the physical educator should allow for some flexibility when adapting activities.

The effect of cognitive fatigue should also be considered. Some individuals with a disability, such as cerebral palsy, brain injury, and processing disorders, expend a great amount of cognitive energy just trying to coordinate body parts. Therefore, their concentration may diminish more quickly than other students. When students show cognitive fatigue, they should be provided with more frequent rest periods. One way to provide cognitive rest is to alternate an instructional-level task with an easier task, such as one that is targeted for skill maintenance.

Use of substitutions

Rotating one person with another or using two players together "as one" are examples of substitution. Alternating an individual with a cardiac condition with a student with asthma during a vigorous game or sport is a viable solution to meet their individual needs for limited participation time, the demands of the game, and the needs of the others in the class. Substitution can be used with any students, whether or not they have a disability.

Adaptation of a skill

Changing the skill or motor requirements of an activity to fit the needs of the student may be necessary. In some cases, adapting a skill also requires modifying the rules. An individual with atrophied upper arm muscles may be allowed to "palm" the ball or bounce and catch the ball in basketball; an individual with paraplegia may be allowed to hit or dribble (soccer style) the ball with a crutch; a young student with severe mental retardation may be allowed to catch the ball after one bounce instead of catching the ball in flight.

MAKING CONNECTIONS

Accommodating a Student's Cognitive Fatigue

Mrs. Akino is conducting a lesson on throwing with her primary-level special day class students by having small groups go through a series of stations. She groups two students with mild cerebral palsy and one student with traumatic brain injury together while other students work in pairs. The group of three students takes five throws per turn, while students in pairs take ten throws per turn. The shorter turns and less frequent turns allow more rest time for the students who are susceptible to cognitive fatigue.

In all cases, it is important to strive for the development of the most efficient movement patterns and motor skills possible. Children with hemiplegia, cerebral palsy, spina bifida, or a lower leg amputation may never be able to execute a motorically perfect jump, but they may be expected to become proficient within their limitations. It may sometimes be appropriate for a student who is mentally retarded, but is not physically limited to be encouraged until able to develop a mature jumping pattern.

Adaptation of equipment

At some time, you may need to use special equipment or adapt the equipment used in physical education programming. Equipment modification is a means of meeting the needs of students with a disability to allow their participation in physical activity. Some general ideas for adapting equipment include:

1. Use brightly colored objects for students with visual impairment.
2. Use auditory cues, such as a bell inside a ball, for students who are blind.
3. Use longer or shorter striking implements for individuals with a physical impairment.
4. Lower nets.
5. Use suspended or stationary objects for striking or kicking.
6. Use lightweight objects such as balloons instead of balls.
7. Use assistive devices such as ramps, rails, and supports.
8. Attach side barriers to table games for students using wheelchairs.

Further discussion and examples regarding modification of equipment may be found in Chapter 13.

Adaptation of rules

When adapting activities to include students with disabilities, the saying that "rules are made to be broken" often applies. Although rules should not be adapted or changed so much that the purpose of the game is lost, rule changes should be considered part of the learning process. Simple rule changes might include allowing one bounce instead of an in-flight catch, ten players on a baseball team instead of the usual nine, two steps after catching a basketball pass, base runners to walk when the ball is fielded by a player with a disability, and each team's turn at bat to consist of every person on the team batting once.

TASK ANALYSIS

Task analysis is *a method used to determine the components of a given task (skill or ability) and the prerequisite behaviors.* Task analysis is important when determining the level of a child's ability, the appropriate level to begin instruction, the most natural and meaningful progression (i.e., sequence of events), and the written performance objectives. When conducting a task analysis for students with a disability, it may be helpful to think of three subcomponents: skill progression analysis, individual mechanical analysis, and environmental analysis. These subcomponents combine to form an individualized instructional progression (see Table 10.2).

1. **Skill progression** refers to *the appropriate component parts and sequence of events of the targeted skill necessary to perform the skill effectively.* Examples of a written skill progression analysis are found in Tables 10.2 and 10.3. Note the detailed task analysis in Table 10.2 and the shorter skill progression in Table 10.3. Writing such an in-depth analysis is not always necessary, but skilled physical educators do go through these steps mentally. They know the prerequisite skills or abilities, then break the task into its component parts and order the steps.
2. The next step is to analyze the individual's mechanics by observing the student's performance, or attempted performance, of the targeted task. This leads to identifying the influence of the disability (as well as prior learning) on the motor performance.
3. The third step is to analyze environmental influences on the student's performance.

TABLE 10.2 *Task analysis.*

TASK: THE JUMP—two-footed take-off and two-footed landing.

1. **Starting position.**
   A. Standing:
      - Feet 3 inches apart and parallel
      - Toes pointing forward
      - Body erect
      - Arms at sides of body (arms straight and relaxed)

2. **Preparation for the jump.**
   A. Feet:
      - Firm on ground
      - Pointing forward
   B. Legs:
      - Ankles flexed
      - Knees flexed and bent straight forward over toes so force exerted on extension can pass straight through the joint and not at an angle
   C. Body:
      - Hips flexed
      - Trunk leaning slightly forward (about 3 degrees)
   D. Head:
      - Tilted slightly forward (about 3 to 5 degrees)
   E. Arms:
      - Elbows flexed with arms swung back
      - Wrist relaxed with equal contraction between flexors and extensors
      - Fingers flexed in easy fisted position

3. **Take-off.**
   A. Start momentum:
      - Head tilted forward
      - Body leaning forward
      - Arms swing forward, then backward (elevation can be affected by increasing forcefulness of upward swing of the arms)
   B. Elevation of body:
      - A forceful contraction of all extensor muscles to extend all joints flexed (wave summation of all joints in action)
      - Arms thrust upward, head thrusts up (The momentum of the arm swing is transferred to the upper body and, if timed with leg extensions, adds force to the jump; center of gravity is lower when arms are down, so swinging them upward raises the center of gravity and causes the body to rise higher.)
      - Final force applied by ankles and toes being forcefully extended (The more force produced against the floor, the greater the counterpressure that projects the body [deeper the crouch] and the more force obtained. However, the body must be lifted through the distance that it is lowered; more work is done when a low crouch is used. Optimal depth of the crouch depends on the strength of the leg muscles.)

4. **Landing.**
   - Before touching the ground, spread feet to about shoulder width for better balance
   - Toes first, then heels touch the ground
   - Relax knee and hip joints enough to help absorb landing shock
   - Arms come down slowly to aid in balancing
   - Body extensors slowly contract to stabilize body to standing position (The forceful extension of legs in jump for height leaves them in position directly below the center of gravity of the body so that equilibrium on landing is no problem and, being extended, they are in position to flex at all joints on contact with the floor to reduce the downward momentum gradually and absorb the force of landing without injuring the body.)

Source: Irma Pack, Class assignment, California State University, Los Angeles.

TABLE 10.3 — Skill progression for jumping.

STARTING POSITION	PREPARATION FOR JUMP	TAKE-OFF	LANDING
■ standing	■ foot placement	■ start momentum	■ feet spread
	■ leg position	■ elevation of body	■ toes first
	■ body position	■ final force	■ relaxed knees
	■ head position		■ arms assist
	■ arm position		

By combining and analyzing the information obtained in these three steps, the physical educator can determine and plan the appropriate instructional progression.

Through these thought processes, the physical educator can analyze performance systematically, thus building the foundation upon which good physical education programs for individuals with a disability can be based. Table 10.3 divides the task of jumping as outlined in the task analysis into time sequence-related subtasks. Figure 10.11 illustrates the task of throwing by identifying the subtasks, and then shows the underlying sensory processes (prerequisite movement components) that are needed to complete the task. In some cases, task analysis involves more than a mechanical analysis of the movements. For example, verbal communication between teammates may be included in some games, determining the direction in which to move may be part of the task, or

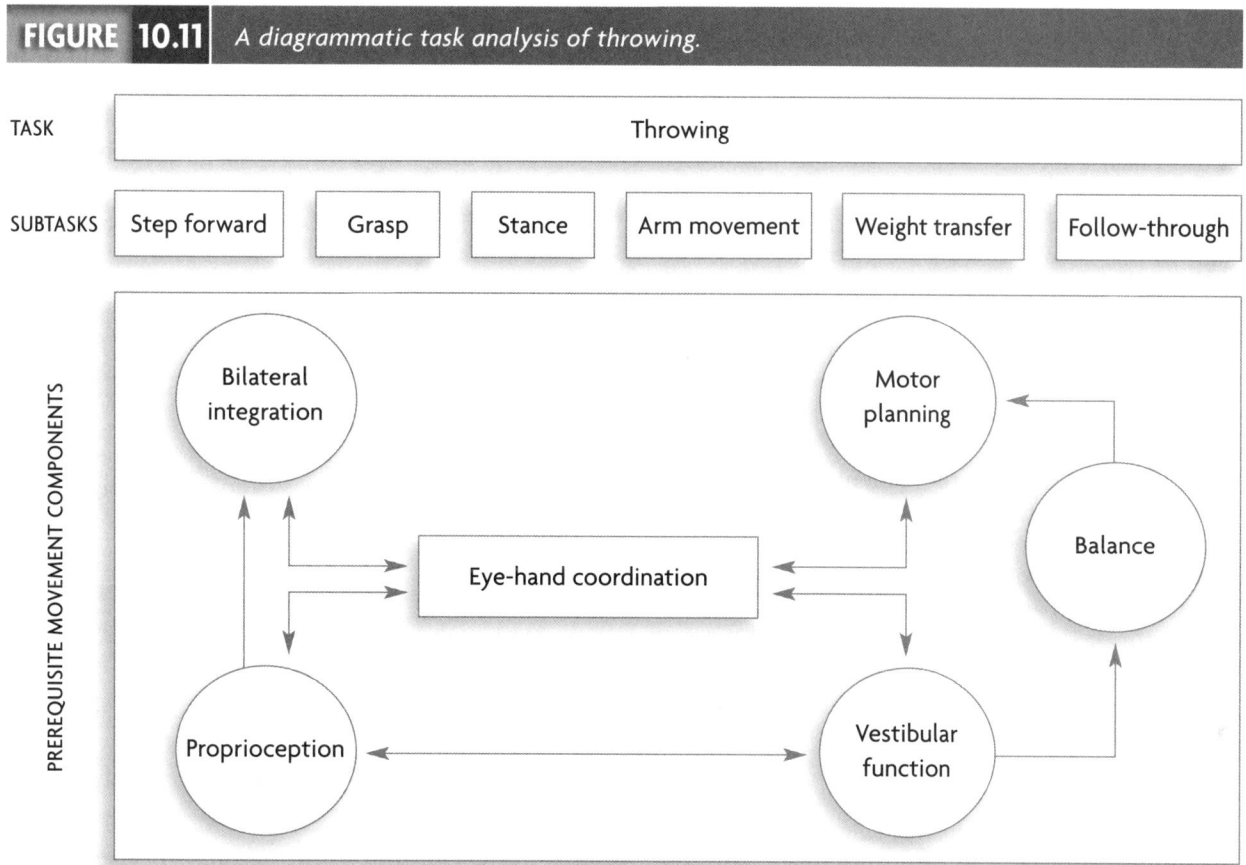

FIGURE 10.11 A diagrammatic task analysis of throwing.

Teaching Tip

SHARING THE TASK ANALYSIS • Share the task analysis information for a specific skill with paraeducators and support personnel, as well as with parents, so that they can use it to practice skills and activities when the adapted physical education specialist is not on campus or when the student is at home.

variables influencing the selection of appropriate equipment may have to be analyzed. Table 10.4 defines the elements of task analysis and applies them to the example of a student with hearing impairment catching a fly ball.

Task analysis is critical when the teacher is using various techniques such as chaining, partial participation, and successive approximation.

Chaining

Chaining is *a procedure through which simple behaviors are combined into more complex behaviors*. Three types of chaining are forward, backward, and global. *Forward chaining* is used to teach the first component of a complex task before continuing to the next component of that task. The teaching progression follows the task analysis sequentially from the first step to the last. If the teacher is using this strategy to teach a forward roll, the student would first learn to squat on his toes.

Backward chaining starts with the final component of the task and works sequentially backward toward the first step. With this strategy, the student who is learning to roll might begin by lying prone on a large bolster or ball that is pushed forward, while the teacher guides the roll by holding on to the student's feet. The last step, standing up, would be the first one the student learns to do independently.

With *global chaining*, the student begins by doing the easiest part of the task, with the teacher performing or providing physical guidance for all other parts. As the student becomes proficient at the easiest part, the next easiest part is added, and so on. Using global chaining to teach the forward roll might entail starting the student prone on the ball and teaching her first to take weight on her hands independently. Then the teacher might guide her through the rest of the movement, but have her stand up by herself at the end. The advantages of global chaining include providing early success and ensuring that the student understands or is familiar with the whole task before the most difficult elements are attempted.

MAKING CONNECTIONS

Global Chaining, Partial Participation

When batting in a softball game, Jim, a student with cerebral palsy, might be able to hold the bat in a modified position and, with physical help, hit the ball from a tee. Then, the person helping Jim tags a peer who runs the bases for him. Using global chaining, Jim learns to perform the next easiest task, which might be swinging the bat to hit the ball. He may never be able to run the bases at a competitive rate, even after he has learned to perform most of the parts of batting independently. Jim still plays the game using partial participation.

Partial Participation

Partial participation is another method that can be effective when teaching individuals with a disability. The principle of **partial participation** involves *the student participating in all of the parts of the task or activity in which he or she can be successful. Accommodations such as alternate rules, peer assistance, or physical guidance are used for the parts of the activity or task that the student cannot successfully perform otherwise*. Partial participation and global chaining can often be used together effectively to facilitate inclusion and to enable the student with a disability to participate in an activity while continuing to learn some of the skills required for full, independent participation.

Successive Approximation

Successive approximation is an instructional method similar to the progressive part method. **Successive approximation** involves *having students learn and practice skills that are increasingly similar to the target skill*. For example, teaching a student to jump rope is often done through successive approximation:

1. Jump over a line or stationary rope on the ground.
2. Jump over a low rope with a little swing.
3. Jump over a rope with a wide swing.
4. Jump over a rope with one full overhead swing at a time.
5. Jump over a rope swinging rhythmically overhead.

Within the behavior modification theory, successive approximation is referred to as *shaping*. **Shaping**

TABLE 10.4 Task analysis of catching.

TASK: CATCHING A FLY BALL

Subcomponent/Description	Example
Skill progression analysis: Analyzing the appropriate sequence of events of the targeted skill. Looking at all of the component parts required to perform the skill effectively.	■ Visual tracking of the ball, moving into the projected line of trajectory, maintaining a ready position to adjust whole body position, timing movements to intercept ball with hands, grasping ball, absorbing force of ball with bend of arms, and maintaining a balanced body position and control of the ball.
Individual mechanical analysis: Analyzing each individual's movement pattern during attempts of the targeted skill and observing ways in which the disability (or other factors) may influence the motor performance.	■ An individual who is hearing impaired is observed to respond slowly because she does not hear the bat hit the ball and has difficulty adjusting her body position adequately to maintain a balanced and stable position for receiving the ball.
Environmental analysis: Analyzing the effects of the environment and setting surrounding the performance of the targeted skill. Individuals with a disability may be particularly sensitive to many of the environmental elements typically present in the physical education setting, such as: noise level, distractions, personal space, extraneous movements, language, and social/emotional climate (including competition, disability awareness, attitudes, and performance anxiety).	■ A student with hearing impairment is observed to be distracted by other players moving within his line of sight to the ball and by the opposing team's attempts to distract with loud noises or movements. Although he can catch fly balls in practice or isolated situations, his performance is greatly reduced in a game setting, indicating possible social distraction or performance anxiety.
Instructional progression: Using information from all of the elements of the task analysis of a targeted skill and determining the appropriate instructional elements for a specific individual.	■ Modify the typical teaching progression to include a brightly colored ball. Train the student to watch the ball attentively as it is pitched. ■ Emphasize advanced balance techniques such as wide stance while moving from side to side or forward and backward, exaggerated knee bend (to lower center of gravity), and restricted head movement (to limit shifting of center of gravity). ■ Privately interview the student regarding his feelings about playing in team game situations in the general physical education class, and discuss possible accommodations or interventions (e.g., practicing in small groups, playing lead-up games, and understanding teamwork with an emphasis on team roles and cooperation; teaching teammates simple sign language or gestural cues to enhance communication).

refers to *reinforcing behaviors that are successively closer to the target behavior.*

CREATING A POSITIVE ENVIRONMENT

Motivation

By keeping students motivated and focused on a goal, physical educators can support students in exhibiting positive behaviors. **Motivation** refers to *the state of being roused into action; it is the urge to push toward a specific goal.* Three general sources of motivation are factors within the task, factors within the individual, and factors external to the task and individual (Waggoner, 1973).

1. Factors within the task. Several factors affect motivation within the task. The first is the *novelty* of the task, which might include a new task, a unique task, new equipment, or a change in an old familiar activity. Doing something familiar in an unfamiliar way can also be quite motivating.

The second factor is the *complexity* of the task. Tasks that are too complex lead to frustration, and frustration leads to behavior problems. Students with a disability who are frustrated by the complexity that typical educational tasks present to them may find relief by exhibiting behaviors that cause them to be removed from the situation. Other students with a disability may find complexity an exciting challenge. Tasks that are too simple can easily bore anyone, and behavior problems may result. The complexity of the task should vary with the student's ability to be motivated by it and handle it. For example, when presenting a cup stacking activity to the group, the teacher may instruct a student with lower cognitive functioning to use the pattern of 3–3 while others are performing 3–3–3. A student with higher cognitive functioning may use the same pattern but repeat the cycle two or more times. Alternatively, she may perform the same sequence with three different sets in the same amount of time. Another example is presenting stunts and tumbling activities to a class. A student with Down syndrome may perform the pencil roll (both for safety and for strength) while the other students are introduced to the egg roll (repeatedly turning to the side in a small, tucked body position) or a forward roll.

Closure is another factor within the task that motivates some people. **Closure** *involves seeing something to completion.* Completing a crossword puzzle or climbing to the top of a mountain, for example, are activities that some people enjoy because these activities both involve a recognizable end point and provide the satisfaction of seeing a task to completion. Students with some types of disabilities, such as autism spectrum disorders, developmental disability, or emotional disturbance, may be particularly motivated by visual closure. For example, when such a student is practicing a motor skill for 15 minutes, the teacher might place a beanbag on one of five poly spots (or in rings, hoops, etc.) at approximately three-minute intervals to mark the time visually until the end of the practice period. This is a physical and visual way for the students to mark time and see that they are approaching a goal.

2. Factors within the individual. Intrinsic motivators—*motivational factors within the individual*—include internal satisfaction from successful achievement, the level of aspiration set by the individual, and a knowledge of the results. To help

---

MAKING CONNECTIONS

Using a Closure Strategy

The following examples take advantage of closure motivation in a physical activity setting. Some involve visual closure, which should be used when students need visual supports or are developmentally young.

- Ask a student to toss beanbags into a bucket and to fill it rather than asking her to throw the beanbags at various types of targets. (Closure is seen when all of the beanbags are in the container.)
- Ask a student to throw all the beanbags in the bucket to targets of his choice before changing tasks. (Closure is seen when the bucket is empty.)
- Ask a student to jump in 10 consecutive hoops and pick up a marker in each one rather than asking the student simply to jump in the hoops. (Closure is seen when all of the hoops are empty.)
- While the student is using a scooter board in sitting position, ask her to put a floor puzzle of the human body together by carrying one piece at a time from a box, around some cones, to the puzzle area. One or two students can do the task this way with their own equipment, while others may be able to do it as a small group activity. (Closure is seen when the puzzle is complete.)
- Simply telling a student the number of times to do a task and counting verbally, backward, helps to structure the time. Counting backward is effective when the student has learned that something happens or stops when the numbers get to zero.

establish intrinsic motivation, reinforcement and knowledge of results should be given to all students.

Gauthier (1981) found that students with a disability in general physical education classes were less likely than their peers without a disability to receive feedback (knowledge of results) following a movement response. Physical educators should be careful to provide adequate feedback to all students.

Aspiration levels do affect motivation, and individuals with a disability frequently have difficulty setting appropriate levels of aspiration for themselves. A skilled teacher who has conducted an accurate task analysis can help students set realistic aspirations, thereby increasing motivation and skill improvement.

3. Factors external to the task and individual. *The factors external to the task and to the individual* are known as **extrinsic motivators.** Social reinforcers and tangible reinforcers are two examples of extrinsic motivators. Learners are more apt to perform effectively (and to behave appropriately) when they receive positive reinforcement in the form of praise, acknowledgment, tangible reinforcement, or other factors external to the task and individual.

Class Rules

The physical educator must manage many types of rules in order to conduct a class successfully. Game rules, safety rules, and school rules are a few of the categories involved. The effective use of class rules can be a powerful strategy for providing structure and consistency, and thereby preventing or limiting undesirable behavior. The effective use of class rules has two main elements: setting class rules and responding to broken rules.

Setting class rules. Class rules might be thought of as the framework of the overall class structure. Well-constructed, easily understood rules can help to make any class run more smoothly. The following guidelines increase the effectiveness of class rules:

1. Involve the class in setting the rules to enhance the students' "buy in" and understanding of the rules.
2. State the rules briefly and clearly.
3. State the rules positively. Avoid rules that start with the word "no" or "don't." Rules that tell the student what to do and that are incompatible with undesirable behavior serve as behavioral teaching tools. For example, "Keep your hands and feet to yourself" is more effective than "No hitting, kicking, or pushing"; "Hold the ball while the teacher is talking" is more effective than "Don't bounce the ball while the teacher is talking."
4. Find ways to praise or reinforce rule-following more often than you call attention to rule-breaking.
5. Rules may have to change depending on the situation and activity. However, everyone must understand the rule change, and it is often important for students to understand why a rule has been changed.
6. Rules should be actively taught to the students and reviewed often. Physical educators should not assume that students understand what rules mean or when they should be applied.
7. Rules should be posted whenever possible. They may be posted in the form of a written or pictorial sign or symbol, as long as students understand the meaning of the picture or symbol. Posted rules serve as a nonpersonal reminder to follow the rules. When the rules cannot be posted, they should be reviewed more often.

Responding to broken rules. Before a student actually breaks a rule, teachers should think about how to respond effectively to broken rules or misbehavior. You may find it helpful to develop these four habits:

1. Move toward the person, which will enhance personal contact. Do not attract peer attention to misbehavior by handling it publicly when it can be handled gently, in private.
2. Use nonverbal, visual cues such as facial expressions (e.g., smile, frown) and gestures (e.g., point, extend hand to indicate "stop"). These are helpful with most students, but they

---

Teaching Tip

POSTING RULES • Ways to post rules in physical activity settings include:

- Clip rules on a clipboard. Hang the clipboard on a wall or fence or prop it on a chair, ledge, or box.
- Laminate a poster. Hang it on a fence using a binder ring or bolt snap clip (the type of clip found on the end of a leash).
- Tape the rules to the side of a bucket, large cone, or equipment cart.
- Tape the rules to a door or wall that students must pass on their way to the activity (e.g., exit from the locker room).

may be particularly useful with students with a language disability, hearing impairment, developmental disability, or attention deficit.

3. Label the misbehavior after a reprimand, and direct the student toward the desired activity or behavior. For example, the teacher may hold her hand up toward the student and say, "Susie, stop! You may not run on the pool deck. Walk to the pool stairs." Use reprimands sparingly to maintain their effectiveness.

4. Direct any consequence toward the specific person who broke the rule. When students feel that rules are enforced fairly, they are more likely to be motivated to follow them. Group consequences are rarely effective unless everyone in the group broke the rule.

POSITIVE BEHAVIOR SUPPORT

Positive behavior support (PBS) refers to *a comprehensive set of strategies that are meant to redesign an environment so that problem behaviors are minimized or prevented*. It also focuses on teaching students new skills in order to make problem behaviors unnecessary. A synthesis of more than 100 research articles (ERIC Clearinghouse on Disabilities and Gifted Education, 1999) that involved individuals with various cognitive disabilities found the following:

- Positive behavior support is widely applicable to individuals with serious challenging behaviors.
- Research in PBS is rapidly contributing to our knowledge of how to use the results of assessments and how to correct environmental deficiencies.
- PBS is effective in reducing problem behavior by 80 percent in two-thirds of the cases.
- Success rates are higher when intervention is based on prior functional assessment.

Positive behavior support considers the communicative intent of a behavior, along with the environmental factors that occur just before and just after the behavior that sustain it or cause it to occur again. Then, accommodations, supports, or instruction of new skills are designed to address the specific features of the behavior. Functional assessment helps to determine the function that the behavior serves for the individual, leading to interventions that teach or reinforce a functionally equivalent (but more desirable and effective) replacement behavior. Functions of behaviors can be categorized in several ways; however, most behaviors fall into the categories of protesting something or trying to get something. Examples of protesting functions include screaming to protest work that is too difficult, walking away from the area to protest uncomfortable conditions, or hitting to protest an abrupt transition. Examples of trying to get something include grabbing to get a toy, sitting and rocking to get vestibular stimulation, or making irritating noises to get attention. Refer to the references for this chapter for readings on positive behavior support.

Positive behavior support and intervention is a field of study that involves much research and technical knowledge. The intent of this section is simply to provide some information useful in the physical education program. Positive approaches to behavior intervention are not only the most effective but also the most appropriate, ethical, and efficient for educational settings. Although mild punishment may be used in education, the skilled teacher uses it sparingly—emphasizing instead positive approaches such as positive reinforcement, contingency management, and shaping.

Physical educators must clearly understand the principles of antecedents and consequences and their effect on behavior. Considering the situations described in How Would You Respond? and The Authors Respond will help to promote an under-

MAKING CONNECTIONS

Addressing Aggressive Behavior

Monique is a seven-year-old girl who started walking a year and a half ago and is just beginning to vocalize some words by repeating a verbal/sign cue. She displays some aggressive behaviors, such as reaching, hitting, kicking, pinching, and pushing others. During physical education class, she tends to move close to peers and tries to pull at their hair bows or push them, and then she will lie down on the floor or ground. The adapted physical education specialist has interrupted this behavior by saying, "Quiet hands" and placing her own hands at her side to show Monique what to do. Then, when Monique begins to reach, hit, or kick again, she is asked to walk around the group activity and re-enter it to play again. At that time, the adapted physical education specialist again demonstrates and cues Monique with "quiet hands." This serves as a stimulus change that interrupts the aggressive behavior chain and cues the replacement behavior of quiet hands. In this case, it was determined that the function of the aggressive behaviors was to protest waiting and to gain the attention of the adult to relieve Monique's boredom. Within a week Monique started to vocalize an approximation of "quiet hands."

standing of the relationship between behavior and its consequences. Although the embarrassment of being singled out in situation A might cause Bill not to disrupt again, the teacher's response (providing the attention that Bill sought) is just as likely to increase the chance that Bill will repeat that behavior. In situation B, what happens to John's behavior when he is asked to dress himself? Is the purchase of a toy in situation C an effective means of extinguishing the pestering behavior? How long will Steve's complaining behavior stop in situation D if the teacher dismisses Steve from the class?

Of course, preventing behavior problems from occurring in the first place is the most effective approach. Effective, well-planned teaching strategies and lessons that match not only the curriculum but also the skill level, needs, developmental level, and interests of the students will go a long way in preventing behavior problems. Educators can use many of the strategies and techniques described in subsequent parts of this section proactively to prevent behaviors from becoming problematic.

Behavior Modification

Behavior modification, based on the concept of operant conditioning, is considered *an educational approach that applies theories of learning to the teaching of selected behaviors.* Reinforcement is the key strategy used when behavior modification is aimed at eliciting or maintaining behaviors that are controlled, constructive, predictable, and orderly.

Reinforcement is a procedure that ultimately *increases the frequency of occurrence of a given behavior that it follows.* The increase in behavior is a result of the *presentation of a desirable stimulus* (**positive reinforcement**) or the *removal of an undesirable stimulus* (**negative reinforcement**) following the given behavior. (Note that negative reinforcement and punishment are very different, yet people often confuse the two.)

It is very important to have a clear understanding of the difference between a reinforcer and a reward. Mistakenly using a reward instead of a reinforcer may render your behavior intervention ineffective. Wright, Gurman, et al. (1998) explain the difference as follows:

> Reinforcement is said to have occurred when a consequence to a behavior results in that behavior increasing or maintaining its frequency. Thus, the behavior is reinforced—made stronger and more resistant to elimination because the individual desires the reinforcer and associates the behavior with desirable outcomes. A reward, on the other hand, is given by an observer to some-

one for having met some criterion established by the observer. Frequently, the giver assumes the recipient will like the outcome. The reward may actually be hated by the receiver (e.g., "You did that sheet of problems so beautifully that you get to do another one as a reward"). A reward is what you think will work, while a reinforcer is what is proven to work. (p. 81)

Positive reinforcement follows behavior and has the effect of increasing the probability of that behavior recurring (e.g., smile, food, token). Negative reinforcement also increases the behavior it follows, but works by removing an aversive stimulus. Examples include removing the close proximity of a teacher—moving away from the student after he stops being silly and begins to perform the directed task—or

---

How Would You Respond?

THE RELATIONSHIP BETWEEN BEHAVIOR AND CONSEQUENCES

The scenarios below present some behaviors, typical responses, and the likely results of the response. In each case, the response may provide a short-term solution to the behavior problem, but it will not prevent the problem from recurring. After reading each scenario, develop a strategy you might employ to prevent the child from repeating the behavior.

A. Bill causes a disruption in class.
   Teacher yells, "Bill, sit down and be quiet. You know better than that."
   If Bill was disruptive to get attention, the behavior probably will continue.

B. When asked to dress himself, John has a tantrum and bites his wrists.
   Institution staff dresses him.
   John is not likely to be interested in learning to dress himself.

C. In the grocery store, Jane pesters her mother relentlessly to buy her a toy.
   Mother buys the toy.
   The pestering stops, but it will probably recur.

D. Steve complains about participating in physical education class because he gets tired and sweaty.
   Teacher dismisses Steve from class for the day.
   Complaining stops in this situation, but it will probably recur in another.

allowing a child to leave her bedroom after her homework is completed. A baby who stops crying when his parent picks him up is providing negative reinforcement to the parent by ceasing the aversive stimulus of crying.

Positive reinforcement is usually used in behavior modification, and it is a powerful tool for successful behavior management and for instruction. As presented in Table 10.5, positive reinforcers are classified as social, activity, token, or material (also called tangible).

The maintenance of desirable behavior is often related to the following aspects of reinforcement: the amount of reinforcement, the delay of reinforcement, and the schedule of reinforcement (continuous or intermittent). Delaying the reinforcement often causes a slippage of the behavior in the learning process. Reinforcement is most effective when it is given immediately after the expected behavior. An efficient practice is to provide continuous reinforcement (i.e., provide a reinforcer immediately after each time a behavior is displayed) until the response is well established, and then gradually change to intermittent reinforcement. Behavior learned in this way is highly resistant to **extinction** (*reduced strength or rate or a complete absence of the behavior when reinforcement is withdrawn*).

Analyzing Behavior

The various models for analyzing behavior may each be effective in different situations. The effectiveness of a behavior analysis model may depend on the population, activities, resources, educational philosophy, teaching style, and severity of behavior. In most models, targeting a specific behavior and analyzing the forces that cause it to occur or recur (its function) are essential steps in selecting an effective intervention.

Applied behavior analysis (ABA) is one prominent method for analyzing behavior. ABA is *the process of systematically applying interventions based upon the principles of learning theory, to improve socially significant behaviors to a meaningful degree and to demonstrate that the interventions employed are responsible for the improvement in behavior* (Sulzer-Azeroff & Mayer, 1991). A functional behavior assessment (FBA) is often used within ABA as an ongoing assessment tool. A **functional behavioral assessment** is *a precise description of a behavior, its context, and its consequences, with the intent of better understanding the behavior and the factors influencing it* (Wallin, 2001–2004). An FBA is a highly effective strategy for discovering the reasons why a behavior occurs (functions) and designing specific interventions to address those reasons. When the physical educator is studying behavior intervention, the functional analysis of behavior is an area that is important to cover. The adapted physical educator who works with students with severe behaviors will find it imperative to understand functional analysis of behavior.

Positive behavior support requires analyzing the interaction between the individual and the group and environmental forces that act on the individual. The physical educator must consider the student's developmental level, intellectual ability, and language development level and adjust behavior expectations accordingly. For example, if a student has a cognitive developmental level similar to that of a typical three-year-old, it may be ineffective to expect the student to follow a contract or a "token" reinforcement system, or to work for several hours before receiving reinforcement. This is not to suggest

TABLE 10.5 Types of reinforcers.

TYPE	CHARACTERISTICS	EXAMPLES	WHEN TO USE
Social	Interactional	Praise, smile, handshake, hug, encouragement	Continuously
Activity	Performed by student	Game, project, movement	When social reinforcers are ineffective
Token	Visual Manipulable	Check mark, happy face Poker chip, sticker, coin	When social reinforcers are ineffective When activity or material can't be given immediately
Material	Manipulable Consumable	Prize, toy Food	When social, token, and activity reinforcers are ineffective in controlling behavior

The Authors Respond

THE RELATIONSHIP BETWEEN BEHAVIOR AND CONSEQUENCES

Situation A: The teacher might find it more effective to use a strategy that draws less attention to Bill after his disruption, such as moving closer to him and staying there until he settles down or praising other students who are behaving appropriately.

Situation B: Tantrums and biting are serious behaviors. Staff may be selecting the safest approach by dressing John instead of asking him to get dressed. If independent dressing is a goal for John, teachers will need to consider carefully the components of task analysis, particularly motivation, in designing an instructional plan for this skill.

Situation C: Buying a toy following pestering will stop the pestering in the short run, but it is actually reinforcing the pestering behavior. A good alternative would be to take a more proactive approach such as telling Jane that she won't get a toy regardless of how much she pesters her mother. But if she refrains from pestering, she will get a small treat or favorite activity at the end of the shopping trip.

Situation D: This situation is similar to C. The teacher can turn Steve's complaining behavior around by ignoring the complaining, while reinforcing an incompatible replacement behavior such as exerting gradually increasing amounts of effort in physical activities. Other motivators should be considered as well, such as personal improvement that can be made evident to Steve through regular feedback on his skills or physical fitness.

that a teenager with this cognitive profile should be taught with the same methods and materials as a three-year-old. Both the developmental and the functional skill approaches must be examined to individualize physical education instruction for older students with a developmental delay.

Some disabilities are associated with specific behavioral characteristics. Therefore, the physical educator should learn and understand not only the motor characteristics likely to be present in individuals with a disability, but also the behavioral characteristics. Although each individual presents a unique set of characteristics, regardless of their disability, a physical educator's understanding of common behavior patterns is an important basis for a proactive approach. To research disability-related behavioral characteristics and suggested interventions, physical educators should seek public, private, or personal libraries, websites, and disability-specific advocacy organizations. The references at the end of this chapter will get you started. Some behavioral characteristics associated with specific disabilities that are relevant to physical activity are listed in Appendix C.

Behavior Support Strategies

The physical educator must be able to support the students' positive behavior and be consistent with any behavioral programs implemented in the classroom and the students' living environments. Consistency is one of the most important contributions that the physical educator can make to supporting positive behavior. The physical educator will use one or more global strategies to teach new behaviors, maintain behaviors that have been taught, strengthen existing behaviors, and reduce inappropriate or undesirable behaviors. Such strategies include antecedent management, motivation, behavior modification, contingency management, class rules, and mild punishment. Below we discuss the strategies not discussed earlier.

Antecedent management

Antecedent management is an intervention strategy that focuses on preventing a behavior from occurring (or reducing its frequency and strength) by *focusing on the antecedents: those events that occur immediately prior to the behavior and serve to trigger the behavior.* It is usually more effective and easier to control antecedents than consequences, yet this approach is often overlooked. For example, when the physical educator tells the class to "get ready to run a lap," Martin, a child with a developmental disability, sits down. In this case, telling the children to "get ready to run a lap" is the antecedent to Martin's behavior of sitting down. This behavior might be prevented by telling the children "you get to run now" or having a peer buddy walk Martin to the track and begin running with him while the teacher directs the rest of the class. Another example might be to have the children "play" using a new way to run around the field such as "Follow the Leader" or "Team Runners" (five students running in line, with the last person running to the front and exchanging places with the leader without stopping the flow of movement). Martin's teacher asked the children to "play a new way to run" because she had analyzed the function of sitting behavior and determined that Martin didn't run because it was boring. She increased the interest level

MAKING CONNECTIONS

Examples of Reinforcers and Rewards

Reinforcer Example 1: Mary improved her physical fitness by 25 percent in all categories, scored at the top of her age group on fitness testing, and became a very valuable player on her intramural water polo team. This is a reinforcer because she chose to join the water polo team and her fitness level has contributed to her success in this endeavor.

Reward Example 1: Mary's physical education teacher decided to give bonus points to anyone scoring at the top level on their fitness tests. Therefore, Mary received an "A" grade in physical education. This was a reward, because she only needed a passing grade and would have gotten it without the bonus points.

Reinforcer Example 2: Jimmy is a very active and energetic seven-year-old. His physical education teacher regularly allows students to play on the mats and soft tumbling equipment when they have completed their "practice" activity. Jimmy always tries hard during the practice activity because he wants to earn the privilege of playing on the tumbling equipment.

Reward Example 2: One day, Jimmy's teacher knows her class time will be short. So, she tells the class she will give them each an oatmeal cookie instead of play time when they finish their practice activity. Jimmy doesn't like oatmeal cookies as well as play time. Therefore, he doesn't try to finish his practice activity.

Reward and Reinforcer Example: Sally is in the same class as Jimmy. She works hard every day to complete her practice activity, whether she earns play time or a cookie. She likes the teacher and likes to have the approval of the teacher. When a substitute teaches the class, Sally is very subdued and doesn't work very hard to complete her practice assignment. Therefore, play time and cookies are rewards for her, but her reinforcer is approval from her teacher.

---

to provide motivation based on the function (avoiding boredom) of the inappropriate behavior.

Another example is Rafael, a student with language delay and processing difficulties. If Rafael is asked to follow a three-part direction given to the group, he is likely to be confused and frustrated and to engage in some type of inappropriate behavior such as screaming, walking away, or disrupting the class. An effective alternative may be to change the antecedent to reduce Rafael's frustration by pairing him with a peer who can repeat each part of the direction when it is time to perform it. This points out the critical importance of understanding the whole child in order to provide effective physical education programming.

Other antecedent management strategies have been discussed previously. For instance, removing distracting items may involve covering or putting away extra equipment in the room. Providing a consistent class routine (e.g., warm-up exercise, instruction, practice, then game) can enhance the students' feeling of security and predictability, which supports positive behaviors.

Antecedent management is often the best place to start when the educator is looking for ways to improve behavior. The structure of the class, class rules, and type of instructional strategy are the sources of most behavioral antecedents in a school setting.

Contingency management

Contingency management is a *behavior modification strategy in which the consequences for a behavior are clearly stated (prior to the opportunity to engage in the behavior) and controlled by the teacher (or other person attempting to modify the behavior) in order to strengthen or weaken the targeted behavior.* Seven guidelines are important to contingency management (Rushall & Siedentop, 1972):

1. Behaviors must be defined in observable and measurable terms.
2. Terminal behaviors must be clearly stated.
3. Continuous measurement is necessary.
4. The target behavior must be the one that is reinforced.
5. Contingencies must be clearly stated and understandable by the student.
6. Contingencies must be fair.
7. Tasks should be small and reinforcement frequent at the beginning.

Contingency management systems are often classified into three categories: simple *task–reinforcer systems*, *token systems*, and *contract systems* (see Table 10.6 for a brief description of the three systems). The simple task–reinforcer system involves immediate reinforcement after the completion of the task. Under the token system, the reinforcer is a token that can be exchanged for other items. This can be a very effective system in a class in which students prefer different tangible or activity reinforcers. However, students must be able to understand the mathematics of the system, have the persistence to earn and save tokens

TABLE 10.6	Contingency management systems.
CATEGORIES	EXAMPLE
Task–reinforcer system	Teacher says, "When you have completed running the mile, you may play basketball."
Token system	When students display target behaviors, they receive poker chips, points, or marks with token status. The tokens then act as powerful reinforcers because they can be exchanged for a variety of desirable items (e.g., toys, activities, privileges, food).
Contract system	The student and teacher enter into an agreement (verbal or written) that states the reinforcer that the student will receive after displaying a target behavior.

over a period of time, and be patient enough to wait for their item or activity. The third and most sophisticated form of contingency management is the contract system. It is most effective when used with older students, as it requires some insight, forethought, and the ability to accept a delay between exhibiting the behavior and receiving the reinforcement.

As previously mentioned, positive approaches are most effective in educational settings. However, mild punishment is another type of contingency management that can be effective. Immediate punishment may be necessary in order to halt a potentially dangerous or significantly disruptive behavior.

Punishment is *an aversive stimulus applied following a behavior that you want to stop or decrease.* It can be used in contingency management, as when schools provide a list of punishments such as detention or suspension that will be applied for serious infractions of rules. The length of time a student is receiving punishment is an important variable to consider. Table 10.7 compares punishment and positive strategies and may help teachers determine which approach to use. It is important to note the lasting negative effects punishment can have on the student–teacher relationship and even the student's participation in school.

TABLE 10.7	Comparison of punitive and positive procedures.
PUNISHMENT PROCEDURES	POSITIVE PROCEDURES
■ Rapidly stop behavior.	■ Slowly stop behavior.
■ Provide immediate relief for teacher.	■ May not provide immediate relief to the teacher.
■ Teach the student and peers what not to do.	■ Teach the student and peers how to behave.
■ Decrease positive self-statements (self-concept).	■ Increase positive self-statements (self-concept).
■ Decrease positive attitudes toward school and school work.	■ Increase positive attitudes toward school and school work.
■ Cause withdrawal (e.g., going off-task, tardiness, truancy, dropping out).	■ Promote enhanced participation.
■ Increase the likelihood of aggression (toward property or people).	■ Decrease the likelihood of aggression.
■ Teach students to respond in a punitive manner.	■ Teach students to recognize the positive.
Result: Suppression, not elimination, of undesirable behavior.	Result: Alternative, positive behavior to replace maladaptive behavior.

Other Behavior Support Techniques

Some other behavior support techniques and methods are listed below and have been discussed by many authors (Axelrod & Hall, 1999; Sulzer-Azeroff & Mayer, 1991).

1. *Planned ignoring*—ignoring noncontagious behavior. For example, the teacher ignores a student who calls out without raising her hand.

2. *Signal interference*—using cues (nonverbal, eye contact, facial expression, and body postures) to transmit to the child the feeling of disapproval and control (see Figure 10.12). For example, the teacher gives eye contact and puts one finger to her mouth to communicate to a student who is talking too much.

3. *Proximity control*—moving into the immediate vicinity of the child to control behavior. For example, the teacher walks toward and stands near a student who is bouncing a ball during instruction, which causes the student to remember that the teacher has asked him to hold the ball.

4. *Reduction of tension through humor*—using humor or making light of a tense situation. For example, the teacher smiles and laughs when he trips and falls over the tumbling mats in front of the class; a student remembers a joke to tell everyone about "losing all the marbles" after another student accidentally loses the last usable ball.

5. *Hurdle lesson*—restructuring the activity or task to lessen frustration and disruption and to enhance the possibility of success. For example, the teacher notices that one student has not hit the target at all. She allows that student to stand closer to the target.

6. *Restructuring the classroom program*—making a change in the program to enhance desirable behavior. For example, the class practices a skill in pairs on their own, rather than individually with teacher direction, so that the teacher can give more attention to students who are not participating.

7. *Verbal removal*—telling a child verbally to leave the room or the area in an effort to get the child temporarily out of the area, but not necessarily for punishment. For example, a child who can't stay still during verbal instruction is asked to get a ball from a storage area.

8. *Physical restraint*—physically controlling an individual who is violent and out of control. (Physical restraint should be used *only* as a last resort and *only* after specific training in safe, nonharmful methods.)

The Influence of Sensory Responsiveness on Behavior

Because sensory processing is an integral part of the sensory-integrative-motor-sensory-feedback system (SIMSF, as explained in Chapters 3 and 4), unusual sensory responses can affect all types of behaviors. Understanding differences in an individual's sensory responsiveness, and how these differences may affect behavior, can help the teacher plan effective behavior support strategies. Refer to Chapter 3 for a description of the five sensory modalities or systems. In addition to the vestibular, tactile, proprioceptive, visual, and auditory modalities, some models include the gustatory–olfactory (taste and smell) modality, but this modality has minimal impact in educational settings unless the person has an extreme hypersensitivity to taste and smell.

Everyone (with and without a disability) has a general state of arousal and responsiveness to sensory stimuli that can be placed on a continuum from most to least responsive. Various biological, environmental, developmental, and emotional components interact to determine the level and to cause changes in the level at any point in time. These factors often interact in individuals with a disability to place them at the extreme ends of the responsitivity continuum. Individuals falling toward the most responsive end of the continuum can be categorized as overresponsive or hypersensitive. Behaviors related to this level are interpreted as sensory-avoiding. Individuals who fall toward the

FIGURE 10.12

This teacher is using signal interference to quiet the class.

opposite end of the continuum, the least responsive, can be categorized as underresponsive or hyposensitive. Behaviors related to this level are interpreted as sensory-seeking. Disabilities that are frequently associated with sensory-seeking and sensory-avoiding behaviors include autism, traumatic brain injury, developmental delay, learning disability, and other neurological disorders.

Individuals who are hypersensitive (sensory-avoiding) have a low tolerance for sensory stimuli that others consider harmless or nonirritating. They learn to avoid or protest the stimuli to which they are sensitive. For example, a child may cover her ears during a large group game because the amount of noise from peers talking feels very loud and is irritating. Individuals who are hyposensitive (sensory-seeking) have a high tolerance for sensory stimuli and often seek out extensive amounts of one or more types of sensory stimulation. For example, a child may repeatedly rock or spin, touch certain textures, make noises, twirl or flick fingers or objects near the eyes, or bump into people and objects. To others, these may seem to be unnecessary and annoying behaviors; however, the child exhibiting the behavior may be using it to gain needed sensory stimuli, which, in turn, may increase attention or concentration on the task. However, these behaviors may also distract the student from the task; therefore, the teacher should analyze the effect of the behaviors at any point in time.

It is important to understand that both sensory-seeking and sensory-avoiding behaviors may be present in the same individual. They may even occur in relation to the same types of stimuli because the responsivity level fluctuates, because the child develops more tolerance for the stimuli, or because the child can tolerate stimuli when he can control them. For example, a student may be observed to touch peers frequently, rub smooth textures repeatedly, and hold an object in his left hand while writing with his right hand. However, when standing in line, the same individual overreacts to light touches from peers, and he pushes teachers away when they attempt to use physical guidance. This individual is seeking tactile stimulation that he can control while avoiding tactile stimulation controlled by others.

Sensory stimulation can have a cumulative effect in some people. That is, they are tolerant of a stimulus until it reaches a certain threshold, at which time it becomes irritating. Almost everyone has a threshold for the loudness (pitch and decibel level) of sound or the intensity (number, speed, and brightness) of moving objects in their visual field. Avoiding these stimuli when they are at high levels is considered an acceptable and healthy strategy and generally does not interfere with daily living. An individual who is sensitive to auditory stimuli may tolerate a group game well in the morning, but not in the afternoon after she has experienced several hours of listening in the classroom, recess play, the school bell ringing, music instruction, and lunchtime activities. In this case, the reduced level of tolerance for noise in the afternoon can be considered to be a result of the cumulative effect of listening to sounds all morning.

Physical activity professionals should also understand the calming and alerting effects of certain types of sensory stimuli. With this knowledge, the teacher can plan activities and accommodations to assist individuals with self-regulation (e.g., calming themselves when overly stimulated or increasing their attention when lethargic or distracted).

In general, stimuli that tend to be calming for most people include the following (Wright, Gurman, et al., 1998):

1. Deep-pressure touch, such as massage; lying between two beanbag chairs; or bouncing, either energetically or slowly and rhythmically
2. Neutral warmth, as in retaining the body's heat with a blanket or jacket
3. Chewing, sucking, or licking
4. Vibratory stimuli that are large in amplitude and low in frequency, as experienced when riding in a car
5. Decreased physical activity
6. Slow, rhythmic movement such as slow swinging or rocking
7. Quiet music with a definite, predictable rhythm (e.g., instrumental or orchestral music with no vocals)

In general, stimuli that tend to be alerting for most people include the following (Wright, Gurman, et al., 1998):

1. Light touch, such as tickling, wiping skin with a soft cloth, or light brushing or stroking
2. Cold or chilling activities such as touching ice cubes or standing in a cold breeze
3. Spinning
4. Fast vibration, such as therapy vibrators with about 300 cycles per second

Table 10.8 gives suggestions and examples to help the physical education teacher identify interventions appropriate for sensory-seeking and sensory-avoiding behaviors in physical activity settings. For additional information, Table 4.1 gives examples of sensory-seeking and sensory-avoiding behaviors related to specific sensory stimuli.

TABLE 10.8 *Basic sensory interventions useful in physical activity settings.*

CATEGORY/TYPES OF INTERVENTIONS	EXAMPLES
Sensory-Seeking	
Provide a "sensory diet" (various sensory-based activities scheduled into a child's day to help meet the child's individual sensory needs)	■ Child jumps between stations rather than walking (providing additional proprioceptive and vestibular stimulation) ■ Child is allowed to perform the rocking chair exercise while waiting at the station (providing additional vestibular stimulation) ■ Child wears keychain with tactile toy attached to belt at all times; specific toy is rotated daily (providing availability of tactile stimulation)
Teach replacement behaviors (more acceptable methods for gaining the same type of stimulation)	■ Child learns how to clasp his own hands and count to 10 instead of touching student next to him ■ Child uses Theratube bracelet to chew instead of chewing on shirt ■ Child gets vibrating pillow to use instead of hitting head
Use reinforcers that provide preferred sensations	■ Child is allowed to run across the field following 10 focused trials of throwing for accuracy (vestibular reinforcer) ■ Student uses a personal, portable tape player while completing the distance walk or run (auditory reinforcer) ■ Child is allowed to go to the slide for two turns after completing the warm-up exercise routine (vestibular reinforcer)
Determine calming sensations and use them when appropriate	■ Following a music or movement activity, child wraps herself into a parachute or sits under a small mat (providing deep-pressure touch)
Provide accommodations to allow for sensory-seeking behavior	■ Child is allowed to stand in a hula hoop instead of on a poly spot to provide more (but limited) space for movement during exercises
Sensory-Avoiding	
Reduce or eliminate irritating stimuli in the environment	■ Large group counts silently or uses sign language instead of a loud, group cadence ■ Student stands at the back of the line or sits at the end of a semicircle to avoid unwanted touch from peers
Provide accommodations to reduce the effects of irritating stimuli	■ Teacher touches student where clothing provides a buffer ■ Child stands close to teacher to eliminate visual distractions from peers
Teach coping strategies	■ Child asks adults or peers to speak softly ■ Child self-selects a quiet area of the gymnasium or field for skill practice ■ Teacher uses a timer, watch, or verbal cue to reassure child of limited exposure to irritating stimuli
Schedule breaks in a bland or calming environment	■ Teacher excuses child from class a few minutes early to get a drink of water or sit in a quiet place before going to the next class ■ Teacher allows the child to finish bouncing a ball to a partner 10 times, then sit away from the group and watch the others as they complete the task several more times
Refer to therapist for desensitization program	■ School requests nonthreatening strategies to reduce a child's fear of climbing on playground apparatus ■ Teacher contacts therapist to discuss parts of a desensitization program that could be infused into the physical education program

SUMMARY

To individualize instruction, it is necessary to understand the process of learning and the factors affecting learning, and to develop strategies appropriate for meeting individual needs. The motor-learning literature identifies 10 factors affecting learning: amount and type of practice, methods of learning, meaningfulness of activity, activity versus passivity, knowledge of results, transfer of learning, plateaus, retention, motivation, and feedback. These factors tend to affect the learning of individuals with a disability in unique ways, and educators should understand them well in order to individualize instruction.

Styles of teaching and techniques and methods of instruction are many and varied. A teacher may employ one or more of the following instructional methods: part and whole method, explanation and demonstration, guided discovery, and movement exploration. The educator may individualize instruction by modifying the instruction, the learning environment, or the activity. These strategies should be used along with task analysis and behavior support techniques. Eclectic and creative strategies with a foundation in the developmental approach are necessary to meet the varied needs of individuals with a disability.

Educators should understand and use behavior support strategies and principles, including behavior modification, antecedent management, contingency management, and motivation. Positive approaches to behavior support are not only the most effective, but are also the most appropriate, ethical, and efficient for educational settings. In addition, the educator should consider the effect of different levels of sensory responses on behavior for children with a disability.

CHAPTER 10

Learning Activities

10.1 Choose a game or physical activity (e.g., volleyball, locomotor skills, aerobic fitness) and write it at the top of a piece of paper. Make a chart with three rows and three columns. Label each column with an age range (not more than a three-year span, e.g., 6–8 years, 3–4 years). Label each row with a student need or difficulty, such as difficulty processing language, paraplegia, avoids tactile stimuli, uses visual communication system, or similar issues. Fill in each blank square with at least two ways you might modify the instruction, the environment, or the activity for a student of that age with the listed need.

10.2 Using five note cards, on each card briefly describe one undesirable behavior that might occur in a physical education or adapted physical education class. Exchange cards with a partner. Write down one to three behavior support strategies that the teacher could use to address the behavior or reduce the negative effects it may have on the class. Discuss your ideas with your partner. To guide your discussion consider:

- Was this task difficult? Why or why not?
- Were any behaviors left blank? Why or why not?
- What resources did you use, and what are some other possible resources?

10.3 Observe some children with a disability such as an autism spectrum disorder, developmental disability, or Tourette Syndrome. List some behaviors that you think may have a sensory function. Be prepared to discuss your reasons or rationale with your class.

REFERENCES

Axelrod, S., & Hall, R. V. (1999). *Behavior modification: Basic principles* (Managing behavior, Pt. 2, 2nd ed.). Austin, TX: Pro-Ed.

Browning Wright, D., Kraemer, B., & Morton, K. B. (1997). *Prompting.* Unpublished paper, Diagnostic Center Southern California, Los Angeles.

Caraulia, A. P., Wyka, E. T., & Christiansen, S. (Eds.). (1997). *Nonviolent crisis intervention: Learning to defuse explosive behavior.* Milwaukee, WI: CPI.

Cheatum, B. A., & Hammond, A. A. (2000). *Physical activities for improving children's learning and behavior.* Champaign, IL: Human Kinetics.

Cook, L., Cullinan, D., Epstein, M. H., Forness, S. R., Hallahan, D. P., Kauffman, J. M., et al. (1991). Problems and promises in special education and related services for children and youth with emotional or behavioral disorders. *Behavioral Disorders, 16,* 2999–3013.

Copple, C., & Bredekamp, S. (1997). *Developmentally appropriate practice in early childhood programs (rev. ed.).* Washington, DC: National Association for the Education of Young Children.

Deci, E., Nezlek, J., & Sheinman, L. (1981). Characteristics of the rewarder and intrinsic motivation of the rewardee. *Journal of Personality and Social Psychology, 40*(1), 1–10.

Donnellan, A. M., La Vigna, G. W., Negri-Shoultz, N., & Fassbender, L. (1998). *Progress without punishment: Effective approaches for learners with behavior problems.* New York: Teachers College Press.

ERIC Clearinghouse on Disabilities and Gifted Education, 1999.

Frost, L. A., & Bondy, A. S. (2001). *PECS—The picture exchange communication system training manual.* Bethesda, MD: Woodbine House.

Gauthier, R. A. (1981). A descriptive analytic study of teacher–student interaction in mainstreamed physical education classes. *Dissertation Abstracts International, 41*(8), 3474-A.

Hall, R. V., & Hall, M. C. (1998). *How to select reinforcers (How to manage behavior series, 2nd ed.).* Austin, TX: Pro-Ed.

Hill, G. M. (March/April 2001). Should kids "pick the team" in K–12 physical education classes? *Strategies, 14*(4), 26.

Hunt, P., Haring, K., Farron-Davis, F., Staub, D., Beckstead, S., Karasoff, P., et al. (1993). Factors associated with the integrated educational placement of students with severe disabilities. *Journal of the Association of Persons with Severe Handicaps, 18,* 6–15.

King, L. J. (1986). *Calming-alerting activities.* Paper presented at a seminar titled "Attention deficits in learning disorders and autism" with Temple Grandin, Ontario, CA, sponsored by Division of Innovation and Development, Continuing Education Programs of America.

Koomar, J., Kranowitz, C. S., et al. (2005). *Answers to questions teachers ask about sensory integration.* Las Vegas: Sensory Resources.

Lavay, B. W., French, R., & Henderson, H. (2006). *Positive behavior management in physical activity settings.* Champaign, IL: Human Kinetics.

Lawther, J. D. (1978). *The learning and performance of physical skills.* Englewood Cliffs, NJ: Prentice Hall.

Mayer, G. R. (1999). Constructive discipline for school personnel (statistical data Included). *Education and Treatment of Children, 22,* 36.

McGhie, S. (January/February 2002). Late again? Developmentally appropriate methods for forming teams. *Strategies, 15*(3), 35.

Morton, K. B., & Wolford, S. (1994). *Analysis of sensory behavior inventory (rev. ed.).* Arcadia, CA: Skills with Occupational Therapy.

Mosston, M. (1989). *The spectrum of teaching styles: From command to discovery.* Belmont, CA: Wadsworth.

Mosston, M., & Ashworth, S. (1994). *Teaching physical education* (4th ed.). New York: Macmillan.

Omoto, K. (1985). *People to People.* Unpublished.

O'Neil, R. E., Horner, R. H., Albin, R. A., Storey, J., & Sprague, J. (1997). *Functional assessment and program development for problem behavior: A practical handbook.* Baltimore: Brookes.

Pack, I. J. (1974). *Adapted physical education at San Fernando Junior High School.* Unpublished paper, California State University.

Parish, L., & Treasure, D. (2003). Physical activity and situational motivation in physical education: Influence of the motivational climate and perceived ability. *Research Quarterly for Exercise and Sport, 74,* 173.

Prusak, K. A., & Darst, P. W. (2001). The effect of choice on the motivation of adolescent females in physical education. *Research Quarterly for Exercise and Sport, 72,* A-76.

Robb, M. D. (1972). *The dynamics of motor skill acquisition.* Englewood Cliffs, NJ: Prentice Hall.

Rushall, B. S., & Siedentop, D. (1972). *The development and control of behavior in sport and physical education.* Philadelphia: Lea & Febiger.

Seaman, J. A. (1973, Summer). Right up their alley. *Teaching Exceptional Children, 5*(5), 20.

Sulzer-Azeroff, B., & Mayer, G. R. (1991). *Behavior analysis for lasting change.* New York: Holt, Reinhart & Winston.

Thorndike, E. L., Bregman, E. O., Tilton, W. J., & Woodyard, E. (1928). *Adult learning.* New York: Macmillan.

Waggoner, B. E. (1973). Motivation in physical education and recreation for emotionally handicapped children. *Journal of Health, Physical Education, and Recreation, 44,* 73–76.

Wallin, J. M. (2001–2004). *Functional behavior analysis.* Oak Harbor, WA: www.polyxo.com/fba/.

Wilbarger, P., & Wilbarger, J. L. (1991). *Sensory defensiveness in children aged 2–12: An intervention guide for parents and other caretakers.* Santa Barbara, CA: Avanti Educational Programs.

Wright, D. B., & Gurman, H. B., et al. (1998). *Positive intervention for serious behavior problems (rev. ed.).* Sacramento: California Department of Education.

CHAPTER 11

Effective Programming
DEVELOPMENTAL ACTIVITIES

Guiding Questions

1. What are some examples of activities for sensory stimulation and discrimination?

2. What types of special activities and equipment can be used for the development of motor patterns and motor skills?

3. What are some factors to consider when planning activities for preschool children?

4. What are some examples of when the physical educator should transition to providing a combination of developmental and functional type activities?

5. How are cognitive learning and language development incorporated into the physical education program?

6. How can the physical education teacher encourage language use and development through physical education activities?

7. What are the ways physical activities can enhance socialization and affective growth?

PLANNING FOR DEVELOPMENTALLY APPROPRIATE ACTIVITIES

When planning lessons and presenting activities, the physical educator must select the appropriate types of activities, make adaptations or modifications in accordance with the individual's needs and challenges, and apply the principles of learning suggested in this text. It is important to remember that planning involves the consideration of a variety of factors, many of which have already been presented (e.g., philosophy, program goals, curriculum models, accommodations, and necessary supports). The activity should not be one that just fills time and space or keeps the students occupied, but one that meets the needs of the individual students and the group as a whole. Each teacher should think about the skills that are required when playing a game or participating in an activity so that each student has a successful experience. This means that lead-up games and activities, the "give-and-take" process of learning how to take turns or share equipment, and emphasizing the differences between cooperation and competition are important elements in the teaching process.

The National Association for Sport and Physical Education (NASPE) standards (refer to Chapter 9) provide a "roadmap" to follow when planning the general physical education program. The goals and benchmarks from each individualized education program (IEP) provide a more specific direction, as well as program focus, for specific students. These three components (standards, goals, and focus) guide the professional in planning an effective and fun program of physical education for all students.

The program focus for physical education is easily organized for different age groups based on the developmental model. Remember that, at a certain point, a decision must be made to focus more on a combination of the developmental and functional approaches to activities that are age-appropriate for the students. For example, hopping on one foot is not an appropriate developmental task to continue to teach a student who is 10 or 13 years old. But stepping off a height or over obstacles or alternating the foot pattern might be more functional for accessing the bleachers for a ball game, using the escalator at the mall or airport, or crossing a street. The educator should not plan activities for the sake of "keeping everyone active or busy" but should instead choose activities based on the importance of each activity and the reason for teaching it to the students. A guiding question that teachers can ask is, "Does the student have the skills for the activity?" For example, if the goal for the student is to take turns and cooperate, then the lead-up activity may be just as effective as the game itself.

When considering a focus of the activities to present to a class of students, the physical educator can begin with moving from simple to complex: setting a foundation (reflex activity), then moving toward motor patterns and skills. The activities as presented here are neither modified nor suggested for any specific disability grouping. The physical educator must select the appropriate types of activities and make adaptations or modifications in accordance with each individual's challenges and unique needs, and the principles outlined in this text.

Activities for Reflex Development and Inhibition

At the base of the developmental model (Seaman & DePauw, 1995) are the innate neural capacity and reflex and survival behaviors of the young child. With the inclusion of individuals with a disability in physical education classes, it is necessary for teachers to incorporate activities for reflex development or inhibition within the curriculum. This should be done only after consultation with medical personnel or physical (PT) or occupational therapists (OT). You are advised to attempt these activities with the utmost caution and a sound experiential base. The reason the team approach is so successful is that each person can contribute to the lesson from a different knowledge base, perspective, and experience. This adds to the enrichment of program goals and objectives as well as the lesson provided for all students.

Appendix H describes reflex development, inhibition, and contraindications. The reflexes addressed include:

- Hand grasp reflex
- Startle reflex
- Crossed extension reflex
- Asymmetrical tonic neck reflex (ATNR)
- Symmetrical tonic neck reflex (STNR)
- Tonic labyrinthine reflex (TLR:P for prone and TLR:S for supine)
- Support
- Righting reactions
- Protective extension

Activities such as animal walks, angels-in-the-snow, and balance board activities, as well as effective movement experiences for young children (preschool and primary students), are discussed later in this chapter (and in Appendix H).

Activities for Sensory Stimulation and Discrimination

The need for sensory stimulation is well documented in the literature. For growth and development, the child requires sensory-stimulating activities coupled with motor responses. Each sensory system has a developmental sequence that progresses from gross sensation to discrimination. The activities presented for each sensory system are designed to provide sensory stimulation and, later on, to require discrimination and the refined use of sensory input. The sensory modalities described in Appendix H include:

- Tactile (stimulation, discrimination)
- Vestibular
- Proprioceptive
- Auditory
- Visual, including ocular training activities and space and form perception

Activities for Enhancing Sensorimotor Responses

The student must be able to organize and use sensory information for motor action. This process involves integration that results in sensorimotor responses, including:

- Praxis (motor planning)
- Integration of both sides of the body
- Balance and equilibrium responses
- Eye–hand and eye–foot interaction and coordination
- Crossing the midline of the body
- Body awareness

Activities for Enhancing Motor Patterns and Motor Skills

Activities at this level of the model include those that help to provide individuals with a repertoire of basic movement experiences. Joint range of motion (ROM) activities and basic body movements occur in conjunction with normal motor development and other basic motor experiences; thus, they need not be isolated. For students who are very young or those with a severe disability, ROM, body positioning, and early motor experiences may not occur naturally or sequentially. Some of the activities listed here can help facilitate movement opportunities for these students.

Examples of developmental activities included in Appendix H are listed in the following categories:

1. Early motor experiences and motor patterns:
   - ROM
   - Head control
   - Rolling over
   - Crawling (on stomach, reciprocal action of limbs)
   - Creeping on hands and knees
   - Sitting
   - Kneeling
   - Standing and walking
   - Stair climbing
   - Hand and arm use
2. Activities for motor pattern development (locomotor):
   - Walking
   - Running
   - Jumping
   - Hopping
   - Sliding
3. Activities for motor pattern development (manipulative):
   - Rolling ball
   - Throwing
   - Bouncing ball
   - Catching
   - Striking
   - Kicking
4. Activities for motor pattern development (non-locomotor):
   - Bending
   - Reaching and stretching
   - Turning and twisting
   - Pushing and pulling
5. Activities for locomotor skills development:
   - Galloping
   - Skipping
   - Leaping
   - Combinations
6. Special equipment and activities:
   - *Equipment*—balance beam, balance board, hula hoops and carpet squares, parachute, jump ropes, scooter boards, T-stools, tin can stilts, mini trampoline and rebounder
   - *Activities*—angels-in-the-snow, animal walks, wrestling games, relaxation, stunts, therapeutic activities

SELECTING APPROPRIATE ACTIVITIES FOR DEVELOPMENTAL NEEDS

The effective teacher creates opportunities for children to move by planning and organizing developmentally appropriate and meaningful activities. This section discusses the general principles involved in selecting activities at various developmental levels. Appropriate activities often overlap two age groups. It is important for the physical educator to remember that although development occurs sequentially, it does not occur at exactly the same rate for all children. When planning learning activities for a group of children, the physical educator must consider the various rates of development of the children in the group. In general, when selecting developmentally appropriate activities (especially when considering the needs of the whole class and those of the student with a disability), the physical educator should be prepared to plan a variety of opportunities for movement. The variety or variation of movement experiences brings meaning and purpose to the lesson, while also addressing NASPE standards, IEP goals, and the program focus.

Infants

Infants come into this life using all of their senses (e.g., smell, taste, sight, hearing, and touch) to explore, interact with, and learn about the world around them. One of the first ways that an infant will learn is through his or her own body. The parent, caregiver, or teacher can facilitate the child's natural curiosity about the world by guiding the infant to discover and become aware of the workings of his or her senses. As professionals, we want to encourage children to be curious and eager to discover what their senses can tell them about their environment. It is primarily through the process of awareness and learning about the body and how it moves that the infant learns. It is also during this process of exploration and learning that the child notes differences in the uses of the senses. The child can explore the uses of the senses when presented with alternatives that relate to the child's own body and the surrounding world.

Thus, we can assume that it is mainly through play that a child learns. Play is "learning," and it is one of the most effective kinds of learning. The young child is one of the best learners because he or she learns more, at a faster rate, than at any other time in his or her life. A child first learns by becoming aware of himself or herself, then he or she is ready to explore and learn about others around him or her. First, the child relates to the mother and father (or primary caregiver) and then to others. Objects of play, such as dolls and toys, widen the field of recognition and learning. As the child crawls and moves around in the environment, he or she becomes aware of space and how he or she relates to the space. The child observes differences in shapes, textures, sizes, weights, colors, and so on. As the child manipulates objects, he or she begins to learn how they are related to each other and develops the perception of distance—how far to reach to pick up an object. As learning extends to climbing in and out, up and down, under, over, and around objects, the child learns and becomes more skilled, doing more and more for himself or herself. This learning process is the same for all children. For a child with a disability, caregivers and teachers provide help and assistance for learning that is not easily acquired so that the child can reach his or her potential.

When determining how best to facilitate learning for infants, it may be helpful to ask the following questions:

1. What components (patterns) of movement does the infant need in order to master the new skill?
2. What future skills incorporate this important component (pattern) or skill?
3. What areas of cognitive and language development can be facilitated by this movement?

The baby's mental ability grows naturally and experientially. His or her learning process thrives on encouragement, challenge, and a sense of pleasure. The best and most effective type of learning environment, whether provided by the parent or by educators, is one in which the child is accepted and encouraged to develop at his or her own rate, primarily through opportunities for engaging in a broad variety of experiences.

For the educator who is providing this type of environment, it is important to remember:

1. Young children learn from concrete and active experiences.
2. Young children learn at their own level of ability and readiness.
3. Young children have different and individual learning styles.
4. Young children typically learn from exposure to a task or activity (e.g., hearing, seeing, or feeling it) and then attempting to perform it themselves.
5. Young children master a skill by repeating it many times, often by incorporating it into their play experiences.

For the infant and many students with multiple disabilities or a severe disability, activities involving reflex development and inhibition are the first step in building a foundation for further motor skill development. (Refer to Appendix B.) Of course, proper training on the part of the physical educator is necessary, and consultation with medical personnel, such as physical or occupational therapists, is often essential. When working with infants, it is particularly important to collaborate with other professionals. The physical educator is advised to attempt activities with the utmost caution and a sound knowledge base.

Preschool and Primary Grades

Often, young children do not participate in school programs for extended periods of time. Thus, parents can help their children acquire motor skills at home. It is often said that parents are a child's first teachers. Assistance from professionals can help parents plan activities appropriate for the particular needs of their child. Professionals consulting with parents should keep the home environment in mind. Parents usually appreciate suggestions of activities that do not require expensive equipment and that can be incorporated in the typical daily and weekly schedules of family activities.

Most motor activities designed for young children with a disability prepare them for participation in physical activities enjoyed by their same-age peers. These activities are consistent with the philosophy, curriculum, and equipment used in developmentally based preschool programs. Parents and teachers should be generous in making available activities that are creative and interesting to the children in their care.

Research has indicated that young children with a disability must often be taught skills that other preschool-aged children incidentally acquire through participation in enriched and stimulating activities and environments. Children with a disability may need to be motivated to pursue activities that increase their perceptual awareness of the world around them. They may need assistance with learning how to cope in the school environment. Most of all, they must be given feedback that leads to feelings of self-worth and confidence.

When determining how best to facilitate learning for preschool-aged children, it may be helpful to ask the following questions:

1. What movement experiences (physical activities) are important for this child and his or her same-aged peers?
2. How much time should be devoted to physical activity at home? At school?
3. What activities or experiences can be provided to allow the child to enlarge and expand his or her learning?
4. How can physical activities enhance this child's language and cognitive learning?

Movement makes a difference in all of our lives. For the young child with a disability, it helps her develop the basic skills essential to learning in other domains. For example, the ability to perform the simple movement of reaching out to touch an object will allow the child to gain information about the object's size, color, shape, texture, and position. Movement can help the child become confident and independent. When a child is able to crawl, slither, roll, or use a scooter, tricycle, or crutches, he has increased his control over the environment, rather than being controlled by it.

Movement is learning: When a child manipulates blocks, toys, puzzles, or balls or looks at books, movement is involved. Movement can mean freedom when the child is able to negotiate around obstacles, climb, move, or dance. Movement can mean safety when the child can run, walk, crawl, or roll away from dangerous situations.

Movement is communication: Joy, acceptance, and pleasure (fun) can be communicated when a child can nod her head "yes" or "no," clap her hands, or jump. Frowning, crying, or dropping one's shoulders can communicate unhappiness. Children who have been taught alternatives in movement or who have mastered a variety of movements are more easily accepted by peers and know that they have achieved success on their own.

The teacher's general goal is to guide the child through many movement patterns in various positions (e.g., prone, supine, sitting, kneeling, standing). When children participate in numerous opportunities to develop movement skills, they can progress at their own rate and experience different feelings about each movement experience—confidence, understanding, curiosity, or even inadequacy, fear, and frustration. It is the teacher's role to guide the children through these experiences and feelings and allow them to learn through practice, problem solving, and creativity.

Elementary School Grade Levels

Teachers must be aware of the developmental milestones and progressive stages of development through which children pass on their way to achieving mature movement patterns. In the elementary age levels, children refine their ability to perform basic movement patterns and typically achieve what we call *mature patterns*. Keep in mind that children with a disability who are in the primary grades of elementary school may be functioning developmentally at a preschool level.

The environment and experiences provided in school facilitate learning and the development of the skills necessary to move toward the top of the developmental model. In other words, learning through physical activities in the elementary school age ranges helps the child start to apply movement skills to culturally determined forms of movement. By being aware of milestones in development and analyzing movement patterns, the teacher can present realistic and progressive movement challenges to the students. One of the important characteristics of an effective teacher is the ability to pose problems or present challenges so that children are motivated to move. This ability is especially important when providing purposeful program planning for children with a disability. All children have the potential for movement and should be provided with support and opportunities to experience and solve movement challenges and acquire skills.

When providing these learning experiences for children at the elementary school level, the physical educator may wish to consider the following possibilities:

1. Use different positions, equipment, and environmental spaces to:
    - Teach vocabulary concepts to build understanding and progression.
    - Vary the space and equipment used, the obstacles encountered, and the complexity of the task presented.
    - Encourage the student to try all tasks and help his or her learning by providing definite and specific directions and feedback.
2. Use a variety of learning experiences and games so that the child will:
    - Understand the task and skills to be performed.
    - Have an opportunity to participate as much as he or she would like (active movement).
    - Have successful attempts in learning skills and playing with other children.
3. Use different teaching strategies to help the child perform a task by:
    - Conveying to the student what it is that he or she needs to do in order to learn, correct, or improve his or her performance and skills.
    - Changing the objectives to meet individual needs, such as making an adaptive response or increasing skill levels.

> ## *Teaching Tip*
>
> **SPECIFIC EXPLANATIONS** • How will you explain to the child what to do?
>
> The teacher must focus on the language and the specific explanations provided to each student. Are you telling them *how* to do something (e.g., *how* to balance, *how* to kick a ball, *how* to hop, *how* to run, *how* to turn the rope)?
>
> "Try hard," "keep going," "practice"—all are easy to say and use, but none clearly identifies *what* the child should be doing. It might be more helpful to think about what to say to the child that describes what he should be doing, how he can do it, and what to think about when he is moving his body (e.g., "lift your feet higher," "bend your knees," "look at the object coming," "bend your arms to catch the ball").

4. Use specific organizational patterns for effective lessons that provide for:
    - Several smaller groups, to increase the number of children who are active at one time.
    - Varied pacing, to allow for active participation, slower processing, relaxation, practice, and so on.
    - Building a progression from simple to complex and sequencing skills, concepts, and rules of play.
5. Use task analysis to assist the student's learning process by recognizing the elements necessary to complete a task.

Middle School and Junior High School

Middle and junior high school students focus on applying motor skills to a variety of culturally determined forms of movement. Exposure to a wide variety of activities is important to help students understand their preferences, strengths, and physical fitness needs. At this age, most students have acquired adequate cognitive and language skills for learning to apply important concepts of health-related fitness to daily physical activities. Students who excel in sports and physical activities emerge and often gain significant attention from their peers. It is important for the physical educator to remember that *all* students must become physically educated. The emotional development of children at this age often involves experimenting with independence from adults and risk taking. With increased independence, students may be more sensitive to criticism, embarrassment, praise, and attention; this sensitivity is sometimes accompanied by a strong need for acceptance among peers. Students may be more willing to take physical risks than social risks.

Programming that helps students to explore their physical abilities safely through guided physical challenges is often effective. Many sports provide a natural environment to facilitate this type of learning, such as:

- Gymnastics and wrestling
- Physical fitness and martial arts
- Track and field
- Aquatics
- Traditional team sports

When selecting activities and designing learning experiences, the physical educator should keep motor and emotional milestones in mind, as well as other areas of development. To facilitate learning for students in middle school and junior high school, it may be helpful for the teacher to ask the following questions when planning activities:

1. How can a broad and balanced variety of physical activities be provided?
2. How can fitness concepts be taught and experienced?
3. How can learning experiences support emotional development?
4. How do group norms and values affect the selection of learning experiences?
5. How can individual preferences and interests be incorporated into the movement curriculum?
6. How can healthy lifestyle choices be encouraged throughout the curriculum?

In this age range, physical education programming for students with a disability often must shift away from teaching students to perform developmentally lower motor patterns and skills and move toward applying learned skills to chronologically age-appropriate movement activities. The student with a disability should focus on helping to select and apply appropriate accommodations, adaptive devices, and compensatory strategies. Learning self-advocacy skills is often important to support the student's growing need for independence and peer acceptance.

Secondary or High School

Within the secondary school program, the student is provided with a comprehensive and contemporary physical education and sport program. The student usually experiences a well-balanced and varied program of sport opportunities and receives information on skill and technique acquisition, safety, scoring, rules and etiquette, strategy, equipment, and related terminology. Additionally, the student is usually provided with programming in health and fitness concepts and in leisure and recreational activities that the student can pursue for a lifetime. Career opportunities in physical education and sport are also explored.

For the student with a disability, this is a time to develop more refined and skilled performances in selected activities. Listed below are some considerations when planning at the secondary level:

- Student preferences
- Lifetime sports and activities
- Regional sports and games (e.g., skiing, surfing, rock climbing, kayaking)
- Alternative sports and activities (e.g., Frisbee, earth ball, cooperative games)
- Safe risk-taking experiences (e.g., rock wall climbing, stunts and tumbling, diving, ropes courses)
- Activities that are accessible in the community (e.g., swimming, bowling, golf, skating)
- Disability sport opportunities

MAKING CONNECTIONS

Students Initiating Use of an Adaptive Device or Accommodation

1. Jonathan is a student who uses a wheelchair and enjoys being with his peers, especially a friend, Tom, who enjoys playing kickball. Because Jonathan is proficient at rolling a ball off a bowling ramp, he is placed as pitcher for the team. Another team player is assigned to be a "creeper," assisting Jonathan in catching or deflecting the kicked ball and in placing the ball on top of the ramp for the next pitch. When it is Jonathan's turn to kick, he asks a teammate to be a "kicker" for him and then he propels his chair around the bases.
2. Marcie is a student with spina bifida who uses a wheelchair and enjoys playing volleyball. She tells her volleyball team that she would like to have a rule change for her position: Allow her to serve the ball from the mid-court area and to use the volleyball trainer during the game. All players agree to the rule change and use of the trainer ball.

MAKING CONNECTIONS

Students Apply an Adaptation to Recreational Activity with Peers

1. Dylan is a student with Down syndrome. He has recently started playing basketball at the local park with his friends. One day a few new players came. Dylan and his friends explained the rule changes that they use. The rules of play are that Dylan is allowed to dribble the ball without opposition before passing to a teammate. He is also able to shoot from any position within the key area without a time penalty. Scoring is as follows: one point when the ball touches the net, two points when it touches the rim or backboard, and three points when he makes a basket.

2. Susan is a student with spina bifida who enjoys playing tennis with her family and friends. She is able to maneuver her wheelchair around the court easily, but explains to her friends that she likes to play with the following rule changes: allowing two bounces before she strikes the ball and allowing her to perform a drop serve over the net rather than an overhead serve.

Transition to Adult Programs

The transition from child to adult is exciting and challenging for every adolescent and family. This is a time to prepare for the future, as well as to face the new challenges of a demanding time of life. Varied and consistent opportunities for participation in physical activity settings provide exposure to peers and provide role models for social interaction and appropriate behaviors, as well as developing physical skills necessary for any young person, whether or not the person has a disability. A "special friend" can provide invaluable opportunities for sharing and learning. This person could be a neighbor, sibling, other family member, or volunteer from the community.

The physical education teacher has a unique opportunity to support and encourage participation in community programs, whether through programs at the local community college or university or through recreational programs. The individualized transition plan (ITP), usually started when the student is 16, provides a vehicle to plan and prepare for adulthood. Individuals with a disability may be enrolled in school programs beyond the typical age at which most youth complete their high school education. In addition, some individuals with a disability continue to need the support of adapted physical education while enrolled in a postsecondary program. Physical education programming at this developmental level should focus on refining and completing instruction that enables the individual with a disability to participate in physical activities in the community with adults. Some individuals may continue to need support and assistance throughout life, but the ultimate goal is for each person to be as independent as possible in pursuing a general program of health-related physical activity. Examples of some successful outcomes include:

- A person with a physical disability who directs a personal assistant to assist with positioning for physical fitness activities.
- A person with a visual impairment who independently travels to a local recreation center to participate in a community-based physical activity.
- A person with mental retardation who chooses to continue to participate in a Special Olympics sport.
- A person with a brain injury who regularly participates with friends or family members in fitness walking.

INCORPORATING ALL LEARNING DOMAINS INTO THE PHYSICAL EDUCATION PROGRAM

Much has been written about the importance of movement and learning and about how learning can take place through the medium of movement. Recent attention to action-based learning and the multiple intelligences has broadened the possibilities for incorporating other learning domains into the physical education program. Planned physical activities can supplement and expand classroom content. The teacher's role is to select, plan, implement, and evaluate learning activities that incorporate concepts about movement. Within this role are vast opportunities to infuse the cognitive, language, social, and affective aspects of the school curriculum into the movement and physical education program. Although physical education teachers must consider their specific facilities, equipment, resources, and educational objectives, some general guidelines can be helpful when planning activities for children.

The effective teacher plans, designs, and implements realistic, enriching, and appropriate learning experiences for students. Creating opportunities for the student to make connections between the movement activity and a fact or idea learned in another curricular area heightens interest and facilitates learning. Activities can be sequenced so that they are linked toward achieving a special goal or objective. Linking the activity presented in physical education with language arts, mathematics, science, or history in an "interdisciplinary" approach usually enhances learning in each subject area. A team of teachers, two teachers from different subject areas, or the physical educator alone can conduct an interdisciplinary teaching lesson.

Cognitive Learning

Movement provides a natural medium through which individuals discover and explore their environment and learn about the world. Movement allows the opportunity for physical growth and social interactions, is enjoyable, and provides for a release of tension. It is no wonder that philosophers from Plato to Rousseau and educators from Itard to Montessori have argued for the inseparability of sensorimotor and educational experiences, postulating that movement experiences enhance and enrich intellectual attainment.

Learning through movement is not a new idea to the physical educator. Jessie Feiring Williams coined the phrase "education through the physical" in the early 20th century. Mosston, Kiphard, Cratty, and Humphrey have used this concept in physical education programming. More recently, Graham, Holt-Hale, and others have addressed how cognition and movement can be combined in the physical education program. Although diverse in content and approach, their programs have all yielded positive results when physical activity and cognition were combined.

A variety of categories may guide the cognitive learning process. Students can be provided opportunities for learning based on knowledge, comprehension, application, analysis, synthesis, and evaluation. The activities presented can easily be focused on each of those categories to meet the challenge of assisting students to become lifelong learners. The focus is not merely on accomplishing "things" or "games," but on providing a process through which students may fulfill their potential. This is an exciting and ever-changing task, requiring that we consider the developmental model, the curriculum focus, and the activities to present to students to meet their individual needs.

Cognitive skills activities

Simple recognition skills can be taught through physical activities. Letter, number, color, and shape recognition activities are easily incorporated into a physical education program. For example, the teacher can ask the students to perform the following activities:

1. Stand on the letter "A."
2. Jump on the number "1."
3. Walk on the lines that form a triangle.
4. Sit on the blue carpet square.
5. Position your bodies into the shape of a circle.
6. Hop two times.
7. Make an "I" with your bodies.
8. Find the diamond shape.

Letter or number grids, painted or taped on the ground or floor, can be used for these activities. Other equipment and supplies might include flashcards of numbers, letters, colors, and shapes; colored carpet squares and hula hoops; jump ropes for making shapes; and blocks of various colors, shapes, letters, and so on.

Depending on the ability of the student, the recognition skills practiced can be expanded to include spelling, reading, counting, and simple arithmetic activities. For example, the teacher can ask students to perform the following activities:

1. Spell your name by stepping on each letter in sequence.
2. Use a locomotor skill and spell its name.
3. Tell your age by jumping on the number(s).
4. Add, subtract, multiply, or divide using the number grid.

MAKING CONNECTIONS

Learning Across the Curriculum

Mrs. Swanson divided her class into five groups and explained to students that they could build their own culture. She asked them: "What language(s) would the people speak? What dances would they do? Be prepared to show us one dance. What music will your culture like? Name some musical instruments (or make some up) that you would take along to this culture. What games would they play? List two games or sports that will be the favorites of your culture. Teach these to the rest of the class. Make some up if you would like. What will be the ten most common foods? Will these comprise a nutritional diet as we know it based on the food pyramid we learned in class?" Predictably, students drew heavily from the various cultural backgrounds represented by students in each group, and some of their creations represented a melding of two or more cultures.

EXTEND YOUR KNOWLEDGE
Understanding Cognitive Development

Understanding cognitive development will add teaching tools to the physical educator's repertoire. Cognitive development includes the areas of information processing, intelligence, language development, and memory. Development of cognition follows stages, just as motor development does. The ways in which motor skills are taught, including communication techniques, group interaction, selection of games and activities, and the amount of practice needed, are all influenced by the teacher's understanding of cognitive development. Therefore, the physical educator who is able to identify and understand the cognitive development of students will be better able to select effective teaching strategies and activities.

Jean Piaget, a Swiss psychologist who lived from 1896 to 1980, was a leading researcher in the field of cognitive development. His theory of cognitive development recognizes four stages, which are subdivided into several periods or segments. The following is a short summary of Piaget's stages of cognitive development.

1. *Sensorimotor Stage—birth to approximately age 2.* Reflexive behaviors gradually turn into intelligent behaviors as the child matures and interacts with the environment. An infant develops means—end problem-solving behavior, and by age two, the child can solve sensorimotor problems through representation.
2. *Preoperational Thought—approximately 2 to 7 years of age.* A rapid increase in the development of representational skills occurs, including spoken language, along with an increase in conceptual development. Egocentric thought and reliance on the perceptual components of a problem are hallmarks of this stage. By age seven the child is pre-logical. Moral reasoning emerges, and the child begins to reason about rules and justice, although the concept of intentionality has not yet developed.
3. *Concrete Operations—approximately 7 to 11 years of age.* The ability to use logical thought develops, including growth in the concepts of seriation and classification. The ability to understand the concept of conservation (e.g., of number, mass, liquid) to solve problems is another hallmark. In this stage the concept of intentionality develops, leading to the ability to begin to consider the motives of others when making moral judgments.
4. *Formal Operations—approximately 11 to 15 years of age.* Structurally, the child is cognitively mature and can apply logical thought to all categories of problems, including hypothetical problems and those involving the future. Idealistic feelings emerge as the teenager has difficulty coordinating his or her ideals with reality. Personality formation occurs as the adolescent begins to adapt to the adult world. (Wadsworth 1989, pp. 143–144)

Studying Piaget's theory or those of others such as Barbel Inhelder, Lev Vygotsky, and Jerome Bruner can reveal important concepts that are useful to the teacher. For example, students who are still working through the stage of preoperational thought are not yet able to take the other person's point of view. Therefore, they may have difficulty participating in activities that involve teamwork and competition. By approximately age 7, most typically developing children have completed this stage. However, many students with a disability may take longer to complete this (or any) developmental stage. Another example is of younger children, who have not yet mastered one-to-one correspondence. Even though these students may be able to say numbers in order, they typically cannot count one number each time they do a repetition of an exercise or a jump.

Sources for Further Reading in Cognitive Development:

Furth, H. G., & Wachs, H. (1975). *Thinking Goes to School: Piaget's Theory in Practice.* New York: Oxford University Press.

Gallagher, J. M., & Reid, D. K. (1981). *The Learning Theory of Piaget and Inhelder.* Belmont, CA: Wadsworth, Inc.

The Psi Café provides links to high-quality websites that emphasize psychological issues. The site contains a section on cognitive development. www.psy.pdx.edu/PsiCafe.

Vygotsky, L. S. (1980). *Mind in Society: The Development of Higher Psychological Processes.* Cambridge, MA: Harvard University Press.

Vygotsky, L. S., & Kozulin, A. (1986). *Thought and Language* (rev. ed.). Cambridge, MA: The MIT Press.

Wadsworth, B. (1989). *Piaget's Theory of Cognitive and Affective Development.* White Plains, NY: Longman.

5. Play word scramble: With word cards placed between two teams, one member from each team scrambles to find a specified letter or word to complete a sentence or to answer a question.

The physical educator also can connect content from physical activity to mathematics, social studies, or anatomy by providing related activity and movement experiences.

Almost any academic subject can be brought into the physical education program. In addition to reading, spelling, and math, activities might include telling time or learning a lesson in history by participating in the sports of the time, such as jousting, cricket, or running. Dancing games are an interesting way to introduce history and geography (see Appendix H for additional ideas).

Movement activities for teaching concepts

Concepts (e.g., small, large, over, under, on, around, through, flat, round, right, left) can be taught or reinforced through movement experiences and physical activities. Group and individual exploration of such concepts is made concrete through physical movement.

Because distinct concepts are easier to teach and reinforce through physical education than subtle ones, distinct concepts should be taught first, with instruction in subtle concepts following. Distinct concepts include big–little, large–small, fast–slow, up–down, top–bottom, and high–low. Subtle concepts include round–flat, right–left, wide–narrow, around–through, and in–out. Concepts can be taught through movement activities specific to the concept, movement exploration activities, and obstacle courses involving the concepts (see Figure 11.1).

Movement activities specific to a concept vary according to the teaching approach. For example, to teach the concepts of big–little, the physical educator can ask students to perform the following activities:

1. Make your bodies as big as you can.
2. Make your bodies as little as you can.
3. Bounce a big (little) ball.
4. Make a big (little) movement of the arm.
5. Take a big (little) step.

To teach the same concepts with a movement exploration approach, the teacher might include the following question–performance activities:

1. How big (little) can you make your body?
2. Show me two or three big (little) parts of your body.
3. How many ways can you move a big (little) part of your body?

FIGURE 11.1

Movement concepts of on top, across, through, between, or middle can be taught with a simple obstacle course activity.

4. Show me how you can make a big (little) movement.
5. Show me how you can run in a big (little) space.

The same concepts can be taught using a cooperative or problem-solving approach and asking the group to work together in small groups or as a whole class.

Obstacle courses can provide the experience of several stations for the concept of big and little. For example:

1. Climb big (little) steps or stairs.
2. Make a big (little) circle with a jump rope.

3. Crawl through a big tunnel and then through a little tunnel.
4. Bounce a big (little) ball.
5. Throw a little (big) ball to a big (little) target.

Activities can be designed that are specific to the concept. Initially, it is advisable to work on or include only one concept and its opposite in the physical education lesson (this will vary with age and ability level). Other concepts can be added periodically throughout the program and reinforced singularly or in combination, using the methods discussed previously. For example, specific activities could include:

1. Bounce a large (small) ball quickly (slowly).
2. Make your body large and flat.

Movement exploration activities could include:

1. How quickly (slowly) can you move in a circle?
2. Show me how you can be round and wide.

Obviously, obstacle courses can be planned to reinforce or introduce any number of concepts. Varying the type of movement and the concept affords the opportunity to teach a variety of motor patterns and skills as well as a variety of concepts. Spatial relationships and the associated language are particularly important to teach using movement, because movement is a primary modality for making these concepts concrete to the learner. Examples in an obstacle course might include:

1. Walking around a triangle
2. Jumping over a small object (see Figure 11.2)
3. Crawling under an object
4. Climbing on a large box

Words from every part of speech and their meaning can be reinforced or made concrete through movement experiences. Prepositions such as *over, under, around, through, on, into,* and *out* can be demonstrated through movement. Adjectives and adverbs can best be understood through action (e.g., *quick(ly), slow(ly), strong(ly), weak(ly), thin, flat, round*). Some of the more complex nouns (e.g., *game, circle, space, area*) and verbs (e.g., *fling, toss, rotate, twist, flex, extend*) are more easily understood when put into movement than without the kinesthetically felt motor performance.

Problem-solving activities

Physical education programs can help all students to enhance their ability to solve problems. As with other aspects of cognitive learning, the process of problem solving can be made more concrete

FIGURE 11.2

This student is working on the jumping pattern and learning the concept "over" by jumping over a line.

through actual experience. There are at least five types of activities that encourage problem solving:

1. Task-specific
2. Movement exploration
3. Group problem solving
4. Individual problem solving
5. Guided discovery

Once again, moving from simple to complex activities and varying the activities as appropriate for the students' age and ability are important principles. Examples include:

1. Finding the fastest way to get from "A" to "B"
2. Finding the most direct route from "A" to "B"
3. Finding the most efficient way of moving
4. Determining the best way to modify a game or piece of equipment so students with a disability can participate

Task-specific activities are directed at solving a particular problem specified by the teacher. For example, the task is to solve the problem in terms of speed: the fastest way to get from "A" to "B," the fastest way to move around a given area, or the fastest way to complete a game.

The *movement exploration* approach allows the group or individual to solve a given problem in a variety of ways:

1. Show me one way in which you can move quickly from "A" to "B." Show me another way. Which is faster?
2. Show me some ways to move around space.
3. What are some ways you could finish (or complete) a game?

Any or all of these methods can be incorporated into physical education programs, depending on your teaching style and the age and ability of the students. Not only can the concept of "over" be taught during a jumping activity, but through the technique of guided discovery (as discussed in Chapter 10), the student can also figure out how high he can really jump.

Memory activities

Memory plays an important role in cognitive learning. It is necessary for learning to be retained, to provide a base for further learning. Memory, or retention, is just as important for learning in the motor domain. Motor experiences can help to enhance memory, as learning by doing adds another modality to concepts learned by seeing or by listening. For students with a disability that involves a sensory impairment or processing difficulty (e.g., auditory or visual processing delay), movement may be the primary modality for learning all concepts.

The physical education program may call upon either general memory or specific memory. **General memory** in physical education refers to *the ability to remember learned motor skills and physical activities* (including games, sports, dance, and play). Memory can also include the ability to remember the rules of games, parts of dances, warm-up exercises, and the like. Activities repeated quite frequently can provide the opportunity for overlearning, which tends to increase retention.

Memory ability may often be impaired in a person with a disability, especially among those with mental retardation, multiple disabilities, traumatic brain injury (TBI), or a learning disability. Thus, it is important for teachers to be aware of the potential for an impaired memory ability and to include time for reinforcing learning (i.e., overlearning) in an effort to increase retention.

Specific memory activities in the physical education program can be of *several subtypes such as motor memory, visual memory, auditory memory, sequential memory, and symbolic memory.*

1. **Motor memory** is *the ability to remember and accurately repeat a motor pattern*. Individuals with poor motor memory may need more than the usual practice and cuing. Examples of tasks requiring motor memory include:
   - Remembering precisely how high to lift your foot in order to clear each step when going up stairs.
   - Remembering a specific motor sequence such as the step–hop pattern for skipping.
   - Remembering precisely how to move body parts to approach, take off, and perform a swan dive from a three-meter board versus a five-meter board.
   - Remembering how far to duck your head (so you don't bump it) when going under the cover at the top of a playground slide.
2. **Visual memory** involves *remembering what you have seen, such as an object or a motor pattern you are trying to imitate*. Modeling and imitation alone may not be effective teaching techniques for individuals with poor visual memory. Other techniques, such as auditory and tactile cues and physical guidance, may be needed to supplement visual teaching strategies.
3. **Auditory memory** involves *remembering what you hear*. It is often associated with language difficulties. In the physical education setting, individuals with poor auditory memory may have difficulty remembering verbal directions and the names of objects and people.
4. **Sequential memory** refers to *remembering items in a series or sequence*. Examples of tasks requiring sequential memory include:
   - Two directions (e.g., *run* to the fence and *run* back) with the same motor demand (run).
   - Three or more directions with a single motor demand.
   - Two directions with multiple motor demands (e.g., *run* to the tree and *walk* to the fence).
   - Three or more directions, with multiple motor demands.
5. **Symbolic memory** refers to *the ability to respond to stimuli of a coded nature*. For example, if students are asked to jump whenever they hear the sound of a bell and walk at the sound of a whistle, they must respond motorically based on a preset, memorized coding system. For example, students can:
   - Perform a different motor task for a specified auditory cue (e.g., jump for bell sound; walk for whistle).

- Perform different motor tasks for a specified visual cue (e.g., walk when hands are held up).
- Perform the appropriate motor task based on a visual or auditory cue presented randomly by the teacher.
- Memorize a sequence of cues and then perform the associated motor tasks.

Activities for encouraging creativity

Human creative ability often lies dormant, and this is particularly the case with students with a disability. Whenever possible, physical education teachers should incorporate creativity into their programs. Ways of encouraging creativity include:

1. Movement exploration
2. Creative rhythms and dance
3. Inventing new games and activities

The key to encouraging creativity is to involve the student in the learning process. The teacher should encourage the student to find a new way of moving or to do something different or unique. (See Figure 11.3.) Encouraging creativity often requires that the teacher provide initial guidance or structure through environmental manipulation and class discussions. The following questions and tasks can stimulate students' creativity:

1. How many ways can you make yourself large (small, flat, round, and so on)?
2. Can you balance on two similar body parts? Can you balance on two different parts? Three, four, or more parts?
3. Given a topic, plan and execute an expressive movement or series of movements. This can be done individually or in a group. Topics might include anger, joy, windy day, silence, slow-moving animals, busy city, inventions, washing machine, calculator, snow, the ocean, and so on. (Refer to Table 11.4 on page 273.)
4. Move body parts or the total body to music. Music can be varied from loud to soft, heavy to light, fast to slow, and so on. This can be done individually or in a group.
5. Given a type of music, move individually or as a part of a group to the music, according to personal feeling.
6. Tell a story through movement, with or without music.
7. Create a new activity or new game. The teacher might initially set some guidelines (e.g., one person with no equipment, using a locomotor pattern; more than one person, two types of locomotion; a ball and beanbag as equipment, no other stipulations; a balloon and two teams of students who must not use their hands). (See Table 11.4.)

FIGURE 11.3

Creative movement can use a variety of different pieces of equipment and music for all children.

Language Learning

Language development is fostered by a language-enriched physical education environment. A language approach to teaching physical activity is a method whereby concepts, words, meanings, and language are incorporated into physical education instruction. At times, it is important to place special emphasis on language acquisition and its use in physical education. All children can benefit from a language-enriched learning environment. This emphasis, however, is most beneficial to children with speech or language impairment, autism, learning disabilities, and mental retardation.

A language-enriched atmosphere requires a conscious effort by teachers to adjust their language to the level of the student, to monitor the amount and quality of language used, and to encourage language use by the student. Initially, the development of a language-enriched physical education program may not be easy; ultimately, it can become an integral part of the physical education program and a natural part of the teacher's repertoire. Language development can be stimulated through:

1. Verbalization by students
2. Identification and naming
3. Reinforcement of language concepts through movement
4. Use of sensory channels
5. Use of language games (see Tables 11.2 through 11.5 later in this chapter)

Language games, commonly referred to as signal–response games, are an effective and fun teaching tool. Signal–response games are those involving a signal given to the group verbally (or with a gesture or sign) to which the group responds motorically. Popcorn is a popular playground signal–response game (sometimes referred to as "four-corner exchange"). Players stand on the corners and intersections of the four-square pattern on the playground. The person in the middle must give words in a category (e.g., foods, cards, toys, colors, games). When he or she says "popcorn," all players must "pop" and run to a new corner or intersection. The person in the middle position tries to get to a corner or intersection before another player. The object of the game is to maintain the outside positions and not to get into the middle. Middle players can change after several turns in the middle, or the group can help with words until the player is ready to say "popcorn." Gestures and signs are another fun component to add to the game. (This game was adapted from the Magic Word game.) Other examples of signal–response games are:

- Run, Sheep, Run
- Midnight
- Red Light, Green Light
- Steal the Bacon (when played with partner teams)

Verbalization and vocalization by students

All students, especially those with speech and language impairments, should be encouraged to speak during physical education. Physical activities can be designed to include a need to speak, sign, or communicate in some way. This need to vocalize is especially applicable to students with autism or severe disabilities and students with moderate mental retardation—at least it often can motivate them to approximate a meaningful sound or word. A relatively easy way for a teacher to encourage verbalization is by direct inquiry.

Teacher asks:	*Student answers:*
1. What are you going to do?	1. Run tree; run back; go outside; line up; find ball.
2. What did you do?	2. Ran tree; ran back; stood on line; got ball.
3. Where did you go?	3. Trees; outside.
4. How did you move?	4. Ran; walked; rolled.
5. What did Sally do?	5. Ran; walked; she ran; she walked.
6. What color is the ball?	6. Blue; red.

A similar method is to have students repeat directions as best they can. Initially, the students might repeat simple directions, progressing toward verbal repetition of several directions or complex tasks. The students can be encouraged to greet the teacher and other students, lead the warm-up exercises, and interact verbally with others.

The quality of the verbalization must be considered. Consultation with the speech-language pathologist (SLP) or classroom teacher will reveal the quality of language production, appropriate for each student, that should be expected during physical education. When working with students whose programs emphasize language, the physical educator should collaborate closely with the classroom teacher and other specialists for consistency of language use, quality of language production, and reinforcement of language.

Identification and naming

A specific way to encourage language use is through the identification and naming of objects, body parts, directions, actions, sizes, shapes, colors, and so on; the list is endless. Parts of speech including nouns, verbs, prepositions, adverbs, articles, and adjectives can all be used in this fashion. The student might be asked to describe the action before, during, and after the actual motor performance. Emphasis can be placed on the correct usage of the parts of speech in relation to the motor performance: *ran quickly*, *moved around the large space*, *jumped on top of the round object*, and so on.

Initially, it is best to have the students understand and use nouns, verbs, and some adjectives. The concept or meaning of all of the parts of speech, especially prepositions, adverbs, articles, and adjectives, can be reinforced or made concrete through movement. Activities for language development include the following:

1. Name the body parts

Teaching Tip

ADAPTATIONS FOR TUG-OF-ROPE • Playing tug-of-rope can be a fun activity that children enjoy (see Figure 11.4). The creative educator can adapt the game into several different variations using bicycle tires. Some suggestions include:

1. Using small mountain bike tires, two players pull against each other toward a designated line or cone. It is even more fun with the class divided into teams with all of the partners pulling against each other at the same time.
2. Using a large racing bicycle tire, one partner pulls the other, who is riding prone on a scooterboard in a fully extended body position.
3. Using any size bicycle tire, have four players pull at the same time toward designated cones. Each team can be designated a specific color, with a corresponding colored deck ring around their cone. Grabbing and holding up the ring indicates first place or a number of points scored for the team.

Hint: It is helpful to stuff each tire with plastic bags to thicken the inside and then surround the entire tire with duct tape or some other type of durable rubberized tape.

FIGURE 11.4

Pulling or "tug-of-rope" activities can have partners using a scooterboard and pulling with a bicycle tire or hula hoop.

2. Name objects in the physical education environment
3. Name actions or movements, or verbalize a choice of these (e.g., run, walk, roll, hop)
4. Name contrasting qualities of objects or movements (e.g., fast–slow, big–little, long–short)
5. Identify directions, shapes, colors, and so on
6. Name combinations of the above (e.g., red ball, big step, fast run, little finger)

Use of sensory channels

Although much of the previous discussion has naturally centered on auditory input, language acquisition, production, and use can and should be encouraged through other sensory channels, including multisensory input. Visual input is a valuable channel in language development, and all of the previously mentioned activities can easily be modified to include visual input. Many activities using this type of input were included in the discussion on teaching cognitive skills and teaching concepts; all of them can also be used to increase language acquisition and use.

Learning grids and other types of activities that involve students moving appropriately in marked areas of the playground or floor can be modified to facilitate language. Activities such as asking students to spell words by jumping into the various letter squares or answering questions asked by other students allow students to become more involved in the learning process. Games of these types can be created by the students themselves, with myriad variations.

Auditory coding has excellent application for children at higher cognitive levels. Students assign an auditory cue (e.g., clap, whistle, or spoken word) to a motor activity (e.g., one hop, two jumps, or a somersault). One student gives the series of auditory cues, and the other students must decode them into physical movement.

The ABCs of movement

The ABCs of Movement is a fun project for any age group in the physical education setting, especially as a rainy day activity. The object is to come up with as many words as you can for each letter of the alphabet, according to the category given. The following categories are usually best for movement experiences: animals; actions (including position in space, tempo, movements, directions, patterns, or pathways); and favorite toys, colors, or games. The list is as long as the imaginations of the children. For example, Table 11.1 was modified from ideas shared in the *Great Activities Newsletter* (1996) by Kathleen Popp, an adapted physical education teacher in Nassau, New York.

TABLE 11.1 The ABCs of movement.

LETTER	ANIMALS	ACTIONS (include position in space, tempo, directions, patterns, pathways, etc.)	GAMES OR TOYS
A	alligator, ape	around, agitate	archery
B	bear, baboon	behind, bend, backward	baseball, basketball, bocce ball, badminton
C	cat, caterpillar, crab	criss-cross, circle	canoeing, cricket
D	dog, dragon, dinosaur	down, decline	diving
E	elephant, eel	elevate	equestrian, earthball
F	frog, fly	fast, far, forward	fencing, Frisbee
G	giraffe, goat	gallop, grapevine	golf, gymnastics
H	hamster, hog	half turn	hockey, handball
I	insect, inchworm	in, incline	ice skating
J	jaguar, jackrabbit	jump, jackknife	jump rope, judo, jacks
K	kangaroo	karaoke	kayaking
L	lamb, lion, lynx, lobster	leap, line	lacrosse
M	monkey, manatee, mallard	move	marbles
N	nautilus	near, next to	Naughts and Crosses
O	octopus	out, over	Over the Line, Old Maid
P	pig, pigeon, platypus	pass, parallel, play	polo, paddleball, pool
Q	quail	quick, quiver, quiet	Quoits
R	rooster, rhinoceros	run, rhythm, row, roll	racquetball
S	snake, seal, seahorse	share, skip, side slide, slow, squat	swimming, scuba, skiing, skating, soccer, softball
T	turtle, tarantula, toucan, terrier	toss, turn, twist, through	tennis, tag
U	unicorn, urchin	up, under, unroll, undulate	"Untie" the knot, Ultimate Frisbee, "Up Jenkins!"
V	vulture	v-sit, vault, vibrate	volleyball
W	worm, walrus, wasp, woodpecker, weasel	walk, wag, wobble	weight lifting, wrestling
X	tyrannosaurus rex	x (formation)	X-games
Y	yak	yawn	yoga
Z	zebra, zebu	zigzag, zoom	Ziginette

Source: Adapted and modified from Kathleen Popp's Action Alphabet, *Great Activities Newsletter,* January/February 1996. Used with permission.

> ## Teaching Tip
>
> **INCORPORATING LANGUAGE** • The following are some suggestions for incorporating language into the physical education program:
>
> - Using bulletin boards
> - Using the alphabet to present and review a variety of words during movement activities (e. g., physical fitness terms from A to Z; jump rope rhymes using the alphabet)
> - Playing the game Microphone and sequencing numbers; letters of the alphabet; or categories such as animals, cars, or games (depending on the age and level of the students)

Socialization

Physical education provides an effective means for encouraging and developing socialization skills. By its very nature, physical education offers individuals a variety of social experiences and social interactions. Physical education teachers and other physical activity professionals are advised to vary social situations and to provide opportunities for students with a disability to experience diverse aspects of human interaction.

Students with a disability may lack the skills necessary to relate to others or to respond appropriately to a given social situation. The student's behavior may be due, at least in part, to the lack of opportunity. Thus, the physical educator can provide social situations and guide those who need assistance through the variety of social experiences available in physical education.

As much as possible, students with a disability should be provided the opportunity to participate in partners or pairs, small groups, and large groups. Additionally, individual and team competitive experiences can be valuable. Opportunities for socialization include the following:

- Experiencing winning and losing
- Participating as a member of a team
- Functioning in various leadership roles—captain, co-captain, and leader of exercises or warm-up
- Participating in dance activities
- Practicing appropriate personal space
- Participating in specific activities—taking turns, obeying rules, exercising self-control, social awareness of others
- Participating in class discussions of appropriate and inappropriate social behavior
- Using alternative behaviors instead of withdrawal or antisocial or aggressive behavior

Affective Learning

Affective learning refers to *changes in or the development of the student's emotional response to situations.* This type of learning usually occurs in conjunction with changes in other areas of development. Increases in appropriate social behavior are often concomitant with affective development.

Often, the first noticeable changes in the behavior of students with a disability occur in the affective domain. Increased mental and physical ability often lead to increased confidence, more assertive behavior, and increased feelings of self-worth. Although the primary goal of physical education for individuals with a disability is not to increase affective development, it is frequently a byproduct. It is important to note that changes in a student's confidence, self-concept, and self-worth can and do occur often, and are influenced by the physical education experience. Readers can probably think of activity experiences in their own lives that helped them to learn specific appropriate behaviors. Examples include learning how to become involved in an activity that others are playing, while showing respect for and protection of others during play, following rules, becoming self-directed and setting personal goals, being sensitive toward others (cooperation, group decisions, teamwork), and allowing for the full participation of all persons regardless of differences.

The old adage "nothing succeeds like success" is applicable here: Success in physical education activities fosters emotional growth (enhanced self-concept, confidence, and self-worth) and fosters development in the motor domain. Students with a disability generally have experienced failure more often than they have success. Thus, care must be taken to ensure some measure of daily success. This must not be done at the expense of growth or challenge, however; there is much to be learned by making mistakes. Learning through success and mistakes should not be evenly balanced; rather, lessons should be planned to include much learning by success, sprinkled with a little learning through small mistakes.

The student with a disability usually needs a modicum of structure and routine that allows for a feeling of security and predictability. Eventually, structure and routine must give way to change, challenge, and additional demands, and it is in this process that development and learning take place.

FIGURE 11.5 *Sportsmanship group: Focusing on social skills in a game setting.*

Instruction in social skills that can be applied to games and physical activities is usually the responsibility of the physical education teacher, recreation leader, or recreation therapist, and sometimes the coach. Learning social skills in adult-structured physical activities may be a critical component in learning to "play" with peers at recess or other child-structured play times. Of course, directed teaching for the generalization of skills from one setting to another may be necessary.

One way to help children acquire and practice social skills and language in a social setting is to use a game format called Sportsmanship Group (Tibbetts & Morton, 2001). The purposes of a Sportsmanship Group include:

- To teach specific physical education skills and knowledge of motor activities and games.
- To provide an opportunity to practice social and motor skills in a situation where it is possible to model, imitate, and practice without adverse social consequences (e.g., teasing or ridicule from peers).
- To improve the quality of interaction between peers within a structured setting.
- To increase acceptance of self and others despite differences in motor skill levels.

Appendix G contains a complete description of Sportsmanship Group and a sample lesson plan. In summary, Sportsmanship Group encompasses specific praise and token reinforcement for the display of positive social behaviors. It includes a three-part framework for lesson planning so that positive social skills are previewed, practiced, and reviewed:

1. Pregame review or discussion of the four sportsmanship rules: use friendly talking, keep hands and feet to self, try your best, cheer for your team. (These rules can be modified as appropriate for the group by using the guidelines for making class rules contained in Chapter 10.)
2. The game play, during which the teacher (and other assistants, if possible) reinforces individuals for displaying specific behaviors consistent with the sportsmanship rules.
3. Post-game discussion, in which students nominate a peer for "Best Sport of the Day" by saying what that peer did that was considered good sportsmanship (e.g., "I like the way Tommy gave me a high five and said good job when I hit the ball" or "Sally was a good sport by not getting mad when the ball beat her to the base").

Sportsmanship Group is most often effective with upper elementary students but can be adapted for older students. It is not generally appropriate for students with a cognitive developmental level below about seven years, as developmentally younger children have not generally developed the ability to take the other person's point of view. (In fact, team sports and complex group games are often difficult for young children for the same reason.)

One of the greatest results of physical education programming is the student with a disability who wants to, can, and will actively participate in physical activity, who seeks out and accepts challenges, and who feels confident and worthwhile as an individual. A positive physical education experience can help the child to reach this goal and enhance the child's growth in the affective domain.

Incorporating Multiple Learning Domains

When examining the ways to incorporate the learning domains into the physical education lesson, the reader should remember to keep the program goals and objectives in mind, especially when adapting an activity and emphasizing another aspect of the game. The physical educator might use one game and just keep adapting or modifying it to change the focus or purpose; or she could use several games to focus on one aspect of learning, such as the social or language component. The possibilities are endless, limited only by the professional's desire to create and the amount of time available. To help the reader get started, the games and activities shown in Tables 11.2 through 11.5 provide examples of diverse and purposeful lessons.

The next chapter addresses effective planning for the culturally determined forms of movement and how to modify or adapt these activities.

TABLE 11.2	Tire pull game.
GAME	DESCRIPTION
Tire Pull	Two students stand facing each other while holding opposite sides of a bicycle tire. When a signal is given, both students pull (using both hands with an overhand grasp) in opposite directions until one player is touching the target cone or crosses the middle line. The distance of the target cone depends on the age group, but is usually placed behind them approximately 8 to 10 feet away. Time limit is called after 30, 45, or 60 seconds if students have not reached the target cone or pulled their opponent across the middle line. At the end of the game, players drop the tire in the middle, shake hands, and say "good try". Sometimes this game is played in teams: four teams, with one from each team playing each round. A different-color cone is set up for each player. All four players move to the middle of a mat or playing area and stand in position to grasp the tire. On a signal or the word "pull" or "go," the players attempt to pull the tire and touch or knock down their cone and score a point for their team. If a player lets go of the tire and hits or kicks the cone, it does not count—the player must have at least one hand on the tire to win the point. After the round, concluded by a handshake, the teams reposition the cones and the next four players come out and repeat the task.

Suggestions for incorporating cognitive, affective, social, and language experiences

Cognitive:	▪ Ask students to use strategies such as timing, consistency, and balance for pulling in a controlled manner. ▪ Use memory by calling names or numbers for the partners to move to the tire and begin pulling.
Language:	▪ Ask students to say "good try" while shaking hands with partners. ▪ Ask other students to be good spectators by cheering for the participants (usually four or five partner sets) with "pull" or "go, team, go" or by calling out the players' names.
Social:	▪ Ask students to shake hands at the end of the game.
Affective:	▪ Encourage students to attempt the task with different-size partners or with an increased time limit.

TABLE 11.3	Parachute play.
GAME	DESCRIPTION
Parachute Play	Students stand around the edge of a parachute and grasp the sides. The movements of the parachute will assist in many of the learning domains depending on the focus or emphasis of the teacher's lesson (see Appendix H).

Suggestions for incorporating cognitive, affective, social, and language experiences

Cognitive:	▪ Ask students to use an overhand grasp with the right or left hand and to move around the circle with extended arms. ▪ Use memory by calling names or numbers for partners to exchange places by moving under the lifted parachute. ▪ Ask students to identify the location and name of a muscle group when performing conditioning activities using the parachute.
Language:	▪ Have students exchange places when you call assigned numbers or names. They must greet each other with a hand shake or compliment in the middle under the canopy.
Social:	▪ Work as teams on each half of the parachute to shake balls off onto the other side. ▪ Work as a group to produce a wave or roll a ball around the edge (e.g., plane traveling the equator).
Affective:	▪ Ask a "panel" (half of the group) to observe and "judge" the merry-go-round, calliope, mountain, or mushroom based on form and style (ratings are #1: best, #2: excellent, and #3: good), then switch the groups.

TABLE 11.4 — Inventions.

GAME	DESCRIPTION
Inventions	Students are divided into groups of three to five each. Their task is to create an invention of their own or something that they know about in their home, school, or environment and mimic it in movement. Give each group five minutes to create their invention and prepare it for presentation to the class. Each invention must include all members of the group moving together. Present the invention to the class to guess what the invention is.

Suggestions for incorporating cognitive, affective, social, and language experiences

Cognitive:	■ Ask students to use different speeds, levels, directions, and body shapes for the movement. ■ Provide task cards with inventions listed for each group to pick from or just ask the group to "make up" their own invention. ■ Ask students to choose several pieces of equipment to use with their invention (adding a hula hoop, carpet square, ball, rope, or poly spot can provide another dimension to the invention idea).
Language:	■ Incorporate language concepts of force, direction, or levels.
Social:	■ Emphasize cooperation and creativity.
Affective:	■ Focus on cooperation and having each student in the group contribute at least one movement or idea for the invention.

TABLE 11.5 — Human tic-tac-toe.

GAME	DESCRIPTION
Human Tic-Tac-Toe	Students stand in line on both sides of the "playing board." Each team alternates turns, taking a position on the "playing board" until one of the teams achieves "three in a row." Remember you can score in a vertical, horizontal, or diagonal line. The "playing board" is a space in the middle of the room, gymnasium, or playing field that has tape, hula hoops, tires, carpet squares, or poly spots designating the nine "squares" on the tic-tac-toe board. Efforts should be made to have the players take their places quickly, without touching other "squares" and without the assistance of their teammates. (This game is an effective indoor or rainy day activity because the children can play without talking.) *Variation:* Add four spaces for Score Four game.

Suggestions for incorporating cognitive, affective, social, and language experiences.

Cognitive:	■ Ask students not to verbally assist or point to squares for teammates. ■ Have students specify the number of the square they want to occupy before moving to the square. ■ Track the number of "wins" for each team with tally marks and count totals at the end of the game. ■ Ask students to identify the position of the line that completes the three in a row (vertical, horizontal, or diagonal) and then add the compass point (north, south, east, or west).
Language:	■ Use 3 x 5 cards (or hold right hand above head using the "x" and "o" sign language) to identify teams. ■ Have students use sign language for "x" and "o" with arms extended above head. ■ Have teammates help players by indicating sign language numbers for the specific square to occupy (without verbal communication).
Social:	■ Have teams shake hands at the end of the game or give "silent" cheers for the teams. ■ Divide class into teams of any size.
Affective:	■ Have students determine type of "cheer" made for others on the team. ■ Ask students to identify different ways to assist players who do not understand how to play the game or a new strategy of play.

SUMMARY

Effective programming is contingent on a thorough understanding of the needs, abilities, challenges, and interests of all children. The teacher of physical education must consider not only the needs of the class, but also the unique needs of each student. Effective programming includes appropriate goals and objectives, a variety of teaching strategies and curriculum focus for instruction, and appropriate modifications or accommodations for all students. Activities must be chosen from the reflex level to the motor skills level of the developmental model, according to each student's challenges. A number of enjoyable games and activities can be included in the program to stimulate students to develop the necessary motor-sensory responses, motor abilities, and motor skills.

Educational experiences in other than the motor domain can be provided through physical activity. Using movement as the medium, the teacher can reinforce cognitive learning, encourage language development, provide social experiences, and create opportunities for affective learning. Motor, cognitive, social, language, and affective developmental experiences should and can be easily incorporated into the physical education setting to develop effective programs for the whole person.

CHAPTER 11

Learning Activities

11.1 Observe a group of young children participating in gross motor activities at a preschool or in a play group. Which child uses verbal language the most? Which child seems to be the leader? Which child displays the most mature and accurate motor skills? For each of these questions, describe how you arrived at your answer.

11.2 Select a specific motor skill or task you might want a developmentally young student or a child with language delay to perform (e.g., overhand throw at a target, curl-up, broad jump, leap over a line). Write down how you would communicate what you want the child to do. Discuss in class or with a small group.

11.3 In a small group (3 to 5 students), discuss the ways in which you could teach a familiar game or activity while incorporating other learning domains. For example, pick a tag game and incorporate math and directional concepts, or balance tasks involving the use of fulcrums and science concepts, or partner tasks involving basic knowledge of anatomy (e.g., muscles and bones).

REFERENCES

Adams, R. C., Daniel, A. N., McCubbin, J., & Rullman, L. (1982). *Games, sports, and exercises for the physically handicapped.* Philadelphia: Lea & Febiger.

Balderson, D., & Sharpe, T. (September/October 2004). Promoting positive social behavior in physical education. *Strategies, 18*(1), 17.

Bates, A., & Hanson, N. (1996). *Aquatic exercise therapy.* Philadelphia: Saunders.

Beller, J. M., & Stoll, S. K. (1993, August). Sportsmanship: An antiquated concept? *JOPHERD,* 74–79.

Bredekamp, S., & Copple, C. (Eds.). (1997). *Developmentally appropriate practice in early childhood programs* (rev. ed.). Washington, DC: National Association for the Education of Young Children.

Cheatum, B. A., & Hammond, A. (2000). *Physical activities for improving children's learning and behavior.* Champaign, IL: Human Kinetics.

Clements, R. L. (1995). *My neighborhood movement challenges—Narratives, games, and stunts for ages three through eight years.* Reston, VA: National Association for Sport and Physical Education.

Clements, R. L., & Schiemer, S. (1993). *Let's move, let's play! Developmentally appropriate movement and classroom activities for preschool children.* Reston, VA: National Association for Sport and Physical Education.

Dean, B. (July 2005). New dimensions in movement and fitness through integration. *Teaching Elementary Physical Education, 16*(4), 17.

Earwood, C. (1997, March). *Geometric language and movement*. Paper presented at a workshop session during the Los Angeles County Office of Education Adapted Physical Education Conference, Los Angeles, CA.

Eldar, E., Morris, D., DaCosta, R., & Wolf, T. (March/April 2006). "Are You Square?" A game for developing self-control and social skills. *Strategies, 19*(4), 17.

Furth, H. G., & Wachs, H. (1975). *Thinking goes to school: Piaget's theory in practice*. New York: Oxford University Press.

Gallahue, D. (2002). *Developmental physical education for today's children*. Champaign, IL: Human Kinetics.

Garcia, C., Garcia, L., et al. (1996, May). The value of integration—activities that get children involved. *Teaching Elementary Physical Education, 7*(3), 20–22.

Graham, G. (2001). *Teaching children physical education—Becoming a master teacher*. Champaign, IL: Human Kinetics.

Graham, G., Holt-Hale, S. A., & Parker, M. (1998). *Children moving: A reflective approach to teaching physical education* (4th ed.). Mountain View, CA: Mayfield.

Great Activities Publishing Co. (1994). *The best of great activities—K-6 physical education games and activities (A select collection of the best fitness activities, ideas, and games from Great Activities' first ten years)*. Durham, NC: Author.

Gustafson, M. A., Wolfe, S. K., & King, C. L. (1990). *Great games for young people*. Champaign, IL: Human Kinetics.

Hellison, D. (2003). *Teaching responsibility through physical activity*. Champaign, IL: Human Kinetics.

Hengstman, J. G. (2001). *Movement ABCs—An inclusive guide to language development*. Champaign, IL: Human Kinetics.

Herman, A., & Wiener, D. (September/October 2003). Design and implementation of a motor skills practice course for K–1 students. *Strategies, 17*(1), 23.

Hutchinson, G. E., & Mercier, R. (September 2004). Using social psychological concepts to help students. *Journal of Physical Education, Recreation, and Dance, 75*(7), 22.

Jacobson, E. (1991). *You must relax*. New York: McGraw-Hill.

Lepore, M., Gayle, G. W., & Stevens, S. F. (1998). *Adapted aquatics programming: A professional guide*. Champaign, IL: Human Kinetics.

Lichtman, B. (1993). *Innovative games*. Champaign, IL: Human Kinetics.

Lins, C., Miller, J., Summers, D., & Winckler, C. (1995, July/Aug.). *1, 2, + 3. Let it be in P.E.* Paper presented during a workshop session at the United States Physical Education National Conference, Orlando, FL.

Maeda, J. K., & Randall, L. M. (July/August 2002). A physical education program for preschoolers of all abilities. *Strategies, 15*(6), 21.

Marston, R. (March 2004). An early childhood movement laboratory model: Kindergym. *Teaching Elementary Physical Education, 15*(2), 6.

McCall, R. M., & Craft, D. H. (2000). *Moving with a purpose—Developing programs for preschoolers of all abilities*. Champaign, IL: Human Kinetics.

Morris, G. S. D., & Stiehl, J. (1999). *Changing kids' games* (2nd ed.). Champaign, IL: Human Kinetics.

Mosston, M., & Ashworth, S. (1994). *Teaching physical education* (4th ed.). New York: Macmillan.

Pangrazi, R. P. (2001). *Dynamic physical education for elementary school children* (13th ed.). Boston: Allyn & Bacon.

Pangrazi, R. P. (2001). *Lesson plans for dynamic physical education* (13th ed.). Boston: Allyn & Bacon.

Peake, P. (2004). *Making boards tutorial for Boardmaker and Speaking Dynamically Pro*. Solana Beach, CA: Mayer-Johnson LLC.

Pica, R. (2000). *Moving and learning: Toddlers*. New York: Thompson Delmar Learning.

Pica, R. (1991). *Special themes for moving and learning*. Champaign, IL: Human Kinetics.

Picture Communication Symbols, The. (1981–2004). Mayer-Johnson LLC. Boardmaker Application Software. (1989–2004). Mayer-Johnson LLC. Speaking Dynamically Pro Application Software. (1990–2004). Solana Beach, CA: Mayer-Johnson LLC.

Popp, K. (1996). Action alphabet. *Great Activities Newsletter, 14*(3), 19–20.

Psi Café, The. www.psy.pdx.edu/PsiCafe.

Robert, D. L., & Yongue, B. (March 2004). Developing quality preschool movement programs: CHAOS and KinderPlay. *Teaching Elementary Physical Education, 15*(2), 9.

Sanders, S. W. (2002). *Active for life: Developmentally appropriate movement programs for young children*. Champaign, IL: Human Kinetics.

Schiemer, S. (2000, August). *Brain-based learning; Multiple intelligences; Active learning; Differentiated learning; Interdisciplinary teaching*. Workshop presentations at 27th Annual Cal Poly Elementary Physical Education Workshop, sponsored by California Polytechnic State University, San Luis Obispo, in cooperation with the California State Department of Education, and supported by CAHPERD.

Schiemer, S. (2000). *Assessment strategies for elementary physical education*. Champaign, IL: Human Kinetics.

Seaman, J. A., & DePauw, K. P. (1995). *Sensory motor experiences for the home: A manual for parents*.

Reston, VA: American Alliance for Health, Physical Education, Recreation, and Dance.

Stevens-Smith, D. (September/October 2004). Movement and learning: A valuable connection. *Strategies*, 18(1), 10.

Stillwell, J. (1996, May). Know your learner—Plan curriculum with your students' developmental characteristics in mind. *Teaching Elementary Physical Education*, 7(3), 18–19.

Tibbetts, T., & Morton, K. (2001). *Sportsmanship group* (Rev.). Unpublished paper, California Department of Education, Diagnostic Center, Southern California.

Wadsworth, B. (1989). *Piaget's theory of cognitive and affective development*. White Plains, NY: Longman.

CHAPTER 12

Effective Programming

INCLUSIVE PRACTICES AND APPLYING MOTOR SKILLS IN CULTURALLY DETERMINED FORMS OF MOVEMENT

Guiding Questions

1. What is the benefit of providing a noncategorical approach to activities presented in physical education?

2. What are some of the benefits of using inclusive practices when planning the daily lesson for students?

3. What are some of the adaptations that can be implemented when teaching culturally determined forms of movement?

4. How are relaxation techniques used effectively in physical education programs, and why?

PHILOSOPHICAL APPROACHES TO PROGRAMMING

Effective programming encompasses the broad range of ideas presented in Chapter 11, as well as the application of motor skills in culturally determined forms of movement. We believe that four overriding philosophical approaches should guide programming: (1) inclusion in general education, (2) the **noncategorical** (*not using a disability or a diagnosis as the basis of a category*) grouping of students and selection of activities, (3) universal design of lessons so that all students, whether identified as having a disability or not, can learn and demonstrate skills using one of an array of methods, and (4) a commitment to using inclusive and noncategorical programming principles when teaching culturally determined forms of movement.

Inclusive Programming

It is the responsibility of all professionals to determine their own style of inclusive practices for effective and efficient lessons. As mentioned in Chapter 11, a single activity may be used to teach several concepts or include several domains of learning, or the professional may choose to use a variety of activities to teach one concept or skill.

Inclusion is more than a "placement": it is an attitude. The trend in educational programs and legislation has been toward making the educational setting a more inclusive environment where all children can and do learn. The expected attitude is one in which all people are treated with respect and value. This attitude leads to thoughtful planning of activities that enable people to exemplify the character traits of kindness, honesty, courage, friendship, perseverance, responsibility, and respect. Stereotyping based on gender, race, culture, size, or disability is not practiced. A wide variety of learning activities and instructional strategies is used, and students have the opportunity to make choices to meet their individual needs and preferences.

Characteristics of ideal inclusive practices and programs for students include those adapted from the PEERS (Providing Education for Everyone in Regular Schools) project sponsored by the California Department of Education, Special Education Division (1992):

1. Students are members of chronologically age-appropriate general physical education class activities in their "home" school, magnet school, or school of choice.
2. Students progress with peers to subsequent grades and participate in all activities within the school (e.g., use of locker room for middle school students, intramurals).
3. Students participate in a "special class" only for enrichment activities as provided for all students (not isolated in a different "class").
4. The type or severity of the disability does not preclude involvement in the inclusive program.
5. All teachers and staff collaborate to ensure:
    a. The student's participation as a member of the class.
    b. The instruction of the student's individualized education program (IEP) goals and objectives.
    c. The appropriate adaptations or modifications of the physical education curriculum and equipment to facilitate student learning and participation.
6. Effective instructional strategies (e.g., cooperative learning, activity-based instruction, varied teaching styles) are supported and encouraged in the general physical education class setting.
7. Class size and staff-to-student ratio are appropriate for the group.
8. Supplementary instructional services (e.g., physical therapy, occupational therapy, orientation and mobility, adapted physical education) are provided through a team approach in the general education setting (including physical education), natural settings, and the community as needed.
9. Regularly scheduled collaborative planning meetings are held with school staff and support personnel to support smooth entry, ongoing program development, monitoring, and transition.

The attitude, perspectives, knowledge base, and training of each professional guide or direct the program planning. The desire to teach each individual is to be highly regarded. Just as the physical educator prefers to have choices regarding where to teach a lesson, what materials to use, and how to instruct students, students at all levels prefer to have choices about where to move, what equipment to use, and how to participate. Providing a slanted rope for jumping and Mosston's continuum of styles of teaching are effective for the same reason: They transfer decision-making and choice-making from the teacher to the student. Examples of careful planning for inclusive practices include:

1. Editing jump rope rhymes to exclude violent language or gender biases.

2. Including the social practices, cultural games, or holiday celebrations from a wide variety of cultures or religions.
3. Eliminating all exclusionary games (e.g., musical chairs, tag with one person "it" and everyone standing "out" until everyone is caught), rules (e.g., three strikes you are out), and practices (e.g., captains choosing up teams in front of the group) from the activities presented.
4. Using creative methods for allowing all students to participate fully in the activities presented.

Specific methods for creating an inclusive environment are as diverse as each situation. The following situations, activities, and techniques have worked for some physical educators and are provided as a resource to stimulate thinking:

- When an all-school track meet is planned, the physical education teacher and adapted physical education specialist collaborate to plan for the inclusion of students with a disability.
- When scheduling and planning for physical education are discussed at an IEP meeting, the physical education teacher is invited. If he or she is not present, an information form is immediately filled out and given to the physical education teacher after the meeting. When it is known in advance that the physical education teacher will not be present at the IEP meeting, the adapted physical education specialist asks for verbal or written input to present for the physical education teacher.
- The adapted physical education specialist invites the whole class when providing direct services to a classmate with a disability.
- Adapted physical education students are allowed to invite one or two general education students to attend the adapted physical education lesson.
- The adapted physical education specialist provides services in the general physical education class, which involves a review of the unit plans before the student with a disability begins to attend the class.
- The adapted physical education specialist teaches parallel lessons with half of the general physical education class (including half of the students with a disability who are enrolled in the class). Prior to the lesson, the two teachers meet briefly to share plans and strategies.
- The adapted physical education specialist helps students with a disability perform a dance for a school talent show.
- The adapted physical education specialist organizes a special event for the whole school, such as "Gummy Bear Field Day" or "International Games Day," or inclusive activities for "All Children Exercising Simultaneously (ACES) Day," "Family Fun Nights," or "Physical Education and Sport Week."
- The adapted physical education specialist provides resource information, materials, equipment, and ideas for lessons by providing charts, test alternatives, scoring procedures, and so on.
- The adapted physical education specialist provides in-service training experiences for school staff, support personnel, and volunteers on accessing playground activities and equipment for students with a disability.
- The adapted physical education specialist provides suggestions for bulletin boards that include photographs of students with a disability participating in physical activity or of the types of adaptations used.
- The adapted physical education specialist provides information regarding the IEP process, laws, types of disabilities or congenital syndromes, and the specific motor needs of individual students to other members of the IEP team.

Noncategorical Programming

Using a noncategorical approach means viewing the student as an individual person and providing individually appropriate programming. This is the opposite of grouping students by the category of disability (a categorical approach) and providing programming based on group needs.

Although it may be helpful to know some of the characteristics to expect to find in an individual with a particular disability, it is unethical (and probably technically illegal) to group students and provide programming based only on the expectations of their disability. Furthermore, there are so many ways that an individual with a disability can compensate or accommodate for a disability that an expected characteristic often does not translate into an inability to perform. For example, a person using a wheelchair might be expected to be unable to walk; however, many are able to stand, stand with support, walk short distances, walk slowly, or walk using personal or mechanical assistance. It should be fairly easy to see that grouping all students who use a wheelchair together and providing programming based on the expectation that they cannot walk is very likely to limit the students' opportunities to stand and walk. Programming that limits movement is antithetical to the purposes and goals of physical education. The noncategorical approach goes hand in hand with inclusive practices because both are based on the provision of equal opportunity.

Universal Design

The term *universal design* originated in architecture and was originally applied to enabling physical access to environments by people with different abilities. The classic example is curb cuts. They were designed to enable individuals who use a wheelchair to access sidewalks and street crossings. In practice, they are used just as much by people pushing a stroller or riding a skateboard. Electronic captioning was first used to enable individuals with a hearing disability to use television monitors. However, it also enables everyone in a noisy environment such as an airport or restaurant to utilize monitors as well. In the context of learning, **universal design** is defined by the Council for Exceptional Children as follows:

> the design of instructional materials and activities that makes the learning goals achievable by individuals with wide differences in their abilities to see, hear, speak, move, read, write, understand English, attend, organize, engage, and remember. Universal design for learning is achieved by means of flexible curricular materials and activities that provide alternatives for students with differing abilities. These alternatives are built into the instructional design and operating systems of educational materials—they are not added on after-the-fact. (*Research Connections in Special Education*, 1999)

Following are examples of instructional methods that employ principles of universal design (adapted from Burgstahler, 2001–2004):

1. *Inclusiveness.* Create a class environment that respects and values diversity. Avoid segregating or stigmatizing any student. Respect the privacy of all students.
2. *Physical access.* Assure that instructional areas are accessible to individuals with a wide range of physical abilities and disabilities.
3. *Delivery methods.* Use multiple modes to deliver content. Alternate delivery methods, including verbal, demonstration, peer-assisted, and discovery activities. Make sure each lesson is accessible to students with a wide range of abilities, disabilities, interests, and previous experiences.
4. *Interaction.* Encourage different ways for students to interact with each other and with you.
5. *Feedback.* Provide effective prompting during an activity, as well as feedback when the lesson or assignment is complete.
6. *Assessment.* Provide multiple ways for students to demonstrate skills and knowledge. For example, besides traditional tests, consider group work, demonstrations, portfolios, and presentations as options.

Culturally Determined Forms of Movement

It is particularly important to keep the principles of inclusive and noncategorical programming in mind when teaching culturally determined forms of movement. As the name states, these activities are culturally determined. There is often a tendency to look at the cultural norm and judge people by comparing them to it. For example, a common initial reaction is: "A person using crutches can't play soccer because soccer, by definition, involves fast running, agility, and balance." It is the responsibility of the physical activity professional to help people replace that thought with an approach that is inclusive and noncategorical. When faced with an individual with a disability who is participating in sport, the initial reaction should be to ask, "What can we all do to include this person in the activity?"

When thinking about culturally determined forms of movement, it is important to consider not only a developmental approach but also a "top-down" approach. The developmental approach allows the achievement of lower-level skills to support the performance of the skills at subsequent levels. However, this is not the only way to learn or to perform higher-level skills, especially when compensatory techniques and accommodations are used. A "top-down" model begins by assessing performance at the most complex and refined skill level and progressing downward along a continuum (as in an intra-skill progression or task analysis). A top-down approach is most often used for a specific skill, sport, or activity (e.g., performing a long jump, shooting baskets, a tennis rally), whereas a developmental model is most often used for broad categories of skill (e.g., balance, locomotion, throwing a variety of objects).

The advantage to using a top-down approach is that it often enables the student to participate in an activity at a more complex and refined level in a shorter amount of time. It is based on the student's abilities, not disability. It takes advantage of the student's innate capacity and previously learned compensatory strategies and accommodations. The advantages of using a developmental approach include building foundational skills and creating a repertoire of motor skills that can be generalized to many activities. However, the developmental approach is generally a slower process when the ultimate goal is learning a sport or other culturally determined form of movement. Table 12.1 compares the use of the developmental and top-down approaches when teaching a tennis ball rally.

TABLE 12.1 *Comparison of developmental and top-down approaches for teaching a tennis ball rally.*

TOP-DOWN	DEVELOPMENTAL
1. Demonstrate rallying on a court with a partner.	1. Teach grip, stance, swing, ball control, etc., and have student practice until proficient at each.
2. Student is given a ball and racket and attempts rallying with a partner.	2. Rally against a wall.
3. If successful, the student can move ahead to learning how to play a game of tennis.	3. Increase rally distance.
4. If not successful, teacher makes suggestions and may have student practice rallying against a wall.	4. Rally over short distance with a partner.
5. If still not successful, teacher identifies problem areas (e.g., grip, stance, swing, accuracy, etc.) and teaches them.	5. Gradually increase distance with instruction for refining grip, stance, swing, ball control, etc., as necessary.
6. If still not successful, teach simple drills for ball control and re-teach grip, stance, swing as necessary.	6. Rally on a tennis court with a partner.

SELECTING APPROPRIATE ACCOMMODATIONS

The physical activity professional must look at the curriculum and determine how the individual with a disability can be successful. Many times, individuals with a disability have already developed the modifications or adaptations necessary to participate in specific activities in the physical education curriculum. However, when the student has difficulty or does not know how to make the necessary adjustments, the physical activity professional can provide assistance or support.

There is really no limit to the accommodations available. The creativity of the physical activity professional is an important asset in this regard. However, trying to develop a repertoire of accommodations for activities can be overwhelming. Therefore, many physical educators find it helpful to develop accommodations by using the methods discussed next.

Types of Curriculum Adaptations

Table 12.2 presents nine types of curriculum adaptations. Physical educators can use one or more types when adapting activities to include all students. As the "How Would You Respond?" activity suggests, the teacher should attempt varying degrees of adapting the lesson so that the least restrictive level of participation is available for the student. The process presented in Table 12.3, which is another example of a top-down model, represents a different framework for adapting a curriculum. Of the various frameworks, choose one that fits your personal teaching style and use it. You may also wish to try several types systematically and then use them selectively depending on the situation (e.g., age of students, environment, activity).

Adapting the Lesson or Game

Any skill, activity lesson, or game can be adapted for students. Usually the process of adapting involves changing various components of the lesson. For example, Chapter 10 presented several suggestions that will help the physical educator adapt a lesson. The Program Adaptations for General Physical Education (refer to Table 9.2) or the Adaptations Commonly Needed for Children with a Specific Disability (refer to Table 9.3) are just a few examples of strategies that can be used.

The physical education curriculum has been developed to meet the movement and health needs of all students. The intent is to match the benefits and strengths of the lesson activities with the instructional needs and individualized educational goals of the student with a disability. This is the time for the physical education teacher and the adapted physical education specialist to collaborate and share ideas. Team planning allows all interested people to provide input for a "student-centered" program of lessons. The student's abilities and challenges identified through the assessment and IEP process can then be addressed within the activity

TABLE 12.2 *Nine types of curriculum adaptations.*

QUANTITY*

Adapt the number of items that the learner is expected to learn or complete. For example:

- Reduce the number of push-ups a learner must perform at any one time
- Reduce the number of rules required to know before taking a post-test

TIME*

Adapt the time allotted or allowed for learning, task completion, or testing. For example:

- Individualize a timeline for completing a task; pace learning differently (increase or decrease) for some learners
- Adapt rules to require other players to count to five before acting (give a head start)
- Increase time allotted to finish an endurance run or swim

LEVEL OF SUPPORT*

Increase the amount of personal assistance with a specific learner. For example:

- Assign peer buddies, teaching assistants, peer tutors, or cross-age tutors
- Increase use of verbal or visual cues
- Provide extra opportunities for practice

INPUT*

Adapt the way instruction is delivered to the learner. For example:

- Use different visual aids, enlarge the boundary markers, plan more concrete examples, provide "hands-on" activities, and place students in cooperative groups

DIFFICULTY*

Adapt the skill level, the problem type, or the rules on how the learner may approach the work. For example:

- Allow the use of an adaptive device, simplify task directions, change rules to accommodate learner needs (e.g., hitting ball with crutch in soccer, using ball ramp in bowling)
- Use equipment to make the task easier, such as a batting "T" or a foam ball

OUTPUT*

Adapt how the student can respond to instruction. For example:

- Instead of answering questions verbally, allow a gesture or sign response; use a communication book for some students; allow students to show knowledge with "hands-on" materials

PARTICIPATION*

Adapt the extent to which a learner is actively involved in the task. For example:

- In a jump rope activity, have a student hold the rope and turn while others jump
- Assign the student to play the same position from day to day in a game or sport
- Allow the student to perform only part of the task (e.g., student with a disability bats but student without a disability runs the bases)

ALTERNATE GOALS**

Adapt the goals or outcome expectations while using the same materials. For example:

- In volleyball, expect a student to be able to serve the ball over the net from mid-court line using a two-handed overhand throw while others learn to serve overhand from back boundary line
- As an endurance goal, student swims five laps of pool wearing flotation device, while others run the mile

SUBSTITUTE CURRICULUM**

For example:

- During fitness testing, one student practices playground apparatus activities for climbing, swinging, or sliding
- During a track unit, a student with spastic quadriplegia participates in adapted aquatics
- During a soccer unit, an individual with a heart condition participates in a walking unit with individual goals

*This adaptation is an *accommodation* if the student can demonstrate mastery of the standard on an assessment. The key concept is: Will the student ultimately master the same material but demonstrate that mastery in alternate ways or with alternate supports? If standards are not fundamentally or substantially altered, then this adaptation is an accommodation to a learning or performance difference.

**This adaptation is a *modification* if the student will not demonstrate mastery of the standard on an assessment. If routinely utilized, these adaptations are modifications and require individualized goals and assessment.

Source: Adapted from C. Deschenes, D. G. Ebelling, and J. Sprague (1994), *Adapting Curriculum & Instruction in Inclusive Classrooms: A Teacher's Desk Reference,* Bloomington, IN: The Center for School and Community Integration, Institute for the Study of Developmental Disabilities. Used with permission.

TABLE 12.3 *Steps for adapting the curriculum.*

ASK...

1. Can the student do the same activity at the same level as peers; for example, running the field or catching a ball?

IF NOT...

2. Can the student do the same activity but with adapted expectations; for example, running a shorter distance or catching a larger ball from a shorter distance?

IF NOT...

3. Can the student do the same activity with adapted expectations and materials; for example, walking to a cone or the fence and returning or trapping the ball rather than catching?

IF NOT...

4. Can the student do a similar activity but with adapted expectations; for example, walking to a designated position and stopping, or bouncing a ball to a partner and receiving the ball with both hands when rolled back?

IF NOT...

5. Can the student do a similar activity but with adapted materials; for example, walking along a line with a partner, or trailing a wall or fence, or pushing a wheel toy for support, or catching the Geoball from a shorter distance?

IF NOT...

6. Can the student do a different, parallel activity; for example, using a smaller group for a relay walk or jog task; or rolling a large ball, weight ball, or bell ball with a partner or small group using a large ball?

IF NOT...

7. Can the student do a different activity in a different section of the room or field area; for example, using basketball court lines to walk or jog around, or working with a partner at the end of the line away from distractions?

IF NOT...

8. Can the student participate in a portion of the activity (e.g., partial participation); for example, only serving the ball for a game of volleyball or playing goalie with a peer?

IF NOT...

9. Can the student do a functional activity in another part of the room or field area; for example, standing up and sitting down to retrieve an object or, in a seated position, pushing a ball away from the body instead of playing catch?

Source: Adapted and modified from M. A. Falvey and Richard Rosenberg (1998, March). *Infusing A-PE activities into a community based program for students with severe handicaps.* CAHPERD 55th Annual Conference. Used with permission.

---

lesson. Through collaboration and planning, the teacher and specialist can identify the supplementary services and supports needed, as well as determine the accommodations required to meet the diverse needs of the students in class (e.g., teaching and learning styles, formations and equipment used, cooperative and multicultural games).

Through this process (assessment, IEP meetings, and collaboration), the physical educator's knowledge base and teaching skills are validated. They can then be applied to quality programs that include individuals with a disability. Often, teachers who have been hesitant to approach a student with a disability find that, with a little encouragement and information, they meet a fun, friendly, and motivated student—a student with similar hopes and desires for movement experiences and participation to those of others in class.

When planning effective program lessons, the physical educator must always be informed, aware, and mindful of the contraindicated activities for individuals with a disability. These vary with each student and activity, and the educator should discuss them with other professionals. How the student will access the activities should also be considered. Of course, it goes without explanation that safety is always the primary focus for all students.

Whether for safety reasons or to enable all students to participate in an activity lesson, it may be helpful to adapt a task, skill, or activity. The educator can assist individual students by providing any of the following:

- A basic knowledge of the game rules, boundaries of play, and strategies needed for dual or team sport activities
- Choices regarding the amount of time, type of equipment, or groups to play with
- Individual cues or assistance from a peer
- Adapted equipment and instruction in its use

How Would You Respond?

NINE TYPES OF CURRICULUM ADAPTATIONS

The following are examples of adaptations used within physical education. This exercise can help the reader to become familiar with the adaptations that can be applied for any or all students served in a general physical education setting. For each example, determine which one of the nine curriculum adaptations presented in Table 12.2 is exemplified. To check your answers, see The Authors Respond on page 287.

Michael pushes a volleyball trainer upward and forward when tossed to him by a partner (and then tosses the ball to his partner) while the class works in groups of five to seven with a leader.

Briana is allowed to have the ball bounce two or three times before contacting the ball during a four-square game.

Alex will step on the opposite foot and throw a softball overhand using his preferred hand for a distance of 10 feet or more to a target area or person. The other students are working in pairs, throwing overhand (using opposition) and measuring the distance of each throw.

Tim collects all the poly spots or cones after the skill practice activity while his peers are getting into groups or partner sets for the next activity. He does not complete the next activity.

Garrett works on the fine motor skills of grasping and reaching a suspended balloon or ball while his classmates are playing catch.

Ashley will remain in the front corner position for volleyball during the rotation and be ready to serve from that position when it is her turn to serve.

Lisa walks or jogs around one-half of the field area while her classmates walk or jog around the full field area.

Ryan, a third grader, is placed between age-appropriate peers for warm-up exercises and partner tasks so his friends can cue him (or assist as needed) to remain with the group and imitate the movements.

Jenny is nonverbal. She is provided with two pictures that she can point to, to indicate her preferences of equipment, partners, or activity station.

David performs sit-ups at his own pace (without stopping) while his classmates complete them to a 1, 2, 3, 4 cadence.

Bre'onte is allowed to finish running a lap on the field quickly and then choose a free-time activity or get a drink of water while his classmates take longer to complete the task.

Jamie has a hearing impairment and ADHD. He stands near the teacher when she explains the task or skill to the class and receives an extra demonstration from a peer buddy just before he attempts the skill or task.

Sebastian has a learning disability and limited achievement in reading. His physical education class is organized into cooperative groups that rotate through various skill stations. Someone else in the group reads the task card out loud at each station. This enables Sebastian to understand the task.

Adapted from *Success With the Difficult Learner*, in-service training by Diana Browning Wright. Adapted from Deschenes, C., Ebelling, D., and Sprague, J. (1994), *Adapting Curriculum & Instruction in Inclusive Classrooms: A Teacher's Desk Reference*. Used with permission.

- A wide variety of activities and movement experiences appropriate for the age group
- Assistance and supports that emphasize the student's abilities

The reader is reminded that any adaptation used may not be necessary forever. Many adaptations aid skill development. The physical activity professional should remember to plan for a systematic fading of prompts and cues. A more detailed discussion of prompting and reducing prompts can be found in Chapter 10.

An Example of Adapting Activities Based on a NASPE Standard

To illustrate the ideas in this chapter, Table 12.4 provides examples of adaptations for students having difficulty completing a task. For general categories of the physical education curriculum, this table lists activities related to NASPE Standard 1. The table lists the category, describes the activity, and, finally, suggests an application for a student with a disability. General examples are offered for planning lessons and considering how to provide successful

TABLE 12.4

NASPE Standard 1: Demonstrates competency in many movement forms and proficiency in a few forms.

SKILL AREA: JUMPING	APPLICATION FOR STUDENT HAVING DIFFICULTY WITH TASK
Category: AQUATICS	
Activity: Jump from the side of the pool feet first into the water and then hold the wall to regain stable upright position.	■ Jump or bob on bottom of pool. ■ Jump off first step at entry into pool. ■ Jump off first step of ladder into pool. ■ Jump off side of pool with an adult in the pool to guide student to the side. ■ Jump off side of pool holding flotation object such as a noodle.
Category: DANCE	
Activity: Tinikling (pole dance): follow pattern of dance in coordinated timing with movement of the long poles. Straddle jump (apart and together movements) is used, with a pattern of: 1. Beat #1: straddle jump outside poles 2. Beat #2: jump between poles with both feet together 3. Beat #3: jump between poles with both feet together 4. Beat #4, #5, #6: repeat pattern 5. Beat #7, #8, #9: repeat pattern with 180-degree turn in middle to face opposite direction	■ Allow for slower movement of poles for cadence. ■ Allow for lower height and wider opening of poles. ■ Allow student to practice using lines on floor or jump bands before using poles. ■ Allow student to perform only the "holder" position, using the poles rather than jumping. ■ Allow student to perform with peer for stability and timing. ■ Prompt peers to provide verbal support for jump pattern.
Category: PHYSICAL FITNESS	
Activity: Jump for distance (long jump): running long jump is used during a track and field unit.	■ Walk and jump into sand pit and increase speed of walking pattern. ■ Shorten stride of running pattern prior to jump. ■ Allow student to run and leap. ■ Provide visual cues for takeoff position. ■ Provide auditory cues for last three steps (e.g., "1, 2, 3, jump"). ■ Allow student to mark landing position and measure distance. ■ Provide guide line (rope) for "trailing" by student with a visual impairment.
Category: STUNTS AND TUMBLING	
Activity: Jump and touch stunt: students stand in place on mats in personal space and jump upward, bringing knees upward in flexed position to touch outstretched hands placed about waist height.	■ Touch one knee (right hand to right knee). ■ Touch one knee while hopping on one foot. ■ Jump down from height (jump box) and touch knees. ■ Lower position of hands. ■ Have student count number of jumps for partner.

(continued)

TABLE 12.4	Continued.
SKILL AREA : JUMPING	APPLICATION FOR STUDENT HAVING DIFFICULTY WITH TASK

Category: GAMES AND SPORTS

Activity: Basketball (jump ball): starting position with a short forward stride, whole foot on floor for balance, knees bent, and arms at sides. Jump upward with full extension of all joints, including wrists, fingers, and arms. After ball is tossed, tap with fingers.	■ Stand and tap a suspended ball. ■ Stand and tap a mark on the wall (vertical jump). ■ Vertical jump. ■ Toss brightly colored ball. ■ Vary height of toss. ■ Verbally prompt student to jump prior to releasing toss. ■ Have partner stand farther away from ball.

learning experiences for all students. Using these examples, educators can make specific changes for various age groups.

Many more categories and activities could be included in Table 12.4. We have selected only a few in order to help the reader understand the connection between NASPE standards, curriculum areas, and adaptations.

INCLUDING ALL STUDENTS IN CULTURALLY DETERMINED FORMS OF MOVEMENT

The following sections offer suggestions for applying motor skills in specific activity areas when planning the physical education program. It is not intended as a complete listing of considerations or activity areas, just a small sample of some of the options.

Traditional Physical Education Activity Areas

Aquatics

Access, safety, and the level of supports required are concerns for all students participating in water activities. The size of the group and amount of supervision may be factors to consider when providing instruction to an individual with a disability, but these are dependent on the teacher's and student's experiences, comfort, and level of skill in the water. The formations used, fitness levels of participants, activities provided, equipment used, and skills addressed can all be valuable contributions to the water experience and learning for students. A full curriculum is provided in the Adapted Aquatics programs offered by such organizations as the American Red Cross, AAHPERD, and your local Parks and Recreation aquatic programs.

Most people enjoy water experiences and can develop water safety skills. For example, Michella, a student with deaf-blindness and cerebral palsy, was provided access to a community pool each week for a recreational swim. After the second lesson, she was moving from the shallow end of the pool down to the deep end to "sit" on the bottom because she enjoyed feeling the bubbles rising to the surface. Her parents told the adapted physical education specialist that Michella enjoyed taking a bath and that they thought swimming would be a water experience in which the family could participate with Michella. Eventually, Michella's father bought an underwater camera just to take pictures of Michella diving from the board and going to the bottom of the pool, something she achieved by the end of the school year.

Dance

The inclusion of students with a disability into rhythm and dance activities is easily accomplished through the use of partners and small groups, such as those required for line or square dances and interpretive dances. All individuals with a disability are unique in how they respond to and enjoy music and dance, and need only the opportunity to express their responses in their own manner.

Tracy, a student with spastic cerebral palsy, wanted to attend school dances but was hesitant to go until the adapted physical education specialist and the physical education teacher provided some practice opportunities in class with her peers. Using a scarf for the partners to hold, several partners took turns learning how to push and pull, spin and twirl,

The Authors Respond

NINE TYPES OF CURRICULUM ADAPTATIONS

Quantity*
Adapt the number of items that the learner is expected to learn or complete. For example:
- Lisa

Time*
Adapt the time allotted or allowed for learning, task completion, or testing. For example:
- David
- Bre'onte

Level of Support*
Increase the amount of personal assistance with a specific learner. For example:
- Ryan
- Michael

Input*
Adapt the way instruction is delivered to the learner. For example:
- Jamie
- Sebastian

Difficulty*
Adapt the skill level, the problem type, or the rules on how the learner may approach the work. For example:
- Briana

Output*
Adapt how the student can respond to instruction. For example:
- Jenny

Participation*
Adapt the extent to which a learner is actively involved in the task. For example:
- Ashley
- Tim

Alternate Goals**
Adapt the goals or outcome expectations while using the same materials. For example:
- Alex

Substitute Curriculum**
For example:
- Garrett

*See Table 12.2.
**See Table 12.2.

---

and "dip" Tracy's wheelchair safely (under Tracy's command and watchful eye). The enjoyment Tracy gained from the practice experience was enough of an incentive for Tracy to go to a dance and participate. She became the "belle of the ball" at the subsequent dances because everyone wanted a chance to be her partner, twirl her wheelchair, and "glide" or "boogie" on the dance floor.

Physical fitness

The wealth of information regarding physical fitness activities and assessment procedures, tools, and alternatives for individuals with a disability allows the teacher to provide a wide variety of experiences. In addition, many test items are available for use in developing a fitness profile for all students (e.g., FITNESSGRAM [Cooper Institute, 2004] and the *Brockport Physical Fitness Test Manual* [Winnick & Short, 1999]).

The inclusion of individuals with a disability in physical fitness programs can be one of the first curricular areas in which the teacher and student develop confidence and skill because of the success and fun the programs provide. This curricular area can provide a forum for learning how to use individual adaptations and implement other teaching strategies effectively. The students can participate in activities that are developmentally appropriate and based on their own unique abilities and challenges. The physical fitness program allows students to practice and to develop health-related fitness skills and behaviors.

The challenge facing the physical educator is usually one of access to alternative testing or adapting the activities or test items to meet the individual needs of each student with a disability. However, all classes have students with varying fitness levels, such as the taller student who has not developed the upper body strength to support his or her body weight (e.g., for tasks such as the flexed arm hang, push-ups), the obese student who tires easily and has difficulty running, or the student with a limited attention span who has difficulty following the route designated for the distance run. The student using a wheelchair or the student with a visual impairment may face some of the same challenges. The correct adaptations provide opportunities for all students to participate successfully in the fitness activities, whether or not they have been identified as having a disability.

The physical educator must become aware of, expand his or her knowledge about, and consider the vast array of options that can be used for fitness testing that includes all students in the program. Testing is a large component of the fitness curriculum and can be implemented by all those involved in educating students with a disability. Working closely with the team members, especially the doctor, nurse, and parent, can be critical when providing an individualized fitness program for a student.

Regular physical activity in a developmentally appropriate and planned physical education program can make an important contribution to the physical fitness of all participants. Because planning is an integral part of providing meaningful activities for students, the physical educator should identify and implement activities that lead each student to become a "physically educated person"—activities that provide for maximum involvement, as well as develop the necessary physical, social, and cognitive skills needed for physical fitness. Class organization, behavior support, motivation, and the goals of the fitness program are some of the areas teachers should address when helping students develop a "healthy fitness attitude."

MAKING CONNECTIONS

Improving Acceptance of Individuals with a Disability in General Physical Education Fitness Programs

Mr. Morris has been a physical education teacher at a large urban high school for over 15 years. He is chair of the department and a mentor teacher. He was reluctant to accept Stan, a child with Down syndrome, in his class for a physical fitness unit, primarily because he didn't think he had the knowledge or time to give Stan the individual attention he would surely need. Mr. Benjamin, the adapted physical education teacher, met with Mr. Morris to explain some of Stan's individual challenges, which mainly fell in the areas of muscle strength, endurance, and some mild coordination problems. Mr. Benjamin also explained that Stan's strengths included a good ability to imitate motor skills, a love of sports and physical activity, and an ability to work cooperatively with peers. Mr. Morris quickly realized that other students already in his class had similar or greater challenges when participating in the fitness unit. The meeting and the information he learned relieved Mr. Morris's concerns, and Stan was successfully included in the class.

The goals of the physical fitness component of the curriculum often depend on the time available for teaching the children. In other words, a physical education program that meets five days a week for 30 minutes each day has different goals than a program that is limited to meeting only one or two days a week for 30 or 45 minutes. This is why lessons that provide for vigorous activity, personal decision making, self-responsibility, and learning about health-related physical fitness are important.

Choosing a fitness test can be instrumental in providing for the needs of each participant. For a thorough discussion of testing, see Chapters 5 and 6. When selecting a test specifically to measure fitness, consider the Cooper Institute's FITNESSGRAM. It was designed for the inclusion of all students, has reporting forms (also available in Spanish), and is based on a philosophy that focuses on "what the students can do," not on "what they cannot do." The Brockport Physical Fitness Test is another valuable resource because it is designed for fitness testing of youths with physical and mental disabilities.

Teachers should select materials that encourage students to take personal responsibility for fitness and to develop a personal training or exercise program for use both in and out of school. Because current technology has "user friendly" reporting forms, it is easy for the physical educator to track student performance and progress. Fitness data can be monitored throughout the student's school career. In addition, fitness data are usually easily understood by others and, therefore, are an excellent public relations instrument for use with families, school administrators, and the community.

The adaptations listed earlier in this chapter can be applied to the fitness testing and activity portion of each lesson. For example, the distance (quantity) of the mile run may be adapted to be appropriate for the student's developmental level. It is appropriate for young students to finish the quarter mile, for fourth graders to run for eight to ten minutes and determine the distance completed, and for any age group to use the PACER (Progressive Aerobic Cardiovascular Endurance Run from Prudential FITNESSGRAM), as it enhances motivation and attention by having students work in groups or with partners.

When changes or adaptations are made, they should allow the students to be more successful and to feel confident about their own levels of health and fitness. Students should be encouraged to compare current performance to their previous performances rather than comparing it to the performances of peers. Improving and maintaining their fitness level should be the goal. For example, an excellent lead-up to performing a flexed arm

MAKING CONNECTIONS

Using Personal Interests in a Physical Fitness Program

Lindy, who is an obese student with developmental delays and a congenital syndrome, is very interested in music. She is allowed to leave class when her academic work is complete and walk around the field area wearing her radio with headset, which helps motivate her to increase the distance she can walk in a period of time. She was accompanied by an instructional aide until she learned the routine, and then student volunteers from the adjacent middle school were assigned to provide support and companionship while she exercised. Lindy's time, distance, and behaviors are recorded on a chart kept on a clipboard along with the schedule that the volunteers use each day. The data reveal that this is an effective and successful intervention for Lindy—it increased her aerobic capacity (i.e., walking faster and longer distances) and eventually allowed her to participate in walking field trips with her class. More important, it allowed her to participate with her family in shopping trips to the mall and walking trips on the beach. As a byproduct of this exercise routine, Lindy also lost weight.

---

hang or pull-up is using the straight arm hang on a horizontal bar with overhand grasp. Measuring increased hang time, up to 30 seconds or more in one year, is often an appropriate place to start. In addition, this allows the elementary school-aged student who is cautious or fearful of playground apparatus to gain confidence to attempt and practice the task.

Choices (or options) of specific test items are available for aerobic capacity, body composition, flexibility, and muscular strength and endurance (both upper and lower body). Another helpful option is to have the students identify the types of activities in which they participate, wish to perform, or can access outside school, so that the amount of activity can be increased. A program (associated with the FITNESSGRAM) called Activitygram uses the form of a questionnaire to identify the amount and type of activity in which individuals engage. The participant receives feedback regarding the types of activities to continue. In addition to these resources, the adapted physical educator can supply information about other fitness tests that can be adapted.

Games and sports (including cooperative games)

A vast amount of educational literature on developmentally appropriate games and activities is available. The Council on Physical Education for Children (1992) developed *"Rules" for Using Developmentally Appropriate Games in the Curriculum* that can be used by all students in the physical education class. This publication is an excellent guide for planning and implementing lessons. "Tried and true" rules (or guidelines) for the physical educator who is using games in a developmentally appropriate physical education program include:

1. Use selected or modified games to provide students with maximum opportunities for skill improvement and participation.
2. Modify official, adult rules to match the students' skill levels.
3. Use games and activities that continually involve all students, rather than games that eliminate players.
4. Form teams randomly or cooperatively instead of having captains choose teams publicly or dividing by gender.
5. Use smaller teams to provide the students with maximum practice.
6. Use activities and games that enhance self-improvement and emphasize cooperation rather than competition.

Stunts and tumbling

Safety, spotting, and a well-planned and arranged environment are key to a successful unit of instruction for stunts and tumbling activities. Some activities, however, are contraindicated, such as those that put pressure on the neck of a child with Down syndrome and repetitive flexion exercises by a student with spasticity. The physical educator should be aware of these and plan accordingly. Adequate space and mats, movement sequences, smooth and organized transitions, and effective supervision all support safe, meaningful, and fun experiences.

At one elementary school, the physical education teacher enjoyed gymnastics and tumbling activities and was able to bring that knowledge and interest into the school curriculum by providing activities for stunts, tumbling, and the use of some equipment (e.g., balance beams, balance boards, rebounders, and a vaulting box). A class for children with visual impairments that was located on campus participated in many of the activities with supervision and support from the adapted physical education specialist. As part of the unit of instruction, a field trip was arranged to a local gymnasium where the students were able to observe an Olympic Rhythmic Gymnastics demonstration. In addition, the students were able to sample the different pieces of gymnastics equipment—the rings, parallel bars, vaulting horse, jumping pit, trampoline, and different heights of balance beam. The experience was memorable. Some of the children with a disability signed up for a tumbling class with peers.

Relaxation activities

Many children need help to learn how to calm themselves or just relax. Children feel stress every day, just as adults do. Behaviors indicating stress can be exhibited as anxiety; irritability; or such bodily responses as headaches, upset stomach, or muscle tension. Relaxation and stretching activities involve poise, balance, and concentration as used in tai chi and yoga. The emphasis is on performing movements slowly in order to promote health and relaxation and stimulate energy. It is recommended that each physical education session include some form of relaxation. For active students, relaxation activities might be beneficial at the beginning of the class; for all students, relaxation activities are beneficial at the end.

Teachers can incorporate stress reduction routines into physical education at the end of class as a "cool-down" activity or during class as a "change of pace" between activities. A stunts and tumbling unit is an especially appropriate time to introduce relaxation techniques. Partners can "check" each other for tension and release during exercises, mirror each other in a "slow motion" activity, or just lie down on the mats for a rest while focusing on deep, slow breathing.

When students understand the relationship between contraction and relaxation and movement, they can begin to apply this knowledge to their skill performances. **Relaxation** is a motor skill that must be learned. It is *the release of the tension from a specific muscle or a group of muscles.* Relaxation is important to learn for several reasons:

- It helps to maintain good mental and physical health.
- It relieves tension and pressure (real or imaginary) that may have caused frustration, fatigue, poor health, or undesirable behaviors.
- It teaches the pairing of opposing muscles for contraction and relaxation, which assists with balance, symmetry, skill development, and refined muscle control.
- It teaches the recognition of tension and the ability to differentiate between the feelings of tension and relaxation, which is helpful to students who are coping with their own behaviors, peer interactions, or other stressors.
- It helps when coping with negative, as well as positive, stress such as competition, risk taking, and excitement.

Yoga postures can be easily assimilated into the physical education curriculum, program goals, objectives, and activities. The purpose of yoga is to stretch the body, breathe rhythmically, and become relaxed in order to swim better, run faster, or perform other physical activities more efficiently and smoothly. The fanciful names used in yoga (e.g., "rag doll," "elephant trunk," "dolphin," "butterfly," and "sunflower") are amusing and enjoyable for young children and may help them visualize relaxation. High school or college students can easily incorporate the postures into their fitness or activity class or personal training routines.

The use of imagery is often helpful when teaching relaxation to students in the upper elementary grades or higher. Descriptions of specific locations that are serene and calming, such as a stream floating by a green meadow in the mountains, are helpful. Imagery might include the following:

- Descriptions, such as "rag doll," "cat," "being very sleepy like a baby, puppy, or kitten," "float like a cloud," "fall into the sand and let it hold you until you make an impression," "fill your stomach with air like a balloon and let it out slowly," or "bend like Gumby."
- Contrasting opposite feelings, such as "march like a wooden soldier and then be Raggedy Ann," or "make yourself tall like a tree and then small like a flower."
- Isolating different body parts, such as "be a tall flower and have the petals sway in the breeze," "fly like a dove with one broken wing."

Relaxation routines can include:

- Progressive muscle relaxation (refer to Appendix H).
- Listening to slow, quiet music and slowing the breathing rhythm.
- Slowly counting while concentrating on rhythmic breathing or a calm, serene environment.
- Yoga exercises.
- Mirroring the slow movements of a partner or the teacher.
- Early morning stretching and a slow walk around campus before class.
- Identifying vocabulary and role-playing using words that describe how the body feels, looks, acts, and moves when relaxed or tense.

TABLE 13.1	*Lesson plan examples: Meeting IEP goals and objectives.*
EXAMPLE 1	**Grade level:** Kindergarten–primary grades **Activity:** Directional concepts & pathways
NASPE Standard 1	Demonstrates competency in motor skills and movement patterns needed to perform a variety of physical activities.
Physical Education Curriculum	■ Student will move in different directions (i.e., forward, backward, sideways). ■ Student will follow different pathways (i.e., straight, curved, zigzag). ■ Student will move in different levels (i.e., low, medium, high). ■ Student will be able to move safely within general space while maintaining his or her own personal space.
Class Size:	30 first graders plus 8 children from special needs classes with IEP goals and objectives
Formation:	Basketball courts, playground space, or flat area where lines can be drawn
Equipment:	Chalk; beanbags, deck rings, and pinnies
Lesson Focus	Directional concepts and pathways: ■ Directions—forward, backward, sideways ■ Pathways—straight, curved, zigzag ■ Levels—low, medium, high Given verbal instruction from teacher, students practice different pathways, directions, and levels while performing a walking movement in open space on playground blacktop. Play Pac Man.
Goals and Objectives	*Student 1:* Learn to stay in line and follow peers. *Student 2:* Ask peer to be sighted guide and follow pathways with partner. *Student 3:* Learn to move backward and where to look to avoid bumping into people or obstacles. *Students 4 & 5:* Stay with the group for specified period of time (i.e., lesson practice—10 minutes or game activity—5 minutes). *Student 6:* Maneuver wheelchair around peers and follow pathways. *Student 7:* Match word concept to movement (i.e., label movement or level and demonstrate the movement or level given term and model; or demonstrate movement or level given term or verbal prompt). *Student 8:* Learn to avoid tag by moving in opposite direction from opponent (tagger).
Pac Man Game	Best played on basketball court using lines. Make additional lines drawn with chalk to make connections around the playing area. Pick 6 students to be the "ghosts." Each wears a pinnie (colored jerseys) so that the other students can see who the "ghosts" are and who the "Pac Men" are. The "ghosts" must start in the middle of the playing area (usually in the center circle). All the "ghosts" count out loud to 10 while the other students scatter around the play space, following the lines of the court and the lines that you have made with chalk. The "Pac Men" and the "ghosts" will walk in the correct direction, given by the teacher. (After learning the game walking, progress to running and other locomotor patterns.)

(continued)

TABLE 13.1	Continued.

When a "ghost" tags a "Pac Man," the "Pac Man" must go to a designated area and do a stretch or an exercise for a specific number of times and then re-enter the game to continue to play. The "ghosts" must work together to get the "Pac Men."

Give each round about 3 to 5 minutes. When watching the game, see who is following directions, showing good sportsmanship, and so forth. Those students will be the next "ghosts."

Other rules:

- Look up when walking (or running).
- Do not push people in front of you.
- Stay on lines rather than jumping across lines.

EXAMPLE 2	**Grade level:** Upper elementary grades, third–fifth grade **Activity:** Physical fitness lesson—5 components of fitness
NASPE Standard 4	Achieves and maintains a health-enhancing level of physical fitness.
Physical Education Curriculum	■ Student will participate in selected activities to develop and maintain or improve fitness levels. ■ Student will record performance achieved, such as number of curl-ups or continuous jumps with rope. ■ Student will complete activity for each component of physical fitness.
Class Size:	60 fourth graders plus 14 children from special needs classes with IEP goals and objectives
Formation:	Station activities on grass field area near playground or blacktop space where apparatus is located
Equipment:	Medicine balls, aerobic steps, dyna-bands, various sizes of individual jump ropes, and music
Variations:	■ Some students may repeat station if time is needed to finish task or for more practice. ■ Some students may not record scores at the station.

Lesson Focus	Station practice:
	1. Medicine ball curl-ups with partner
	   ■ Raise and lower body while partner counts.
	   ■ Raise and lower body to cadence for 1 minute.
	2. Aerobic steps (to music)
	   ■ Increase heart rate level.
	   ■ Count pulse.
	   ■ Create routine of steps using forward, backward, and sideways movements.
	3. Dyna-bands (3 strength tasks)
	   ■ Perform horizontal pull 10 times.
	   ■ Perform vertical pull 10 times.
	   ■ Perform diagonal pull 10 times.
	4. Apparatus—horizontal bar (pull-ups using overhand grasp)
	   ■ Identify grips.
	   ■ Perform flexed arm hang.
	   ■ Perform pull-up.

(continued)

- Providing a script and routine of movements to use when tense (e.g., after coming in from recess or physical education, students close eyes, squeeze and release a fist, and take deep breaths).

Back relaxation exercises are important to older students and adults for maintaining strength and flexibility. The purpose is to perform slow motion exercises using the weight of the legs to assist the movement. For example, lying supine on a mat, slide the knees up toward the chest and hold the knees gently. The pressure of the weight of the relaxed legs affects the back. Several movements can be done slowly and easily to relieve tension in the lower back (e.g., rocking slightly back and forth or from side to side, or just holding the knees without movement and then extending one leg at a time by sliding the foot on the mat to rest with a rolled towel under the knees).

Recreation therapists, medical personnel, and physical therapists are helpful team members for identifying relaxation exercise routines, specific movements, and exercises that can be incorporated into the general physical education curriculum.

Multicultural Games and Activities

It is important for a person to understand the history and cultural significance of the games and activities in which he or she participates. Therefore, the physical educator should take the time to point out and incorporate these features into the curriculum. Several examples are provided in Chapter 11 and Appendix H (e.g., Sumo wrestling). Games such as these contribute to a foundation for understanding cultural diversity. Multicultural games and activities can be occasions for celebrating differences and delivering educational information. Table 12.5 presents some goals and activities for incorporating multicultural games.

Many games and activities from different countries have already been incorporated into the physical education curriculum (e.g., hopscotch, games from Africa), and others have evolved from past cultures. Different countries, regions, or cultures may use different implements or field arrangements to play a game, or they may have another name for a game that is similar (e.g., cricket and baseball, soccer and football). Oftentimes, a game can turn into a sport over time. For example, lawn tennis was played in 1905 by women wearing long, full skirts, long sleeves, and straw hats as a social event for fun. Almost 90 years later, it is a game played by highly trained athletes engaged in competition for monetary prizes, and wearing a very different type of clothing. This parallels the history of changes in the status of women in Western culture. Participating in a variety of games and activities from other countries can contribute to a deeper understanding and insight into the contributions of various groups and cultures around the world. In addition, multicultural activities allow students to focus on enjoyment and learning about different populations or groups.

Learning how nutritional needs are met in another culture and what types of foods are used can be effectively incorporated into a lesson or game. Another adaptation of the nutrition idea is to incorporate the diet and nutritional needs of children with diabetes. For example, when playing "Shipwreck" (see the Teaching Tip on page 293), the sailors sent to the galley to eat could identify specific foods for the country they are visiting or the types of foods or precautions that are necessary for people with diabetes. In this way, curricular areas such as health and diabetes awareness may be integrated. Another example is to use a map to find the specific location of the country where a game originated and determine its physical relationship to the United States or North America. The class might discuss directional positions, as well as the foods grown and used in that country.

Disability Awareness Activities

The challenge of inclusion is to create environments where differences are celebrated rather than viewed as difficulties or deficits to overcome. This understanding is then applied to all individuals.

There are many different kinds of diversity—ethnic, cultural, gender, and so forth. One of the most important areas of diversity to address when individuals with a disability are involved in physical activities is that of individual differences. Activities that help individuals understand their own strengths and challenges, as well as the strengths and challenges of others, often contribute to the development of an accepting attitude toward individuals with a disability and enhance the inclusive environment.

Young children, in particular, benefit from brief, direct information about the disability of a student with whom they interact. This is also true regarding any specialized equipment that an individual with a disability uses (e.g., crutches, braces, wheelchair, augumentative communication device, helmet). It is ideal when the person with a disability is able to help provide the information. Parents of children with a disability should have the opportunity to participate in disability awareness

TABLE 12.5 *Goals and activities to consider for multicultural games.*

GOALS	POSSIBLE ACTIVITIES
Demonstrate knowledge of world, country, state, community, and school diversity.	■ Play games and sports from around the world. ■ Participate in an International Field Day event. ■ Study how plants and herbs vary in use from culture to culture (e.g., jump rope to "red hot peppers" and discuss how pepper is used in foods and medicine around the world).
Demonstrate understanding of the ways in which group participation and membership contribute to the values, attitudes, and behaviors of individuals in the group.	■ Study and perform ethnic dances. ■ Discuss the meaning of specific movements and activities. ■ Invite groups to perform. ■ Organize a Special Olympics sporting event. ■ Infuse patriotism into some activity, rhyme, or dance.
Demonstrate skills (e.g., social skills) for effective interaction between individuals of different genders, cultural backgrounds, and abilities.	■ Discuss sportsmanship skills, sports etiquette, and behaviors that can be demonstrated during an activity. ■ Discuss differences and participate in lessons and activities that require an exchange of social greetings, cultural preferences, or communicating without using oral language. ■ Present activities from around the world (e.g., games, dances, rules of etiquette). ■ Provide for all students to participate within their "interest" areas without gender stereotyping (e.g., girls in football and weight lifting, boys in dance and aerobics).
Demonstrate understanding of the influences, dynamics, and consequences of discrimination, bias, prejudice, and stereotyping.	■ Analyze health products, clothing, or sporting advertisements that discriminate and redesign the ad or product. ■ Simulate and discuss a physically or mentally challenging situation and discuss feelings and experiences about that situation. (Caution: Remember that no one can "know" what it is like to have a disability through a simulation, but we can talk about the movement or physical experience during activity and possible compensations for it.)
Demonstrate understanding of our interdependence or dependence on others and our responsibility as an individual, a school citizen, a family member, a community participant living in the state, country, and world with others.	■ Discuss environmental issues that affect health and access to physical activity opportunities. ■ Participate in designing and making recommendations for accessibility to a school, community, playground, park, or activity.

activities as well. They may be willing to speak to a small group of children or adults about a specific disability or disabilities in general. In all disability awareness activities, the emphasis should be on what the individual *can* do, rather than what he or she cannot do. In other words, a disability must be viewed within the context of the whole child.

People who have little experience with people with a particular disability or with disabilities in general may have a tendency to place undue attention on the disability. Some people without a dis-

Teaching Tip

SHIPWRECK • The game of Shipwreck is popular in physical education classes. It offers a variety of options for teaching that can be adapted to meet the specific and individual needs of each student, as well as to meet the goals or objectives of the lesson. Students respond to instructions given by the teacher (captain of the ship) either verbally or through the use of pictures. The instructions are as follows:

FULL SPEED AHEAD:	Students power walk around the room.
ALL ENGINES STOP:	Stop and freeze.
ANCHOR AWAY:	Push-up position near a wall.
SCRUB THE DECK:	Hands and knees position; scrub the ground using both hands.
INSPECTION:	Line up against the wall (or a line) side by side and salute with the right hand (port, starboard, stern or aft, and bow can also be used for positions to line up before saluting).
LIFE BOATS:	Partners sit facing each other in "L" fashion while holding hands and sing "row, row, row your boat" while teacher sprays water across the group.
BOY OVERBOARD:	Boy lies down prone on ground; girl stands next to him with hand near forehead looking outward.
GIRL OVERBOARD:	Girl lies down prone on ground; boy stands next to her with hand near forehead looking outward.
MATES IN THE GALLEY:	Sit in circle of five and pretend to read the menu.
HOIST THE SAIL:	Groups of three form pyramid with top person moving arms and hands to "hoist" the sail (students can also do individually by standing and moving arms/hands to "hoist" the sail).
GENERAL QUARTERS:	All students lie on floor in head/toe alternate positions (e.g., head to head and toe to toe across/around gymnasium).
BATTLE STATIONS:	Groups of three: #1 lies prone on ground (torpedo); #2 straddles torpedo and forms rocket; #3 straddles torpedo and forms backward gun.
HIT THE DECK:	Everyone lies prone on ground.
BRIG:	The "brig" is a taped circle in the middle of the room/gymnasium (this helps students move around the room in one direction); any students who walk or run into the "brig" have to stay there; students in the "brig" do a push-up and join the group at the next command.

MENU:	BRIG MENU:
Cheeseburgers	Squid sandwich with peanut butter
French fries	Octopus tentacles
Pizza	Frog eye soup
Strawberry cake	Shark kidney pie
Root beer float	Tuna liquid

Variations:

- Change the menu for each country visited: Italy is spaghetti, Mexico is tacos, etc.
- Incorporate several words from the language of each country visited: numbers, colors, animals, movements, etc.
- Movement alternatives. Anchor Away: mimic the movements of pulling in a heavy anchor by using left/right hands alternating the pulling action; Life Boats: everyone uses "V" sit position with partner or holding hands with student using a wheelchair and rowing back and forth together; Hit the Deck: everyone holds isometric push-up position or must be in a push-up position next to three other "sailors" shoulder to shoulder; etc.
- Additional activities for the lesson can include dances, music, and games from the country visited.

Source: Adapted from ideas shared by Gerald Kearney, physical education teacher, Hoggard Magnet Elementary School, Las Vegas, Nevada. Used with permission.

ability, particularly teens and adults, are fearful or apprehensive about interacting with an individual with a disability because they don't know what to say, don't want to hurt the person's feelings, and don't want to feel embarrassed because they don't know how to interact. In addition, they may harbor misconceptions about the disability. Examples of some common misconceptions are:

- All people with physical disabilities are fragile and can be hurt by being touched.
- All people with mental illness are violent and dangerous.
- Many disabilities are contagious.
- You should never look at people with a disability because they will think you are staring at them.

Therefore, the first step in "ability awareness" activities is to provide simple, basic information—to help people feel comfortable when interacting and find appropriate ways to talk about a disability. One way to help people become more aware and comfortable when interacting with individuals with disabilities is to conduct disability awareness exercises. The goal of this type of activity is to realize that we all have individual differences and that we must consider the feelings and needs of others in order to work together. Exercises that include simulating a disability can be helpful, but it should always be explained that it is impossible to simulate a disability fully; that is, the feelings of an individual with a disability can never be simulated, nor can the challenge presented by the ongoing and usually permanent nature of a disability.

There is, however, value in attempting to play wheelchair basketball in order to understand some of the motor (and sensory) demands on an individual with a disability and become a better teacher or teammate. The difference is that this experience is a "practice opportunity" to enhance understanding and improve instruction and interaction. If you choose to use a simulation activity, it must be carefully planned so that all participants understand and achieve the true purpose. One simulation that is often used is to blindfold a sighted person and have a "sighted guide" lead the person through an obstacle course or over a travel pathway. One of the reasons that this is not actually the experience of a visually impaired person is that visual impairment encompasses so many different levels of light and sight perception, changes in the visual field, and experiences related to the onset of the impairment. However, a structured discussion following this simulation can help sighted individuals gain insight that will help them, for example, to perform more adequately as a sighted guide, or to better understand rule modifications used for an individual with a visual impairment in the class. In addition, it is sometimes helpful to have a person with a disability such as visual impairment come and discuss the disability and answer questions regarding their experiences in sport or physical education activities, especially relating to leisure time and recreational activities or playground games with peers. Table 12.6 presents several examples of disability awareness activities.

Community-Based Instruction Programs

Community-based instruction is an important and functional aspect of the physical education curriculum, especially for helping students adapt their motor skills to culturally determined forms of movement. Community-based instruction includes bringing the students into the community and bringing the community into the classroom.

Going out into the community

Instruction that takes place in the community provides opportunities for students to experience skills in different, realistic settings. It may be difficult to include this type of instruction in the general physical education class because of the class size or the adopted curriculum, but creative planning and support from other programs can provide valuable lessons and experiences for all students. The adapted physical educator can often help facilitate community-based instruction by:

1. Providing ideas for the family to use at home, at a park, at a recreation venue, or in a school community (e.g., family night bowling, shopping, or going to the mountains for the day). Ideas can include how the student could access, perform, and participate with others.
2. Providing ideas and support to the classroom teacher when a field trip or community-based activity is planned (e.g., riding the bus, going to the zoo, going to a restaurant, or attending a concert). Ideas can include how the student could access the bus, carry food at the restaurant, negotiate environmental obstacles (e.g., curb, hill, bump, turnstile), or find a seat in the audience.
3. Providing support by planning and implementing community-based instruction around physical activities (e.g., using a public swimming pool, skating rink, or gymnastics club).

TABLE 12.6 Disability awareness activities.

THE DIFFERENCES AMONG US

A. *Purpose:* To be aware that everyone is unique and that we all have limitations and challenges. People with a disability are people first. Labels and predetermined attitudes can create barriers.

B. *Setting:* Training room, classroom, any gathering place.

C. *Activity:* Identify three or four areas of the room as area A, B, C, D. Ask all people who wear glasses to go to area A. Ask all people who are left-handed to go to area B. Those who are left-handed and wear glasses should shift to area B. Ask all those who cannot remember an appointment without writing it down to go to area C (again, those already in area A or B should shift if necessary). Ask all those who have difficulty following driving directions from one place to another to go to area D. By this time, many people have shifted groups. Next, the participants should return to their original seats and the leader should ask for a show of hands as to how many groups each person was in. Ask the group to share comments or feelings, then make the points stated above in the purpose statement.

DISABILITY AWARENESS FOR PARENTS

A. *Purpose:* To understand that all parents have preferences about how their child will be treated. To communicate respect for each other by acknowledging that parents know their children and the things that bring out the best in their child.

B. *Setting:* Training room, classroom, any gathering place. Mixed group of parents of children with and without a disability, teachers, staff.

C. *Activity:* In small groups, parents list key phrases or behaviors they would like teachers and staff to use with their children. Give age-appropriate examples to get them started (e.g., for young children, get down to eye level when talking to my child; for older children, move close to my child and speak in a calm voice, don't yell across the room or playground; for teens, briefly explain why an assignment or activity is being used). Share and discuss phrases and behaviors with the larger group. Write some on large paper strips and post them in key places in the classroom, school, gym, or waiting area.

SIMULATION WITHIN A TEAM

A. *Purpose:* To gain awareness of how teamwork can change the effect of a disability on team outcomes.

B. *Setting:* Divide participants into groups and give each group the same materials for building a model structure (e.g., house, vehicle, playground structure). Physical education equipment can be the materials used, to assist in the application to physical activity environments. Other types of materials that can be used include classroom supplies (e.g., paper, glue, tape, pipe cleaners, straws), recycled items, or natural objects collected outside (e.g., sticks, leaves, pebbles, bark). Assign one or two individuals in each group a disability role. Examples of disability roles include:

- Cannot talk
- Cannot hear
- Cannot see
- Cannot stand or walk
- Cannot use hands
- Cannot count or read
- Uses only one-word sentences

C. *Activity:* Ask the groups to build the structure. Allow at least 15 minutes for building time. Ask each group to share their experience and use the following guiding questions:

- Were you successful in building a structure? Why? Why not?
- What contribution was made by the individuals with a disability role?
- Were any assumptions made that created a barrier for participation or task completion?
- What accommodations or compensations did your group use, and were they helpful?
- What did you learn? Would you do anything differently if faced with this situation again?

Source: Adapted from A. Carr, S. Eyrich, S. Amos-Green, and M. Moberg (1997), *Connections Project: Learning Communities for All Children.* A training project developed by the California Institute on Human Services, Sonoma State University, and sponsored by the California Department of Education.

Table 12.7 provides examples of some physical activity programs often available in the community and summaries of their program content.

When a student with a disability is involved in a sport in the community, physical educators and community members must work together effectively to enable the student's participation. Examples of accommodations applied to a specific sport are described in the box on page 297 titled "Making Connections: Accommodations for a Student with Dwarfism."

Bringing the community to the classroom

Introducing community resources by bringing in speakers or demonstrations can help students prepare for community outings. For example:

- Professional athletes (or high school or college athletes) visit the school prior to the students attending a tennis, basketball, hockey, or baseball event.
- A lifeguard from a local pool or beach comes to talk about water safety.
- The teacher shows a video about skiers who are disabled or another disability sport and provides resources.
- A bicycle safety rodeo at school could include tandem bicycles, three-wheeled bikes, and maps of local bike paths.

In order to complete some activities, individuals must perform many components of motor skills in the community, such as access to the elevator or escalator (agility), crossing streets by stepping up and

TABLE 12.7 *Examples of content for some community physical activity programs.*

PHYSICAL ACTIVITY PROGRAM	SUMMARY OF PROGRAM CONTENT
Basketball day camp for 8- to 17-year-olds	Basketball skills at various levels, including game play
YMCA swimming lessons	Swimming skills from water adjustment to advanced strokes, and diving taught in progressive ability-level and age-level classes
Health club or community recreation aerobics class	Individual improvement or maintenance of aerobic endurance through aerobic dance activities
Youth soccer league	Soccer skills and competitive game play by age groupings
City softball league	Competitive softball games for adults
Senior center tai chi class	Individual improvement or maintenance of physical fitness for older adults through slow stretching, mobility, balance, and concentration activities, as well as relaxation
Local adapted bowling league	Turn taking, strength development, scoring procedures, and timing for eye–hand coordination through team bowling league for individuals with a disability
Recreational bicycling club	Safely negotiating travel pathways, endurance and strength for pedaling, balance and coordination, leisure time activity as a tandem rider
Boating or fishing	Paddling canoe, kayak, or boat and understanding currents; types and styles of fishing poles and fish; geographical locations and laws for fishing
Recreational skating (roller, ice, or in-line)	Donning shoes and skates, balance and coordination, push and slide of skate, stops, turns, and safe falls; partner skating, dances, and group participation, leading to independent or supervised participation in "open rink" or park skating
Walking club	Orienteering, social interaction, geographical differences, safety precautions, fitness
Recreational golf lessons	Etiquette, striking, estimating, fitness (endurance and strength), social interaction, scoring, rules of play

MAKING CONNECTIONS

Monthly Roller Skating School Event

Becker Elementary School holds a monthly roller skating "party" after school for all students. David, a student with Down syndrome, wants to participate with his peers and siblings. David has difficulty with strength, balance, and endurance and needs some practice prior to participating. A suggestion was given to his parents on how David could practice the "sliding" movement at home by using one piece of finger-painting paper for each foot and "sliding" across the floor. (Another excellent practice material for sliding and skiing movements is a mouse pad with a smooth plastic finish.)

During physical education class, several peers were asked if they were going to the roller skating event and were willing to take turns being "peer partners" for David. The adapted physical education specialist arranged to be present for support at the event to make suggestions and provide assistance.

MAKING CONNECTIONS

Accommodations for a Student with Dwarfism

Mr. Woods, who is an avid golfer and is also employed as a security guard on campus, coaches the Alexander Middle School golf team. The team uses a local community golf course that requires players to be at least 18 years of age in order to drive a golf cart. The golf league prohibits the use of golf carts in competition, but the rules do not state a reason. Kyle, who has dwarfism, joined the team in seventh grade. The large amount of walking for practice and competition gave him severe hip pain. Kyle walks between classes at school and for other relatively short mobility tasks, but he uses a motorized scooter chair for long walks such as shopping at a mall or going to an amusement park. Kyle participates in the general physical education program with swimming substituted for track and any other units requiring large amounts of running. Kyle's doctor was consulted and said that the pain was due to a skeletal anomaly in the hip area and would likely get worse with increased walking. He did not feel it would respond to conditioning.

Kyle's coach and parents consulted Kyle's physical education teacher, who scheduled a meeting with the adapted physical education teacher. The adults worked together to give the golf course and golf league a medical explanation of need for Kyle to use his motorized scooter chair on the golf course. Kyle demonstrated his safe driving skills to the golf course staff. The league and golf course were reminded of the requirement to provide equal access to all. Kyle participated on the golf team for two years and continues to play on his high school team.

---

down a curb and traveling distances (endurance), carrying items (strength), or counting and exchanging coins and money (fine motor).

Scheduling staff coverage for community-based instruction is often challenging, but it can be done by making adaptations, assisting others when working with the student with a disability, coaching peers, providing direct instruction, and facilitating positive interactions among students. The challenge is in providing the necessary support. This is when collaboration and the team approach work best, because all members of the team can communicate their support needs for specific activities, including the community-based instructional activities. Flexible scheduling for the itinerant teacher, university student and parent volunteers, or peers can provide the support needed, depending on the situation and the goals, objectives, and needs of the student. One benefit of using peers to support inclusion and community-based instruction is that this provides more opportunities for social interaction and integration. In fact, for community-based instruction, it is important to have several peers provide support to a student with a disability so that it is a more realistic, normalizing "real-life" or "real-world" experience. For example, going bowling is more realistic when four or five students with mixed abilities gather at the bowling alley instead of a large group of students who all have a disability.

In a school setting, many adults may organize, supervise, or lead physical activities. In many cases, the administrator or physical educator provides guidance and consultation to the activity leader when an individual with a disability is participating. "Making Connections: Lunch-Time Soccer" presents the suggestions provided to a parent volunteer who led a lunch-time recreational soccer program during the school year.

The most powerful strategy, for inclusion as well as community-based instruction, is to encourage and support the general physical education teacher in assuming instructional responsibility for all students. This is a challenging task at times. It helps immensely when a leader (such as a principal) sets the tone of acceptance and responsibility for all children, because the whole school community is encouraged to follow the philosophy and adopt the attitude of acceptance. Another key may be the relationship established between the general physical education teacher and the adapted physical education specialist. When this relationship is one of mutual support and collaboration, inclusion and acceptance of students with a disability are greatly enhanced.

PLANNING ACTIVITIES THAT DEVELOP STUDENT INTERESTS

Lifelong participation in physical activities and the development of an active lifestyle as an adult are supported by positive feelings related to physical activities. Adults usually develop an interest in certain types of activities and independently pursue them. Children and teens, especially those with a disability, may not have been exposed to a wide enough variety of activities to know their own interests. For some students, instruction in fitness and movement concepts may not have been adequately applied to their activities of interest. Others may find physical edu-

MAKING CONNECTIONS

Lunch-Time Soccer

An elementary school posted an open sign-up for any students in the fourth and fifth grades who wanted to play soccer during lunch recess. Dakota, a student with a visual impairment, was very interested in playing and signed up. The "coach" volunteer approached the principal of the school and was concerned about how to handle the "situation." The principal said that everyone at school was able to participate and that support could be provided. A discussion with the adapted physical education specialist and physical education teacher resulted in a list of suggestions to be followed when the volunteers were on campus. The result was that Dakota was able to participate fully and received the "certificate of participation" at the end of the program. The suggestions were as follows:

Accommodations/modifications for students with visual impairments participating in lunch-time recreational soccer program:

1. *Always Think Safety:*
   a. Ensure that students wear helmet and safety goggles during play activities.
   b. Fullback position in soccer is best, or a wing if playing a forward position.
   c. Assign a peer to be a sighted guide with student for running, if needed.
   d. Change type of ball used, if possible, to brightly colored, soft, or with sound.
   e. Identify boundaries of play using large cones or brightly colored objects (make sure that the field area is clear of obstacles or equipment).

2. *"Anchor" Student to the Play Area:*
   a. Provide consistency in position on field and direction of goal.
   b. Identify teammates or players sitting or standing next to the student so that he or she can know where to line up or position himself or herself for play.
   c. Use "position specific" language for directing student on field (both coach and players should do so) and especially giving verbal warning of a pass to student.

3. *Be Prepared with Specific Verbal Directions and Physical Assistance (when needed):*
   a. Describe position or direction to goal area and distance frequently, especially in practice trials, for making corrections and having feedback that is helpful.
   b. Be explicit about the movements to make or position of the body in relation to other players, object (ball), and goal.

4. *Ensure Safe and Successful Participation:*
   a. Use special equipment, if needed.
   b. Make any rule changes, such as a time (or slow count) when student is in possession of ball, to allow for passing and participation.
   c. Ask student for the modifications/adaptations that he or she would like to have (self-advocacy is an important life skill).

cation unsatisfying because activities of interest to them have not been offered.

Nontraditional Curriculum Resources

The list of activities for students at any level on the developmental model can be as long or short, diverse or restricted as the physical educator chooses, and he or she should attempt to expose students to as much variety as possible to stimulate their interest. In doing so, educators may wish to consult nontraditional curriculum resources. For example, the activities listed in professional journals (e.g., *Journal of Health, Physical Education, Recreation, and Dance*; *Strategies*; *Adapted Physical Education Quarterly*) or available from local and state professional organizations, as well as on the Internet, can provide suggestions for a wide array of movement experiences. Examples of some nontraditional sources of activities include:

1. Yoga exercises and tai chi movements learned at the local recreation center.
2. Leisure time and recreational activities or sports such as bocce ball or shuffleboard experienced on a travel or cruise experience.
3. Conditioning exercises and walking programs from the local hospital's cardiac rehabilitation seminar programs.
4. Rules and histories of games and sports from school, local, or professional libraries and the Internet.
5. Dance and rhythms or rhymes for hand and rope games from the radio, television, local dance studios, contemporary artists, music instruction, and the students themselves.

We encourage the reader to be creative and resourceful and to learn from each movement opportunity.

Instructional Tips

It is the physical educator's responsibility to help students develop an interest in physical activities and to tie physical education instruction to student interests. Tips for accomplishing this include:

- Encourage students to participate in all activities presented in class, even when something new is presented, so that they can experience the "feel" and "fun" of the movement.
- Expand the number of games and activities that students experience in the physical education curriculum (e.g., using a wide variety of throwing objects and striking implements and explaining their use in games).
- Plan demonstrations, presentations, or participation in the school "talent show" featuring games, dances, and recreational activities from other cultures and asking students to bring, wear, or share their individual costumes and equipment.
- Provide students (and parents) with a physical education interest survey so that the student (and family) preferences can be identified and explored.
- Use specific books, literature, news articles, special events (e.g., the Olympics, or soccer and tennis tournaments), and television shows to explore activities.
- Provide inclement weather experiences by using board games, fine motor games, cooperative games, and videos that demonstrate a wide variety of activities or sporting events from other countries.
- Ask students to create their own games and activities using specific types of materials and equipment or playing areas.
- Combine multicultural activities within the lesson.
- Ask younger children to look through magazines and library books and draw pictures of some of the activities they would like to try or to do more often.
- Assign homework to the older students that requires them to attend a sporting event or watch a television presentation on some activity in which they have not previously participated.

SUMMARY

The full range of physical activities can and should be used when programming physical education for individuals with a disability. The principle of inclusion and a noncategorical approach will enhance the experience of all students. An effective physical education professional implements appropriate strategies and adaptations for each individual and provides the necessary supports, techniques, and developmentally appropriate lessons to guide students' progress in learning culturally determined forms of movement.

CHAPTER 12 Learning Activities

12.1 Select one of the disability awareness activities from this chapter and use it in class. Write a paragraph describing how this activity could be used with students with various types of disabilities, and why it would be beneficial.

12.2 Choose one developmental level. For a class that includes five students with ADHD and three students with a learning disability, at the level chosen, write a short lesson plan for three fitness activities emphasizing adaptations to include all students. Follow up with a class presentation and discussion.

12.3 Present an inclusion scenario and discuss the following items with the class:

- Types of support the student or students might need
- Types of support the general physical education teacher might need
- Types of support the adapted physical educator might need

REFERENCES

Ability awareness kit—Helps make everyone aware of the challenges faced by differently abled children. Norcross, GA: SPORTIME (Item #1-26513). www.sportime.com.

Anderson, B. (2000). *Stretching: 20th anniversary.* Bolinas, CA: Shelter Publications.

Barbarash, L. (1997). *Multicultural games.* Champaign, IL: Human Kinetics.

Bennett, J. P., & Riemer, P. C. (1995). *Rhythmic activities and dance.* Champaign, IL: Human Kinetics.

Block, M., & Conatser, P. (May/June 2002). Adapted aquatics and inclusion. *Journal of Physical Education, Recreation, and Dance, 73*(5), 31.

Block, M. E. (2000). *A teacher's guide to including students with disabilities in regular physical education* (2nd ed.). Baltimore: Brookes.

Branner, T., Goebel, G., & Young, D. (2004). *The safe exercise handbook.* Dubuque, IA: Kendall Hunt.

Burgstahler, S. (2001–2004). Universal design of instruction. www.washington.edu/doit/Faculty/Strategies/Universal.

California Department of Education, Special Education Division. (1992). *PEERS (Providing Education for Everyone in Regular Schools).* Sacramento, CA: Author.

Carr, A., Eyrich, S., Amos-Green, S., & Moberg, M. (1997). *Connections project: Learning communities for all children.* A training project developed by the California Institute on Human Services, Sonoma State University, and sponsored by the California Department of Education.

Clancy, M. E., & Rubin, T. R. (1998). Adapting games for diverse student needs. *Teaching Elementary Physical Education, 9*(5), 9.

Claxton, D., Grube, D., & Young, J. (September/October 2001). Using initiative games to build community, cooperation and trust. *Strategies, 15*(1), 35.

Conkell, C. S., & Pearson, H. (1995, September). Do you use developmentally appropriate games? *Strategies,* 22.

Cooper Institute for Aerobics Research. (2004). *Prudential FITNESSGRAM/Activitygram test administration manual.* Champaign, IL: Human Kinetics.

Council on Physical Education for Children. (1992). *Developmentally appropriate physical education practices for children: A position statement of the Council on Physical Education for Children (COPEC).* Reston, VA: National Association for Sport and Physical Education.

Davis, K. (1998). Integrating children with disabilities into gross motor activities. *Teaching Elementary Physical Education, 9*(5), 10.

Davis, R. W. (2002). *Inclusion through sports: A guide to enhancing sport experiences.* Champaign, IL. Human Kinetics.

Davis, R. W., & Stanton, K. (1998). Public Law 105-18: New implications for regular physical education. *Teaching Elementary Physical Education, 9*(5), 5.

DePauw, K. P., & Karp, G. G. (1994). Integrating knowledge of disability throughout the physical education curriculum: An infusion approach. *Adapted Physical Activity Quarterly, 11,* 3–13.

DePauw, K. P. (2000). Social-cultural context of disability: Implications for scientific inquiry and professional preparation. *Quest, 52*, 358–368.

DePauw, K. P. (1996). Students with Disabilities in Physical Education. In S. J. Silverman & C. D. Ennis (Eds.), *Student learning in physical education—Applying research to enhance instruction* (pp. 101–124). Champaign, IL: Human Kinetics.

Deschenes, C., Ebelling, D. G., & Sprague, J. (1994). *Adapting curriculum & instruction in inclusive classrooms: A teacher's desk reference.* Bloomington, IN: The Center for School and Community Integration, Institute for the Study of Developmental Disabilities.

ERIC Clearinghouse on Disabilities and Gifted Education. (Fall 1999). *Research connections in special education,* Number 5 (p. 2). http://ericec.org/osep/recon5/rc5sec1.html.

Falvey, M. A. (1991). *Inclusive education.* Handout from California State University, Los Angeles, CA, School of Education, Division of Special Education.

Falvey, M. A., & Rosenberg, R. (1998 March). *Infusing A-PE activities into a community based program for students with severe handicaps.* CAHPERD 55th Annual Conference.

Hannes-Metzker, A., & Martinez, R. (1999). The handy-band workout. *Strategies, 12*(3), 5–8.

Happel, K. (1998). To ski or not to ski? That is the question. *Teaching Elementary Physical Education, 9*(5), 13.

Hinson, C. (1995). *Fitness for children.* Champaign, IL: Human Kinetics.

Houston-Wilson, C., & Lieberman, L. J. (1999). The individualized education program in physical education. *JOPERD, 70*(3), 60.

Johnson, J., & Pierce, J. R. (September 2000). Creating an ability awareness day in physical education. *Journal of Physical Education, Recreation, and Dance, 71*(7), 16.

Kasser, S. L. (1995). *Inclusive games—Movement fun for everyone.* Champaign, IL: Human Kinetics.

Kasser, S. L., & Lytle, R. (2005). *Inclusive physical activity—A lifetime of opportunities.* Champaign, IL: Human Kinetics.

Koehler, G. (November/December 2001). Stress management exercises for teachers and students. *Strategies, 15*(2), 7.

LeFevre, D. N. (2002). *Best new games.* Champaign, IL: Human Kinetics.

Lepore, M., Gayle, G. W., & Stevens, S. F. (1998). *Adapted aquatic programs: A professional guide.* Champaign, IL: Human Kinetics.

Lichtman, B. (1999). *More innovative games.* Champaign, IL: Human Kinetics.

Lieberman, L. J., & Houston-Wilson, C. (2002). *Strategies for inclusion: A handbook for physical educators.* Champaign, IL. Human Kinetics.

Lieberman, L. J., James, A. R., & Ludwa, N. (May/June 2004). The impact of inclusion in general physical education for all students. *Journal of Physical Education, Recreation, and Dance, 75*(5), 37.

Morris, G. S. D., & Stiehl, J. (1999). *Changing kids' games* (2nd ed.). Champaign, IL: Human Kinetics.

National Association for Sport and Physical Education. (2005). *Active start: A statement of physical activity guidelines for children birth to five years.* Reston, VA: American Alliance for Health, Physical Education, Recreation, and Dance.

Nelson, C. (November/December 2003). Yoga for elementary students. *Strategies, 17*(2), 26.

Nichols, D. R. (November/December 2001). Kayaking—An activity for integrating students with disabilities. *Strategies, 15*(2), 31.

Pangrazi, R. P. (2001). *Dynamic physical education for elementary school children* (13th ed.). Boston: Allyn & Bacon.

Pangrazi, R. P. (2001). *Lesson plans for dynamic physical education* (13th ed.). Boston: Allyn & Bacon.

Peterson, S. C., & Cruz, L. M. (November/December 2000). Using small-sided games in traditional activities. *Strategies, 14*(2), 19.

Poppen, J. D. (1995). *Fitness zone ahead.* Bend, OR: Maverick Publications.

Research connections in special education. (1999). No. 5, Fall, p. 2.

Sawicki, T. (2000). Developmentally appropriate activities using games modification. *Strategies, 14*(2), 22.

Sinibaldi, R. (March/April 2001). PEERS: Partners & equals, exceptional & regular students. *Strategies, 14*(4), 9.

Tripp, A., Piletic, C., & Babcock, G. (2004). *A position statement on including students with disabilities in physical education.* Reston, VA: Adapted Physical Activity Council of the American Association for Active Lifestyles and Fitness.

Virgilio, S. J. (1997). *Fitness education for children—A team approach.* Champaign, IL: Human Kinetics.

White Jr., G., Cosebolt, K., & Hull, S. (November/December 2004). Low-organized games: An approach to inclusion. *Strategies, 18*(2), 27.

Winnick, J. P., & Short, F. X. (1999). *The Brockport physical fitness test manual—A health-related test for youths with physical and mental disabilities.* Champaign, IL: Human Kinetics.

Wright, D. B. (1998). Success with the difficult learner. Adapted from D. Deschenes, D. G. Ebelling, & J. Sprague (1994), *Adapting curriculum & instruction in inclusive classrooms: A teacher's desk reference.* Bloomington, IN: The Center for School and Community Integration, Institute for the Study of Developmental Disabilities.

Chapter 13

Organizing the Instructional Program

Guiding Questions

1. What steps should be taken when organizing the instructional program?

2. What are some of the factors to consider when establishing the schedule for the itinerant adapted physical education specialist?

3. What should be considered when selecting, adapting, or constructing equipment?

4. What are some modifications that can be made to existing facilities for physical activity to make them accessible or more easily used by individuals with a disability?

5. What are some safety precautions for individuals with a disability that should be considered in addition to those for individuals without a disability?

PLANNING AND ORGANIZATION

When organizing the physical education program to include students with a disability, the physical educator must consider numerous factors and perform many steps prior to the actual lesson implementation and contact with students. This may seem to be a monumental task, but breaking it down into categories and steps will help to make it manageable.

The planning portion of organizing the instructional program has five major components: (1) orientation and communication, (2) scheduling, (3) lesson planning, (4) evaluation, and (5) organizational strategies. Each of these components is an essential ingredient for a successful program of physical activity. Evaluation is covered in Chapter 5. The other four components of planning are discussed next.

Orientation and Communication

The following list outlines the adapted physical education specialist's major tasks and strategies, especially if the specialist is assigned an itinerant schedule. The general physical educator should incorporate many of these tasks and strategies when individuals with a disability are in the class.

- Determine the locations (addresses) and telephone numbers of assigned schools, and introduce yourself to the staff. It is usually best to use a district map showing the location of schools, especially for rural or highly populated urban areas.

- Identify the number of students on your caseload at each school, locate the individualized education programs (IEPs) and referrals, and schedule times for the physical education classes. General physical educators should also review the IEPs of any students with a disability in their classes.

- Learn and follow district procedures for work activities, such as check-in and check-out procedures for each school, attendance, use of substitutes, mileage reimbursement, conference or workshop attendance, and budgeting and purchasing procedures.

- Establish a communication trail for accountability that includes IEP schedules, the location of your mailbox and contact numbers for messages at each school, requests for resources, observations and referrals, and conference or workshop attendance.

- Determine what spaces are available for activities, the times that the various spaces are available to you, and the number of students you will have in class at a given time.

MAKING CONNECTIONS

Professional Support Group

Ms. Chang, an itinerant adapted physical educator, and several of her colleagues, who are the only adapted physical educators in the district, often have felt isolated. They decided to meet regularly at one of the district offices to make connections and contacts with each other to share information, to provide support, and to facilitate professional development. Topics of discussion have included lessons, student behaviors, general everyday events, and special projects. In addition, members have exchanged strategies learned at workshops or conferences that some have attended. One year, they decided to choose a topic of focus for each meeting, such as assessment, behavior management, or equipment modification. Occasionally, they invite outside speakers from the local university, but mostly the group provides support for the teachers and an opportunity to share problems and solutions with one another.

- Make connections with peers for support and to share lesson ideas and strategies, equipment, and conference and workshop information that will facilitate professional development. General physical educators and adapted physical education specialists should make contact even before the start of the school year, sharing schedules, telephone numbers, and other contact information. Once school begins, they should maintain regular contact.

- Determine safety and security procedures on each campus, as well as between schools (e.g., walkie-talkie on campus, pagers, district picture ID card, or other technology needed).

- It is usually helpful to have the district print business cards for identification and sharing with parents, teachers, and staff so that it is easy for them to contact you. In addition, the itinerant specialist may want to keep copies of her or his schedule handy to give to staff and parents.

Scheduling

Schedules and scheduling variables may be quite different from one physical educator to the next. The most obvious differences are between a physical educator who is at one school site and an itinerant physical educator who travels to several schools in one day (or week). In addition, the schedules for elementary and secondary schools are different because of the amount of time allotted for physical education classes, as well as the types of schedules used by the schools. The weekly schedule for the adapted physical education specialist can usually be determined by the first or second week of school, depending on the number of referrals and assessments required at the beginning of the year. That schedule will usually change a few times during the school year (usually in October or January, and sometimes in the spring, when referrals and transfers are common).

Another component of scheduling for the adapted physical educator concerns the transition from elementary to secondary schools in a district or county program. Often, it is helpful and necessary for the adapted physical educator to approach the receiving secondary schools at the end of a school year and discuss the students who are making the transition to middle or high school. Some students have to schedule their physical education class early or late in the day (e.g., because of fatigue, attention span, difficulty dressing, or athletic team participation). It is much easier for secondary schools to meet these needs if they are informed before the end of the year (or end of the "track" in year-round calendars), so they can be considered when all students in the school are scheduled. Block scheduling presents a different challenge for the student transitioning from elementary to secondary school. The adapted physical education specialist should investigate the specific scheduling parameters at the secondary school a student will attend and be involved in advance planning with the staff at the receiving school.

Although school assignments are the main factor affecting the typical schedule, adapted physical educators must consider numerous other variables, including the following:

1. Time necessary for:
   - Processing referrals and planning assessments.
   - Conducting assessment activities, especially for team assessments and report writing.
   - Traveling the distance between school sites, including travel pattern, routes, traffic, time of day, geographic locations (e.g., rural versus urban).
   - Instruction (e.g., contact minutes and number of sessions for each student).
   - Collaborating, team teaching, etc.
   - Locating and storing equipment, and performing any duties as a faculty member at the school site.
   - Providing resources to school staff (e.g., equipment, materials, ideas for activities for the inclusion of students with a disability) and scheduling requests for in-service training (e.g., physical fitness training and testing for a student with a disability; special activities such as Jump Rope for Heart or Hoops for Heart, All Children Exercising Simultaneously [ACES], Physical Education and Sport week, assemblies or talent shows).

2. Coordination and implementation of:
   - Research and information gathered regarding rare conditions, multiple disabilities, new approaches, and so on.
   - Procedures for tracking students, such as designing a database for attendance tracking, monitoring IEP dates, and recording information for progress reports.
   - The schedule for the training, assignment, work hours, and duties of physical education assistants, peer tutors, and volunteers.
   - Team assessments, parent interviews, and phone calls.
   - Procedures for equipment orders, care and repair, and inventory, and providing resources when requested.

3. Preparation for transitions—infant to toddler to preschool, preschool to elementary, elementary to secondary, and secondary to adult programs. Activities to support transitions may include visits to the new program with or without the student, planning meetings and collaboration between current and receiving staff, and facilitating parent input and support.

Lesson Planning

Presentation of lessons to students is the most important component of the instructional program, influencing student learning on a daily basis. This chapter focuses on general suggestions related to planning developmentally appropriate lessons and how they will help to meet the goals and objectives for students with a disability.

All teachers should prepare and organize their lessons in a manner that fits their own personality and teaching philosophy. For example, some teachers like to have many forms and descriptions on the computer; some teachers use the "copy it and go" method; some teachers complete the district's required forms for lesson planning with their own "shorthand" notes. Whatever the method, the focus should be on a progression of developmentally appropriate activities that enable success for all students.

Effective teachers manage their time wisely—they never find themselves "winging it" or using the "throw out the ball" approach to teaching. This approach usually fails with students with a disability because it does not provide enough continuity or repetition for the students to learn skills adequately. Often, the unpredictability of the lesson itself creates a challenge for some students to attend and manage appropriate behaviors.

The developmental model will easily fit into the scope and sequence, philosophy, goals, and objectives of any curriculum framework. For example, for children between two and seven years of age, the basic focus will be on the fundamental movements; for those between eight and 10 years of age, the introduction of general sport skills will be incorporated into the lessons; for students between 11 and 13 years of age, more specific sport skills should be taught, leading to specialized sport skills for those age 14 to adult. Some physical education textbooks print yearly allotted times or percentages that should be spent on specific activities at each grade level, to guide the educator in making general decisions about the schedule and lesson plans. However, student interests, progress, and time spent in physical activity directly influence lesson planning.

The teacher who has aligned lessons with the NASPE standards and the district or school curriculum is well positioned to become proficient at identifying the activities that will best assist students in learning the skills and behaviors required to become competent movers. The examples in Table 13.1 show the relationship between planning lessons based on the NASPE standards, following district curriculum, and meeting the individual needs of specific students in class.

Teaching Tip

SCHEDULE DISTRIBUTION • It is helpful to distribute to each school site monthly schedules that include the following information:

1. Your personal identification and contact numbers (e.g., pager, cell phone, home school site)
2. Date of schedule and revision dates
3. Days and times you provide services (and sometimes the type of service in codes, such as D for direct or C for collaboration)
4. Locations and site names with a telephone number and contact person at each school site
5. Grade level of classes

(Caution: Do not use the students' names on the schedule—just classroom teacher's name or the time of class.)

Organizational Strategies

Effective teachers use key organizational strategies. These are critical to the smooth implementation of the other components of the program plan. This section addresses basic organizational strategies that are applicable to most general physical education and adapted physical education programs. Teachers must implement other organizational strategies based on their assignment and local circumstances, policies, and procedures. The refinement of organizational strategies seems to be a never-ending task; however, organization is an essential ingredient to being prepared to perform all job duties and managing job-related stress. Managing paperwork, time, equipment, behavior, information resources, stress, and communication, as well as providing a safe environment and individualized instruction, all require the use of organizational strategies.

Managing paperwork

General physical educators and adapted physical education specialists generate and receive many documents informing them about their students, schools, districts, and so forth. An important aspect of both jobs is learning to organize such paperwork as IEPs, portfolios, homework, and grades for easy access and referral. Strategies for managing paperwork include:

- Align IEP objectives with grading so that information collected is useful for both.
- Align IEP objectives with grading timelines.
- Plan to send out progress reports when grades are sent out.

Managing time

Physical educators need to have good time-management skills in order to complete assessments in a timely manner, schedule IEP meetings, plan lessons, meet with parents, and so forth. Strategies for managing time include:

- Find out who schedules IEPs and establish a communication system so you are informed of upcoming meetings as far in advance as possible.
- Establish a weekly time period in your schedule to be used for assessment and IEP preparation.
- Prepare a yearly calendar listing the IEP due dates, and identify those that are triennial IEPs, so that you are prepared in advance, especially considering vacation, staff development days, and, for year-round schedules, the track-out times.

(continued on p. 312)

TABLE 13.1	Continued.
	5. Individual jump rope 　■ Increase number of jumps. 　■ Perform jumps with partner.
Goals & Objectives	*Student 1:* Reach and pass medicine ball to partner from standing position. *Student 2:* Assume bent-knee seated position and slowly lower body while holding medicine ball. *Student 3:* Find partner and verbally ask to work together. *Student 4:* Start and stop with music. *Student 5:* Place step near environmental support or peer and step up (right foot, left foot) and then step down in front (right foot, left foot) to learn to descend stairs. *Student 6:* Identify body parts to touch while holding with dyna-band. *Student 7:* Make a choice of appropriate tension (color of band) to use. *Student 8:* Increase number of repetitions and record on chart number completed. *Student 9:* Use wheelchair to approach low horizontal bar and grasp bar with both hands for 10 seconds in extended position. *Student 10:* Use overhand grasp and lift feet off ground to support body weight. *Student 11:* Perform straight arm hang for more than 10 seconds. *Student 12:* Follow demonstration and verbal prompts to "step and turn rope." *Student 13:* "Grip and flip"—sequencing movements of grip, flip, and step over rope or jump loop. *Student 14:* Facing partner, imitate partner jumps while jumping in front of but outside of jump rope.
EXAMPLE 3	**Grade level: Middle School, sixth and seventh grade** **Activity: Swimming**
NASPE Standard 2	Demonstrates understanding of movement concepts, principles, strategies, and tactics as they apply to the learning and performance of physical activities.
Physical Education Curriculum	■ Student will perform front crawl with correct body position and breathing technique across 1 lap of pool. ■ Student will perform back crawl with correct body position and breathing technique across 1 lap of pool. ■ Student will make choice of flotation device and practice arm or leg action for 1 lap of pool. ■ Student will make choice of stroke and complete 2 laps of pool.
Class Size:	40 seventh graders plus 5 children from special needs classes with IEP goals and objectives
Formation:	Locker room and pool area
Equipment:	Flotation devices (pool noodles, kick boards, etc.)
Lesson Focus	1. Preparation and dressing skills 　■ Use of locker room and combination lock 　■ Dressing in timely manner

(continued)

TABLE 13.1	*Continued.*	

	2. Safety awareness
	  ■ Choosing flotation device
	  ■ Choice of partner
	  ■ Location in pool for practice
	3. Stroke performance
	  ■ Label and body position for stroke	

Goals & Objectives	*Student 1:* Use key lock to maintain possession of clothing. *Student 2:* Demonstrate appropriate body position for stroke given verbal prompt. *Student 3:* Make choice of appropriate flotation device to use for kicking practice. *Student 4:* Walk independently in shallow end of pool across width of pool and pick up objects from bottom of pool. *Student 5:* Follow partner during lap swim and imitate strokes.	
EXAMPLE 4	**Grade level:** High School, tenth–eleventh grade **Activity:** Pickleball	
NASPE Standard 2	Demonstrates understanding of movement concepts, principles, strategies, and tactics as they apply to the learning and performance of physical activities.	
Physical Education Curriculum	■ Student will be able to grasp racket correctly. ■ Student will be able to perform forehand or backhand volley correctly. ■ Student will volley ball over net successfully. ■ Student will be able to successfully participate in cooperative activity with partner.	
Class Size:	40 eleventh graders plus 5 children from special needs classes with IEP goals and objectives	
Formation:	Tennis courts or inside with courts set up with nets	
Equipment:	Pickleball paddles and balls	
Variations:	May want to use adaptive racquet or ball size, if needed	

Lesson Focus	1. Paddle use
	  ■ Grip—forehand, backhand
	  ■ Striking ball upward (volley)
	  ■ Bouncing ball on ground back to paddle (waist height)
	  ■ Control force of ball coming off paddle; upward, bounce
	  ■ Partner hitting—5 feet away: volley game. How many hits can you hit back and forth with partner?
	2. Format
	  ■ Individual practice
	  ■ Practice with partner over net
	  ■ Practice with partner against two other people	

Goals & Objectives	*Student 1:* Approach peer and ask partner to work together and volley ball over net (verbal exchange).	

(continued)

TABLE 13.1 Continued.

Student 2: Track ball and make contact when given verbal prompt.

Student 3: Explore amount of force applied to ball so that ball will travel farther distance, or closer distance with accuracy.

Student 4: Recognize teammates and stay with group or partner for 15 minutes.

Student 5: Exchange turns and demonstrate appropriate sportsmanship (i.e., attitude, verbal comments, sharing ball, or to keep trying).

EXAMPLE 5	**Grade level: Any age group** **Activity: Dance**
NASPE Standard 5	Exhibits responsible personal and social behavior that respects self and others in physical activity settings.
Physical Education Curriculum	■ Student will perform dance steps to cadence or beat of music. ■ Student will perform correct steps in movement sequence.
Class Size:	40 seventh graders plus 5 children from special needs classes with IEP goals and objectives
Formation:	Floor space, small gymnasium, dance room, or multipurpose room
Equipment:	Music CD and player; Cowgirl Stomp—music "I Feel Like a Woman" by Shania Twain
Lesson Focus	Students partner off and face each other. 1. Back 3 steps and clap, forward 3 steps and clap (8 counts). One partner goes forward to start and one goes backward to start—they move together! 2. Repeat. 3. Grapevine right-clap (4 counts). Partners are moving away from each other. 4. Jump forward and hold for 1 count, jump back and hold for 1 count (4 counts). 5. Two heel clicks (2 counts). 6. Right toe touch forward two times (2 counts). 7. Step right-forward around to face partner in opposite direction (4 counts). 8. Touch right heel with partner, stomp down, repeat with other foot (4 counts). 9. Step right-forward around to face partner in starting position (4 counts). 10. Repeat.
Goals & Objectives	Student 1: Identify starting floor position, partner, and body position to begin dance. Student 2: Clap and move to the beat of music. Student 3: Demonstrate understanding of direction and levels used in dance by imitating partner from side-by-side position. Student 4: Perform with physical prompt correct directions of left, right, forward, backward, while facing partner. Student 5: Perform isolated part of given command independently after presented with demonstration. Student 6: Sequence two movements in stationary position with partner.

> ## Teaching Tip
>
> **INSTRUCTIONAL TIME** • Make good use of instructional time by:
>
> - Maximizing time on task
> - Focusing on student attention and needs
> - Communicating the purpose of the lesson clearly
> - Using a variety of teaching strategies
> - Providing effective instructions and feedback
> - Following yearly, monthly, weekly, and daily plans for developmentally appropriate activities that are purposeful, sequential, and meaningful to the student
> - Providing age-appropriate learning experiences

- Place protocols of frequently used tests in a file box for easy access on testing days (see the Teaching Tip titled "All Utility Items" later in this chapter.

Managing equipment

Managing the equipment (supplies and materials) means ordering, maintaining an inventory, and caring for and repairing the items (further information is provided later in this chapter). Strategies for managing equipment include:

- Keep an updated listing or inventory of items (be sure to include ball bags and storage carts in your order and inventory).
- Develop a check-out procedure for sharing with other specialists or teachers and students.
- Identify equipment location, and develop organization and storage procedures.
- Arrange for safe and efficient transporting of the items, such as from the storage location to the activity site, from one school to another, or from the car to the activity location on each school site.

Providing positive behavior support

Organization in the class, including establishing and following rules and routines, often helps to prevent undesirable behavior. Below are organization strategies for behavior support. (Refer to Chapter 10 for further information on behavior support strategies.)

- Use appropriate strategies without interfering with instructional time; use consistent strategies that are efficient, as well as age-appropriate, and that can be used throughout the school day.
- Teach the appropriate behaviors or rules to follow, and frequently give praise and reinforcement for following them:
    a. Make a statement of praise to the student (e.g., "You made an accurate throw to your partner").
    b. Be specific about what was good (e.g., "I like the way you looked at your partner and made a step with the opposite foot").
    c. Connect the specific comment to a skill, personality trait, or character strength (e.g., "Your ability to focus on the target and follow through will help in the baseball game next week").
    d. Assist the student with handling his or her anger, upset, and frustrations through a variety of techniques that are specific to each student but fit with the class rules and routines (e.g., providing an opportunity to remove self from the situation and get a drink of water; reminding the student that anger is a natural emotion but hitting is not an acceptable way to handle anger or frustration).
- Teach students self-responsibility, individually and as a group, as an effective tool for positive behavior support.
- Use creative alternatives for warm-up exercises, lining up, groupings or team divisions, and distribution and retrieval of equipment.

Managing smooth transitions

Planning for and facilitating smooth transitions between activities is a critical organizational strategy for all teachers, but it is particularly important for adapted physical education teachers. Many children with a disability need significant support during transitions, especially those who have difficulty with attention, language, sequencing, social skills, and memory. The teacher must have a clear idea of the intent of the lesson activities and the behaviors and performances expected. This includes the behaviors and performances expected during transitions from one activity to another. Teachers who fail to plan for effective transitions between activities often find they are wasting important learning time on reorganizing students and dealing with discipline problems. Smooth transitions between activities allow for increased learning time, and they provide students with opportunities to increase independence, gain a sense of responsibility, and develop social interaction skills.

It is often necessary and time efficient to specifically teach transition skills to students, especially at the beginning of a semester or unit. Examples of transition skills in physical education include the ability to move from:

- One location to another quickly and efficiently (e.g., to get into position for the next activity).
- One piece of equipment to another by retrieving from and/or returning to a specific container or location (e.g., to pick up a ball after putting away poly spots).
- One formation to another smoothly (e.g., from a scattered formation for exercises to a partner or small group activity).
- One instruction to the next (e.g., listening and focusing on speaker or language used).

The teacher's responsibility is to plan, organize, and teach the appropriate transition strategies so that the students use their learning time wisely. Additional transition strategies include the following:

- Songs and hand movements or arm exercises help children focus while moving from one location to another, queuing up before or at the end of class, or following in line. For example, students might sing the "follow the leader" song with arms extended, making circles forward and backward, while moving to class.
- A set routine of "warm-up" activities prior to lesson instruction helps to provide consistency and focus. For example, from a line-up position with classroom teacher, on the signal "go," students run one at a time to the physical education teacher and give "high fives," jump short ropes 25 times, and then toss an object with a partner 20 catches prior to lining up or going into a classroom for instruction.
- Place 3 x 5 cards with individual students' names into a pocket on a wall, fence, or cart to indicate their presence in class (for roll call) and/or for a choice of activities or partners.
- Use a "cheer" at the end of class in a circle formation for review of the lesson, cool down, and preparation to transition back to the classroom.
- Tires and hula hoops are effective for many activities; young children can use them as a steering wheel for driving their car or bus, or students can roll them as they run to the line.
- Consistently locate equipment for specific activities in the same place, organized and ready for use before the lesson.
- Use the task of putting items away as a natural transition activity; for example, throwing beanbags into the middle hoop or basket at the end of an activity helps students practice target accuracy and accomplishes collection of objects.
- Strategies for dividing partners and teams are innumerable based on the ages and needs of the group. For example, divisions may be made according to colors of clothing, birth months, or "ducks and cows," or students may give a handshake to another student to choose partners.
- Apply multiple intelligences strategies to transition between activities; for example, ask a small group to identify how music is used in physical education or to locate geometric shapes within the environment and use them as a target location, and so on.

Managing information resources

As discussed in Chapter 2, many resources are available in the school, district, community, and state for working with students with a disability. Physical educators should be able to find these resources quickly and easily when they are needed. Following are strategies for managing these resources:

- Establish office space (if you are itinerant, having it at the school where you spend most time may be helpful).
- Maintain a filing system for information on topics such as medical conditions, positive behavior support strategies, curricular areas, special events, community recreation programs, and physical activities.
- Find out if there is a district curriculum resource room or curriculum library and learn how to use it.
- Identify district reporting periods and other data for all grade levels and schools. This will be helpful in timing your collaboration with other professionals for purposes of recording progress and grades.
- Establish sources for medical information such as the school nurse, occupational and physical therapists, a local medical library, or websites.
- Establish your own resource library (those old textbooks may come in handy someday!).
- Join local, state, and national professional organizations.
- Subscribe to online physical education or adapted physical education bulletin boards and newsletters.
- Get to know local colleagues and establish monthly or quarterly meetings to share ideas and information.
- Attend conferences.

- Prepare a yearly professional development plan in which you set a few personal goals in areas such as curriculum focus, behavioral support techniques, communication, or lesson planning (this can help you focus on a few key topics at a time and keep you from feeling overwhelmed by information overload).
- If you are itinerant, keep a list of important school and district phone numbers with you.

Stress management

Today's educators are challenged by large classes, public scrutiny, changing educational policies, and more. Whether you are a general physical educator or an adapted physical education specialist, the job can be stressful. Following are strategies for managing stress:

- Engage in personally satisfying recreation and leisure activities such as regular exercise, relaxation, socializing, hobbies, or reading.
- Find a friend or family member who is a "good listener" and willing to listen to you vent your frustrations.
- Start "professional support group meetings," allowing 10 to 15 minutes to eat a snack, discuss daily frustrations, and problem solve solutions together.
- Model and discuss your own stress-management strategies with students as appropriate for their developmental level.

Managing communication

Good communication is essential to the collaboration required in developing the IEP and in working with teachers, specialists, and administrators. Ongoing communication can be especially challenging if you have an itinerant assignment. Below are organizational strategies for enhancing communication. (Also see Chapter 2 for more information.)

- Make a habit of checking for messages and mail each time you visit a site.
- Get to know key staff at each site, such as office personnel, custodian, and general physical educator (or department chair for physical education in secondary programs).
- Make a written schedule and distribute it at each school; keep extra copies handy to give to parents or others as necessary (include instructional and office times, locations and phone numbers, and contact persons at each school).
- Try to stick to your schedule, but when you must deviate, inform others (especially classroom teachers for children you serve) as soon as possible, preferably in writing.
- Establish a working relationship with other school or agency staff who serve the same children, such as physical therapists, occupational therapists, speech-language specialists, psychologists or mental health providers, school psychologists, and instructional assistants.
- Introduce yourself to parent group leaders such as the PTA president.
- Locate the master calendar for each school site and check it frequently (if a monthly calendar is published, make sure the person preparing it knows that you want to receive a copy).
- Get business cards (or make a flier) to let parents and school site staff know how best to get in touch with you (consider including an e-mail address).

Individualized instruction

Providing individuals with the instruction they need requires organization. Below are organization strategies that help make individualized instruction possible.

- If you are itinerant, keep a copy of each of your students' IEP goals and objectives with you.
- Know the medical history of each of your students.
- Plan lessons that meet the needs of many students.
- Follow any behavior plans that are in effect for a student.

SAFETY

Safety for all students participating in an instructional or recreational program is of primary importance. The attitudes of the teacher and the students about movement, play, and work, as well as their understanding of how to protect themselves and others when engaged in physical activity, often determine the success of an organized instructional program.

Good instructional organization contributes to safety. Organizational strategies that help create a safe environment, where the educator is aware of ways to prevent, recognize, and respond to emergencies, include:

- Learn district and school disaster preparedness and medical emergency procedures.
- Keep first-aid and personal safety supplies in your car (if itinerant), office, or equipment bag.

- Obtain a copy of each school's list of students with specific health issues and procedures (e.g., for seizure, extreme temperature, bee stings).
- Earn and maintain certificates in adult and child CPR (cardiopulmonary resuscitation), use of AEDs (automated external defibrillators), first aid, and relief of choking.
- Assist the Safety Committee on your campus or school location with procedures and precautions for emergencies, such as fire drills, shelter-in-place practice, or other unsafe situations. For example, assign "traveling buddies" to students who use a wheelchair. Engage the pairs in practicing evacuation along the routes with wheelchair access to facilitate speed and safety.

Safety Factors to Consider in the Education Program

Several factors contribute to safe physical education programming, including (1) assigning and teaching responsibility for safety, (2) reviewing lessons and activities for safety, (3) teaching safety skills, and (4) ensuring the safety of equipment and the environment.

1. Responsibility for safety. A key ingredient of a safe and successful program is for the teacher to be aware of, understand, accept, and implement safety precautions and use preventive measures as much as possible. The physical education teacher is cautioned not to rely too quickly on students to be responsible for their own safety. There is no substitute for adequate adult supervision in physical activities.

The types of activities planned for the lesson, the age level and maturity of the students, and their experience in movement are key safety factors to consider. For developmentally younger children, adults are responsible for all safety precautions and procedures. As students mature, they can take responsibility for an increasing number of safety issues, including such behaviors and skills as responding to "start" and "stop," listening to instruction, working cooperatively with a partner or in small groups, using personal space, interacting with general space and equipment, managing accidents when they occur, and, in some cases, lifting and carrying techniques. For some individuals with a disability who use personal medical or mobility equipment (e.g., wheelchair, crutches, colostomy bag), specialized safety skills and behaviors must be taught; examples include getting assistance with transfers from a wheelchair, using crutches responsibly during game play, and avoiding certain positions or activities that are contraindicated. Of course, it is imperative that all adults who work with children with a disability understand, teach, and consistently model safety principles and behaviors.

When students are taught to develop responsible play behaviors, especially for space awareness (the use of personal and group space) and interacting with equipment, they are better prepared for safe play. It does not help the learning process to "overprotect" the students by eliminating certain games, activities, or pieces of equipment; setting too many rules of play; or using only one type of formation for movement because it is "organized" and safe. For example, consider the elementary physical education teacher who always uses lines or circles with students moving in a counterclockwise direction instead of a scatter formation for locomotor movements. The students are not provided the opportunity to learn how to move safely in other contexts (e.g., walking in crowds, encountering a student who uses a wheelchair or is visually impaired, or taking a modern dance class). Learning to move safely in a variety of ways and under a variety of circumstances is helpful throughout the school career of all students and should be part of the instructional plan.

2. Safety review of lessons and activities. Of course, some units of instruction require more safety-conscious behaviors than others, and each lesson and activity should be reviewed for safety elements and precautions (e.g., water safety, heat exhaustion). Some things to look for when reviewing a lesson or activity for safety are:

- The need for "spotting" partners in tumbling and gymnastics.
- Protecting a student with a disability, such as visual impairment or traumatic brain injury from objects that are thrown.
- Weather conditions, especially sun exposure and extreme temperatures (cold and hot).
- Contraindicated exercises or activities, especially for students with a disability such as spastic cerebral palsy, atlantoaxial instability (AAI), or a heart condition.
- Space available for use when practicing skills or moving quickly.
- Obstacles and hazards such as sprinkler heads, uneven surfaces, and trash such as pet "deposits" or glass (usually found after the weekend).
- The possibility of collisions with people, equipment, or objects during movement because of a rapid change of direction.
- Methods for entering the movement environment (e.g., gym, field) to prevent students from impulsively and dangerously accessing equipment (e.g., several students running in and

jumping on gymnastics equipment, standing on balance boards without spotting, or crashing scooterboards into people or objects).

- Safe methods for taking equipment out of the storage space.
- Medically necessary equipment or precautions, such as helmets or reduction of static electricity for students with a cochlear implant.

3. Safety skills. Safety skills may be taught to students (especially at the beginning of the school year) through direct instruction, practice, and specific routines. For example, the teacher might focus on the routine for retrieving and returning equipment by practicing the "routine" of passing individual equipment to the leader of a small group, stacking it in front of the line, or returning it to a specific location (e.g., bucket, cart, area of the room). A common example of a safety problem occurs when several students run to retrieve an object of play, such as a ball, that has moved away from the group. When three or four students run to get the ball, they usually have a "tussle" over who will carry it back to the group. The effective teacher should predict this, and similar situations, and instruct students early in the year or unit to follow a specific procedure for retrieving equipment. For example, teach them to identify the closest person to the object, who is then designated to retrieve it (one person, one ball rule). These routines help eliminate unsafe situations and teach the students responsible behaviors that they can use throughout their lifetime.

4. Equipment and environment safety. The physical educator should establish a regular schedule of checking and identifying equipment and apparatus that need care, maintenance, or repairs. The physical education professional can contribute to the whole school environment by participating on the school safety committee and discussing the following topics:

- Playground rules, surfaces, and schedules of student play (e.g., young and older students separated in space or time).
- Spacing equipment and activities on the playground and field spaces in order to avoid collisions.
- Indicating travel pathways, lines of people "traffic," and danger zones on the playground surface, especially around specific pieces of equipment.
- Ways to encourage compliance with playground safety rules, such as by posting rules and color-coding play areas and the start and stop areas of equipment use (e.g., painting a red line on the playground to indicate out-of-bounds areas for recess, painting one end of an overhead ladder green for go and the other end red for stop to indicate the flow of traffic from green to red).
- Methods for providing adequate supervision and communication between adults on the playground.

The physical educator can reduce problems on the playground with strategies such as the following:

- Identify play areas for use during the instructional program and during play times with paint designs.
- Create a "recess" or "playground" rule handbook that includes instructions for playing games, rules of play, equipment needs, and adaptations; provide it to teachers, playground supervisors, and other staff. You may also wish to create a copy of the handbook with laminated pages in a binder and keep this copy in a designated spot on or near the playground.
- Develop in-service training programs to provide training for volunteers, teaching assistants, and other persons involved in playground supervision. Topics might include access for a student with a disability, inspections, sun exposure, observations, management of seizures, conflict management, and supervision of play activities.

> ## Teaching Tip
>
> **STUDENT RESPONSIBILITY FOR PLAYGROUND EQUIPMENT** • It is usually helpful to involve students in an adult-structured system for the use and care of play equipment, whether at recess or during physical education class. For example:
>
> - Student council members rotate the duty of checking equipment in and out to students at recess. The physical education teacher and playground supervisors provide oversight and guidance.
> - Each physical education class has one or more equipment monitors, a privilege earned through good citizenship and effort.
> - The classes rotate the responsibility for checking equipment in and out at recess.
> - Recess playground equipment is assigned to classes and color coded by grade level. Playground supervisors award an extra recess each month to the class that has not lost or broken any equipment (normal wear and tear is expected and considered).

> ## Teaching Tip
>
> **PREVENTING COMMON PLAYGROUND BEHAVIOR PROBLEMS**
>
> - Do not allow "benching" at recess for classroom infractions unless an adult can be assigned the sole responsibility of supervising benched children. Playground supervisors are generally too busy supervising a large number of students in a large area.
> - Set up a system for students to help other students with conflicts over game rules. For example, use "rule masters"—students who pass a test on the rules of a particular game (e.g., four-square, handball, basketball) and are designated a "rule master" for helping to resolve disputes in that game.
> - Start a program for training designated students to facilitate conflict resolution, such as "Peace Patrol" or "CRT" (conflict resolution team).
>
> Other resources and examples of these types of programs can be found in the library or on the Internet under the topics of character education, peer mediation, and conflict resolution.

Playground Safety Standards and Guidelines

More than 200,000 children are injured each year on the playground. In 1995, the National Program for Playground Safety (NPPS) was established to address the needs and concerns of playground safety. The program is located at the University of Northern Iowa and serves as a public resource for current information on injury prevention and safety on playgrounds.

Playground problems and injuries can be reduced and even eliminated through careful planning for a safe play environment. Because physical education classes are frequently taught on school playgrounds, this is an area in which physical educators can be of particular help. The NPPS suggests the following four areas of focus:

- S: supervision
- A: age-appropriate design
- F: fall surface
- E: equipment

S. *Supervision* should be present, visible, and actively involved in observing all students. Key items for playground supervisors to address include:

- Checking students' clothing for hazards such as untied shoes and scarves or hoods that pose a choking risk if caught on climbing equipment.
- Maintaining a focus on and implementation of the rules of play and safe movements (e.g., walking near the drinking fountain, walking around game courts where other students are engaged in play).
- Preparing for emergencies (e.g., accident, injury, illness, strangers, dangerous objects left on the playground overnight or by work crews).
- Observing student interactions, such as teasing or bullying, that can escalate to a fight.
- Informing themselves about students who are particularly vulnerable to accidents on the playground (e.g., those with a seizure disorder, orthopedic disability, or traumatic brain injury).
- Checking the condition of playground equipment and surfaces daily.

A. *Age-appropriate design* means that thought has been given to an accessible and developmentally appropriate design of the playground so that the equipment and apparatus provide for safe play experiences for all students.

F. *Fall surfaces* under climbing and moving equipment are an important factor. Improving the type, depth, and coverage of shock-absorbing surfaces under and around the equipment increases safety in the event a student falls off the equipment.

E. *Equipment* should be checked daily for such things as splinters, worn areas, loose parts, slippery spills, and trash left by weekend visitors to campus. In some areas, special circumstances require careful inspection (e.g., poisonous snakes at schools that are adjacent to desert or mountain areas, or slippery ice patches that remain in shaded areas after an overnight freeze).

Playground structures and design options are numerous and varied and can be as creative as the architect or the desires of the community. Although funding is a consideration, the cost of equipment may be less important than the long-term safety of the users. Partnerships and team decisions (including teachers, parents, administrators, vendors, and community leaders) are usually the best when planning a playground that will provide positive experiences for all children, including those with a disability. Finally, instructing students in how to use equipment for safe and responsible play further contributes to a safe and fun play environment. For more tips on playground safety, visit www.playgroundsafety.org.

> ## Teaching Tip
>
> **SIGHT LINES** • It is always helpful to paint "sight" lines around poles on the blacktop and school campus—not only for students with a visual impairment, but also for students who are just playing around and not paying attention. A "sight" line is a band of brightly colored paint around the pole (e.g., basketball, tetherball, support beam) at the approximate "sight" level of students on campus (lower for elementary than secondary).
>
> One day a third grade girl was playing tag with her friends and did not notice that there were new poles around the gate and trash receptacle area. As she was running, she collided with the pole at face height; she was knocked down with a bloody nose and was a little stunned by the force of the contact. This accident could have been avoided with cones around the new obstacle until it was painted, closer supervision by the adults in the areas of play, and the student's attention on where she was moving.
>
> In another case, a student with a visual impairment stood next to the wall nearest his classroom every day at recess. He refused to play with his peers even when personally invited. When staff intervened, they discovered he was afraid to play on the playground because he bumped into the poles frequently—the poles were gray, and he couldn't see them against the gray background of the asphalt. Once the poles were painted, he was able to move safely and efficiently.

FACILITIES

Accessibility Guidelines

In recent years, the Americans with Disabilities Act (ADA) and the United States Access Board have increased public awareness of issues of access to programs for people with a disability. We believe in and advocate for the participation of individuals with a disability in all types of movement and physical activity. The United States Access Board is a federal agency committed to the accessible design of programs. The ADA Accessibility Guidelines provide standards for barrier-free, accessible environments, including play areas, recreational facilities, outdoor areas, and public rights-of-way. These published standards are provided to help planners design facilities for inclusion and to serve as a template for implementing programs that are accessible to individuals with a disability. Additional requirements of the ADA concern employment (e.g., hiring and making reasonable accommodations for workers with a disability), public services and transportation (e.g., provision of transportation to enable participation in and access to sports programs), public accommodations (e.g., private agencies that are open to the public must implement changes in policy and improve access opportunities for individuals with a disability), and telecommunications (e.g., telephone relay services for individuals with deafness). These guidelines affect the physical education program primarily in regard to accessible routes and unobstructed pathways to the physical education instructional program and activities.

Of course, the adapted physical activity professional (e.g., adapted physical education specialist, recreation therapist, physical therapist, occupational therapist, or coach of a disability sport) can offer assistance to the facility administrator regarding general accessibility issues. The adapted physical activity professional should focus carefully on the accessibility of sport, play, and fitness facilities.

An important factor in the accessibility of the playground, whether the kindergarten size or the regular playground for older students, is the accessibility of platforms. Stairs and ladders, rungs and handgrips, and handrails are all features that can be either an obstacle or a bridge to "play" with others. Sometimes, the equipment has a transition point for those students using a wheelchair, or protective barriers and guides are provided for students with visual impairment. (Refer to NPPS for specific guidelines on playground access.) Consider the following examples:

- A student with a visual impairment who is learning to run uses guide wires (lines or ropes) that have been added to the apparatus or environmental supports around the play area (e.g., fence and pole under shaded structure). See Figures 13.1, 13.2, and 13.3.
- A student with traumatic brain injury is given additional supervision when playing only on selected apparatus.
- A student with autism is taught a movement script to say to other students in order to access the slide and jungle gym.
- A student who uses a wheelchair moves across the sand on a wooden platform built by PTA volunteers until a permanent ramp can be installed; then, the student is able to crawl and climb on the equipment and even uses the slide to re-enter the apparatus.

Providing information and support to programs that provide services and opportunities to students with a disability is an important aspect of the adapted physical education program. In providing sup-

FIGURE 13.1

To make a guide wire, use a three-quarter-inch rope and attach at each end an interlocking clasp (same as used on a tetherball line). Tightly wrap each end of the rope around a structure or post over a distance of 50 to 60 yards. Tie a knot near each end to give a tactile cue to the student to stop before reaching the end. Attach a carabiner to the rope and a short loop-type handle (8" to 10" in size) to the carabiner. Ask the student to hold the loop with his or her preferred hand and run along the guide wire. To return to the starting position, the student will move under the guide wire, turn around, and return using the preferred hand again.

FIGURE 13.2

A girl with visual impairment runs using a guide wire.

FIGURE 13.3

Learning to run with a guide wire, this student with visual impairment has not yet learned to stride. With practice she will relax her arm and take larger, faster strides.

port to the program, the adapted physical educator can make the program more accessible and more visible to the parents and participants. Sharing information, providing demonstrations, and conducting information training with staff, as well as teaching the skills students may need to be successful, are key elements of such support. The accessibility skills that students learn are likely to help them succeed in physical activities throughout life.

All persons, regardless of disability, deserve appropriate recreational and leisure opportunities throughout their lifetime. When these experiences are provided in the least restrictive environment possible, then the best of services is being provided. Often, finding the least restrictive environment involves creating additional opportunities that are in line with the needs and interests of the individual. In addition to the direct physical benefits of participating in group and individual physical activities, the indirect results may include promoting a positive self-concept and fostering social interaction and group cooperation. Adapted physical educators can do much to facilitate participation in leisure and recreation programs by:

- Knowing what is available and what could be made available.
- Teaching students about the importance of wise use of leisure time.
- Helping students explore and develop new interests.

Legislated Standards for Accessibility

As mentioned earlier, numerous pieces of legislation have addressed the problem of making facilities and programs accessible to individuals with a disability. Serious efforts have been made in both the public and private sectors to modify existing facilities and provide new facilities with mechanisms for accessibility. These mechanisms and modifications include ramps; handrails; wider bathroom stalls with grab bars; lower telephones, sinks, and drinking fountains; automatic door openers; and Braille characters on a variety of directional and informational signs. Two pieces of legislation, the Rehabilitation Act of 1973 and the Architectural Barriers Act of 1967, are primarily responsible for these kinds of physical changes becoming evident in the community. Since these laws were enacted, serious efforts have been made, in both public and private sectors, to meet minimum standards of accessibility to educational facilities. These standards can be summarized as follows:

1. Establish the size, shape, and location of spaces within or adjacent to a building such as parking and stairs.
2. Control the size, shape, and location of such objects as door handles, rest rooms, toilets, water fountains, and control knobs.
3. Indirectly place limits on the personal energy used by the person with a disability by limiting the angles of ramps and on the degree of any hazard that might be encountered by modifying the door hardware design to alert people that doors lead to hazardous spaces.
4. Specify the size and nature of the signs and signals that guide a person entering and using a building.

Although a specific administrator in an educational agency is ordinarily designated to conduct an evaluation of facilities for accessibility and to initiate modifications to bring the agency into compliance, the physical educator also may be asked to give some input when alternatives are available. Thus, physical educators should not only be aware of some of the architectural barriers in the physical education setting, they should also be aware of modifications that could be made to improve accessibility (see Table 13.2).

TABLE 13.2 *Examples of facility modifications.*

- Install ramps, especially for access to activity areas (e.g., from building to blacktop, blacktop to field).
- Make curb cuts in sidewalks and entrances (for all school locations).
- Widen doorways.
- Add raised markings on elevator buttons and campus buildings and doorways.
- Install grab bars in toilet stalls.
- Increase maneuvering space in toilet stalls and raise seats for transfers.
- Lower mirrors to the height of people using wheelchairs, especially for dance class.
- Slant mirrors over wash basins.

- Texture cement floors to help prevent slipping, especially in pool and locker room areas.
- Lower towel and soap dispensers.
- Lower light switches, fire alarms, and drinking fountains for people using wheelchairs.
- Install flashing lights and augment the audible bell alarms for individuals with a hearing impairment.
- Provide lighted and audible directional markings and exit signs for individuals with a visual impairment.
- Provide a removable row of bleachers for "seating" people who use wheelchairs.
- Reduce excessive pressure needed to operate doors, especially when focusing on functional and/or increased independence.

Source: Adapted from LaRue, R. J. (2002), Designing for inclusion: A historical, conceptual, and regulatory guide to planning an accessible environment. In T. H. Sawyer (Ed.), *Facilities Planning for Health, Fitness, Physical Activity, Recreation, and Sports: Concepts and Applications* (10th ed.). Champaign, IL: Sagamore. Used with permission.

Using Available Space

Knowing what desirable and ideal facilities and conditions are and actually having them are often two different matters. Adapted physical educators at the elementary school level (whether permanent or itinerant) and at the secondary school level often find that the space they use for instruction is space left over after everyone else takes their share. At the elementary level, the adapted physical educator—especially the itinerant teacher—is often vying for space with the music teacher, art teacher, psychologist, nurse, speech therapist, special assemblies, and many other itinerant and intermittent programs. At the secondary level, the adapted physical educator's claim on space may present slightly different problems, not necessarily problems of less magnitude. At least at the secondary level, there are clearly identified teaching stations for which all staff members put in a bid, and decisions are made based on curriculum and student needs. If instructional units for adapted physical education can be designed to coincide with the instructional unit time frame of the general physical education program, then the rotation of facilities can be made at the same time during the school year.

When considering alternate locations for conducting class, consider the space needs of all students in each class. Sometimes, the leftover space is truly more appropriate and functional than the space that the physical educator originally preferred. Students who are distractible may function far better in a barren hallway or small room than they would in the open space of the gymnasium or playing field. Some children with autism, an emotional disturbance, or a behavioral disorder, for example, tend to become agitated and lose their orientation in larger open spaces. Students with a history of running away from the group may also attend better to the task and be less inclined to stray from the group if the limits of their play area are clearly defined by the walls of a room.

The stage in an elementary school provides a well-defined activity area with a certain muting effect on noise, and hence behavior, because of the surrounding draperies. Small classes could meet on the school stage on a regular basis; for some groups, that might be the most desirable area of the entire school facility. A young teacher at a special education school reports using a portion of a very wide hallway to conduct her adapted physical education classes with students with mental retardation. To avoid distractions and frequent interruptions, she uses gymnastics mats standing on edge to screen off the activity area from the portion of the hallway used for traffic. Except for the noise created when another class goes by, this is a reasonable solution to a situation in which space is limited. Another alternative for effective use of space is for the adapted physical educator to co-teach with the general physical educator in the same space. This alternative not only accommodates smaller groups but also facilitates social interaction with peers and the learning of motor skills within a game setting.

Outdoor Facilities

Outdoor facilities fall into one of two categories: space and structures. The size of the space available for use can seldom be altered unless the school district owns adjacent undeveloped property. Thompson (1976) recommends 60 square feet per student, but this is often not available on the school grounds. Adjoining or nearby property such as parks and open fields may provide additional needed space. Many communities have worked jointly with the local school district to develop park property immediately adjacent to the school grounds.

This arrangement not only provides a satisfactory means of expanding the use for both agencies, but also ensures that both facilities are used for greater amounts of time. The community recreation program, for example, can use school property during school vacations when the school would otherwise sit idle. This joint arrangement also allows, at least in the development period, an opportunity to avoid the duplication of equipment and use features. For example, the school playground may contain swinging and climbing equipment, and the adjacent park may provide equipment that offers supplemental experiences for exploring, crawling, and imaginative play (see Figure 13.4).

Outdoor structures that may require modifications include pools; stadiums; playing courts for tennis, basketball, volleyball, and handball; and multipurpose playing fields. One major modification that might be desirable is the enclosure of some of these structures. Portable, air-filled enclosures are available and in use in many parts of the country to extend the time that the structures (e.g., pools and playing courts) can be used. These are relatively inexpensive compared to permanent enclosures, and may be acquired through a federally or privately funded project or as a major project for local community groups.

Minor modifications of outdoor structures include adding a ramp or lift, handrails, and grab bars in and around the edge of the swimming pool. The physical educator and the responsible administrator should be aware of such minor barriers as thresholds or steps leading onto playing courts,

FIGURE 13.4

These creative play areas provide opportunities for children to practice all the movement patterns.

fields, and asphalt-surfaced play areas. Attention should also be given to the width of the gates to play areas for accessibility by a wheelchair. The grass on playing fields should be kept short and, whenever possible (depending on the growing conditions), should be a hard-surfaced grass that does not retain or require a great deal of water (e.g., Zoysin, St. Augustine, Bermuda, or Fescue). This kind of surface is much easier for moving wheelchairs and walkers. Remember that access to the field area is sometimes difficult for students using a wheelchair. Sometimes, alternate routes can be made available that also improve the accessibility of the school campus for all students.

An opportune moment to discuss changes with the school administrators is when the school is preparing to receive a new student with a disability. For example, the adapted physical education specialist may be working with a student at the elementary school who will make the transition into the middle school the next school year. Preparations for receiving the student may include modifications that make the campus facilities and instructional program more accessible to all students.

Outdoor asphalt playing surfaces are often marked for regulation volleyball and basketball or, in the elementary schools, for circle games, four-square, obstacle courses, and other games. Often, so many lines are painted on the playing surface that students have difficulty distinguishing one set of game lines from another. For students with visual figure–ground perception difficulties, a premarked playing surface presents an insurmountable visual task. If space permits, it is desirable to avoid overlapping lines completely. If this is not possible, the lines for each game or sport should be painted in different colors. This may help, at least in a small way, with the visual figure–ground problems.

Indoor Facilities

An ideal type of indoor physical education facility is a motor lab. Motor labs are especially useful at the elementary level, but can be implemented at the secondary level as well. A **motor lab** is *a room containing specialized equipment necessary for individuals with a disability, but that can and is used by all students.* Such equipment might include mirrors (that can be covered); stall bars; wall-pulley weights; a scale for measuring body weight and height; hanging and chinning bars; a ramp for riding scooterboards; large crash pads; wedge mats; physio-balls; suspended equipment (e.g., swing, soft balls on a rope); parallel bars for gait training, gymnastics, and arm and upper body development; and perhaps a bicycle ergometer.

FIGURE 13.5 Elementary school motor lab.

In a motor lab (see Figure 13.5), some of the equipment should be movable to provide for individual needs and creative lesson planning. Many physical educators using a motor lab prefer to rearrange or "redecorate" the room monthly based on seasonal themes or unit plans. At the elementary level, a motor lab is usually set up to facilitate the learning of developmental motor patterns and motor skills. At the secondary level, a motor lab may be designed to address physical fitness and skills related to culturally determined forms of movement. Although an adapted physical education specialist may be responsible for the setup and maintenance of a motor lab, it should be made available to all teachers for movement activities as much as possible.

All facilities at a school should be available for use by all students, including indoor physical education facilities (e.g., dance studio, weight room, gymnasium, multipurpose room, and swimming pool). Because students with a disability are enrolled in both general and adapted physical education classes, all facilities must be accessible and set up to enable adaptations. The adapted physical education teacher and classes should be included in facility rotations just as the general physical education teacher and classes are included.

EQUIPMENT

To facilitate learning in physical education, it is often necessary to modify the learning environment. This can be done in two areas: the purchase, adaptation, and construction of equipment and the construction, modification, and use of facilities and other play spaces. Although physical educators infrequently have the opportunity to influence the construction of new facilities, they usually can influence the acquisition of equipment. Educators are encouraged to be as frugal and as

MAKING CONNECTIONS

Middle School Accessibility

John, a student with cerebral palsy, recently started using a wheelchair at the end of fifth grade. The transition to middle school required his learning the use of the wheelchair and negotiating around campus. But eventually he is going to transfer to the high school, which is an older campus where some of the buildings do not have ramps or elevators. After a short walk around the campus, school administrators and district personnel determined that John would not be able to attend physical education or any of the science classes. There is no ramp to get him down to the gymnasium, and he would have to be driven in a vehicle to enter from the back side, then wheel around to the front of the building for class, which is not time-efficient, practical, or appropriate.

In addition, all science classes are on the second floor of a building that does not have an elevator. The discussion about the accessibility of the campus two years prior to John's enrolling was helpful to the school administrators and district personnel. The adapted physical educator discussed the use of a "Z" pathway to access the physical education class and taught John how to use the pathway. The discussion expanded to include installing elevators in the future for easier access to some buildings and classrooms.

MAKING CONNECTIONS

Elementary School Motor Lab

Marie is an adapted physical education specialist assigned to one elementary school and two high schools. She has developed a motor lab at the elementary school and uses it for adapted physical education instruction on Mondays and Wednesdays. On Friday mornings, she uses it to conduct assessments. On Tuesdays, Thursdays (when Marie is at the high schools), and Friday afternoons, general education teachers sign up to use the lab for general physical education. It is closed one day a month for "remodeling," and that is when Marie sets it up for a new unit, based on seasonal themes used in the classrooms.

---

clever as possible when obtaining materials and equipment, as long as safety is not compromised.

For purposes of this text, **equipment** is defined as *those pieces of apparatus or "heavy" items that are purchased and used for several years before needing replacement* (e.g., tumbling mats, jump ropes, volleyball nets). **Supplies** are defined as *those items that are consumed or worn out relatively easily and must be replaced frequently* (items that last one to two years, such as playground balls, hula hoops, and playground chalk, and very short-term items such as marking tape, office supplies, cleaning supplies, and test protocol sheets). These supplies are used for the instructional program, as well as on the playground for recess, and should be listed in the school budget.

Developing the Equipment List

The physical educator must make some projections into the future to acquire and develop material resources that will serve the school and students over an extended period of time. The average expected life span for a piece of equipment being used in the public schools on a daily basis is only three to five years. Thus, it is hardly necessary to project more than that period of time. The teacher should maintain a list of equipment and facility needs as the program progresses, adding to it whenever facilities or equipment are unavailable for an activity the teacher would have liked to conduct.

A list should be made for equipment, supplies, materials, and facilities that itemizes everything thought necessary (see Table 13.3). The next step is to determine where items can be obtained. Generally, the adapted and general physical education programs should be able to use the same equipment as long as there is enough for both programs on a daily basis. Of course, it is up to the teachers to develop an organized system for communicating who wants to use what and when. Some schools provide a certain amount of office supplies for each faculty member, which should include the adapted physical education teacher. Some teachers may have playground equipment that can be borrowed, and even the school nurse may be able to lend items periodically (e.g., a scale and tape measure). The district may have a system for "checking out" large pieces of equipment (e.g., incline mats, balance beams) for a period of time. Parent groups are often willing to collect items to be used in physical education, such as gallon milk jugs to be made into scoops, bread bags for making jump ropes, or scraps of material to be made into scarves. Using existing resources such as these may significantly reduce the amount of equipment that must be purchased.

Physical educators using the developmental approach should have access to equipment and facil-

TABLE 13.4 *Basic equipment useful for each developmental level.*

Reflex development and inhibition

- Pans, trays, or buckets of sand, beans, Styrofoam pellets, wood beads, sponges
- Small balls, blocks, sponges
- Small bright objects, rattles, noisemakers
- 35mm film cans with varying weights inside
- Stuffed animals, dolls, toys, beanbags, or hand puppets
- Mats or body-sized carpet pieces—1 per student
- Bolsters, large cushions, padded barrel
- Large pieces of fabric of varying textures
- Large cardboard boxes or plastic forms for crawling through
- Scooterboards—1 per student
- Rope (½" diameter x 15')—2 per class
- Parallel bars for walking
- 36" cage ball
- Cloth tunnels of various heights and lengths

Sensory stimulation and discrimination

- Water hose with a variety of nozzles and a variety of sprinkler heads
- Wading pools or large buckets—1 per 3 students
- Buckets, sponges, squeeze and squirt toys, washcloths
- Beach balls
- Wading pool filled with sand
- Modeling clay, Silly Putty
- Tempera paint, liquid detergent, shaving cream, cornstarch
- Blindfolds—1 per student
- Tactile box with armholes and various objects inside
- Swings, slides, swinging tire, net, hammock, incline ramp
- Tricycles, scooterboards, bicycles
- Mini-trampoline, "Jumpin' Jiminey"
- Climbing equipment—stall bars, ladder, jungle gym
- Rhythm instruments—tambourine, bell, ratchet, rhythm sticks, drum, blocks—1 per student
- Parachute
- Suspended balls of various sizes and colors
- Flashlight
- Hula hoops—1 per student
- Wall mirrors—6' x 10'

Enhancing sensorimotor responses

- Record player and records, tape player and tapes, CD player and CDs
- Beads and string—1 set per student
- Peg board, pegs, rubber bands—1 set per student
- Clothespins, container
- Beanbags, yarn balls, sponge balls, scoops—1 per student
- "Play-Buoy" or "zoom ball"—2 per class
- T-stools—1 per student
- Balance boards—1 per 2 students
- Inner-tube barrel, lined (padded) barrel
- Roller skates—1 pair per student
- Commercial games—Twister, Funny Bones, Simon (electronic game)
- 4" balance beam (low and high, or adjustable)
- Tin can stilts—1 pair per student
- Tumbling mats
- Rubber balls—1 per student, various sizes
- Grids on roll plastic with letters, numbers, shapes, colors
- Soap bubbles—1 bottle per student
- Small objects for sorting—nails, clips, screws, nuts, bolts
- Butcher paper—1 body-sized piece for each student

(continued)

TABLE 13.4 Continued.

Enhancing motor patterns and skills

- Set of stairs with handrail
- Pull toys, wagon—2 or 3
- Boundary markers (traffic cones)—2 dozen
- Poly spots
- Milk cartons, plastic or wooden bowling pins—2 dozen
- Medicine ball
- Whiffle balls
- Pinnies or flags
- Throw-down bases
- Tennis balls, baseballs, softballs, soccer balls, footballs (foam and regular)—1 per 2 students
- Frisbees—1 per 2 students
- Batons, bats, sticks, racquets—1 per student
- Inner-tube stripes
- Balls with various types of tactile or gripping surfaces

Culturally determined forms of movement

Aquatics	■ Submergible toys for retrieving ■ Flotation devices—floaties, belts, life jackets, inner-tubes, tennis balls	■ Kickboards ■ Hydraulic lift for pool
Conditioning	■ Individual jump ropes ■ Chinning bar	■ Free weights, bars ■ Wrist weights
Dance and rhythms	■ Ribbons, flags, scarves	■ Disco, rock, and other dance music
Fitness	■ Universal gym, wall weights, weighted boots, suspended ropes ■ Bicycle ergometer ■ Pedometer	■ Heart rate monitors ■ Sit and reach box ■ FITNESSGRAM kit, ACTIVITYGRAM kit ■ Track and field equipment (e.g., batons, shotput, hurdles)
Games and sports	■ Equipment for table tennis, chess, checkers, croquet, shuffleboard, tetherball, box hockey	■ Equipment for angling, archery, badminton, indoor bowling, fencing, golf, tennis, bocce ball ■ Sport-specific balls and equipment

Durability. The durability of a piece of equipment is important if the equipment is to be useful. Some significant considerations when judging how durable a piece of equipment must be include the age and size of the students using it; the frequency of its use; how it is to be used; and whether it will be used in structured, directed, or unstructured activity. Although the students may have been taught the safe and careful use of equipment and other materials, vigorous play will inevitably contribute to the destruction of some pieces.

Economy. The cost of the construction or purchase and maintenance of equipment is an important consideration. Economy is important, but "economical" does not always mean "cheap"; if a piece of equipment is available from several manufacturers, the least expensive of the choices may not be the most economical. Also, if a piece of equipment is likely to be used frequently by several classes, it will sustain more wear and tear. The durability of a piece certainly contributes to its economy.

The maintenance required for a piece of equipment may detract from the economical value of a lesser price. If an item has moving parts or mechanical or electrical components that can malfunction, the availability and cost of service should be computed into its price.

Size. The appropriate size of a piece of equipment depends on the space in which it is to be used and the physical body size and developmental levels of the students using it. The available activity space, as well as the space available for storage, may dictate both the size and the number of pieces that can realistically be obtained. The students' size, of course, is important in terms of the appropriateness and durability of a piece of equipment. The developmental level of the students plays an important role; for example, older students with cerebral palsy who are developmentally young may need a larger ball (10 or 12 inches) than would ordinarily be used with this age group (see Figure 13.6). The durability of the ball may also be a factor if students' motor control is so poor that they cannot control the force applied when catching, kicking, or throwing the ball. Ordinarily, a small beach ball might be appropriate for this population, especially if ocular tracking and catching abilities are poor. If the beach ball is smashed every time it is caught, however, a more durable, lightweight foam ball of the same size might be more appropriate. Although the more durable ball may initially be more expensive, it may be more economical than purchasing a beach ball every week.

Diversity. The diversity or range of use of equipment may be a major consideration when working with a school population that has very diverse needs. If a piece of equipment can be used to achieve a variety of goals and objectives, it is probably more practical than a similar piece having a limited application. Basic tumbling mats are useful and practical items that can be used for a variety of activities and lessons. The mats can be placed in the open position for lying down and performing many stunts and tumbling activities, such as the Superman, airplane, or rocking chair activities. They can also be stacked on top of each other in the folded position for jumping off a height or jumping onto when jumping down from a height. They can be placed outside next to a wall for the "wall walk" exercise and for some physical fitness test items, such as curl-ups, sit and reach, and push-ups. One physical education teacher uses the mats with markings that identify the hand and foot placements for the cartwheel. They are also useful when performing some of the "fun" activities involving problem solving and games, such as "Islands." The uses of this one piece of equipment are limited only by the students' and teacher's creativity.

FIGURE 13.6

A great variety of ball sizes and types should be kept on hand to accommodate differences in body sizes and developmental levels. This variety also allows you to address the specific objectives of an activity and to individualize activities for students of differing abilities.

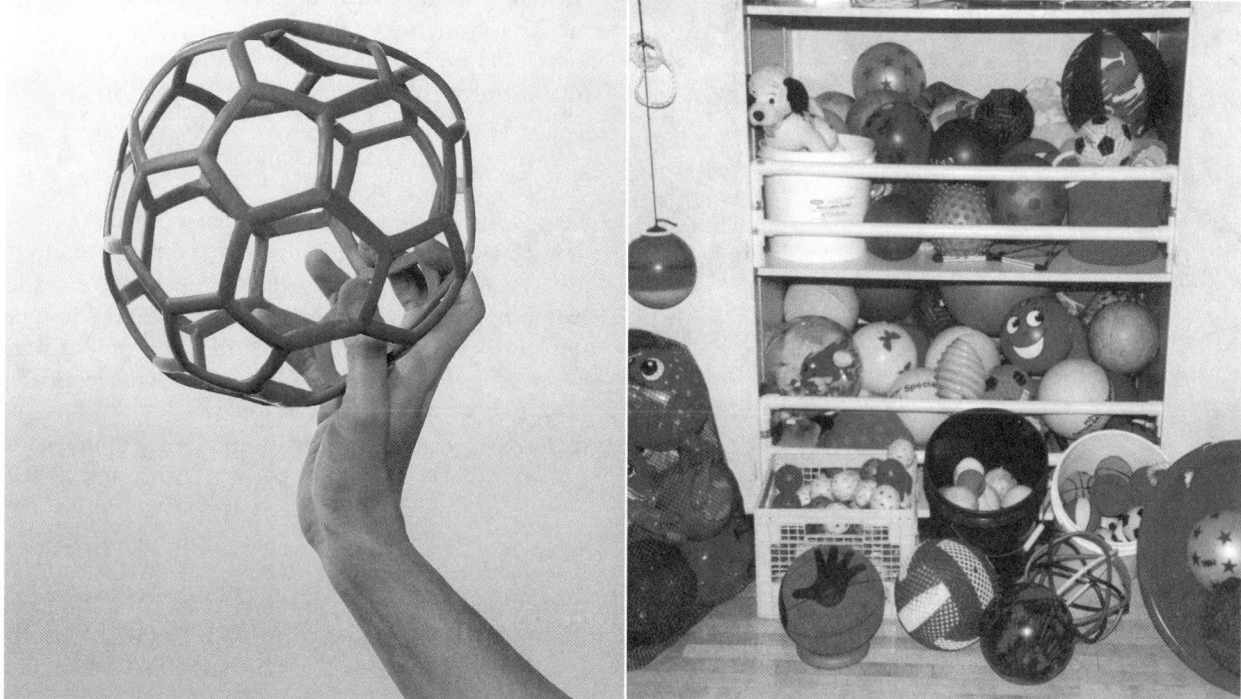

FIGURE 13.7

Unique equipment having a variety of uses in adapted physical education includes bolsters of various sizes, balance beams, airflow and incline mats, and large foam shapes; T-stools with different size bases; and scooterboards.

Safety. Of course, planning for safety is very important. In addition to the safety considerations previously discussed relative to playgrounds, some of the potential dangers related to equipment and supplies (especially when you are modifying or making your own equipment) that should be considered are:

- Choking on small items or pieces that are easily broken off. Use a bathroom toilet paper roll core as a guide. If an item can fit through the tube, it is a potential choking hazard, especially for developmentally young students or those who put things in their mouths frequently.
- Allergic reactions caused by scented items, paints, or glues. Frequently check your list of students with health problems, including allergies and asthma. If there is a question about an item, consult a health professional or the student's parents. Be aware of individuals who have an allergy to latex, which is an ingredient in many plastics.
- Injuries from falling on sticks or sharp objects
- Worn, chipped, or frayed parts (These may cause injuries themselves or may be a warning of impending equipment breakdown.)
- Worn, broken, or missing surfaces under playground or indoor climbing equipment
- Inappropriate clothing or shoes that can get caught in equipment or lead to falls

Adapting Equipment

Although a great deal of good, appropriate equipment is available in the marketplace, a particular piece may not be quite right for the physical educator's context, the population to be served in general, or any specific student. In addition, some pieces of equipment may be too expensive because of the quantity needed. A similar item can sometimes be adapted or made (e.g., making balls out of wadded newspaper and masking tape may be more economical when the teacher has to use 30 at a time and ball rebound is not necessary). Therefore, adaptations of existing or newly acquired equipment may be necessary. Some of the features discussed in the previous section may be obtained or enhanced through equipment adaptation. Nonportable items can be made portable by attaching removable wheels or by constructing a transport dollie. For example, most companies making trampolines also manufacture removable wheels made of tubular steel, which can easily be attached to the frame of the trampoline to move it from one place to another. A large piece of equipment such as a vestibular board, a therapy ball (i.e., physio-ball, Kinball, or rolled towel, or some similar material. These materials then may be removed depending on the needs of each child. Modifying a piece of equipment to make it larger might be done by wrapping it with foam rubber tubing or threading a tubular sleeve onto the handle of a bat or racket for use by a student whose grip strength is adequate only in the wider ranges of finger extension.

Many types of equipment can be made more stable by adding Velcro or anti-skid matting under or on the equipment; for example, place a Velcro strap across the shoes of the child trying to ride the tricycle or bicycle so that the feet will remain on the pedals, or place pieces of rubber matting (or other textured material) across the top of the scooterboard so that the child can remain on the top without sliding off when pulling across the rope. The diversity of a piece of equipment may be enhanced by adding features or qualities to the existing piece. See Figure 13.8 for examples of equipment adaptations.

When adapting equipment, often the first consideration is a particular student's unique needs relative to the use of that equipment. Adding a weighted ring to the end of a baseball bat as used by athletes during warm-up enhances proprioception and, therefore, may help with a student's awareness of where the bat is in space. Other adaptations commonly used to increase the usability of a piece of equipment by all students include the addition of straps, weights, textured materials, bright colors, or other visual cues. Straps of Velcro attached to the equipment or wrist cuffs worn by the student can substitute for grip strength on such equipment as archery bows, wall pulleys, racket and paddle handles, or cue sticks. Students with minimal hand strength and control may be able to guide a pool or shuffleboard cue if given the opportunity to maintain contact with the equipment. Commercially available gloves with a flap that wraps around a stick, bat, or racket and attaches back onto the glove could also be used. These items can be "home-made" with Velcro, canvas, and other materials and a little creativity. Weights attached to striking implements or sewn into cuffs worn on the wrists or ankles can enhance proprioception in students with poor kinesthetic awareness. Very few ounces of weight are needed for this purpose. Items such as large washers or drapery weights provide just enough stimulation to help students become more aware of where the implement or their body parts are in space. The goal, of course, is to reduce the amount of weight gradually as awareness and skill increase.

Wrist and ankle cuffs, commonly used in the rehabilitation setting, have had only limited use in the physical education program. These items, usually made of leather with a metal ring firmly riveted

---

Teaching Tip

USE OF TUMBLING MATS

1. *Wall walk.* Students lie down prone on mats with feet placed next to wall. Mats are placed close to the wall to give a cushioned "floor" for the hands and a safe landing place for the body. Partners stand across from student at top of mat on sidewalk ready to exchange turns when time is up. The objective is to "walk" feet upward on the wall (in backward movement) and hold position for 30 seconds. Position is similar to a hand-stand but propped on the wall. Further difficulty can be provided by changing the height of the foot placement or having the student slowly lower and raise the body by bending the elbows.

2. *Islands.* This is a fun team game played with scooterboards and tug-o-ropes. The object of the game is for each team to transfer the team members from one island to another without touching the water (the floor between the mats) with their bodies. Each team has one scooterboard and two mats approximately 10 to 15 feet apart. One player is on one mat and the rest of the team members are on the opposite mat. They must toss the rope across the "ocean" and then transport the team members from one "island" to the other by pulling them across on the scooterboard. If a player "falls" into the ocean, then the player must begin again. Cooperation and strategies are involved in deciding who will be the first and last player on the "islands" and the best way to move the scooterboard back and forth.

---

cage ball) or mushroom, or even a softball backstop can be transported by building a dollie on which to place the equipment or by having a dollie attached to the equipment in such a way that it can be used easily. The washability of a piece of equipment may be improved without changing its function by fashioning a vinyl or fabric cover that can be removed and washed.

In practice, the size of most pieces of equipment can more easily be reduced than expanded. Of course, this possibility may vary with each individual piece. Equipment that is intended to hold a student in place—a swing, chair, or wagon—can easily be modified by filling the space not filled by the student's body with foam rubber, Styrofoam, pillows, a

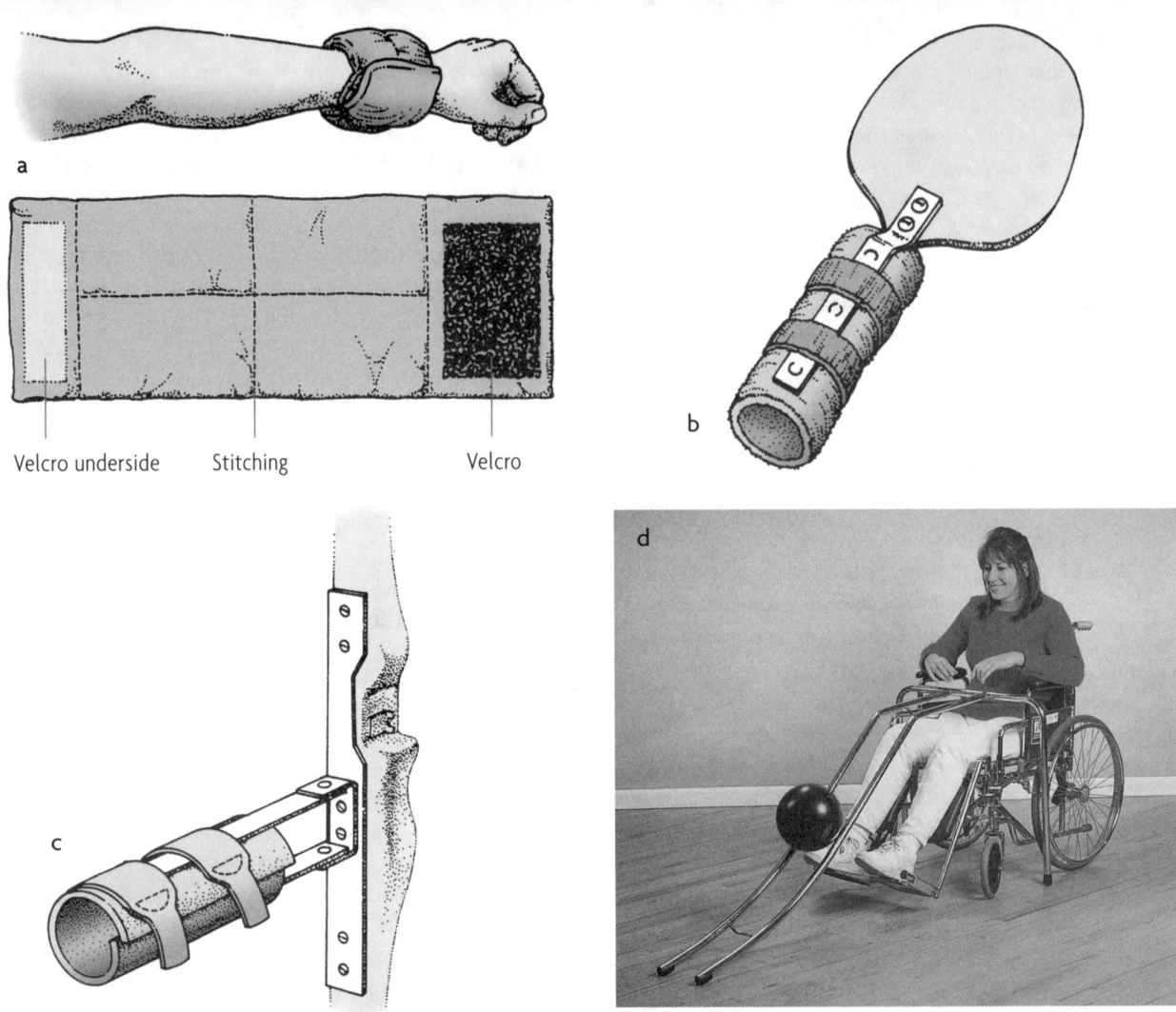

FIGURE 13.8 Examples of equipment adaptation include (a) weighted wrist cuff for a student who is unable to grip a weight, (b) an adapted table tennis racket for a student with a sensitive skin condition, (c) an adapted archery bow for a student with a paralyzed hand, and (d) an adapted ramp for bowling.

Source: Jim Cowart (1977), *Instructional Aids for Adaptive Physical Education.* Hayward, CA: Alameda County School Department.

to the midpoint, provide a student with quadriplegia access to resistive exercises and activities. The equipment to be moved, such as a wall pulley, is clipped to the metal ring so the student can use upper or lower limb movement to exercise active muscle groups.

The texture of a piece of equipment with which a student has contact may be altered to enhance the student's tactile awareness. For youngsters with poor tactile perception, a football may be altered with a handprint (applied with a rubberized silicone substance) outlining the position of the hand required to pass the ball effectively. This works quite successfully when teaching students the hand position—it allows them to keep their eyes on the target instead of visually checking the hand position.

The visual stimuli provided by a piece of equipment can easily be adapted by painting or applying bright colors, as with the boundary lines on the playground. Yellow playground balls are commercially available and are helpful to many students with a visual impairment. Other brightly colored playground balls and equipment can also be used to serve the needs of the students with a visual impairment or visual imperception who may have difficulty with ocular tracking, visual discrimination, or visual attending. Circles of yellow or red vinyl or contact paper can be applied, for example, to a basketball backboard indicating the spot where the ball must hit in order for it to go into the basket. Just as we use the trademark on the baseball bat to indicate the most correct and safest position of the bat, a brightly colored circle of contact paper on a softball bat can mark the place where the ball should make contact. This again can serve the purpose of focusing visual attention on the point of contact.

Working with Minimal Equipment

Despite this lengthy discussion on the acquisition and adaptation of equipment, an elaborate inventory of equipment is not necessary to deliver appropriate services. Certainly, a few minimal basic pieces are necessary to provide a variety of movement experiences, just as a minimal amount of space is required for the children to move. Lack of equipment, however, is no excuse for an inappropriate program. Often, a physical educator can implement an effective and developmentally appropriate program with the use of several long ropes (15 to 20 feet in length), used bicycle tires (from the local bicycle repair shop), traffic cones, and tennis balls (from the local tennis club). Whether beginning a program with a limited budget or just maintaining a program, it is the resourcefulness of the professional that will determine the amount and types of equipment, supplies, and materials to be used. For example, for starting a program at a new school, the physical education budget might be higher than in future years. The physical educator who is transferring to a program that is already established may find a variety of resources available for the students to use because the previous teacher was careful and resourceful—or there may be nothing because care, security, or budget was lacking. Whatever the circumstances, it will always be important for the physical educator to plan lessons without much equipment, as well as maintain an ongoing list of items needed or desired for the program.

Making Equipment

Raw materials to construct equipment can be obtained through many means. If it is possible to patronize local merchants by purchasing raw materials using school district, PTA, or community funds, that source should be exhausted first. When funds

---

> ## *Teaching Tip*
> **ALL UTILITY ITEMS**
>
> *Equipment and materials:* Poly spots, small cones, 2 long ropes (15'), 2 short ropes (6–8'), Koosh balls, tennis balls, foam ball, soccer ball, stopwatch, beanbags, masking tape, chalk, parachute.
>
> *Object control items:* An assortment of balls (if space is available) such as a basketball, soccer ball, or playground ball (8.5"), and bat (plastic or aluminum depending on age of students).
>
> *Assessment:* A small duffel bag with items that are used for a specific assessment. This is an easy way to carry the test items, as well as the protocols that might be needed on a moment's notice.
>
> *Clerical:* Clipboard that includes a carrying case for paper clips, stick-on notes, mileage and attendance records, and lesson plans.

---

run out, alternative means should be explored. One such means is the use of discarded and recycled items. Merchants, community groups, and parents will be willing to save castoffs once the needs of the physical education program are made known to them.

Carpet samples, cardboard tubes used to hold roll carpeting or linoleum, bleach and milk jugs, milk cartons (both large and small sizes), coffee cans, canvas scraps, PVC pipe, and scraps of wood are all readily available at no charge. Specific materials that may not fit into the category of discarded or recycled items may be donated by local merchants through direct contact or service clubs. As with the "wish list" discussed earlier, the list should be carefully evaluated in terms of what pieces of equipment can be made and what must be purchased. All items donated and purchased must be carefully inspected and considered for safety prior to student use.

The only limit to the equipment that can be made is the creativity of the professional and his or her colleagues and students, as long as safety is ensured. "Homemade" equipment should meet the same criteria as commercially made equipment for portability, washability, durability, economy, size, diversity, and safety. Edges should be smoothly sanded, wood should be sealed with varnish or lacquer, and any metal edges should be carefully masked to avoid injury or harm to the student. Any equipment made according to printed instructions should follow the specifications to the letter to avoid problems with liability. Resources for homemade equipment

FIGURE 13.9 Examples of equipment that can be made.

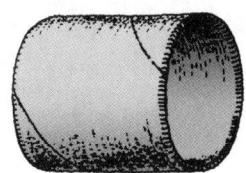

Barrel roller. Barrel of any size with carpet, burlap, sheep skin, or other fabrics attached inside and out. Stitch pieces together to cover and line the barrel, then punch holes near the top and bottom rims and sew to barrel using nylon cord and overhand stitch.

Sample objective: Child will roll in a barrel a distance of 10 feet.

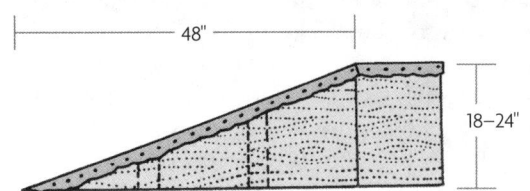

Incline mat. Wedge-shaped construction with 3/4" plywood top and sides. Top should be padded or carpeted. Supporting ribs of 1" or 2" should be equally spaced inside for durability.

Sample objective: Child will roll up and down incline in 3 pieces of textured fabric.

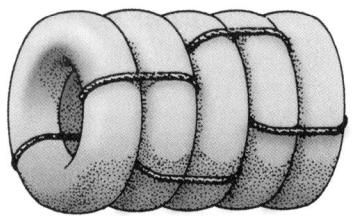

Inner-tube. Inflate 4 or 5 inner-tubes and tie together in twos as shown.

Sample objective: Child will roll in inner-tube in both directions a distance of 10 feet.

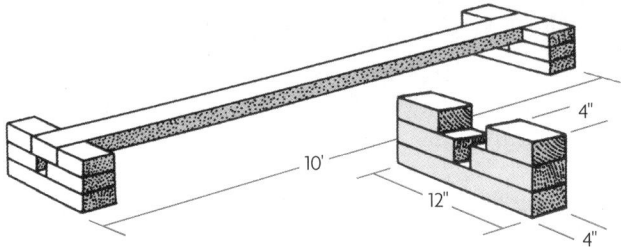

Balance beam. 2" x 8" x 10' hardwood board can be used flat on the floor or on supports made from the same material. Notches in supports are 2" and 4" to hold beam flat or on edge for variations in balance challenges. A third support may be used in the center for heavier children.

Sample objective: Child will walk length of beam unassisted in 3 out of 5 trials.

(continued)

---

are included in the reference section at the end of this chapter. Figure 13.9 gives examples of equipment that can be made.

Any number of venues can be used for funding—low incidence funds, discretionary funds, district supplies, and educational or PTA accounts. The district worksheets and catalogues will usually list equipment items with a description, size, and the cost. These items should be used first when making the request because they are easily and quickly obtained from the district warehouse. Then, catalogues of equipment distributors such as *Flaghouse*, *GOPHER*, or *Sportime* may be used.

Purchasing and Maintaining Equipment

Discussions with your supervisor and general physical education teachers and a review of the IEPs for your caseload will help you make an appropriate list of items that will meet the needs of all students. Sometimes, it is helpful for the general physical education teacher and adapted physical education specialist to combine their budgets and order more items. This can also work well with the other specialists in the district, region, or county and is an effective and efficient way to exchange (share) equipment and supplies (refer back to Tables 13.3 and 13.4).

Once the order has been made, the teacher should keep a copy for an accurate record of the items as they are acquired, repaired, or lost. The teacher's priority list of items should be kept up to date during the year so purchases can be made as funds become available or other sources are identified.

Once the equipment, supplies, and materials have been acquired, then the responsibility for inventory, care and repair, and maintenance should be scheduled as part of the duties of the physical education teacher. Physical education "from the

TABLE 13.3 *Equipment supply list for physical education.*

ITEM	NUMBER (MIN.)	ITEM	NUMBER (MIN.)
Equipment			
Adjustable basketball hoop	1	Jerseys or pinnies (various colors to identify teams)*	Dozen of each color
Balance beam (4" wide)	2		
Balance board	2	Medicine ball*	1–2
Baton (relay, track)*	6–8	Plastic whiffle bat (black)	4–6
Batting tee	4–6	Poly spots	30
Bowling pins and ball(s)*	1–2 sets	Potato sacks*	4–6
Cage ball	2	Scoops*	30
Discus	1–2	Scooterboards (various sizes)	20
Football flag—detachable (yellow, red)	Dozen of each color	Shot put	1–2
		Softball/baseball bases (home plate and 3 bases)	2 sets
Frisbee	30	Softball bats (various lengths)	4–6
Gymnastics ribbons and streamers*	30	Tennis racquets (and/or paddles)	30
Hockey sticks, puck, and no-bounce balls	1 set	Tinikling sets (poles and beat boards)*	5–8 sets
Jump rope and jump band (long)*	4	Therapy or Kinballs (various sizes)	5–10
Jump rope (short—various sizes)*	30	Traffic cones (12", 18", 24")	24
Lummi sticks*	30	Tug-o-rope	1–2
Parachute (small and large)	1 each	Tumbling mats	6–8
Supplies			
Playground ball 5"	20	Beach balls (various sizes)	6–8
Playground ball 8.5"	32	Tennis balls*	80–100
Playground ball 13"	20	Beanbags*	30–40
Playground ball 16"	20	Targets (various sizes, shapes, colors)	5–8
Basketball	12–15	Carpet squares*	30
Football	12–15	Hula hoops (24", 30", 36" sizes)*	30
Kickball	12–15	Masking tape/floor tape (variety of colors and widths)	2–3 rolls
Soccer ball	12–15		
Volleyball	12–15	Scarves	80–100
Tetherballs	6–8		
Materials			
Fine motor items such as scissors, small manipulatives, etc.		Equipment bags	4–6
Rhythm and music tapes and CDs		Measuring tape (100')	1
Video tapes (sports, movement, games, jump rope)		Stopwatch	2
Records and record player		Textbooks for reference	
Audiotape recorder and CD player		Computer, printer	
Drum	1–2	Answering machine	
Tambourine	1–2	Assessment tools and protocols	4–5 kits (as needed)

*Items that can be made, donated, or provided at low cost.

ities that provide experiences and opportunities for learning along the entire developmental continuum. The exact type of equipment or facilities necessary may vary depending on the student population, number of students in class, and their individual needs. For example, a school campus with students with a physical disability probably requires different equipment for providing tactile experiences than an elementary school campus with students with deaf-blindness.

As you develop the equipment list, compare it to the developmental model. Are equipment and facilities available to provide experiences at each level? Remember, particularly when evaluating equipment relative to the sensory systems, that certain sensory systems have demands placed on them simply by the way the equipment is used. Therefore, it is necessary to evaluate the inventory list on the basis of the primary intended use or actual use of the items on the list. For example, a softball places demands on the tactile and proprioceptive systems, but it is not intended, nor is it primarily used, to provide a tactile experience or enhance tactile development. It is, of course, primarily used for activities at the top of the developmental model in the area of culturally determined forms of movement; that is, the sport of softball. The use of softballs of varying weights can enhance proprioception. This kind of creative use of common equipment is encouraged. Once you have evaluated the inventory in terms of the developmental model and made a tally of the needs met by existing resources at each level of the model, go back to the list of items still needed. Compare the "still-needed" list with the levels of the model for which few resources are available, and prioritize these items at the top of a "final request list." After the school district funds are depleted, begin to seek supplemental funding and support and use your creativity for other materials. Table 13.4 lists a variety of equipment and materials that have been used successfully to achieve goals and objectives at each level of the developmental model.

Selecting Equipment

Selecting equipment, supplies, and materials can be both enjoyable and frustrating. Sometimes, the equipment the physical educator has in mind is not available or has not been invented or constructed yet. In this instance, brainstorming with colleagues may be helpful. Do not hesitate to ask the physical and occupational therapists, speech therapist, or classroom teachers if they have seen or heard of the piece you seek. Professional conferences and conventions for physical education and special education are good places to learn about available equipment. The exhibitors usually supply literature and are eager to discuss newly marketed educational supplies and equipment.

When selecting and ordering equipment and supplies, there are seven primary features to consider:

1. Portability
2. Washability
3. Durability
4. Economy
5. Size
6. Diversity
7. Safety

Portability. The portability of a piece of equipment is most important for those teachers who travel from school to school. It may also be a significant factor within a school, depending on the ambulation of the students, space available for the program, and climatic conditions.

If a room or gymnasium is available for the physical education program, it may not be necessary to have equipment that is easily transported, because the students can be brought to the activity room. Consider the amount of space available for storing large, nonportable equipment; the possibility of covering distracting equipment when it is not in use; the ambulation and mobility of the students; and the space available for instruction. If weather conditions are such that outdoor space can be used a great deal of the time during the school year, this may be the deciding factor for choosing between a portable and nonportable piece of equipment.

Washability. The washability, or the ability to keep a piece of equipment clean and hygienic, is important for health and safety. Students who drool or are likely to have bowel or bladder movements during activity may be lying or sitting on the equipment, and all students must be protected from the spread of germs and bacteria by the equipment. Developmentally young children put their hands in their mouths and can spread germs with their hands at a rapid rate; therefore, systems for the control of bacteria, viruses, allergens, and other irritating substances must be in place. A great deal of physical education equipment is available with plastic, vinyl, or other washable coverings. The washability of existing or handmade equipment should be maintained by regularly sanding and lacquering the surfaces. Smaller toys and equipment should be regularly washed in a dishwasher or washing machine, or sanitized by soaking in a bleach solution, rinsing, and air drying.

FIGURE 13.9 Continued.

Boomer ball bat. Use an old baseball bat and a large water bottle (or other type of large bottle). Shave off the top portion of the bat so that it will fit into the opening of the bottle. Secure with washer, bolt, and screw on the outside end and tape around the opening for the "handle." Students often will hold closer to the opening depending on their hand and upper body strength. Lighter-weight boomer bats can be made with plastic dowels and large soda bottles attached in the same manner.

Sample objective: Child will bat pitched ball resulting in a long projection into the field area and a loud noise.

Six-pack net. Collect the plastic ring holders from six-packs of soda. Connect the corners of the ring holders with plastic ties from the hardware store, fishing line, or durable string, or crochet together for a colorful alternative. Join as many as you need to form your net and then fasten to the goal posts. A clothesline rope can be woven through the top of the ring holders to hold the six-pack net and attach to posts for volleyball.

Sample objective: Students will be able to use the net for volleyball, tennis, as a target or boundary line, or for jumping and leaping across when placed on the ground.

Source: J. S. Seaman and K. P. DePauw (1995), *Sensory–Motor Experiences for the Home.* Reston, VA: American Alliance for Health, Physical Education, Recreation, and Dance. *Six-Pack Net Replacers.* Brett D. Mills, Chair, Department of HPES, St. Andrews College, 1700 Dogwood Mile, Laurinburg, North Carolina 28352.

trunk of your car" is often a reality for many itinerant specialists. Managing equipment sometimes means planning what can be transported in the district's or personal vehicle. Therefore, the specialist can be effectively prepared by carrying several "all utility" items so that they can be used when needed. See the Teaching Tip titled "All Utility Items" on page 333 for items that might be useful when working "from the trunk of your car."

SUMMARY

Careful and thorough planning is critical to conducting a successful physical education program for individuals with a disability. Lesson planning, unit planning, scheduling, and coordinating with IEPs are major components. Safe and enjoyable movement experiences will result from careful planning. As with other aspects of the physical education program, the acquisition, adaptation, and use of equipment and facilities should be approached systematically and creatively. The needs of the population to be served should provide the foundation for this process so that the best use may be made of available resources. Securing sources of funding outside the educational context is an important step in maintaining quality services. Even with little or no resources, the adapted physical educator has the responsibility to provide appropriate educational experiences. Thus, imagination and creativity can pave the way for new and different solutions to challenges on a daily basis.

Learning Activities

13.1 Obtain a daily and weekly schedule from an adapted physical education specialist. For the following items, compare and contrast the schedule with those obtained by classmates:

a. Different age groups (e.g., preschool, elementary, middle, and high school schedules)
b. Itinerant versus single-school assignments
c. Rural versus urban assignments
d. Different types of assignments that serve a variety of disability categories (e.g., classes with students with a hearing impairment versus those with students who are nonambulatory)

13.2 Tour a gym, physical education building, or sport facility. Make a list of the accessible and inaccessible features for a person with:

a. Blindness
b. Paraplegia who uses a wheelchair
c. Quadriplegia who uses a power wheelchair
d. Deafness

13.3 Pick your favorite movement skill, activity, or game and create a lesson to present to the class. Include the following information in your lesson format:

a. Specific age group
b. Equipment and space needed
c. Lesson focus (goals and objectives as they relate to NASPE standards and district curriculum)
d. Practice and game activity
e. Additional goals and objectives that can be met (as on IEPs)
f. Safety precautions and procedures, if needed
g. Closure experience and discussion

REFERENCES

Almquist, S. (May/June 2001). The emergency plan. *Strategies, 14*(5), 30.

Brady, B., & Sanders, C. (January/February 2004). A study in teaching CPR to a disabled student. *Strategies, 17*(3), 13.

California Department of Education, Special Education Division. (August 2001). *Adapted physical education guidelines in California schools.* Sacramento, CA: Author.

Cowart, J. (1997). *Instructional aids for adaptive physical education.* Hayward, CA: Alameda County School Department.

Faigenbaum, A. D., & Cloutier, G. (May/June 2002). Medicine ball training for children. *Strategies, 15*(5), 15.

LaRue, R. J. (2002). Designing for inclusion: A historical, conceptual, and regulatory guide to planning an accessible environment. In T. H. Sawyer (Ed.), *Facilities planning for health, fitness, physical activity, recreation, and sports: Concepts and applications* (10th ed., pp. 65–71). Champaign, IL: Sagamore.

Marston, R. (1994, October). Constructing equipment from recycled materials. *JOPERD*, 44–47.

NASPE & GSSI. (September/October 2002). 10 essentials for avoiding dehydration. *Strategies, 16*(1), 18.

Russell, A. C. (2000, August). *Beating the budgetary blues: Free and inexpensive equipment.* A presentation at the 27th Annual Cal Poly Elementary Physical Education Workshop, San Luis Obispo, California, syllabus 301–305.

Seaman, J. S., & DePauw, K. P. (1995). *Sensory-motor experiences for the home.* Reston, VA: American Alliance for Health, Physical Education, Recreation, and Dance.

Steele, E. (1994). *Peace Patrol: Creating a new generation of problem solvers and peacemakers.* Spring Valley, CA: Innerchoice Publishing.

Unruh, N., Unruh, S., & Scantling, E. (August 2002). Heat can kill: Guidelines to prevent heat illness in athletics and physical education. *Journal of Physical Education, Recreation, and Dance, 73*(6), 36.

Additional Resources

National program for playground safety. School of Health, Physical Education & Leisure Services, WRC 205, University of Northern Iowa, Cedar Falls, IA 50614-0618, 800-554-PLAY, www.uni.edu/playground.

CHAPTER 14

Connections and Transitions

Guiding Questions

1. Who are some of the professionals that adapted physical educators are likely to encounter in the community, and what are their roles?

2. What are some local service organizations that could be approached to share their resources with individuals with a disability?

3. What are some of the ways the physical educator can interact with the family to support the student's participation in physical activity?

4. How can volunteers be used successfully in the adapted physical education program?

5. What are some communication methods that would help to increase support and interest in your physical education program?

Physical educators often must look beyond the educational environment for services that will enhance the education and growth of students with a disability. Services available in the school and in the community may be listed as related services on the individualized education program (IEP). Other services, which may not qualify as related services, are available to complement the educational program.

The adapted physical educator often has the occasion to interact with professionals delivering services to students outside the educational context and with parents providing home activities. For example, the educator may occasionally consult doctors of pediatrics, orthopedics, and neurology to ensure that the student is participating in safe and healthful physical activities. Other medical professionals, such as nurses, clinical psychologists, rehabilitation nurses, occupational therapists, and physical therapists, may be treating the child within or outside of the educational system. This chapter provides a brief overview of some of the community service providers that adapted physical educators commonly encounter (see also Chapter 2). This will provide a sampling of the variety of services available and will clarify the role of the professionals involved. However, each community is different because of local and state laws and procedures as well as cultural norms. Therefore, the adapted physical educator should investigate the specific related services available in the community in which the person with a disability lives.

Additionally, it is important to involve the family of the person with a disability. The family is the core of a person's support system, both legally and culturally in the United States. For many individuals with a disability, one or more family members take on the role of lifelong advocate. Consulting, informing, and educating the family regarding physical activities that are available and accessible greatly enhances their ability to support the person with a disability, thereby increasing the success and quality of participation in physical activities.

TRANSITION FROM SCHOOL TO ADULT PROGRAMS

It is recognized, both philosophically and legally, that educators have a responsibility to plan for a smooth and successful transition to adult life for individuals with a disability. Of course, this includes physical educators. IDEA '04 sets the foundation for educational programming related to the transition to adult life. It clearly identifies that its primary purpose is to "ensure that all children with a disability have available to them a free, appropriate education that emphasizes special education and related services designed to meet their unique needs and prepare them for employment and independent living" [20 U.S.C. 33, Subchapter 1, sec. 1400 (d)(1)(A) (2004)]. This is consistent with the general goals of any physical education program—to teach students a broad range of skills that will enable them to maintain a healthy, active lifestyle across the life span.

Planning a program that will enable the individual with a disability to maintain an active lifestyle as an adult begins in early childhood. Throughout the individual's school program, the foundation for lifelong activity should be established. Educators accomplish this by implementing the developmental model and focusing instruction on achieving functional motor goals.

Throughout the school career of the individual with a disability, he or she should be provided experiences in the application of physical education knowledge and skills to activities outside school. Whether people have a disability or not, they will find it easier to maintain an active lifestyle outside the school setting if they have had practice applying physical education knowledge in a variety of settings. However, beginning by age 16, additional emphasis should be placed on teaching the student to apply physical education knowledge in a variety of settings.

Individualized Transition Plan

IDEA '04 requires that when a student reaches age 16, the IEP include a statement of the child's transition service needs, which must be updated at least annually. This statement must identify the interagency responsibilities or linkages that are needed. Therefore, the IEP for secondary students is often referred to as an Individualized Transition Plan or ITP. (State and local policies and procedures will determine whether the document is referred to as an IEP or ITP; in some cases the terms are used interchangeably. For purposes of this chapter, ITP will refer to the IEP for a student aged 16 or older.)

Generally, the ITP focuses on the areas of instruction, related services, community experiences, the development of employment and other post-school adult living objectives, and, when appropriate, acquisition of daily living skills and functional vocational evaluation. Goals and objectives for physical education can fall within any of these areas. For example, physical recreation and leisure skills are important for community living. Physical and motor fitness skills are necessary to support vocational and employment demands, personal health, and daily living activities. Therefore, the ITP

> ## Teaching Tip
>
> **TEACHING PRACTICAL ASPECTS OF BOWLING** • Teaching students their shoe size, how to ask for rental shoes, and how to put them on is just as much a part of bowling in the community as rolling the ball down the lane. Students may also need to be taught how to ride public transportation in order to get to the bowling lanes for a Saturday morning junior bowling league.

team should consider the student's needs for physical education in relation to these areas of adult living. If necessary, the ITP team should write goals and objectives, which will generally fall in the categories of physical fitness, functional motor skills, and recreation and leisure skills. (See Chapter 8 for a comparison of types of IEPs.)

In addition, the ITP should emphasize the student's preferences. Including a preference interview or checklist in the physical education assessment when developing the ITP is good practice. (See Chapter 6 for a discussion of alternative methods of collecting data.)

PARTNERSHIPS WITH COMMUNITY ORGANIZATIONS

Most communities have a variety of organizations, both private and public, that directly provide physical activities, are willing to adapt physical activities, or engage in various methods for supporting and facilitating participation in physical activities for individuals with a disability. Some organizations that directly provide physical activity programs for youth include YMCA/YWCA, Boys and Girls Clubs, municipal recreation departments and aquatics programs, and sport-specific clubs or camps.

One or more of the following service clubs may be found in nearly every community in the United States: local chambers of commerce, Jaycees, Kiwanis, Knights of Columbus, Optimists, Lions, Rotary International, 20–30 Clubs, YMCA/YWCA, Altrusa, Soroptimists, and Lady Jaycees. Youth groups include Assisteens, Boy Scouts and Girl Scouts, Boys and Girls Clubs, college and university sororities and fraternities, Kiwanettes, Letterman's clubs, and Rotary Annes. These organizations may be contacted to provide a variety of services. Some clubs endorse or sponsor a specific project on a regular basis. For example, the Lions have been noted for their sight-saving program. Historically, in every community in which the Lions are located, they provide services and funding for children with visual impairments and sponsor special annual events such as car rallies, partner surfing, Braille Olympics, or tandem bicycle rides. Services may range from providing eye examinations and transportation, to purchasing corrective lenses for students in need. Other clubs, if approached with a specific project such as sponsoring a Special Olympics team, may be encouraged to do so on a continuing basis.

Youth groups tend to provide human resources more often than financial resources. The vigor and enthusiasm that high school- and college-aged service-oriented individuals can bring to your program is rarely matched. Specific fund-raising projects are often within the purview of youth organizations. Youth organizations often tackle with enthusiasm the task of raising money through a jog-a-thon, rope-jumping-a-thon, or bike-a-thon.

Employing a service club member as a volunteer in the physical education program can also provide enrichment for the students. Using volunteers of any age, however, requires some concerted effort on the part of the adapted physical educator. (Some of the skills involved in working with volunteers are discussed later in this chapter.)

The physical educator must be well informed about community organizations in order to:

- Select learning experiences that will transfer to activities provided by community organizations (e.g., specific sport and physical activity skills, social skills related to participation in physical activities, use of locker rooms and other facilities, and check-in and check-out procedures).
- Assist students with a disability to find and select activities and organizations of interest, such as Unified Sports, Blaze Sports, AYSO VIP soccer, or Challenger Little League.
- Teach advocacy and other activity-related skills that will enable the individual with a disability to access community organizations (e.g., appropriately requesting needed services and adaptations; determining schedules, transportation, and personal equipment needs; sampling available activities).
- Assist parents and family members to gain information and establish communication with various community organizations.

Suggested activities to develop and maintain partnerships with community organizations include:

- Keeping a list, card file, or electronic file of community resources and updating it periodically (see the example in Figure 14.1).

> **FIGURE 14.1** *Sample record of community resources.*
>
> Name and location of program: Springdale Recreation Center
> 2201 Cedar Ave., Springdale
>
> Contact person: Heather Marks, (704) 555-1212
>
> Type of program: Adapted aquatics taught in eight-week sessions. Classes meet twice weekly with some classes scheduled in the evening and some weekends. Call for current schedule.
>
> Participants served: All ages and disabilities.
>
> Eligibility criteria for admission: Persons lacking bowel and bladder control must wear protective garments.
>
> Cost: $10 per session for people outside of Springdale; no fee for residents.
>
> Last updated: 1/13/07

- Visiting community organizations that directly or indirectly support participation in physical activities for individuals with a disability.
- Contacting organizations that provide physical activities for individuals without a disability and asking about opportunities available (some organizations will create opportunities for individuals with a disability when they know there is a need).
- Offering to explain and demonstrate some specific adaptations that the organization could implement to enable access and participation by individuals with a disability.
- Working in one or more community organizations as a volunteer.
- Taking students on field trips to community organizations and facilities for physical activities (e.g., gym, health club, skating rink, bowling alley, gymnastics club, dance studio, youth sport competition, ski slope, park facility).
- Inviting the employees of community organizations to visit and observe your classes when appropriate and related to their programs.
- Writing a short description of your adapted physical education program and sharing it with community contacts.
- Surveying parents or caregivers about the successful experiences their children have had in leisure or recreation activities, day camps, or after-school programs and listing the specifics (e.g., people, places, and programs) to share with other families; helping parents connect with other families to participate in similar activities or share transportation to events.

Advocacy Within Community Programs

When enrolling a child with a disability in a community program, it may be helpful to set up a two-way communication system of reciprocal advocacy. It doesn't matter who begins the process. The goal is to share the information and expectations for the program and the child with a disability—for example, what does the recreation leader need to know about the child with a disability to provide the best experience for all participants? Information to exchange might include the following:

1. From the program leader's perspective:
   - Identification of behaviors to support, especially if the child is nonverbal.
   - Supports needed for safe and successful participation.

- Strategies or reinforcements that are effective.
- Assistance needed with self-care (e.g., toileting and bathroom needs, eating or nutritional needs, medications).
- Medical needs and procedures for emergency.

2. From the parent's perspective:
   - How to help the child participate fully in a safe and fun environment.
   - How to facilitate the child's social interaction (e.g., making friends, verbal interaction, learning appropriate behaviors in different environments, following rules and other adults).
   - How to provide safe and appropriate behavior support.
   - Contact numbers for emergency.

A modified version of the Dreams and Fears Inventory (see Figure 14.5) can help the parents communicate with staff of community programs. This tool can be especially helpful to open up the dialogue between the recreational staff leaders and the parents about expectations and supports that the child needs for a successful experience.

MAKING CONNECTIONS

Collaborating with a Parent

Julie, a single parent with two children with autism, both age 10, wants her boys to go to the community recreation center after school for the activity programs. She enrolls them in the program for swimming and sports activities. But during the first day, behaviors escalate. Jonathan refuses to participate, begins to yell and scream, and then starts to move toward other peers, apparently intending to hit or kick them. Julian begins to become agitated, says "Stop," and starts to run away from the group. One staff member intervenes but is not able to calm the boys; he changes the activity for the rest of the group while another staff member tries to contact Julie. When Julie comes to pick the boys up, the recreation leader approaches her and asks if they could talk about the expectations and needs of the staff and participants.

Their challenge will be to find the best solution for all participants. This will take ongoing, open communication. Julie explains how she supports her children's behavior and what happens in other programs in which they are successful. The leader now feels he knows where to start.

Professional Services

Professional services may be available through government-supported agencies or private agencies. These services are often available at residential care facilities, but this chapter focuses on services most commonly available to individuals with a disability who live in their own home or a foster home and attend school in the public sector. In addition, although many different types of professional services may be available in a larger community, this discussion is limited to those most closely related to or likely to affect physical education.

Therapeutic recreation. The American Therapeutic Recreation Association defines **therapeutic recreation** as follows:

> "*the provision of treatment services and the provision of recreation services to persons with illnesses or disabling conditions.* The primary purposes of treatment services, which are often referred to as recreational therapy, are to restore, remediate or rehabilitate in order to improve functioning and independence as well as reduce or eliminate the effects of illness or disability. The primary purposes of recreational services are to provide recreation resources and opportunities in order to improve health and well-being. Therapeutic recreation is provided by professionals who are trained and certified, registered and/or licensed to provide therapeutic recreation." (American Therapeutic Recreation Association, 2005)

The commonality between adapted physical education and therapeutic recreation lies primarily in the medium of the physical activities and the use of evaluation, goal planning, and activity analysis. In addition to physical activities, therapeutic recreation provides program activities that go beyond those typically included in physical education programs: creative arts, camping and outdoor recreation, hobbies, excursions, horticultural activities, social recreation, and table games.

By communicating regularly with the recreation therapist in the community or residential facility, the adapted physical educator can ensure that the child with a disability gains experiences to complement or supplement the skills taught in the educational context. It may, however, become the responsibility of the adapted physical educator to make the initial contact with the recreation therapist or recreation program director to open lines of communication. Once this has occurred, a relationship can develop that will meet the needs of individual students.

MAKING CONNECTIONS

Collaborating with Another Professional

Mr. and Mrs. Morgan want their son Ben to participate in the Safe-key program before and after school. Ben is seven years old and has cerebral palsy, seizures, and limited head and arm movements and control using a wheelchair. He is very social and likes to interact with peers during class time. It takes extra time for him to speak one or two words, but he is able to communicate his desires and needs to peers. The staff is unsure how to include him in the program, which consists of outdoor activities (e.g., four-square, hopscotch, playground apparatus), puzzles, and breakfast in the morning; and homework completion, snack, outdoor activities, and board and musical games indoors in the afternoon.

The leader asks the adapted physical education specialist and parents to meet to discuss how Ben could participate successfully in the activities with the group, especially in outdoor games. Lots of good ideas were shared. The adapted physical education specialist agreed to provide some equipment and adapted game rules so the leader could teach the other children.

Dance therapy. Based on the assumption that body and mind are interrelated, **dance or movement therapy** is defined by the American Dance Therapy Association as *"the psychotherapeutic use of movement as a process, which furthers the emotional, social cognitive, and physical integration of the individual"* (American Dance Therapy Association, 2005). Dance or movement therapy causes changes in feelings, cognition, physical functioning, and behavior. Dance therapy, which emerged in the 1940s from the impact of World War II, seeks to change one's self-concept, self-awareness, behavior, and interpersonal interactions, as well as changing the body itself and providing opportunities for the release of tension and anxiety. In this process, the therapist serves as a catalyst and facilitator.

Dance therapy sessions, like physical education, begin with warm-up activities. During this time, the therapist assesses the group needs and rhythm. Unlike physical education, the activity portion of each session usually consists of movement experiences based on themes and the group's interaction and needs at that point in time. Often, the final part of each session strives toward the resolution of conflict and the restoration of the self-concept for each individual. Although dance, like recreation, can have therapeutic value for all people, dance therapy is primarily used in conjunction with psychotherapy for individuals who have emotional, social, or cognitive problems.

Other services in the community. Other services are also available in the community, including social work, rehabilitation counseling, art therapy, therapeutic horseback riding (hippo therapy), and music therapy. Because adapted physical educators do not typically come in contact with the professionals who provide these services, we do not discuss their roles. Physical educators are encouraged to seek information about services such as these available in the local community. Many can be beneficial and may reinforce physical education goals and lessons. Information about such services and even an occasional field trip to facilities can assist students with a disability to enhance their fitness, recreational interests, and independence.

Private organizations and businesses. A number of organizations have evolved to provide services where there were none and to supplement educational and community services. Some of these organizations grew out of parental and community concern; others emerged as a result of a need felt by professionals to pool their resources. Some organizations act primarily as advocates for a specific population; an example is The Arc (formerly the National Association for Retarded Children).

In many areas of the country, there is still a need for some of these organizations to provide educational services. Adapted physical educators should be aware of organizations outside the schools that can serve as resources for providing a fuller, more enriching experience for individuals with a disability. Organizations at the local level that provide supplemental therapy, recreation, and summer or year-round camping opportunities should be explored. Examples of national organizations include: United Cerebral Palsy (UCP), Learning Disabilities Association (LDA), Epilepsy Foundation of America, National Braille Association, National Easter Seal Society, March of Dimes Birth Defects Foundation, and Autism Society of America. Most of these organizations have local chapters in many geographic areas, and other similar organizations may exist at the state and local levels.

Private businesses should not be overlooked as sources of physical activity for individuals with a disability. Just as people without a disability use health clubs, private gyms, sport clubs, personal trainers, and fee-for-service athletic facilities, so can individuals with a disability. Some facilities provide adaptive devices as might be necessary. For example, most bowling alleys provide bumpers to block the gutters, skating rinks may have large buckets or other balance-enhancing devices that can be borrowed, and aquatic centers may have ramps, lifts, and other adaptive aquatic equipment.

THE ROLE OF THE FAMILY

Communication with the significant persons in the home environment can be of value to the physical educator, especially the adapted physical education specialist. Although the generalist has less occasion and time to interact with the parents, guardians, and families of students with a disability, the information provided in this section might prove useful as resource material.

The IEP process formalizes communication between the home and school, and these channels should be kept open. In the past, much of the communication with the home has been of a negative nature, and educators have clearly communicated that parents should "stay out of my domain." We hope that this trend has begun to change, and that the change can be facilitated by the individual efforts of teachers. Communication and interaction between the home and school is a two-way street, and teachers must make it clear that they welcome contact from parents.

Benefits of Family Involvement

Communication and interaction with the people in the student's home environment (parents, guardians, foster parents, siblings, surrogate families, and others living or interacting in the home) can be most informative and enlightening. An initial positive experience will greatly enhance the interaction. Although eligibility for special education and adapted physical education is based on a deficit model, physical educators should always look for, report, and discuss the individual's abilities and strengths first. These positive attributes are the resources for participation, movement, and success in physical activities. Most families are already well aware of the difficulties and challenges that their family member faces. A collaborative team effort can be established with the family when the professional focuses on the individual's abilities and strengths.

The following are some of the values and benefits of home–school interaction:

1. Sharing information leads to more effective decisions regarding appropriate physical education programming.

FIGURE 14.2

This adolescent with a disability is regularly included in family play.

2. The consistency, continuity, and reinforcement of skills and behaviors between the home and school programs are enhanced.
3. Interest and participation in physical activities by the family are stimulated, and the value of motor activity for individuals with a disability is underscored.
4. Situations and activities that facilitate family–child interaction are created (see Figure 14.2).

Obtaining Information from the Family

The whole individual must be considered in physical education programming, and information obtained from the family can be valuable in creating a total picture of the student. Often, parents' knowledge of their child's capabilities and limitations is better than the information that can be obtained from an assessment or interviews of other educators and service providers. Individuals in the home environment can be specifically questioned about the student's hidden abilities, likes and dislikes, preferred mode of communication, motivators, and so on. Gathering all possible information allows the physical educator to design the most appropriate and individualized program. The inventory in Figure 14.3 may help to gather information from parents and others who live with the child.

A detailed parent interview form is provided in Figure 14.4 to help you gain information from parents or caregivers. This particular format works well

FIGURE 14.3 — Interest questionnaire for parents and students.

INTEREST QUESTIONNAIRE

1. What types of activities, sports, or leisure experiences does your family enjoy? (Examples: go for walks, attend baseball games, play card or board games, do puzzles, gardening, swimming)

2. What types of activities, sports, or leisure experiences does your child enjoy? Avoid? Repeat? Engage in for an extended period of time?

3. What do you feel or think are your child's strengths and needs in the area of sport and physical education skills?

4. What community programs does your child participate in, or which ones would you like him or her to participate in (e.g., soccer, baseball, swimming, skiing, Special Olympics)?

5. What are the needs of your family related to leisure or recreation for your child (e.g., transportation, peer assistance)?

6. What are your goals for leisure or recreation for your child?

7. What skills do you think your child needs to learn in order to participate in physical activities with peers and family members?

8. What are your safety concerns for your child's participation in leisure or recreational activities?

9. What are your long- or short-term wishes for your child regarding play, leisure, sport, and physical activity?

10. What are obstacles to participating in leisure activities (e.g., cost, transportation, time available)?

FIGURE 14.4 *Parent interview form.*

PARENT INTERVIEW

As a member of the IEP team, you are a valuable information provider and a helpful participant for the other team members who are assessing and evaluating your child. Your candid, accurate, and thorough responses will help in the preparation of the assessment setting and program planning. Thank you for your assistance in completing the following information. (Comment: This interview can also be done in person or on the telephone if the parent prefers.)

Name of student _____ Date _____

CATEGORY	RESPONSES

Medical Information

Diagnosis: _____

Medications: _____
_____

Seizures: ☐ Yes ☐ No   Type: _____

Endurance: ☐ Low ☐ Medium ☐ High

Allergies: ☐ Yes ☐ No   Types (insect, medications, foods, other): _____

Special concerns: _____

Other: _____

Weekday Schedule of Activities

What activities does the student like to play?

Indoors: _____

Outdoors: _____

What skills does the student perform?

Locomotor: _____

Ball skills: _____

What assistance is needed?   Adult supervision: _____

_____   Adaptive equipment: _____

Family Activities

Weekday: Indoors: _____   Outdoors: _____

Weekends: Indoors: _____   Outdoors: _____

Preferences: Indoors: _____   Outdoors: _____

Desires/hopes: _____

(continued)

FIGURE 14.4 Continued.

Communication

Receptive (What communication forms are used for input?): _____

Expressive (What communication forms are used for output?): _____

Pragmatics (What forms are used for social interaction?): _____

Language (Priority vocabulary?): _____

Behavior Management

Positive behaviors: _____

Challenges: _____

How do you handle behaviors that are of concern? _____

Student preferences: Tangibles: _____   Praise: _____

Basic Skills

Please check issues that are of importance at this time and circle specific areas of need.

- ☐ Motor — Gross motor skills, fine motor skills, range of motion, bearing weight, balance, physical fitness, motor planning, use of special equipment, play skills, other: _____
- ☐ Mobility — Orientation, mobility, need for adaptive equipment, other: _____
- ☐ Cognitive — Learning style, problem-solving strategies, reasoning, other: _____
- ☐ Academic — Reading, writing, math, Braille, specific subject areas, other: _____
- ☐ Perceptual — Processing visual, auditory, tactile, olfactory, kinesthetic, vestibular, and gustatory information, other: _____
- ☐ Eating — Finger feeding, use of utensils, tolerance of textures, drinking from a cup, use of special equipment or procedures, other: _____
- ☐ Personal Care — Toileting, hygiene, tooth brushing, grooming, self-help with clothing, blowing nose, other: _____
- ☐ Social — Interactions with others, self-esteem, cooperation, other: _____
- ☐ Work Habits — Self-initiation, attention span, response to authority, productivity, neatness, speed, accuracy, independence, time on task, other: _____
- ☐ Behavior — Self-management, excesses, assertiveness, advocacy, other: _____

Other comments

Include any comments regarding the movement and play skills you observe or would like to have your child perform, as well as behaviors, language, or preferences that you would like to share with the team:

_____

_____

Name of person completing form _____   Date _____

when given to the parent to fill out, but it should always be followed by a phone call or meeting to review the contents. Some adapted physical education specialists find it helpful to use this interview for an initial assessment. Subsequently, they use one of the two forms in Figures 14.3 and 14.4 for annual and triennial reviews.

Some families, unfortunately, have learned "the hard way" what activities and situations will and will not work for their child. Their experiences may have led to the formulation of "dreams" and "fears" for their child. It may be helpful to discuss these dreams and fears with the parents when planning a physical education program for their child. Figure 14.5, "Dreams and Fears Inventory," is offered to assist the adapted physical educator in that regard once a relationship with the parent has been established.

Figure 14.6, "The Grief Process," is included to help educators better understand this important topic.

Sharing Information with the Family

Consistency is vital in the educational process. With effective communication, adults at home and school can provide continuity and consistency in all aspects of educational programming. For example, specific behavior management techniques can be shared and applied in both environments. Family members can reinforce skills taught at school, and vice versa. Thus, an increased awareness of the student's performance is fostered. With an experience of effective, open communication, parents and family members are more likely to communicate with service providers outside the school, such as after-school program staff, to further enhance consistency and continuity.

Students with a disability, especially those with a more severe disability, often do not participate in or know how to play or enjoy leisure activities outside of those sponsored by the school. Often, the person with a disability cannot play independently and requires the assistance of or supervision by someone else in the home. The parent or family member may be ill-equipped to help or intervene with the child unless the adapted physical educator has shared the methods and techniques found to be successful at school. The family members can be taught strategies and techniques of movement intervention and play to use at home, and, in turn, some may volunteer at school or in related services. They can also be given information on community and organizational resources and opportunities of which they may not be aware.

Information shared about the physical education program may stimulate the family's interest and participation in general physical activities in the after-school hours. The value of movement to the student with a disability can be instilled in parents and other family members. Information on community activities, available motor programs, special workshops, and the like can be provided to families, which may, in turn, encourage the whole family to participate.

Physical activities can foster increased family–child interaction. Casual or more general opportunities include family outings and games; playtime; leisure time activities; trips to the playground, park, swimming pool, or bowling alley; or even watching selected television shows together. Other opportunities include participation in organized movement and physical activity programs (e.g., Special Olympics, scouting programs, therapeutic recreation or adapted sports programs, church groups, camps). Both the child and the family benefit from participation in any of these programs.

A home program of physical and movement experiences can be designed and implemented to strengthen the child's areas of weakness and enhance development. Through involvement in a home program, family members can learn the basic play skills and needs of the child—what to do and how to do it. The capabilities of the child become more apparent, and family members develop a deeper understanding of the child's physical and motor needs. The success of the home program is related to the level of communication between the physical education teacher and individuals in the home.

Methods of Communication

Once the communication channels are open, the physical educator should strive to keep them open. Parental support and interest in the physical education program can be a valuable asset. The following suggestions may help you initiate and foster communication with the student's family:

1. Send letters home about the general physical education program.
2. Explain, in written form, how the specific goals of the IEP will be met through physical activity.
3. Make phone contact with parents at least once per year. (When possible, discuss areas of need with the child's parents before the IEP meeting.)
4. Provide parent or family workshops, in-service training, and play nights.
5. Hold parent conferences on a regular basis.
6. Sponsor and hold play days, festivals, and demonstrations.
7. Provide "homework"—activities to practice at home, or an activity of the week designed to meet specific goals.

FIGURE 14.5 *"Dreams and Fears" Inventory.*

DREAMS AND FEARS

To the Parent: In the following categories, please describe your child and some of the key experiences of your life together. These may change over time, but knowing what they are today will help you plan for the future and explain to the professionals what you would like for your child. Be creative and enjoy the process of dreaming and identifying what you want for your child. Also, be realistic when determining what your fears might be like.

Strengths, gifts, and talents (e.g., affectionate, social, curious, helpful, good stamina and high energy level, accepting of his or her challenges):

Medical history (e.g., diagnosis [if known], surgery, medications, therapy services needed, medical procedures pending):

Educational history (e.g., schooling programs, early intervention programs, outside services provided, current placement in school):

Parents' dreams (e.g., self-esteem, worth and sense of belonging, have friends, be happy, acceptance of difference by peers, go to neighborhood school, be with neighborhood friends, be invited to peer activities such as birthday parties, play and work on computers independently, be part of the community, acquire skills and an education, have a good job, be self-supporting):

Parents' fears (e.g., no sense of belonging to neighborhood or community, being lonely, rejected because of differences, living in isolation from peers with no friends, no exposure to good role models as he or she matures, acquires inappropriate behaviors, financially dependent, no recreation or leisure activities, no skills or ability to live independently after parents' death):

Supports needed (e.g., to communicate more clearly, to have friends, extra help from teacher, a good education, toileting assistance, assistance or prompts to control drooling, learns best in a structured environment):

Likes (e.g., being with other children, playing games, learning, pleasing others, playing with neighborhood children, computers, looking at books or being read to, wanting people to be proud of him or her, playing ball):

FIGURE 14.6 The grief process.

To improve interactions, communication, and empathy with the family, it is helpful to understand the grief cycle and the effect it may have on the family of a child with a disability. Individuals may experience the process of grieving at different times in their life, triggered by many things—failing an important exam, moving, ending a significant relationship, or the loss of a friend or family member. This process is often triggered by change, which demands a shift in perceptions or expectations. The chart illustrates the stages of the grief cycle that everyone experiences, but how and when each person reaches each stage is unique to that individual.

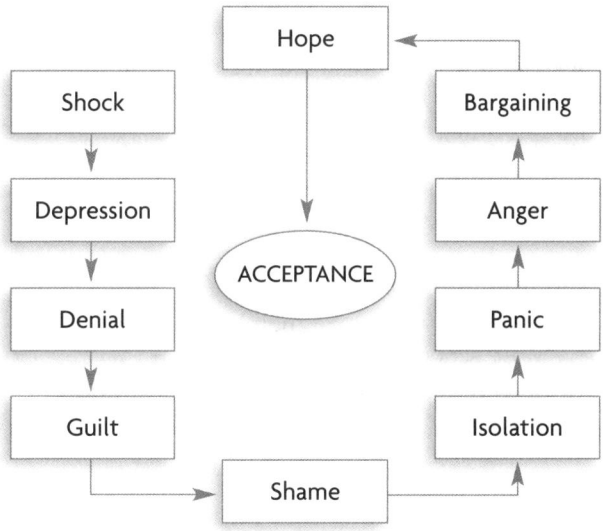

It is important to recognize that the grief cycle is not a linear process and that people experiencing loss may return to a previous stage—just as they think they have reached a level of acceptance or hope, something happens and they again become angry or panicked, or feel isolated. For example, a parent of a child with a disability, before he or she was born or before the disability was diagnosed, had beliefs, expectations, and dreams about who that child would become. Although most parents eventually come to realize that their child will not fulfill all of their dreams, it is a gradual process that occurs over 18 or more years. There may be sudden onset of a behavior or a specific event that forces the parents of a child with a disability to face the loss of their dreams for their child all at once. A parent may again feel a sense of grief at significant times in the developmental process—while some parents are celebrating their child's first dance, first little league game, or getting a driver's license, the parents of a child with a disability may grieve for their child again if the child is not participating in such events. The adapted physical educator can help parents build new dreams by sharing resources for other activities, such as wheelchair sports programs or Special Olympics.

Educators may experience the grief process with families as well; for example, when working with a child who has a progressive disability. It is certainly complicated, or perhaps impossible, for a physical educator to determine exactly where a parent or other family member may be in the grief cycle; however, it is important to understand that the family member's behavior may change as he or she goes through the various stages in the cycle. Also, the educator should remember that experiencing the grief cycle is a normal psychological process that may be an important coping mechanism. Therefore, a supportive approach is usually the best. For example:

- Support, rather than push, the parent in moving through the stages.
- Listen a lot.
- Be prepared to say the same thing repeatedly in a tactful and patient manner.
- Show respect for the parent.
- Show respect and caring for the child.
- Be positive; state positive information first; communicate positive messages about the child more frequently than negative messages.
- Use good consultation techniques, as you would with other educators.
- Show a willingness to try things the parent suggests or requests.

The purpose of understanding the grief cycle is not to label parents or others, but to develop an appreciation of the process we all go through when handling difficult challenges in our lives. An adapted physical educator who understands this process and the benefits that each stage can contribute toward personal growth can empathize and support parents by listening and providing resources as needed. The family system is critical in the education of any child, and it is important to recognize that a disability affects each member of the family, as well as the professionals who serve them, in different ways.

8. Send special notes home whenever appropriate—"good job" note, completion of objective note, or certificate of award. Send positive information home more frequently than negative information.
9. Provide to the parents a list of community organizations, books, sports programs, related services, and resource people.
10. Be visible and available at open house and back-to-school night.
11. Use a photo display to explain the program. Attend special events when possible.
12. Use parents as volunteer aides for the physical education program.

Developing Home Programs

Occasionally, adapted physical educators need to develop a home program for a child with a disability. Home programs are most often based on recommendations from an infant or preschool assessment team. Home programs are effective when the infant or preschooler has motor needs and the parent and family members are learning how to play with their child and help the child develop some of the basic reflexes and motor responses. A collaborative approach by all professionals working with an infant or preschooler is the best practice. The adapted physical educator should always collaborate with other professionals, especially any occupational (OT) and physical therapist (PT), who are providing services to the young child. (Most of the time, an OT or PT will be providing services to a very young child with significant motor needs.) It is important to remember that the adapted physical education specialist is not usually expected to go to the child's home; rather, he or she provides support to the family and young child through discussion and modeling that usually takes place at the school or sometimes an agency site. Some of the services that the adapted physical education specialist might provide include:

- Suggesting play activities or songs and games that will help the child explore the environment and interact with others.
- Providing resources (e.g., catalogues, equipment, toys).
- Suggesting methods to help the child use equipment or toys already in the home.
- Collaborating and consulting with other professionals.
- Suggesting methods to embed motor activities in regular daily activities.

Special Olympics programs offer a variety of materials to help parents in planning sport activities, including a manual for parents and teachers on topics such as bowling, swimming, ball skills, tumbling, weight lifting, and track and field. *Tool Chest* (Henry, 1998) and *Sensory–Motor Experiences for the Home* (Seaman & DePauw, 1995) are resources for parents that list many activities and experiences (adapted or designed specifically for the home environment) that enhance the sensorimotor development of children with a disability.

VOLUNTEERS

The use of volunteers requires some extra effort on the part of the physical educator, but can serve to enhance the physical education program. Volunteers are special individuals who must be cared for and nurtured. Volunteers usually offer their help because they have a need to contribute something to others. Each must be handled with respect and care—as though they were a rare gem. Many organizations need people who can give their time for free, and these agencies are competing for their services. Therefore, unless the physical educator makes volunteers feel as though what they are doing is important, they will take their services elsewhere.

Most schools and school districts have established policies and procedures for volunteers. The physical educator should learn and follow them. Guidelines for using volunteers will be similar to those for paraeducators found in Chapters 2 and 9.

SUMMARY

From the increasing visibility of individuals with a disability and the response of the community to their needs comes a greater circle of resources for enhancing the quality of life for this population. Specialists in adapted physical education often become the pivot point for coordinating movement experiences for students in their charge. Thus, they must be familiar with resources and opportunities outside the educational context. General physical educators often are asked about opportunities in the community. Whether the physical educator is working closely with professionals in related services, parents, or volunteers, the constant driving energy should be the desire to provide appropriate, satisfying movement experiences for students with a disability and to prepare them to transition into a healthful and active adult lifestyle.

CHAPTER 14

Learning Activities

14.1 Plan an interview of a parent of a child with a disability or a professional who serves individuals with a disability (e.g., recreation therapist, coach of adapted sport athletes, dance therapist). Select four or five questions from Figure 14.3 (Interest Questionnaire) or Figure 14.4 (Parent Interview). Modify the questions as appropriate for the person you will interview. Conduct the interview and summarize it in a three-minute oral report to the class.

14.2 Divide into small groups of two to four students. Select a type of community resource (e.g., health club, youth sport league, recreation program, club) to research. Each person in the group should find three community resources, programs, or businesses in the community where you plan to teach that provide opportunities for individuals with a disability to participate in physical activities. Communicate with other group members to avoid duplication.

Write each resource on paper or a card and photocopy them for other members of the class (see sample format in Figure 14.1). Share the resources with the class so that each class member has a file of community resources to begin their teaching experience.

REFERENCES

The American Dance Therapy Association Inc. (2005). 2000 Century Plaza, Ste. 108, Columbia, MD 21044. www.adta.org.

American Therapeutic Recreation Association (ATRA). (2005). 1414 Prince Street, Ste. 204, Alexandria, VA 22314. www.atra-tr.org.

The ARC of the United States. (2002). 1010 Wayne Ave. Ste. 650, Silver Springs, MD 20910. www.thearc.org.

Autism Society of America. 7910 Woodmont Ave. Ste. 300, Bethesda, MD 20814-3067. www.autism-society.org.

Davis, R. W., & Stanton, K. (1998). Public Law 195-17: New implications for regular physical education. *Teaching Elementary Physical Education, 9*(5), 5–8.

Easter Seals. (2005). 230 W. Monroe St. Ste. 1800, Chicago, IL 60606. www.easterseals.com.

Falvey, M. A. (1986). *Community based curriculum: Instructional strategies for students with severe handicaps.* Baltimore: Brookes.

Henry, D. (1998). *Tool chest: For teachers, parents and students handbook.* Youngtown, AZ: Henry Occupational Therapy Services.

Hill, G. M., & Cleven, B. (July/August 2005). Using student survey to help choose physical education activities. *Strategies, 18*(6), 6.

Individuals with Disabilities Education Act Amendments of 2004. United States Code (2004). Chapter 33, subchapter 1, section 1400 (d)(1)(A).

Individuals with Disabilities Education Act Amendments of 2004. United States Code 20, Chapter 33, subchapter II, Section 1414, (d)(1)(A)(vii)(I) and (II).

Learning Disabilities Association of America. (2005). 4351 Garden City Dr., Landover, MD 20785. www.ldanatl.org.

March of Dimes. (2005). 1275 Mamaroneck Ave., White Plains, NY 10605. www.marchofdimes.com.

Seaman, J. A., & DePauw, K. P. (1995). *Sensory–motor experiences for the home* (2nd ed.). Reston, VA: American Alliance for Health, Physical Education, Recreation, and Dance.

United Cerebral Palsy. (2005). 1660 L St. NW Ste. 700, Washington, DC 20036. www.ucp.org.

15

Lifelong Physical Activity and Sport

Guiding Questions

1. What is the importance of health promotion and the prevention of secondary conditions for individuals with a disability?

2. How can physical educators promote physically active lifestyles among individuals with a disability?

3. How has disability sport changed in the past 50 years?

4. What opportunities exist for individuals with a disability who wish to participate in sports at the local level, at the state level, and at the national level?

5. What international competition exists for the elite athlete with a disability?

Being physically active is important to all individuals, including individuals with a disability. As we have emphasized throughout this book, physical education should provide the foundation for active participation in physical activity throughout the life span. Numerous recreation, fitness, and sport opportunities for individuals with a disability exist "beyond the schoolyard fence" (see Chapter 14 for a discussion of available professional services and community resources). It is important that physical educators become knowledgeable about these opportunities so that they can encourage individuals with a disability to participate in community recreation programs, fitness programs, and sport competitions, including elite sport.

To complement the information presented in this chapter, physical educators should identify local and regional resources that provide community recreation, outdoor recreation, and fitness and sport programs accessible to individuals with a disability. The National Center on Physical Activity and Disability (NCPAD) provides searchable directories of organizations, programs, and facilities that provide opportunities for accessible physical activity; contact information for adaptive equipment vendors; and lists of books and videos (access NCPAD at www.ncpad.org).

In addition, students with majors in kinesiology or exercise science seeking jobs outside the public schools will find professional opportunities to work with individuals with a disability in fitness centers, recreation programs, rehabilitation centers, and sport settings. Thus, it is important that you become aware of programs for health promotion and fitness, as well as sport and recreational programs, through the levels of elite competition. For more detailed information about fitness and health promotion for individuals with a disability, see NCPAD (2001) and Rimmer, Braddock, and Pitetti (1996).

HEALTH PROMOTION AND FITNESS

The World Health Organization (WHO) has been very active in promoting health, well-being, and physical activity among all segments of the world's population. Specifically, WHO (1997) concluded that physical activity is an essential component of everyday life and seems to be the single most effective means whereby all individuals can influence their own health and functional ability. WHO (2001) has undertaken an initiative to develop a framework for describing the functional, health, and disability status of all people (International Classification of Functioning and Disability—ICIDM-2). The approach de-emphasizes the "disability" per se, focusing on the functional ability of all persons, and aligning with the disability rights movement (see Chapter 1 for further discussion).

Health promotion for individuals with a disability must remain a major focus. According to Rimmer (1999), preventing secondary health conditions by empowering individuals with a disability to take control of their own health is a cost-effective strategy. Health care professionals should join in this effort to enrich the lives of individuals with a disability. It could truly be an exciting era if rehabilitation professionals extend their services into community-based fitness centers and facilitate the promotion of good health practices for the more than 50 million Americans with disabilities.

One of the major themes underlying the independent living movement (disability rights) is the inclusion and participation in all aspects of society, including the right to maintain good health. Also influenced by the Americans with Disabilities Act (ADA), health promotion for individuals with a disability is now being addressed by several major agencies, including the Institute of Medicine, the Centers for Disease Control and Prevention, the National Center for Medical Rehabilitation Research, the National Institutes of Health, and the National Institute on Disability Research.

Further evidence of the trend toward health promotion comes from two U. S. Department of Health and Human Services reports entitled *Healthy People 2000* and *Healthy People 2010*. *Healthy People 2000* states that "a clear opportunity exists for health promotion and disease prevention efforts to improve the health prospects and functional independence of people with disabilities" (1991, p. 41).

As described by the President's Council on Physical Fitness and Sports (PCPFS, 2001), *Healthy People 2010* is a goal-oriented roadmap to society's health. An essential ingredient for the highest quality of life for everyone is an active lifestyle, and the goals are written to promote this lifestyle. According to Rimmer (2005), the definition of health promotion for individuals with a disability consists of four parts:

1. The promotion of healthy lifestyles and a healthy environment
2. The prevention of health complications (medical secondary conditions) and further disabling conditions
3. The preparation of the person with a disability to understand and monitor his or her own health and health care needs
4. The promotion of opportunities for participation in commonly held life activities.

(For more information, see *Healthy People 2010* at www.health.gov/healthypeople.) In sum, the focus of *Healthy People 2010* and the international classification initiative (ICIDM-2) is on functional ability, healthful lifestyles, and active living for all persons.

As a result of efforts such as those described above, the definition of health has changed. "When health is viewed not as the absence of disability or chronic conditions, but as the ability to function effectively in given environments, to fulfill needs, and to adapt to major stresses, then, by definition, most people with disabilities are healthy" (NCPAD, 2001). This perspective requires a shift from disability prevention to health promotion (Rimmer, 1999). This approach (health promotion and the prevention of secondary health conditions) is applicable not only to school-age individuals with a disability, but also to individuals with a disability as they age.

As the paradigm shifts from disease and disability prevention to the prevention of secondary conditions in individuals with a disability, many professionals can play an important role in the integration of health promotion into the fabric of a community. One such approach is the community-based health promotion model that identifies the future role for fitness centers (Rimmer, 1999). Included among the tasks of this model are the identification and elimination of barriers, the development of meaningful fitness programs, education about the role of nutrition in health promotion, and the adoption of behavior that fosters healthful living and active lifestyles.

As the continuum of rehabilitation moves further into the community, trained exercise specialists (e.g., physical therapists, exercise science majors) will have a growing number of opportunities to serve as consultants to local fitness centers. In addition, personnel is needed in the full range of public and private facilities, including senior centers, park districts, and local YMCAs. It is important to note here that the major components of a health-related fitness program for individuals with a disability are the same as for the general population: aerobic capacity, strength, body composition, and flexibility. What may vary, however, are the types of activities used to improve fitness and the intensity, frequency, and duration of the activities.

Despite an increased awareness of the benefits of physical activity and fitness, habitual physical activity remains a missing component in the lives of most people who have a physical or mental disability. Several reasons for the inactive lifestyle are often found among individuals with a disability, including:

- A lack of knowledge concerning the importance of exercise to healthy living
- Limited access to transportation to and from the exercise site
- Inaccessible facilities and equipment
- The perception by some that some individuals are not able to (or should not) exercise because they have a disability

Thus, physical educators play an important role in encouraging fitness and physical activity as a regular part of every student's life. Physical educators should encourage all students to become involved in community-based health and fitness programs, especially as students with a disability prepare for the transition beyond high school.

To reflect changing perspectives on disability and physical activity and health, it is important that general physical educators and adapted physical education specialists incorporate a philosophy and practice of physical education that emphasizes health promotion and the prevention of secondary health conditions when working with students with disabilities. This philosophy should reach programs that extend into the community and continue throughout the life span. With a shift from the medical or rehabilitation model to a model of interdependence (Condeluci, 1995), it follows that individuals with a disability will have more autonomy and independence. If this philosophy persists across all programs, individuals with a disability will assume more responsibility for themselves instead of relying on professionals to make decisions for them. It is incumbent upon physical educators, including exercise scientists and therapists, to provide these individuals with the necessary information and resources to make informed choices about living active, healthy lifestyles.

Inasmuch as physical activity and exercise are critical components of active living, sport and recreation are perhaps the most common avenues for pursuing active, healthy lifestyles. Although these have been more readily available to typically developing children, opportunities for individuals with a disability are increasing at a steady pace. Such oppor-

---

Teaching Tip

UPPER EXTREMITY ERGOMETER • An upper extremity ergometer can be used to test and improve aerobic capacity in a person with a lower extremity disability. For a person with limited upper body control, a recumbent bicycle, in place of a stand-up bicycle, can be used for testing and improving aerobic capacity.

tunities can be found in separate programs as well as inclusive sport programs for all individuals.

SPORT

Sport is a familiar and highly visible entity in today's society, with roots that extend back in history for thousands of years. As sport evolved across the centuries, not only did new forms of sport emerge, but the participants changed as well. Today, sport is a viable option for individuals with a disability—one that spans from recreational sport to elite competitive sport. It is important that physical educators understand the continuum of sport opportunities and encourage their students to consider active participation. Athletes who participate in the Paralympic Games, Special Olympics, and the Deaflympics serve today as successful examples for youth with a disability.

In addition to gaining knowledge of elite competitive disability sport, it is important for physical educators to become aware of the opportunities available to individuals with a disability and to help them get started by providing information to all students, especially those who show interest. Contact local schools and recreation departments for a list of local recreation and sport programs, especially those accessible to individuals with a disability. National disability sport organizations (DSOs) can provide informational brochures, newsletters, videos, and more. Many DSOs sponsor sport development programs for youth interested in sport and have a listing of programs on the local, state, and regional levels. Limited interscholastic and intercollegiate sport programs for athletes with a disability exist. Appendix F contains physical activity and disability sport resource information.

Sport equipment including specialized wheelchairs and sport prostheses are available to assist individuals with a disability in sport participation. For specific information about sport and sport equipment, please contact the disability sport associations identified in Appendix F.

Unified Sports

The Unified Sports program was developed by Special Olympics to provide a means whereby youth (8 years and older) and adults with an intellectual disability could train with and compete alongside individuals without intellectual disabilities (known as partners). A total of 26 sports are available year round, ranging from alpine skiing to volleyball. Unified Sports enables individuals to learn new sports, develop higher-level sport skills, participate in a meaningful inclusive environment, socialize with peers, and participate in community settings. These sport programs are often initiated by local parks and recreation departments, community sport organizations, and various local clubs. Physical educators could play an integral role in the development and implementation of the Unified Sports program. Although Unified Sports is a specific program of Special Olympics, the concept is one that could be modified to the particular needs and interests of all students.

> **EXTEND YOUR KNOWLEDGE**
>
> *"Athletics"*
>
> The term *athletics* is used in international sport arenas to refer to track and field competition.

Defining Disability Sport

The term **disability sport** is used to refer to *sport that has been designed for or is specifically practiced by athletes with a disability* (DePauw & Gavron, 2005). Disability sport encompasses sports initially designed for a specified disability group (e.g., goal ball for athletes with visual impairments, wheelchair basketball for those athletes with physical impairments who use a wheelchair, sitting volleyball for athletes with lower limb impairments). Disability sport also includes those sports practiced by individuals without a disability that have been modified or adapted to include athletes with a disability (e.g., wheelchair tennis, tandem cycling), as well as those that require little or no modification (e.g., athletics, wrestling, swimming). Thus, disability sport in its broadest context encompasses many sport opportunities and competitions for athletes with physical, sensory, and intellectual impairments.

The history of disability sport can be traced to the Sports Club for the Deaf founded in Berlin in 1888. Early in the 20th century, the first International Silent Games (for the Deaf) were held in France in 1924, and the British Society of One-Armed Golfers was founded in 1932. The aftermath of the World Wars brought the notion of the rehabilitation of disabled veterans to the forefront and laid the foundation for disability sport as we know it today (see DePauw & Gavron, 2005). Disability sport is now recognized by the International Olympic Committee, and regional, national, and international competitions are available to athletes with a disability. For the early history and significant milestones of disability sport, see Table 15.1.

TABLE 15.1 *Early chronology and significant milestones of disability sport.*

YEAR	EVENT
1888	First Sports Club for the Deaf founded in Berlin.
1924	1st International Games for the Deaf (also referred to as International Silent Games; now Deaflympics) held in Paris.
1932	British Society of One-Armed Golfers founded.
1935	First U.S. participation in 4th World Games for the Deaf.
1944	Sir Ludwig Guttmann establishes the Spinal Injuries Centre at the Stoke Mandeville Hospital in Aylesbury, England.
1945	American Athletic Association of the Deaf founded.
1946	First wheelchair basketball game in the United States played by war veterans at Veterans Administration Hospitals in the California and New England chapters of Paralyzed Veterans of America.
1948	1st Stoke Mandeville Games for the Paralyzed, Aylesbury, England. Karoly Takacs, competing on the Hungarian Olympic team at the Olympics in London, wins the gold medal in rapid-fire pistol event, using his left hand after loss of his right hand. The Flying Wheels of California win the 1st National Paralyzed Veterans of America Wheelchair Basketball Championships.
1949	1st Annual Wheelchair Basketball Tournament, University of Illinois (U.S.). 6th International Games for the Deaf (Deaflympics), Copenhagen. 1st World Winter Games for the Deaf (Seefeld, Austria). National Wheelchair Basketball Association founded.
1952	Liz Hartel (postpolio) wins silver medal in dressage at Summer Olympics, representing Denmark. First international wheelchair athlete tournament (became identified as the International Stoke Mandeville Games).
1955	CISS officially recognized by the IOC in June.
1956	First athletic scholarships in the United States for athletes with a disability (blind wrestlers). National Wheelchair Athletic Association founded (later to become Wheelchair Sports, USA).
1957	1st U.S. National Wheelchair Games, Adelphi College, New York.
1960	9th Annual International Stoke Mandeville Games (would become known as the 1st Paralympic Games; also referred to as 1st International Games for Disabled) in Rome. United States sends a team to participate in these games for the first time. International Stoke Mandeville Wheelchair Sports Federation founded.
1964	International Sports Organization for the Disabled founded.
1967	1st Pan American Games for spinal cord–injured athletes. National Handicapped Sports and Recreation Association formed to govern U.S. winter sports for athletes with disabilities.
1968	International Special Olympics founded by Eunice Kennedy Shriver; first competition held in Soldier Field, Chicago (1st Special Olympics World Summer Games). International Cerebral Palsy Society founded; sponsors the first international games for individuals with cerebral palsy in France.
1969	North American Riding for the Handicapped Association formed in Virginia.
1972	4th International Games for the Disabled (4th Paralympic Games) held in Heidelberg; first quadriplegic competition added.
1974	1st National Wheelchair Marathon, Ohio. U.S. women's basketball team competes against another U.S. team for the first time.
1975	First women's National Wheelchair Basketball Tournament. 1st Gold Cup Tournament/World Championship (wheelchair basketball), Bruges, Belgium. Bob Hall, first wheelchair entrant in Boston Marathon, finishes in 2:58. 4th Special Olympics World Summer Games held in Mt. Pleasant, Michigan; Games broadcast nationwide on CBS-TV's *Sports Spectacular*. *Sports 'n Spokes* magazine founded.
1976	The Olympiad for the Physically Disabled (5th Paralympic Games in Toronto) includes blind and amputee athletes.

(continued)

TABLE 15.1 Continued.

YEAR	EVENT
	1st International Winter Games for the Disabled (1st Winter Paralympic Games), Omskoldsvik, Sweden.
	United States Association of Blind Athletes (USABA) formed.
	UNESCO conference establishes right of individuals with a disability to participate in physical education and sport.
	National Foundation of Wheelchair Tennis founded.
1977	First female wheelchair entrant to the women's division of Boston Marathon (3:48).
	First national championships of USABA, Macomb, Illinois.
	University of Illinois hosts the 1st Intercollegiate Wheelchair Basketball Tournament.
	1st Special Olympics World Winter Games in Steamboat Springs, Colorado. CBS, ABC, and NBC cover the Games.
1978	PL 95-606, the Amateur Sports Act of 1978, passed by Congress.
	National Association of Sports for Cerebral Palsy (NASCP) founded, now known as U.S. Cerebral Palsy Athletic Association.
	Cerebral Palsy–International Sports and Recreation Association organized.
1979	United States Olympic Committee (USOC) Handicapped in Sports Committee (later to be known as the Committee on Sports for the Disabled) formed, chaired by Kathryn Sallade (representing the American Athletic Association of the Deaf).
1980	Olympics for Disabled (6th Paralympic Games), Arnhem, The Netherlands. Cerebral palsy athletes (ambulatory) included for the first time.
	Sit-skiing introduced at Winter Skiing Championships in Winter Park, Colorado.
	Curt Brinkman finishes Boston Marathon in under 2 hours using a wheelchair.
1981	First annual World Wheelchair Marathon Championships held with Orange Bowl Marathon.
	International Blind Sports Association formed in Paris.
	United States Amputee Athletic Association founded; first annual national games held in Nashville.

YEAR	EVENT
	First wheelchair athletes, George Murray and Phil Carpenter, cross the United States.
	United Nations International Year for Disabled Persons.
	USOC and IOC issue formal statement rejecting use of term "Olympics" for competitions involving disabled athletes except for Special Olympics.
1982	Blind women compete for the first time in the World Goal Ball Championships at Butler University, Indianapolis, Indiana.
	Karen Farmer, a single-leg amputee, attends college on athletic scholarship for women's track at Eastern Washington University.
	Linda Downs, Class 5 cerebral palsy athlete, finishes the New York Marathon (11:15).
	International Coordinating Committee of the World Sports Organizations formed in Leysin, Switzerland.
1983	Six wheelchair racers finish a mile in less than 4 minutes.
	Seven wheelchair racers finish Boston Marathon in less than 2 hours.
	1st International Women's Wheelchair Tournament, France.
1984	Neroli Fairhall (New Zealand) is first wheelchair athlete to meet eligibility and compete in Olympics in women's archery.
	First wheelchair races as demonstration events for 1984 Olympics (1,500 meter won by Paul Van Winkle of Belgium in 3:58.50; 800 meter won by Sharon Rahn Hedrick in 2:15.50).
	First disabled skiing events included within the program of the 1984 Olympics in Sarajevo.
	One venue of the International Games for the Disabled (7th Paralympic Games) held for the first time in United States (Hofstra University, Hempstead, New York). The second venue is held at the International Stoke Mandeville Games in Stoke Mandeville, England. Wheelchair marathon takes place for the first time.
	George Murray (wheelchair marathoner) pictured on Wheaties cereal box.

(continued)

TABLE 15.1 *Continued.*

YEAR	EVENT
	First full-length article in commercial magazine, *Runner's World,* about female athlete with a disability: Linda Downs for the 1982 New York Marathon.
	The term "Paralympic Games" approved by the IOC.
	Palaestra, forum for sport, physical education, and recreation for those with disabilities, founded.
1985	15th World Games for the Deaf held in United States (Los Angeles) for the first time.
	U.S. Olympics Sports Festival includes athletes with a disability for the first time: 16 females and 26 males.
	National Cerebral Palsy/Les Autres Games includes dwarf athletes and physically disabled athletes with conditions other than cerebral palsy.
	Dwarf Athletic Association of America formed to organize sport for dwarf athletes.
	3rd Special Olympics World Winter Games, Park City, Utah.
	USOC Committee on Sports for the Disabled (COSD) establishes a special research committee.
1986	Prize money for competitors in the push rim wheelchair division introduced at the Boston Marathon.
	The International Sports Federation for Persons with Mental Handicap formed in Spain.
	The NASCP reorganized as the United States Cerebral Palsy Athletic Association.
	United States Les Autres Sports Association formed.
1987	Rick Hansen finishes his two-year Man in Motion World Tour. Hansen wheeled 24,901.55 miles across 34 countries and raised $26.1 million for research.
	Arnhem Seminar, held March 14 in Arnhem, The Netherlands, to discuss the creation of a new structure for international disability sport (later to be named the International Paralympic Committee).
	Candace Cable wins the Boston Marathon for the fifth time; Andre Viger wins for the third time; John Brewer wins the quad division for the seventh time.
1988	Winter Olympics in Calgary includes demonstration events (three-track alpine, blind Nordic) for males and females.

YEAR	EVENT
	Summer Olympics (South Korea) includes wheelchair races as demonstration events (1,500 meter for males; 800 meter for females). Sharon Hedrick wins second gold medal in Olympic wheelchair 800 meter (2:11).
	Successful 8th Summer Paralympic Games held in Seoul; staged similarly to Olympics. Olympic Organizing Committee assists Paralympic Organizing Committee.
	The IOC officially recognizes Special Olympics and agrees to cooperate with Special Olympics as a representative of the interests of athletes with mental retardation.
1989	Seven females and seven males named the first U.S. Disabled Athletes of the Year.
	International Paralympic Committee formed in Dusseldorf, Germany.
	Robert D. Steward elected to serve as the first president of the IPC.
1990	Shirley Platt becomes the first female (Deaf) executive secretary of American Athletic Association of the Deaf (AAAD, now known as the USA Deaf Sports Federation).
	Dr. Donalda Ammons appointed the first Deaf female director of the World Games for the Deaf U.S. team.
	Diana Golden, three-track skier, signs sponsorship agreement with Subaru and also becomes spokesperson for ChapStick Challenge for Disabled Skiers.
1991	Jean Driscoll becomes the first athlete with a disability to be named the Sudafed Female Athlete of the Year.
	Sue Moucha is the first athlete with a disability to attend the International Olympic Academy.
	Jan Wilson named the first coordinator, Disabled Sport Programs, USOC.
	Active Living magazine founded in Canada.
1992	9th Summer Paralympic Games held in Barcelona; IOC President Samaranch attends and endorses the Games, establishing the connection between the Olympic and Paralympic Games for the future.
	U.S. men's wheelchair basketball team stripped of its gold medal due to positive drug test.

(continued)

TABLE 15.1 Continued.

YEAR	EVENT
	1st Paralympics for Persons with Mental Handicaps held in Madrid.
	5th Winter Paralympic Games held in Tignes-Albertville, France, immediately following the Winter Olympic Games.
	Connie Hansen and Candace Cable become the only two women to compete in all Summer Olympic exhibition events to date.
	Tanni Grey (Great Britain) named the Sunday Times Sportswoman of the Year by Her Majesty The Queen.
	Tricia Zorn (USA) wins 12 medals (10 gold, 2 silver) at the Summer Paralympic Games in Barcelona (also had won 12 in 1988 Paralympics in Seoul).
1993	The COSD reorganized, with USOC allowing for greater participation of athletes with a disability in governance of disability sport.
	IPC establishes the Sport Science Committee.
1994	Brighton Declaration on Women and Sport calls for equity and equality in society and sport including women with disabilities.
	Monique Kalkman (The Netherlands) earns the title of Amsterdam's Sportswoman of the Year.
	Mark E. Shepherd, Sr., becomes the second coordinator, USOC Disabled Sport Services.
1995	The USOC officially designated at the U.S. National Paralympic Committee.
1996	The IPC officially hosts the 10th Summer Paralympic Games in Atlanta and assumes responsibility for the Games in the future. First Paralympics to attract worldwide sponsors.
	Jean Driscoll (USA) becomes the first person to win the Boston Marathon for the seventh time (all divisions).
1998	1st World Blind Sports Championships held in July in Madrid.
1999	Official opening of the IPC headquarters in Bonn, held September 3. IOC President Samaranch attends.
	USOC forms the Paralympic Athletes Council and the Paralympic Sport Organizations.
2000	Cooperation agreement signed by IOC President Samaranch and IPC President Steadward in Sydney.
	11th Summer Paralympic Games, Sydney.
	Marla Runyan (legally blind) competes in the Paralympics and the Olympics in Sydney.
	The COSD is reorganized again, allowing for the formation of the U.S. Paralympic Corporation as the representative body for athletes with a disability in the United States.
	Jean Driscoll wins a record-breaking eighth Boston Marathon.
2001	Phil Craven elected as the second president of the IPC, the first athlete with a disability to serve in this capacity.
	Laureus World Sports Awards includes Sportsperson with a Disability award to Vinny Lauwers, an Australian paraplegic yachtsman.
	The International Sports Federation for Athletes with Intellectual Disability suspended from membership in the IPC after an IPC investigation commission finds that the process of assessment and certification of athletes with an intellectual disability for the Sydney 2000 Paralympic Games had not been properly carried out (athletes without an intellectual disability competed and received medals in events for athletes with intellectual disability).
2002	8th Winter Paralympic Games, Salt Lake City, Utah.
	Commonwealth Games in Manchester includes official disability sport events (160 athletes from 20 countries and five sports).
2003	IPC President Phil Craven elected as a new IOC member (#123) at the 115th session of the IOC in Prague.
	The IPC signs the World Anti-Doping Code and revises the IPC Anti-Doping Code to comply with the World Anti-Doping Code and WADA's standards.
	15th Deaflympics, Sundsvall, Sweden.
	11th Special Olympics World Summer Games, Dublin (first time the Games are held outside the United States).
	European Commission designates 2003 the European Year of People with Disabilities; IPC introduces International Paralympic Day 2003.
	International Association of Athletics Federation (IAAF) 2003 Athletics World Championships includes IPC exhibition events.

(continued)

TABLE 15.1 Continued.

YEAR	EVENT	YEAR	EVENT
	Marla Runyan finishes fifth among sighted runners in the Boston Marathon.	2006	9th Winter Paralympic Games, Torino, Italy.
	Jean Driscoll serves as commentator for the official coverage of the Boston Marathon.	2007	16th Winter Deaflympics scheduled for Park City, Utah.
2004	12th Summer Paralympic Games, Athens.		12th Special Olympics World Summer Games scheduled for People's Republic of China.
	Randy Snow, wheelchair tennis player, inducted into the U.S. Olympic Hall of Fame; first Paralympian to be honored. Paralympian category to continue as a permanent class of the Hall of Fame.	2008	Summer Paralympic Games scheduled for Beijing.
		2009	21st Summer Deaflympics scheduled for Taipei, Taiwan.
	U.S. women's goal ball team becomes the first disability sport team to move into the Olympic Training Center resident program.	2010	Winter Paralympic Games scheduled for Burnaby and Vancouver, Canada.
2005	20th Deaflympics, Melbourne.		
	8th Special Olympics World Winter Games, Nagano, Japan (first time for the Games to be hosted in Asia).		

Source: Adapted, by permission, from K. P. DePauw & S. J. Gavron (2005). *Disability Sport.* (Champaign, IL: Human Kinetics), 277–287.

Deaf Sport

Deaf Sport is *"a social institution within which people who are deaf exercise their right to self-determination through organization, competition, and socialization surrounding Deaf Sport activities"* (Stewart, 1991, p. 2). On one level, Deaf Sport can be defined as sport in which athletes who are deaf compete, a parallel entity to able-bodied (hearing) sport in which individuals with hearing impairments participate. On another level, Deaf Sport should be viewed from a cultural perspective. Not only is Deaf Sport a celebration of community among Deaf people, but it is a microcosm of the Deaf community (Stewart, 1991).

DISABILITY SPORT

Disability Sport in the United States

A significant event in the history of the U.S. disability sport movement was the passage of the Amateur Sports Act of 1978. The enactment of this Act (now known as the Ted Stevens Olympic and Amateur Sports Act of 2000) led to the inclusion of the following purpose in the constitution of the United States Olympic Committee (USOC):

> To encourage and provide assistance to amateur athletic programs and competition for amateur athletes with disabilities including, where feasible, the expansion of opportunities for meaningful participation by such amateur athletes in programs of athletic competition for able-bodied amateur athletes. (www.olympic-usa.org/ASA2000.pdf)

To achieve this objective, a category of membership for disability sport organizations and a Committee on Sports for the Disabled (COSD) were developed. The COSD served a coordinating role for disability sport within the USOC until the development of the U.S. Paralympic Corporation assumed that role in 2001.

The disability sport groups have continued to evolve over time—many have changed names, and some have dissolved or combined functions. In addition to the disability sport associations, selected sport organizations have incorporated athletes with

> **EXTEND YOUR KNOWLEDGE**
>
> *"Deaf Sport"*
>
> When capitalized, Deaf Sport refers to sport as a specific cultural event in which athletes with hearing impairments participate. When capitalized, Deaf refers to the community of individuals with hearing impairments who choose to adopt a cultural identity as Deaf.

a disability within their association. Many of these sport associations serving individuals with a disability are listed in Appendix F. The major disability sport associations are listed below:

- Disabled Sports USA (DS/USA)
- National Disability Sports Alliance (NDSA, formerly the United States Cerebral Palsy Athletic Association, Inc.)
- National Wheelchair Basketball Association (NWBA)
- Special Olympics International (SOI)
- USA Deaf Sports Federation (formerly American Athletic Association for the Deaf)
- United States Association of Blind Athletes (USABA)
- United States Paralympic Corporation (USPC, formerly known as USOC Committee on Sports for the Disabled)
- Wheelchair Sports, USA (WSUSA)

International Paralympic Committee

The International Paralympic Committee, formed in 1989, is the umbrella multi-disability organization for elite sport for athletes with a disability. As such, the primary responsibility of the IPC is to organize, supervise, and coordinate the Paralympic Games—an international elite competition for athletes with physical and visual impairments—and other multi-disability competitions on the elite sport level. The IPC is an international nonprofit organization currently run by more than 160 National Paralympic Committees and five disability-specific international sport federations. The specific purposes of the IPC include the following (adapted from the IPC Web page, www.paralympic.org):

- Organize Paralympic and Multi-Disability World Games and World Championships.
- Serve as liaison with the International Olympic Committee (IOC) and all other relevant international sports bodies.
- Seek integration of sports for athletes with a disability into the international sports movement while always safeguarding its own identity.
- Supervise and coordinate the conduct of the Paralympics and other Multi-Disability World and Regional games.
- Coordinate the calendar of international and regional competitions with the guarantee to respect the sport technical needs of the individual disability groups.
- Assist and encourage educational programs, research, and promotional activities.
- Promote, without discrimination for political, religious, economic, sex, or racial reasons, the practice of sport for individuals with a disability.
- Expand the opportunities for individuals with a disability to participate.

Throughout its history, the Paralympics have been connected to the Olympic Games and the IOC. Initially, an attempt was made to hold the Paralympic Games in the same country (and city if possible) and year of the Olympic Games (e.g., Rome, 1960; Tokyo, 1964; Germany, 1972; Canada, 1976). The Olympic flag first flew over the International Games for the Disabled held in New York in 1984. Although this arrangement was somewhat informal, the connection of the Olympic Games and the Paralympic Games became more apparent four years later at the 1988 Summer Paralympic Games in South Korea. These Games utilized the same facilities, housing, competition sites, media relations, and support facilities as the 1988 Olympic Games. The opening and closing ceremonies were identical. Since 1988, the Summer and Winter Paralympic Games were formally scheduled to be held in the same city, following shortly after the Olympic Games and using the same facilities (Barcelona, Spain, 1992; Lillehammer, Norway, 1994; Atlanta, USA, 1996; Nagano, Japan, 1998; Sydney, Australia, 2000; Salt Lake City, USA, 2002). This practice will continue given the fact that the bidding process for hosting the 2008 Olympic Games includes a formal bid for hosting and organizing the Paralympic Games.

The formal relations between the IPC and IOC gained strength in 2000. At the Paralympic Games in Sydney, an agreement between the IOC and IPC was signed by IOC President S. E. M. Juan Antonio Samaranch and IPC President Dr. Robert D. Steadward. The cooperative agreement indicates that the two organizations "share the common belief in the right of all human beings to pursue their physical and intellectual development" (*Paralympian*, 2000, p. 3). Further, the agreement covers specific areas of cooperation, including representation of the IPC on such IOC commissions as Evaluation for the Olympic Games, Coordination for the Olympic Games, Culture and Olympic Education, Athletes, and Women and Sport Working Groups. According to this agreement, the IPC president will become a member of the IOC. Through this agreement, the IOC has demonstrated its support and provided financial assistance for the Paralympic movement.

International Competitions

Sport opportunites for individuals with a disability are plentiful today, including recreational sport programs and activities organized through local recreation centers, youth sport programs, and even interscholastic and intercollegiate programs (including athletic scholarships). Although numerous national and international events and activities are available, only the three major international competitions are presented in this section. Please note that athletes with a physical or visual disability can participate in multi-sport and multi-disability international competitions and other Olympic-type international competitions. Examples include International Wheelchair Basketball tournaments, World Goal Ball championships, World Cup Alpine Disabled Skiing championships, and European Championships for Athletics and for Swimming. These types of competitions and events are also available to athletes competing through Special Olympics and Deaflympics.

Deaflympics

As specified in its constitution, the CISS has the sole responsibility for sports for the Deaf throughout the world. In exercising this responsibility, the CISS sponsors the Deaflympics (formerly known as the World Games for the Deaf). The **Deaflympics** is *a quadrennial event for athletes who are Deaf that includes both summer and winter components* (Stewart & Ammons, 2001). The sports included in the summer games are athletics (track and field), badminton, basketball, cycling, marathon, shooting, soccer, swimming, table tennis, team handball, tennis, volleyball, and water polo. The sports on the winter games program include Nordic skiing, speed skating, alpine skiing, and hockey. These games are not to be conducted during the Olympic year and usually occur the year following the Olympic Games. Deaflympics have been held since 1924 (see www.deaflympics.org).

The Paralympics

The British government opened the Spinal Injuries Center at Stoke Mandeville Hospital in Aylesbury, England, in 1944 and appointed Sir Ludwig Guttman as the center's first director. Guttman's introduction of competitive sports as an integral part of the rehabilitation of veterans with spinal cord injuries led naturally to the founding of the first Stoke Mandeville Games for the Paralyzed in 1948 (Guttman, 1976). These games are considered the forerunner of the Paralympic Games. Fourteen British veterans (including two women) competed in archery at these games (Scruton, 1998).

The competitive events of these Games expanded from one sport (archery) to six sports (archery, netball, dartchery, javelin, snooker, and table tennis) in three years (Scruton, 1998). In 1952, the first international competition for wheelchair athletes was held at Stoke Mandeville with competition between a British team and a team from the Netherlands—they competed in lawn bowling, table tennis, shot put, javelin, and club throw. By 1960, wheelchair basketball, fencing, snooker, swimming, and weight lifting were officially added to the sport program offered under the auspices of the newly formed International Stoke Mandeville Games Federation (ISMGF). The ISMGF, whose purpose was to sanction all international competitions for individuals with a spinal cord injury, provided the foundation for the Paralympic Games and the organizations for disability sport, including the International Paralympic Committee (IPC).

The term *Paralympics* comes from the Latin word "para" meaning "next to" or "with" and the name Olympics. Summer and Winter Paralympic Games are held every four years and currently are held in the same host country as the Olympics. The Games offer many of the same sports found on the program of the Olympic Games. Internationally, the term Paralympic has been used to identify the Games since the 1964 Paralympic Games in Tokyo, Japan.

Special Olympics

In 1968, Eunice Kennedy Shriver founded Special Olympics and hosted the first International Special Olympic Games at Soldier Field, Chicago. Special Olympics was created through the Joseph P. Kennedy, Jr. Foundation for the benefit of individuals with mental retardation. The mission of Special Olympics is to provide year-round "Olympic-type" sports training and competition for children and adults with intellectual impairment in the United States and around the world. The list of official sports, as well as demonstration sports, are found on the website of Special Olympics (www.specialolympics.org/sports). International competitions are held every two years, alternating between the Winter and Summer Games.

SUMMARY

Lifelong physical activity is important to all individuals, including those with a disability. Although physical educators have the primary responsibility to provide quality physical education for individuals with a disability, it is also important that they provide a foundation for individuals to seek physical activity in community settings and with family. Health promotion and the prevention of secondary health conditions are critical to lifelong physical activity. Fitness programs and sport opportunities are becoming increasingly viable options for individuals with a disability.

CHAPTER 15 Learning Activities

15.1 Visit the website of the International Paralympic Committee and find the calendar of events. Identify the number and type of competitions. Identify the variety of sports offered to individuals with a disability. Look for records of athletic achievement among athletes with a disability. Also view the websites for Deaflympics and the Special Olympics.

15.2 Identify local recreation centers, health and wellness programs, fitness centers, and sport centers in your community. Visit or contact these. Inquire about the recreation and sport opportunities available for individuals with a disability. Identify specific physical activity and fitness programs accessible to individuals with a disability. See Chapter 12 for community strategies. Share this information with your classmates.

15.3 Interview individuals with a disability about the barriers to achieving physically active lifestyles. Consider ways in which these barriers can be eliminated. Discuss how you will assist individuals with a disability to achieve their goal of lifelong physical activity. Review Chapter 9 for barriers to inclusion.

15.4 Access the website of the National Center on Physical Activity and Disability at www.ncpad.org. Review the resources on physical activity for individuals with a disability available in your geographic area. Make a list of the information available through this site.

REFERENCES

Active Living Alliance for Canadians with a Disability. (1994). *Moving to inclusion*. Ottawa, Canada: Author.

American College of Sports Medicine. (1997). *ACSM's exercise management for persons with chronic diseases and disabilities*. Champaign, IL: Human Kinetics.

Condeluci, A. (1995). *Interdependence: The route to community*. Winter Park, FL: GR Press.

Deaflympics. (2005). www.deaflympics.com.

DePauw, K. P. (2000). Women with disabilities. In B. Drinkwater (Ed.), *Encyclopedia of sports medicine: Women in sport* (Vol. 8, pp. 301–310). London: Blackwell Science Ltd.

DePauw, K. P. (2001). Disability sport. In K. Christensen, A. Guttmann, & G. Pfister (Eds.), *International encyclopedia of women and sport* (Vol. 1, pp. 326–330). Great Barrington, MA: Berkshire Reference Works.

DePauw, K. P., & Gavron, S. J. (2005). *Disability sport*. Champaign, IL: Human Kinetics.

Disability Today Publishing Group. (1997). *The triumph of the human spirit: The Atlanta Paralympic experience*. Ontario, Canada: Author.

Doll-Tepper, G., Kroner, M., & Sonnenschein, W. (Eds.). (2001). *New horizons in sport for athletes with a disability* (Vols. 1 & 2). Cologne, Germany: Meyer & Meyer Verlag.

Durstine, L. (1997). *ACSM's exercise management for persons with chronic diseases and disabilities*. Champaign, IL: Human Kinetics.

Guttman, L. (1976). *Textbook of sport for the disabled*. Oxford, England: H. M. & M. Publishers.

International Paralympic Committee. Purposes of the IPC. Retrieved May 23, 2002, from www.paralympic.org.

Krotoski, D. M., Nosek, M., & Turk, M. (Eds.). (1996). *Women with physical disabilities: Achieving and maintaining health and well-being*. Baltimore: Brooks.

Lockette, K. F., & Keys, A. M. (1994). *Conditioning with physical disabilities*. Champaign, IL: Human Kinetics.

Miller, P. (1995). *Fitness programming and physical disability*. Champaign, IL: Human Kinetics.

National Center on Physical Activity and Disability. (2001). Available at www.ncpad.org.

Paralympian. (2000). IOC-IPC cooperation agreement. Retrieved May 23, 2002, from www.paralympic.org/paralympian/20004/2000405.htm.

Patrick, D. L. (1997). Rethinking prevention for people with disabilities, part I: A conceptual model for promoting health. *American Journal of Health Promotion, 11,* 257-260.

Pitetti, K. H. (1993). Exercise capacities and adaptations of people with chronic disabilities: Current research, future directions, and widespread applicability. *Medicine & Science in Sports & Exercise, 25*(4), 421-422.

Pitetti, K. H., Rimmer, J. H., & Fernhall, B. (1993). Physical fitness and adults with mental retardation: An overview of current research and future directions. *Sports Medicine, 16*(1), 23-56.

President's Council on Physical Fitness and Sports. (2001). *Research Digest, 3*(9). Washington, DC: U. S. Government Printing Office.

Renwick, R., & Friefield, S. (1996). Quality of life and rehabilitation. In R. Renwick, I. Brown, and M. Nagler (Eds.), *Quality of life in health promotion and rehabilitation*. Newbury Park, CA: Sage.

Rimmer, J. H. (1994). *Fitness and rehabilitation programs for special populations*. Dubuque, IA: Brown.

Rimmer, J. H. (1999). Health promotion for people with disabilities: The emerging paradigm shift from disability prevention to prevention of secondary conditions. *Physical Therapy, 79,* 495-502.

Rimmer, J. H. (2005). *Health promotion: Health promotion for people with disabilities: The emerging paradigm shift from disability prevention to prevention of secondary conditions*. Available through National Center on Physical Activity and Disability at www.ncpad.org/wellness/fact_sheet

Rimmer, J. H., Braddock, D., & Pitetti, K. H. (1996). Research on physical activity and disability: An emerging national priority. *Medicine & Science in Sports & Exercise, 28,* 1366-1372.

Scruton, S. (1998). *Stoke Mandeville: Road to the Paralympics*. Aylesbury, England: The Peterhouse Press.

Seaman, J. A. (1999). Physical activity and fitness for persons with disabilities. *President's Council on Physical Fitness and Sports Research Digest, 3*(9).

Shephard, R. (1990). *Fitness in special populations*. Champaign, IL: Human Kinetics.

Smith, R. (1996). Fitness centers that offer therapy. *Rehabilitation Management, 4,* 79-82.

Special Olympics. (2005). www.specialolympics.org.

Special Olympics Unified Sports. (2005). www.specialolympics.org.

Stewart, D. A. (1991). *Deaf sport*. Washington, DC: Gallaudet University Press.

Stewart, D. A., & Ammons, D. (2001). Future directions of the Deaflympics. *Palaestra, 3,* 45-49.

U. S. Department of Health and Human Services. (1991). *Healthy people 2000: National health promotion and disease prevention objectives*. Washington, DC: U. S. Government Printing Office.

U. S. Department of Health and Human Services. (2002). *Healthy people 2010: Understanding and improving health* (2nd ed.). Washington, DC: U.S. Government Printing Office. Retrieved May 23, 2002, from www.health.gov/healthypeople.

U. S. Olympic Committee Constitution. (2001). Retrieved May 23, 2002, from www.olympic-usa.org.

World Health Organization. (1997). The Heidelberg guidelines for promoting physical activity among older persons. *Journal of Aging and Physical Activity, 5,* 2-8.

World Health Organization. (2001). International classification of functioning and disability—ICIDM-2. Available at www.who.int.

APPENDIX A
Adapted Physical Education National Standards

Adapted Physical Education National Standards (APENS) (Kelly, 2006) is the result of a project funded by the United States Department of Education, Office of Special Education and Rehabilitation Services, Division of Personnel Preparation (#H029K20092). Its development spanned approximately three years and involved 500 adapted physical educators nationwide. The report's scope encompasses 15 broad standards that are based on the roles, responsibilities, and perceived professional needs of practicing adapted physical educators. Each standard is divided into five levels that were subjected to rigorous review by several committees and exhaustive statistical treatment.

The regulations governing implementation of the 2004 amendments to IDEA made significant changes in the definition of who is qualified to deliver educational services to students with a disability. The regulations still identify physical education as special education (Sec. 300.38) and acknowledge the certification of teachers as a "states right," by stating:

> as applied to an elementary school teacher . . . [and for teachers teaching above the elementary level—teachers must] . . . have subject matter knowledge appropriate to the level of instruction being provided, as determined by the State, needed to effectively teach to those standards. (Federal Register: June 21, 2005 [Volume 70, Number 118], p. 35841)

The major change in the regulations is inherent in the law's definition of a special education teacher, identifying qualifications of those professionals separately from professionals within special education who provide specifically defined instruction such as physical education, speech-language pathology, travel training, and vocational education. The new terminology used in IDEA '04 is "highly qualified," and Sec. 300.18 of the regulations define it as follows:

> (i) The teacher has obtained full State certification as a special education teacher (including certification obtained through alternative routes to certification), or passed the State special education teacher licensing examination, and holds a license to teach in the State as a special education teacher, except that when used with respect to any teacher teaching in a public charter school, highly qualified means that the teacher meets the requirements set forth in the State's public charter school law." (Federal Register: June 21, 2005 [Volume 70, Number 118], p. 35838)

These criteria apply to every professional providing instruction, whether it is in the classroom, in the home, in hospitals and institutions, or in other settings, except charter schools, as stated above. Given the changes in federal law in this most recent set of amendments, it seems even more imperative that the APENS be accepted in each state as providing the standards to define a "highly qualified" physical educator. Only 16 states have a teacher certification or endorsement in adapted physical education, so these national standards would provide consistency across the nation in identifying those physical educators most qualified to work with students with a disability.

The APENS project's goals were to:

1. Develop national standards for the field of adapted physical education.
2. Develop a national certification examination that measures an applicant's knowledge of the standards and mastery of that knowledge in order to grant a national certification in adapted physical education (CAPE).

The goal was, and still is, to provide standards that would serve as a guide for curriculum content development to train adapted physical education specialists. Further, it was hoped that the states would either adopt the standards as a framework for state-authorized licensure or certification or accept the national certification in lieu of state licensure to identify adapted physical education specialists "qualified" to provide services to students with a disability.

Based on known factors, the standards were developed to include both the prerequisite content a general physical educator should know and the content an adapted specialist should know. Thus, the standards outline the competencies to be demonstrated by physical educators who teach students with a disability in general physical education (GPE) classes. The content of each standard area is divided

TABLE A.1 — The five competency levels.

Level 1 Standard number and name (e.g., 2. Motor Behavior).

Level 2 Major components of the standard (e.g., 2.02 Understand Motor Learning).

Level 3 Subcomponents—dependent pieces of knowledge of fact or principle related to the major component that *all general physical educators* are expected to know (e.g., 2.02.07 Understand how to organize and schedule practice with emphasis on instructional efficiency).

Level 4 Adapted physical education content—additional knowledge regarding the subcomponents that teachers working with individuals with a disability must know (e.g., 2.02.07.01 Understand how task variation complements skill acquisition in individuals with disabilities).

Level 5 Application of adapted physical education content knowledge from Level 4 to teaching individuals with a disability (e.g., 2.02.07.01.01 Vary practice schedules along dimensions such as distance, speed, and time).

Adapted from: Kelly, L. E. (Ed.). (2006). *Adapted Physical Education National Standards*, 2nd ed. Champaign, IL: Human Kinetics.

TABLE A.2 — Standard element form.

Standard 9	**Instructional Design and Planning**
9.01	Understand the factors needed to develop a systematic overall curriculum plan of instruction
9.01.03	Determine scope (goals and objectives) and sequence (when they will be taught) of the curriculum based on long-term goals, which will serve as the basis for the IEP and IFSP
9.01.03.01	Understand the concept of *"top-down planning"* to establish long-term goals for individuals with disabilities
9.01.03.01.01	Select goals based on projected employment
9.01.03.01.02	Select goals based on living situation
9.01.03.01.03	Select goals based on leisure preferences
9.01.03.01.04	Select goals based on skill potential
9.01.03.01.05	Select goals based on access to facilities and equipment

---

into five competency levels. Table A.1 describes the levels and their requirements. Table A.2 lists the components of a standard element form.

Although it is neither feasible nor appropriate to reproduce the national standards here, we list the content outline of each of the 15 standards here for your information. For students planning to become adapted physical education specialists, it would be useful to obtain both the standards and the study guide, either to study for the certification exam or to ensure that all areas of competence reflected in the standards are being covered by your state's certification process. For students who are planning to be general physical educators, it is important to know Levels 1 through 3 of these standards in order to competently address the needs of students with a disability included in your classes. For university faculty who teach one or more adapted physical education courses, it is recommended that the course content be compared with Levels 1 through 3 for that content needed by generalists in physical education and that Levels 4 through 5 be covered in more advanced courses.

ADAPTED PHYSICAL EDUCATION NATIONAL STANDARDS

elow is a brief description of the content of each of the 15 standards.

Standard 1: Human Development

The foundation of proposed goals and activities for individuals with a disability is a basic understanding of human development and its applications to those with various needs. For the adapted physical education teacher, this implies familiarity with theories and practices related to human development. This standard focuses on knowledge and skills helpful in providing quality APE programs.

Standard 2: Motor Behavior

Teaching individuals with a disability requires some knowledge of how individuals develop. In the case of APE teachers, it means having knowledge of typical physical and motor development as well as understanding the influence of developmental delays and other variants of development on the process of becoming a moving organism. It also means understanding how individuals learn motor skills and applying principles of motor learning during the planning and teaching of physical education to students with a disability.

Standard 3: Exercise Science

Physical educators must understand that modifications to the scientific principles of exercise and the application of these principles may be necessary when teaching individuals with a disability, to ensure that all children with a disability enjoy similar benefits of exercise. While there is a wealth of information in the foundational sciences, the focus of this standard is on the principles that address the physiological and biomechanical applications encountered when working with diverse populations.

Standard 4: Measurement and Evaluation

This standard is one of the foundation standards underscoring the background an adapted physical educator should have in order to comply with the mandates of legislation. Understanding the measurement of motor performance is essential to determining the current level of performance, identifying a scope and sequence of instruction, determining eligibility for special services, and providing quality physical education to students with a disability.

Standard 5: History and Philosophy

This standard traces facts regarding legal and philosophical aspects of current-day practices in adapted physical education. This information is important to understanding the changing contribution that physical education can make in the lives of students with a disability. Major components of each law that related to education and physical activity over the years are emphasized. This standard also covers a review of history and philosophy related to special and general education.

Standard 6: Unique Attributes of Learners: Considerations for Professional Practice

Adapted physical educators must be knowledgeable of the disabilities identified in the Individuals with Disabilities Education Act (IDEA) and found within the school-age population. Material is categorically organized in order to present the information systematically. This organization is not intended to advocate a categorical approach to teaching children with a disability. All children should be treated as individuals and assessed to determine their needs; however, disabilities present their own unique learning challenges.

Standard 7: Curriculum Theory and Development

Concepts for developing curriculum must be based on sound curriculum theory, such as selecting goals based on relevant and appropriate assessments and aligning instruction with those goals. Curriculum development is more than writing unit and lesson plans, and it must be tailored to meet the unique needs of students with a disability as well as the rest of the students in the class. This standard addresses deriving learning objectives, organizing learning centers, and using other innovative instructional tools.

Standard 8: Assessment

This standard addresses the process of assessment, which is commonly taught as part of the basic measurement and evaluation course in a physical education degree curriculum. Assessment goes beyond data gathering to include measurements for the purpose of making decisions about special class placement, related services, and program components for individuals with a disability.

Standard 9: Instructional Design and Planning

Instructional design and planning must occur before an APE teacher can provide services to meet legal mandates, educational goals, and, most important, the unique needs of the individual with a disability. Many of the principles addressed earlier in human development, motor behavior, exercise science, and curriculum theory and development are applied to this standard, to ensure that the educator will successfully design and plan programs of physical education.

Standard 10: Teaching

A major part of any APE position is teaching. This standard covers teaching styles and teacher behaviors, managing student behavior (including increasing desirable and decreasing undesirable behaviors), and preventive strategies for creating an effective and appropriate learning environment for all students.

Standard 11: Consultation and Staff Development

As more students with a disability are included in the general education program, adapted physical education teachers will be asked to provide more consultation and staff development activities for colleagues. This will require sensitivity and excellent communication skills. The dynamics of interdisciplinary cooperation in the consultation process require knowledge of several consultative models. This standard identifies key competencies that an adapted physical educator should have for effective consultation and staff development.

Standard 12: Program Evaluation

Program evaluation involves evaluation of the entire range of educational services. Few physical educators are formally trained for program evaluation, as national standards for programs have only recently become available. Therefore, any program evaluation that has been conducted is typically specific to the school or district, or limited to a small range of parameters such as the number of students scoring at a certain level on a physical fitness test. Adapted physical education programs are almost never considered in this process. Student outcomes, program operations, and consumer satisfaction are, however, included in this standard.

Standard 13: Continuing Education

This standard stresses the necessity of teachers remaining current in their field. A variety of opportunities for professional development are available at local colleges or universities, through professional organizations at the state and national levels, and online. Many school districts also offer in-service training. This standard also covers sources of information in the literature, including several publications available through subscription and resources on the World Wide Web.

Standard 14: Ethics

A fundamental premise of the Adapted Physical Education National Standards Project is that those who seek and meet the standards for certification as adapted physical educators will strive at all times to adhere to the highest of ethical standards in providing programs and services for children and youth with a disability. This standard was developed to ensure that members not only understand the importance of sound ethical practices but also adhere to and advance such practices.

Standard 15: Communication

In recent years, the role of the professional in APE has evolved from that of direct service provider to include communicating with families and other professionals in order to enhance program instruction for individuals with a disability. This standard includes information about ways the APE teacher may communicate effectively with families and other professionals and use a team approach to enhance service delivery to individuals with a disability.

REFERENCES

Federal Register. (2005). Individuals with Disabilities Education Act. Washington, DC: U.S. Government Printing Office. (June 21, 2005: Vol. 70, No. 118).

Kelly, L. E. (1991). *Developing outcome standards for adapted physical education* (Unpublished raw data). Charlottesville, VA: University of Virginia.

Kelly, L. E. (Ed.). (1995). *Study guide for APENS exam.*

Kelly, L. E. (Ed.). (2006). *Adapted physical education national standards* (2nd ed.). Champaign, IL: Human Kinetics.

APPENDIX B

Developmental Schedule

AT BIRTH

I. Reflex Activity
  A. Asymmetrical tonic neck reflex (ATNR) elicited by rotation of the head to one side—extensor tone on the face side and flexor tone on the skull side; one limb flexes, the other extends (DeQuiros & Schrager, 1978)
  B. Moro reflex (DeQuiros & Schrager, 1978), startle reaction (Bobath & Bobath, 1971)—abduction and extension of arms resulting from loud noise, sudden movement, or unsupported head tipping backward
  C. Rooting reflex (in response to stimulus at corner of mouth)—the lower lip drops, tongue moves toward stimulus, and head turns to follow it (Fiorentino, 1972)
  D. Sucking reflex (immediate sucking motion of lips in response to finger placed on lips)—jaw drops and lifts rhythmically (Fiorentino, 1972)
  E. Crossed extension reflex—one leg held in extension and stimulation to the foot results in flexion and extension of the opposite leg and fanning of toes (Fiorentino, 1972)
  F. Withdrawal reflex (with both legs extended and soles of feet stimulated)—extension of the toes and dorsiflexion of the feet, followed by flexion of legs (Fiorentino, 1972)
  G. Labyrinthine righting reflex—with vision occluded, held in prone, supine, and vertical tilt, head moves to normal position (Fiorentino, 1972)
  H. Primary walking—automatic walking (sometimes called step reflex) when held upright (Fiorentino, 1972)
  I. Grasp reflex—pressure in palm of hand results in flexion of the fingers (Fiorentino, 1972)
  J. Placing reaction—infant held up, dorsum of hand brushed against under edge of table results in the infant flexing the arm and bringing clenched fist down on table top (Fiorentino, 1972)
  K. Tonic labyrinthine reflex (TLR)—results in maximal extensor tone when head is about 45 degrees above horizontal in supine and maximal flexor tone when head is about 45 degrees below horizontal in prone (Bobath & Bobath, 1971)

II. Head and Trunk Postures
  A. Head usually turned to side
  B. When pulled to sitting, head sags backward then falls forward onto chest

III. Upper Extremities
  A. Hands fisted most of the time (Banus et al., 1971)
  B. Crude circular movements of arms as reaction to stimuli

IV. Lower Extremities
  Legs flexed, externally rotated, and alternately flexing and extending as response to stimuli

V. Play Behavior
  None

BIRTH TO SIX WEEKS

I. Reflex Activity
  A. Inhibition of crossed extension reflex (Fiorentino, 1972)
  B. Neck righting reflex—turning of the head results in a turning of thorax and torso (Bobath & Bobath, 1971)

II. Head and Trunk Postures
  A. Lifting of head and chin when prone (Jersild, 1954), the beginning of the formation of the cervical curve
  B. Head erect but bobbing when held in sitting position (Covert, 1965)
  C. Uniformly rounded back (Gesell, 1940)
  D. Control of oculomotor muscles (Gesell, 1940)

III. Upper Extremities
  A. Ring retained when placed in hand (Halverson, 1933)
  B. Flexion and extension of arms (Gesell, 1940)
  C. Circular arm movements

IV. Lower Extremities
   A. Reflexive creeping motion when prone (Gesell, 1954)
   B. Unilateral flexion of knee (Gesell, 1954)
V. Play Behavior
   A. Leg thrusting (Shirley, 1933), seemingly a response to pleasurable stimuli
   B. Plays with hands
   C. Brings objects in hands to mouth

SIX WEEKS TO THREE MONTHS

Average height: 22 in. (54 cm.); Average weight: 10 lbs. (4.6 kg.)

I. Reflex Activity
   A. Asymmetrical tonic neck reflex begins to become inhibited (DeQuiros & Schrager, 1978)
   B. Withdrawal reflex inhibited (Fiorentino, 1972)
   C. Primary walking reflex inhibited (Fiorentino, 1972)
   D. Placing reaction begins to become inhibited (DeQuiros & Schrager, 1978)
II. Head and Trunk Postures
   A. Trunk strongly dominated by flexor tone (Fiorentino, 1972)
   B. Head held erect (Ilg & Ames, 1960)
   C. Chest held up when in prone position (Jersild, 1954)
   D. Eyes follow object past 90 degrees (Banus et al., 1971)
   E. Eyes locate on object (Ilg & Ames, 1960)
III. Upper Extremities
   A. First directed arm movements in response to objects (Gesell, 1940)
   B. Reaches and touches from lying or sitting position (Ilg & Ames, 1960)
IV. Lower Extremities
   A. Extended legs and alternate kicking (Gesell, 1954)
   B. Supports a fraction of body weight when held erect (Gesell, 1954)
V. Play Behavior
   A. Holds rattle and glances at it (Gesell, 1940)
   B. Pulls at others' clothing (Gesell, 1940)
   C. Learns by seeing and putting objects in mouth
VI. Social Development
   A. Gratification of body needs
   B. Egocentricity
   C. Solitary play
   D. Responsiveness to people and objects
   E. Playing peek-a-boo and pat-a-cake
   F. Smiling
   G. Seeking attention

THREE MONTHS TO SIX MONTHS

Average height: 24 in. (60 cm.); Average weight: 14 lbs. (6.4 kg.)

I. Reflex Activity
   A. Inhibition of asymmetrical tonic neck reflex (DeQuiros & Schrager, 1978)
   B. Inhibition of Moro reflex (DeQuiros & Schrager, 1978)
   C. Inhibition of rooting reflex (Fiorentino, 1972)
   D. Inhibition of sucking reflex (Fiorentino, 1972)
   E. Inhibition of grasp reflex (Fiorentino, 1972)
   F. Landau reaction (Fiorentino, 1972)—increased extensor tone in prone that stimulates the deep postural muscles of the back and neck required for standing
   G. Appearance and inhibition of symmetrical tonic neck reflex (DeQuiros & Schrager, 1978)—extension of the head causes extension of the arms and flexion of the hips; flexion of the head causes flexion of the arms and extension of the hips
II. Head and Trunk Postures
   A. Complete head control (Shirley, 1933)
   B. Sits with minimal support (Gesell, 1940), begins the development of the lumbar curve
   C. Lifts abdomen from floor (Ilg & Ames, 1960)
   D. Rolls from supine to side or to prone position (Shirley, 1933)
   E. Tenses for lifting when on back (Ilg & Ames, 1960)
   F. Ocular pursuit in a sitting position (Covert, 1965)
III. Upper Extremities
   A. Both bilateral and unilateral reaching for dangling objects (Gesell, 1954); bilateral activities at midline (Fiorentino, 1972)
   B. Supports self on extended arms (Gesell, 1940)
   C. Simultaneous flexion and thumb opposition (Shirley, 1933)
   D. Releases against resistance or drops (Jersild, 1954)

IV. Lower Extremities
      A. Momentarily supports large part of body weight (Gesell, 1940)
      B. Extends and lifts legs symmetrically when in supine (Gesell, 1954)
      C. Holds knees straight (Gesell, 1940)
   V. Play Behavior
      A. Visually pursues lost toys (Banus et al., 1971)
      B. Grasps feet (Banus et al., 1971)
      C. Rescues toy dropped within reach (Banus et al., 1971)
   VI. Language Development
      A. Exhibits undifferentiated crying
      B. Begins to make differentiated sounds
      C. Attends to person's voice
      D. Experiments with voice
      E. Turns head toward sounds

SIX MONTHS TO NINE MONTHS

Average height: 26 in. (60 cm.); Average weight: 17 lbs. (7.6 kg.)

   I. Reflex Activity
      A. Tonic labyrinthine reflex inhibited
      B. Protective extensor reaction (parachute) appears (Fiorentino, 1972)—forward movement in the upside-down vertical position results in what helps "break one's fall" when losing one's balance
   II. Head and Trunk Postures
      A. Sits alone without support (Ilg & Ames, 1960)
      B. Leans forward from a sitting position without losing balance (Ilg & Ames, 1960); this is assisted by protective extensor reaction for support when leaning forward
      C. Maintains balance when turning from side to side (Gesell, 1940)
      D. Creeps on stomach with reciprocal, rather than bilateral, action of limbs (Banus et al., 1971; Fiorentino, 1972)
   III. Upper Extremities
      A. Props self up on one arm flexed when in prone position (Gesell, 1940)
      B. Has independent use of hands (Gesell, 1940)
      C. Complete thumb opposition, partial finger prehension (Jersild, 1954)
      D. Rotates wrist in manipulation of object (Jersild, 1954)
      E. Drops for release (Gesell, 1940)
   IV. Lower Extremities
      A. Pulls to knees for standing position (Gesell, 1940)
      B. Draws up knees into crawling position (Gesell, 1940)
      C. Stands with support
      D. Begins to crawl (on all fours) (Jersild, 1954)
   V. Play Behavior
      A. Manipulates string of dangling rings (Gesell, 1954)
      B. Reaches for toys out of reach (Banus et al., 1971)
      C. Holds one object, regards and grasps another (Banus et al., 1971)
   VI. Intellectual Development
      A. Learns through the senses
      B. Perceives objects in immediate sensorimotor visual field
      C. Reflex activity
      D. No object permanence

NINE MONTHS TO TWELVE MONTHS

Average height: 27 in. (67 cm.); Average weight: 19 lbs. (8.6 kg.)

   I. Reflex Activity
      Landau reaction very strong (Bobath & Bobath, 1971)
   II. Head and Trunk Postures
      A. Sits indefinitely (Gesell, 1940)
      B. Changes from sitting to prone position (Ilg & Ames, 1960)
      C. Does not tolerate supine position (Gesell, 1940)
   III. Upper Extremities
      A. Grasps with neat pincer grasp (Banus et al., 1971)
      B. Turns pages of a magazine (Shirley, 1933)
      C. Holds cup with assistance (Gesell, 1940)
      D. Drops voluntarily (Gesell, 1940)
      E. Precise poking with extended forefinger (Ilg & Ames, 1960)
   IV. Lower Extremities
      A. Synchronous movement of arms and legs in crawling position (Gesell, 1954)
      B. Alternate flexion and extension when arm and leg on opposite body sides move (Gesell, 1954), action is preparatory to balanced upright locomotion

C. Stands with support and takes steps (Shirley, 1933)
D. Walks when led (Jersild, 1954), but will revert to crawling when efficient locomotion is needed
E. Supports entire weight on soles of feet (Gesell, 1940)

V. Play Behavior
A. Plays pat-a-cake (Shirley, 1933)
B. Retains ball and attempts to throw or roll it (Gesell, 1940)
C. Stands and moves around furniture

VI. Language Development
A. Babbles
B. Imitates sounds; says "da-da," "ma-ma," responds to "no," shakes head "no"
C. Says one word
D. Knows names
E. Gestures
F. Three-word vocabulary at one year
G. Responds to "give it to me"

TWELVE MONTHS TO EIGHTEEN MONTHS

Average height: 28 in. (70 cm.); Average weight: 20 lbs. (9.2 kg.)

I. Reflex Activity
Continued labyrinthine righting, parachute, and Landau reactions (DeQuiros & Schrager, 1978)

II. Head and Trunk Positions
Good balance (Gesell, 1940)

III. Upper Extremities
A. Primitive grasping with wide-open hand (Shirley, 1933)
B. Exaggerated finger extension in throwing (Gesell, 1940)
C. Walking before and after casting (Gesell, 1940)
D. Primitive grasp in writing (Shirley, 1933)
E. Use of butt end of crayon, uses shoulder movement in writing (Gesell, 1940)
F. Poor but improved release (Gesell, 1940)

IV. Lower Extremities
A. Secure in walking (Gesell, 1940)
B. Stands on one foot when held (Jersild, 1954)
C. Steps before and after throwing (Gesell, 1954)
D. Walks a board for 12 in. (30 cm.) (Gesell, 1954)
E. Begins to run (Gesell, 1954)
F. Climbs and stands on chair (Gesell, 1954)
G. Descends from stool 10 in. (25.5 cm.) high (Gesell, 1954)
H. Creeps up flight of six steps and descends by creeping, sitting bumps, and later marking time (Gesell, 1954)
I. Jumps a distance of 12 in. (30 cm.) (Gesell, 1954)
J. Attempts to kick a ball (Gesell, 1954)

V. Play Behavior
A. Builds five-block tower (Shirley, 1933)
B. Inserts key in lock (Gesell, 1954)
C. Puts pellets in bottle (Gesell, 1954)
D. Nests four boxes (Shirley, 1933)
E. Marks with pencil (Shirley, 1933)
F. Hugs doll (Banus et al., 1971)
G. Walks into a ball; tries to kick later in this stage (Banus et al., 1971)

VI. Language Development
A. Points to things wanted
B. Shows variety of emotions
C. Knows three body parts
D. Imitates talking
E. Uses words to indicate needs and wants
F. Ten-word vocabulary

TWO YEARS TO THREE YEARS

Average height: 32 in. (80 cm.); Average weight: 28 lb. (13 kg.)

I. Reflex Activity
No change

II. Head and Trunk Postures
Secure in balance and movement

III. Upper Extremities
A. Reaches for object without supporting self or twisting trunk (Gesell, 1940)
B. Holds spoon by thumb and radial fingers (Fokes, 1971)
C. Folds paper, pulls off socks, finds armholes, strings beads, turns doorknob, holds glass with one hand, builds six-block tower (Gesell, 1940)
D. Holds crayons with fingers (Gesell & Armatruda, 1941)

IV. Lower Extremities
A. Stands alone on either foot (Jersild, 1954)

B. Stands on walking board with both feet (Jersild, 1954)
C. Stands with heels together when shown (Gesell, 1940)
D. Walks in the direction of a line (Gesell, 1940)
E. Walks between parallel lines (Gesell, 1940)
F. Carries large object while walking (Gesell, 1940)
G. Walks on tiptoe (Gesell, 1940)
H. Walks backward 9.9 ft. (3 m.) (Gesell, 1940)
I. Runs on toes (Gesell, 1940)
J. Kicks a ball (Fokes, 1971)
K. Jumps distance of 12 in. (30 cm.) with one foot leading (Gesell, 1940)
L. Jumps from ground with both feet (Gesell, 1940)
M. Ascends a few steps on alternating feet (Gesell, 1940)
N. Ascends and descends steps by marking time (Jersild, 1954)

V. Play Behavior
A. See those suggested in III and IV above
B. Strings beads with needle (Gesell, 1940)
C. Folds paper when shown (Gesell, 1940)
D. Turns pages in book (Gesell, 1940)
E. Draws vertical and circular strokes (Gesell, 1940)
F. Imitates simple actions of others (Gesell, 1940)

VI. Language Development
A. Uses plurals
B. Knows simple songs
C. Gives full name
D. Knows gender
E. Counts to three
F. Can tell a story
G. Uses five- to six-word sentences
H. Names colors
I. 800-word vocabulary

VII. Intellectual Development
A. Preoperational thought through sensorimotor activity
B. Focuses on one characteristic only
C. Has primary classification ability
D. Is not concerned with contradictions
E. Is able to distinguish vertical from horizontal lines

THREE YEARS TO FOUR YEARS

Average height: 38 in. (96 cm.); Average weight: 33 lbs. (15.5 kg.)

I. Reflex Activity
No change

II. Head and Trunk Postures
A. Shoulders erect (Gesell, 1940)
B. Abdomen less protruding (Gesell, 1940)
C. Upright posture characterized by extreme lumbar curve

III. Upper Extremities
A. Leans, extends arms, and twists easily while reaching (Gesell, 1940)
B. Picks up small objects without fingers touching table top (Gesell, 1940)
C. Unbuttons, but cannot button, clothing (Gesell, 1940)
D. Drives nails and pegs (Strang, 1959)
E. Uses both hands to steady block tower (Gesell, 1940)
F. Begins to use scissors (Strang, 1959)
G. Uses shoulders and elbows to throw; guides course of ball with fingers (Gesell, 1940)
H. Rests shaft at juncture of thumb and index finger when writing; extends medius on shaft (Gesell, 1940)
I. Releasing free and easy (Gesell, 1940)

IV. Lower Extremities
A. Uniform walking pattern using heel to toe progression (Jersild, 1954)
B. Walks backward a long distance (Gesell, 1940)
C. Walks 20 to 28 ft. (6 to 8 m.) on walking board in 15 seconds with three errors (Gesell, 1940)
D. Walks in circular path of circle 4.5 ft. (14 cm.) in diameter (Jersild, 1954)
E. Walks on tiptoes 9.9 ft. (3 m.) (Jersild, 1954)
F. Runs easily and smoothly with moderate speed (Gesell, 1940)
G. Hops up to seven times on one foot (Gesell, 1940)
H. Skips on one foot (Jersild, 1954)
I. Uses alternate feet in ascending up to three steps (Jersild, 1954)
J. Rides tricycle (Gesell, 1940)

V. Play Behavior
A. Holds pen between thumb and index finger (Gesell, 1954)
B. Copies circle (Covert, 1965)

C. Makes a square (Gesell, 1940)
D. Builds tower with 9 to 10 blocks (Gesell, 1940)
E. Catches a large ball with arms fully extended (Gesell, 1940)
F. Feeds self without spilling food, laces shoes, and removes clothing (Gesell, 1940)

VI. Social Development
A. Preference of playmates
B. Strong attachment to one other child
C. Parallel play
D. Imitates other children's play
E. Takes turns
F. Plays aggressively
G. May have an imaginary playmate

FOUR YEARS TO FIVE YEARS

Average height: 42 in. (1.3 meters); Average weight: 39 lbs. (18 kg.)

I. Reflex Activity
   No change
II. Head and Trunk Postures
   Balanced and steady (Gesell, 1940)
III. Upper Extremities
   A. Reaching lacks poise; uses arms rather than hands (Gesell, 1940)
   B. Picks up small objects with thumb and index finger (Gesell, 1940)
   C. Puts toys away, washes face and hands (Strang, 1959)
   D. Brushes teeth, undresses with assistance (Gesell, 1940)
   E. Uses preferred hand for throwing; throws forward without regard for height; throws overhand (Gesell, 1940)
   F. Catches a large ball in one out of three trials (Gesell, 1940)
   G. Good precision and timing on release; releases without pressure (Gesell, 1940)
IV. Lower Extremities
   A. Walks and runs long distances (Strang, 1959)
   B. Stops and goes quickly in running (Gesell, 1940)
   C. Balances on toes (Gesell, 1940)
   D. Hops on either foot seven or eight times (Gesell, 1940)
   E. Descends stairs on alternate feet (Jersild, 1954)
   F. Jumps skillfully (Strang, 1959)
   G. Shifts weight in throwing
   H. Slides (Gutteridge, 1939)
V. Play Behavior
   A. Uses play apparatus, will play with others to some degree if guided
   B. Fantasy play with others
   C. Gives life to playthings, talks to them
VI. Intellectual Development
   A. Learns colors
   B. Classifies by emotions
   C. Uses symbols to represent concrete world
   D. Makes intuitive judgments about relationships

FIVE YEARS TO SIX YEARS

Average height: 43.5 in. (1.3 meters); Average weight: 42.5 lbs. (19.5 kg)

I. Reflex Activity
   No change
II. Head and Trunk Postures
   No change
III. Upper Extremities
   A. Precision in use of tools (Gesell, 1940)
   B. Throws skillfully at shoulder level (Gesell, 1940)
   C. Catches ball with hands (Gesell, 1940)
   D. Precise release (Gesell, 1940)
IV. Lower Extremities
   A. Walks long distances on tiptoe (Gesell, 1940)
   B. Balances on toes for several seconds; stands on one foot indefinitely (Gesell, 1940)
   C. Skips on alternating feet (Gutteridge, 1939); skips to music (Strang, 1959)
   D. Climbs easily (Gutteridge, 1939)
   E. Descends long staircase with alternate feet (Gesell, 1940)
   F. Roller skates and rides bicycle (Strang, 1959)
   G. Kicks ball 8 to 10 ft. (2.5 to 3.3 m.) with accuracy (Gesell, 1940)
   H. Broad jumps 28 to 30 in. (70 to 78 cm.) (Gesell, 1940)
V. Play Behavior
   A. See those suggested in III and IV above
   B. Interested in stunts and trapeze type play (Marx, n.d.)
   C. Ice skates (Marx, n.d.)

VI. Language Development
   A. Acquires sounds and structure needed for life
   B. Can follow three commands in sequence
   C. Lacks sensitivity to listener in giving information

SIX YEARS TO SEVEN YEARS

Average height: 46 in. (1.5 meters); Average weight: 48 lbs. (23 kg.)

I. Reflex Activity
   No change
II. Head and Trunk Postures
   No change
III. Upper Extremities
   A. Uses elbows and wrists in throwing; guides path of ball (Gesell & Armatruda, 1941)
   B. Catches tossed ball chest high from a distance of 3.3 ft. (1 m.) in two out of three trials (Gesell & Armatruda, 1941)
IV. Lower Extremities
   A. Uses walk, run, jump in strenuous activities (Gesell & Armatruda, 1941)
   B. Stands on each foot alternately with eyes closed (Gesell & Armatruda, 1941)
   C. Hops 50 ft. (15.5 m.) in nine seconds (Gesell & Armatruda, 1941)
   D. Jumps 12 in. (21 cm.) and lands on toes (Gesell & Armatruda, 1941)
   E. High jumps 8 in. (21 cm.) (Gesell & Armatruda, 1941)
   F. Kicks soccer ball with accuracy 10 to 18 ft. (3.5 m.) (Gesell & Armatruda, 1941)
V. Play Behavior
   A. Likes wrestling, tumbling, crawling, climbing, swinging (Banus et al., 1971)
   B. Enjoys small group games
VI. Social Development
   A. Participates in cooperative play
   B. Accepts adult authority
   C. Boasts
   D. Uses favorite expressions
   E. Seeks group approval
   F. Plays in groups of three

BEYOND SEVEN YEARS

I. Motor Development
   Motor patterns already developed evolve into motor skills and eventually become refined game and sport skills

II. Language Development
   Masters sound patterns; utilizes complex sentence structure; reads; learns multiple word meanings; acquires adult language structures; uses socially oriented language; masters peer language, adult language, and foreign language

III. Social Development
   Identifies with persons of same sex; is loyal to gang; rejects adult authority; participates in large group activities; seeks peer acceptance; develops personality type; is influenced by peer pressure; becomes intrinsically motivated

IV. Intellectual Development
   Organizes environment through direct experiences; perceives consequences of own actions; uses logic; classifies by two characteristics; begins addition and subtraction; comprehends abstract concepts; handles contradictions, thoughts, direct observations; works with theories and abstractions; sees logical relationships; solves problems

REFERENCES

Banus, B. S., Weldon, J. A., & Taylor, E. A. (1971). *The developmental therapist*. Thorofare, NJ: Charles B. Slack.

Bobath, B., & Bobath, K. (1971). *Abnormal postural reflex activity caused by brain lesions*. London: Heinemann.

Covert, C. (1965). *Mental retardation*. Chicago: American Medical Association.

DeQuiros, J. B., & Schrager, O. L. (1978). *Neuropsychological fundamentals in learning disabilities*. San Rafael, CA: Academic Therapy Publications.

Fiorentino, M. R. (1972). *Normal and abnormal development*. Springfield, IL: Thomas.

Fokes, J. (1971). Developmental scales of motor abilities. In B. Stephens (Ed.), *Training the developmentally young* (pp. 31–54). New York: John Day.

Gesell, A. (1940). *The first five years of life*. New York: Harper & Row.

Gesell, A. (1954). The ontogenesis of infant behavior. In L. Carmichael (Ed.), *Manual of child psychology* (pp. 187–246). New York: Wiley.

Gesell, A., & Armatruda, C. S. (1941). *Developmental diagnosis*. New York: Harper & Row.

Gutteridge, M. (1939). A study of motor achievements in young children. *Archives of Psychology, 244*, 5–178.

Halverson, H. M. (1933). The acquisition of skill in infancy. *Journal of Genetic Psychology, 43*, 3–48.

Ilg, F., & Ames, L. (1960). *Child behavior*. New York: Dell.

Jersild, A. (1954). *Child psychology*. New York: Prentice Hall.

Marx, O. (Undated). *Motor activities: Newborn to six years of age*. Washington, DC: American Alliance for Health, Physical Education, Recreation, and Dance.

Piaget, J. (1952). *The origins of intelligence*. New York: Norton.

Shirley, M. (1933). The first two years: A study of 25 babies. *Institute of Child Welfare Monograph*, Series 7, 2.

Strang, R. (1959). *An introduction to child study*. New York: Macmillan.

Weiss, C. D., & Lillywhite, H. S. (1976). *Communicative disorders*. St. Louis, MO: Mosby.

APPENDIX C

Movement Attributes and Etiology of Disabilities

The developmental approach, by definition, requires the educator to look at students from the standpoint of "where they are" developmentally—not what they "have" as a medical diagnosis or condition that carries with it predetermined limitations and expectations. Along with understanding development, understanding the unique movement characteristics or challenges to learning motor skills of individuals with a disability gives the teacher the tools needed to accommodate students in physical education and activity programs. Understanding the etiology or background of a student's disability is useful in order to appreciate the implications for physical activity. You should refrain, however, from referring to students by their disability, as in, "The class of retarded students," "I work with a disabled athlete, Ann," or "The cerebral palsied kids have the most trouble with balance." Although these may be true statements, they give no insight into what these students are capable of *doing*, and further, they relegate the person (or group) to second place behind the disability. This makes the disability the focus, rather than the person. Today, it is appropriate to use "person-first" language (i.e., acknowledging the person first by putting his or her name or the name of the group ahead of the disability). "The class of students who have mental retardation," "I work with Ann, an athlete with a disability," or "Children with cerebral palsy have the most trouble with balance" are more appropriate statements. Students as people and their abilities—not their disabilities—should serve as the basis for planning programs for physical education and physical activity.

Therefore, this appendix is designed to assist you in two ways:

1. To understand the etiology of the 12 most commonly occurring disabilities as defined by the amendments to the Individuals with Disabilities Education Act of 2004 (IDEA '04).

2. To appreciate the unique movement characteristics that present challenges to learning skills and may require adapting some aspect of the curriculum or program to ensure participation and inclusion in physical education.

At the end of the discussion of each disability, a Teaching Tip directs you to strategies most useful for teaching students with that disability. For easy reference, the disabilities and the challenges to learning are listed alphabetically. The 12 disabilities defined by federal legislation include:

- Autism
- Deaf-blindness
- Emotional disturbance
- Hearing impairment, including deafness
- Mental retardation
- Multiple disabilities
- Orthopedic impairment
- Other health impairments
- Specific learning disability
- Speech or language impairments
- Traumatic brain injury
- Visual impairment

DISABILITIES DEFINED IN FEDERAL LEGISLATION

Autism

Although Kanner described autism in 1943, there is still much debate about how broadly the term should be applied and who should be included in this disability type. Usually, students within this disability category are clustered within an **autism spectrum,** meaning *a group of disorders that share some characteristics and behaviors* as originally described by Kanner. According to IDEA '04, the term means:

> A developmental disability significantly affecting verbal and nonverbal communication and social interaction, generally evident before age three, that adversely affects a child's educational performance. Other characteristics often associated with autism are engagement in repetitive activities and stereotyped movements, resistance to environmental change or change in daily routines, and unusual responses to sensory experiences.
>
> (i) Autism does not apply if a child's educational performance is adversely affected pri-

marily because the child has an emotional disturbance. (U.S. Department of Education, regulations, Sec. 300.8 (c) (1), 2005)

The Autism Society of America (ASA) defines autism as follows (abridged):

> Autism is a complex developmental disability that typically appears during the first three years of life and is the result of a neurological disorder that affects the normal functioning of the brain, impacting development in the areas of social interaction and communication skills. Both children and adults with autism typically show difficulties in verbal and non-verbal communication, social interactions, and leisure or play activities. One should keep in mind however, that autism is a spectrum disorder and it affects each individual differently and at varying degrees.
>
> Autism is one of five disorders that falls under the umbrella of Pervasive Developmental Disorders (PDD), a category of neurological disorders characterized by "severe and pervasive impairment in several areas of development."
>
> The five disorders under PDD are:
> - Autistic Disorder
> - Asperger's Disorder
> - Childhood Disintegrative Disorder (CDD)
> - Rett's Disorder
> - PDD-Not Otherwise Specified (PDD-NOS)

(Autism Society of America, 2005)

Each of the five disorders under PDD has specific diagnostic criteria, which have been outlined in the American Psychiatric Association's *Diagnostic and Statistical Manual of Mental Disorders* (2000).

Both the IDEA '04 and the ASA definitions are descriptive and agree on two major characteristics: difficulty developing social relationships and language delays or dysfunction. The ASA definition goes on to include difficulty with leisure and play activities; previously it also included repetitive body movements such as hand flapping and rocking. Some of the characteristics previously attributed to children with autism have been more definitively linked to others of the disabilities under PDD.

Currently, the diagnosis of autism is usually referred to as Autism Spectrum Disorder or autistic-like behaviors. These terms more accurately indicate the range of severity of the symptoms that are demonstrated by individuals with this disability. A unique condition identified more frequently today is **Asperger syndrome.** Originally identified in the 1940s by Hans Asperger, this condition arguably is considered within the autism spectrum. Although repetitive and stereotypic movement characteristics are shared with classic autism behaviors, individuals with Asperger syndrome tend to *differ with more developed language skills and cognitive abilities* (Attwood, 1998). **Autistic disorder (savant)** is the type most typically portrayed in literature and movies such as *Rainman*. Individuals with this type stand out because of their *almost bizarre inconsistencies in ability*. Most have difficulty sustaining a coherent conversation yet can recite trivia or accomplish incredible feats such as instantly counting the number of matches spilled on the floor, playing a piano piece after hearing it only once, or recalling all of the winning lottery ticket numbers for the past year. Individuals with savant qualities that stand out are rare; however, this exemplifies the uneven profile of development that is quite often displayed by individuals with autism. Wide differences in strengths and weaknesses should be considered carefully when planning an educational program for individuals with autism. Two specific behaviors likely to affect motor performance—walking or standing on tiptoes and looking at things out of the corners of the eyes—are particularly common in individuals with autism.

> ## Teaching Tip
>
> **AUTISM** • Understanding behavior management and functional assessment (including the use of a functional analysis in physical education) are key to focusing students with autism on the motor tasks of your physical activity program. In addition, the lesson plan may address the need for structure and consistency, sensory experiences, and completion of task.

Deaf-Blindness

The category of deaf-blindness is defined in IDEA '04 as:

> concomitant hearing and visual impairments, the combination of which causes such severe communication and other developmental and educational needs that they cannot be accommodated in special education programs solely for children with deafness or children with blindness. (U. S. Department of Education, regulations, Sec. 300.8 (c) (2))

The most common cause of deaf-blindness is prematurity (Baldwin, 1995); however, the majority of cases having multiple disabilities have unknown causes. The leading known cause after prematurity is Usher's syndrome, a genetic condition resulting in congenital deafness and progressive blindness. Even

> **Teaching Tip**
>
> **DEAF-BLINDNESS** • Using a multisensory approach to learning and capitalizing on tactile, proprioceptive, and vestibular systems enhances these students' learning in the motor domain. Consistent structure (routine) and expanding familiar skills are useful strategies.

> **Teaching Tip**
>
> **EMOTIONAL DISTURBANCE** • An understanding of behavior management and the ability to maintain consistent class routines and depersonalize behaviors (even when they seem to be personally directed) are key to focusing students with emotional and behavioral disorders on the motor tasks of your physical education program. Motivation and varied lessons are valuable in facilitating participation.

so, only about 5 percent of cases can be explained by this X-linked genetic disorder (Accardo, Whitman, Laszewski, Haake, & Morrow, 1996).

Because both deafness and blindness are measured on a continuum, deaf-blind individuals vary in their functional use of either or both sensory systems. For example, a person with total blindness and severe, but not total, deafness is considered deaf-blind.

Thus, if the deficit in hearing and vision requires special instructional adaptations in both modes for the student to benefit from educational services, the student is considered deaf-blind.

Emotional Disturbance

IDEA '04 uses the term emotional disturbance to mean:

> A condition exhibiting one or more of the following characteristics over a long period of time and to a marked degree that adversely affects a child's educational performance:
>
> - An inability to learn that cannot be explained by intellectual, sensory, or health factors.
> - An inability to build or maintain satisfactory interpersonal relationships with peers and teachers.
> - Inappropriate types of behavior or feelings under normal circumstances.
> - A general pervasive mood of unhappiness or depression.
> - A tendency to develop physical symptoms or fears associated with personal or school problems.
>
> Emotional disturbance includes schizophrenia. The term does not apply to children who are socially maladjusted, unless it is determined that they have an emotional disturbance under paragraph (c)(4)(i) of this section. (U.S. Department of Education, regulations, Sec. 300.8 (c) (4) (ii), 2005)

There are essentially two types of emotional or behavior disorders: externalizing (typically aggressive) and internalizing (typically withdrawn). Externalizing behaviors tend to be identified first and most frequently because these are the behaviors that disturb others (e.g., aggression and delinquency). Internalizing behaviors, although just as serious, often go undetected because the child turns inward, and his or her behavior is not disruptive or disturbing to others. Anorexia and bulimia (eating disorders), depression, and anxiety are examples of internalizing behavior disorders. Physical educators should be aware of both types of emotional disorders because they are often in a unique position to witness the manifestation of these characteristics.

Emotional and behavioral disorders can almost always be traced to biological or environmental factors. Researchers continue to learn more about the lasting emotional effects of fetal alcohol syndrome and prenatal exposure to crack cocaine and other illegal and legal drugs, some of which are common household products. Home and community influences, such as poor role models, abuse, neglect, and trauma, can contribute to emotional and behavioral disorders.

Hearing Impairment and Deafness

Federal law uses the term "deafness" to identify the lack of ability usefully to perceive sounds in the environment, with or without a hearing aid for use as the primary means of gaining information. Children with residual hearing also receive special education services. The amount and type of hearing loss, as well as the time in a person's life when the hearing loss was acquired, significantly affect motor performance and the need for accommodation and support in the learning environment.

Hearing loss is usually broken down into the following levels:

- *Hard of hearing.* The person has residual hearing that, with the use of a hearing aid, is sufficient to enable the successful processing of linguistic information.
- *Prelingually deaf.* The condition was present at birth or occurred early in life, prior to the individual acquiring speech or language.

> **Teaching Tip**
>
> **HEARING IMPAIRMENT AND DEAFNESS** • Teachers are encouraged to acquire at least minimal sign language skills in order to communicate with students using manual communication. Otherwise, teaching students with hearing loss and deafness can follow the same progression and utilize the same strategies as teaching students without hearing loss. Lesson presentation should emphasize visual demonstrations and specific, concrete explanations.

- *Postlingually deaf.* Deafness occurred in a person following the acquisition of speech and language.

It appears that about 35 percent of childhood deafness in the United States can be attributed to heredity. Up to 55 percent of causes are unknown or unreported, with the balance caused by such sources as rubella, prematurity, Rh incompatibility, meningitis, otitis media, high fever, infection, measles, mumps, and trauma. Medical advances have all but eradicated most of the preventable causes of hearing loss in the United States. Approximately 22 million people in the United States have trouble hearing. While most people with hearing loss are older folks who have lost hearing with age, approximately 12 out of every 1,000 persons with hearing impairment are under 18 years of age, based on the most recently available National Center for Health Statistics figures. That means that the chances are excellent that at least one student in your school will have a hearing loss.

There are two general types of hearing loss: conductive and sensorineural. We have all experienced some level of conductive hearing loss from time to time when up in an airplane or when we have a cold or sinus infection. Because of the high frequency of head colds in children, approximately 50 to 80 percent of children are likely to have a conductive hearing loss at some time. A **conductive** loss results from a *blockage of or damage to the outer or middle ear that prevents sound waves from being conducted to the inner ear.* **Sensorineural** losses occur when there is *damage to the inner ear or auditory nerve.* This damage cannot be reversed, and improvement with the use of hearing aids is often difficult (Boothroyd, 1998). Any hearing loss is reason for concern to physical educators because the headquarters of vestibular function is housed in the middle ear, and infections and other causes of hearing loss may create balance difficulties at the same time.

Mental Retardation

Whereas the term *mental retardation* is used in IDEA '04 and in most educational literature and state statutes, other terms are still in use or emerging to refer to the same disability. Terms such as *mental handicap, mental deficiency, cognitive disorder,* and *intellectual limitations* are commonly found throughout the literature in education, the social sciences, and medicine. A new term, *intellectual disability,* is being used more and more in clinical medicine, in behavioral and social science literature, and relative to adults in post-secondary education and the work force. Executive Order 12994, signed April 25, 2003, by President George W. Bush, renamed the president's advisory committee on mental retardation as the President's Committee for People with Intellectual Disabilities. The term *intellectual disability* and the other alternative terms are synonymous with mental retardation, regardless of the context. *Mental retardation* is used throughout this textbook, as this is still the principal term used in education.

Mental retardation has had several definitions over the years, the most commonly accepted being that developed by Grossman (1983), which focuses on deficits and relies heavily on a measurement of "sub-average" intelligence by a traditional IQ test such as the Weschsler Intelligence Scale for Children, Woodcock-Johnson Tests of Cognitive Ability, or the Kaufman Assessment Battery for Children (additional discussion of instruments can be found in Chapter 6, under "Measures of Intelligence"). Grossman's definition was accepted by the American Association on Mental Retardation (AAMR) and was the most widely used description of mental retardation. In recent years, however, a paradigm shift has been supported by the profession, changing the orientation from the negative deficit viewpoint to a more positive perspective with emphasis on adaptive skills (Luckasson et al., 1992). This definition is as follows:

> Mental retardation refers to substantial limitations in present functioning. It is characterized by significantly subaverage intellectual functioning, existing concurrently with related limitations in two or more of the following applicable adaptive skill areas: communication, self-care, home living, social skills, community use, self-direction, health and safety, functional academics, leisure, and work. Mental retardation manifests before age 18. (Luckasson et al., 1992, p. 1)

Although IQ tests have long been recognized as flawed in identifying the functional capacity of individuals, they are still often used as one of the measures of intellectual functioning. Figure C.1 shows the distribution of IQ scores and the typical demarcations between degrees of retardation.

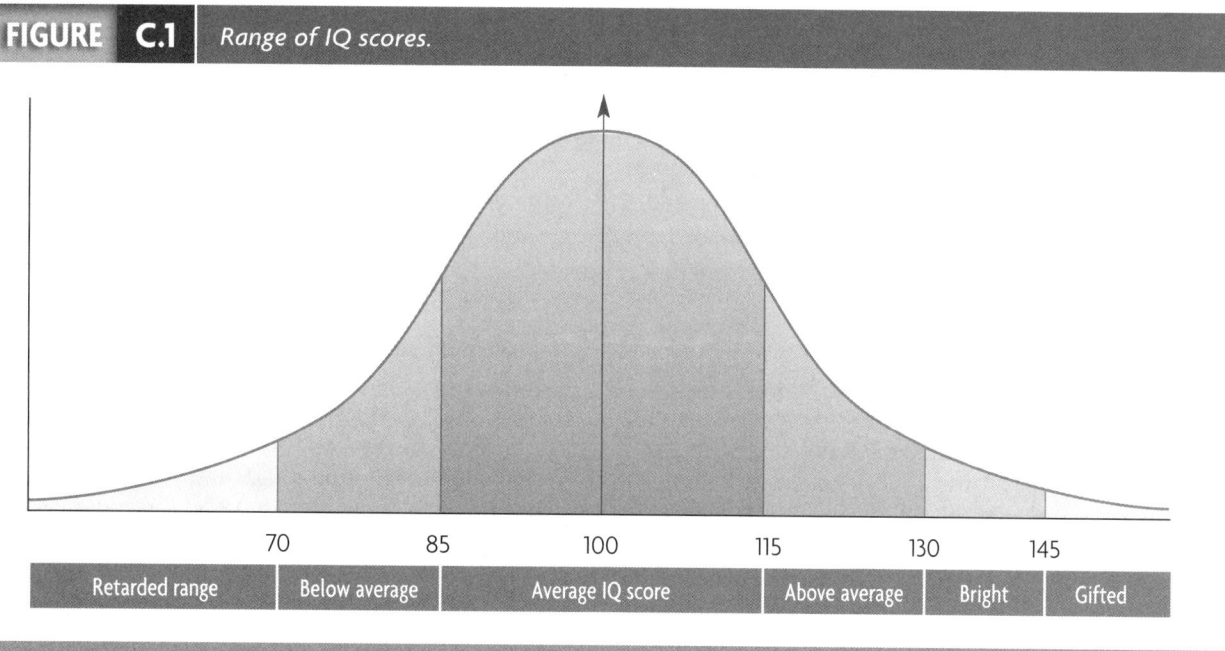

FIGURE C.1 Range of IQ scores.

Recently, the AAMR has placed more emphasis on adaptive skills. Those skills listed in the definition developed by Luckasson et al. (1992) are explained in Table C.1.

The AAMR established a system in 1992 that classifies the amount of support needed by the individual in four categories, from least intense to most intense: intermittent (I), limited (L), extensive (E), and pervasive (P). These levels refer to the services and supports that individuals may require, regardless of their IQ, in order to function in the environment. Students with intermittent support receive it

TABLE C.1 Adaptive skills defining mental retardation.

ADAPTIVE SKILL AREA	EXPLANATION
Communication	Understanding and expressing messages through symbolic or nonsymbolic behaviors
Self-care	Toileting, eating, dressing, and grooming skills; hygiene
Home living	Home environment skills relating to housekeeping, property maintenance, cooking, budgeting, home safety, and scheduling
Social	Skills related to social exchanges, including interaction with others, as well as the initiation and termination of interaction
Community use	Use of appropriate community resources, such as traveling in the community, shopping, purchasing services, and using public transportation
Self-direction	Skills related to making choices, completing tasks, seeking assistance, and resolving problems
Health and safety	First aid, physical fitness, illness identification, and safety skills
Functional academics	Skills related to learning in school, such as basic reading, writing, and practical mathematics
Leisure	Recreational interests and activities that may involve social interaction, mobility skills, taking turns, and playing appropriately
Work	Employment (job) skills, such as task completion, money management, attention, and cooperation

Source: Adapted from B. R. Bryant, R. L. Taylor, & D. P. Rivera (1996), *Assessment of Adaptive Areas (AAA): Examiner's Manual* (pp. 2–3), Austin, TX: Pro-Ed. Used with permission.

> **Teaching Tip**
>
> **MENTAL RETARDATION** • Sequence instruction based on appropriate developmental level, age appropriateness, and the student's interest level. Be patient, and provide consistent and firm structure and class rules.

> **Teaching Tip**
>
> **MULTIPLE DISABILITIES** • Address the disability that interferes most with motor performance. Sequence instruction appropriately and accommodate secondary conditions as you are able.

on an "as needed" basis, meaning for example that they may have an aide for certain classroom activities, but not for physical education. Pervasive supports may include an attendant who stays with the student at all times during the school day.

The causes of mental retardation are numerous; it may result from either a single factor or multiple factors. Although the AAMR has identified general causal groupings for mental retardation (see Table C.2), the vast majority of cases result from unknown causes. Of those causes associated with treatable health-related problems, the cause itself may be treatable, minimizing the retardation, or the fetus or infant may be treated, minimizing or eradicating the retardation altogether.

Multiple Disabilities

IDEA '04 states:

> Multiple disabilities means concomitant impairments (such as mental retardation–blindness, mental retardation–orthopedic impairment, etc.), the combination of which causes such severe educational needs that they cannot be accommodated in special education programs solely for one of the impairments. Multiple disabilities does not include deaf-blindness. (U.S. Department of Education, regulations, Sec. 300.8 (c) (7), 2005)

More than 90,000 youth were reported as having multiple disabilities in the last census (1996). Children with multiple disabilities may exhibit a wide range of characteristics, depending on the combination and severity of disabilities, and the student's age. They may share certain traits, however, including:

- Limited speech or communication
- Difficulty in basic physical mobility
- Tendency to forget skills through disuse
- Trouble generalizing skills from one situation to another
- A need for support in major life activities, e.g., domestic, leisure, community use, vocational (NICHCY, 1997)

TABLE C.2 *Causes of mental retardation.*

CAUSAL GROUPING	EXAMPLES
Infections and intoxicants	Rubella, syphilis, meningitis, encephalitis, Rh incompatibility
Metabolism and nutritional disorders	Phenylketonuria (PKU), Tay-Sachs disease, Hurler's syndrome, cretinism, Prader-Willi syndrome
Gross brain disease	Tuberous sclerosis, Starge-Weber-Dimitri's syndrome, Recklinghausen's disease
Unknown prenatal influence	Microcephalus, hydrocephalus, Apert's syndrome, Cornelia de Lange's syndrome
Chromosomal abnormality	Down syndrome, Klinefelter's syndrome, Turner's syndrome
Trauma or physical agents	Injury to mother or developing fetus, excessive X-ray radiation, anoxia, perinatal injury from birthing, prolonged labor, postnatal infections, high fevers, poisons, convulsions, electric shock
Genetic causes	Fragile X syndrome (FXS) associated with retardation resulting from a mutation on the X chromosome
Environmental influences	Sensory deprivation, neglect, abuse, unknown

Orthopedic (Physical) Impairment

Although IDEA '04 refers to this category of disabilities as "orthopedic impairment," it includes conditions that, in the strictest sense, are not orthopedic. Orthopedic, technically, refers to conditions affecting the bones and joints. As Table C.3 shows, under IDEA '04, there are other disabilities that manifest themselves as "physical" impairments (i.e., affecting the body's mechanics, but not strictly affecting the bones and joints). The federal government defines orthopedic impairment as a condition

> that adversely affects a child's educational performance. The term includes impairments caused by congenital anomaly (e.g., clubfoot, absence of some member, etc.), impairments caused by disease (e.g., poliomyelitis, bone tuberculosis, etc.), and impairments from other causes (e.g., cerebral palsy, amputations, fractures, or burns causing contractures). (U. S. Department of Education, 2005, regulations, Sec. 300.8 (c) (8))

Physical educators must address the challenges to the students' use of biomechanics regardless of whether the impairment is caused by a disease or birth anomaly, whether only the bones and joints are affected, and whether there is a neurological basis for the condition.

The causes of orthopedic impairments range from illness to injury. Certainly, diseases such as polio and measles have virtually been eliminated as a cause in America, but these are still sources of disability in other countries around the world. Motor vehicle accidents, water and diving accidents, sports injuries, child abuse, poisoning, premature birth, infectious diseases, genetic sources, seizures, and hydrocephaly are all possible causes of the impairments listed in Table C.3.

Other Health Impairments

The U.S. Department of Education defines "other health impairment" as

> having limited strength, vitality or alertness, including a heightened alertness to environmental stimuli, that results in limited alertness with respect to the educational environment, that—
> (i) Is due to chronic or acute health problems such as asthma, attention deficit disorder or attention deficit hyperactivity disorder, diabetes, epilepsy, a heart condition, hemophilia, lead poisoning, leukemia, nephritis, rheumatic fever, and sickle cell anemia; and
> (ii) Adversely affects a child's educational performance. (U.S. Department of Education, 2005, regulations, Sec. 300.8 (c) (9))

Although the federal government identifies attention deficit disorder and attention deficit hyperactivity disorder as "other health impairments" due to the "heightened alertness to environmental stimuli," the challenges to teachers more closely resemble those of children with learning disabilities; thus, we

---

Teaching Tip

ORTHOPEDIC IMPAIRMENTS • Conduct a functional assessment (or authentic assessment) of what students can do, and build on their strengths while providing a fun and safe environment. Knowledge of adaptive devices and equipment (as well as the teacher's own creativity) will facilitate inclusion in the movement activities and physical education curriculum.

TABLE C.3 *Orthopedic impairments.*

Neurological conditions	Musculoskeletal conditions	Bone and joint conditions
Cerebral palsy	Rheumatoid arthritis	Dwarfism
Epilepsy and seizure disorders	Juvenile rheumatoid arthritis	Congenital and traumatic amputations
Multiple sclerosis	Still's disease	Legg-Calve-Perthes
Muscular dystrophy	Arthrogryposis	Postural deviations
Poliomyelitis	Contractures from burns or other causes	Osteogenesis imperfecta
Spina bifida		Osteomyelitis
Spinal cord injuries		Osgood-Schlatter's condition

discuss these impairments below, along with learning disabilities. Only a few of the most commonly occurring health conditions are presented here.

Asthma. Asthma is *a chronic respiratory condition in which the individual experiences repeated episodes of breathing difficulty.* The incidence of asthma has risen in recent years, with slightly more males being affected than females. Exercise, stress, and environmental factors can bring on an "attack" of bronchial tube spasms and swelling and an excessive secretion of mucus accompanied by coughing and wheezing. The condition can usually be controlled by medication, modifying the environment, monitoring the amount and type of exercise, and reducing exercise as soon as an "attack" begins. Some students are able to identify their own "triggers" (conditions that bring on an attack) and are encouraged to manage their exposure to these conditions.

Cystic fibrosis. Cystic fibrosis is *an inherited childhood disease characterized by chronic respiratory and digestive problems.* An abnormal secretion of the membranes that line internal organs and excessive salt loss in perspiration are ever-present characteristics. Health care interventions, including replacing enzymes for aiding digestion and aggressive care of lung infections, have helped prolong the life of individuals with this condition.

Diabetes. A metabolic disturbance, diabetes is *a hereditary or developmental problem of sugar metabolism, resulting in insufficient insulin in the bloodstream.* Diabetes can be managed through diet, exercise, and insulin treatment. Individuals with diabetes learn very early what their limits are and carefully monitor the critical factors. New advances in medicine have resulted in oral medication and insulin pumps, freeing many people with diabetes from taking insulin by injection. Diabetic control in children is sometimes more difficult than with adults. The physical education teacher should be aware of the warning signs and appropriate insulin or "count" levels when planning or scheduling movement activities. Teachers should also learn and review the warning signs and medically recommended first aid for insulin shock and diabetic coma.

Cardiovascular disorders. Cardiovascular disorders include a broad range of heart, blood, and blood vessel conditions. *Congenital heart defects* can result in school absences and often require that the student take medication during the school day. *Hemophilia,* a rare, sex-linked disorder of the blood, is transmitted through a recessive gene from the mother to male children. A deficiency of a clotting factor in the blood is a principal characteristic and often precludes students from participating in contact sports. *Rheumatic fever,* although not as common in the United States as it once was, has lasting effects on the heart, which warrant its inclusion here. It usually is preceded by strep throat and is accompanied by a painful swelling and inflammation of the joints, brain, or heart.

Childhood cancer. Cancer among children is a substantial public concern. Each year in the United States, approximately 12,400 children and adolescents younger than 20 years of age are diagnosed with cancer. Approximately 2,300 children and adolescents die of cancer each year, making cancer the most common cause of disease-related mortality for children 1 through 19 years of age (National Cancer Institute, 1999).

Although the mortality rate among children has decreased over the past 20 years, the incidence of cancers in children has slowly increased—especially diagnoses of melanoma. Among all age groups, the most common childhood cancers are leukemia, lymphoma, and brain cancer. As children enter their teen years, the incidence of osteosarcoma (bone cancer) also increases. Leukemia causes an abnormal increase in white blood cells. Lymphomas are malignant growths and cause enlargement of the lymph glands. Melanomas, or skin cancers, are spots on the skin caused by exposure to the sun.

Children undergoing treatment for any of these conditions are often drained of energy and limited in their ability to participate in school activities. Physical educators can play a role in making all children aware of the dangers of the sun's rays through lecture and by requiring sun-safety practices such as wearing sunscreen and hats when participating in outdoor activities.

HIV and AIDS. HIV and AIDS result from a viral disease that attacks the body's disease-fighting immune system. *Human immunodeficiency virus (HIV)* is a potentially fatal viral infection that, in school-aged children, almost exclusively is transmitted from an infected mother or through infected blood products. *Acquired immune deficiency syndrome (AIDS)* is the result of the HIV developing to full-blown AIDS. Careful monitoring of the student's general health is required to avoid any exposure to infections that the immune system is unable to fight. The United States Centers for Disease Control (CDC) recommend that most children with HIV/AIDS be admitted to school without restriction, stating that they pose no threat to classmates.

Hepatitis B. Hepatitis B is a highly infectious viral disease. It causes inflammation of the liver and is characterized by jaundice and fever. Cases of this strain and *Hepatitis A* are on the increase in the United States.

Obesity. Although not typically included in a listing of disabilities, obesity is the major health-threatening condition in America among the school-aged population. Obesity is defined in terms of body fat and is expressed by the percentage of actual body weight that is made up of fat. For children to age 12, if 20 percent or more of the body weight is fat, the child is considered obese. Physical educators have an important role in teaching lifestyle behaviors that control body weight and encouraging students to adapt and use them into adulthood.

Hematologic disorders: sickle cell disease (anemia). Sickle cell disease is a genetic blood disorder that affects the hemoglobin of approximately one in 375 African Americans born in the United States each year. Hemoglobin's role is to deliver oxygen to the cells of the body; sickle hemoglobin (Hemoglobin S) causes the blood cells to bend into a sickle or crescent-shaped form, which is rigid and has difficulty passing through small vessels. When sickle-shaped cells block small blood vessels, complications can occur, including pain, convulsions, and stroke.

Sickle cell disease is an inherited disorder. In the United States, the disease is more prevalent in African Americans; however, worldwide it is distributed among all races in Central and South America, southern Europe, central and southern India, and Africa. If one parent has the sickle cell trait and one parent has another hemoglobin trait, there is a one in four chance that the child will be born with sickle cell disease.

Treatment strategies include red blood cell transfusions, medication, and bone marrow transplantation. While medical treatment may be ongoing, teachers should be aware of the difficulties children with this disorder may encounter in physical education.

Because the oxygen-carrying mechanism in the blood (red blood cells) is damaged in children with these disorders, it is not efficient at oxygenating the muscles. Transport of oxygen is important to sustained activity; thus, these children will show signs of fatigue before other children. Create an environment where children have permission to self-regulate—rest as needed—or place them in roles where the demands are less vigorous, such as a first base player in softball or setter in volleyball. The rules or game protocols may be altered to accommodate the need to be less active while keeping all children "in the game."

Specific Learning Disability

The number of students identified as having a specific learning disability varies considerably from state to state, from district to district, and from one school intervention team or service committee to the next. Although most definitions are based on that established by the federal government, the proportion of students identified is reported by the Department of Health and Human Services as 7.5 percent to 9 percent of boys and 6 percent of girls (Dey & Bloom, 2005). Dey and Bloom present some interesting data:

- Six percent of children ages 3 through 17 with learning disabilities had attention deficit hyperactivity disorder (ADHD).
- Boys are twice as likely as girls (9 percent vs. 4 percent) to be diagnosed with this disorder.
- When compared with children with excellent or very good health status, children with fair or poor health are four times more likely to have a learning disability (26 percent vs. 6 percent).
- Children with fair or poor health are also three times more likely to have ADHD (17 percent vs. 6 percent).

The U. S. Department of Education's definition of specific learning disabilities is found in the regulations for IDEA '04:

> "Specific learning disability" means a disorder in one or more of the basic psychological processes involved in understanding or in using language, spoken or written, that may manifest itself in an imperfect ability to listen, think, speak, read, write, spell, or do mathematical calculations, including conditions such as perceptual disabilities, brain injury, minimal brain dysfunction, dyslexia, and developmental aphasia. Specific

---

Teaching Tip

HEALTH IMPAIRMENTS • Understanding the principles of physical conditioning and safety as related to students' medical status and modifying activities to accommodate students who may need frequent rest periods, more fluid consumption, or control of body temperature will go a long way toward inclusion of students with health impairments in regular physical activities.

> **Teaching Tip**
>
> **LEARNING DISABILITIES** • Understanding behavior management, using functional assessment and observation skills, frequently changing activities, and supporting a variety of learning styles are key to focusing students with learning disabilities on the motor tasks of your physical education program.

learning disability does not include learning problems that are primarily the result of visual, hearing, motor disabilities, mental retardation, emotional disturbance, or environmental, cultural, or economic disadvantages. (U.S. Department of Education, 2005, regulation, Sec. 300.8 (c) (10))

One of the defining characteristics of students with a learning disability is unexpected underachievement. In other words, these children do not have mental retardation, yet they perform well below the expectations of teachers and parents.

There is no standard means of classifying or clustering individuals with a specific learning disability, so Table C.4 identifies categories of behaviors or characteristics that interfere with learning, particularly in the motor domain, that are common among individuals with learning disabilities. Students may have any combination of these characteristics.

Unfortunately, not much is known about the causes of learning disabilities. Some students have proven brain damage from head injury or anoxia; some may have inherited this disability. Diet and various other environmental factors have also been suggested as causes of learning disabilities, but few have gained widespread acceptance. More is being learned about genetic factors as technology improves.

Speech or Language Impairments

Although classified in federal legislation as one category, these impairments are really two separate but related disabilities. *Language* is the communication of ideas through symbols we call words. *Speech* is the vocal production of language. A student who has difficulty communicating thoughts and ideas at age-appropriate levels has a language disorder. Another whose speech is unintelligible or unpleasant and interferes with communication has a speech impairment.

Speech disorders. Speech disorders are divided into three categories: articulation, voice, and fluency or speech flow. Individuals may have problems in more than one of these areas simultaneously. *Articulation disorders* relate to the intelligibility of an individual's speech. Interfering qualities may include omissions—leaving out a sound or letter in pronouncing words; substitutions—using one sound in place of another; additions—adding extra sounds to words; or distortions—sounds that only approximate the correct sound. Because speech is a fine motor activity, many children with speech disorders also have other movement disorders. *Voice disorders* refer to variations in pitch, loudness, and the quality of the sound. Monotone speech, stereotyped inflections, and breaks or cracks of the voice are considered disorders of pitch. Nasality and hoarseness are two examples of disorders of the quality of voice. *Speech flow or fluency disorders* are associated with the rate and flow pattern of a person's speech. Stuttering is one type. It includes abnormal repetitions, hesitations, or prolongation of speech sounds, syllables, or movements required for articulation (Hallahan & Kauffman, 2005). Young children often exhibit dysfluencies and articulation disorders in the course of normal speech development. Hesitating in the middle of the sentence, repeating parts of the sentence or words, or inserting fillers such as "umm" or "you know" are very common, as are substitutions, such as saying /w/ instead of /r/, as in "wobin" instead of robin. Dysfluency in young children is often the result of being excited, stressed, or in unfamiliar situations and normally resolves itself with maturation.

Language disorders. Language disorders include problems in receptive language—deriving meaning from what is heard; and in expressive language—expressing oneself in a meaningful way with words. Three aspects of language can be disordered in children: form, content, and use.

> **Teaching Tip**
>
> **SPEECH OR LANGUAGE DISORDERS** • Planning a structured program with class routines and instructional learning cues will provide an effective learning environment for students with speech or language disorders. In addition, language can be embedded into the lesson, such as movement vocabulary, positional concepts, and social language. Appropriate teaching strategies for anyone with difficulty processing language include multisensory instruction, simplifying language, ample use of visual communication methods, and reducing reliance on auditory memory and auditory sequencing.

TABLE C.4 Characteristics common to individuals with a specific learning disability.

Perceptual, perceptual–motor, and general coordination problems
- Visual perception disabilities
- Auditory perception disabilities
- Perceptual–motor dysfunction
- Underdeveloped body image
- Poor spatial orientation
- Clumsiness
- Poor fine motor coordination
- Poor balance
- Poor eye–hand coordination
- Motor-planning problems or inaccurate motor responses

Disorders of attention and hyperactivity
- Short attention span
- Distractibility
- Hyperactivity
- Impulsiveness
- Perseveration
- Hyporesponsiveness

Language problems
- Expressive language problems
- Receptive language problems
- Auditory sequencing difficulties
- Auditory retention problems

Disorders of memory and thinking
- Memory deficit
- Impulsivity
- Lack of concept development
- Dissociation

Emotional ability
- Lack of emotion
- Frequent changes in mood
- Social maladjustment
- Low self-esteem
- Frustration

Neurological problems
- EEG irregularities
- "Soft" neurological signs
- Hypo- or hyperresponsiveness to sensory stimuli

Academic achievement
- Achievement potential discrepancy
- Uneven development
- Problems in reading, writing, spelling, and arithmetic

The rule systems used in oral language are referred to as *form*. Three rule systems comprise form in language: phonology—the sounds used; morphology—the structure of words; and syntax—how the word is placed in a sentence. It is in language form that most people who speak English as a second language have difficulty. They often substitute a sound used in their native language for sounds used in English, use the wrong tense of a word, or use the words in the wrong order for English syntax. Children with form disorders are likely to commit some of these same rule violations.

The second aspect of language, *content*, relates to the meaning of spoken language. Semantics is the system that determines the meaning of the content. Unless the speaker and listener share the same meaning for a given word, an entirely different message may be heard. As an example, the use of slang or "inside jargon" is often the place where teens and parents fail to communicate—certain "inside words" used to communicate between teens often have a different meaning to their parents. This is a matter of difference in semantics. Children with delayed language may understand only one meaning of a word or only the most simple and concrete meaning.

The third aspect, *use*, concerning pragmatics or how language is used, is based on context. Students with this type of disorder are likely to be inappropriate in their speech, using language that is appropriate for one context in another context in which it is not. Again, as an example, words that teens use among themselves to communicate may be totally inappropriate if used at home or at a church meeting. Teens use jargon or lingua intentionally to exclude listeners other than their "inside group." This makes it ever so much more important for the educator to stay current with the latest jargon so that inappropriate uses can be eliminated from the classroom. Teachers must know whether "totally rad" or "she dissed me" is appropriate talk for school. (It is equally important to know whether Bart Simpson is a legitimate student signing into after-school detention!)

Etiologies of speech and language disorders are many, varied, and sometimes unknown. They include brain damage, malfunction of the respiratory or speech mechanisms, and malformation of the articulators as in cleft lip or palate. Individuals with hearing impairments and those who have chronic ear infections experience interruptions in hearing language and thus are at a disadvantage when learning to replicate it.

Traumatic Brain Injury

In the past, professionals directing programs for adults and seniors have been most likely to encounter individuals with traumatic brain injury (TBI) resulting from motor vehicle accidents, assaults, sports accidents, and other causes (Hux & Hacksley, 1996). Schools have seen an increase in individuals with TBI in the past 40 years. More than 100,000 children and youth between birth and age 21 are hospitalized each year with head injuries. It is estimated that 1 in 500 develop continuing learning and behavioral problems (Katsiyannis & Conderman, 1994). As a result of modern medicine, more children are surviving serious head injuries, and experts estimate that nearly one third of those who sustain injury acquire lifelong disabilities (Singer, Glang, & Williams, 1996). Therefore, Congress added TBI to the list of special education categories in 1990 and defines this disability in IDEA '04 as:

> an acquired injury to the brain caused by an external physical force, resulting in total or partial functional disability or psychosocial impairment, or both, that adversely affects a child's educational performance. The term applies to open or closed head injuries resulting in impairments in one or more areas, such as cognition; language; memory; attention; reasoning; abstract thinking; judgment; problem solving; sensory, perceptual, and motor abilities; psychosocial behavior; physical functions; information processing; and speech. The term does not apply to brain injuries that are congenital or degenerative, or to brain injuries induced by birth trauma. (U. S. Department of Education, 2005, regulations, Sec. 300.8 (c) (12), p. 35837)

Teaching Tip

TRAUMATIC BRAIN INJURY • Be mindful of a student's ongoing medical condition and address learning challenges as they present themselves. Functional assessment and observations of motor performance for safe and successful participation will facilitate the transition of students with TBI back into school as well as contribute to their rehabilitation. Always focus on what the student *can do*, while accommodating or making allowances for processing delays.

In many ways, individuals with TBI may be more challenging to teach because of the change in performance they experience. Attempts to perform tasks—physical or mental—once found to be easy can become frustrating and confusing. Unlike individuals with mental retardation or other disorders present from birth, these children once knew how to function normally, and following the trauma, must learn all over again. During the healing and learning process, they also will grieve the loss of normal functioning and demonstrate anger at the present situation. Family members and teachers undergo the same grieving process, discussed in more detail in Chapter 14.

The most common causes of TBI are falls, domestic accidents, motor vehicle accidents, pedestrian and bicycle accidents, assaults, and sports injuries (Hux & Hacksley, 1996). Whereas these causes are more common among older children and adults, sadly the most common cause of TBI among children under age two is child abuse.

Visual Impairment

Professionals recognize several classifications of visual impairment. The generally accepted definition of legal blindness is:

a level of visual impairment that has been defined by law to determine eligibility for benefits. It refers to central visual acuity of 20/200 or less in the better eye with the best possible correction, as measured on a Snellen vision chart, or a visual field of 20 degrees or less. (American Foundation for the Blind, 2006)

States and school districts vary in determining the range of visual acuity that will qualify students for special education services. Typically, students with visual acuity measuring 20/70 to 20/200 in the better eye with correction are considered to have low vision (Heller, Alerto, Forney, & Schwartzman, 1996). The movement in defining disabilities is more toward function—in this case, use of residual vision—so educationally, *blind* includes those who have such a severe visual impairment that they have no functional use of vision for learning and use Braille for reading. Students with low vision can see large print and usually require special materials or assorted magnifying devices. Visual impairments are usually classified in terms of visual acuity as measured by a Snellen chart. This chart measures one's ability to see relative to the normal eye. Most individuals who are legally blind have some useable vision—that is what the Snellen chart score measures: a person who is legally blind can see at 20 feet what the normal eye can see at 200 feet; thus, the person's vision is said to be 20/200.

The behavior of individuals with a visual impairment varies depending on the extent of sight loss and the age at onset of the impairment. Those who have a severe visual disability that was present at birth have *congenital blindness*. They have no visual reference to the physical world. Individuals who acquired a severe visual disability after the age of two have *adventitious blindness*. They may have an orientation to the physical world that helps "ground" them and give them a visual reference. The older an individual is when he or she loses sight, the more experience the person has to reference as he or she navigates through life.

Nearly all blindness in school-aged children results from accidents or prenatal factors such as heredity, prematurity (low birth weight), or infection in the mother (e.g., Rubella during pregnancy). Genetic factors in retinitis pigmentosa have been identified, taking medical research one step closer to finding a cure.

CHALLENGES TO LEARNING MOTOR SKILLS

When using the developmental model in planning instruction, teachers should consider each student's level of motor development along with the learning challenges or characteristics that he or she brings to the learning environment. Because students with varying disabilities present these learning challenges, this section discusses the learning challenges with reference to the disabilities in which they manifest. The developmental model is also woven into the discussion to retain orientation to motor development.

Aggressive behavior. The typical middle and high school curriculum includes a variety of activities of competition, such as sport, that can precipitate aggressive behavior in students who have a disability of which aggressive behavior is a characteristic. Students with autism, emotional disturbance, and behavioral disorders may strike out at others or engage in self-injurious behavior with seemingly little provocation. These students are capable of developing advanced skills and culturally determined forms of movement but may require repeated and clearly defined statements of acceptable behaviors across the curriculum.

Attention deficit. Although attention span increases with age in the normal course of development, students with autism, emotional disturbance, mental retardation, specific learning disability, attention deficit hyperactivity disorder, and TBI have persistent challenges to maintaining attention and on-task behavior. Short segments of activity in increasing lengths and effectively used back-to-task cues are necessary. Most of these students are capable of developing advanced motor skills and engaging in culturally determined forms of movement, although some may require some form of prompting.

Auditory perception disorder. Beyond hearing acuity, students with autism, hearing impairment, speech and language impairments, deaf-blindness, mental retardation, learning disabilities, and TBI

Teaching Tip

VISUAL IMPAIRMENT • Providing consistent activity area setup and routines, and objects that contrast with the environment; taking the time to introduce the student to the movement area ("anchoring"); and assigning a "peer buddy" will assist students with a visual impairment to be safe and successful in the physical education class. In addition, using position-, direction-, and action-specific language in instructions is often most helpful to those students in performing the movement task.

may have breakdowns in processing and interpreting sounds—especially language. Words that sound alike get confused, parts of a set of instructions may get lost, and other distractions can complicate understanding. Although some of these students can develop advanced motor skills, the severe forms of deaf-blindness, mental retardation, and TBI may preclude students from developing beyond the developmental level of motor patterns.

Brittle bones. Students with cancer and some orthopedic impairments such as osteogenesis imperfecta either become fragile or are fragile as a result of their disability. Whereas, developmentally, these children should develop motor skills normally, they often must follow medical restrictions on activity, which results in a lack of experience or opportunity to develop skills or participate at all.

Control of physiological functions. Individuals with certain health and orthopedic impairments may have personal hygiene and personal care needs. For example, the effects of certain medications on muscles of the bladder, sweat glands, and intestines may require the student to change clothing or may affect participation in aquatic activities. Some examples include water temperature triggering seizures, a need to avoid situations that could rupture an external collection bag, and a need for extra privacy when changing diapers. Although those who wear diapers or an external collection bag may not be seen often in general physical education classes, their participation is not precluded. Most issues regarding personal care can be resolved by working with the student, parents, and other school personnel.

Fatiguing easily. Some students fatigue easily as a direct result of their disability (e.g., sickle cell disease, congenital heart defects, hemophilia, rheumatic fever, or muscular atrophy). Others fatigue easily as an indirect result of their disability, such as students with visual impairments or deaf-blindness, because they often lack the opportunity to participate in vigorous activity and condition their cardiovascular systems. Moving extra weight in appliances and other assistive devices challenges students with leg braces and other orthopedic impairments. Students can develop motor skills to the extent that their use of space permits, but frequent rest periods may be required. Efforts to improve strength and endurance can be charted easily in physical education class or in a homework project using gradually increasing goals.

Hypertonia. Too much muscle tone is common among individuals with cerebral palsy, contractures, hyperactivity, and certain neurological conditions or syndromes. Advanced levels of motor skills and culturally determined forms of movement can be acquired, but this is limited by the students' range of motion, on-task time, and ability to learn.

> ## Teaching Tip
>
> **HYPERTONIA** • Regular muscle stretching and flexibility exercises are important for individuals with hypertonia. It will often be necessary for the physical educator to work collaboratively with an occupational or physical therapist who also works with the student with hypertonia.

Hyper- and hyporesponsiveness to sensory stimuli. Some level of disrupted transmission of sensory stimuli accompanies most disabilities in the category of neurological impairments. Students with sensory impairments such as deafness and hearing impairment, visual impairment, deaf-blindness, or paralysis (spinal cord injuries) clearly cannot respond to stimuli they cannot receive. Other neurological "soft signs" seen in students with autism, emotional and behavioral disorders, specific learning disabilities, and TBI are often accompanied by reduced responsiveness or overresponsiveness to some forms of stimuli. Whether the reason is obvious and explainable or not, the physical educator has the responsibility to plan activities at age-appropriate levels to help the student manage or cope with stimuli that interfere with learning and participation.

Hypotonia. Students who are obese or who have mental retardation (especially Down syndrome and Prader-Willi syndrome), multiple sclerosis, an autism spectrum disorder, poliomyelitis, spina bifida, spinal cord injuries, or muscular dystrophy may have flaccid muscles or low muscle tone resulting from their disability. Other students with flaccid muscles include those with visual impairments and deaf-blindness, in part because their level of activity tends to be limited, but these students can fully develop advanced motor skills given the opportunity and guidance. Hypotonia usually refers to a neurologically based condition of the muscles that is not considered changeable through exercise, whereas flaccid muscles refers to weakness and low tone that is a result of inactivity. However, many people with hypotonia have limited activity for many reasons. Therefore, they can improve their muscle strength and decrease the flaccid condition of their

> **Teaching Tip**
>
> **HYPOTONIA** • When working with individuals with low muscle tone, the physical educator should plan muscle strengthening and toning programs that are based on individual potential for improvement.

muscles to some degree. Individuals with flaccid muscles due exclusively to inactivity can achieve greater improvement through exercise.

Joint dysfunction. Most orthopedic disabilities classified as musculoskeletal conditions or orthopedic impairment are accompanied by joint dysfunction. Students with joint dysfunction acquire motor skills normally but may be limited by range of motion or pain. New medical treatments for pain and disease management are helping these children live more typical, active lives.

Language impairment. Difficulty with receptive and expressive language accompanies a number of disabilities in addition to speech or language impairment. Students with autism, hearing impairments, deaf-blindness, emotional disturbance and behavioral disorders, mental retardation, learning disabilities, and TBI may require some of the same adaptations for instruction as students whose primary disability is a speech or language impairment.

Low fitness. Students who have limited movement experience and opportunity (e.g., those with visual and hearing impairments, deaf-blindness, autism, or mental retardation) will probably remain in the low fitness range unless a concerted effort is made to increase self-initiated activities. Students with other disabilities, such as asthma, cardiovascular disorders, obesity, and muscular dystrophy, can be conditioned through slow, methodical incremental increases in aerobic, strength, and flexibility demands. Except for the most severely involved students, all can gain health benefits from fitness activities.

Memory and understanding. Although memory and understanding difficulties often result in a lack of response or an inappropriate motor response, they are related, but separate, challenges. For students who have difficulty understanding as a result of mental retardation, autism, language impairment, hearing impairment, or TBI, the educator can aid their understanding by providing a different form of input (stimuli), teaching smaller "chunks" of information at once, and using experiential learning and increased repetition. Students with memory difficulties such as those listed earlier and children with learning disabilities may have central processing disorders and can learn strategies that will help them recall certain kinds of information.

Poor balance. Students with poor balance include individuals with hearing impairments, deaf-blindness, muscular dystrophy, hydrocephalus, and cerebral palsy. They may not engage in activities at heights as in beam walking and using other gymnastics apparatus. In some cases, they may need to wear protective headgear. Their development of motor skills in other areas, however, may be limited only by their experience and opportunity.

Poor coordination. Students with a disability presenting the most obvious challenge to learning are those with cerebral palsy. Because of damage to the cerebellum, the mechanism of the brain most responsible for coordinating movement is impaired. Students with speech disorders, mental retardation, a specific learning disability, TBI, and other neurological disorders also show varying but lesser degrees of motor awkwardness. The development of culturally determined forms of movement is expected in all but the most severe cases; however, competitive activities are not likely to be highly motivating to some of these students.

Primitive reflex retention. Interference from primitive reflexes (those that should be integrated or inhibited) is more common among students with a disability than physical educators may realize. Students with "soft" neurological signs such as those with autism, speech and language impairments, learning disabilities, and TBI often demonstrate reflexes that interfere with throwing, tumbling, and catching. Students with cerebral palsy usually retain primitive reflexes because of the pathology of the disability.

Proprioceptive disorder. When students do not receive proprioceptive information (kinesthetic awareness) or receive inaccurate proprioceptive information, their motor accuracy is impaired. They often do not know where their body parts are in space or how to plan a sequence of movements. This disorder appears most often among students with speech disorders, mental retardation, neurological impairments, learning disabilities, and TBI. This interference with kinesthetic awareness often prevents these students from refining advanced motor skills and developing skill in culturally determined forms of movement.

Repetitive and stereotypic movements. For the teacher who is not aware that movements such as hand flapping, head banging, perseverating on an object, and other similar behaviors may be presented, they can be unnerving. Students with autism, visual impairments, and deaf-blindness often demonstrate repetitive, seemingly purposeless movements. Replacing these behaviors with more acceptable and appropriate behaviors is usually the goal of the entire educational team as well as the parents. The development of motor skills, however, is limited only by the student's experience and opportunities to participate.

Seizures. Seizure disorders can be anticipated to accompany all disabilities that result from head injury, as well as many of those accompanied by neurological "soft signs." This includes students with mental retardation, neurological impairments, learning disabilities, and TBI. Most seizures can be controlled through the use of medication. The physical educator should know the procedures recommended by the school district or agency, as well as each student's unique idiosyncrasies. For some students who have persistent forms of seizure disorder, it may be necessary for the physical educator to know the medically recommended first-aid procedures for grand mal seizures, which involve the whole body and can result in loss of consciousness. Whenever a student with a seizure disorder is enrolled in a physical education class, the teacher should check for any medically restricted activities. More subtle forms of seizures, such as petit mal (neurological staring spells) and complex partial seizures, may present a safety and teaching challenge in physical education because they include short periods during which the student is unaware of sights, sounds, and movement in the environment. Medical information is usually available to help the physical educator understand the student's unique patterns and type of seizures.

Tactile system disorders. Tactile disorders, just like other disorders in the earlier-maturing systems, tend to interfere with the acquisition of motor skills. Students with autism, neurological impairments, specific learning disabilities, and TBI tend to exhibit some level of impaired tactile sensation. Some respond only to deep touch; others are hyperresponsive and cannot tolerate tactile stimuli at all. Good tactile perception is thought to contribute to the development of spatial and body awareness. The tactile system is relied upon to learn a skill, such as throwing a ball with seams or laces, wrestling, tag, or gymnastics, and a deficit in this system can seriously impair learning.

> **Teaching Tip**
>
> **BODY TEMPERATURE REGULATION** • The physical educator should facilitate the individual's efforts to control body temperature environmentally (e.g., the student may need to wear more or less clothing or exercise out of the sun or in an air-conditioned room).

Temperature regulation difficulties. Temperature regulation difficulties can lead to hypo- or hyperthermia. Students with spinal cord injuries, spina bifida, poliomyelitis, or TBI may have damage to the nerves controlling the autonomic nervous system, reducing the body's ability to shiver when cold or perspire when overheated and creating a dangerous situation. Some cardiovascular disorders that inhibit circulation may also contribute to difficulties.

Vestibular system disorders. Although vestibular system disorders may manifest in poor balance, other effects such as dizziness, lack of spatial awareness, and approach or avoidance of movement also present learning challenges. Students with autism, hearing impairments, deaf-blindness, mental retardation, neurological impairments, learning disabilities, or TBI may show signs of disorders in this earlier-maturing system. Students who engage in repetitive, stereotypic movement may seek movement in the form of swinging or spinning. Children who become dizzy or disoriented as a result of this disorder may avoid movement or any activity in which they lack control over the rate of movement, such as riding a merry-go-round, swinging, and sometimes tumbling activities.

Visual perception disorder. Students with autism, visual impairment, deaf-blindness, mental retardation, learning disabilities, or TBI may have breakdowns in processing and interpreting visual stimuli. Being unable to distinguish an object, such as a ball, from the background (visual figure–ground), predict

> **Teaching Tip**
>
> **HELPING ALL CHILDREN** • It is important to remember that the "CAN DO" attitude is best practice for ALL students. When a child shows an interest in learning a skill, then a provision should be made for developing that specific skill through the developmental model.

visual characteristics of an object that is partially hidden (visual closure), remember a sequence of visually presented items (visual sequential memory), or sustain visual attention, as well as other interferences such as attention deficit, can complicate the acquisition of motor skills. For example, the ability to catch a chest pass in basketball is hampered when the student with reduced visual figure–ground ability cannot distinguish the ball from the body of the person throwing the ball. Although some students with visual perception disorder can develop advanced motor skills, the severe forms of deaf-blindness, mental retardation, and TBI may prevent students from developing beyond the developmental level of locomotor patterns.

QUICK REFERENCE

Table C.5, a quick reference to common attributes of specific disabilities, is offered to help you prepare quickly, review, or look up the challenges to learning that are most common to specific disabilities.

TABLE C.5 *Quick reference of common attributes of specific disabilities.*

CLASSIFICATION OF DISABILITIES	Aggressive behavior	Attention deficit	Auditory perception disorder	Bowel and bladder problems	Brittle bones	Fatiguing easily	Hypertonia	Hyper- or hyporesponsiveness	Hypotonia	Joint dysfunction	Language disorder (receptive/expressive)	Low fitness	Memory and understanding problems	Poor balance	Poor coordination	Primitive reflex retention	Proprioceptive disorders	Repetitive and stereotypic movements	Seizures	Tactile system disorders	Temperature regulation problems	Vestibular system disorders	Visual perception disorder
Autism	X	X	X					X			X	X	X				X		X		X		X	X
Deafness/Hearing Impairment			X					X			X		X										X	
Other Health Impairments				X	X	X					X		X							X			
Speech/Language Impairments			X								X					X	X	X					
Visual Impairment					X		X	X			X							X					X
Deaf-Blindness			X			X		X	X		X	X	X					X				X	X
Emotional Disturbance	X	X					X		X														
Mental Retardation			X	X					X		X	X	X		X		X		X			X	X
Orthopedic Impairment				X	X	X	X	X	X	X		X		X	X					X	X	X	X
Learning Disability		X	X				X	X			X		X		X	X	X		X			X	X
Traumatic Brain Injury	X	X	X					X			X		X		X		X		X	X	X	X	X

CHALLENGES TO LEARNING MOTOR SKILLS

REFERENCES

Accardo, P. J., Whitman, B. U., Laszewski, C., Haake, C. A., & Morrow, J. D. (1996). *Dictionary of developmental disabilities terminology*. Baltimore: Brookes.

American Foundation for the Blind. (1963). *Blindness: Some facts and figures*. New York: Author.

American Foundation for the Blind. (1999). *Prevalence estimates of blindness and visual impairment in the United States*. New York: Programs and Policy Research.

American Psychiatric Association. (2000). *Diagnostic and statistical manual of mental disorders*. Arlington, VA: Author.

Attwood, R. (1998). *Asperger's syndrome: A guide for parents and professionals*. Philadelphia: Jessica Kingsley Publishers.

Autism Society of America. (1999). *Autism Society of America* (brochure). Bethesda, MD: Author.

Bailey, D. B., Jr., Aytch, L. S., Odom, L. S., Symons, F., & Wolery, M. (1999). Early intervention as we know it. *Mental Retardation and Developmental Disabilities Research Reviews, 5*, 11–20.

Boothroyd, A. (1998). Recruitment and dynamic range in sensorineural hearing loss. *Hearing Loss, 19*, 11–13.

Bryant, B. R., Taylor, R. L., & Rivera, D. P. (1996). *Assessment of adaptive areas (AAA): Examiner's manual* (pp. 2–3). Austin, TX: Pro-Ed.

Dey, A. N., & Bloom, B. (2005). *Summary Health Statistics for U.S. Children: National Health Interview Survey, 2003*. National Center for Health Statistics, Vital Health Stat 10(223). Washington, DC: U.S. Government Printing Office.

Greenspan, S. (1997). Dead manual walking? Why the 1992 AAMR definition needs redoing. *Education and Training in Mental Retardation and Developmental Disabilities, 32*, 179–190.

Grossman, H. J. (Ed.). (1983). *Classification in mental retardation*. Washington, DC: American Association on Mental Retardation.

Hallahan, D. P., & Kauffman, J. M. (2005). *Exceptional learners: Introduction to special education*. Needham Heights, MA: Allyn & Bacon.

Heller, K. W., Alerto, P. A., Forney, P. E., & Schwartzman, M. N. (1996). *Understanding physical, sensory, and health impairments*. Pacific Grove, CA: Brooks/Cole.

Hux, K., & Hacksley, C. (1996). Mild traumatic brain injury: Facilitating school success. *Intervention in School and Clinic, 31*, 158–165.

Individuals with Disabilities Education Act. (1997). Public Law No. 105-17, 111 Stat. 37.

Kanner, L. (1943). Autistic disturbances of affective contact. *Nervous Child, 217*–250.

Katsiyannis, A., & Conderman, G. (1994). Serving individuals with traumatic brain injury: A national survey. *Remedial and Special Education, 13*, 319–325.

Kauffman, J. M. (1997). *Characteristics of behavioral disorders of children and youth* (5th ed.). Columbus, OH: Merrill.

Lester, G., & Kelman, M. (1997). State disparities in the diagnosis and placement of pupils with learning disabilities. *Journal of Learning Disabilities, 30*, 599–607.

Luckasson, R., Coulter, D. L., Polloway, E. A., Reis, S., Schalock, R. L., Snell, M. E., Spitaluik, D. M., & Stark, J. A. (1992). *Mental retardation: Definition, classification, and systems of supports*. Washington, DC: American Association on Mental Retardation.

MacMillan, D. L., Gresham, F. M., & Bocian, K. M. (1998). Discrepancy between definitions of learning disabilities and school practices: An empirical investigation. *Journal of Learning Disabilities, 31*, 314–326.

National Cancer Institute. (1999). *Cancer incidence and survival among children and adolescents*. U.S. SEER Program 1975–1995, N.I.H.: Washington, DC.

National Information Center for Children and Youth with Disabilities. (1997). Fact Sheet Number 10 (FS10). Washington, DC: Author.

Norris, L. (1999). Disorders of hearing in adults. In E. Plante & P. M. Beeson (Eds.), *Communication and communication disorders: A clinical introduction* (pp. 117–146). Boston: Allyn & Bacon.

Singer, G. H. S., Glang, A., & Williams, J. M. (Eds.). (1996). *Children with acquired brain injury: Educating and supporting families*. Baltimore: Brookes.

Tuttle, D. W., & Ferrell, K. A. (1995). Visually impaired. In E. L. Meyen & T. M. Sktic (Eds.), *Exceptional children and youth: An introduction* (4th ed., pp. 487–532). Denver, CO: Love.

United States Department of Education. (1999). Assistance to states for the education of children with disabilities and the early intervention program for infants and toddlers with disabilities: Final regulations. *Federal Register, 64*(48), C.F.R. Parts 300 and 303. Washington, DC: U. S. Government Printing Office.

APPENDIX D

Measurement and Evaluation Review

Chapter 5 covers measurement concepts that are important to understanding the process of assessment. Ultimately, future professionals should complete a measurement and evaluation course if they have not done so at this point. This appendix is intended to provide a brief introduction to some of the descriptive statistics discussed in Chapter 5. It is hoped that this more detailed coverage will supplement the chapter and further clarify the concepts presented.

STANDARDS

The point is made in Chapter 5 that standards are available for identifying students who should be considered for special class placement, for determining whether a student has met his or her annual goals and objectives, and for deciding when it is appropriate to recommend that a student be moved from an adapted physical education class to general physical education. To make these decisions using formal testing, it is important to understand the difference between criterion-referenced and norm-referenced standards. *Norm-referenced standards* are developed by gathering data on a large number of individuals who have specifically defined characteristics. For motor performance, the important characteristics tend to be age and sex because of the differences that emerge between boys and girls as children get older. The data are organized statistically, and performance standards called norms are constructed. Comparing a performance with norms results in a hierarchical ordering of individuals. Table D.1 shows a sample table of norm-referenced standards for performances of high school female volleyball players.

Criterion-referenced standards state an explicit definition of a task or score that must be attained to declare a level of accomplishment. Any given description or score represents the minimal level of competence or the ideal level to which the task is mastered. Comparing a performance to the criterion results in a description of the student's approximation to the criterion rather than a hierarchical order-

TABLE D.1

Sample norm-referenced standards.

HIGH SCHOOL PLAYERS

Percentile	Height	Vertical Jump	20-Yard Dash	Basketball Throw
99	74.0	22.0	2.87	70.8
95	71.0	18.5	3.04	64.5
90	70.0	17.8	3.12	60.0
85	69.0	16.5	3.17	57.0
80	68.0	16.0	3.20	55.0
75	67.5	15.7	3.23	52.8
70	67.0	15.3	3.26	51.5
65	66.5	15.0	3.28	50.5
60	66.0	14.5	3.32	49.0
55	65.5	14.2	3.34	48.4
50	65.5	14.0	3.37	47.2
45	65.5	13.7	3.42	46.0
40	65.0	13.5	3.46	44.5
35	65.0	13.3	3.47	43.5
30	64.0	13.0	3.50	42.0
25	64.0	12.5	3.53	40.8
20	63.0	12.3	3.57	39.2
15	62.5	12.0	3.60	37.8
10	62.0	11.5	3.67	36.4
5	61.5	11.0	3.80	33.5

Source: Data used with the permission of James G. Disch, Rice University, Houston, TX.

ing of that student's performance relative to other similar students. Table D.2 shows one form of criterion-referenced standards.

Another form of criterion found on health-related fitness tests is a threshold score that a student should achieve to have gained health benefits from physical activity on that parameter (see Table D.3).

SCORES

Types. The two types of scores most commonly used are continuous and discrete. *Continuous scores* have a potentially infinite number of values (i.e., along a continuum), depending on the ability or accuracy of the tool used in the measurement. The following are continuous scores for students running a 100-yard dash:

Student A	11.2 secs.
Student B	10.9 secs.
Student C	9.3 secs.
Student D	10.2 secs.
Student E	9.9 secs.

It can be seen that these scores could have been more precise if they were timed with a watch that registered 100ths of a second. There also could have been many more scores between the high of 11.2 seconds and the low of 9.3.

In contrast, *discrete scores* have a limited number of specific values and usually have no obtainable scores between these values. Performances such as curl-ups or push-ups generate discrete scores because there is no measurable performance between a complete curl-up or push-up. The following are scores on these performances made by the same five students:

Student A	20 curl-ups	12 push-ups
Student B	22 curl-ups	15 push-ups
Student C	25 curl-ups	25 push-ups
Student D	18 curl-ups	26 push-ups
Student E	23 curl-ups	22 push-ups

Classification. Scores can be classified as ratio, interval, ordinal, or nominal. *Ratios* have a common unit of measure between each score and a true zero point. The number of curl-ups, push-ups, or feet jumped are examples of ratios. *Interval scores* have a common unit of measure between each score, but do not have a true zero point. Intelligence or knowledge tests generate interval scores because each score reflects one more question answered correctly than the next lower score, but a zero score does not reflect absolute lack of intelligence or knowledge. A zero score, in this instance, simply means that no questions were answered correctly. *Ordinal scores* do not have a common unit of measure. Class rankings are ordinal because they are "ordered"—the best-skilled student in class is given a rank of 1, the second best a rank of 2, and so on. For example, based on the times from the earlier 100-yard dash, the students are ranked here from best to worst.

Student C	#1
Student E	#2
Student D	#3
Student B	#4
Student A	#5

The student ranked #1 ran .6 seconds faster than #2, and #2 ran only .3 seconds faster than #3, yet there is only one ranked position between each

TABLE D.2

Sample criterion-referenced standards for locomotor patterns.

PERFORMANCE	CRITERION
Walking	Walks distance of 10 feet
Running	Runs length of gym
Throwing	Throws overhand with weight shift
Jumping	Jumps with feet together

TABLE D.3

Sample criterion-referenced standards for health-related fitness items.

| | PERCENT FAT | | CURL-UPS | | PUSH-UPS | |
AGE	BOYS	GIRLS	BOYS	GIRLS	BOYS	GIRLS
5	10–25	17–32	2–10	2–10	3–8	3–8
6	10–25	17–32	2–10	2–10	3–8	3–8
7	10–25	17–32	4–14	4–14	4–10	4–10
8	10–25	17–32	6–20	6–20	5–13	5–13
9	10–25	17–32	9–24	9–24	6–15	6–15
10	10–25	17–32	12–24	12–24	7–20	7–15
11	10–25	17–32	15–28	15–28	8–20	7–15
12	10–25	17–32	18–36	18–36	10–20	7–15

of them. A disadvantage to class ranks is that the identity of each individual score is lost and the ranks make the students' abilities appear as though they are equally distributed across the spectrum. *Nominal scores*, which are names, cannot be hierarchically ordered, but they can provide useful information for the adapted physical educator in the assessment process. It is useful to know which students are right-handed, which cannot eat peanuts, and which are subject to seizure.

Organization. Scores can be organized in a number of different ways depending on how they are to be used. A simple *frequency distribution* is a table with all of the scores (x) listed in descending order from best to worst. Opposite each score is the frequency (f) or number of times that score occurs (i.e., the number of students making each score). The highest score is usually the best score (except in timed events, in which the lowest score is best). Table D.4 shows a sample frequency distribution.

If this table represented a group of students being considered for Special Olympics competition, it is easy to see from the organization of scores which students are the most likely candidates to compete in the softball throw. Because the softball throw for distance is suggested as a measure of shoulder strength and arm speed, Table D.4 also helps identify students who need work in those areas.

Table D.5 shows the distribution of scores on the 50-yard dash. Because the 50-yard dash is a running event, the lowest score (i.e., fewest seconds) is the best score. Again, it is easy to get a picture of this group of students in terms of running speed. The teacher can readily identify students who need work in this area.

Another simple method of organizing scores is by *graphing*. This method gives a literal picture of the similarities and differences within a group on any given measure. For example, to graph the softball throw scores represented in Table D.4, the scores are listed on the horizontal axis and the frequencies on the vertical axis. A dot is placed on the graph above each score and opposite the frequency or number of students making that score. When the dots are connected with lines, a frequency polygon is completed. A smooth line drawn through the majority of the scores gives an even better picture of the distribution (see Figure D.1).

A graph of the 50-yard dash times (shown in Table D.5) gives a different picture of this group of students (see Figure D.2). The long, low tail of the curve to the left of the graph, which shows that relatively few students ran slowly, characterizes a negatively skewed distribution. If the long tail were to the right, it would be positively skewed. As discussed in Chapter 5, simple polygons of students' performances will tell you very quickly how similar or different students in your class are on any given parameter.

DESCRIPTIVE STATISTICS

Mean

Although the frequency table and polygon help to characterize the group, other descriptive values are significant when describing specific characteristics.

TABLE D.5
50-yard dash measured in seconds (ratios).

X	F	X	F	X	F
7.2	1	8.1	9	9.1	1
7.3	1	8.2	12	9.3	2
7.4	1	8.4	9	9.5	1
7.6	1	8.6	9	9.6	1
7.7	2	8.7	7	9.9	1
7.9	1	8.8	2	10.1	1
8.0	2	8.9	1	10.3	1

TABLE D.4
Softball throw measured in feet (ratios).

X	F	X	F	X	F
169	1	115	2	87	5
154	1	112	2	85	3
152	2	110	5	70	2
149	3	107	7	65	2
130	1	105	12	64	1
128	1	103	10	50	3
127	1	100	5	41	1
125	2	98	3	30	1
123	3	95	2	27	1
120	1	91	2	15	1

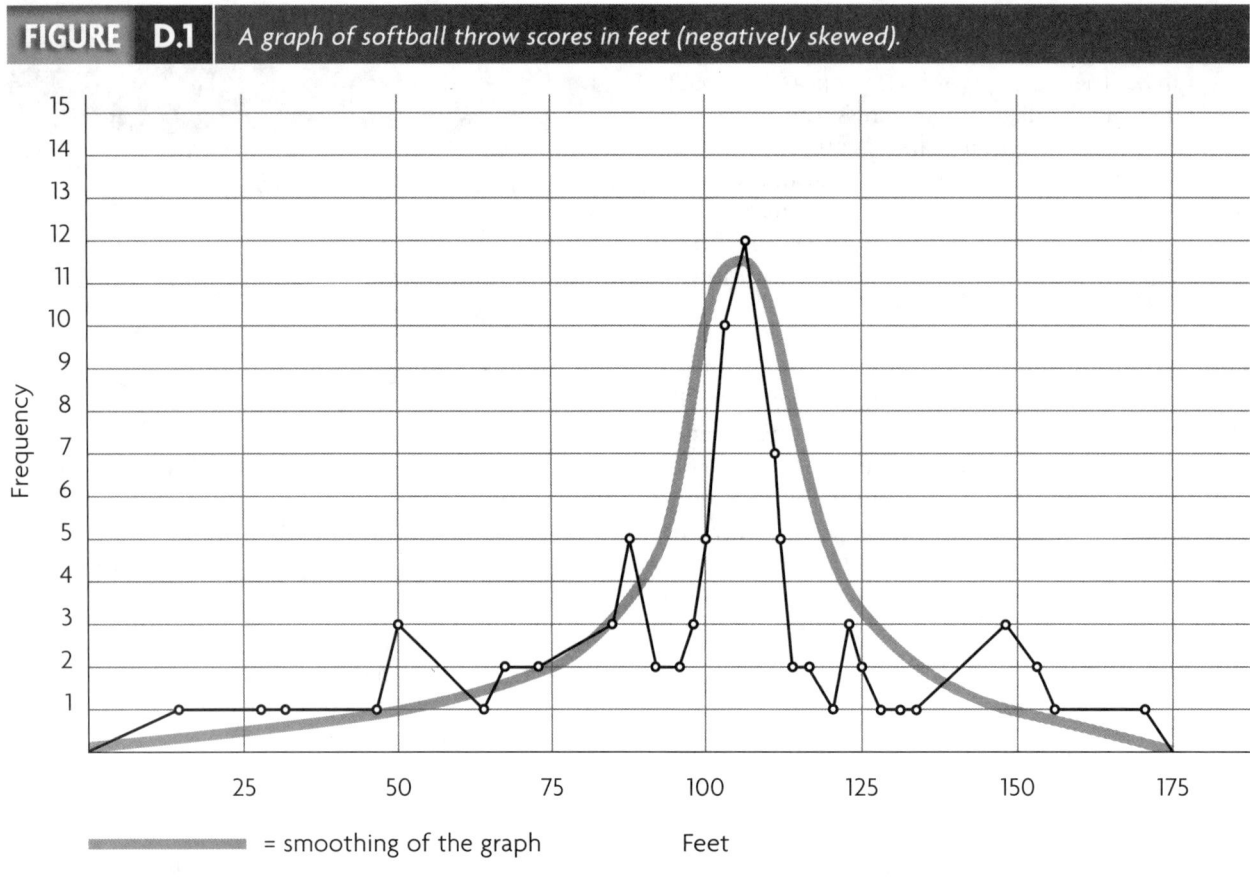

FIGURE D.1 *A graph of softball throw scores in feet (negatively skewed).*

= smoothing of the graph   Feet

Measures of central tendency are among the most important descriptive statistics, the most commonly used being the mean.

The *mean* is the arithmetic average score of all the scores and is influenced by the position and value of any single score in the group. Adding all of the scores in the group and dividing that sum by the number of scores in the group produces the mean. For example, the sum of the softball throw scores divided by the number of scores is:

$$\frac{8,708}{86} = 101.26 \text{ for the average or mean score}$$

The formula for calculating the mean is:

$$\bar{x} = \frac{\Sigma x}{n}$$

$\bar{x}$ = mean; n = the number of scores in the group; x = a score; and Σ = summation

Median

The *median* is the absolute middle score—half of the scores fall above this score and half fall below. To find it, the scores must be listed in order from best to worst. The median of the softball throw scores in Table D.4 is 105 because out of 87 scores, 43 scores are greater than 105 and 43 less than 105. Notice that the median is affected only by the position of each score and not the value.

The formula for finding the median is:

$$M = n - 1 + \frac{1}{2}$$

M = median and n = the number of scores in the group

Mode

The *mode* is the score in a group that is most frequently obtained. For the softball throw scores, the mode is 105. The mode is seldom used in test development and reporting. It is the least stable measure of central tendency because a change in one score (in some cases) changes the value of the mode. If only two more students had thrown the ball 103 feet, the distribution would be bi-modal—having two modes. Or, if three of the students throwing the ball 105 feet had thrown it 104 feet, suddenly 103 feet would be the mode.

In a normal curve (i.e., frequency polygon), the mean, median, and mode are the same (see the normal or bell-shaped curve shown in Figure 5.4). The highest point on the curve is where the most students scored. This high point is also in the exact middle of the distribution. In a negatively skewed curve, such as Figure D.1, the mean is less than the median and the mode because its value is influenced (it is drawn down) by the extremely low scores. In a positively skewed curve, the situation is reversed.

Standard Deviation

Another value often used to describe a group of scores is the standard deviation. As a measure of variability, it indicates the spread of the scores—the homogeneity or heterogeneity of the group.

The *standard deviation*, used with the mean, is the most common measure of variability reported in ready-made tests. It describes the average amount by which all of the scores differ or deviate from the mean. Looking at the two frequency polygons (Figures D.1 and D.2) showing the softball throw and the 50-yard dash, it is easy to see that the standard deviation for the softball throw is going to be much larger than for the 50-yard dash because this polygon is more spread out. A large standard deviation describes a rather heterogeneous group of scores; a small one describes a homogeneous group.

The standard deviation is very useful in interpreting measurements, as you have seen in Chapters 8 and 9. A formula for calculating the standard deviation is:

$$SD = \sqrt{\Sigma \frac{(\bar{x} - x)^2}{n}}$$

SD = standard deviation; $\bar{x}$ = mean; Σ = summation; n = number of scores in the group; and x = a score

Range

The range, used with the mode, is the easiest statistic to determine. The *range* is the difference between the lowest and highest scores and tells much about impending challenges to a teacher planning group activities. Like the mode, it is not a very stable measure because a change in either of the extreme scores could significantly affect the range. It can readily be

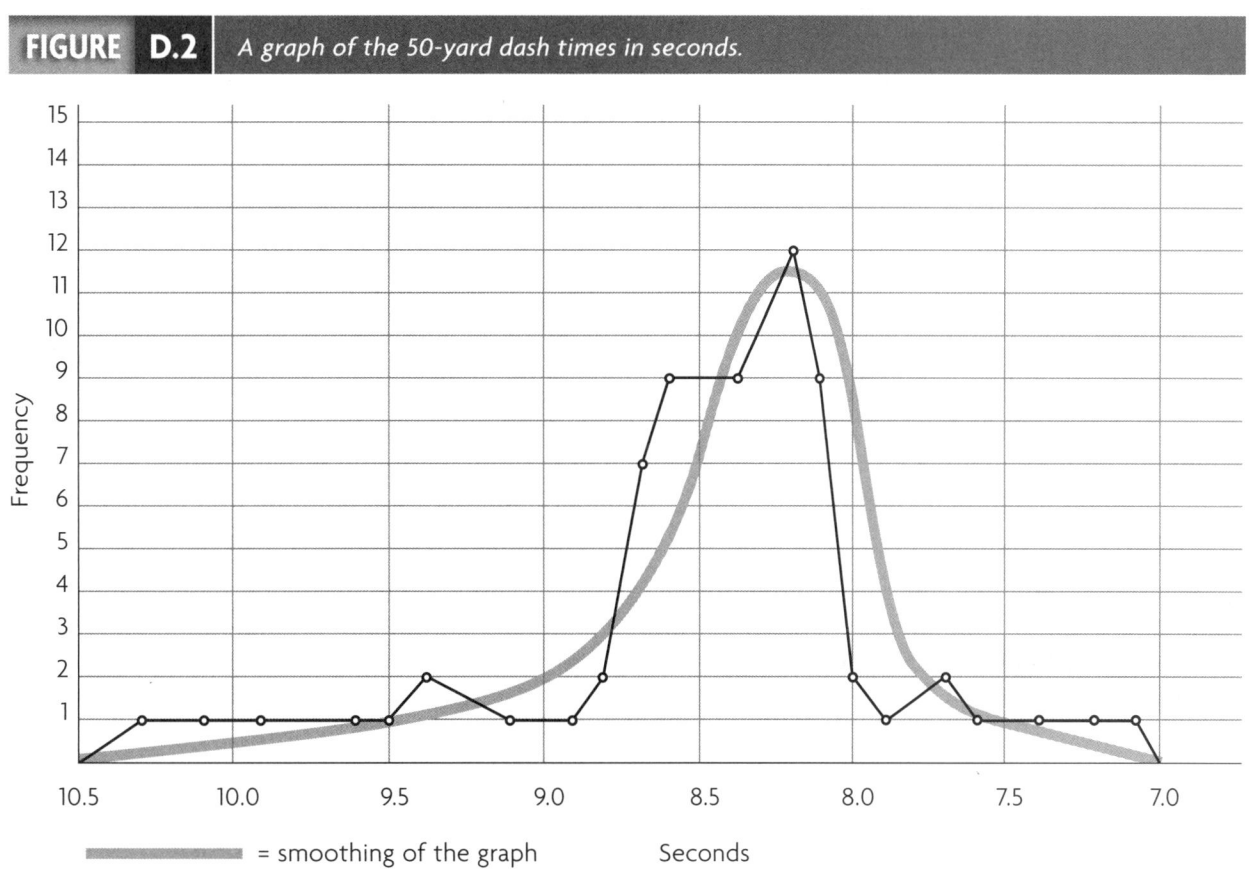

FIGURE D.2 A graph of the 50-yard dash times in seconds.

= smoothing of the graph   Seconds

determined that the range for the softball throw scores (Table D.4) goes from the high score of 169 to the low score of 15, for a range of 154! This difference is as great as the total distance the second-best thrower threw the ball!

Rank

A student's score may be more meaningful when considered in the context of the group. The score takes on further meaning when the mean and standard deviation are also known. Because these values represent the group of which the student is a part, a parent or professional can see generally how the student compares (*ranks*) either with a nationally derived group as expressed in percentile ranked norms or with a group of local peers as in the student's own class. More precise methods are used in ready-made tests to explain the position of a given score, and it is important for the adapted physical educator to be familiar with them in order to use them when interpreting a particular score.

Correlations

Determining the relationships (*correlations*) between scores is another way to ensure that the interpretation of measurements will net a quality assessment. An easy-to-use correlation formula is the Spearman Rho formula. It is not as accurate as other formulas because the scores are first reduced to ranks, thus losing the actual value of the individual scores. It is easier to calculate by hand, however. The differences between the ranks of the two measures are used in the formula:

$$R = 1 - \frac{6\Sigma d^2}{n(n+1)(n-1)}$$

R = Rho (the correlation); Σ = summation; d = difference between the ranks of each pair of scores; and n = the number of pairs of scores

Standard Scores

When trying to describe a student's overall performance, sometimes it is necessary to reduce the scores to one common scale in order to make sense out of them.

The z score scale has a mean of zero and a standard deviation of ±1. This means that all of the scores below the mean are negative numbers and all above are positive. Using z scores has several disadvantages: the teacher must handle many fractional values; half of the scores will be negative; and parents or others who are unfamiliar with this scale may be confused by the fractional and negative scores.

The following formula converts a raw score to a standard z score:

$$z = \frac{\bar{x} - x}{SD}$$

z = the standard score; $\bar{x}$ = mean; x = a score; and SD = standard deviation

The defined mean of zero on the z score scale can easily be seen in this formula. If, for example, a score of 12 (x = 12) were at the mean in a distribution ($\bar{x}$ = 12), the difference is zero. Zero divided by the SD is zero, the mean on the z score scale.

T scores are on a scale of 20 to 80, with a mean of 50 and a standard deviation of 10. Like percentiles, T scores are easier to understand than z scores and are expressed in whole numbers. T scores are also easier to explain to parents because the numbering system used has a base of 10. A T score of 60 or 70 is more meaningful to most parents than a z score of 1 or 2. The T score formula is:

$$T = 50 \pm 10\frac{(\bar{x} - x)}{SD} \quad \text{or} \quad T = 50 + 10z$$

T = the standard score; $\bar{x}$ = mean; x = a score; SD = standard deviation, and z = a z score

If z scores are already provided, the physical educator may want to convert to T scores using the second formula. This avoids the fraction (decimal) and moves the score relative to the T score's mean of 50.

z and T scores can be used in calculations, making it possible to combine scores of two very dissimilar measures such as a ratio (e.g., timed event) and a discrete score (e.g., curl-ups). To combine or even compare a performance scored in seconds with one scored in completed tasks requires converting to some form of common unit of measure such as a standard score.

APPENDIX E

Annotated Summary of Available Tests

REFLEX TESTING

MILANI-COMPARETTI TEST OF REFLEX DEVELOPMENT

Available: Munroe-Meyer Institute
985450 University of Nebraska
Medical Center
Omaha, NE 68198-5450

Validity: None reported

Reliability: Inter-rater and test–retest reliability (stability) reported in manual

Scoring: Check-off by months

Population: Infants 0–24 months; functioning at that age; those suspected of having residuals of reflexes

Performances (parameters) measured: Primitive reflexes, righting reactions, parachute reactions, tilting reactions, postural control, and active movement

Economy: Individual administration

Norms: Expressed in months that reflex should be present

SENSORIMOTOR TESTING

MVPT MOTOR-FREE VISUAL PERCEPTION TEST, THIRD EDITION (MVPT-3)

Available: Academic Therapy Publications
20 Commercial Blvd.
Novato, CA 94949-6191
www.academictherapy.com

Validity: Median correlation of 0.49 for construct validity determined by age differentiation, within and among parameters measured

Reliability: 0.86 on test–retest basis

Scoring: Dichotomous raw scores (right or wrong); convert to perceptual age and standard scores

Population (norming sample): More than 2,000 individuals 4–80+ years

Performances (parameters) measured: 36 items measure spatial relationships, visual discrimination, figure–ground, visual closure, visual memory; subject points to selection from multiple choices; new items for adults

Economy: Individually administered in 20–25 minutes; required materials include multiple-choice templates, score sheet

Norms: Expressed in perceptual age scores and standard scores

Note: Test has been expanded with new plates added to the top end of the existing test in order to measure the visual–perceptual functioning of normal and head-injured adults to 80+ years of age

QUICK NEUROLOGICAL SCREENING TEST, REVISED EDITION

M. Mutti; N. Martin; H. Sterling; N. Spalding

Available: Academic Therapy Publications
20 Commercial Blvd.
Novato, CA 94949-6191
www.academictherapy.com

Validity: With educational classification for 88 pairs of learning-disabled and typically developing children

Reliability: 0.41–0.93 for items on test–retest basis one month apart

Scoring: Rating scale with criteria; total score determines an overall, criteria-based indicator of the person's performance

Population (norming sample): Based on 2,239 typically developing, learning-disabled, and undifferentiated children 6.5 to 18.3 years of age

Performances (parameters) measured: 15 tasks common to standard pediatric neurological and neuropsychological batteries, includes measurement of balance, visual–motor integration, fine- and gross-motor control, sound discrimination, and other developmental tasks

Economy: Individually administered in approximately 20–30 minutes; equipment required includes test manual, protocol sheets, cue cards (which provide scoring instructions), geometric figure reproduction sheets, and developmental activities forms

Norms: Criterion-referenced tables showing age at which 25, 50, and 75 percent of norming sample met criterion per item

Note: Training video available from San Jose State University, Dept. of Special Education, San Jose, CA, (408) 924-3700

BEERY VMI, FIFTH EDITION

Available: Pro-Ed
8700 Shoal Creek Blvd.
Austin, TX 78757-6897
www.proedinc.com

Validity: 0.95 with Visual Motor Integration; 0.67 with Motor Free Visual Perception Test

Reliability: Reliable for all ages and unbiased with regard to gender and race; has internal consistency reliability of 0.90 or above for all ages and provides numerous examples for practice scoring

Scoring: Scoring criteria for drawings are clearly stated and highly objective on a 4-point scale

Population: Representative sample of more than 2,500 students

Performances (parameters) measured: Child copies series of increasingly complex geometric forms to document the presence and degree of visual–motor difficulties in individual children

Economy: Short format and full format, less than 10–15 minutes each

Norms: Reported in standard scores, percentiles, and age equivalents for children 2 to 18 years

PSYCHO-EDUCATIONAL PROFILE, THIRD EDITION (PEP-3)

Available: Pro-Ed
8700 Shoal Creek Blvd.
Austin, TX 78757-6897
www.proedinc.com

Validity: With intelligence test scores ranging from 0.85 with the Merrill-Palmer Scale to 0.24 with the Leiter International Performance Scale

Reliability: Inter-rater reliability is 0.92

Scoring: Nominal is appropriate, mild, severe for behavioral scale; passing, emerging, failing for developmental scale

Population: Most appropriately used with children with autism functioning at or below the preschool range and within the chronological age range of 6 months to 7 years

Performances (parameters) measured: Developmental functioning in imitation, perception, fine motor, gross motor, eye–hand integration, cognitive performance, and cognitive verbal areas; includes Behavioral Scale and new caregiver report

Economy: Testing time ranges from 45 minutes to 1.5 hours. Administered individually

Norms: Age range estimates

DEVELOPMENTAL TEST OF VISUAL–MOTOR INTEGRATION (VMI-5)

Available: Pro-Ed
8700 Shoal Creek Blvd.
Austin, TX 78757-6897
www.proedinc.com

Validity: 0.89 between VMI scores and chronological age

Reliability: See *Visual–Motor Integration* (monograph) by Keith E. Beery, Follett Publishing, 1967

Scoring (objectivity): Discrete scores on 15 items

Population (norming sample): Children ranging in age from 2 to 18 years, 11 months

Performances (parameters) measured: Ability to imitate drawings of various forms (e.g., copying vertical lines, horizontal lines, circles, vertical-horizontal cross, right oblique line, square, left oblique line, etc.)

Economy: Administered individually or in groups in 15–20 minutes; visual perception and motor coordination tests less than 5 minutes; required equipment includes test booklet for each student, administration and scoring manual, pencils

Norms: Expressed in age-equivalents for children 2 through 18 years

PERCEPTUAL-MOTOR ASSESSMENT FOR CHILDREN (P-MAC)

Available: McCarron-Dial Systems, Inc.
PO Box 45628
Dallas, TX 75245
www.mccarrondial.com

Validity: The reliability and validity of each P-MAC trait depends on its constituent measure. Several components of the P-MAC are validated against commonly used tests based on traditional views in clinical psychology, neuropsychology, and education such as the WISC-R, WRAT, and Wechsler. Basically, the perceptual–motor components of these tests correlate in a range from 0.84 to 0.90 to similar subtests on these other instruments.

Reliability: Test–retest reliability ranges from 0.84 to 0.98 for the six subtests

Scoring (objectivity): Scores are ratio and timed; a software program is included to analyze overall functioning

Population (norming sample): Test can be used with individuals 4 to 15 years

Performances (parameters) measured: Placing beads in a box, finger tapping, nut and bolt assembly, hand strength, standing on one foot, finger–nose–finger sequence

Economy: Individually administered in 45 minutes

Norms: Computer program generates a report analyzing performance on subtests with recommendations for teaching; encourages activities developing muscular strength and flexibility such as weight lifting, jogging, hiking, walking, and stretching

MOTOR DEVELOPMENT PROFILES

DENVER II

Available: Denver Developmental Materials, Inc.
PO Box 371075
Denver, CO 80237-5075
www.denverii.com

Validity: Standardization used regression analysis and a goodness of fit test to determine accuracy of the curves; validity was based on this for 2,096 children from Denver City and County, CO

Reliability: Inter-observer reliability determined; of 149 items: 141 = 1.0; 7 = 0.90–0.99; 1 = 0.83

Scoring: Pass–Fail

Population (norming sample): Standardization included 2,096 children ranging in age from birth to six years. One third of norming sample were Anglo, one third African American, one third Hispanic. One third of the children have mothers with less than 12 years of education, one third had 12 years, and one third had more than 12 years. Children were evenly divided between boys and girls. Each item was administered to an average of 783 children to determine separate norms for each subgroup when they differed by a clinically significant amount.

Performances (parameters) measured: 125 test items selected represented personal–social, fine-motor–adaptive, and language tasks to identify delays in development

Economy: Time needs depend on the age of child and number of items passed; administered individually; equipment required includes small toy, rattle, piece of yarn, paper and pencil for scribbling and drawing, box of raisins, eight small cubes, pictures of familiar objects, small ball

Norms: Chart showing at what age level 25, 50, 75, and 90 percent of children can perform specific tasks. Norms divided by ethnic groups and level of mother's education. Non-Denver group was divided into three residence categories—rural, suburban, urban—and further divided by maternal education. Separate norms were established for each subgroup. When they differed by a clinically significant amount, their separate norms are shown in the *Denver II Technical Manual*. The test has been normed and re-standardized in six other countries.

PRESCREENING DEVELOPMENTAL QUESTIONNAIRE II (PDQ II)

Available: Denver Developmental Materials, Inc.
PO Box 371075
Denver, CO 80237-5075
www.denverii.com

Validity: Based on Denver II

Reliability: Based on Denver II

Scoring: Maternal report to questions using dichotomous responses of "suspect" or "non-suspect"

Population (norming sample): Standardization included 2,096 children ranging in age from birth to six years

Performances (parameters) measured: 125 test items selected represented personal–social, fine-motor–adaptive, and language tasks to identify "likely to be suspect" on the longer Denver II test

Economy: Time needed for parent to complete questionnaire, approximately 10 minutes; scoring, 3 minutes; only equipment needed is scoring sheet

Norms: Uses Denver II norms

GUIDE TO EARLY MOVEMENT SKILLS (GEMS)

Available: NFER-Nelson Publishing Co. Ltd.
Darville House, 2 Oxford Road East
Windsor, Berkshire SL4 1DF, England
www.nfer-nelson.co.uk

Validity: N/A

Reliability: N/A

Scoring: Checklist

Population: Typically developing children birth to 24 months

Performances (parameters) measured: Four elements, developmental sequences of movement skills categorized as gross and fine motor skills

Economy: Untimed; occasional use of readily available equipment

Norms: Based on normal development at specific ages

Note: Includes teaching activities for each skill listed and adult behaviors appropriate to each developmental level

DEVELOPMENTAL SCHEDULES

DEVELOPMENTAL INDICATORS FOR ASSESSMENT OF LEARNING, THIRD EDITION (DIAL-3)

Available: American Guidance Service
4201 Woodland Road
PO Box 99
Circle Pines, MN 55014-1796
(800) 328-2560
www.agsnet.com

Validity: .79

Reliability: Inter-rater = .90; Test–retest = .86

Scoring: Observational

Population: 3 years through 6 years, 11 months

Performances (parameters) measured: Motor, concepts, language, self-help development, social development

Economy: 20–30 minutes

Norms: Criterion

Note: Also available in Spanish

BATTELLE DEVELOPMENTAL INVENTORY, SECOND EDITION (BDI-2)

Available: Riverside Publishing
425 Spring Lake Dr.
Itasca, IL 60143, (800) 323-9540
www.riverpub.com

Validity: Not reported

Reliability: Not reported

Scoring: 3-point scoring system for 341 items for complete test and 96 items for screening test provides a sensitive measure for screening, diagnosis, and evaluation of early development

Population: Birth to 7 years, 11 months; stratified random sample based on U. S. Census guidelines; 800 children

Performances (parameters) measured: Personal–social, adaptive, motor, communication, and cognition; in the motor domain the following are measured: muscle control, body coordination, locomotion, fine muscle, perceptual motor

Economy: Complete BDI: 1–2 hours; screening test: 10–30 minutes

Norms: Percentile ranks, standard scores, and age equivalents

Note: Also available in Spanish

PEABODY DEVELOPMENTAL MOTOR SCALES (PDMS-2)

Available: Pro-Ed
8700 Shoal Creek Blvd.
Austin, TX 78757-6897
www.proedinc.com

Validity: Valid for a wide variety of subgroups as well as the sample in its entirety

Reliability: Not reported

Scoring: Not reported

Population: Birth to 5 years; more than 2,000 children representative of the current U. S. population

Performances (parameters) measured: Reflexes, balance and equilibrium, locomotion, object manipulation, grasping and visual–motor integration; test is divided into a Gross Motor Quotient Scale and Fine Motor Quotient Scale

Economy: 45–60 minutes (20–30 minutes per scale)

Norms: Scaled scores in the form of z scores, T scores (developmental motor quotient for each scale and a composite), age equivalents, basal and ceiling age levels

Note: Test accompanied by software that performs all scoring conversions and generates a report suitable for inclusion in a student's permanent record. Also available is the P-MAP: Peabody Motor Activities Program, ordered developmentally by skill areas that coincide with parameters measured.

INFANT–TODDLER DEVELOPMENTAL ASSESSMENT (IDA)

S. Provence, J. Erikson, S. Vater, S. Palmeri (1995)

Available: Riverside Publishing
425 Spring Lake Dr.
Itasca, IL 60143, (800) 323-9540
www.riverpub.com

Validity: Not reported

Reliability: 0.90 to 0.96 for ages 0–18 months, 0.78 to 0.96 for ages 19–36 months

Scoring (objectivity): Percentage delay

Population (norming sample): Birth to 3 years

Performances (parameters) measured: Gross motor, fine motor, relationship to inanimate objects, language/communication, self-help, relationship to persons, emotions and feeling states, and coping

Economy: Varies

Norms: Performance age range that describes the child's developmental level; percentage delay can be computed

MOTOR ABILITY TESTS

TEST OF GROSS MOTOR DEVELOPMENT (TGMD-2)

Available: Pro-Ed
8700 Shoal Creek Blvd.
Austin, TX 78757-6897
www.proedinc.com

Validity: Construct validity provided in manual

Reliability: Coefficients for the Locomotor subtest average 0.85; for Object Control subtest average 0.88; Gross Motor composite average 0.91

Scoring (objectivity): Ratings of 12 skill performances in two subtests and a composite score

Population (norming sample): Children 3 to 10 years, 11 months keyed to projected 2000 census

Performances (parameters) measured: Locomotor subtest includes: run, gallop, hop, leap, horizontal jump, slide. Object Control subtest includes: striking a stationary ball, stationary dribble, catch, kick, overhand and underhand throw

Economy: Administered individually in 15–20 minutes; equipment needed includes running space, chalk or other marker, 4- to 6-inch lightweight ball, plastic bat, 8- to 10-inch playground ball, 6- to 8-inch sponge ball, 3 tennis balls, wall space

Norms: Percentiles, standard scores, age-equivalents, and a composite Gross Motor Quotient for children 3.0 to 10.11 years if both subtests are completed

PHYSICAL FITNESS TESTS

THE ROCKPORT WALK TEST

Available: G. M. Kline et al. (1987). Estimation of $\dot{V}O_2$ Max from a one-mile track walk, gender, age, and body weight. *Medicine and Science in Sports and Exercise, 19,* 253–259

Validity: Provides a means of estimating $\dot{V}O_2$ Max from heart rate response to walking speed; not valid for individuals in good physical condition who cannot walk fast enough to get their heart rate above 120 bpm

Reliability: 0.88

Scoring: Multiple regression equations estimate $\dot{V}O_2$ Max for men and women

Population (norming sample): Adults 20 years+

Performances (parameters) measured: Aerobic fitness by way of a mile walk

Economy: Track and heart rate monitor or watch with second hand to measure heart rate following walking

Norms: Regression equations considering age, weight in pounds, time to complete mile walk, and exercise heart rate

U OF H NON-EXERCISE TEST

Available: A. S. Jackson and R. M. Ross (1997). *Understanding exercise for health and fitness* (3rd ed.). Dubuque, IA: Kendall/Hunt

Validity: Underestimates aerobic fitness of those over 55 ml/kg/min, but this constitutes about 5 percent of adult population; most accurate for people with an aerobic fitness below 55 ml/kg/min

Reliability: N/A

Scoring: $\dot{V}O_2$ Max is estimated without testing using individual's age, sex, body composition, and self-report level of aerobic exercise; self-rating scale of 1–7 allows the individual to describe his or her general activity level for the previous month

Population (norming sample): Based on data on employees and astronauts at NASA/Johnson Space Center in Houston, TX, between 1987 and 1997

Performances (parameters) measured: Zero on rating scale describes level of activity as "Avoid walking or exertion, e.g., always use elevator, drive whenever possible instead of walking"; 7 on rating scale describes level of activity as "Run over 10 miles per week or spend over 3 hours per week in comparable physical activity."

Economy: Actual self-rating takes very little time; data on age, sex, and body composition must be gathered at some point

Norms: $\dot{V}O_2$ Max estimated using a formula developed by Jackson and Ross provides a means of comparing men and women with standards for aerobic capacity published by the American College of Sports Medicine (1991)

FITNESSGRAM

Available: Human Kinetics Publishing
PO Box 5076
Champaign, IL, 61825-5076
www.humankinetics.com

Validity: Not reported

Reliability: Not reported

Scoring: Criterion-referenced

Population (norming sample): 5–17+ years

Performances (parameters) measured: Back and leg flexibility, shoulder flexibility, aerobic capacity, body composition, and upper body strength

Economy: Administered in groups in two class periods

Norms: Boys and girls 10–17 years

ISOMETRIC STRENGTH TEST: HAND DYNAMOMETER

Available: online search: handgrip dynamometer
www.itinscales.com

The hand dynamometer assesses grip strength or the intensity of the voluntary movements of each hand. This test takes approximately five minutes to administer and is highly reliable. Age- and gender-stratified norms are available for ages 5.0 through 70.0 years. Grip strength measures subtle motor impairment, lateralization of brain injury, and the functional integrity of the two cerebral hemispheres.

* * *

Available: online search: handgrip dynamometer www.itinscales.com

Validity: 0.78–0.93, depending on measuring tool and joint angle

Reliability: 0.94 for each test

Scoring: Weight lifted for average of two trials

Population (norming sample): Originally used with adults for pre-employment testing for physically demanding jobs, but also used for general fitness testing

Performances (parameters) measured: Various lifts using an instrument with an electronic load cell, chain, and handle for arm flexion, shoulder lift, torso pull, and leg strength (extension)

Economy: Administered individually in 30–45 minutes, or each subtest could be administered separately in 10–15 minutes

Norms: Expressed in percentile ranks for men and women of college age and older

ISOTONIC 1-RM STRENGTH TESTS

Available: L. R. Gettman (1993). Fitness testing. In *Resource Manual for Guidelines for Exercise Testing and Prescription.* Philadelphia: Lea & Febiger

Validity: Construct of muscular strength of the arms or legs

Reliability: Unreported

Scoring: Maximum amount of weight that can be lifted with a single repetition (1-RM = one repetition maximum) divided by body weight to give relative strength/weight ratio

Population (norming sample): Men and women 20 years of age and older

Performances (parameters) measured: Several different performances can be used, but the most common are bench press and leg press

Economy: Considering time for warm-up and light weight trials, 20–30 minutes and weight equipment required

Norms: Nominal referencing standards (poor, fair, average, good, excellent) for men and women in 10-year intervals from 20 to 60+ years

COMPREHENSIVE MOTOR PERFORMANCE TESTS

ADAPTED PHYSICAL EDUCATION ASSESSMENT SCALE II (APEAS II)

Available: Los Angeles Unified School District
333 S. Beaudry
16th Floor, Adapted P.E.
Los Angeles, CA 90017, (213) 241-8052

Validity: Face with literature; not racially, culturally, or sexually biased

Reliability: Variable per item; 10 items > 0.70 on test–retest basis

Scoring (objectivity): Eight items use ratios representing distance or repetitions, eight items use ratings, and two items generate categorical data; 0.39–0.96 with median of 0.63

Population (norming sample): Stratified nationally drawn random sample of students ages 5–18 years based on age, disability, sex, and ethnicity

Performances (parameters) measured: Perceptual motor function, object control, locomotor skills, physical fitness, and adaptive behavior

Economy: Administered individually or in small groups in about 20–30 minutes per student; required equipment includes 8.5" and 10" rubber ball, 18-inch ruler or yardstick, five 6" x 6" beanbags, stopwatch, test manual, chalk, score sheets; secondary version: tape measure, wood paddle, 2 tennis balls, 12" softball, soccer ball, basketball, pencil with eraser, whistle

Norms: Expressed in percentile ranks at six-month intervals for 5–7.11 years and one-year intervals for 8–18 years, based on sex*. Preschool version also available

*Eligibility criteria for APE: significantly reduced performance of two or more years or 1.5 standard deviation below mean; equal to or less than 7.5 percentile

Note: Soon to be available from AAHPERD

BRUININKS-OSERETSKY TEST OF MOTOR PROFICIENCY, SECOND EDITION (BOT-2)

Available: American Guidance Service
P. O. Box 99
Circle Pines, MN 55014-1796
www.agsnet.com

Validity: 0.57–0.78 with age; item relationship to subtest 0.65 to 0.87 for internal consistency

Reliability: 0.60–0.89 for items on long form; 0.86 for short form on test–retest basis for 126 children

Scoring: Ratios generated for time, repetitions, and errors; some items scored pass–fail

Population (norming sample): 800 typically developing children; 80 in each age group 0.5–14.5 years

Performances (parameters) measured: Complete battery consists of eight subtests comprising 46 separate items. The short form consists of 14 items from the complete battery. Overall, the test measures running speed, agility, balance, bilateral coordination, strength, upper limb coordination, response speed, visual–motor coordination, upper limb speed, and dexterity.

Economy: Individually administered in approximately 45–60 minutes for complete 46-item battery; 15–20 minutes for 14-item short form; required equipment for standardized administration included in test kit, stopwatch not included

Norms: Expressed in standard scores converted from z scores, percentile ranks, and stanines

CARE-R CURRICULUM, ASSESSMENT, RESOURCES, EVALUATION

Available: L.A. County Office of Education
Adapted Physical Education Office,
Lincoln Annex
600 E. Grand Ave.
San Gabriel, CA, 91778
(626) 286-6802, E-APE@lacoe.edu

Validity: Face with literature

Reliability: None reported

Scoring: Age referenced

Population: Birth to 17 years, varies for each area

Performances (parameters) measured: Curriculum-based assessment measuring gross motor, object control, health and physical fitness, perceptual–motor and fine motor

Economy: Time needed to administer varies based on student needs

Norms: Age equivalencies (age ranges)

DEVPRO MOTOR SKILLS ASSESSMENT

Available: C & D Kofahl Enterprises
15892 Standish Lane
Huntington Beach, CA 92647
(714) 898-0676
www.devprosoftware.com

Validity: Face with literature

Reliability: None reported

Scoring: Criterion-referenced

Population: Birth to 11 years

Performances: Measures basic skill development with a database of more than 950 skills arranged by developmental age level into 22 subtests. Subtests are classified as: pre-ambulatory skills, balance skills, locomotor skills, object control skills and body awareness

Economy: Time needed to test each student individually is 20–40 minutes; updating student performance in existing student record takes about 5–8 minutes. DEVPRO computer software produces a variety of reports including comments, medical background and data from other tests.

Norms: Criterion-referenced

APPENDIX F

Lifelong Physical Activity and Disability Sport Resources

In addition to the resources identified here, please contact your local schools, fitness centers, recreation centers, and city or county parks and recreation departments for programs that provide opportunities for individuals with a disability. Many of the national disability sport associations have regional and state organizations.

PERIODICALS (MAGAZINES, JOURNALS)

Active Living: The Health, Fitness and Recreation Magazine for People with Disability, Disability Today Publishing Group

Adapted Physical Activity Quarterly, Human Kinetics

American Journal of Health Education, www.aahperd.org/aahe/

American Journal of Sports Medicine, www.sportsmed.org

Archives of Physical Medicine and Rehabilitation, www.physiatry.org/publications

Journal of Leisurability, www.lin.ca/resource/html/jofl.htm

Journal of Pediatric Exercise Science, www.humankinetics.com/products/journals

Journal of Physical Education and Sport and *Journal of Physical Activity and Health*, www.humankinetics.com/products/journals

Journal of Physical Education, Recreation and Dance, www.aahperd.org/aahperd/joperd_main.html

Medicine and Science in Sports and Exercise, www.ms-se.com

Palaestra, Challenge Publications

The Paralympian: Newsletter of the International Paralympic Committee, IPC headquarters in Bonn, Germany

Research Quarterly for Exercise and Sport, www.aahperd.org

Sports 'n Spokes, Paralyzed Veterans of America, www.sportsnspokes.com

Strategies, www.aahperd.org

Teaching Exceptional Children, www.journals.sped.org

Therapeutic Recreation Journal, http://scolar.vsc.edu

INTERNET RESOURCES

Valuable links are also available on each of the following sites.

AccessLife.com

ADAPT-TALK, www.lyris.sportime.com/adapt-talk-index.html

Adapted Physical Activity Council (AAHPERD), www.aahperd.org/aaalf/

Adapted Physical Education National Standards, www.cortland.edu/apens/

Deaflympics, www.deaflympics.org

International Council on Sport Science and Physical Education (ICSSPE), www.icsspe.org

International Federation of Adapted Physical Activity, www.ifapa.net

International Paralympic Committee, www.paralympic.org

National Ability Center (NAC), Park City, Utah, www.nac1985.org

National Center on Physical Activity and Disability, www.ncpad.cc.uic.edu/home.htm

National Sports Center for the Disabled (NSCD), Winter Park, Colorado, www.nscd.org

Palaestra, www.palaestra.com

P.E. Central, www.pecentral.org

PELINKS4U, www.pelinks4u.com

Special Olympics, www.specialolympics.org

Sport Information Resource Centre (SIRC), Ottawa, Canada

SPORT ASSOCIATIONS (U.S.)

See *Sports 'n Spokes* magazine for a complete listing of wheelchair sport associations and current contact information.

American Wheelchair Table Tennis Association, 23 Parker St., Port Chester, NY 10573

Disabled Sports USA (DS/USA), 451 Hungerford Dr., Suite 100, Rockville, MD 20850, www.dsusa.org

National Disability Sports Alliance (NDSA; formerly the United States Cerebral Palsy Athletic Association), 25 W. Independence Way, Kingston, RI 02881

National Wheelchair Basketball Association, 710 Queensbury Loop, Winter Garden, FL 34787, www.nwba.com

National Wheelchair Softball Association, 1616 Todd Ct., Hastings, MN 55033, www.wheelchairsoftball.com

North American Riding for the Handicapped Association (NARHA), P.O. Box 33150, Denver, CO 80233, www.narha.org

Ski for Light, Inc., 1400 Carole Lane, Green Bay, WI 54313

Special Olympics International, 1325 G St. NW, Suite 500, Washington, DC 20005, www.specialolympics.org

United States Association of Blind Athletes (USABA), 33 N. Institute St., Colorado Springs, CO 80903, www.usaba.org

United States Disabled Alpine Ski Team, P.O. Box 100, Park City, UT 84060, www.usskiteam.org

United States Paralympic Corporation (USPC; formerly known as USOC Committee on Sports for the Disabled), USOC Headquarters, Colorado Springs, CO 80909

United States Quad Rugby Association, 101 Park Place Circle, Alabaster, AL 35007, www.quadrugby.com

United States Tennis Association (USTA), 70 W. Red Oak Lane, White Plains, NY 10604, www.usta.com

United States Wheelchair Swimming, Inc., c/o Wheelchair Sports, USA (WSUSA), 3595 E. Foundation Blvd., Colorado Springs, CO 80910

United States Wheelchair Weightlifting Federation, 39 Michael Place, Levittown, PA 19057

USA Deaf Sports Federation (formerly American Athletic Association of the Deaf), www.usadsf.org

Wheelchair Archery, USA, c/o Wheelchair Sports, USA (WSUSA), 3595 E. Foundation Blvd., Colorado Springs, CO 80910

Wheelchair Sports, USA (WSUSA), 3595 E. Foundation Blvd., Colorado Springs, CO 80910

Wheelchair Track and Field–USA (WTFUSA), 2351 Parkwood Rd., Snellville, GA 30039

Women's Sports Foundation (WSF), Eisenhower Park, East Meadow, NY 11554, www.WomensSportsFoundation.org

World T.E.A.M. Sports, 2108 S. Boulevard, Charlotte, NC 28203, www.worldteamsports.org

REFERENCE BOOKS AND ARTICLES

Active Living Alliance for Canadians with a Disability. (1994). *Moving to Inclusion.* Ottawa, Canada: Author.

Block, M. E. (2000). *A Teacher's Guide to Including Students with Disabilities in General Physical Education (Teachers' Guides to Inclusive Practices).* Champaign, IL: Human Kinetics.

Davis, R. W. (2002). *Inclusion Through Sports: A Guide to Enhancing Sport Experiences.* Champaign, IL: Human Kinetics.

DePauw, K. P., & Gavron, S. J. (2005). *Disability Sport.* Champaign, IL: Human Kinetics.

DePauw, K. P. (2000). Female Athletes with Disabilities. In B. Drinkwater (Ed.), *Encyclopedia of Sports Medicine: Women in Sport.* London: Blackwell Science Ltd.

Disability Today Publishing Group. (1997). *The Triumph of the Human Spirit: The Atlanta Paralympic Experience.* Ontario, Canada: Author.

Doll-Tepper, G., Kroner, M., & Sonnenschein, W. (Eds.). (2001). *New Horizons in Sport for Athletes with a Disability, Vol. 1 & 2.* Cologne, Germany: Meyer & Meyer Verlag.

Durstine, L. (1997). *ACSM's Exercise Management for Persons with Chronic Diseases and Disabilities.* Champaign, IL: Human Kinetics.

Hodge, S. R., Murata, N. M., Block, M. E., & Lieberman, L. J. (2003). *Case Studies in Adapted Physical Education: Empowering Critical Thinking.* Scottsdale, AZ: Holcomb Hathaway.

Jourkowsy, A., Rothstein, L., & Reeve, C. (2002). *Raising the Bar: New Horizons in Disability Sports.* New York: Umbrage Editions.

Kasser, S. L. (1995). *Inclusive Games.* Champaign, IL: Human Kinetics.

Kasser, S. L., & Lytle, R. K. (2005). *Inclusive Physical Activity: A Lifetime of Opportunities.* Champaign, IL: Human Kinetics.

Krotoski, D. M., Nosek, M., & Turk, M. (Eds.). (1996). *Women with Physical Disabilities: Achieving and Maintaining Health and Well-being.* Baltimore: Brooks.

Lieberman, L. J., & Cowart, J. F. (1996). *Games for People with Sensory Impairments: Strategies for Including Individuals of All Ages.* Champaign, IL: Human Kinetics.

Lieberman, L. J., & Houston-Wilson, C. (2002). *Strategies for Inclusion: A Handbook for Physical Educators.* Champaign, IL: Human Kinetics.

Miller, P. (1995). *Fitness Programming and Physical Disability.* Champaign, IL: Human Kinetics.

Paciorek, M., & Jones, J. (1994). *Sports and Recreation for the Disabled: A Resource Manual* (2nd ed.). Indianapolis, IN: Benchmark.

Rimmer, J. H. (1994). *Fitness and Rehabilitation Programs for Special Populations.* Dubuque, IA: Brown.

Seaman, J. A. (1999). Physical Activity and Fitness for Persons with Disabilities. *President's Council on Physical Fitness and Sports Research Digest,* 3(9).

Shephard, R. (1990). *Fitness in Special Populations.* Champaign, IL: Human Kinetics.

Sherrill, C., & DePauw, K. P. (1997). Adapted Physical Activity. In J. D. Massengale & R. A. Swanson (Eds.), *The History of Exercise and Sport Science.* Champaign, IL: Human Kinetics.

Stark, R., Rogers, M., Johnson, J.-M., & Chiasson, G. (Eds.). (1990). *Sport and Recreation for the Disabled: A Bibliography.* Ottawa, Canada: SIRC/CDS.

Steadward, R., Nelson, E., & Wheeler, G. (Eds.). (1994). *The Outlook.* Edmonton, Canada: Rick Hansen Centre.

Steadward, R. D., & Petersen, C. (1999). *Paralympics: Where Heroes Come.* Edmonton, Alberta: One Shot Holdings.Steadward, R. D., Wheeler, G. D., & Watkinson, E. J. (2004). *Adapted Physical Activity.* Edmonton, Alberta: University of Alberta Publication Services.

Steadward, R. D., Wheeler, G. D., & Watkinson, E. J. (2004). *Adapted Physical Activity.* Edmonton, Alberta: University of Alberta Publication Services.

APPENDIX G

Sportsmanship Group: Sample Lesson Plan

LESSON PLAN	EXAMPLE BEHAVIOR
A. Adult briefly explains game and calls on student to state the four rules of good sportsmanship: 1. Try your best 2. Cheer for your team 3. Hands and feet to self 4. Friendly talking	Adult: "Today we will play kickball. Who can raise their hand to tell me the four rules of sportsmanship that we've been working on? The first two to get them all correct will be our captains today." (calls on first child) Child: (repeats only two rules) Adult: "Think about it for a little longer, and I'll try to get back to you. Who can help him?" (continues calling on students until two students correctly identify the four rules; they stand up beside the adult as captains)
B. Students are divided into teams by adult. (Do not have captains "choose" teams.)	Students line up behind their captains and the group waits for the next instruction.
C. Adult instructs students where to go (which team is up, who assigns positions, etc.).	Students go to their positions and the game begins.
D. Adult rewards students immediately for exhibiting behaviors that fall in one of the four categories of good sportsmanship rules by giving out stickers. Adult ignores behaviors considered poor sportsmanship unless flagrant. Students are also encouraged to ignore any name-calling if it occurs.	As the students play the game, child A tells another, "That was a good try!" Adult immediately rewards A with a sticker and says, "Good cheering for your team, A!" Child B, who is in the field, runs to catch a fly ball. She drops it, but an adult immediately gives her a reinforcer, saying, "You are really trying your best, B. You are trying to catch the ball with both hands."
E. Stop game and instruct the group to sit together. Students nominate good sports, and adult then selects the best sport of the day, who may then be awarded a special sticker.	Adult: "Who can raise their hand and tell me who was a good sport today?" (calls on student J) J: "F was a good sport today." Adult: "What did F do that shows good sportsmanship?" J: "She tried her best by trying to catch all the balls that came to her." Adult praises J's statement and continues until all students who desire to participate have had a turn. Adult, after consultation with other staff, then states, "The best sport of the day award goes to M." M is given a special sticker, and all students and adults applaud.

A HIERARCHY OF DESIRED SOCIAL SKILLS IN THE SPORTSMANSHIP GROUP SETTING

It should be noted that the hierarchy listed below is not all-inclusive. Gaps may be noted, and the simultaneous teaching of skills may be necessary.

I. Turn taking
   A. Child understands basic concept.
   B. Child waits for a short time for his or her turn.
      1. Uses concrete materials to identify individual waiting space such as chair, carpet square, rope, mat, hoop, etc.
      2. Uses representational materials to identify individual waiting space such as a line or shape drawn on the ground
      3. Uses spatial relationship to natural landmark to identify individual waiting space (e.g., being between two other students in line, next to a building wall, in one area of the court, by a tree)
   C. Child waits for several minutes for a turn.
      1. Uses concrete materials to assist waiting (see I.B.1)
      2. Uses representational materials to assist waiting (see I.B.2)
      3. Uses spatial relationships to assist waiting (see I.B.3)
   D. Child can accurately identify whose turn it is.
      1. Identifies when it is his or her turn without prompting
      2. Identifies turn of person before him or her
      3. Identifies turns of all children in the group
   E. Child takes only his or her own turn.
      1. Is able to stay in line in correct order
      2. Allows all other group members to have a turn before repeating own turn
      3. Shares equipment with team members during game activity
II. Team Playing
   A. Child demonstrates team membership
      1. Identifies a group of players as a team
      2. Identifies which group is his or her team
      3. Identifies all others on his or her team
      4. Identifies others not on his or her team
      5. Performs his or her assigned team role only when it is helpful to the team
      6. Always performs assigned team role when it is helpful to the team
      7. Performs only the team member role assigned (does not monopolize play)
      8. Assists teammate in making a goal or point
   B. The child performs the special role assigned to the captain.
   C. The child performs social skills necessary for cohesive interaction with his or her team members.
      1. Keeps hands and feet to self
      2. Attends to activity and attempts to perform skills
         a. Stays with group
         b. Watches activity and listens to instructions without being easily distracted
         c. Initiates movements without prompting
         d. Follows directions
         e. Ignores negative comments/actions made toward him or her
         f. Displays frustration appropriately (e.g., no put-downs, yelling, etc.)
         g. Accepts compliments appropriately
         h. Discusses misunderstandings with peers or adults constructively
         i. Accepts minor changes in rules or routine when notified in advance
         j. Attempts to incorporate suggestions to improve skills
         k. Supports the efforts of others (e.g., cheers for team)
         l. Makes constructive suggestions or cues other team members

APPENDIX H

Effective Programming: Developmental Activities

DEVELOPMENTAL ACTIVITIES

The activities in this appendix are presented according to their level in the developmental model, starting with reflex activity and activities for the development of motor patterns and skills and ending with activities for applying motor skills in culturally determined forms of movement. The activities are not modified or suggested for any disability grouping. The physical educator must select the appropriate type of activities, making adaptations in accordance with the individual's movement characteristics and needs and the principles suggested in this text (see Appendix C). Some activities listed may be appropriate only for a small group or direct service adapted physical education. Others can be easily incorporated into the general physical education class activities and may provide new and varied experiences for all students.

Reflex Development and Inhibition

This section presents activities for reflex development and reflex inhibition, as well as contraindications. The physical educator is advised to attempt these activities with the utmost caution and a sound experiential base. With the inclusion of individuals with a disability into the general physical education class, it is necessary for physical education teachers and adapted physical education specialists to collaborate so that activities for reflex development or inhibition are included in the program. This should be done only after proper training and, whenever possible, consultation with medical personnel or physical or occupational therapists.

A brief description of the various reflexes is presented, followed by a list of appropriate activities and a list of contraindications (the lists are not meant to be all-inclusive). Activities such as animal walks, angels-in-the-snow, and balance board activities are discussed later in this appendix.

Grasp reflex. The grasp reflex refers to *an automatic grip movement occurring upon stimulation of the palm; voluntary release is difficult.*

1. Offer a variety of tactile experiences for the hands, including play with textures and in a sandbox.
2. Place objects (e.g., blocks, ball) in the hand in such as way that the hand is kept partially open.
3. Place objects in front of the student and encourage the grasp reflex.
4. Have the student build towers or stack objects.
5. Use progressively weighted objects for grasping.
6. Use a variety of sizes of objects.
7. Have the student use one or both hands to grasp and hold objects.

Contraindications/Precautions

1. Do not force the child's hands open.
2. Do not pull on the child's fingers to straighten them; rather, stroke or gently massage the back of the hand and encourage relaxation.

Startle reflex. The startle reflex refers to *automatic abduction, then adduction of limbs in response to sudden noise, movement, or change in environment.*

1. Provide auditory stimulation for the student who knows it will occur, with a variety of sounds (e.g., clap, bell, rattle, voice) increasing in intensity.
2. Provide opportunities for the student to move limbs in a variety of body positions and assist him or her to do so.
3. While the student is positioned over a bolster (e.g., in a sitting position), place objects in front of him or her to encourage voluntary movement.

Contraindications/Precautions

1. Avoid making quick movements or sounds without the student being aware of it first.
2. Ensure safety when the student is known to have the startle reflex. Don't leave such a student unattended.
3. Don't expect learning to occur in noisy, busy environments.

Crossed extension reflex. The crossed extension reflex is *observed in the supine position; when one leg is flexed, the opposite leg extends.*

1. Provide opportunities for the student to flex both legs at the same time, and slowly assist him or her to do so.

2. Provide opportunities for the student to extend both legs at the same time, and slowly assist him or her to do so.
3. Have the student roll up in a variety of textured materials (e.g., parachute, blanket, tarp, towels).

Contraindications/Precautions
1. Avoid activities that stimulate only one side of the body.
2. Avoid sudden, quick changes in leg positions.

Asymmetrical tonic neck reflex (ATNR). The presence of ATNR is exhibited by what resembles the fencing position. The ATNR is elicited *when the head is turned to the side, causing extension of arm on face side and flexion of arm on skull side to occur.*

1. In either prone or supine position, the student rotates the head from side to side and looks at objects while holding a ball or fairly large object with two hands.
2. While supine, student brings arms to the midline of the body.
3. While supine, student reaches for objects above body but at midline.
4. Student rolls with arms at sides or above head.
5. Student rolls in barrel.
6. Student crawls and creeps forward, focusing on object directly ahead (e.g., following a pattern or line on floor).
7. In hands and knees position, student maintains balance while turning head only.
8. Student creeps with head turned sideways.
9. Student maintains 3-point balance position while turning the head toward the side with a raised extremity.
10. While standing with weight supported by extended arms against the wall, student rotates head, keeping elbows straight.
11. Student stands with arms outstretched and swivels head from side to side, with no movement of arms.

Contraindications/Precautions
1. When ATNR is known to be present, avoid activities that allow flexion and extension on opposite sides of body. Present materials and activities at front midline.
2. Do not allow the student to remain in the ATNR position; reposition whenever possible using relaxation techniques and moving items of interest to midline. (Consult physician or occupational therapist for other positioning techniques.)

Symmetrical tonic neck reflex (STNR). STNR is exhibited by the following: *with flexion of the head, upper limbs flex, lower limbs extend; with extension of head* (caution: not too far back to avoid tension and pressure to spine), *upper limbs extend, lower limbs flex.*

1. Student assumes and maintains creeping position, flexes and extends head. Position student if necessary.
2. Student creeps forward, maintaining the proper position with head flexed or extended.
3. With the body supported by extended arms against wall, student flexes and extends head.
4. Standing with arms outstretched in front, student moves head up and down with no change in arm position.
5. Student may perform most animal walks and wrestling games.

Contraindications/Precautions
1. Student should avoid prolonged "bunny-scooting."
2. Student should avoid rocking forward and backward while in creep position.

Tonic labyrinthine reflex: prone. TLR:P is *exhibited by increased trunk flexion when prone and increased trunk extension when supine.*

1. Student rolls with arms over head or at sides (e.g., pencil roll, log roll).
2. Student rolls in a padded tube.
3. Prone, student raises head only and looks toward ceiling.
4. Prone, student raises chest, head, arms, and legs off the floor and holds the position.
5. Prone with extended arms, student lifts head and chest off the floor.
6. Prone, student lifts legs only, then arms only.
7. Prone on scooterboard, student propels forward and holds extended position.
8. Student pulls self forward using a rope while prone on scooterboard.

Tonic labyrinthine reflex: supine. TLR:S is *exhibited by increased trunk extension when supine.*

1. Student rolls with arms over head or at sides (e.g., pencil roll, log roll).
2. Student rolls in a barrel (or large tire tube).
3. Supine, student lifts head off floor and looks at toes with hands placed on thighs.
4. Student rolls in a ball from supine position.

5. Supine, student holds large, soft objects with arms and legs.
6. Supine, student wraps hands and arms around knees bent to chest and rocks back and forth in balanced position with head and feet off the floor as in a "rocking chair" (see Figure H.1).
7. While sitting on a scooterboard, student propels forward with arms.
8. While supine on scooterboard, student pulls self along suspended rope holding hips at 90 degree angle.

Contraindications/Precautions

1. When TLR is known to be present, avoid teaching the forward or backward roll; proceed slowly when teaching any roll.
2. Avoid prolonged prone-lying or supine-lying positions.

Support. Positive support in standing is *exhibited by extension of legs and plantar-flexion of feet;* **negative support** is *exhibited by a lack of weight bearing;* and the **stepping reflex** is *automatic, high stereotypic walking when placed in standing position.*

1. Place the student in standing position, encouraging proper stance and position if necessary.
2. Increase amount of weight bearing in the standing position by gradually increasing time spent standing.
3. Provide proprioceptive stimulation (i.e., pressure) to the bottom of feet while the student is supine, ensuring dorsiflexion of feet and extension of both legs.

Contraindications/Precautions

1. Do not leave the student unattended in standing position.
2. Avoid "walking" without weight bearing.
3. Check with medical personnel, occupational therapist, or physical therapist for precautions (e.g., circulatory changes, joint stability) before standing any individual who spends a prolonged amount of time in sitting or lying positions.

Righting reactions. Righting reactions include **neck righting** (*trunk rotates with head*), **body righting** (*log rolls*), and **optical righting** (*head orients to midline of body in either vertical or horizontal position*).

1. Student rolls with arms over head or at sides (caution: segmental roll is best—see below).
2. Student rolls in a barrel (or large tire tube).
3. Student rolls up and down an incline.
4. Student creeps forward and backward, keeping eyes fixed on an object in front of the student.

FIGURE H.1

Performing a supine "rocking chair" stunt helps to integrate the tonic labyrinthine reflex: supine.

5. Student maintains balance and vertical head position while on a tilt board.

Contraindications/Precautions

1. Avoid reinforcing or practicing log rolls; substitute with segmental rolling.
2. Ensure safety in balancing activities.

Protective extension. Protective extension is exhibited by *extension of arms and abduction and extension of fingers in response to falling.*

1. Prone with arms extended, student pushes chest and head off floor.
2. Student supports weight on arms while tilted forward over bolster.
3. Student extends arms while rolled forward and downward on cage ball (see Figure H.2).
4. Student extends arms and supports self while being gently pushed forward from kneeling and sitting positions.
5. Teacher rocks student slowly forward, backward, and sideways while in prone or sitting position on large bolster or cage ball.
6. Student maintains extension of arms while prone over bolster.

Contraindications/Precautions

1. Protect student from precarious positions that could cause loss of balance and falling.
2. When protective extension reflex is not present, do not leave the student unattended on balance apparatus.
3. Remove obstacles to prevent tripping and falling.
4. Protect student's head from injury.

FIGURE H.2

Supporting weight on the arms while tilted forward over a cage ball helps to develop protective extension.

Activities for Sensory Stimulation and Discrimination

The need for sensory stimulation is well documented in the literature. For growth and development, the student is in need of sensory-stimulating activities, coupled with motor response. Each sensory system has a developmental sequence that progresses from gross sensation to discrimination. The activities presented below for each sensory system are designed to provide sensory stimulation and, later on, to require discrimination and refined use of sensory input.

Tactile system. The tactile system uses the touch receptors of the skin. It has both an arousal and calming effect on the central nervous system (CNS) and has a profound effect on the sensorimotor process. The following activities are included initially to provide stimulation and then to require use of that tactile information for discrimination.

Tactile Stimulation
1. Tactile play with sponges, soaps, washcloths, tactile toys (e.g., Koosh balls).
2. Water play in a small wading pool, sprinkler, water table, or other water play toys.
3. Water play in search of objects.
4. Sandbox play: student looks for hidden objects; buries objects; covers hands, feet; builds castles (see Figure H.3).
5. Mud play; play with Styrofoam pellets.
6. Tactile play for hands in a container of edible items (e.g., oatmeal, rice). This is a very good substitution for the sandbox for young children or students who put non-edibles in their mouths.
7. Play with modeling clay, dough, or putty.
8. Hand, foot, or body painting.
9. "Dry off" or roll up in blankets or assorted cloths with various textures (e.g., silk, net, burlap).
10. Shaving cream play: student paints body, hands, and feet and slides and rolls in shaving cream. (Comment: this is usually done with younger children as an exploration activity rather than as part of the physical education class.)
11. Draw cornstarch images on arms after spreading powder on body.

Tactile Discrimination
1. Draw shapes, numbers, or letters on student's back using index finger, and ask student to identify.
2. While blindfolded, student locates the partner's touch, either single or two simultaneous touches.
3. Feeley bag: objects are concealed in a bag or box, and student must identify each by touch.
4. Tactile box with textures, shapes, or letters; match them only by feel.
5. Blindfolded, student identifies shapes cut out of paper, tagboard, or foam.
6. Carpet squares: use for sitting, standing, kneeling, lying on, rolling over, and so on.

FIGURE H.3

Searching for objects in a sandbox stimulates the tactile system and helps develop tactile discrimination.

7. Rope route: student follows a rope maze or obstacle course purely by touch, using hands or feet, or by moving on scooterboards.

Vestibular system. Vestibular input is an extremely powerful source of sensory stimulation. Vestibular input is received when there is whole body movement through space or a tilting of the head. Once received and organized, vestibular stimulation can be used to enhance balance and equilibrium responses. Although there is an element of vestibular stimulation in almost everything we do, the following activities are suggested for their high degree of vestibular input.

1. Student swings in a playground swing, hammock, net, tire, or swing. This can be done sitting, prone, kneeling, and so forth.
2. Sliding down a decline. (Caution: check school playground rules and safety at bottom of slide prior to instruction.)
3. Scooterboards, skateboards, skates, bicycles, and so forth provide a great deal of vestibular stimulation. (See Figure H.4.)
4. Rolling, somersaulting, and trampolining.
5. Riding down an incline on a scooterboard.

FIGURE H.4

Riding a scooterboard in prone position provides students with a great deal of vestibular stimulation.

Proprioceptive system. Proprioceptive input comes from deep pressure and vibration, providing stimulation that helps the person to use information about where one's body is in space; it also serves to enhance balance. Proprioceptive stimulation is included in almost all activities found in physical education. Only a few examples are cited here.

1. Reaching and stretching activities.
2. Pushing, pulling, lifting, squeezing, and carrying objects with hands and feet.
3. All animal walks and wrestling games.
4. Tug-of-rope activities.
5. Climbing ropes, ladders, and jungle gyms.
6. Tumbling and trampolining activities.
7. Pressure applied directly to student's legs, arms, and other body parts to increase the amount of proprioception received from partner:
   - Pushing down on upward extended legs while supine
   - Pushing on extended arms
   - Pushing against person in sitting position to elicit resistance (e.g., have the student imitate an immovable object such as a "rock" or "bench," or have student sit on a scooterboard with "seat belt" fastened by placing hands on sides of scooterboard and holding tightly without releasing once the "car" is moving. Partner "drives the car" by pushing on shoulders to steer. This is easily incorporated into a dramatic play activity involving "driving cars" and people in the community, such as crossing guards and policemen)

Auditory system. A great deal of information from the environment comes in the form of sounds. Additional experiences in discrimination and listening skills assist with the processing of auditory information.

1. Naming various sounds while blindfolded (e.g., bell, ball bouncing, whistle, clap, stomp).
2. Identifying the direction of the sound (localization); student hears and must point in the direction of the sound.
3. Playing blind-man's bluff or blind tag: object is to play the game relying solely on auditory input.
4. Identifying words or directions spoken over background noise (auditory figure–ground).
5. Performing a motor activity or sequence when given an auditory cue (e.g., clap means jump, whistle means stop).

Visual system. Visual input is used in most physical education activities. It is advisable to include activities specific to the visual system to enhance processing.

Ocular training activities

1. Following a swinging or moving ball with just the eyes.
2. Hitting a swinging ball with a stick, using both hands, one hand, and alternating hands.

FIGURE H.5

Finding one's way through an obstacle course can teach space and form perception.

3. Hitting a suspended ball toward a given target.
4. Following a flashlight beam in a darkened room with eyes and with body.

Space and form perception

1. Making one's body into various shapes (e.g., circle, triangle, letters), individually or in groups.
2. Navigating through a maze on the ground.
3. Moving through an obstacle course involving small and large spaces (see Figure H.5).
4. Moving through large containers (e.g., old refrigerator boxes) cut into various shapes (e.g., crawl through the square, go backward out the diamond).
5. Distinguishing a given letter or shape from a maze of lines on the ground.
6. Using jump ropes to make letters, shapes, and numbers (e.g., use short, long, or Chinese ropes).
7. Moving through hula hoops suspended in the air or placed at different positions and heights.
8. Playing follow-the-leader.
9. Making mirror images (two students, facing one another, perform identical movements).

Activities for Enhancing Motor-Sensory Responses

The student must be able to organize and use sensory information for motor action. This process involves integration resulting in motor-sensory responses, including the following:

1. Praxis (motor planning ability)
2. Integration of both sides of the body
3. Balance and equilibrium responses
4. Eye–hand and eye–foot interaction and coordination
5. Crossing the midline of the body
6. Body awareness

Praxis (motor planning). Motor planning—*the ability to plan and execute purposeful, nonhabitual movement*—is required in most activities in a physical education program. The following activities are presented for their content relative to demands on motor planning.

1. Rolling, crawling, creeping, walking, running up and down an incline, over and under objects, forward and backward, and so on.
2. Performing any or all locomotor movements in a sequence, moving quickly from one to the other.
3. Moving through an obstacle course blindfolded or with eyes closed.
4. Following a rope maze blindfolded.
5. Performing angels-in-the-snow.
6. Performing animal walks and wrestling games.
7. Following a serpentine rope.
8. Playing "tag" games.
9. Imitating postures and positions quickly and slowly.
10. Playing follow-the-leader.
11. Moving to different beats of a drum or music.
12. Performing balance tasks or stunts (see activities for balance and equilibrium responses).
13. Performing novel movement tasks (e.g., snapping fingers, shooting marbles).
14. Performing mirror images with partner.
15. Stringing beads.
16. Duplicating pegboard or rubber band board patterns.
17. Dropping clothespins into containers.
18. Participating in puppet play.
19. Putting one's body into various shapes (e.g., statues).
20. Following a specified line in a maze.
21. Following a rhythm using rhythm sticks (or cups exchange).

Integration of both sides of the body. It is important for the body sides to work together efficiently, as well as to work independently. The following activities enhance both *bilateral* and *reciprocal action* of the body sides.

1. Jumping through hula hoops placed in different patterns and at varying distances apart (e.g., vertical, horizontal, diagonal, alternating).
2. Jumping on trampolines, inner tubes, tires, and so on.
3. Prone, propelling oneself forward on scooterboard, using arms.
4. Pushing cage ball with both feet together or both arms together.
5. Catching a ball with two hands.
6. Clapping hands together (or using clap, clap, snap rhythm).
7. Catching beanbags or yarn balls with scoops.
8. Bilateral play with ribbon sticks.
9. Pulling oneself up an incline by rope, hand over hand.
10. Alternate hopping.
11. Riding a tricycle.
12. Hitting a suspended ball, alternating hands (e.g., tetherball).
13. Hitting a suspended ball with a stick held horizontally (hands at ends and hands together in the middle).
14. Performing animal walks.
15. Participating in wrestling games.
16. Participating in balance activities.
17. Playing wheelbarrow with partner(s).
18. Moving specified limb (specified by touch or name of part) without moving any other body part.
19. Hitting balloons with two hands together, then alternating hands.
20. Playing tug-of-rope.
21. Climbing ropes, ladders, jungle gyms.
22. Using a "Play-Buoy" (sometimes referred to as a "zoom" ball).
23. Performing parachute activities.

Balance and equilibrium responses.
1. Maintaining balance in side-lying, sitting, kneeling, hand and knee, and standing positions.
2. Maintaining balance while sitting on a T-stool.
3. Maintaining a variety of body positions on a tilt board or balance board.
4. Rolling in an inner-tube barrel or texture-lined barrel.
5. Maintaining body positions while gently being pushed by teacher.
6. Participating in trampoline or rebounder activities (see Figure H.6 and also section on trampoline/rebounder activities later in this appendix).
7. Playing Twister; playing Funny Bones.
8. Balancing various body parts identified by name or number.
9. Roller skating.
10. Skateboard activities.
11. Scooterboard activities.
12. Balance beam activities.
13. Participating in animal walks and wrestling games.
14. Sliding down an incline on a carpet square.
15. Following footsteps painted or placed on floor.
16. Walking on a specified line.
17. Stepping on newspaper (or hula hoops, carpet squares, etc.) placed throughout room.
18. Walking on tin can stilts or blocks of wood, traveling across the room (see Figure H.10 on p. 440).
19. Participating in tumbling activities.
20. Climbing on playground apparatus.
21. Balancing in various positions with eyes closed.
22. Forming pyramids with several children.
23. Locomoting on an uneven surface.
24. Balancing beanbags on various body parts (e.g., shoulder, knee, back of hand, elbow).
25. Balancing beanbags and moving around the room.
26. Moving oneself through a hula hoop while holding it with left, right, or both hands.

Eye–hand and eye–foot interaction and coordination.
1. Reaching for object with hand.
2. Stacking objects.
3. Building towers.
4. Nesting objects.
5. Hitting suspended ball with hands.
6. Hitting suspended ball with feet.
7. Pushing objects with one foot, with two feet together.
8. Participating in kicking, catching, bouncing, striking, and throwing activities.
9. Keeping balloons in the air as long as possible.
10. While sitting or supine, keeping balloons in the air with feet.
11. Clapping hands to music.
12. Beating drum to a rhythm.
13. Using rhythm sticks.
14. Rolling ball up and down and around body.
15. Walking through a ladder (or tires) placed on the ground.
16. Forming shapes (e.g., letters, numbers) with rope.

FIGURE H.6 Using a rebounder and physical assistance to help a child develop equilibrium and balance responses.

17. Tracing letters, numbers, shapes, and so on.
18. Throwing beanbags onto letter grids.
19. Kicking or rolling ball around room or space.
20. Playing pat-a-cake, ice cream, or tic-tock hand clap rhymes.
21. Catching and blowing soap bubbles.
22. Sorting and matching small objects (e.g., marbles, clips, beads, screws).

Crossing midline of body.

1. Imitating postures, positions, or movements that require crossing the midline of the body (fun partner play activity):
    a. Hand on opposite ear, eye
    b. Hands on opposite knees, thighs, feet
    c. Cross-over walking pattern
2. Hitting a suspended object using hand contralaterally, forcing hand across midline.
3. Rolling segmentally up and down incline.
4. Rolling in a barrel (or large tire tube).
5. Catching small objects two-handed (e.g., bean bags, balls) that are thrown at side of body.
6. Reaching with both hands to left foot, then to right foot.
7. Stacking objects on one side of the body.
8. Keeping suspended ball in motion, alternating hands for striking.

Body awareness.

1. Identifying and performing or moving the body in different planes (front, back, side, top, bottom) and body parts:
    a. Back of body
    b. Back of hand
    c. Side of head
    d. Top of foot
    e. Front of leg
2. Identifying planes in relation to objects or partner(s):
    a. Place back on ground
    b. Place top of head against wall
    c. Place bottom of hand on ball
3. Touching specified body parts on self.
4. Touching specified body parts on others (e.g., People to People game—see Chapter 10, Figure 10.3).
5. Identifying body parts and their movements:
    a. Lift arm above head

b. Point toe toward ground
   c. Wiggle nose
6. Identifying right and left on self and others.
7. Moving toward the right and left of self and objects.
8. Assuming basic body positions (e.g., supine, prone, long-leg sit, crossed-leg sit, kneel, squat, hands and knees) on command.
9. Performing angels-in-the-snow.
10. Moving body in specified pattern:
    a. Walk in a circle
    b. Make triangle with elbow
    c. Draw a figure-eight with hand
11. Moving body in relation to object:
    a. Both feet in hula hoop
    b. Hands on carpet square
    c. Total body over hula hoop
12. Playing Simon Says or One Behind.
13. Playing Hokey Pokey.
14. Playing Twister or Funny Bones.
15. Tracing entire body on paper, then coloring and cutting it out.

Activities for Enhancing Motor Patterns and Motor Skills

Activities at this level of the developmental model include those that provide individuals with a repertoire of movement experiences.

Early motor experiences and motor patterns

Range of motion (ROM). When a student is unable to perform voluntary movement, activities to elicit ROM can sometimes be incorporated in the physical education setting. However, the physical therapist should always be consulted before performing the passive movements with a child. The adapted physical educator can collaborate with other professionals, especially the physical education teacher, on ideas for incorporating movements into the class activities. Sometimes, these activities are listed as accommodations or modifications required by the IEP for students with a disability.

1. Flex both legs up; lower one leg slowly, then the other.
2. Abduct one leg out to the side, then the other.
3. Flex legs, turn knees in, then out; return to straight-leg position.
4. Move feet in a circular pattern around ankle.
5. Flex legs, rotate both knees, and lower legs to each side.
6. Raise one arm overhead, then the other.
7. Raise arm out to side, then arm over head, repeat with other arm.
8. With arm flexed and held at shoulder height, move hand and lower arm above shoulder and then below; repeat with other arm.
9. Extend arm.
10. Rotate extended arm inward and outward; repeat with other arm.
11. Extend wrist through entire ROM by turning palms up and down.
12. Move hand in circular pattern around wrist (ask student to move suspended object in a circle).

Head control. Head control is *the ability to hold the head in position when other body parts move.*

1. With student prone over bolster, visually stimulate student to lift head by holding colorful object in front of him or her.
2. With student prone over bolster, stimulate back of neck to assist in head raising by touching the neck.
3. With student in sitting position, visually stimulate him or her to raise head by talking or using a sound-activated toy.
4. Have student pull slowly (or grasp and hold hands on dowel for assistance) from supine position to sitting to initiate head control.
5. With student supine, place head in correct alignment for back-lying position.
6. When correct head position is achieved, hold shoulders to help student maintain head position.

Rolling over. In each of the following activities, place objects within the reach of the student or stimulate auditorily to elicit the rolling-over pattern.

1. Student rolls from side-lying position to supine with and without assistance.
2. Student rolls from side-lying to prone position with and without assistance.
3. Student rolls from prone to supine position with and without assistance.
4. Student rolls from supine to side-lying to prone position with and without assistance.
5. Student rolls from supine to prone position with and without assistance.
6. Assist student in rolling from prone to supine and supine to prone with arms extended over head.
7. Assist student to roll in texture-lined barrel.
8. Assist student to roll in inner-tube barrel.

9. Assist student to roll up in textured materials.
10. Assist student to roll up and down an incline.

Crawling. The crawl consists of *reciprocal action of limbs while moving along on stomach.* It is advisable to place objects or position the teacher directly in front of the student to encourage crawling.

1. Crawling, both arms pull together, legs still.
2. Crawling, both arms pull together, legs use reciprocal action.
3. Crawling, both arms use reciprocal action, legs still.
4. Crawling, both arms use reciprocal action, legs use reciprocal action.
5. Crawl over, under, around objects.
6. Crawl up and down an incline.

Creeping. The creep consists of *forward movement on hands and knees, in the 4-point position for locomotion.*

1. Place student over bolster in creep position, student bears weight on arms.
2. Place student over bolster in creep position, student bears weight on legs.
3. While over bolster in creep position, student bears weight on arms and legs.
4. In creep position, student bears weight on arms and legs with and without support from teacher.
5. Creep forward.
6. Creep over, under, around, and through objects.
7. Creep through tunnels.
8. Creep up and down an incline.
9. Creep in or on a specified pattern.

Sitting.

1. While in crossed-leg sit, hands at sides, student maintains position with and without support. Student should avoid sitting in the "W" sitting position.
2. While student is in crossed-leg sit, place student's hands in lap; student maintains position with and without support.
3. While student is sitting, place objects in front of him or her within reach, and encourage reach and grasp while returning to upright sitting position.
4. Sitting on bolster, student bears weight on legs without and with support.
5. Sitting on (straddling) bolster, with weight equally distributed between legs, student maintains position.
6. Sitting in chair, student plays with objects positioned in front of him- or herself.

Kneeling.

1. Student kneels in upright position using arms on object (e.g., table, bolster) for support, maintains position, and reaches for toys.
2. Student kneels in upright position with one-arm support.
3. Student kneels in upright position without assistance.
4. Student walks forward on knees.
5. Student walks on knees up and down incline, through obstacle course, and so on.

Standing and walking.

1. Student stands in upright position, leaning or with arms supporting body.
2. Student stands with one-arm support.
3. Student stands without support.
4. Student walks along objects (cruising).
5. Student walks from object to person.
6. Student walks from person to person.
7. Student walks forward and backward with and without assistance.

Stair climbing.

1. On hands and knees, student creeps up stairs.
2. Student sits on top step and descends by sitting on each step on the way down.
3. Student creeps up forward and creeps down backward.
4. Using one step, student steps up on platform, turns around, and steps down with and without support; repeats with other foot.
5. While holding handrail, student ascends each step one at a time with both feet placed on each landing, same lead foot.
6. Student descends, both feet on each step.
7. With support, student ascends each step alternating lead foot; descends with same lead foot.
8. Student ascends each step alternating lead foot; descends with alternate feet with and without support.
9. Vary height and width of steps used for stair climbing.

Hand and arm use. Provide access and opportunities for students to explore and assist as needed.

1. Provide a variety (diverse array) of objects to grasp and place in hands.
2. Place student's hands in tactile box for play.
3. Place objects in front of student; encourage reaching and grasping (palmar then pincer grasp).

4. Play pat-a-cake.
5. Imitate hand movements.
6. Stack blocks.
7. Nest items.
8. Hit suspended ball, balloons.
9. String beads.
10. Pick up tiny objects (e.g., marbles, dice, pick-up sticks, dominoes).
11. Open and close clothespins.
12. Place pegs in holes.
13. Stretch, reach, bend arms.
14. Push and pull large cage ball, large beach ball.
15. Pull objects (e.g., pull-toys).
16. Push small carts while walking.
17. Pull oneself up incline using rope.
18. Grasp parachute handles, sides of parachute, or cooperation bands.

Activities for motor pattern development: Locomotor

Walking. Walking is *progressive alternate leg action and continuous contact with supporting surface; one foot moves ahead of the other with heel of forward foot touching ground before toe of opposite foot pushes off, and the arms and legs move synchronously in opposition* (Wickstrom, 1977).

1. Walk with assistance.
2. Walk with support.
3. Walk quickly from one stable object to another over a short distance (a few feet).
4. Walk forward from one point to another.
5. Walk backward from one point to another.
6. Walk between parallel lines drawn on floor.
7. Walk on single line on floor (vary width of line, such as 6", 4", 2", etc.).
8. Walk following curved line, figure-eight, or any specified pattern.
9. Walk up and down incline.
10. Walk through a ladder or tires on ground.
11. Walk on footprints, following a specified pattern.
12. Walk on tiptoes.
13. Walk through obstacle course.
14. Walk with a variety of tempos (e.g., quickly or slowly).

Running. Running is *a natural extension of walking in which each leg goes through a support phase and a recovery phase, and the full sequence produces two periods of nonsupport; trunk leans forward and arm swings in opposition to leg action.*

1. Run forward or backward.
2. Run up and down an incline.
3. Run along a straight line or zigzag course.
4. Run through traffic cones set in various positions.
5. Run for distance.
6. Run and show ability to change directions quickly.
7. Run, stop, and move on command.
8. Run with a variety of tempos (e.g., quickly, slowly).

Jumping. Jumping is *a forward, explosive propulsion of the body off the ground with both legs.* From a crouch position, with body weight forward, the arms swing forward and upward; hips, legs, and ankles flex and extend at takeoff; knees bend at landing; body weight moves forward and downward at landing.

1. Rise on toes.
2. Bounce on mini-tramp or rebounder.
3. Coordinate rising on toes with knee and hip extension.
4. Jump down from step, increasing the height of takeoff platform.
5. Jump forward.
6. Jump over line, over rope.
7. Jump forward and backward over rope raised slightly off the ground, gradually increasing height.
8. Perform a series of forward and backward jumps.
9. Jump into a designated space (e.g., hula hoop, carpet square).
10. Jump up to reach object over head with one hand, then both hands.
11. Jump sideways over line or rope.
12. Jump over moving rope.
13. Jump with a variety of tempos (e.g., quickly, slowly).
14. Jump with feet together, with feet apart.
15. Straddle jump.
16. Teach jump rope starting with long rope and then using short ropes:
    a. Step over rope (slant rope is an effective adaptation for the horizontal rope so that all students can decide which height to attempt and be successful in stepping over the rope).
    b. Jump over rope moving forward and backward.
    c. With rope passing over head, step over rope.
    d. With rope passing over head, jump over rope.

e. Jump over rope twice in a row.
f. Increase number and tempo of rope turns.

Hopping. The hopping action consists of *a slight body lean forward with weight supported on one foot and nonsupport leg bent at knee; arms move upward; landing on toes, weight is transferred to ball of foot, then to heel; upright balance is maintained.*

1. Initiate hop of the preferred foot with and without support.
2. Hop forward one hop.
3. Perform a series of hops on preferred foot.
4. Hop on the nonpreferred foot.
5. Alternate feet for hopping.
6. Hop in a variety of directions (e.g., forward, backward).
7. Hop through an obstacle course.
8. Hop through hopscotch pattern in correct number sequence (use preferred, then nonpreferred foot).

Sliding. Sliding consists of *sideways locomotion; one foot is brought sideways close to contact with other foot, which then moves sideways away from the body; weight shifts from side to side in one direction.*

1. Step sideways on line (i.e., step together, step together—sometimes referred to as side slide).
2. Step sideways in one direction, then the other.
3. Increase speed of slide with more weight on balls of feet.
4. Slide to a rhythm.
5. Alternate direction and lead foot of slide (e.g., agility practice using arm signals for direction).

Activities for motor pattern development: Manipulative

Rolling ball.

1. While seated, roll ball away from self with both hands together (e.g., hands under ball, hands on top, hands on side).
2. Roll ball toward object or person (use long-sitting straddle or crossed-legged positions).
3. While kneeling or squatting, roll ball underhand with one and both hands, away from self.
4. Roll ball toward object, person, or specified direction (e.g., call name of person first).
5. Vary the distance of the roll.
6. Vary the size, weight, and type of the ball.

Throwing. Throwing is a movement sequence that involves *thrusting an object into space, initiated by a forward step with contralateral leg, followed by hip and trunk rotation, whipping action of propelling arm, and followthrough after release of ball.*

1. Hurl small objects (e.g., paper balls, yarn balls, rubber balls, tennis balls).
2. Throw small objects underhand without specified speed, force, direction, and so on.
3. Throw underhand, specifying target area (e.g., to knock down pins or cones).
4. Throw, specifying speed, distance, or direction.
5. Teach student the backswing, step forward, and followthrough for underhand throw.
6. Vary the size, weight, type, and shape of the object to be thrown (e.g., beanbag, ball, balloon, medicine ball, bowling ball).
7. Throw toward moving target (e.g., a rolling hula hoop).
8. Throw while moving.
9. Roll hula hoop toward object using underhand pattern; vary speed, direction, force, quality, and so on.
10. Repeat items 1 through 9 using overhand throw.
11. Throw various objects (e.g., beanbags, baseball, small balls, football) using overhand pattern.
12. Throw objects sidearm, varying factors as appropriate.
13. Throw a Frisbee (step forward with homolateral foot).

Bouncing ball.

1. Grasp rubber playground ball with two hands, drop and catch with two hands.
2. Vary size of ball for drop–catch.
3. Push ball downward (bounce) with two hands and catch with two hands.
4. Vary size, weight, and type of ball.
5. Use one hand to bounce ball and catch two-handed.
6. Perform continuous bounce while standing in place (stationary).
7. Walk forward while bouncing ball (dribbling).
8. Bounce ball over line to partner (e.g., 2-square format).
9. Vary the locomotor pattern while dribbling.
10. Dribble around cones, following a figure-eight pattern.
11. Vary size, weight, speed, and force while dribbling.
12. Bounce a ball two-handed toward a person or object (bounce pass).
13. Vary the height of the bounce.
14. Vary the direction of the bounce.

15. Vary the length and speed of the bounce.
16. Two-handed bounce pass to moving or stationary object, person, or target.

Catching. Catching consists of *using the hands to stop and control an aerial ball; arms are raised in front of body; hands are cupped; hips and knees are flexed; hands contact and grasp ball; limbs bend to absorb force.*

1. Trap a rolled ball with two hands while sitting in long straddle position.
2. Catch a ball after dropping it (drop–catch).
3. Catch a bounced ball at chest height with two hands.
4. Vary type of ball (e.g., rubber ball, beach ball, basketball).
5. Vary speed, direction, or force of bounced ball.
6. Catch tossed ball by trapping it.
7. Catch tossed ball with arms and hands, then with two hands.
8. Catch tossed ball with two hands only.
9. Play catch with another student, varying the size of the ball, length of throw, and speed.
10. Catch balls thrown over objects.
11. Catch objects with one hand (e.g., beanbags, Frisbees, balls).
12. Catch while moving through space.
13. Play Hot Potato.
14. Circle ball toss (group juggling).

Striking. Striking consists of *contact with an object (ball) by an implement (bat, hands, foot); body weight is shifted (step) in direction of intended hit; hips and trunk rotate (turn); arms swing around and forward (swing)* (Wickstrom, 1977).

1. Hit suspended object (e.g., ball, balloon) while kneeling or standing.
2. Try to keep a balloon in the air with hand.
3. Vary the height of the object to be struck.
4. Hit object toward a target.
5. Vary hitting object hard or easy, fast or slow.
6. With striking implement (e.g., baton, bat, stick), hit object suspended at head, chest, waist, or knee height, and on ground; use one or both hands on implement.
7. Hold stick horizontally with two hands, hit suspended ball.
8. Strike playground ball with both hands and rebound off wall, then attempt to catch ball.
9. Specify direction, speed, and force of strike.
10. Vary size of implement and object to be hit (large–large, large–small, small–large, medium–medium).
11. Strike appropriate (stationary) objects with baseball bat, hockey stick, racquet, and so on.
12. Strike appropriate object, moving with implement (e.g., baseball bat, hockey stick, tennis racquet, badminton racquet).

Kicking. Kicking consists of *contact with an object by the foot: step forward on support leg; swing kicking leg forward; extend lower leg into object; swing opposite arm forward in reaction.*

1. Push ball away from the body with preferred, then nonpreferred, foot.
2. Kick ball away from the body with preferred, then nonpreferred, foot.
3. Kick stationary ball toward target in specified direction or back and forth between partners.
4. Vary speed, distance, and height of kick.
5. Vary the size, weight, and type of ball.
6. Kick a stationary ball with side of foot (soccer style).
7. Run to stationary ball and kick.
8. Dribble (i.e., continuously kick ball) forward in specified direction or through obstacle course.
9. Dribble between partners.
10. Kick a variety of stationary balls (e.g., football, kickball, soccer, playground) in appropriate manner.
11. Kick a moving ball.

Activities for motor pattern development: Nonlocomotor

Bending.
1. Bend the body forward.
2. Bend the body backward.
3. Bend the body sideways.
4. Bend (flex) the body parts—one leg, both legs, one arm, knees, both arms, arms and legs, hands, and so on.

Reaching and stretching.
1. Reach with one and two hands to touch object overhead while standing.
2. Touch toe or floor with one and two hands from standing position.
3. Reach (stretch forward, backward, and to each side) from standing position.
4. Stretch forward to touch toes with both hands from long-sitting position.
5. Bend from long-sitting straddle position and touch each foot with one and two hands.
6. In supine position, point toes and extend legs as far as possible; extend arms over head.

Turning and twisting.
1. Rotate each body part around axis (e.g., foot, arm, leg, and hand circles).
2. In upright position, turn entire body in a small circle.
3. In upright position, twist upper body in one direction, then in opposite direction while maintaining stable lower body position.
4. In supine position, bend knees and rotate to one side, then the other.
5. Jump and turn body one-quarter, one-half, three-quarters, and full turn in each direction.
6. From side-lying position, rotate upper and lower body in opposite directions.

Pushing and pulling.
1. In sitting position, push large cage ball away with one and two hands or one and two feet.
2. In supine position, push cage ball with hands or feet or both.
3. In prone position, push body off floor.
4. In upright position, push against heavy or light object; against stationary or movable object.
5. Walk forward while pushing object (e.g., cage ball, cart, box).
6. In hands and knees position, push another person with entire body (e.g., wrestling games).
7. Prone on scooterboard, propel forward and backward using feet or hands on wall or floor.
8. Prone or supine on scooterboard, pull oneself along suspended rope.
9. Pull oneself up incline in prone position.
10. In upright position, pull objects on string toward oneself using reciprocal arm action.
11. Walk forward and pull objects along behind.

Activities for motor skill development

Motor skills emanate from motor patterns; that is, skills are the more accurate and specific uses of motor patterns and combinations of patterns. Each of the motor experiences and motor patterns discussed in the previous section included activity suggestions for the development of skill, although they were not specified as such. A few additional examples are presented here.

As variables are manipulated in an attempt to refine motor ability, the activities generally are said to be for enhancing motor skills. Varying the activity's speed, rhythm, quality, direction, surface, or area requires that the pattern be refined into skill. Examples include:

1. Walk, run, hop, and so on, forward in a straight line as fast as possible.
2. Walk backward blindfolded on a balance beam.
3. Jump over an object and land on one foot, or jump into a specified area.
4. Throw at a target.
5. Run through an obstacle course.
6. Hop, under control, downhill.

Combinations of motor patterns result in motor skills. A gallop is a combination of a step and slide, a skip is a step–hop, and a leap is an airborne giant step (initial part of hop with landing on opposite foot).

Galloping. A gallop is *forward motion of the body in which the same foot leads on each stride, and the opposite foot is brought adjacent and parallel; step–slide action.*
1. Walk forward on a line with same foot in front.
2. Speed up the "lead leg walk" into a gallop.
3. Walk forward with the nonpreferred foot in front.
4. Gallop with the nonpreferred foot forward.
5. Gallop along a path (e.g., circle, line, zigzag, or shape patterns).
6. Alternate the lead leg for gallop.

Skipping. Skipping is *an alternate step and hop action with each foot; weight shifts forward with step; arms move in opposition.*
1. Follow footsteps for teaching step–hop.
2. Perform a step–hop with one foot, repeat.
3. Perform a step–hop with other foot, repeat.
4. Perform step–hop with one foot, then with other foot, repeating pattern.
5. Increase the number of alternating patterns; step–hop right, step–hop left, and so on.
6. Increase the speed of repetition.
7. Skip using a variety of tempos (e.g., quickly and slowly).
8. Skip in a circle or along a pathway.
9. Skip to music.

Leaping. Leaping consists of *pushing forward with support leg and catching with opposite leg; arms move alternately during leap; weight shifts forward and upward on takeoff, then downward and forward on landing.*
1. Take a very large step forward with the preferred foot forward.

2. Take a large step quickly.
3. One-foot takeoff into air, take large step quickly.
4. Perform leap with one foot takeoff, land on opposite foot.
5. Repeat items 1 through 4 with nonpreferred foot.
6. Alternate lead foot; alternate leaping.
7. Leap over low object such as line, rope, shoes.
8. Leap as high as possible.
9. Leap as far as possible (e.g., long distance).
10. Run and leap to music or rhythm.

CULTURALLY DETERMINED FORMS OF MOVEMENT

Many books, card files, and articles describe activities for individuals with a disability, including games, sports, athletics, dance, and so on. The following sections list activities in aquatics, dance, fitness, games and sports, and special equipment and activities. These listings are examples of appropriate activities and are not intended to be all-inclusive.

Aquatics

The water is a wonderful medium for movement for individuals with a disability. Almost every individual can participate in water learning activities, and many can learn to swim. The American Red Cross has identified five safety skills that every person with a disability should be taught:

1. Turning over from prone to supine
2. Changing directions
3. Prone float
4. Supine float
5. Breath control

These skills should be taught to individuals with a disability as soon as possible for their own safety and the safety of others. Keep in mind that individuals can participate in many water activities that may not lead to the acquisition of swimming skills.

Water adjustment: On-deck wading pool.

1. Walk into water and gradually increase depth to knees.
2. Sit in water and gradually increase depth to waist height.
3. Splash water by slapping hands or fists in water or pushing and pulling water with partner.
4. Wash face with water by cupping both hands and bringing up to face.
5. Water play: pour water with bucket; squeeze sponges, splash balls, etc.
6. Retrieve objects (e.g., deck rings, tennis balls, splash balls, chips) from water.

Water adjustment: In-water swimming pool.

1. Sit on step.
2. Splash water on body and face.
3. Move down steps into water.
4. Wade in waist deep, assisted.
5. Wade in waist deep, unassisted.
6. Wade in chest deep, assisted.
7. Wade in chest deep, unassisted.
8. Move forward, backward, and sideways, unassisted.
9. Bend knees and submerge to chin.
10. Put parts of head (i.e., chin, ears, cheeks, forehead, nose, mouth, eyes) into water.
11. Quickly place nose and mouth into water and recover.
12. Place whole face into water and recover.
13. Submerge body to ears.
14. Submerge with head under water (e.g., "1, 2, 3, under" or tea party).

Breath control.

1. Out of water: inhale, exhale.
2. With body in chest-deep water, easy inhale, slow exhale.
3. Blow ping-pong ball across pool.
4. Blow bubbles using straw and shorten length gradually.
5. With mouth in water, slowly exhale into water, making bubbles.
6. With face in water, blow bubbles.
7. Submerge and blow bubbles.
8. Rhythmic bobbing, 3- or 4-second intervals.
9. Exhale through nose into water.

Body control.

1. Walk slowly through water; walk rapidly.
2. Jump while in water.
3. Squat under water.
4. Sit on bottom of pool.
5. Kneel on bottom of pool.
6. Lie prone (or supine) on bottom of pool.
7. Roll over while on bottom of pool.

8. Combine movements (e.g., knees to sitting, sitting to prone) while on bottom of pool.
9. With hands on steps, bring legs up to floating position, unassisted recovery.
10. With hands on steps, prone float position, unassisted recovery.
11. With hands on steps, prone float position, kick with legs.
12. With hands on steps, kick slowly (or rapidly).
13. While held in prone position in chest-deep water, recover to standing with assistance, then without assistance.
14. While held in supine position in chest-deep water, recover to standing with assistance, then without assistance.
15. While being pulled in prone position, maintain relaxed body position.
16. Retrieve objects (e.g., diving rings, chips) from two to three feet of water.
17. Jellyfish float: float with arms, legs, and hands extended toward bottom of pool and back rounded.
18. Turtle float: grab legs, feet off bottom, and float.
19. Prone float and recovery.
20. Supine float (knees bent) and recovery.
21. Roll over from prone float to supine float.
22. Roll from supine float to prone float (see Figure H.7).

FIGURE H.7

Adaptive devices such as this mat can help a person learn to float.

Basic skills.
1. Steamboat: kick while being pulled through water.
2. Prone glide with assistance.
3. Prone glide to steps and recover.
4. Prone glide to instructor (two feet away from steps), assisted recovery.
5. Prone glide to instructor (three or four feet from steps), unassisted recovery.
6. Prone glide width of pool (6 to 10 feet).
7. Kick glide to steps (three feet).
8. Kick glide to instructor (three or four feet), assisted recovery.
9. Kick glide (three or four feet), unassisted recovery.
10. Kick glide the width of pool (6 to 10 feet).
11. While in supine position, finning and sculling* with hands.
12. Beginning armstroke with underwater recovery of arms.
13. Armstroke: hand over hand.
14. Beginner's stroke with kick.
15. Front crawl without breathing.
16. Change directions while swimming.
17. Swim two widths of pool (15 to 20 feet).
18. Jump into chest-deep water.
19. Jump into head-deep water and swim 15 to 20 feet.

*Finning and sculling use only hands for movement. **Finning** is done *supine with hands at sides, moving in finning motion; body moves head first.* **Sculling** is done *supine with arms over head; body moves feet first.*

Swimming skills.
1. Front crawl with breathing.
2. Swim under water (five to eight feet).
3. Jump into deep water and swim 30 feet.
4. Tread water with arms and legs.
5. Dive into pool from sitting position.
6. Dive into pool from one knee.
7. Dive into pool from crouch position.
8. Dive from standing position.
9. Elementary backstroke.
10. Breaststroke.
11. Back crawl.
12. Side stroke.
13. Dive from low board.

Creative movement.
1. Somersaults forward (or backward) in water.
2. Log rolls in water.
3. Egg rolls in water.
4. Handstands in shallow water.
5. Elbow stands in shallow water.
6. Walk on hands in shallow water.
7. Corkscrew swimming (turning body with each stroke as in a spiral).
8. Shark swim (swim in circle with one hand on hip, elbow out of water).
9. Swim without using arms, legs only.
10. Swim without using legs, arms only.
11. Swim without using legs or arms.
12. Swim through hula hoops.
13. Retrieve objects from bottom.
14. Rhythmic bobbing in deep water.

Group activities.
1. Inner-tube tag.
2. Inner-tube relay races.
3. Kickboard relays and races.
4. Marco Polo.
5. Water volleyball.
6. Water polo.
7. Water basketball.
8. "Jump-Dive."
9. Jump and catch.
10. Water ballet.
11. Synchronized swimming.
12. Academic and language games.

Conditioning.
1. Standing in shallow water:
    a. Alternate toe touch
    b. Side-straddle hop
    c. Stride hop
    d. Toe bounce
    e. Side bend
    f. Standing crawl
    g. Walking twists
2. Holding side of pool:
    a. Knees up
    b. Knees-up twists
    c. Leg crosses
    d. Leg circles
    e. Ankle circles
    f. Prone, supine, and side-lying flutter kick
3. Bobbing:
    a. Simple bobbing
    b. Alternate leg rearward bobbing
    c. Alternate leg sideward bobbing
    d. Leg astride bobbing
    e. Progressive "bunny hop" bobbing
    f. High bobbing (from deep water)
4. Treading water:
    a. Simple treading water
    b. One-hand high treading
    c. Two-hand high treading
    d. Lookout treading
5. Other exercises:
    a. Sculling forward, backward
    b. Sculling with knee(s) up
    c. Pedaling in water
    d. Leg raises from side-lying position
    e. Alternate leg raising during sculling
    f. Lap swimming

Dance and Rhythms
1. Clap to music.
2. Keep time to music with instruments.
3. Walk (move) to drum beat (fast, slow, loud, soft, and so on).
4. Walk to music.
5. March to a specified beat.
6. Play London Bridge, Hokey Pokey, I'm a Little Teapot, Farmer in the Dell, and so on.
7. Use commercial records, tapes, or CDs.
8. Circle dances (Circasian Circle, Teton Mountain Stomp); line dances (e.g., Hora, Bunny Hop, Cotton-Eye Joe).
9. Square dance (Virginia Reel).
10. Run and leap to music.
11. Imitate partner in time to music.
12. Slow mirroring of partner in time with slow music.
13. Interpretive dance.
14. Dance with ribbons, sticks, flags, clubs, and scarves.
15. Orff-Schulwerk chants.
16. Exercise to music (e.g., leader exchange or aerobics).
17. Jump rope to music and chants.
18. Combine exercises to make a routine set to music.

Teaching Tip

HOMEMADE MEDICINE BALL • Make your own medicine ball by recycling flat playground balls (or any other kind) in any size. Cut a hole around the valve. Fill them with extra rubber from old balls, sand, or anything else to weight the ball. Finish by stuffing tightly with plastic bags for stability and cover the ball with duct tape. Using different ball sizes and colors of tape is a fun way to have several balls for use in class.

19. Swedish gymnastics.
20. Explore different styles and formations of dancing:
    a. Country or square dance using line or circle formation
    b. Disco dance with partners or in shuttle line
    c. Rock and roll in scatter formation or with partner(s)
    d. Aerobic dance in squad lines or using step benches

Physical Fitness Activities

An important objective of any physical education program should be to improve the physical fitness of those participating. The following activities should be included as an integral part of the program.

1. Aerobic activities:
   a. Running in place or for distance (e.g., walking or running programs for mileage completed)
   b. Jump rope activities and games
   c. Aerobic rhythms and dance activities
   d. Par courses and fitness trails
   e. Pedal cycle ergometers, arm cycler
2. Body composition:
   a. Skinfold measurements
   b. Body mass index calculations
3. Flexibility:
   a. Slow stretching exercises
   b. Nonlocomotor movements of bend, twist, stretch, etc.
   c. Stretching different body parts (comfortable discomfort levels only)
4. Muscular strength and endurance:
   a. Pull-up, push-up, sit-up, curl-up, etc.
   b. Rope or pole climbing, climbing walls, climbing cargo nets, etc.
   c. Specific exercises (isometric, isotonic, isokinetic)
   d. Medicine ball activities (see Figure H.8)
   e. Resistance activities using inner-tube strips, surgical tubing, or Theraband
   f. Weight training using weights, Nautilus machines, etc.

Games and Sports

Some games and sports will need adaptations for individuals with a disability, but many can be played without any adaptations. The following are examples of games and sports.

1. Team sports:
   a. Basketball
   b. Football
   c. Hockey (e.g., field, ice, box, roller, or air hockey)
   d. Soccer
   e. Softball, baseball, T-ball
   f. Track and field (e.g., cross-country running)
   g. Volleyball (e.g., stand up or sit down, lead-up games such as Prisoner or Keep It Up)
2. Dual sports:
   a. Badminton
   b. Handball
   c. Ping pong (table tennis)

FIGURE H.8

Passing the medicine ball from one student to another can be a conditioning exercise and provide additional balance challenges.

d. Tennis
   e. Wrestling
3. Individual sports:
   a. Archery
   b. Bowling
   c. Cycling (e.g., 10-speed, mountain, tandem)
   d. Fencing
   e. Golf (e.g., miniature, 9-hole, 18-hole)
   f. Gymnastics
   g. Martial arts and self-defense (e.g., karate)
   h. Skiing
   i. Skating (e.g., ice, roller, in-line skating)
4. Leisure activities:
   a. Board games (e.g., chess, checkers, caroms)
   b. Boating (e.g., kayaking, canoeing)
   c. Bocce ball
   d. Camping, hiking, backpacking
   e. Croquet (e.g., table top or grass)
   f. Horseback riding
   g. Mountain or rock climbing
   h. Shuffleboard (e.g., playing area or table top)
   i. Yoga or Tai Chi
5. Playground games and activities:
   a. Handball
   b. "Heads Up, Seven Up" (throwing small ball against backboard with partner)
   c. Line and circle games (e.g., Drop the Handkerchief, Pop Goes the Weasel)
   d. Four-square
   e. Jump rope (long, short, or Chinese ropes)
   f. Tag
   g. Tetherball (e.g., miniature)

SPECIAL EQUIPMENT AND ACTIVITIES

Variations of obstacle courses, other games, special activities, and special equipment assist in the development and refinement of motor patterns and motor skills. The following are offered as activity suggestions and are not intended to be all-inclusive. Many of them have been suggested in previous sections of this appendix.

Special Equipment

Balance beam (walking board) activities.

1. Walk sideways across board leading with right foot.
2. Walk sideways across board leading with left foot.
3. Walk sideways across board carrying a weight in both hands.
4. Walk sideways across board changing weight from hand to hand.
5. Walk sideways across board with a chalkboard eraser (or beanbag or koosch ball) on top of a shoulder and carrying weight in the hand.
6. Walk sideways down board with weight in hands; in middle of board, turn around and continue backward to end of board.
7. Walk across board with arms extended to sides; then with arms to the front, to the back, and both to one side; then with both arms to other side.
8. Walk across board with arms extended in front, arms to back, arms to opposite sides, both arms to one side, both arms to the other side.
9. Walk forward, heel to toe, across board with eyes on target.
10. Walk forward across board carrying a weight in the left hand.
11. Repeat item 10 with a weight in the right hand.
12. Walk forward across board and change the weight from hand to hand.
13. Walk backward across board.
14. Walk forward across board with a chalkboard eraser (or beanbag or koosch ball) balanced on a shoulder.
15. Walk backward across board with a chalkboard eraser (or beanbag or koosch ball) balanced on a shoulder.
16. Walk forward across board with a chalkboard eraser (or beanbag or koosch ball) balanced on a shoulder, and carrying a weight in the hand.
17. Walk across board and throw a beanbag at a target on command.
18. Walk across board and catch a beanbag and throw it back.
19. Walk across board bouncing and catching a ball.
20. Walk forward with left foot always in front of right; combine activities in items 1 through 19.
21. Repeat item 20 with right foot always in front of left.
22. Walk backward with right foot always in back of left.
23. Walk backward with left foot always in back of right.
24. Walk forward and pick up a chalkboard eraser from the middle of the beam.
25. Walk backward and pick up a chalkboard eraser from the middle of the beam.

26. Walk sideways, leading with left side, and pick up a chalkboard eraser from the middle of beam.
27. Walk sideways while leading with right side and pick up a chalkboard eraser from the center of beam.
28. Repeat items 24, 25, 26, and 27, but this time pick up the chalkboard eraser, place it on top of a shoulder, and continue to end of beam.
29. Have partner hold a wand 12 inches over center of beam. Walk to center, step over the wand, and continue to end of beam.
30. Randomly repeat items 1 through 28 using a wand. Increase height of step necessary to clear the wand, *but only high enough.* (Be sure to tell the child if he or she steps *too high.*)
31. Walk across beam in various ways. Teacher stands at end of board with target; student keeps eyes on target while moving across the board.
32. Repeat item 31 with student keeping eyes on target as target is moved. Call student's attention to the fact whenever he or she has lost the target or looked away.
33. Randomly repeat items 1 through 32 and include the task of going over and under the wand.
34. Walk forward with arms out, palms down, with a chalkboard eraser on the back of each hand.
35. Repeat item 34, but walk backward.
36. Walk board in various directions with weight on the balls of the feet.
37. Walking on the balls of the feet, carry various weights across board and change weight from hand to hand while walking. Be sure student is looking at a definite target while walking.
38. Walk to center of board, kneel on one knee, straighten other leg forward until heel is on board and knee is straight. Stand and walk to end of board.
39. Student walks to center of board and stops. Teacher goes to end of board, facing the student. Teacher moves arms and legs in various positions and student imitates. If position is not correct, call the student's attention to the fact.
40. Student walks to center of board. Teacher throws the student a beanbag and student throws it back to teacher or at a target. On direction, student moves to various positions on the board while teacher stays in one place. Student throws the beanbag to the target and to teacher.
41. Walk board while keeping time to beat of drum or clapping of hands.
42. Walk length of board while keeping eyes closed.
43. Partners join hands and one person walks forward and one walks backward the length of the board.
44. Partners start at opposite ends of the board, walk forward slowly to center of board, pass each other, and continue walking to ends of board.
45. Partners start walking forward slowly on two separate boards; they pass a ball back and forth while continuing to walk.
46. Partners start at opposite ends of two separate walking boards and walk toward each other, attempting to toss and catch a beanbag back and forth.

Balance board. Each of the following activities can be done on any size balance board, starting with the largest base and largest platform and progressing to the board with the smallest base and platform.

1. Sit on balance board and maintain balance.
2. Balance on hands and knees on board:
    a. Lift one leg, then the opposite leg.
    b. Lift one arm, then the opposite arm.
    c. Lift one arm and the opposite leg.
    d. Lift arm and leg on same side of body.
3. Maintain kneeling balance.
4. Maintain standing balance.
5. While balanced in any of the above positions, keep beanbag positioned on various body parts (e.g., head, shoulder, back of hand).
6. While balanced, throw and catch beanbag or ball with partner(s).
7. Vary direction, speed, height, and type of object thrown to individual on balance board.
8. While balanced in any position, hit suspended ball with and without stick, two hands together, or each hand alternately.

Hula hoops and carpet squares. The following activities can also be performed with newspaper sections, areas designated on the ground, jump ropes formed into shapes, poly spots, mouse pads, and so on. One of the initial purposes for using hula hoops or carpet squares is to help students identify their own personal space.

1. Vary position (e.g., stand, sit, kneel, lie down, and so on) on carpet square or in hula hoop.
2. Move around space on command and return to hula hoop or carpet square.

3. Use locomotor patterns and skills in conjunction with hula hoop:
    a. Jump over, jump in, jump around.
    b. Run around.
    c. Straddle hoop, then jump in and out with feet moving apart and together as in jumping jack motion (in and out of the hoop).
    d. Stand in front of hoop.
    e. Crawl or climb through hoop.
4. Place hula hoop or carpet square in front, behind, and to the side of the body.
5. Move around space while carrying hula hoop or carpet square; when signaled to stop, quickly sit (jump, lie down, kneel, and so forth) on or in the hoop or square.
6. Move through an upright hula hoop.
7. Use hula hoop as jump rope.
8. Climb through a maze of hula hoops held upright or at different angles.
9. With hula hoops or carpet squares placed in a specific pattern, locomote through course.

Parachute. The parachute, an exciting catalyst for movement, can be used successfully at all grade levels. An entire class can be continuously and vigorously involved in parachute activities, and all students can participate. (See Figure H.9.)

Group stunts

1. *Inflation.* Hands are at waist level holding canopy. On signal to begin, students squat and seal chute on floor. On command "one–two–stretch," the arms are thrust overhead. The object is to get as much air as possible under the canopy. When the center of the canopy comes down and touches the floor, repeat the stunt, trying to get an even better inflation. This stunt is the basic pattern for other stunts listed here.

2. *Tenting.* The students inflate the chute as in item 1, then walk forward three steps toward the center. (Teacher may wish to cue the students by saying, "In! 1–2–3.") Students hold onto the parachute and as it starts to descend, the teacher can give the command, "Out! 1–2–3."

3. *Mushroom.* The idea of this group stunt is to inflate the parachute and then quickly pull the edges down to the floor (or ground), sealing off the rapid escape of air. The class should continue to hold the edges down tight until the center of the canopy descends to the floor. Teacher may wish to have a contest between two teams to see which one can keep the mushroom inflated the longest. The name "mushroom" comes from the shape of the canopy when sealed with air inside. Have the class try it both from a stationary position and walking three steps in before sealing it.

FIGURE H.9

Groups of students play with a parachute.

4. *Hide-away.* In this stunt, the participants seal themselves inside the canopy. The parachute is inflated and the students walk three steps forward. They quickly turn and re-grasp the chute on the inside edge, then kneel down, holding the edge against the ground. The students remain sealed inside the chute until it begins to descend, then they stand, holding the chute, and duck under to the outside. Teacher may wish to try numbering the students by twos, with one group sealing themselves inside and one group sealing themselves outside.

5. *Sunflower.* The parachute is inflated and the students take three steps forward. They quickly bring the parachute down and kneel on the outside edge. (The chute should be sealed in the shape of a mushroom.) All students should now join hands, and on the commands "In" and "Out," lean forward and back to represent a sunflower opening and closing.

6. *Fly away.* The parachute is inflated and the participants take one step forward. On the command, "Release!" they let go of the canopy, which should remain suspended in the air for a few seconds before floating to the ground.

7. *Grecian flurry.* Eight students grasp a designated arc (side) of the parachute, using the right hand only, and hold it high in the air. On the command, "Forward, run!" they travel a designated distance, keeping the right arm up high. A new group of eight students should be waiting at the finish line to repeat the stunt. You may wish to use eight squads in shuttle formation so that each person gets a turn in order.

Conditioning

1. *Bicep builder.* With one leg forward, students plant their feet firmly and lean back, using palms-up grip, with arms almost fully extended. On a signal to begin, students pull the chute toward themselves without moving their feet or jerking the chute. They should continue to pull as hard as possible for six seconds. Teacher should count aloud and offer encouragement for holding it. Use palms-down grip for variation.

2. *Wild horse pull.* Students turn with their backs to the chute and grasp the edge of the canopy with a palms-down grip. With one foot forward and one back, they plant their feet firmly on the ground and lean forward. On a signal (e.g., whistle), they should pull as hard as they can. Teacher may wish to make team competition out of the exercise by seeing if one half of the students can pull the other half in their direction.

3. *Ocean waves.* Participants hold the parachute at waist level and, on a signal, slowly begin shaking the chute up and down. The tempo should gradually be increased. Have the participants pull back on the chute as they shake it. A variation for greater arm action is to have the students kneel (or sit in the cross-legged position) and shake the chute up and down.

4. *Sky high pull.* Participants start with the parachute held at waist level using a palms-down grip. They should spread their feet for balance and on signal, slowly lift the parachute up until their arms are fully extended overhead. Using just the arms and shoulders (feet, waist, and back do not move), all pull back and hold firmly for six seconds. Use the palms-up grip for variation.

5. *Wrist roll.* The parachute is held at waist level (arms extended) with a palms-down grip. On a signal to begin, all participants begin slowly rolling the edge of the canopy toward the center. Stress that the group stays together, and at the same time, they must keep the canopy tight by pulling a little before each roll of the wrists.

6. *Straight arm pullover.* Starting position is with the parachute held at waist level using a palms-down grip and feet shoulder distance apart. On a signal to begin, the arms are extended slowly overhead. Participants should breathe in slowly in rhythm with the arm lift. At the point of full extension, the arms are slowly lowered to the starting position and participants should exhale. Repeat this complete action at an even tempo for a given number of repetitions.

7. *Bend and stretch.* Students hold chute at waist level with palms-down grip. On a signal to begin, they bend forward, touching the edge of the canopy to their toes (count 1). On count 2, they extend arms overhead, stretching as far as possible. On count 3, the students bend forward at the waist and again touch toes. They return to overhead extended arm position on count 4. This represents one completed repetition of the exercise.

8. *Push-ups.* Students inflate chute and form a mushroom by sealing the edges to the ground. They take the push-up position with hands holding the edges tight on the ground. Students perform push-ups on command from the teacher with the chute inflated in the shape of a mushroom.

9. *Modified squat thrusts* (sometimes referred to as "grasshopper"). Performed in same manner as item 8 (push-ups), except that students extend legs straight back from squat position on count 1 and return to squat position on count 2. On count 3, legs are again extended straight back, and return to squat position on count 4. This is one complete repetition. Students do not come to a standing position as in a regular squat thrust.

10. *Tug-of-rope.* The parachute is first rolled into one long unit similar to a rope. Two teams are selected, and one team lines up along each half of the parachute. The activity is then conducted as a regular tug-of-rope, with the students pulling on a given signal to begin. The nylon chute is extremely strong and can be used safely for this activity.

Parachute games

1. *Ball shake.* The class is divided into two equal teams, with each team gripping one half of the canopy at the edges. A number of light balls are placed on top of the canopy (e.g., rubber balls, volleyballs, beach balls). On a signal to begin, each team attempts to shake the balls off on the other team's side of the chute. Participants may not use

their hands to keep the balls from leaving the canopy. One point is awarded each time a ball leaves the chute and touches the ground (see Figure H.9)

2. *Numbers exchange.* The students are numbered by fives or sixes, depending on the size of the class. The chute is inflated and, as it reaches the maximum height, the teacher calls out a number. (Colors of the parachute can also be used.) All students with that number must leave their places and change places with another student having the same number. All exchanging takes place under the canopy. Students must get to another place before the chute descends and touches their body. Penalties may or may not be imposed. Younger students will probably have difficulty getting the chute high enough to run under. For extremely large groups, it is better to use more numbers so that fewer students are moving about under the parachute. Running, skipping, hopping, jumping, and other locomotor movements can be incorporated into this game.

3. *Numbers race.* The class is divided into two equal teams. Each team counts off consecutively. The parachute is inflated and the teacher calls a number. The person on each team whose number is called must travel around the outside of the parachute and return to his or her place before the center of the chute touches the ground. The teacher should vary the type of locomotor skill used in moving around the chute. The teacher may wish to award one point to the first player returning to his or her own position.

4. *Steal the bacon.* A beanbag or other small object is placed under the chute at approximately the center of the canopy. The class is divided into two equal teams, and each player has a team number. The parachute is inflated and, at its highest point, the teacher calls a series of numbers. The players whose numbers are called must attempt to secure the beanbag and get back to their position without being tagged by an opponent. Also, if the chute descends on them while under the canopy, no points are awarded. A player who successfully gets back to his or her team position without being tagged or touched by the descending chute scores one point for the team. (Caution: remind students to keep arms extended and *not* try to "catch" runners with the chute by pulling it downward rapidly.)

Basic locomotor movements using the parachute

1. *General approach.* Students grasp the edge of the parachute at a seam and use one hand (right or left) designated by the teacher. The teacher has many options regarding the direction that may be used, including circle forward; circle backward; circle forward and, on a signal, change gripping hands and reverse direction; circle forward and, on a signal, move backward; move in toward the center of the chute and back out; and other combinations.

2. *Locomotor skills.* Stress the use of walking, running, hopping, jumping, leaping, skipping, galloping, and sliding.

Special activities for the parachute

1. *Tumbling activities.* Mats are placed under the parachute. Members of the class hold the chute in the inflated position while other pupils perform forward rolls, backward rolls, animal stunts, and so on.

2. *Pyramids.* The class is divided into teams of six. The chute is inflated and each team tries to build a pyramid under the parachute before it comes down and touches them. Mats are placed under the chute for the students to perform on. Teams must be allowed time to practice their pyramids without the parachute so that each member of the team knows exactly what to do before going under the canopy.

3. *Self-testing activities.* Students can be given the challenge of ball bouncing, rope jumping, and so on under the inflated chute.

4. *Long jump rope.* The parachute can be rolled up in the form of a long jump rope. When it is held off the ground, students can run and jump over it, and then crawl under it coming back. They can also hop and jump back and forth over the chute when it is lying on the ground. Many other movement patterns can be presented using the chute in this manner.

5. *Dance steps.* Basic dance steps such as the schottische, step-hop, two-step, polka, and mazurka can be practiced using the parachute as a stimulus for movement. Music will add greatly to this activity.

Ropes.

1. Use short (or long) jump ropes to make different shapes.
2. Form jump ropes into letters, numbers, and so on.
3. Use ropes formed in items 1 and 2 for activities suggested for hula hoops and carpet squares.
4. Make shapes with ropes and place body in the same shape inside the rope.
5. Use short ropes, but have students combine with 2, 3, or 5 partners and repeat designs, shapes, or numbers together as a group.

6. Use long ropes for the activity in item 5 and draw pictures or write in cursive (e.g., one letter, a spelling word, names, or picture of airplane, bird, etc.).
7. Use rope at different heights for jumping over or going under.
8. Jump over serpentine or swinging rope.
9. Follow rope maze with and without blindfolds.
10. Follow rope maze by walking or using a scooterboard.

Scooterboards.
1. Ride prone down ramp.
2. Ride prone down decline; then strike or grab a suspended object.
3. Ride prone down decline; then pick up objects.
4. Ride prone down decline, pick up beanbags, and place in containers.
5. Ride prone down decline, dismount safely, turn, and roll onto mat.
6. Prone, follow line (rope) maze.
7. Prone, follow rope maze blindfolded.
8. Prone, follow maze by memory.
9. Prone or supine, push off wall and glide (e.g., like Superman—with arms extended in front of body; or airplane—with arms extended to sides of body; or rocket—with arms held close to body near hips).
10. Prone or supine, pull self along suspended rope.
11. In sitting position (or prone, supine, or kneeling), maintain balance while being pulled by teacher with an inner-tube strip or old bicycle tire.
12. In sitting, kneeling, or prone position, propel self in a given direction using a plumber's helper.
13. Play tag on scooterboard.
14. Play scooterboard soccer, volleyball, basketball, hockey, etc.

T-stool. A T-stool is a one-legged stool. Provide variety by using different base widths and leg heights.
1. Sit and maintain balance with and without eyes open.
2. Imitate postures while seated (e.g., statues and hand designs).
3. Lift one leg, then other while seated.
4. Balance beanbag on body parts while maintaining balance.
5. Kick ball while sitting on T-stool.
6. Throw and catch ball while balanced.
7. Play handball while seated on T-stool.
8. Play T-stool four-square.
9. Reproduce hand rhythms or patterns.
10. Practice any arm exercise while seated.

Stilts. Stilts may be made out of tin cans or small wooden blocks (see Figure H.10).
1. Stand and maintain balance on stilts.
2. Walk forward on stilts.
3. Walk sideways.
4. Walk backward.
5. Walk along a specified pattern.
6. Step over objects.
7. Play foot races.

Trampoline or rebounder. Use proper spotting techniques and safety measures at all times for any trampoline or rebounder activities (see Figure H.6).

FIGURE H.10

Tin can stilts are fun to walk on and easy to make.

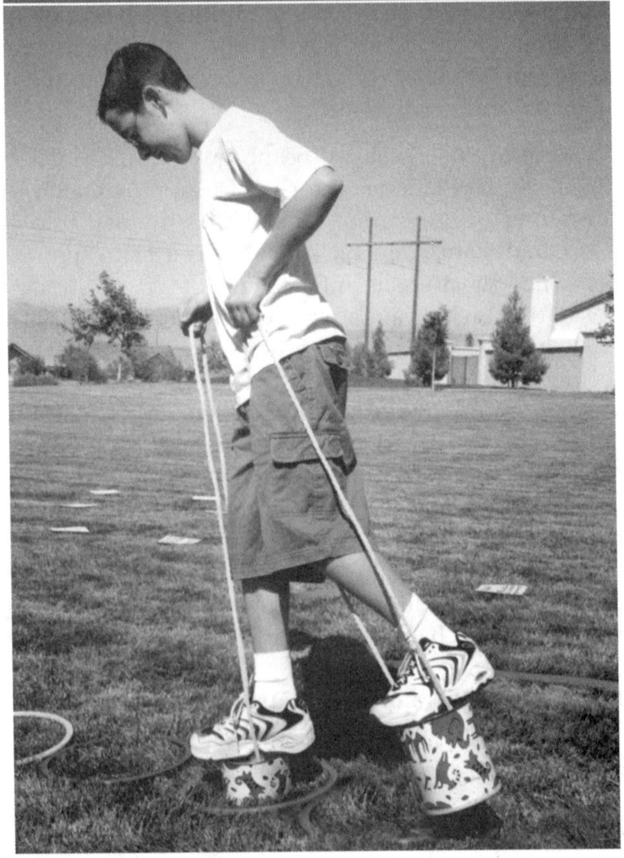

1. Lie prone or supine while being bounced by partner.
2. Roll over and sit up while being bounced.
3. Roll along the bed of the trampoline.
4. Crawl, creep, walk on trampoline.
5. Jump in center of trampoline.
6. Jump as high as possible.
7. Jump as long as possible without losing control.
8. Alternate jumping with feet together, feet apart.
9. Jump and touch toes.
10. Perform knee drop, then return to standing.
11. Perform seat drop, then return to standing.
12. Perform front drop, then return to standing.
13. Perform back drop, then return to standing.
14. Jump with one-quarter, one-half, and full turn.
15. Perform swivel hips with as many repetitions as possible.
16. Perform two tasks in a sequence (e.g., seat drop to knee drop).
17. Perform three-task sequence (e.g., knees to seat to knees).
18. Perform multitask sequence.
19. Perform specified task on verbal or written command.
20. Read letters (numbers, words, actions) while jumping.
21. Read command and perform task.

Special Activities

Angels-in-the-snow. For all activities, the child lies supine.

1. Imitate bilateral movements:
   a. Move both arms along the floor until they touch above head simultaneously and return to side of body.
   b. Move both legs apart and then together, arms stationary.
   c. Move all four limbs apart and together.
   d. Move any three limbs apart and together while the other remains stationary.
   e. Move arms quickly or slowly, legs stationary.
   f. Move legs quickly or slowly, arms stationary.
   g. Move both arms and legs quickly or slowly.
2. Imitate unilateral movements:
   a. Move the right arm and right leg simultaneously, left limbs remain stationary.
   b. Move the left arm and leg simultaneously, right remain stationary.
   c. Alternate right and left limbs moving.
   d. Move quickly or slowly.
3. Imitate cross-lateral movements:
   a. Move right arm and left leg apart and together while other limbs are stationary.
   b. Move right leg and left arm apart and together.
   c. Move opposite limbs quickly or slowly.

The preceding activities can also be done in the prone position. The commands can be given verbally, in printed form, or by touching the specified limb(s). Initially, it may be valuable to move the student passively through the positions to assist recognition of the correct movement.

Animal walks.

1. *Snail.* Move any way one wishes but very slowly.
2. *Busy bee.* Move any way one wishes but very fast.
3. *Snake.* Slither along the ground both prone and supine.
4. *Elephant.* Stand on feet, bend at the waist with hands together hanging down. Move slowly around room, letting arms sway like the trunk of an elephant.
5. *Lion.* On hands and feet, walk around room with head held high.
6. *Bear.* On hands and feet, move around room with the right hand and right foot moving together; left hand and left foot move together.
7. *Seal.* In semi-push-up position with weight supported on hands and legs straight and dragging behind (toes pointed), move forward, alternating hands and dragging legs behind (see Figure H.11).
8. *Crab.* Hands and feet on ground with chest toward the ceiling and back toward the floor, move forward, back, and sideways keeping buttocks off the floor (see Figure H.11)
9. *Inchworm.* Start with hands and feet on ground almost touching each other (legs and arms extended in toe-touch position); keep feet stationary while hands "walk" forward until in push-up position, then "walk" feet forward to starting position; continue across room.
10. *Kangaroo hop.* Hold object between knees, jump with feet together.
11. *Chicken.* While balancing on knees, hold feet off the ground with hands; walk around the room without letting go of feet.
12. *Rabbit.* In crouch position, knees bent, hands and feet close together, lean forward, stretch

FIGURE H.11

The seal (above) and crab (below) walks are two of the many types of animal walks that provide opportunities for sensory and motor experiences.

arms out in front on ground and quickly push off with feet together, then "hop" feet back to starting position.

13. *Alligator.* Move in a prone position, with body completely in contact with floor; pull body along with arms, leaving the tail (that is, the legs) to drag along behind.
14. *Dog.* Move on all fours.
15. *Three-legged dog.* Move using only three limbs.
16. *Crazy dog.* Move in a 4-point walk, but with arms crossed in front of body.
17. *Frog.* Assume a semi-squat position and spring forward to another semi-squat position.

Wrestling games. The following activities are meant to be fun and not highly competitive. Choose appropriate activities according to the students' ability.

1. *Elephant wrestle.* On hands and knees, two students put shoulders or sides together (not heads) and attempt to push each other off the mat or out of the prescribed area.

2. *Alligator wrestle.* In push-up position, two students face each other and attempt to pull each other's hand out from under the body until one falls to the ground.

3. *Arm wrestle.* Opponents face each other across a table, each one with an elbow on the table and forearm straight up. Clasping hands, each tries to push the other's arm down onto the table.

4. *Indian wrestle.* With the outside of the same foot touching, and same hands grasping each other, two students attempt to cause each other to lose balance or to move feet. This works best when performed on two low four-inch balance beams (or lines can be drawn with tape on the floor). The partners face each other on the beams and grasp with a wrist hold to push or pull partner until one steps off beam. (Comment: This is a perfect teaching moment, when considering other cultures or international games, to talk about the Native American culture and how this type of wrestling started on logs raised high above the ground.)

5. *Partner touch.* Partners stand facing each other. Teacher identifies body part, such as right shoulder, left knee, or ankle, and each partner attempts to "touch" opponent without being touched. Partners can keep score of the number of touches made successfully.

6. *Slap hands.* Two students stand facing each other at arm's length with palms facing partner. Each pushes (not holds) and lightly slaps the other's hands until the opponent moves feet or loses balance. (Another version of slap hands is when partners face each other with palms up for partner 1 and palms down for partner 2. Object is for partner 1 to lightly slap or touch the top of partner 2's hands before partner 2 can move his or her hands away, without stepping off balance beam or balance boards. Then, when hands are touched or one partner steps off, the partners exchange positions and play begins again. This is a good opportunity to introduce the concepts of offense/defense, advance/retreat, or aggressive/protective.)

7. *Leg wrestle.* Two students lie on their backs with waists together and heads at opposite ends. They hook elbows and lay hands on their own stomach. Raise inside leg three times and touch opponent's foot; on third raise, hook legs at the knees and try to pull leg to the ground, thus forcing opponent to go over backward.

8. *Thumb wrestle.* Opponents grasp each other's right hand with curled fingers and thumbs extended upward and try to "pin" the opponent's thumb down.

9. *Finger wrestle.* Use 12 to 15 inches of plastic jump rope that has been cut from broken or old ropes. (This is an economical and useful way to recycle materials.) Partners face each other while lying prone (face to face) with elbows on floor. Each partner grasps "rope" between index finger and thumb and they play tug-of-rope until one player releases "rope" or lifts elbow off floor.

10. *Push-up hockey* (need four players). Partner couples face each other in push-up position, approximately five to six feet away from each other. Each partner couple crosses inside hand position to be able to have shoulders as close as possible. Using outside hand only (right hand for partner on right, left hand for partner on left), each player attempts to slide hockey puck through or past the arm position (imaginary line) to score a goal. When a goal is scored, partners exchange places with each other in order to use the opposite hand for the next turn. When one partner couple has three points, the game is over. The game can also be played using a time limit or higher score.

11. *Sumo wrestling.* Sumo wrestling is played on a mat (basho) with a 15-foot-diameter circle drawn with tape. Each player has one ball (e.g., kickball or basketball). Partners face each other across the mat with the balls on the mat between them. Each partner follows a routine of protocol prior to wrestling: throwing rice, clapping hands, extending arms to sides and turning palms upward to show no concealed weapons, and lifting each leg and stomping foot loudly on mat. Then, the players pick up the balls, hold them in front of their bodies, and push against each other until one player touches the floor with something other than his or her feet or leaves the ring before the opponent. Each player bows at the end. This activity can be used in a tournament format.

Relaxation. In general, activities that involve deep pressure, slow stretching, or a slow rocking motion tend to be relaxing. Eliminating extraneous stimuli such as sounds or light may assist the process of relaxation training.

1. *Deep breathing* (in comfortable sitting or supine position):
   a. Count the number of breaths for given period of time.
   b. Feel the rise and fall of chest during breathing.
   c. Actively attempt to slow down breathing pattern.
   d. Inhale and exhale slowly and completely to a specific count (e.g., inhale, 2, 3, 4; hold 2; and exhale 2, 3, 4 until the pattern can be inhale for five counts, hold for five, and exhale for eight).
   e. Continue slow, deep breathing for several minutes.
2. *Rag doll.* Student makes entire body as limp as possible in whatever position is desired:
   a. Stand with feet about shoulder width apart and raise arms above head.
   b. Slowly bend forward as far as possible and keep head down.

Tension and relaxation techniques

Begin the physical education session with yoga exercises or routine. To cool down from exercise or physical activity, do some tension and relaxation exercises—these exercises provide both a calming and a cooling effect (see Figure H.12).

Remember to *exhale* each time you release and deep breathe to relax between contractions. Continue with random combinations at least 10 minutes daily for adults. The idea is to learn control of your body through your mind, and to observe how the body responds to what you tell it.

Progressive relaxation

Lie supine in a warm, comfortable room with eyes closed and quiet surroundings (maybe soft, low music). Begin with the toes and tense/release each body part. Let it relax and stay in its position without moving. Go through the entire body—toes, feet, ankles, calf, knees, thighs. Continue with random combinations at least 10 minutes daily. Feel like you are floating or that your body is making an impression in the sand—the clouds or sand is holding you up and will never let you go.

Stunts.
1. *Knee scale.* Support body on one knee and lower leg, raise head and arms, and point non-support leg backward.
2. *Front scale.* Support body weight on one foot and balance in arched position over that foot.
3. *Side scale.* Support weight on hand and foot on the same side, keeping body rigid.
4. *Shoulder stand.* Support weight on back of shoulders and arms, extend legs into air.
5. *V-sit.* Balance weight on buttocks while extending legs and trunk in air; body resembles a V.
6. *Angel balance.* One student in fully extended prone position balances on upward extended legs of supine student.

TABLE H.12 Tension and relaxation exercises.

DIRECTION TO STUDENT	TEACHER/PARTNER CHECKS FOR RELAXATION OF:
Contract right arm and release.	Left arm, legs, neck, and shoulders.
Contract left arm and release.	Right arm, legs, neck, and shoulders.
Contract right leg and release.	Left leg, arms, neck, and shoulders.
Contract left leg and release.	Right leg, arms, neck, and shoulders.
Contract right arm and right leg. Release.	Left arm, left leg, neck, face, and shoulders.
Contract left arm and left leg. Release.	Right arm, right leg, neck, face, and shoulders.
Contract right arm and left leg. Release.	Left arm, right leg, neck, face, and shoulders.
Contract left arm and right leg. Release.	Right arm, left leg, neck, face, and shoulders.
Contract shoulders and left leg. Release shoulders; release left leg.	Both forearms, right leg, and face.
Contract neck and right arm. Release neck; release right arm.	Left arm, both legs, and face.
Contract right arm, left arm, and right leg. Release left arm; release right arm; release leg.	Left leg, neck, and shoulders.

7. *Head stand.* Balance upside down on head using the hands to form a triangle with the head for support.
8. *Hand stand.* Balance upside down on hands only.
9. *Forward somersault.* Complete a forward roll from crouched position over the head and hands.
10. *Backward somersault.* Roll over backward from crouched position.
11. *Egg roll.* In prone position, grasp feet with hands and perform sideways roll in crouched position.
12. *Tip-up.* Balance on hands only, with elbows tucked inside knees for support.
13. *Dive-n-roll.* Dive over an object or another child (or children) into a forward roll.
14. *Pyramid building.* Several children in hands-and-knees position side by side form the base for the next layer of children in hands-and-knees position (one leg and arm on the back of one child, the other arm and leg on the adjacent child) to form a pyramid.
15. *Back-to-back stand.* Two children, back to back with elbows entwined, rise to standing from sitting position.
16. *Turk stand.* Sit in crossed-leg fashion with arms folded on chest, rise to standing position while keeping arms folded.
17. *Stork stand.* One-legged stand.
18. *Statues.* Move around room, then freeze on command like a statue.

Therapeutic activities.

Exercises for arthritis

1. *Deep breathing.* Stand or lie on back with hands spread beneath lower ribs; inhale and contract abdominal muscles, spreading fingers outward with ribs; hold ribs in extended position and exhale as abdomen is drawn in and up; repeat.
2. *Finger exercise.* Sit with back of hand resting on table or other support; oppose each finger to thumb; extend each finger after each contact with thumb; repeat with each hand.
3. *Finger spread.* Any position where hand is unobstructed; spread fingers as far apart as possible; relax and repeat.
4. *Foot exercise.* Lie on back with legs straight or sit on a stool; dorsiflex the feet; plantarflex the feet; make a circle with foot, stressing inward movement; repeat with other foot.

5. *Leg exercise.* While sitting, feet are dorsiflexed and inverted; toes in plantarflexion; "pedal" with legs, but do not raise higher than 10 inches off floor.
6. *Abdominal exercise.* Lie on back, hands above head, knees bent; swing hands up and toward knees; slowly lower back to floor; repeat.
7. *Bridging.* Lie on stomach with ankles supported, hands at side; lift head and shoulders off floor; return to starting position; repeat.
8. *Shoulder exercise.* Sit in an erect position with hands clasped behind head; keeping elbows at shoulder height, thrust them backward as far as possible; hold; relax and repeat.

Asthmatic exercise program

1. *Abdominal breathing exercise.* Start in hook-lying position with hands on upper abdomen; contract abdominal muscles and exhale as hands sink in toward spine; relax abdominal muscles while taking short breath.
2. Trunk bending and rotation to mobilize spine.
3. Relaxation exercises and activities.
4. Blowing bits of paper or a ping-pong ball across a table.
5. *Side-expansion exercise.* Sit with hands on lower ribs, feet apart; breathe out through mouth slowly, sinking chest and lower ribs; squeeze ribs to expel all air; breathe in, expanding lower ribs; relax.
6. *Forward-bend exercise.* Sit with legs apart; exhale and bend trunk forward; take a quick breath and raise trunk; exhale slowly and let head drop downward and chest sink inward; take a quick breath and return to erect position.
7. *Sidebend exercise.* Stand with feet apart; exhale slowly, bending trunk to one side; inhale and raise trunk; repeat four to six times; repeat on opposite side.
8. *Wave exercise.* Start in supine position with paper or cardboard placed on abdomen; breathe in and out, making paper go up and down.

Deep-breathing exercises

1. In supine position with hips and knees flexed, feet on floor, inhale through nose to maximum; hold briefly, exhale through mouth with hissing sound.
2. In supine position with hips and knees flexed, feet flat on floor, place one hand on chest, other on abdomen; inhale through nose, elevate chest only; hold briefly; exhale through mouth.
3. In supine position with hips and knees flexed, feet flat on floor, place one hand on each side of ribs; inhale through nose; elevate chest only; hold briefly; exhale through mouth; push hands together during expiration.
4. In supine position with hips and knees flexed, feet flat on floor, place folded towel around chest; grasp ends of towel; inhale through nose, elevate chest only; hold briefly; pull towel tight during expiration.
5. Sitting in chair, arms at sides, slowly flex at waist and exhale through mouth while flexing toward floor; hold briefly; slowly sit up; inhale through nose; hold at sitting position.
6. Divide chest into three parts—upper, middle, lower; inhale deeply, then exhale completely in each part.

Weight training (free weights).

1. *Two-arm curl.* Stand, body erect, with feet about 12 inches apart and arms at sides; grasp bar with undergrip, palms up, shoulder width apart; keeping elbows at hips, slowly lift bar by flexing elbow and bringing weights toward shoulders; hold; lower to starting position; repeat.

2. *Two-arm press.* Stand with feet about 12 inches apart, bar on floor in front of feet; bend knees, grasp bar with overgrip, shoulder width apart; bring bar to chest in one motion by flexing elbows and straightening knees; hold weight at chest level; slowly push bar overhead; hold; lower slowly to chest; repeat overhead repetitions; lower to starting position.

3. *Two-arm reverse curl.* Stand with body erect and feet 12 inches apart, arms at sides; grasp bar at thigh height with overgrip, extend wrist to maximum; flex elbows, lifting bar to chest; hold bar at chest level, lower bar to thighs; hold; repeat; return to starting position.

4. *Supine press.* Lie in a supine position, shoulders comfortable, on floor or bench with bar resting behind head; grasp bar; lift bar upward; straighten elbows so that arms are perpendicular to floor; slowly lower bar to chest; slowly push bar upward until elbows are straight; repeat; return to starting position.

5. *Rise on toes.* Stand with heels together, toes turned out; place bar behind the neck; grasp bar with hands at shoulder width; slowly rise up on toes as high as possible; hold; lower slowly; repeat; return to starting position.

6. *Curl-up.* Lie in a supine position with bent knees, ankles supported; place bar across chest; grasp

bar at shoulder width; slowly come to sitting position; hold; return; repeat.

7. *Rowing.* Stand with feet 12 inches apart, bar resting on floor in front; flex trunk at waist, grasp bar with overgrip; flex elbows, bringing bar to chest; hold; lower to straight elbow position; repeat.

8. *Quadriceps lift.* Sit on table, grasping front of table with hands, with small rolled towel under knee, knee flexed 10 to 20 degrees, foot with weight attached resting on stool; extend knee to lift weight; hold at full extension; return to starting position; repeat.

9. *Forward raise.* Stand with feet 12 inches apart, bar in front; grasp bar with overgrip, bring bar to thigh level; lift bar forward and overhead, keeping elbows extended; lower weight; repeat.

10. *Shoulder shrug.* Stand with feet 12 inches apart, arms at sides; grasp bar with overgrip, bar at thigh level with elbows extended; shrug shoulders; lower shoulders to starting position; repeat.

11. *Regular dead lift.* Stand with feet 12 inches apart; flex hips and knees; grasp bar with overgrip; with back flat, slowly straighten knees until body is straight; return bar to floor; repeat.

12. *Straddle lift.* Stand with feet straddling bar; flex knees, keeping back straight; grasp bar with front hand overgrip, rear hand undergrip; slowly stand upright, lifting weights off ground; hold; flex knees; return to starting position.

13. *Straight-arm pullover.* Lie in a supine position with hips and knees straight, arms extended overhead; grasp bar resting on floor behind head, raise bar slowly above head; hold; return bar to floor.

14. *Triceps press.* Lie supine with hips and knees straight, arms straight, elbows extended toward ceiling; bar is placed in hands; grasp with overgrip; lower bar to bridge of nose, keeping elbows pointed to ceiling; slowly straighten elbows; repeat.

15. *Back lift.* Stand with feet 12 inches apart with bar behind heels; flex hips and knees; grasp bar with overgrip; slowly return to standing position; repeat.

16. *Lateral raise.* Stand with feet 12 inches apart, arms at sides; grasp one dumbbell in each hand; slowly raise dumbbells to shoulder level, keeping elbows extended; hold; lower weights; repeat.

17. *Forward raise.* Stand with feet 12 inches apart, arms at sides; grasp one dumbbell in each hand, dumbbells resting on thighs; raise dumbbells directly overhead, keeping elbows straight; hold; lower weights; repeat.

18. *Alternate curl.* Stand with feet 12 inches apart, arms at sides; grasp one dumbbell in each hand; slowly flex right elbow and supinate hand; bring dumbbell to right shoulder; slowly extend right elbow and pronate hand, returning to starting position; as right is lowered, left dumbbell begins curl; repeat; alternate.

Weight training (apparatus).
1. Bench press
2. Bicep curl
3. Deltoid pull
4. Dip
5. Hip abduction and adduction
6. Hip extension and flexion
7. Lateral pulldown
8. Leg press
9. Leg squat
10. Knee extension and flexion
11. Fly
12. Pullover
13. Pull-up
14. Row
15. Shoulder shrug
16. Sit-up
17. Toe raise
18. Triceps pulldown

Childbirth training. Women who are pregnant should continue to be active. The physical educator can recommend special exercises that can be practiced in class and at home. Examples of these are listed below.

Prenatal

1. *Sitting tailor fashion.* Sit on a hard surface, knees bent and widely separated, dropped as close to floor as possible, ankles crossed; chest is lifted, back straight; ribs open and reaching forward; hands rest easily on legs; sit often in this fashion.

2. *Pelvis rock on hands and knees.* On hands and knees, hands directly under shoulders, back flat, rock pelvis (tuck buttocks under), rounding back; tighten abdominal muscles; gradually relax back and abdomen; breathe naturally during exercise.

3. *Costal (rib) breathing.* Sit tailor fashion or lie in supine position, knees bent, feet slightly separated; place one hand on abdomen and other on ribs; inhale, spreading ribs; exhale, feeling rib cage shrink; breathe in through nose and out through mouth; repeat five times.

4. *Kegel (vaginal contractions).* Lie in a supine position, knees flexed, or sitting position; tighten muscles used to hold urine back; hold; repeat often throughout day.

5. *Rocking the pelvis on back.* Lie supine on floor with knees flexed and apart, soles of feet on floor, head resting on pillow; tuck buttocks under, flattening lumbar spine against floor; tighten abdominal muscles; return to starting position; relax.

6. *Side relaxation position.* Lie with torso prone and legs on side; place one arm behind with elbow bent 90 degrees; place pillow under head with shoulder on floor; one leg above and slightly forward, both knees bent; relax completely.

7. *Flexing and extending the legs, seated.* Sit on floor with legs extended diagonally; lift one knee slightly, flex ankle, and increase knee flexion; extend both knee and ankle, pointing toes and pushing back of knee into floor; repeat with other leg; repeat each leg five times.

8. *Tension and relaxation on back.* Lie supine with knees flexed and apart; tilt pelvis; inhale deeply and hold breath; tense entire body; exhale quickly, relax all muscles completely; repeat four times.

9. *Abdominal strengthening.* Lie supine, shoulders on floor, head resting on pillow, knees flexed, feet flat on floor, arms at sides; lift head off pillow, moving chin toward chest; raise right arm and extend toward left knee (only right shoulder and head are lifted); return to starting position; repeat with other side.

10. *Spine stretching.* Sit on floor, soles of feet together, knees apart, hands grasping knees; rock pelvis slowly; gradually straighten elbows; lift chest and return to sitting tall; repeat.

11. *Rock the pelvis standing.* Stand arm's length away from counter, hands grasping edge, elbows straight; lean body forward, lumbar spine arched; rock pelvis, tucking buttocks under; return to starting position.

12. *Sitting in chair and rising.* Stand in front of chair; lower hips, keeping them under shoulders; reach down to feel chair with hands; transfer weight to front edge of chair; rise to standing.

13. *Sit and stretch position.* Sit with soles of feet together, as close as possible to body; push knees down on hands placed on floor; repeat several times.

14. *Knee to chest.* Lie supine with legs straight, pillow under head; pull one knee up to chest; stretch and slowly bring leg straight down; repeat with other leg; repeat.

15. *Blow out the candle.* Lie supine with knees bent, feet flat on floor, and pillow under head; take a deep breath and let it out naturally; purse lips and continue blowing until there is no more air to blow; repeat.

Postnatal

1. *Kegel (vaginal contractions).* See item 4 above.
2. *Rocking the pelvis on back.* See item 5 above.
3. *Prone rest with pillows under pelvis.* Lie prone with abdomen on pillow; can be used for sleeping or resting.
4. *Abdominal strengthening.* See item 9 above.
5. *Torso stretch.* Stand with chin lifted, looking at ceiling; extend both arms up from shoulders; rock pelvis; stretch one arm fully, simultaneously elevate opposite heel so that it raises the left hip; repeat on opposite side.
6. *Flexing and extending the legs, seated.* See item 7 above.
7. *Upper hip roll.* Lie supine and flex knees and hips until knees are close to nose; spread arms out at shoulder level, resting on floor; drop both knees together to right, then to left, touching the floor on each side; repeat.
8. *Rock the pelvis standing.* See item 11 above.

REFERENCES

Jacobsen, E. (1991). *You must relax.* New York: McGraw Hill.

Wickstrom, R. L. (1977). *Fundamental motor patterns.* Philadelphia: Lea & Febiger.

Author Index

Accardo, P. J., 381
ACSM, 125
American Alliance for Health, Physical Education, Recreation, and Dance (AAHPERD), 2, 108, 114, 208, 283
American College of Sports Medicine (ACSM), 125
American Foundation for the Blind, 391
American Therapeutic Recreation Association, 342
Ames, L., 372
Amos-Grees, S., 295
Armatruda, C. S., 374, 377
Attwood, R., 380
Autism Society of America, 380
Axelrod, S. 248

Baldwin, V., 380
Banus, B. S., 371, 373, 374, 377
Baumgartner, T. A., 91, 92, 100, 144, 156
Block, M., 10, 130, 160
Bobath, B., 54, 77, 371, 373
Bobath, K., 54, 77, 371, 373
Boothroyd, A., 382
Braddock, D., 354
Bradley, D. F., 16, 17
Bray, G. A., 124
Burgstahler, S., 280
Burton, A. W., 156

California Department of Education, 160
California Department of Education, Special Education Division, 161, 178, 278
California State Board of Education, 201
Chappell, A. L., 4
Clarke, K. C., 7
Collier, D., 16
Conatser, P., 33
Condeluci, A., 4, 355

Conderman, G., 390
Connor-Kuntz, F., 160
Cooper Institute for Aerobics Research (CIAR), 93
Council on Physical Education for Children, 289
Covert, C., 371, 375
Cuddihy, 136

Davis, L. J., 4
Davis, R.W., 10
DePauw, K. P., 3, 4, 7, 10, 57, 58, 254, 335, 350, 356, 361
DeQuiros, J. B., 371, 372
Deschenes, C., 282, 284
Dettmer, P., 18, 19
Dey, 387
Disch, J. G., 397
Doll-Tepper, G., 3, 4, 10
Drubach, D., 44
Dunn, W., 138, 193

Ebelling, D. G., 282, 284
Eisner, E. W., 93
Eric, 242
Eyrich, S., 295

Fairfax County Public Schools (FCPS), 96
Falvey, M. A., 283
Fiorentino, M. R., 54, 55, 77, 78, 117, 371, 372, 373
Fitzsimmons, M. K., 92
Fokes, J., 375
Friend, M., 18, 20, 22, 27
Frost, L. A., 227

Gansneder, B., 33
Gauthier, R. A., 241
Gavron, S. J., 356, 361, 363
Gersten, R., 16, 17
Gesell, A., 61, 371, 372, 374, 375, 376, 377
Glang, A., 390
Goc Karp, G., 57, 58

Goldman, R., 138
Greenfield, S., 44
Gresham, F. M., 201
Grossman, H. J., 382
Gurman, H. B., 76, 243, 249
Gutteridge, M., 376
Guttman, L., 362

Haake, C. A., 381
Hacksley, C., 390
Hallahan, D. P., 388
Halverson, H. M., 371
Heikinaro-Johansson, P., 33
Henry, D., 350
Hodges, S. R., 10
Howard, P.J., 44
Huettig, C., 160, 161
Hux, K., 390

Ilg, F., 372, 373
Individuals with Disabilities Education Act, 107, 108, 114, 369, 379

Jersild, A., 372, 373, 374, 375, 376

Kassler, S.L., 10
Katsiyannis, A., 390
Kauffman, J. M., 388
Kaufman, A. S., 137
Kearney, G., 293
Kelly, L. E., 33, 93, 200, 367, 368

LaRue, R., 320
Laszewski, C., 381
Lawther, J. D., 221
Lieberman, L. J., 10
Linton, S., 4
Los Angeles County Office of Education, 191
Luckasson, R., 382, 383
Lytle, R., K., 16, 27, 28, 29, 33

Mager, R. F., 185
Marx, O., 376

449

Mayer, G. R., 248
Miller, D. E., 156
Moberg, M, 295
Morrow, J. D., 381
Morton, K., 77, 271
Mosston, M., 223, 261
Mostert, M. P., 20, 27

National Association for Sport & Physical Education (NASPE), 93, 136, 185, 199, 254, 281, 283, 289
National Center on Physical Activity and Disability, 354
National Cancer Institute, 386
Newcomer, P., 138
Novitt-Moreno, A., 44

Oliver, M., 4
Olrich, T. W., 114
Omoto, K., 131, 225

Pack, I. J., 236
Piaget, J., 58, 262
Pitetti, K. H., 354
Popp, K., 268, 269
President's Council on Physical Fitness and Sports (PCPFS), 2, 354

Pyfer, J., 133, 160

Reschly, D., 127
Rimmer, J. H., 354, 355
Robb, M. D., 221
Rosenberg, R., 283
Roth, K., 161
Royeen, C. B., 135
Rushall, B. S., 246

Safrit, M. J., 125
Salvia, J., 98
Schrager, O. L., 371, 372
Scruton, S., 362
Seaman, J. A., 97, 136, 137, 229, 254, 335, 350
Shapiro, J., 4
Sherrill, C., 3, 4, 33
Shirley, M., 372, 374
Short, F. X., 190, 287
Singer, G. H., 390
Smith, D. D., 92
Sprague, J., 282
Stewart, D. A., 361, 362, 363
Stewart, L. 132
Strang, R., 375, 376
Sulzer-Azeroff, B., 244, 248

Thorndike, E. L., 220

Thorndike, R. L., 138
Tibbetts, T., 271

Ulrich, D., 94
U.S. Department of Education, 380, 384, 385, 388, 390

Vetter, P., 171
Vincent, W. J., 144

Waggoner, B. E., 240
Wallin, J. M., 244
Weiss, C. E., 118
Wechsler, D., 137
Whitman, B. U., 381
Wickstrom, R. L., 427, 429
Wiggins, G., 96
William, J. F., 261
Williams, H. J., 45
Williams, J. M., 390
Winnick, J. P., 190, 287
Witt, J. C., 93, 95, 101
Woodcock, R. M., 137, 138
World Health Organization, 354
Wright, D. B., 76, 243, 249

Yell, M. L., 109
Yocum, D. J., 17

Subject Index

AAHPERD, 2, 208, 286
ABCs of movement, 268, 269
Ability awareness, 291–292, 294, 295
Access Board, U.S., 318
Accessibility, 30 (*see also* Accommodations; Adaptations)
    ADA guidelines, 318–320
    inclusion and, 207 (*see also* Inclusion)
    middle school, 324
    of facilities, 318–320
Accommodation Plan, 167
Accommodations, 259, 260 (*see also* Adaptations)
    defined, 208
    for student with dwarfism, 297
    in GPE, 164
    selecting appropriate, 281–286
Achievement dates, determining, 189–193
Action:
    arousal to, 221
    plan, 25
Activities:
    appropriate to developmental needs of adults, 259–260
    appropriate to developmental needs of elementary school grades, 257–258
    appropriate to developmental needs of infants, 256–257
    appropriate to developmental needs of middle school and junior high school, 258–259
    appropriate to developmental needs of preschool and primary grades, 257
    appropriate to developmental needs of secondary school, 258–259
    aquatics, 285, 286
    cognitive skills, 261–266
    dance, 285, 286–287
    dance lesson plan, 311
    developmental, 2, 417–431
    developmentally appropriate, 253–274
    directional concepts and pathways, 307
    disability awareness, 291–292, 294, 295
    enrichment, 278
    for culturally defined forms of movement, 431–435
    for encouraging creativity, 266
    for enhancing motor patterns and motor skills, 255, 425–431
    for enhancing motor-sensory responses, 255, 422–425
    for fostering language learning, 266–270
    for reflex development and inhibition, 254
    for sensory stimulation and discrimination, 255, 420–422
    for socialization, 270
    for teaching concepts, 263–264
    identification/naming, 267–268
    jumping, 285
    locomotor, 427–428
    manipulative, 428–429
    memory, 262–263
    movement, 263–264
    multicultural, 291, 292, 293
    nonlocomotor, 429–430
    parachute, 437–439
    physical fitness, 434
    physical fitness lesson plan, 308
    pickleball, 310–311
    problem solving, 264–265
    reflex development and inhibition, 417–420
    relaxation, 290–291
    safety and, 315–316
    special equipment and, 435–447
    special, 441–447
    stunts and tumbling, 285, 289–290
    swimming lesson, 309–310
    that develop student interests, 298–299
    therapeutic, 444–445
Activity:
    adapting, 234–235
    analysis, 202–203
    lifetime physical, 338–339
    meaningfulness of, 220–221
    model, 201
    placement of individual in, 234
    vs. passivity, 221
Activity reinforcers, 244
Acuity:
    auditory, 82
    visual, 80
Adaptations, 208–214, 281–286, 287
    curricular, 281, 282–283, 284, 287
    environmental, 30
    for children with specific disabilities, 212–214, 282–284
    initiated by students, 259, 260
    innovative teaching techniques and, 229
    making concepts concrete, 227
    of a skill, 234–235
    of activity, 234–235
    of class format, 232–233
    of equipment, 235, 330–333
    of facilities, 231
    of language, 224, 226
    of learning environment, 231–233
    of participation time, 234
    of rules, 235
    sequencing tasks and, 227–228
    techniques for, 224–235
    to facilities, 320 (*see also* Facilities)
    to lesson or game, 281, 283–284
    using multisenses and, 228–229
Adapted Aquatics, 286
Adapted physical activity, defined, 3
Adapted physical education:
    adaptation and, 224–235 (*see also* Adaptations)

assessment and, 90–110 (*see also* Assessment)
collaborative teams and, 15–40 (*see also* Collaborative teams)
consultant model, 33
co-teaching and, 37–40
defined, 2–3
developing and implementing the program, 197–217
developmental activities, 417–447
developmental approach to teaching, *see* Developmental approach
developmental model and, 58–67
educator as resource person, 33–37
eligibility criteria for, 160–161
evaluation and, 93, 96–98 (*see also* Assessment; Evaluation)
facilities for, 318–323
historical perspectives, 3
inclusive programming and, 278–279 (*see also* Effective programming)
incorporating all learning domains, 260–273
individualized education program and, 7 (*see also* IEP)
legislative mandates and, 107–109
levels of programming for, 65–67
noncategorical approach, 8–10
noncategorical programming and, 278, 279 (*see also* Effective programming)
paraeducators and, 215–217
preparation of the IEP, *see* IEP
pre-referral checklist, 172–173
professional roles in, 10–11
resource request, 24
selecting appropriate accommodations, 281–285 (*see also* Accommodations)
strategies for meeting individual needs, 219–251
supporting positive behavior, 240–250
Adapted Physical Education Assessment Scale (APEAS), 126, 160
Adapted Physical Education Assessment Scale II (APEAS II), 146, 160, 408
Adapted Physical Education National Standards (APENS), 11, 200, 367–370

Adapted physical education specialist, 11, 66
Adapted physical educator:
  as resource person, 33–37
  attitude and, 35
  roles of, 33–34
  working with, 34–37
Adaptive devices, 259, 260, 385
Additions, deviations and, 128
Adequate sampling, 115
ADHD, 299
Administration:
  ease of for tests, 114
  of tests, 114–116
  standardized, 115
Administrative support, program plan and, 204
Administrator, as member of IEP team, 32–33
Adult programs, transition to, 260, 338–351
Advocate, adapted physical educator as, 33–34
Aerobic capacity, 146
Affective learning, 270–273
Age-appropriate design, 317
Aggressive behavior, 242, 391
AIDS, 11, 386
Alphabet, using, 261, 268–269, 270
Alternative teaching, 39
Alternative testing, 90–92
Amateur Sports Act of 1978, 361
American Alliance for Health, Physical Education, Recreation, and Dance (AAHPERD), 2, 108, 114, 208, 286
American Association on Mental Retardation (AAMR), 382–383
American Dance Therapy Association, 342
American Red Cross, 286
American Therapeutic Recreation Association, 341
Americans with Disabilities Act, 318, 354
Analysis:
  environmental, 239
  functional, of behavior, 244
  individual mechanical, 239
  skill progression, 239
  task, 235–240
Angels-in-the-snow, 441
Animal walks, 441–442
Ankle cuffs, 331–332

Annual goals, IEP, 182–195 (*see also* Goals)
Antecedent management, 245–256
APEAS II, 146, 160, 408
APENS, 11, 200, 367–370
  summary of standards 1–15, 368–370
  the five competency levels, 368
Appropriateness:
  of tests, 114
  seasonal, 204
Approximation, successive, 238, 240
Apraxia, 84, 228
Aquatics, 285, 286, 431–433
  conditioning, 432
  equipment, 328
  group activities, 433
Arc, The, 342
Archery bows, adapting, 332
Architectural Barriers Act of 1967, 320
Arithmetic average, 103
Arousal state, disorders in, 79
Array of methods, 44
Arthritis, exercises for, 444–445
Articulation disorders, 388
Asperger, Hans, 380
Asperger Syndrome, 380
Assessment, 11, 98–102 (*see also* Evaluation; Measurement; Testing)
  and evaluation, 93, 96–98
  APENS and, 369
  authentic, 91
  data collection and, 111–140
  defined, 98
  drawing conclusions, 152–153 (*see also* Interpretation)
  eligibility criteria for APE, 160–161
  equipment, 333
  formal testing and, 112–116
  formative, 99
  functional, 95
  in preparing for IEP meeting, 171–173
  interpretation of data, 144–158 (*see also* Interpretation)
  interpreting results of, 174–175 (*see also* Interpretation)
  inventories and, 134, 135
  journals and, 136
  key elements of in IFSP and ITP, 166
  legal requirements of IEP, 167–169

legislative mandates and, 107–109
measurement and, 102–107
native language and, 168
of adaptive behavior, 138
of behavior, 92
of language, 138–139
of student participation, 131
of the whole child, 137–139
portfolios and, 135–136
purposes of, 100–101
rating scales/checklists, 92
report of teacher, 173–175
reporting results, 158–160
scores and, 102–107 (*see also* Measurement; Scores)
self-reporting, 134–136
standards and, 93–95
steps in interpretation, 149–153
summary of available tests, 403–409
testing and, 90–92 (*see also* Testing)
time period for, 167–168
universal design and, 280
Assistive devices, 30, 86
Associated reactions, 119
Association for Children with Learning Disabilities, 342
Associations, sport, 411–412
Asthma, 386
exercises for, 444
Asymmetrical tonic neck reflex (ATNR), 56, 118, 150, 156, 254, 418
Attention:
deficit, 50, 387, 391
focusing, 232
selective, 47, 48, 73
span, 79
Attention deficit disorder (ADD), 50, 387
Attitude, consultants and, 35
Attitude inventories, 134, 135
Attitudes, inclusion and, 207
Atypical performance, 63
identifying sources of, 69–87 (*see also* Process disorders)
Audition, 82
Auditory (*see also* Auditory system):
acuity, 82
assessing skills, 138–139
immature input, 57
input, 46, 52, 53
memory, 265
perception, 82, 83

perception disorder, 391–392
processing, 116, 117
processing difficulties, 53
stimuli, 75
and vestibular processing difficulties, 53
Auditory system, 52, 53, 59, 60–61, 158, 421
developmental disorders and, 82, 83
Authentic assessment, 91
Autism, 83, 146, 202, 211, 341, 379–380, 395
adaptations for students with, 212
spectrum, 379–380
Autism Society of America (ASA), 342, 380
Autistic savant, 380
Automatic movement reactions, 56, 77
Automatic movement reflexes, 119
Automatic righting reactions, 119
Average, 103
Awareness:
ability, 291–292, 294, 295
of disability by parents, 295
Axons, 44–45
AYSO VP Soccer, 339

Back relaxation exercises, 291
Backward chaining, 238
Balance, 423
as pivotal skill, 205
percentile ranks norms, 97
poor, 78, 393
postural, 30
Balance beam, 330, 334, 435–436
Balance board, 435–436
Balancing, 148 (*see also* Balance)
teams, 144
Balls, 329
bouncing, 428–429
medicine, 434
rolling, 428
Barrel roller, 334
Barriers, to inclusion, 207–208
Basal ganglia, 47, 48, 50
Basketball:
day camp, 296
wheelchair, 294
Basketball Skills Test, 156
Batelle Developmental Inventory (BDI-2), 122, 406
Batting, 64

Bayley Scales of Infant and Toddler Development (Bayley 3), 122
Bayley Scales of Motor Development, 115
Beery VMI, 404
Behavior:
aggressive, 242, 391
analyzing, 244–245
and consequences, 243, 245
assessment of adaptive, 138
defined, 184–185
functional assessment of, 92
management strategies, 240–250
playground, 317
positive management of, 312
rating, 173
summarized on IEP form, 180
supporting positive, 240–250, 312
terminal, 184
Behavior modification, 243–244
negative reinforcement, 243
positive reinforcement, 242–244
Behavior support, 312
Beliefs, program plan and, 198–199
Bell-shaped curve, 103
Benching, 317
Benchmarks, 96–97, 144, 161
on IEP, 182–195
Bending, 429
Bicep builder, 438
Bicycle riding, 221
Bicycling, 296
Birth, 446
motor development and, 55–56
neurodevelopment at, 57
Blaze Sports, 339
Blindness, 380–381, 390–391
adaptations for students with, 212
Boating, 296
Body:
awareness, 79, 255, 424–425
composition, 146
control, 431–432
crossing midline of, 424
fat, measuring, 124, 125
management, 200
movements, 20
righting, 56
Body Mass Index (BMI), 124
Bolsters, 330
Bone and joint conditions, 385
Books, reference, 412–413
Boomer ball bat, 335

Bouncing, 264
Bouncing ball, 428–429
Boundaries, using to define space, 231–232
Bowling, 296
　adapted ramp for, 332
　skills checklist, 132
Boys Clubs, 339
Braille, 330, 342
Brain:
　parts of, 45
　sensory stimulation of, 50
　sensory systems and, 51–52
Brain injury, 395
　adaptations for students with traumatic, 214
　traumatic, 390
Brain stem, 45, 55
　reflexes, 56, 77
Breakdown, sites and effects, 70–73
Breath control, 431
Brigance Comprehensive Inventory of Basic Skills, Revised (CIBS-R), 122
Brittle bones, 98, 392
Brockport Physical Fitness Test, 123, 124, 150
Bruininks-Oseretsky Test of Motor Proficiency (BOT-2), 126, 127, 408–409
Bulletin boards, 270, 314
Businesses, community, 342–343

California Department of Education, 160, 161, 178, 278
Cancer, childhood, 386
Cardiovascular disorders, 386
CARE-R Curriculum, Assessment, Resources, Evaluation, 126, 409
　sequence of tasks, 191
Carpet squares, 436–437
Catching, 64, 429
　as pivotal skill, 205
　pattern, 62
　task analysis of, 236
Categorical labeling, 8
Categorical thinking, 8–10
Cells, 44–45
Centers for Disease Control and Prevention, 354
Central nervous system (CNS), 44–58
　brain parts, 45
　developmental disorders and, see Developmental disorders

　disordered, 50
　learning and, 222
　process disorders and, see Process disorders
　proprioceptive system and, 51–52 (see also Proprioceptive system)
　reflex emergence and, 55–56 (see also Reflex)
　reflexes and, 54, 55, 117–120 (see also Reflexes)
　sensory responsivity and, 50–51
　sensory systems and, 51–54
　SIMSF system and, 46–54
　structural interdependence and, 155
　structure and function of, 44–46
Central tendency, measures of, 103–104
Cephalo-caudal motor development, 55
Cerebellum, 45, 46
　damage to, 50
Cerebral cortex, 71
Cerebral palsy, 34–35, 39, 102, 202, 286, 329
　adaptations for students with, 212
Certification, APENS, 11
Certified adapted physical educator (C.A.R.E.), 11
Chaining, 238
Challenger Little League, 339
Chambers of Commerce, 339
Checklists, 131, 132–133
　assessment and, 92
　for evaluation of goals, 193
　identifying students needing APE, 172–173
　inclusion, 99
Chewing, as calming stimuli, 249
Childbirth training, 446–447
Childhood Disintegrative Disorder (CDD), 380
Class format, varying, 232–233
Class rules, 241–242
Class size, 98
　inclusion and, 207
Closure strategy, 240
Clubs, community, 339
Clumsiness, 83–84, 102, 389, 393
CNS, see Central nervous system
Cognitive development, 262
Cognitive fatigue, accommodating, 235
Cognitive learning, 261–266

Collaboration, 39 (see also Collaborative teams)
Collaborative process, 16 (see also Collaborative teams)
Collaborative teams, 15–40
　action plan for, 25
　characteristics of effective, 17–27
　communication and, 17–23 (see also Communication)
　co-teaching and, 37–40
　defined, 16–17
　IEP, 27–33
　personal qualities and, 26–27
　problem-solving skills and, 23–26
Collaborators, characteristics of effective, 17–27
Committee on Sports for the Disabled (COSD), 361
Commonalities:
　clustering by, 151
　determining, 151, 157, 159
　finding, 152
Communication:
　adapting language, 224, 226
　addressing the real message, 34–36
　APENS and, 11, 370
　between general educator and adapted physical educator, 34–36
　building rapport and, 18
　collaborative teams and, 17–23
　congruent message sending and, 22–23
　cultural influences, 21
　frame of reference and, 18
　IEP form and, 180
　ineffective, 20, 21
　instructional program and, 304
　jargon and, 22
　managing, 314
　nonverbal, 20–22
　positive language and, 9
　program plan and, 204
　questioning strategies, 20
　reflective listening and, 18–19
　regarding grief process, 347, 349
　speaking skills, 19
　specific explanations, 258
　teaching vocabulary concepts, 258
　with family, 343–350
Community:
　bringing to the classroom, 296–298

health promotion and, 2
partnership with organizations, 338–339
resources, 339–343
Community-based instruction programs, 294–298
Competencies, professional, 11
Complexity, degree of, 204
Comprehensive motor performance tests, 125–126
Concepts:
activities for teaching, 263–264
making them concrete, 227
movement, 263–264
Conclusions, drawing, 152–153
Concontraction, poor, 78–79
Concrete operations stage, of cognitive development, 262
Conditioning, 432
Conditioning equipment, 328
Conditions, performance standards and, 185
Conductive hearing loss, 382
Confidentiality, inclusion and, 207
Congenital blindness, 390–391
Congruent message sending, 22–23
Consent, informed, 168
Consultant model, 33
Consultants, skills/attitudes of, 35
Consultation, 11
APENS and, 369–370
Consulting strategy, 36
Content standards, 184
examples of, 187–189
Content validity, 146
Contingency management, 246–247
Continuing education, 11
APENS and, 370
program plan and, 204
Continuous scores, 102, 398
Contract systems, 246, 247
Contractures, 30
Contraindicated exercises, 315
Control of motor program, breakdown of, 73
Cooper Institute, 288
Cooper, Kenneth, 123
Coordination, 30
eye–foot, 83
eye–hand, 64, 65, 83, 255, 389
poor, 393
Coordinator, resource, 34
Correlation, 107, 402
Correlation coefficient, 147
Cortex, 46

Cortical equilibrium, 56
reactions, 54, 56, 77
Cost, testing and, 114
Co-teaching, 37–40
Courier, adapted physical educator as, 34
CPR, 315
Crawling, 426
Creativity, activities for encouraging, 266
Creeping, 426
Criteria, performance standards and, 185–186
Criterion-referenced standards, 93, 94–95, 397, 398
Criterion-referenced tests, 115
Cross-disciplinary teams, 16
Crossed extension reflex, 56, 118, 417–418
Crossing midline of body, 424
Cues:
prompting hierarchy and, 230
using, 216
Cuffs, wrist and ankle, 331–332
Culturally determined forms of movement, 62–63, 85, 278, 280, 286–298, 431–435
equipment and, 328
testing and, 125
Cultures, communication and, 21
Cumulative files, 114–115
Curriculum:
access to GPE, 202
adaptations to, 281, 282–283, 284, 287
data-based, 126–127
learning across, 261
nontraditional resources, 299
program plan and, 199–200
substitute, 282, 287
theory and APENS, 369
theory and development, 11
top-down model for, 200
Curriculum-based measurement, 127
Cystic fibrosis, 386

Dance, 285, 286–287, 299, 433–434
equipment, 328
lesson plan for, 311
therapy, 342
Data:
collection of, see Data collection
interpretation of, 144–158 (see also Interpretation)
qualitative, 113

quantitative, 113
Data collection, 111–140
at developmental level, 116–127
checklists, 131, 132–133
health-related physical fitness tests, 123–127
informal testing, 127–134 (see also Testing)
motor patterns, 121–123
problem solving and, 26
reflex testing, 117–120
sensorimotor testing, 120–121
Data-based curriculum, 126–127
Deaf-blindness, 380–381, 395
Deaflympics, 363
Deafness, 380–382, 395
adaptations for students with, 212
Deaf Sport, 361
Declarative statements, 175
Deep breathing, 443, 444, 445
Deep pressure, 75
Deep-pressure touch, 249
Deficit model, 174
Delivery methods, universal design and, 280
Demands, analyzing, 149–151
Demonstration, explanation and, 223
Dendrites, 44–45
DENVER II, 122, 405
Design, age-appropriate, 317
Development:
cephalo-caudal, 55
defined, 44
motor, 55–58, 154–155 (see also Developmental model)
neuro-, 55–58
neurons and, 44–45
of central nervous system, 45–46 (see also Central nervous system)
proximal-distal, 55
reflex, 55–56 (see also Reflexes)
reflex activity and, 54–55 (see also Reflex)
schedule of, 371–377, 406 (see also Developmental schedule)
Development model, for test interpretation, 158
Development Test of Visual Motor Integration (VMI-5), 121
Developmental activities, 2
Developmental approach:
applying the, 63–67

assessment of whole child and, 137–139
central nervous system and, 43–58 (see also Central nervous system)
defined, 44
developmental model and, 58–67 (see also Developmental model)
for tennis ball rally, 281
levels of educational programming and, 65–67
reflexes and, 54–58, 60 (see also Reflexes)
sensory input and, see Sensory input
SIMSF and, 46–54
Developmental disorders, 70, 76–85
defined, 70
reflex activity, 77–78
sensory systems and, 78–82
Developmental Indicators for Assessment of Learning (DIAL-3), 406
Developmental level, 204–205 (see also Developmental model)
Developmental model, 58–67
as framework for program plan, 200
earlier-maturing systems and, 60
for interpretation of measurements, 157–158
graphic depiction, 59
innate neural capacity and, 59–60
later-maturing systems, 60–61
motor sensory responses, 61–62
moving down the, 151
reflex activity and, 60 (see also Reflexes)
testing and, 117
understanding, 63
Developmental needs, appropriate activities by age, 256–260
Developmental order, 151
Developmental schedule, 371–377
at birth, 371
birth to 6 weeks, 371–372
6 weeks to 3 months, 372
3 to 6 months, 372–373
6 to 9 months, 373
9 to 12 months, 373–374
12 to 18 months, 374
2 to 3 years, 374–375
3 to 4 years, 375–376
4 to 5 years, 376
5 to 6 years, 376–377
6 to 7 years, 377
beyond 7 years, 377
Developmental Test of Visual-Motor Integration (VMI-5), 404
Deviations, 128
DEVPRO Motor Skills Assessment, 409
Diabetes, 386
Diagnosis, 100
Diencephalon, 45, 46
Difficulty, adaptation to, 282, 287
Direct measures, 112, 124
Direct verbal prompt, 230
Disabilities (see also Disability):
adaptations for specific, 212–214, 282–284
common attributes of specific, 395
definitions in federal legislation, 379–391
etiologies of, 379–391
multiple, 384
Disability:
awareness activities, 291–292, 294, 295
educational model and, 4
evolving societal context of, 4
legal contexts of, 4–8
lifelong activity and, 354–364
medical model and, 4
organizational resources for, 342
rights, 4–8
social minority model and, 4
superstition and, 4
Disability rights movement, 4
Disability sport, 354–364
associations, 411–412
defined, 356
historical context of, 356–361
international competitions, 363
milestones of, 357–361
organizations (DSOs), 356, 362
Disabled, defined, 5
Discovery, guided, 223
Discrete scores, 102
Discrimination:
sensory, 255, 327
tests and, 114
Disorders:
developmental, 76–85 (see also Developmental disorders)
process, see Process disorders
responsivity, see Responsivity
speech or language, 388–390
Distractibility, 79, 80, 389
Distractions, eliminating, 232
Distribution, normal, 103–104
Diversity:
equipment and, 329
individual differences, 291
Domains, learning, 260–273
Dominating reflexes, 77–78
Down syndrome, 96, 97, 98, 99, 260, 297, 392
adaptations for students with, 213
Dreams and Nightmares inventory, 348
Durability of equipment, 328
Dwarfism, 297
Dynamic strength, 145
Dynamometer, 113
Dysdyodokokinesia, 102
Dysfunction, sources of, 86
Dyslexia, 72
Dyspraxia, 154, 228

Early childhood education programs, 66
Ecological model of student performance, 193–194
Ecology of the learning environment, 193–194
Economy, of equipment, 328
Education:
continuing, 11, 370
free, appropriate public, 7
of individuals with disabilities, 4 (see also Adapted physical education)
Education for All Handicapped Children Act of 1975, 5, 6, 7
Education of the Handicapped Act Amendments of 1986, 5
Educational model, 4
Educational programming, 65–67
Effective programming:
developmental activities, 253–274, 417–447 (see also Activities)
inclusive practices, 277–300
philosophical approaches to, 278–281
Elementary physical education programs, 66
Elementary school grades, activities appropriate to developmental needs of, 257–258

Eligibility, 97
Eligibility Review Team, 159
Emotional ability, 389
Emotional disturbance, 381, 395
    adaptations for students with, 212
English as a second language, 22
Enrichment, 278
Environment:
    adaptations to, 210
    creating a positive, 240–242
    least restrictive, 7
    safety of, 316–318
Epilepsy Foundation of America, 342
Equilibrium, 423
    changes in, 119
    cortical, 56
    poor responses and, 78, 79
Equipment, 323–335
    adaptation of, 209, 235, 330–333
    diversity and, 329
    durability, 328
    economy, 328
    lists, 324–328
    making, 333–334
    managing, 312
    portability, 326
    safety of, 316–318
    selecting, 326–330
    size, 329
    special, 435–447
    washability of, 326
    working with minimal, 333
Ergometer, upper extremity, 355
Ethics, 11
    APENS and, 370
Evaluation, 93, 96–98, 144
    APENS and, 369
    benchmarks, 96–97
    defined, 96
    independent, 169
    measurement and, 397–402
    of goals and objectives for IEP, 193
    placement based on, 168–169
    program, 97–98
    purposes of, 100–101
    rubrics, 96, 97
Evaluation and Planning Team, 159
Exercise science, APENS and, 369
Exercises:
    deep breathing, 445
    for arthritis, 444–445
    for asthma, 445
    for tension/relaxation, 443
    weight-training, 445–446
Exertion, perceived, 125
Explanation and demonstration, 223
Explanations, using specific, 258
Explore-Listen-Do, 226
Explosive strength, 145
External validity, 146
Extinction, of behavior, 244
Extrinsic motivators, 241
Eye contact, 20
    autism and, 211
Eye pursuits, 79
Eye-foot coordination, 83
Eye-foot interaction, 62, 423–424
Eye-hand coordination, 64, 65, 83, 255, 389
Eye-hand interaction, 61, 255, 423–424

Face validity, 146
Facial expressions, 20
Facial stimuli, 75
Facilities, 318–323
    adapting, 231
    indoor, 322–323 (see also Equipment)
    outdoor, 321–322
    using available space, 321
Factual statement, 159
Fall surfaces, 317
Family:
    as members of IEP team, 28, 343
    interest questionnaire for, 344
    involvement in ITP, 343–350
    involving in program, 338
    questionnaire to include, 29
    sharing information with, 347
Fatigue, 392
    cognitive, 235
Feedback:
    breakdown of, 73
    CNS and, 47–50 (see also SIMSF system)
    learning and, 221–222
    universal design and, 280
    utilizing sensory, 49
Figure-ground discrimination, 54, 65
Finning, 432
First-aid supplies, 314 (see also Safety)
Fishing, 296
FIT principles of training, 125
Fitness, 354–356 (see also Physical activity)
    equipment, 328
    low, 393
    physical, NASPE standard 1 and, 285, 287–289
FITNESSGRAM, 93, 124, 148, 149, 150, 157, 288, 289, 407
504 Accommodation Plan, 167
Flexibility, 146
    as pivotal skill, 205
Fluency disorders, 388
Formal operations stage, of cognitive development, 262
Formal testing, 90, 112–116
Format, varying class, 232–233
Formation, adaptations to, 209
Formative assessment, 99
Frame of reference, 18
Framework, for program plan, 198
Fraternities, 339
Free, appropriate public education, 7
Free weights, 445–446
Frequency distribution, 103, 399
Functional analysis of behavior, 244
Functional assessment, 95
Functional mobility, 30
Fund-raising, 339

Galloping, 430
Game statistics, as data source, 131, 134
Games:
    activities, 434–435 (see also Activities)
    adapting, 281, 283–284
    multicultural, 289, 290
    parachute, 438–439
    wrestling, 442–443
Games and sports, 289
    equipment, 328
    NASPE standard 1 and, 285
General educator, as member of IEP team, 30
General memory, 265
General physical education, program adaptations to, 208–214, 282–284
Generalist, physical education, 10–11
Gestural cue, 230
Girls Clubs, 339
Global chaining, 238
Goals:
    adaptation to, 282, 287
    alternate, 282, 287
    and related objectives, 192
    defined, 184

framework for, 193–194
IEP and, *see* IEP
of IFSP and ITP, 166
of program plan, 198–199
prioritizing, 186, 189
targeting appropriate, 193
writing measurable, 185–185
Golf, 296
Golf Skill Test Battery for College Males and Females, 156
Grab bars, 320
Graphing, 103, 106–107, 399 (*see also* Measurement)
Grasp reflex, 56, 77, 417
Grasping, 32
Grecian flurry, 437
Greek era, disability and, 4
Grief process, 347, 349
Grip strength, 145
Gross motor skills, request for support in teaching, 24
Group:
large, 233
mixed, 233
position in a, 104–105
small, 233
Groups:
support, 304
youth, 339
Growth:
of central nervous system, 45–46
reflex activity and, 54–55
Growth and development, facilitating, 44
Guide to Early Movement Skills (GEMS), 122, 405, 435–436
Guided discovery, 223
Guidelines, safety, 317–318
Gymnastics:
medical, 3
rhythmic, 290
spotting partners and, 315
Gymnastics Skills Test for College Women, 156

Hand and arm use, 426–427
Hand dynamometer, 407–408
Handicapped Children's Protection Act, 5
Handicaps, adaptations for students with multiple, 213
Handles, adapting, 332
Handwriting, messy, 83
Head control, 425

Health impairment, adaptations for students with, 213
Health promotion, 2, 354–356 (*see also* Physical activity)
Healthful lifestyles, 2
Health-related physical fitness, 145, 146
measurement, 156–157
tests, 123–127
Healthy People 2000, 2, 354
Healthy People 2010, 2, 354
Healthy People with Disabilities, 354
Hearing, 53, 82, 116, 117 (*see also* Auditory)
Hearing impairment, 39, 202, 381–382 (*see also* Deafness)
adaptations for students with, 213
Heart rate monitor, 136
Hematologic disorders, 387
Hepatitis B, 387
Heterogeneity, of scores, 104
Hide-away, 437
Hierarchical sequence of influence, 155
High school, activities appropriate to developmental needs of, 258–259
High school physical education, 66
HIPAA (Health Insurance Portability and Accountability Act of 1996), 33
Historical perspectives of APE, 3
History, APENS and, 369
HIV, 11, 386
Home programs, developing, 350
Homeostasis, 50
Home–school interaction, 343 (*see also* Family)
Homogeneity, of scores, 104
Honesty, 27
Hopping, 428
Hula hoops, 436–437
Human development, 11 (*see also* Developmental model)
APENS and, 368
Human movement:
central nervous system and, 44–58 (*see also* Central nervous system)
culturally determined forms of, 62–63
developmental model and, 58–67
neurological bases of, 44–58
Human tic-tac-toe, 273

Humor, reducing tension and, 248
Hurdle lesson, 248
Hyperactivity, 80, 387
Hyperreponsivity, 74–75, 81–82
Hyperresponsiveness, 392
Hypertonia, 392
Hypertonicity, 78, 79
Hyporesponsiveness, 389, 392
Hyporesponsivity, 74–75, 81–82
Hypotonia, 392–393
Hypotonicity, 78, 79

I CAN, 127
I statements, 19
IDEA '97, 5, 6, 7
compared to Section 504, 167
IDEA '04, 16, 27, 92, 108, 114, 144, 158, 159, 166, 170, 201, 338, 367, 379
disability definitions, 379–391
Ideas, valuing others', 18
Identification activities, 267–268
IEP (Individualized education program), 7, 144, 163–195, 304
assessment and, 171–173
comparison of IFSP and ITP, 165–166
content of, 173–175
determining achievement dates, 189–193
determining related services, 194
diagnosis and, 100
growth of the process, 170
legal framework for, 166–169
legal requirements and, 159–160
legal requirements related to assessment, 167–169
legally mandated components of, 169
lesson plans meeting goals and objectives, 306–311
managing paperwork and, 306
parents and, 28
performance objectives and, 177, 182–186
preparing for program meeting, 170–175
preparing report of teacher assessment, 174–175
referrals and, 171
sample document, 177–183
significance of, 164–165
team, 16–17, 27–33, 158–160
team meeting notes, 181
types of, 165–166

writing goals for, 177, 182–184
IFSP compared to ITP, 165–166
Ignoring, planned, 248
Imagery, use of, 290
Impaired, 8
Incline mats, 331, 334
Inclusion, 10, 39
   barriers to, 207–208
   checklist for, 99
   defining, 205–206
   guidelines for, 278–279 (*see also* Effective programming)
   in culturally determined forms of movement, 278, 280, 286–298, 431–435
   misuses of, 206
   of students with disabilities in general programs, 37–40
   program planning for, 200–202 (*see also* Effective programming)
   successful, 205–208
Inclusive physical education, defined, 10 (*see also* Adapted physical education)
Inclusiveness, 280 (*see also* Inclusion)
Independent evaluation, 169
Independent living movement, 354, 355
Indirect verbal prompt, 230
Individual family service plan (IFSP), 165–166
Individual needs, strategies for meeting, 219–251
Individualism, 22
Individualized education program, *see* IEP
Individualized instruction, 222–224, 314 (*see also* Adaptations)
   explanation and demonstration, 223
   guided discovery, 223
   problem solving and, 223–224
   whole-to-part-to-whole method, 222
Individualized transition plan (ITP), 165–166, 338–339
Indoor facilities, 322–323 (*see also* Equipment)
Infants, activities appropriate for developmental needs of, 256–257
Infant-Toddler Developmental Assessment (IDA), 406

Inference, 159–160
   statements of, 175
Influence, 155
Informal relationship between scores, 106
Informal testing, 90–92, 127–134
Information (*see also* Assessment; Data collection):
   gathering, 23
   managing resources, 313–314
   obtaining from family, 343–347
   sharing with family, 347
Informed consent, 168
Inhelder, Barbel, 262
Inhibition, reflex, 54
Injury prevention, 316–317 (*see also* Safety)
Inner-tube, 334
Input, 47–50
   adaptation to, 282, 287
   auditory, 47, 52, 53
   breakdown of, 70–72
   proprioceptive, 47, 52
   sensory, 47, 50–54 (*see also* Central nervous system)
   tactile 47, 52–53
   vestibular, 47, 52
   visual, 47, 52, 53–54
Instruction (*see also* Instructional program):
   community-based, 294–298
   individualized, 222–224, 314 (*see also* Individualized instruction)
   methods of, 222–223
   one-to-one, 233
   techniques for adapting, 224–230 (*see also* Adaptations)
Instructional design, 11, 369
Instructional program, 303–336
   equipment and, 323–335 (*see also* Equipment)
   facilities and, 318–323
   managing information resources, 313–314
   managing smooth transitions, 312–313
   organizational strategies, 306–314
   planning and organization, 304–336
   safety and, 314–318
   scheduling, 304–305
Instructional progression, 239
Instructional time, 312
Integration, 422–423

   breakdown of, 71–73
   of both body sides, 84–85
   of students into general programs, 37–40 (*see also* Inclusion)
   reflex, 54
   test of visual-motor, 404
Intellectual development, *see* Development schedule
Intelligence:
   below-average, 9
   measures of, 137–138, 382–383
Interaction, individual-environment, 46
Interdependence, 4
   lateral, 155
   structural, 155
Interdisciplinary teams, 16
Interest boosting, 248
Interest questionnaire, 344
Interests:
   activities that develop students', 298–299
   using student's to design program, 289
Interfering reflexes, 60
International Classification of Functioning and Disability, 354
International Federation of Adapted Physical Activity, 3
International Olympic Committee, 356
International Paralympic Committee (IPC), 362
Internet, resources, 411
Interpretation:
   concepts necessary for, 145–149
   describing performance, 152
   determining commonalities, 151
   developmental model for, 158
   drawing conclusions, 152–153
   model for, 157–158
   of teacher assessment, 174–175
   ordering items developmentally, 151
   performance sampling and, 145
   relationships for test, 153–157
   steps in, 149–153
Inter-rater reliability, 113
Intersensory input, 59
Interval scores, 102, 398
Interventions, sensory, 249–250
Interview, parent, 345–346
Intonation, 21
Intracranial shunt, adaptations for students with, 213

Intrasensory influence, 155
Intrasensory input, 57, 59
Intrinsic motivators, 240–241
Inventions, game, 273
Inventories:
    activity preference, 135
    attitude, 134, 135
Inventory, Dreams and Nightmares, 348
IQ, 137–138, 382–383
Islands, 331
Isometric strength test, 407–408
Isotonic 1-RM Strength Tests, 124, 408
Itard, Jean Marc, 3
ITP compared to IFSP, 165–166

Jargon, eliminating, 22 (*see also* Language)
Jaycees, 339
Joint dysfunction, 393
Journals, 136, 411
    professional, 299
Jump rope, 278
Jumping, 223, 261, 264, 427–428
    skill progression for, 236–237
    standards for, 94
    task analysis of, 236–237

Kaufman Assessment Battery for Children, 138, 382
Kickball, activity analysis, 203
Kicking, 429
Kinesics, 20–21
Kinesthesia, 51
Kiwanis, 339
Kneeling, 426
Knights of Columbus, 339
Knowledge:
    consultants and, 35
    of results, 221

Labeling, 19
    effects of, 8
Labyrinthine righting, 56
Lafayette Skinfold Caliper II, 124
Landmarks, using, 231
Language:
    activities for fostering development of, 266–270
    adapting, 210, 224, 226
    assessment of, 138–139
    content, 389
    expressive, 116, 117
    games, 267

impairment, 393, 388–390
impairment, adaptation for, 224, 226
native, for assessment, 168
person first, 8, 379
positive, 9
problems, 116, 117, 388–390
tip for incorporating, 270
Lateral interdependence, 155
Later-maturing systems, 60–61
Law of effect, 220
Law of frequency, 220
Law of readiness, 220
Leaping, 430–431
Learners:
    evaluation of, 98, 99
    unique attributes of, 369
Learning:
    across the curriculum, 261
    affective, 270–273
    allowing time for, 228
    cognitive, 261–266
    defined, 220
    disabilities, *see* Learning disabilities
    domains, 260–273
    environment, *see* Learning environment
    factors that affect, 220–222
    incorporating multiple domains, 271–273
    language, 266–270
    laws of, 220
    lifelong, 261
    methods of, 220
    movement as, 257
    play as, 256
    process of, 220–222
Learning disabilities, 387–388, 389, 395
    adaptations for students with, 214
Learning environment:
    adapting, 231–233
    evaluation of, 97–98
    program plan and, 204
Least restrictive environment, 7
Left hemisphere, 46
Legal requirements, inclusion and, 207 (*see also* Legislation)
Legislation concerning disability, 5–8
    accessibility guidelines, 318–320
    adapted physical education and, 107–109

disabilities defined in federal, 379–391
Lesson plans:
    sportsmanship group, 415–416
    sample, 307–311
Lessons:
    adapting, 281, 283–284
    pacing, 210
    planning, 305–306, 307–311, 415–416
    safety and, 315–316
Letter grids, 261 (*see also* Continuing education)
Letters, sending home, 347, 350
Level of support, adaptation to, 282, 287
Lifelong learning, 261
Lifelong physical activity, 353–364
Likert Method, 134
Limbic lobe system, 46
Linguistic differences, 21
Lions, 339
Listening, 34
    reflective, 18–19
Lists, equipment, 324–328
Little League, 339
Lobes, brain, 46
Local education agency (LEA), 159, 160
Locomotor activities, 427–428
Los Angeles Unified School District, 160

Magazines, 411
Management:
    antecedent, 245–246
    contingency, 246–247
    time, 306–307
Mandates, legislative, 107–109
Manipulative activities, 428–429
Manual dexterity, measuring, 121
March of Dimes, 342
Material reinforcers, 244
Mats, 329, 331, 334
    tumbling, 331
Maturation, of vision, 53–54
Mean, 103, 399–400
Measurement, 102–107, 109 (*see also* Measurements)
    at developmental level, 116–127
    curriculum-based, 127
    defined, 92
    measures of central tendency, 103–104

SUBJECT INDEX **461**

organization of scores, 103
types of scores, 102–103 (*see also* Scores)
Measurement and evaluation, 397–402
APENS and, 369
Measurements:
health-related physical fitness, 156–157
motor ability, 156
motor development, 154–155
motor skills, 156
sensorimotor, 154
Measures of central tendency, 103–104
Measures of intelligence, 137–138
Measures of variability, 104
Median, 104, 400
Medical model, 4
Medicine ball, 434
Memory, 393
activities for enhancing, 265–266
bank, 71
disorders of, 389
general, 265
sequential, 228, 265
specific, 265
symbolic, 265
visual, 265
Mental retardation, 382–384, 395
adaptations for students with, 213
causes of, 384
IQ and, 382–383
learning and, 221
Message sending, congruent, 22–23
Methods, array of, 44
Midbrain reflexes, 56, 77, 119
Middle Ages, disability and, 4
Middle school accessibility, 324
Middle school/junior high, activities appropriate to developmental needs of, 258–259
Middle school physical education, 66
Migration, cell, 45
Milani-Comparetti Test of Reflex Development, 403
Mobility, functional, 30
Mobility specialist, 32
Mode, 104, 400–401
Modeling, 230
Models, of program planning, 200–202

Modifications (*see also* Adaptations):
defined, 208
facility, 320 (*see also* Facilities)
Modified physical education, 108 (*see also* Adapted physical education)
Montessori, 261
Moro reflex, 56
Morphology, 389
Motivation, 101
behavior and, 240–241
extrinsic, 221
learning and, 221
Motivators, intrinsic and extrinsic, 240–241
Motor ability:
measurement, 156
tests, 122, 406–407
Motor behavior, APENS and, 368–369
Motor control, 230
Motor coordination, 83–84
Motor development, 55–58 (*see also* Development model; Development schedule):
measurements, 154, 156
profiles, 121–122, 405
Motor experiences, early, 425–427
Motor-Free Visual Perception Test (MVPT), 120
Motor function:
at birth, 55–56
from four to seven-plus years, 56, 58
from one month to two years, 56–57
from two to four years, 56, 58
Motor lab, 322–323, 324
Motor learning, natural sequence of experiences, 65
Motor output, 57
Motor patterns, 62, 85
activities for enhancing, 255, 425–431
enhancing, 328
prerequisite levels for, 66
tests of, 121–123
Motor performance:
comprehensive tests of, 125–126
factors of, 148
rating, 172
tests of, 408–409
understanding, 69–87
Motor planning, 422
adaptation and, 228

deficits, 83–84
difficulty in, 80
Motor program:
control of, 48
translating perception into, 48
Motor response, 47, 48
voluntary, 62
Motor-sensory responses, 61–62, 82–85
activities for enhancing, 255, 422–425
equipment and, 327
Motor skills, 62, 117
activities for enhancing, 425–431
challenges to, 391–395
gross, 24
improving, 156
measurement, 156
pivotal, 205
Movement:
ABCs of, 268, 269
as communication, 257
as learning, 257
creative, 432
culturally determined forms of, 62–63, 85, 278, 280, 286–298, 328, 431–435
human, *see* Human movement
knowledge, 201
praxis and, 83–84
repetitive, 101, 394
skills, as goal, 201
therapy, 342
Movement attributes/etiology of disabilities, 379–395
Movement exploration, 223
approach, 265
Moving Into the Future: National Physical Education Standards, 199
Multicultural activities, 291, 292, 293
Multidisciplinary teams, 16
Multiple disabilities, 384
adaptations for students with, 213
Multiple sclerosis, 392
Multisenses, using, 228–229
Muscle contraction, inadequate, 79
Muscles, damage to, 50
Muscle tone, 78, 79, 392–393
Muscular dystrophy, 70, 392
Muscular strength, 146, 149
Musculoskeletal impairments, 385

Mushroom, 437
MVPT-3, 403
Myelination, 45, 53, 57, 59

Naming activities, 267–268
NASPE Standards, 184, 199, 254, 284–286
    examples of goals based on standards, 187–189
    lesson plans and, 306, 307–311
National Association for Sport and Physical Education (NASPE), see NASPE Standards
National Braille Association, 342
National Center on Physical Activity and Disability (NCPAD), 354
National Consortium on Physical Education and Recreation for Individuals with Disabilities (NCPERID), 11
National Disability Sports Alliance, 362
National Easter Seal Society, 342
National Paralympic Committee, 8
National Program for Playground Safety (NPPS), 317
National Society for Autistic Children, 342
National standards, APE and, 11 (see also NASPE standards)
Native language, 168
Natural cue, 230
Neck righting, 56
Needs:
    identifying, 23
    prioritizing, 37
Negative reinforcement, 243
Negative relationship, 107
Negative support, 419
Nervous system, see Central nervous system
Net, six-pack, 335
Neural capacity, 46 (see also Central nervous system)
Neurodevelopment:
    and motor function, 55–58
    at birth, 57
    from four to seven-plus years, 56, 58
    from one month to two years, 56–57
    from two to four years, 56, 58
Neurological conditions, 385
Neurological problems, 389
Neuron, 44–45

Nightmares, dreams and, 348
Nominal scores, 102, 399
Noncategorical approach, 9
Noncategorical programming, 278, 279
Nonlocomotor activities, 429–430
Nontraditional testing, 90–92
Nonverbal communication, 18–20
Normal curve, 103, 401
Norming sample, 115
Norm-referenced criteria, 97
Norm-referenced standards, 93, 94–95, 397
Norm-referenced tests, 112, 144
Number grids, 261
Number of players, adaptations to, 209
Numbers exchange, 439
Numbers race, 439
Nurse, as member of IEP team, 32

Obesity, 124, 289, 387
Objectives:
    adaptations to, 209
    defined, 184
    examples, 192
    framework for, 193–194
    on IEP, 177, 182–195, 304
    prioritizing, 186, 189
Objectivity, 113
Observation, 91, 172–173
Observational reports, 114
Observational techniques, 127–129
Obstacle course, 261
Occupational therapist, 31, 254, 350
Occupational therapy, 118
Ocean waves, 438
Ocular tracking, 54
Ocular training activities, 421–422
Olympic and Amateur Sports Act (OASA), 5, 7–8, 361
Olympic Rhythmic Gymnastics, 286
Omissions, deviations and, 128
Optic nerve, 53–54
Optical righting, 56
Optimists, 339
Oral stimuli, 75
Order effect, 148
Ordinal scores, 102, 398
Organizational strategies, 306–314
Orientation and mobility specialist, as member of IEP team, 32
Orientation, program, 304
Orthopedic impairments, 385, 395

Outdoor facilities, 321–322
Output, adaptation to, 282, 287
Overlearning, 221

PACER, 288
Pac Man game, 307
Pain stimuli, 75
Paperwork, managing, 306
Parachute activities/play, 272, 437–439
Paradigm shift, 2
Paraeducators, 215–217
    as member of IEP team, 30
Paralanguage, 21
Paralympic games, 7–8, 362, 363
Parameter, defined, 145
Paraplegia, 72, 150
Parents:
    as members of IEP team, 28
    collaborating with, 341
    disability awareness and, 295
    interview form, 345–346
    questionnaire to include, 29
Part method, 222
Partial participation, 238
Participation:
    adaptation to, 282, 287
    partial, 238
Passivity, vs. activity, 221
Pathological reflexes, 118
Pathologist, speech-language, 31–32
Patterning, 229
Peabody Developmental Motor Scales (PDMS-2), 122, 406
Peabody Picture Vocabulary Test, 138
Pedometers, 136
Peer teaching, 233
PEERS project, 278
Peers, support from, 304
People to People, activity, 225
Perceived exertion, 125
Percentile rank, 105
Perception, 47, 48, 229
    auditory, 82, 83
    breakdown of, 71–73
    visual, 80
Perceptual-Motor Assessment for Children (P-MAC), 121, 404–405
Perceptual-motor testing, 117, 120–121
Performance:
    atypical, 63
    commonly used tests of, 120–121

describing, 129, 131, 152 (*see also* Assessment; Evaluation)
determining current level of, 167 (*see also* Assessment)
ecological model of student, 193–194
identifying deficits in, 64
motor, *see* Motor performance
objectives, IEP and, 177, 182–186
present levels of, 178, 182–183
prioritizing current level of, 176
sources of atypical, 64–65
standards, 184
testing, 112, 124 (*see also* Assessment; Evaluation)
Periodicals, 411
Personal development, 201
Personal qualities, 26–27
Person first language, 8, 379
Pervasive Developmental Disorders (PDD), 380
Philosophical model, 201
Philosophy:
APENS and, 369
of program plan, 198–199
Phone contact, with family, 347
Photo display, 350
Physical access, universal design and, 280
Physical activity:
disability sport and, 354–364 (*see also* Disability sport)
lifelong, 338–339, 353–364
Physical education, 2
accommodations in, 164 (*see also* Accommodations)
adapted, *see* Adapted physical education
inclusive, 10 (*see also* Inclusion)
incorporating all learning domains, 260–273
modified, 108 (*see also* Modifications)
specially designed, 108
traditional activity areas, 286–291
Physical education generalist, 10–11
Physical education program, developing and implementing, 197–217 (*see also* Program plan)
Physical fitness, 354–356 (*see also* Physical activity)
activities, 434 (*see also* Activities)
health-related testing, 123–127

NASPE standard 1 and, 285, 287–289
tests of, 407–408
Physical prompts, 230
Physical restraint, 248
Physical therapist, 254, 350
as member of IEP team, 30–31
Physiological functions, control of, 392
Piaget, Jean, 58, 262
stages of cognitive development, 262
Pickleball, lesson plan for, 310–311
Picture Exchange Communication System (PECS), 227
Pivotal skills, role of, 205
Placement, 100
considerations for, 160–161
determining, 144
evaluation based on, 168–169
Planned ignoring, 248
Planning:
lesson, 305–306, 307–311
the organizational program, 304–336
Plateaus, in learning, 221
Plato, 261
Play, as learning, 256
Play behavior, *see* Development schedule
Playground, observation checklist, 131
Polio, 70
Popcorn game, 267
Portability, of equipment, 326
Portfolios, 135–136
Position in a group, 104–105
Positioning, 229
Positive behavior support (PBS), 242–250
Positive environment, creating a, 240–242
Positive language, using, 9
Positive relationship, 107
Positive support, 419
Posting rules, 241
Postlingually deaf, 382
Postnatal training, 447
Postural balance, 30
Postural insecurity, 79
PPVT-III, 138
Practice, amount and type of, 220
Prader-Willi syndrome, 392
Praxis, 83–84, 255, 422
Prediction, 100

Prelingually deaf, 381
Prematurity, 380, 385
Prenatal training, 446–447
Preoperational thought stage, of cognitive development, 262
Pre-referral checklist, 172–173
Preschool and primary grades, activities appropriate to developmental needs of, 257
Prescreening Developmental Questionnaire II (PDQ II), 122, 405
President's Council on Physical Fitness and Sports (PCPFS), 2, 354
Primitive reflex retention, 393
Prioritizing needs, 37
Privacy rights, inclusion and, 207
Probability, 159, 175
Problem solving, 23, 26
activities, 264–265
individualized instruction and, 223–224
Process disorders, 70–76
breakdown sites and effects, 70–73
defined, 70
input/reception, 70, 71
responsivity, 74–76
selective attention/arousal, 71
SIMSF and, 70–73
Professional competencies, 11
Professional, services, 341–343
Program adaptations for GPE, 208–214, 282–283
Program effectiveness, determining, 100–101
Program evaluation, 97–98
APENS and, 370
Program, instructional, *see* Instructional program
Program plan:
adaptations for GPE, 209–214 (*see also* Adaptations)
components of an effective, 204
curriculum and, 199–200
determining a meaningful, 198–203
determining appropriate level of, 202–203
developing and implementing, 198–217
for inclusion, 200–202 (*see also* Inclusion)
implementing, 203–204

philosophy, beliefs and goals, 198–199
sequencing activities and, 204–205
Program planning (*see also* Program plan)
worksheet, 38
for lifetime physical activity, 338–339
individual, 101
Programming (*see also* Effective programming):
categorical vs. noncategorical, 8–9
effective, *see* Effective programming
inclusive, 278–279 (*see also* Effective programming; Inclusion)
noncategorical, 279
philosophical approaches to, 278–281
top-down approach, 281
Programs:
adult, 338–351
community-based, 294–298
Progress, determining, 100
Progression, 229
skill, 235–237
Progressive muscle relaxation, 290
Progressive part method, 222–223
Progressive relaxation, 443
Proliferation, cell, 45
Prompting, 229–231
hierarchy, 230
Prone reaction, 56
Proprioceptive difficulties, 51–52
Proprioceptive disorder, 393
Proprioceptive input, 46, 51–52
Proprioceptive system, 51–52, 59, 60, 158, 421
breakdown of, 71–72
developmental disorders and, 79–80
Protective extension, 56, 77, 78, 119, 419–420
Providing Education for Everyone on Regular Schools (PEERS), 278
Proximal-distal motor development, 55
Proximity control, 248
Psycho-educational Profile, Revised (PEP-3), 121, 404
Psychologist, as member of IEP team, 28, 30

Public Law 101–336, Americans with Disabilities Act (ADA), 5
Public Law 101–476, Individuals with Disabilities Education Act of 1990, 5–6
Public Law 105–17 (IDEA '97), 5, 6 (*see also* IDEA '97)
Public Law 108–446, Individuals with Disabilities Education Improvement (IDEA '04), 5–6 (*see also* IDEA '04)
Public Law 93–112, Section 504 of the Rehabilitation Act of 1973, 5
Public Law 94–142, Education for All Handicapped Children of 1975, 5, 6, 7
Public Law 95–606, Amateur Sports Act of 1978, 5, 7–8
Pulling, 430
Pull-ups, standards for assessing, 94
Punishment, 243, 247
Punitive procedures, 247
Pushing, 430
Push-ups, 438
Pyramids, 439

Quadrupedal reaction, 56
Qualitative data, 113
Quantitative data, 113
Quantity, adaptation to, 282, 287
Questioning strategies, 20
Questionnaire, interest, 344
Questions, open-ended, 20
Quick Neurological Screening Test II, 120, 403–404

Racquetball Skills Test, 156
Ramps, 320
Range, 104, 401–402
Range of motion, 79, 425
activities, 255
Rank, 402
percentile, 105
Rankings, 398–399
Rapport, establishing, 18, 147
Rating form, 130
Rating scales, 92, 129–130, 156
Ratios, 102, 398, 399
Reaching, 429
Reactions, 56, 119
associated, 119
cortical-equilibrium, 119
righting, 419
Rebounder, 441

Reception:
breakdown of, 70–72
of sensory input, 47
Reciprocation, 84
Recreation, therapeutic, 341
Red Cross, 286
Referrals, 171
Reflex (*see also* Reflexes):
behavior, testing and, 153
development, 55–56, 327
development and inhibition, activities for, 417–420
disorders, 119
emergence, 56
inhibition, 54
integration, 54, 65, 77
retention, 393
Reflex activity, 54–55 (*see also* Central nervous system; Development schedule; Reflexes):
and developmental model, 60
developmental disorders and, 77–78
Reflexes:
activities for developing, 254
brain stem, 118–119
interference from dominating, 77–78
interfering, 60
lack of assistance from, 78
midbrain, 56, 119
residual, 118
signs of abnormal behavior, 120
spinal level, 55, 118
testing, 117–120, 403
tonic labyrinthine (TLR), 55
tonic neck (TNR), 55
Rehabilitation Act of 1973, 5, 167, 320
Reinforcement, positive, negative, 243–244
Reinforcers, rewards and, 243–244, 246
Related services, determining, 194
Relaxation, 290–291
activities, 443
Reliability:
defined, 107
of tests, 113, 147
Repetitive movement, 394
Report, of teacher assessment, 174–175
Reporting mechanism, 204
Residual spinal reflexes, 118
Resource coordinator, 34

Resources:
 community, 339–343 (see also Community)
 Internet, 411
 journals, 411
 managing information, 313–314
 nontraditional, 299
 organizations, 342–343
 physical activity and disability, 411–413
Responses:
 emergence of, 56 (see also Reflexes)
 motor-sensory, 61–62, 82–85
Responsibility for safety, 315
Responsivity:
 continuum, 74, 248–249
 disorders, 74–76
 sensory, 49
Restraint, physical, 248
Results:
 interpreting, 150
 knowledge of, 221
Retardation:
 adaptations for students with, 213
 mental, see Mental retardation
Retention, learning and, 221
Reticular formation, 45–46, 71
Retina, detached, 72
Rett's Disorder, 380
Reward, 243–244, 246
Rheumatoid arthritis, 39
Rhythmic gymnastics, 290
Rhythms, 433–434
 equipment, 328
Right hemisphere, 46
Righting reactions, 56, 119, 254, 419
Righting responses, 56
Rockport Walk Test, 115, 124, 150, 407
Role release, 16
Roller skating, 297
 skills checklist, 132
Rolling ball, 428
Rolling over, 425–426
Roman era, disability and, 4
Ropes, 439–440
Rotary International, 339
Rousseau, 261
Routine:
 providing, 232
 support from, 248
Rubrics, 96, 97, 144, 161
Rules:
 adaptation of, 209, 235
 class, 241–242
 modifying for student with a disability, 39
 playground, 309
 responding to broken, 241–242
Running, 427
 as pivotal skill, 205

Safe-Key program, 342
Safety, 314–318
 equipment, 330
Sampling:
 adequate, 115
 performance, 145
SAT testing, 100
Savant, autistic, 380
Schedules, developmental, 406 (see also Developmental schedule)
Scheduling, 304–305, 306
Schizophrenia, 381
School Appraisal Review Team, 159
Scooterboards, 440
Scores:
 classification, 398–399
 continuous, 398
 correlation and, 107
 correlation coefficient and, 147
 discrete, interval, ordinal, nominal, 102
 graphing and, 106–107
 informal relationships between, 106
 interval, 398
 looking for clustered, 174
 measures of central tendency and, 103–104
 measures of variability and, 104
 nominal, 399
 ordinal, 398
 organization of, 103, 399
 relationships between, 106–107
 reliability and, 107
 standard, 105–106, 402
 types of, 102–103, 398
 validity and, 107
Sculling, 432
Seaman Attitude Inventory, 135
Seasonal appropriateness, 204
Secondary school, activities appropriate to developmental needs of, 258–259
Section 504, 5, 7, 167
 compared to IDEA '97, 167
Seductive objects, removing, 248
Seizures, 394

Selective attention, 47, 48, 73
Self-determination, 27
Self-esteem, 389
Self-image, as goal, 201
Self-paced independent work, 233
Self-rating scales, 134–135
Self-reporting, 92, 134–136
Semantics, 389–390
Sensorimotor:
 measurements, 154
 stage, of cognitive development, 262
 testing, 120–121
 training, 3
Sensorineural hearing loss, 382
Sensory:
 channels, use of, 268
 information, integration of, 48
 interventions, 249–250
 responses, behaviors related to, 75–76
 responsiveness, influence of, 248–250
 responsivity, 50–51
 stimulation, 249
 stimuli, responsiveness to, 392
Sensory input, 46, 47, 50–54 (see also Central nervous system)
 neurodevelopment and, 59
Sensory-integrative-motor-sensory-feedback, see SIMSF system
Sensory-Motor Experiences for the Home, 350
Sensory stimulation, 66
 equipment and, 327
Sensory stimulation and discrimination, 255
 activities for, 420–422
Sensory systems, 51–54, 78–82
 auditory, 82, 83
 proprioceptive, 79–80 (see also Proprioceptive)
 tactile, 80
 vestibular, 78–79 (see also Vestibular)
 visual, 80–82
Sequential memory, 228, 265
Service clubs, 339
Shaping, 238, 240
Shipwreck, 291, 293
Shriver, Eunice Kennedy, 363
Sickle cell disease, 387
Sight lines, 318
Signal interference, 248
Simple frequency distribution, 103

SIMSF system, 44, 46–54, 248 (*see also* Developmental model)
 impairments of, 86 (*see also* Developmental disorders, Processing disorders)
 process disorders and, 70–73
Sitting, 56, 426
Six-P program, 229
Six-pack net, 335
Size of equipment, 329
Skills:
 adaptation of, 234–235
 adaptive defining mental retardation, 383
 as promoted by SIMSF system, 49
 challenges to motor, 391–395
 cognitive, 261–266
 combination, 200
 communication, 17–23 (*see also* Communication)
 consultants and, 35
 fundamental motor, 200
 gross motor, 24
 lifetime, 200
 listening, 18–19
 motor, 62, 85 (*see also* Human movement)
 preacademic/academic/functional, on IEP, 178
 problem solving, 23, 26
 progression, 235–237
 role of pivotal, 205
 safety, 316
 social, 270, 271, 416
 speaking, 19
 swimming, 432 (*see also* Aquatics)
 testing motor, 122–123
 transition, 311–312
Skipping, 96, 430
Sky high pull, 438
Sliding, 94, 428
Smell, stimuli, 76
Soccer, 296, 298, 339
Social development, 128, 129 (*see also* Development schedule)
Social minority model, 4
Social reform, 4 (*see also* Legislation concerning disability)
Social reinforcers, 244
Social skills, 270, 271, 416
Social support, families and, 28 (*see also* Family)
Socialization, 164, 270, 271 (*see also* IEP)
Society, disability and, 4

Softball, 296
Solutions, generating, 23, 26
Somatosensory mature input, 57
Songs, 313
Sororities, 339
Space:
 adaptation of, 231
 and form perception, 422
 using available, 321
 using creatively, 231–232
Spatial orientation, 80–81, 389
Special educator, as member of IEP team, 30
Special Olympics, 123, 356, 362, 363
Specialist, adapted physical education, 11
Specially designed physical education, 108
Specific memory, 265
Specificity:
 as legal requirement, 168
 test, 147–148
Speech:
 flow disorders, 388
 impairments, 388–390
 problems, signs of, 116, 117
Speech-language impairment, adaptations for students with, 214
Speech-language pathologist (SLP), 31–32, 267
Spina bifida, 260, 392
Spinal cord, 45
Spinal reflexes, 55, 56, 77, 118
Sport:
 activities, 434–435
 associations, 411–412
 disability, 354–364 (*see also* Disability sport)
 and games, 289
Sport skills, testing, 122–123
Sports Club for the Deaf, 356
Sports, unified, 356
Sportsmanship Group, 271
 sample lesson plan, 415–416
Spotting partners, 315
Stability, 30
Staff development, 11
Stair climbing, 425
Standard deviation, 104, 401
Standard scores, 105, 402
Standardized administration procedures, 115
Standards, 93, 94, 95

Adapted Physical Education National (APENS), 11, 200, 367–370
 comparison of approaches, 95
 measurement and evaluation and, 397–398
 NASPE, 187–189, 199, 284–286
 of Learning, 148
 safety, 317–318
Standford-Binet Intelligence Scale, 138
Standing, 426
 as pivotal skill, 205
 reaction, 56
Standing broad jump, percentile table, 190
Stanines, 105
Startle reflex, 118, 417
Statements of inference, 175
Statements of probability, 175
Static strength, 145
Station teaching, 39, 233
Statistics:
 descriptive, 399–402
 game, 131, 134
Steal the bacon, 439
Stepping reflex, 419
Stereotypic movement, 394
Stilts, 440
Stimuli:
 calming, 249
 sensory, 49–54 (*see also* Input; Sensory input)
Stoke Mandeville Hospital, 363
Strategy, teaching, 222
Strength:
 factors that contribute to, 145
 model, 174
 standards for assessing, 94
 tests of, 124
Stress management, 314
Stretching, 429
Striking, 429
Structural interdependence, 155
Structure, providing, 232
Structures, outdoor, 321–322
Student progress, determining, 100
Students, inclusion of, *see* Inclusion
Stunts, 285, 289–290, 444
Substitutions:
 deviations and, 128
 use of, 234
Successive approximation, 238, 240
Sunflower, 437
Superstition, disability and, 4

Supervision, safety and, 317
Supine reaction, 56
Supplies, 324, 325 (see also Equipment)
Support, 419
  adaptation to, 282, 287
  group, professional, 304
  of positive behavior, 312
  reactions, 56
Surfaces, fall, 317
Swimming, 296, 431–432 (see also Aquatics)
  lesson plan for, 309–310
  skills checklist, 132
Symbolic memory, 265
Symbolic prompt, 230
Symmetrical tonic neck reflex (STNR), 56, 119, 254, 418
Synaptic transmission, 45
Syntax, 389
System, central nervous, see Central nervous system
Systems, earlier maturing, 60
Systems, later-maturing, 60–61

T scores, 105–106, 161, 402
Table tennis, 332
Tactile (see also Tactile system):
  defensiveness, 80
  input, 46, 52–53
  processing difficulties, 80
  stimulation difficulties, 53
  stimuli, 75
Tactile-seeking behaviors, 80
Tactile system, 52–53, 59, 158, 394, 420–421 (see also Developmental model)
  developmental disorders and, 80
Tai chi, 296
Target heart rate, 137
Task analysis, 235–240
Task cards, 228
Task-reinforcer systems, 246, 247
Tasks, sequencing, 227–228
Task-specific activities, 264–265
Taste, stimuli, 76
Teacher rating scales, 129–130
Teaching:
  alternative, 39
  APENS and, 369 (see also APENS)
  co-, 37–40
  peer, 233
  stations, 39, 233
  strategies, for all students, 208–214
  strategies, using innovative, 229
  team, 39–40
Team:
  approach, 15–40
  playing, 416
  teaching, 39–40
  evaluation and planning, 159
  IEP, 158–160 (see also IEP)
  interaction, 204
  meeting notes, 181
Teams:
  balancing, 144
  characteristics of effective, 17–27
  collaborative, 16–17 (see also Collaborative teams)
  cross-disciplinary, 16
  effective communication and, 17–23
  IEP, 16–17, 27–33 (see also IEP)
  interdisciplinary, 16
  multidisciplinary, 16
  problem-solving skills and, 23–26
  trandisciplinary, 16
Technology, using to collect data, 136–137
Ted Stevens Olympic and Amateur Sports Act of 2000, 5, 7–8, 361
Telencephalon, 45, 46
Temperature regulation difficulties, 394
Temperature stimuli, 75
Tennis:
  ball rally, 281
  table, 332
Tension:
  exercises, 443
  reducing through humor, 248
Tenting, 437
Test:
  interpretation, relationships for, 153–157
  relationships, 149
  reliability of, 147
  specificity, 147–148
  validity, 146–147
Test of Auditory Discrimination, 138
Test of Gross Motor Development (TGMD-2), 115, 122, 156, 406–407
Test of Visual Motor Integration (TVMI), 121
Testing, 109 (see also Assessment)
  adequate sampling, 115
  administration, 114–116
  and related services, 101
  children with a disability, 157 (see also Assessment; Evaluation; Tests)
  conditions of, 115
  criteria for selecting instrument, 112–114
  data collection and, 112–116 (see also Data collection)
  defined, 90
  deviations and, 128
  direct measures, 112
  formal, 90, 112–116
  health-related physical fitness, 123–127
  informal, 90–92, 127–134
  language and, 116, 117
  motor ability, 122
  motor patterns, 121–123
  motor skills, 122–123
  perceptual-motor, 1201–121
  procedures for, 115–116
  reflexes, 117–120
  resources for, 114–115
  SAT, 100
  sensorimotor, 120–121
  sport skills, 122–123
Test-retest reliability, 113
Tests:
  annotated summary of available, 403–409
  as indicators, 148–149
  commonalities among items, 149
  criterion-referenced, 115
  norm-referenced, 112
  of development, 406
  performance, 120–121
  reflex, 403
  sensorimotor, 403
Tests of Language Development, 138
Theoretical model, 201
Therapeutic activities, 444–445
Therapeutic recreation, 341
Therapist, occupational, 31
Therapist, physical, 30–31
Therapy ball, 330
Thinking, disorders of, 389
Throwing, 92, 428
  collaborative process and, 239
  diagrammatic task analysis of, 237
  pattern, 92, 129
Tic-tac-toe, human, 273
Time:
  adaptation to, 282, 287

effective use, 306–307
Time period, for assessment, 167–168
Tire pull game, 272
Token reinforcers, 244
Token systems, 246–247
Tonic labyrinthine reflex (TLR), 55, 56, 63, 77, 78, 119, 254
  prone, 418
  supine, 418–419
Tonic neck reflexes (TNR), 55, 63, 77, 118
Tool Chest, 350
Top-down approach, 280, 281
Top-down curriculum model, 200
Touch, 52, 53 (see also Tactile)
Training, FIT principles of, 125
Trampoline, 440–441
Transdisciplinary team, 16
Transition:
  family involvement in, 343–350 (see also Family)
  from school to adult programs, 338–351
Transitions, managing smooth, 312–313
Translation, breakdown of, 73
Traumatic brain injury (TBI), 390, 395
  adaptations for students with, 214
T-stools, 330, 440
Tug-of-rope, 268, 438
Tumbling, 285, 289–290
  mats, 331
Turn taking, 416
Turning, 430
20–30 Clubs, 339
Twisting, 430

U of H Nonexercise Test, 124, 407
Understanding, 393
Unified Sports program, 339, 356
Uniqueness of individuals with a disability, 9
United Cerebral Palsy (UCP), 342
United States Access Board, 318
United States Association of Blind Athletes, 362
United States Olympic Committee (USOC), 7–8, 361

United States Paralympic Corporation, 362
Upper extremity ergometer, 355
USA Deaf Sports Federation, 362
Usher's syndrome, 380–381

Vacillating responsivity, 74, 77
Validity, 113
  as legal requirement, 168
  defined, 107
  test, 146–147
Variability, measures of, 104
Velcro, equipment adaptation and, 331
Verbal prompts, 230
Verbal removal, 248
Verbalization, 267 (see also Language)
Vestibular input, 46, 52
Vestibular organs, 82
Vestibular system, 59, 78–79, 158, 421 (see also Developmental model)
  developmental disorders and, 78–79, 394
  difficulties, 52
  processing difficulties, 53
Vibration, stimuli, 76
Vision, maturation of, 53–54 (see also Visual; Visual system)
Visual:
  acuity, 80
  closure, 54
  immature input, 57
  impairment, 390–391, 395
  impairment, adaptations for students with, 214
  input, 46, 52, 53–54
  memory, 265
  perception disorders, 54, 394–395
  perception, 80
  stimuli, processing of, 71, 76
Visual system, 59, 60–61, 158, 421–422
  developmental disorders and, 80–82
Visual-motor integration, test of, 404

Vocal cues, 21
Vocal intonation, 21
Vocalization, 267
Voluntary motor responses, 62
Volunteers, 350
Vygotsky, Lev, 262

Waist circumference, 124
Waist-hip ratio (WHR), 124
Walking, 426, 427
  clubs, 296
Wall walk, 329, 331
Warmth, neutral, 249
Washability, of equipment, 326
Water adjustment, 431
Weak upper body strength, 202
Wechsler Adult Intelligence Scale, 137
Wechsler Intelligence Scale for Children, 137, 382
Weights, 331
Weight training, 445–446
Wheelchair:
  adaptations for students using, 212
  dancing and, 286–287
  student use of, 39, 259
Wheelchair Sports, USA, 362
Whole method, 222
Whole-to-part-to-whole method, 222
Wild horse pull, 438
Williams, Jesse Feiring, 261
Woodcock-Johnson III, 137, 382
Word scramble, 263
Workshops, family, 347
World Games for the Deaf, 363
World Health Organization (WHO), 354
Wrestling, games, 442–443
Wrist cuffs, 331–332
Wrist roll, 438

YMCA, 296, 339
Yoga, 290, 299
Youth groups, 339
YWCA, 339

z score, 105, 161, 402